Introduction to Ethics

Elements of Philosophy

The Elements of Philosophy series aims to produce core introductory texts in the major areas of philosophy, among them metaphysics, epistemology, ethics and moral theory, philosophy of religion, philosophy of mind, aesthetics and the philosophy of art, feminist philosophy, and social and political philosophy. Books in the series are written for an undergraduate audience of second- through fourth-year students and serve as the perfect cornerstone for understanding the various elements of philosophy.

Moral Theory: An Introduction by Mark Timmons

An Introduction to Social and Political Philosophy: A Question-Based Approach by Richard Schmitt

Epistemology: Classic Problems and Contemporary Responses, Second Edition, by Laurence BonJour

Aesthetics and the Philosophy of Art: An Introduction, Second Edition, by Robert Stecker

Aesthetics Today: A Reader edited by Robert Stecker and Ted Gracyk

Introduction to Ethics: A Reader edited by Andrew J. Dell'Olio and Caroline J. Simon

Introduction to Ethics

A Reader

Edited by Andrew J. Dell'Olio and Caroline J. Simon

ROWMAN & LITTLEFIELD PUBLISHERS, INC.
Lanham • Boulder • New York • Toronto • Plymouth, UK

Published by Rowman & Littlefield Publishers, Inc.
A wholly owned subsidiary of The Rowman & Littlefield Publishing Group, Inc.
4501 Forbes Boulevard, Suite 200, Lanham, Maryland 20706
http://www.rowmanlittlefield.com

Estover Road, Plymouth PL6 7PY, United Kingdom

British Library Cataloguing in Publication Information Available

Library of Congress Cataloging-in-Publication Data

Introduction to ethics : a reader / edited by Andrew Dell'Olio and Caroline Simon.
p. cm. — (Elements of philosophy)
Includes bibliographical references and index.
ISBN 978-0-7425-6356-8 (cloth : alk. paper) — ISBN 978-0-7425-6357-5 (pbk.)
1. Ethics. I. Dell'Olio, Andrew J., 1959– II. Simon, Caroline, 1953–
BJ21.I58 2010
170—dc22

2010005875

Printed in the United States of America

To my wife, Jeanine, and my daughter, Joanna

—Andrew J. Dell'Olio

To my husband, Steve, and my sons, Paul and Matt

—Caroline J. Simon

Contents

	Preface	xi
Chapter 1	Ethics: Thinking about Right Conduct	1
Chapter 2	Religion and Morality	6
	The Bible	10
	The Qur'an	15
	The Bhagavad Gita	17
	Kai Nielsen, "God and the Basis of Morality"	23
	Richard J. Mouw, "Commands for Grown-ups"	38
	Parliament of the World's Religions, "Declaration Toward a Global Ethic"	51
	Study Questions	62
	For Further Reading	63
Chapter 3	Moral Relativism	64
	American Anthropological Association, "Statement on Human Rights"	67
	Louis Pojman, "The Case Against Ethical Relativism"	72
	Gilbert Harman, "Moral Relativism Defended"	91
	Loretta M. Kopelman, "Female Circumcision/Genital Mutilation and Ethical Relativism"	106
	Study Questions	123
	For Further Reading	124

Chapter 4	Natural Law Theory	125
	St. Thomas Aquinas, *Summa Theologica*	129
	Alan Donagan, "The Scholastic Theory of Moral Law in the Modern World"	138
	Joseph M. Boyle Jr., "Toward Understanding the Principle of Double Effect"	148
	Philippa Foot, "The Problem of Abortion and the Doctrine of the Double Effect"	159
	Study Questions	169
	For Further Reading	170
Chapter 5	Utilitarianism	171
	John Stuart Mill, *Utilitarianism*	174
	Bernard Williams, "A Critique of Utilitarianism"	181
	Brad Hooker, "Rule-Consequentialism"	188
	Peter Singer, "The Singer Solution to World Poverty"	201
	Study Questions	206
	For Further Reading	207
Chapter 6	Ethics of Duty	208
	Immanuel Kant, *Fundamental Principles of the Metaphysic of Morals*	211
	Marcia Baron, "Kantian Ethics"	224
	W. D. Ross, "What Makes Right Acts Right?"	234
	Judith Jarvis Thomson, "Killing, Letting Die, and the Trolley Problem"	240
	Study Questions	253
	For Further Reading	254
Chapter 7	Virtue Ethics	255
	Aristotle, *Nicomachean Ethics*	259
	Confucius, *Analects*	285
	David Hume, *An Enquiry Concerning the Principles of Morals*	292
	Alasdair MacIntyre, "The Nature of the Virtues"	298
	Thomas E. Hill Jr., "Ideals of Human Excellence and Preserving Natural Environments"	319
	Study Questions	334
	For Further Reading	335
Chapter 8	Challenges to Traditional Moral Theory	336
	Bernard Williams, "Morality, the Peculiar Institution"	340

	Friedrich Nietzsche, "The Natural History of Morals"	359
	Virginia Held, "Feminism and Moral Theory"	371
	Kwame Anthony Appiah, "The Demands of Identity"	389
	Cornel West, "Nihilism in Black America"	394
	Study Questions	401
	For Further Reading	402
Chapter 9	Living a Good Life	403
	Pierre Hadot, "Philosophy as a Way of Life"	407
	Plato, *Phaedo*	419
	Plato, *Republic*	425
	Epictetus, "The Enchiridion, or Manual"	442
	Lao-Tzu, "The Tao Te Ching"	445
	The Dalai Lama, "The Ethic of Compassion"	457
	Study Questions	462
	For Further Reading	463
	About the Editors	465

Preface

Why yet another introductory ethics text? As editors, we saw the need for a collection that ranged from classical to contemporary philosophers, included works from eastern as well as western traditions, and a fair sampling of both female and male authors. We have included the most influential ethical theories, while choosing selections that will not overwhelm the introductory student. While the emphasis is on theoretical ethics, selections on applied ethics are also included. For this reason the text should be useful for a range of ethics courses. The selections are rich and varied enough that the text could be used as a sole text in introductory ethics courses or as a supplement to a text in moral theory for upper-division ethics courses.

Introduction to Ethics: A Reader is divided into nine chapters. The first chapter introduces the nature of moral theory with a brief account of the different moral theories that follow in the text. Chapter 2 concerns the relationship between religion and morality and contains selections from representative sacred texts as well as philosophers with different perspectives on this issue. Chapters 3 through 7 are each devoted to a particular moral theory with readings that represent the position and those that challenge the position. Each of these chapters includes a selection that applies the theory to a particular moral problem. Chapter 8 is devoted to challenges to traditional moral theory from a number of perspectives, while chapter 9 is devoted to readings offering practical guidance on "living a good life." There is an introduction to each chapter that summarizes the major points of the selections with pointers on what to note as the selections are read.

Each chapter is followed by study questions and suggestions for further reading. The study questions can function in a variety of ways, depending on instructor discretion. Some instructors may wish to cull exam questions from the study questions. Other instructors may ask students to write journal entries on selected study questions. Other instructors may encourage students to use the study questions as aids for understanding the material without linking them to mechanisms for grading and accountability. The study questions are designed to generate student interest, guide them in philosophical and critical thinking, and aid in their understanding of each selection. The study questions range from ones that will help students with exposition and understanding of the texts to ones that will help students see connections between the materials and everyday issues in their own lives.

We are grateful to Hope College for the support given through Jacob E. Nyenhuis faculty development grants for several years while we worked on this book. In addition, we would like to thank Ross Miller for his support and encouragement from the onset of the project. Others at Rowman & Littlefield who deserve our thanks include Jonathan Sisk, Darcy Evans, and Janice Braunstein. We would also like to thank Lezlie Gruenler for her editorial assistance and Robin Litscher, Walter Nelson, and Sally Smith for their administrative help. Finally, we are grateful for the loving support of our spouses, Jeanine Dell'Olio and Steve Simon, throughout the process of bringing this book to fruition.

CHAPTER ONE

Ethics: Thinking about Right Conduct

Liz is enjoying her job as a volunteer at her neighborhood association fundraiser. Serving cake gives her something useful to do and also allows her to make friendly conversation with people who share her sense of the importance of building community within the neighborhood. She turns to the next person in line, looks up from placing a piece of cake on his extended plate, and swallows hard. "Hello, Liz. It's good to see you again. How have you been?" For the moment she is too stunned to speak.

Liz recognizes Ron immediately but had not noticed him in the room until now. She had no idea he was back in the neighborhood. The last time she saw him was at the sentencing hearing after his trial. For many years they had been next-door neighbors; she'd thought of him as a friend. She'd especially appreciated his befriending her oldest daughter, Brenda, because her husband, a long-distance truck driver, was often gone. Ron, she thought, made a great father-stand-in for Brenda.

That was before it all came to light. When Brenda was eleven, Ron initiated a sexual relationship with her that lasted until she was fourteen. At the time, Liz had no idea and no way of associating Brenda's increasing withdrawal, sadness and inability to concentrate in school with anything more than adolescent moodiness. Brenda finally talked with Liz about the whole thing only after Ron had been charged on the basis of complaints connected with other teenage girls.

Brenda had agreed to testify at his trial. But the strain of the legal process plunged her even deeper into depression. She'd become suicidal, been briefly institutionalized, and required years of therapy, which was not covered by insurance. She's better now, but a hole had been blown through her life and the ache of it has accompanied her into adulthood. It's no accident that she has chosen to stay close to her mother and lives in the same neighborhood as Liz.

Ron had served three years in prison after his conviction. "Paid his debt to society," some would say.

Now he's back.

This story, which is true (names changed for obvious reasons), raises a host of ethical questions. One of us heard this story directly from Liz, who was seeking advice about what she should do. Should she inform the neighborhood association "block captain" on Ron's street about his past? Or should she assume that his past behavior poses no present danger to children and say nothing? Liz's religious tradition teaches forgiveness. She'd struggled for years to forgive Ron and get over her anger over the damage his actions had done to Brenda. She thought she had forgiven him, but her first instinct on seeing him was to smash some cake into his face. Instead she'd turned away in silence and waited for him to move on. Is she obliged to work harder at forgiving him or is her continuing anger appropriate under the circumstances? Is she obliged to at least be civil to him if they meet again or does she have a right to scream? Should she tell her daughter that Ron is back in the neighborhood or hope that their paths do not cross? Should she confront Ron and insist that he has no right to move back to a place where his presence calls up so many painful memories for others?

Whatever advice you would give to Liz, much of it would be rooted in your sense of right and wrong, good and bad, and what it is to be a person of character and moral excellence. She is, after all, seeking advice about what she *should* do. Ethics (or moral philosophy) is a collection of evaluations of conduct or character based on what human beings, as such, should be and do. Ethical or moral evaluations are based on what human beings, as such, are owed.

One can tell that Liz is seeking ethical advice because she is not just asking about what it would be smart or prudent or self-protective to do. She is thinking about not just herself, and not even about just herself and her daughter, but also about how what she does or does not do will affect neighborhood children, and even about what Ron does or does not deserve. Ethics is the systematic study of a guide to conduct that gives appropriate weight to the interests of all who are affected by what one does.

Ethics contrasts not just with prudence but also with custom and law. Sociology, social psychology and anthropology are fields that strive to give systematic accounts of the actual customs, traditions and taboos of groups within particular societies at particular times. Some of these customs are informal and enforced by interpersonal attitudes. Others are codified into particular codes of law and are enforced by formal systems of penalties. We find out through empirical investigation and careful observation what the customs of a group are at a time.

To find out what the laws of a given society are, we go to trained experts who know which law codes to consult in answering particular legal questions.

Here is another example of when ethical reflection is needed: In a famous passage in Mark Twain's *Huckleberry Finn*, Huck is wrestling with the question of whether he should help his friend Jim escape. Huck lives in the antebellum South and knows that according to the laws of his society, Jim is a slave owned by Miss Watson. He knows that he is committing a crime by helping Jim escape. He knows that the majority of his fellow Southerners, and many U.S. citizens living in the North, disapprove of his aiding Jim's escape. Mark Twain strives to make his readers see that none of that settles the issue of what Huck should do. Twain is assuming that there is a standard for judging systems of customs and values by which we ought to live no matter what the customs and values of our society are. When we engage in ethical reflection we are trying to discern and apply a standard by which actual customs, laws, opinions and behaviors should be judged.

Ethical questions cannot be settled by answering the questions "What is customary?" or "What do most people do?" or "What is legal in this jurisdiction?" Ethics stands back from what we can find out by investigating custom and law and says, "I know it is customary, but is it right?" That's why we cannot just send Liz off to consult an attorney or a social scientist to find out what she should do from an ethical point of view.

There are, of course, significant disagreements about the content of ethics—about what we do owe one another and about what sorts of people we should strive to be. We are heirs to twenty-five hundred years of vital conversation about the nature and content of ethics.

Debates about the content of ethics take place between competing *normative ethical theories*. A central controversy within normative ethics is the disagreement over which is more fundamental to ethics: evaluations of actions or evaluations of the character of those who perform the actions? Several sections of this book contain essays concerning normative ethical theories that take action-evaluations as primary. Examples of such theories are natural law theory, various other forms of ethics of duty and utilitarianism. But as you will see when you read the essays in these sections, in many ways natural law theory and other theories of ethics of duty have more in common with one another than with different types of utilitarian theories. This is because another central controversy within ethics is the relationship of duty to the consequences, either actual or predicted, of actions. Utilitarians hold that examining the consequences of actions is the *basis* of determining what actions are or are not obligatory, while natural law theories and other duty-based ethical theories think that our obligations are *rooted in human nature or in the nature of morality itself*. Such views hold that our duties *limit* the extent to which we can take the consequences of our actions into account, while utilitarians think that our duties are *derived*, either directly or indirectly, from the consequences of our actions.

As deep as the division is between those who think that ethical evaluations of actions are based on consequences and those who think that ethical evaluations limit the extent to which consequences matter, this controversy is based on a common assumption that action-evaluation is of primary importance in ethics. Among the earliest systematic examinations of ethics, evaluations of traits of character were thought to be more fundamental than evaluations of action. The main ethical question for these thinkers was not "What action should I perform in this particular circumstance?" but "What sort of person should I be or become?" The idea is that *right actions* are a natural outgrowth of *being the best sort of person*. For virtue ethics, valuable character traits like honesty, courage, fair-mindedness, generosity, self-discipline, and even-temperedness are to be cultivated; damaging character traits like cruelty, laziness, dishonesty and cowardice are to be avoided.

Normative ethical theories like natural law theory, utilitarianism, duty ethics and virtue ethics are different ways of thinking systematically about the *content* of ethics. But the depth and persistence of the disagreements among normative ethical theories have given rise to questions *about* the ethics. Moral relativists, for example, have questioned whether there is any truth to the matter about what system of evaluating human conduct and character is most adequate. Earlier we said that ethics stands back from what we can find out by investigating custom and law and says, "I know it is customary, but is it right?" Moral relativists doubt that this is a meaningful question. Perhaps custom is the bedrock and our sense that there is something deeper or truer—a vantage point above or below all customs and laws in light of which they can be evaluated—is an illusion. Arguments for and against this view are discussed in the third chapter of this book.

From ancient times up to the present many have thought that ethics is deeply tied to religion. On the one hand, some have thought of ethics as being like law, except that it is God, not human legislators, whose decrees constitute and give a firm foundation to ethics. The famous Russian novelist Dostoevsky has one of his characters claim, "If there is no God then everything is permitted." Is this true? If it is, are we faced with another kind of moral relativism, because different religions make divergent claims about God's decrees? Or can all great religions find a common ground on which to base at least basic claims about duties and human decency? And where would this leave atheists? These debates are examined in this book's second chapter, on religion and morality.

In the same way that there have been challenges to traditional religious belief since the nineteenth century, there have also been challenges to both traditional moral theories and the very notion of morality itself. The selections in chapter 8 present some of these challenges. Some contemporary moral philosophers have been critical of the attempt to reduce the complexities of ethical decision-making to any one over-arching moral theory. These "anti-theorists" in ethics charge the standard moral theories with being abstract, impersonal and too concerned with the special notion of "obligation" to capture the very personal, fragile, situational nature of much of the ethical life. Others, like the iconoclastic Friedrich Nietzsche, challenge the basic assumptions of traditional Western morality and advocate an alternative system of values altogether. And recent cultural developments since the 1960s revolving around civil rights and women's rights have led to intellectual movements like feminism and multiculturalism that have questioned the objectivity of traditional Western moral theory while championing the perspectives of historically excluded groups. One cannot engage in thoughtful reflection about the nature of ethics without careful consideration of the issues raised in these challenges to traditional moral theory.

Ethics, of course, is not only moral theory. As important as it is to think through the foundational issues of morality, the main objective of ethical reflection is not how to theorize about morality, but to how to live well. The final chapter of the book includes a number of selections from the history of philosophy, both Eastern and Western, that offer to teach one the way to live a good human life. Here we find a recurring theme: that right living is the key to living well.

Selections in every chapter of this book invite you to ponder deep questions about how to live. The Greek philosopher Socrates claimed that the unexamined life is not worth living. Perhaps—but perhaps not. Unreflective people may stumble into living well. Yet surely an examined life is enriched by its self-reflection. Moreover, if each of us shapes our lives, and the lives of the communities we inhabit, on the basis of what we learn from grappling with the ideas of the authors represented throughout this book, we are likely to live more flourishing—and more fully human—lives.

For Further Reading

Becker, Lawrence C., and Charlotte B. Becker. *Encyclopedia of Ethics*. New York: Garland Press, 1992.

Donagan, Alan. *The Theory of Morality*. Chicago: University of Chicago Press, 1977.

Frankena, William. *Ethics*. Englewood Cliffs, NJ: Prentice-Hall, 1973.

MacIntyre, Alasdair. *A Short History of Ethics*. 2nd ed. Notre Dame, IN: University of Notre Dame Press, 1998.

Timmons, Mark. *Moral Theory: An Introduction*. Lanham, MD: Rowman & Littlefield, 2002.

CHAPTER TWO

Religion and Morality

If asked, many people would say they got their set of values, their sense of right or wrong, good and bad, from their religious background. Certainly, as a matter of historical fact, human value systems, moral ideals and codes of ethical conduct have been either derived from, or influenced by, religious teachings. But the historical relationship between religion and morality leaves unanswered the *philosophical* question of the origin of ethical principles. The moral philosopher asks, "On what ground does morality rest?"

Many theists would answer that morality is dependent upon religion since it is dependent on God. If there were no supreme being, there would be no objective moral truths. On this traditional view, God determines, either through God's nature, through the nature of God's creation, or by God's decrees, what is good and bad, right and wrong. Ethical principles and codes of right conduct are thus revealed through holy scriptures. For traditional believers, then, it is through the sacred texts of religion that we receive our guidance as to how to act rightly and lead a good life, as well as the moral exemplars that serve as models of good or virtuous persons.

Because of the importance that sacred texts have had in shaping their adherents' ethical views, this section includes brief selections from texts connected with Judaism, Christianity, Islam and Hinduism. Yet there are many more examples from the sacred texts of the world's religions than could be included in the limited space of this section. So before commenting on the selections, a brief survey of the ethical teachings of the principal world religions is in order.

Among world religions, three are monotheistic. **Judaism,** the oldest of the three, is rooted in a covenantal relationship between God and the Hebrew people.

A covenant is a binding agreement between a sovereign and a group of people. God becomes the sovereign of the Jews by rescuing them from oblivion and bondage, in order to make them a special witness to other nations of God's workings in the world. This covenantal relationship is maintained through certain obligations to God and others, revealed in the *Torah* (the first five books of the Hebrew scriptures), which constitutes the law that all Jews must follow. The *Torah* and the teachings of the books of the Hebrew prophets aim to establish justice within society and between human beings and God. **Christianity** grows out of the Jewish tradition and shares Judaism's concern for social justice. It breaks with Judaism theologically over the identity of Jesus, whom Christians believe to be God. While maintaining monotheism, Christians add that God is three-in-one: Creator (God "the Father"), Sustainer (the Holy Spirit) and Redeemer (Jesus Christ). Jesus and his followers, most notably Paul, move the locus of this concern from external rules to internal motivations. Love of God and neighbor becomes the primary ethical principle for Christians, who attempt to model their lives on the self-sacrificing love for others displayed in Christ. **Islam** originates in Arabia through the prophet Muhammad, who received and recited the *Qur'an*, the holy book for Muslims. Islam rejects the Christian notion of the Holy Trinity in favor of a strict monotheistic religion based on belief in Allah, the one God, who creates and governs all things through his will. Obedience to God's law or *shariah*, as revealed in the *Qur'an*, is the foundation of Muslim morality, which like Judaism aims to promote social justice and a right relationship with God. Muslims also find moral guidance in the deeds and sayings of Muhammad, as recorded in the *hadith*.

Two of the religions of the East, **Hinduism** and **Buddhism**, originate in India. While Hinduism is ostensibly polytheistic and Buddhism atheistic, both of these traditions have freedom from suffering as their principal aims, and both have devised sophisticated spiritual practices to enable their followers to achieve this goal, called *moksha* or *nirvana*, respectively. Each tradition also includes ethical teachings, based on the overcoming of selfish desires, as part of the path to spiritual liberation. Hinduism, however, has specific ethical duties for each of its social castes, while Buddhism rejects the caste system based on the inherent equality of all human beings. (We will encounter a contemporary version of Buddhist ethical teachings in chapter 9.)

Two of the religions of China, **Taoism** and **Confucianism**, have been enormously influential to the value systems and codes of conduct of Far East Asia, including Japan and Korea. These traditions are discussed in some detail in chapters 7 and 9 of this book.

Three of the selections that follow are representative sacred texts. The first selection is from the Bible, the source of much ethical thought in the West. The Ten Commandments from the book of Exodus lays out a mix of religious duties and some basic ethical principles. Jews and Christians have thought that all humans are obligated to follow at least the ethical rules about interpersonal behavior. The selection from Proverbs, also in the Hebrew scriptures, or Old Testament, as Christians refer to it, describes some of the qualities or virtues a person of good moral character should possess. The selection from the Gospel of Matthew of the New Testament presents Jesus's Sermon on the Mount, which introduces the Christian ethical principles of peace-making, gentleness, forgiveness, and unconditional love. Notice that Jesus seems to say that more is needed beyond refraining from the behaviors prohibited by the Ten Commandments. Internal attitudes matter as much, if not more, than rule-following. In the selections from 1 Corinthians and Colossians, the Apostle Paul, an important early follower of Jesus, extols various Christian virtues and required attitudes. Note that Paul ranks the virtue of love (*agape*) or charity (*caritas*) above the other principal Christian virtues, faith and hope. These biblical selections show that both duty-based ethics and virtue ethics can trace their root to the Judaic-Christian tradition. Utilitarian John Stuart Mill (see the selection on page 180.) maintained that Jesus's Golden Rule was another way of stating the Priniciple of Utility.

The second sacred text in this section is the *Qur'an*, from which we have chosen the brief opening *sura* (chapter) and a selection from the seventeenth *sura* entitled "The Night Journey." The opening *sura* is particularly important for Muslim practice as it is recited before each daily prayer period. It sums up the Muslim view that right conduct is founded on belief in God and adherence to God's commands. The second selection from the *Qur'an* lays out some basic ethical injunctions for Muslims, which, like the Ten Commandments, require having no other gods but God, respect for one's parents, and prohibitions against murder and adultery. In addition to general exhortations *against* miserliness, vengefulness, acting in ignorance and being prideful, and *for* keeping promises and acting fairly and justly, it also includes guidance for social practice, such as giving alms to those in need, caring for orphans, and refraining from infanticide.

The third sacred text in this section is the Bhagavad Gita (Song of the Lord) of Hinduism. The teachings of the Bhagavad Gita, written around the first century CE, are set against the backdrop of a battle between warring forces: symbolically, the battle of good versus evil. But as the opening line of the text reveals, this field of battle is the field of duty (*dharma*). Despite the fact that the kingdom rightly belongs to him, Arjuna, a warrior, is reluctant to wage war against his cousins, knowing well the evils of destruction, and having renounced the worldly goods gained by victory in battle. Yet, Hinduism teaches that persons are divided into specific social classes or castes, with the four traditional castes made up of priest-teachers, warriors, merchants and workers or servants. Each caste has its own set of prescribed ethical duties. As a member of the warrior caste, it is Arjuna's duty to fight. So Arjuna's reluctance to engage in battle presents an ethical dilemma. How is he to act?

In order to help Arjuna resolve his ethical dilemma, he is instructed by Lord Krishna, the divine incarnation of the god Vishnu, who appears as Arjuna's charioteer. Krishna teaches Arjuna how to reconcile his social duty as a warrior with his religious aspiration for salvation. Krishna does this by teaching that there are three ways (*yogas*) to achieve union with the divine, the ultimate goal of human life. These are (1) the way of *knowledge* (*jnana yoga*) or the ability to discern what is eternally true or real from what is merely transient illusion (*maya*); (2) the way of *devotion* (*bhakti yoga*) or the steadfast love of what is eternally real, namely, God; (3) the way of *detachment* (*karma yoga*) or the selfless attitude of sacrifice with regard to the fruits or consequences of one's actions. A fourth virtue may be added to this list, *discipline*, the word typically used to translate *yoga*. Discipline refers to the self-control or self-mastery that leads to equanimity and stability of mind, both of which are necessary for right action. In general, the Bhagavad Gita teaches that an action is right if it is done for the sake of God. The virtues of knowledge, devotion, detachment and discipline make such action possible.

As natural as it may seem to connect ethics to religion, this connection has been disputed since ancient times. The philosophical question of whether ethics is dependent on the will of a God or gods was raised in Plato's *Euthyphro*: do the gods love it because it is pious or is it pious because the gods love it? In other words, is something right because God wills it, or does God will it because it is right? Philosophers who believe that an ethical principle is right because God wills it espouse what has come to be known as "divine command theory." This ethical theory maintains that ethical principles are not autonomous, but derive from God's will. On this view, murder is wrong because God wills it so, as we discover, for example, in the Ten Commandments.

Of course, there are alternative philosophical ways of seeing the connection between God and morality. Some philosophers, such as St. Augustine, among others, influenced by Platonism, identify God's very being with goodness-itself. On this view, God's commands do not create moral obligation. Rather, God's nature is the ground of goodness, while the relation of creature to Creator is the ground of moral obligation. God's commands may bridge an epistemological gap about what we are obliged to do. This is something like a bridge position between divine command theory and natural law theory (see chapter 4).

In "God and the Basis of Morality," twentieth-century American Kai Nielsen objects to divine command theory on the grounds that it makes morality arbitrary. What if God commanded an act of murder, for example? Would this make murder morally right? For Nielsen, we must use some independent ethical standard to judge that God's commands are, in fact, right or good. On this view, God commands something because it is right, the rightness or wrongness of which is based on some ethical standard outside God's will. For Nielsen, not only is morality independent of God or religion, but, contrary to what some have argued, one does not need to believe in God in order to be a moral person, nor is belief in God necessary to lead a meaningful human life.

In the selection from his book *The God Who Commands*, contemporary philosophical theologian Richard J. Mouw defends the reasonableness of divine command theory. One objection that he addresses is the claim by opponents that divine command theory is a form of "infantile" obedience based on fear of punishment by a harsh, demanding God. Instead, Mouw maintains that divine commands must be seen within the context of the larger story of the kind of person a loving, wise God intends for us to be. In the same way it makes sense to obey any expert who has your best interests at heart, it makes sense to obey God's commands.

But what if divine commands conflict? For example, the selections from the Bible and the Bhagavad Gita seem to present very different ethical visions. This raises the question of ethical relativism. If ethical principles derive from sacred texts, and if there are many sacred texts with different religious teachings, does this mean that ethical principles are relative? Or is there a common core to the ethical principles that arise from the world's religions? The issue of moral relativism is addressed in the next chapter.

The final selection of this chapter is a recent attempt by leading participants in the World Parliament of Religions in 1993, based largely on the work of Swiss Roman Catholic theologian Hans Küng, to articulate some universal ethical principles based on the religious teachings of the world. The "Declaration Toward a Global Ethic" proclaims the intrinsic dignity, equality and unity of all persons grounded in the Golden Rule found in all religions: *What you do not wish done to yourself, do not do to others*. From this principle arise four basic ethical commitments: (1) to non-violence and respect for life, (2) to a culture of solidarity and a just economic order, (3) to a culture of tolerance and a life of truthfulness and (4) to a culture of equal rights and partnership between men and women. This selection is an example of applying ethical principles derived from religious traditions to the practical problems of war, economic injustice, racial and religious intolerance and social inequality.

The Bible*

Exodus, Chapter 20

[1] And God spake all these words, saying, [2] I *am* the LORD thy God, which have brought thee out of the land of Egypt, out of the house of bondage. [3] Thou shalt have no other gods before me. [4] Thou shalt not make unto thee

*King James edition (1611).

any graven image, or any likeness *of any thing* that *is* in heaven above, or that *is* in the earth beneath, or that *is* in the water under the earth: [5] Thou shalt not bow down thyself to them, nor serve them: for I the LORD thy God *am* a jealous God, visiting the iniquity of the fathers upon the children unto the third and fourth *generation* of them that hate me; [6] And shewing mercy unto thousands of them that love me, and keep my commandments. [7] Thou shalt not take the name of the LORD thy God in vain; for the LORD will not hold him guiltless that taketh his name in vain. [8] Remember the sabbath day, to keep it holy. [9] Six days shalt thou labour, and do all thy work: [10] But the seventh day *is* the sabbath of the LORD thy God: *in it* thou shalt not do any work, thou, nor thy son, nor thy daughter, thy manservant, nor thy maidservant, nor thy cattle, nor thy stranger that *is* within thy gates: [11] For *in* six days the LORD made heaven and earth, the sea, and all that in them *is*, and rested the seventh day: wherefore the LORD blessed the sabbath day, and hallowed it. [12] Honour thy father and thy mother: that thy days may be long upon the land which the LORD thy God giveth thee. [13] Thou shalt not kill. [14] Thou shalt not commit adultery. [15] Thou shalt not steal. [16] Thou shalt not bear false witness against thy neighbour. [17] Thou shalt not covet thy neighbour's house, thou shalt not covet thy neighbour's wife, nor his manservant, nor his maidservant, nor his ox, nor his ass, nor any thing that *is* thy neighbour's.

Proverbs, Chapter 16

[1] The preparations of the heart in man, and the answer of the tongue, *is* from the LORD. [2] All the ways of a man *are* clean in his own eyes; but the LORD weigheth the spirits. [3] Commit thy works unto the LORD, and thy thoughts shall be established. [4] The LORD hath made all *things* for himself: yea, even the wicked for the day of evil. [5] Every one *that is* proud in heart *is* an abomination to the LORD: *though* hand *join* in hand, he shall not be unpunished. [6] By mercy and truth iniquity is purged: and by the fear of the LORD *men* depart from evil. [7] When a man's ways please the LORD, he maketh even his enemies to be at peace with him. [8] Better *is* a little with righteousness than great revenues without right. [9] A man's heart deviseth his way: but the LORD directeth his steps. [10] A divine sentence *is* in the lips of the king: his mouth transgresseth not in judgment. [11] A just weight and balance *are* the LORD'S: all the weights of the bag *are* his work. [12] *It is* an abomination to kings to commit wickedness: for the throne is established by righteousness. [13] Righteous lips *are* the delight of kings; and they love him that speaketh right. [14] The wrath of a king *is as* messengers of death: but a wise man will pacify it. [15] In the light of the king's countenance *is* life; and his favour *is* as a cloud of the latter rain. [16] How much better *is it* to get wisdom than gold! and to get

understanding rather to be chosen than silver! [17] The highway of the upright *is* to depart from evil: he that keepeth his way preserveth his soul. [18] Pride *goeth* before destruction, and an haughty spirit before a fall. [19] Better *it is to be* of an humble spirit with the lowly, than to divide the spoil with the proud. [20] He that handleth a matter wisely shall find good: and whoso trusteth in the LORD, happy *is* he. [21] The wise in heart shall be called prudent: and the sweetness of the lips increaseth learning. [22] Understanding *is* a wellspring of life unto him that hath it: but the instruction of fools *is* folly. [23] The heart of the wise teacheth his mouth, and addeth learning to his lips. [24] Pleasant words *are as* an honeycomb, sweet to the soul, and health to the bones. [25] There is a way that seemeth right unto a man, but the end thereof *are* the ways of death. [26] He that laboureth laboureth for himself; for his mouth craveth it of him. [27] An ungodly man diggeth up evil: and in his lips *there is* as a burning fire. [28] A froward man soweth strife: and a whisperer separateth chief friends. [29] A violent man enticeth his neighbour, and leadeth him into the way *that is* not good. [30] He shutteth his eyes to devise froward things: moving his lips he bringeth evil to pass. [31] The hoary head *is* a crown of glory, *if* it be found in the way of righteousness. [32] *He that is* slow to anger *is* better than the mighty; and he that ruleth his spirit than he that taketh a city. [33] The lot is cast into the lap; but the whole disposing thereof *is* of the LORD.

Matthew, Chapter 5

[1] And seeing the multitudes, he went up into a mountain: and when he was set, his disciples came unto him: [2] And he opened his mouth, and taught them, saying, [3] Blessed *are* the poor in spirit: for theirs is the kingdom of heaven. [4] Blessed *are* they that mourn: for they shall be comforted. [5] Blessed *are* the meek: for they shall inherit the earth. [6] Blessed *are* they which do hunger and thirst after righteousness: for they shall be filled. [7] Blessed *are* the merciful: for they shall obtain mercy. [8] Blessed *are* the pure in heart: for they shall see God. [9] Blessed *are* the peacemakers: for they shall be called the children of God. [10] Blessed *are* they which are persecuted for righteousness sake: for theirs is the kingdom of heaven. [11] Blessed are ye, when *men* shall revile you, and persecute *you*, and shall say all manner of evil against you falsely, for my sake. [12] Rejoice, and be exceeding glad: for great *is* your reward in heaven: for so persecuted they the prophets which were before you. [13] Ye are the salt of the earth: but if the salt have lost his savour, wherewith shall it be salted? it is thenceforth good for nothing, but to be cast out, and to be trodden under foot of men. [14] Ye are the light of the world. A city that is set on an hill cannot be hid. [15] Neither do men light a candle, and put it under a bushel, but on a candlestick; and it giveth light unto all that are in the house. [16] Let your light so shine before men, that they may see your good works, and glorify your Father which is in heaven. [17] Think

not that I am come to destroy the law, or the prophets: I am not come to destroy, but to fulfil. [18] For verily I say unto you, Till heaven and earth pass, one jot or one tittle shall in no wise pass from the law, till all be fulfilled. [19] Whosoever therefore shall break one of these least commandments, and shall teach men so, he shall be called the least in the kingdom of heaven: but whosoever shall do and teach *them*, the same shall be called great in the kingdom of heaven. [20] For I say unto you, That except your righteousness shall exceed *the righteousness* of the scribes and Pharisees, ye shall in no case enter into the kingdom of heaven. [21] Ye have heard that it was said by them of old time, Thou shalt not kill; and whosoever shall kill shall be in danger of the judgment: [22] But I say unto you, That whosoever is angry with his brother without a cause shall be in danger of the judgment: and whosoever shall say to his brother, Raca, shall be in danger of the council: but whosoever shall say, Thou fool, shall be in danger of hell fire. [23] Therefore if thou bring thy gift to the altar, and there rememberest that thy brother hath ought against thee; [24] Leave there thy gift before the altar, and go thy way; first be reconciled to thy brother, and then come and offer thy gift. [25] Agree with thine adversary quickly, whiles thou art in the way with him; lest at any time the adversary deliver thee to the judge, and the judge deliver thee to the officer, and thou be cast into prison. [26] Verily I say unto thee, Thou shalt by no means come out thence, till thou hast paid the uttermost farthing. [27] Ye have heard that it was said by them of old time, Thou shalt not commit adultery: [28] But I say unto you, That whosoever looketh on a woman to lust after her hath committed adultery with her already in his heart. [29] And if thy right eye offend thee, pluck it out, and cast *it* from thee: for it is profitable for thee that one of thy members should perish, and not *that* thy whole body should be cast into hell. [30] And if thy right hand offend thee, cut if off, and cast it from thee: for it is profitable for thee that one of thy members should perish, and not *that* thy whole body should be cast into hell. [31] It hath been said, Whosoever shall put away his wife, let him give her a writing of divorcement: [32] But I say unto you, That whosoever shall put away his wife, saving for the cause of fornication, causeth her to commit adultery: and whosoever shall marry her that is divorced committeth adultery. [33] Again, ye have heard that it hath been said by them of old time, Thou shalt not forswear thyself, but shalt perform unto the Lord thine oaths: [34] But I say unto you, Swear not at all; neither by heaven; for it is God's throne: [35] Nor by the earth; for it is his footstool: neither by Jerusalem; for it is the city of the great King. [36] Neither shalt thou swear by thy head, because thou canst not make one hair white or black. [37] But let your communication be, Yea, yea; Nay, nay: for whatsoever is more than these cometh of evil. [38] Ye have heard that it hath been said, An eye for an eye, and a tooth for a tooth: [39] But I say unto you, That ye resist not evil: but whosoever shall smite thee on thy right cheek, turn to him the other also. [40] And if any man will sue thee at the law, and take away thy coat, let him have *thy* cloke also. [41] And whosoever shall compel thee to go a mile, go with him twain. [42] Give to him that asketh thee, and from him that would borrow of thee turn not thou away. [43] Ye have heard that it hath been said, Thou shalt love thy neighbour, and hate thine enemy. [44] But I say unto you, Love your enemies, bless them that curse you, do good to them that hate you, and pray for them which despitefully use you, and persecute you; [45] That ye may be the children of your Father which is in heaven: for he maketh his sun to rise on the evil and on the good, and sendeth rain on the just and on the unjust. [46] For if ye love them which love you, what reward have ye? do not even the publicans the same? [47] And if ye salute your brethren only, what do ye more *than others?* do not even the publicans so? [48] Be ye therefore perfect, even as your Father which is in heaven is perfect.

1 Corinthians, Chapter 13

[1] Though I speak with the tongues of men and of angels, and have not charity, I am become *as* sounding brass, or a tinkling cymbal. [2] And though I have *the gift of* prophecy, and understand all mysteries, and all knowledge; and though I have all faith, so that I could remove mountains, and have not charity, I am nothing. [3] And though I bestow all my goods to feed *the poor*, and though I give my body to be burned, and have not charity, it profiteth me nothing. [4] Charity suffereth long, *and* is kind; charity envieth not; charity vaunteth not itself, is not puffed up, [5] Doth not behave itself unseemly, seeketh not her own, is not easily provoked, thinketh no evil; [6] Rejoiceth not in iniquity, but rejoiceth in the truth; [7] Beareth all things, believeth all things, hopeth all things, endureth all things. [8] Charity never faileth: but whether *there be* prophecies, they shall fail; whether *there be* tongues, they shall cease; whether *there be* knowledge, it shall vanish away. [9] For we know in part, and we prophesy in part. [10] But when that which is perfect is come, then that which is in part shall be done away. [11] When I was a child, I spake as a child, I understood as a child, I thought as a child: but when I became a man, I put away childish things. [12] For now we see through a glass, darkly; but then face to face: now I know in part; but then shall I know even as also I am known. [13] And now abideth faith, hope, charity, these three; but the greatest of these *is* charity.

Colossians, Chapter 3

[1] If ye then be risen with Christ, seek those things which are above, where Christ sitteth on the right hand of God. [2] Set your affection on things above, not on things on the earth. [3] For ye are dead, and your life is hid with Christ in God. [4] When Christ, *who is* our life, shall appear, then shall ye also appear with him in glory. [5] Mortify therefore your members which are upon the earth; fornication, uncleanness, inordinate affection, evil concupiscence, and covetousness, which is

idolatry: [6] For which things' sake the wrath of God cometh on the children of disobedience: [7] In the which ye also walked some time, when ye lived in them. [8] But now ye also put off all these; anger, wrath, malice, blasphemy, filthy communication out of your mouth. [9] Lie not one to another, seeing that ye have put off the old man with his deeds; [10] And have put on the new *man*, which is renewed in knowledge after the image of him that created him: [11] Where there is neither Greek nor Jew, circumcision nor uncircumcision, Barbarian, Scythian, bond *nor* free: but Christ *is* all, and in all. [12] Put on therefore, as the elect of God, holy and beloved, bowels of mercies, kindness, humbleness of mind, meekness, longsuffering; [13] Forbearing one another, and forgiving one another, if any man have a quarrel against any: even as Christ forgave you, so also *do* ye. [14] And above all these things *put on* charity, which is the bond of perfectness. [15] And let the peace of God rule in your hearts, to which also ye are called in one body; and be ye thankful. [16] Let the word of Christ dwell in you richly in all wisdom; teaching and admonishing one another in psalms and hymns and spiritual songs, singing with grace in your hearts to the Lord. [17] And whatsoever ye do in word or deed, *do* all in the name of the Lord Jesus, giving thanks to God and the Father by him. [18] Wives, submit yourselves unto your own husbands, as it is fit in the Lord. [19] Husbands, love *your* wives, and be not bitter against them. [20] Children, obey *your* parents in all things: for this is well pleasing unto the Lord. [21] Fathers, provoke not your children *to anger*, lest they be discouraged. [22] Servants, obey in all things *your* masters according to the flesh; not with eyeservice, as menpleasers; but in singleness of heart, fearing God: [23] And whatsoever ye do, do *it* heartily, as to the Lord, and not unto men; [24] Knowing that of the Lord ye shall receive the reward of the inheritance: for ye serve the Lord Christ. [25] But he that doeth wrong shall receive for the wrong which he hath done: and there is no respect of persons.

The Qur'an*

The Opening Chapter

(I. Mecca)

In the name of the merciful and compassionate God.

Praise belongs to God, the Lord of the worlds, the merciful, the compassionate, the ruler of the day of judgment! Thee we serve and Thee we ask for aid. [5]

---

*The Qur'an. Translated by E. H. Palmer in *Sacred Books of the East*, edited by Max Müller (Oxford: Clarendon Press, 1880).

Guide us in the right path, the path of those Thou art gracious to; not of those Thou art wroth with; nor of those who err.

The Chapter of the Night Journey

(XVII. Mecca)

Verily, this Qur'an guides to the straightest path, and gives the glad tidings to the believers [10] who do aright that for them is a great hire; and that for those who believe not in the hereafter, we have prepared a mighty woe.

Man prays for evil as he prays for good; and man was ever hasty.

We made the night and the day two signs; and we blot out the sign of the night and make the sign of the day visible, that ye may seek after plenty from your Lord, and that ye may number the years and the reckoning; and we have detailed everything in detail.

And every man's augury have we fastened on his neck; and we will bring forth for him on the resurrection day a book offered to him wide open. [15] "'Read thy book, thou art accountant enough against thyself to-day!'"

He who accepts guidance, accepts it only for his own soul: and he who errs, errs only against it; nor shall one burdened soul bear the burden of another.

Nor would we punish until we had sent an apostle. And when we desired to destroy a city we bade the opulent ones thereof; and they wrought abomination therein; and its due sentence was pronounced; and we destroyed it with utter destruction.

How many generations have we destroyed after Noah! but thy Lord of the sins of his servant is well aware, and sees enough.

Whoso is desirous of this life that hastens away, we will hasten on for him therein what we please,—for whom we please. Then we will make hell for him to broil in—despised and outcast.

[20] But whoso desires the next life, and strives for it and is a believer—these, their striving shall be gratefully received.

To all—these and those—will we extend the gifts of thy Lord; for the gifts of thy Lord are not restricted.

See how we have preferred some of them over others, but in the next life are greater degrees and greater preference.

Put not with God other gods, or thou wilt sit despised and forsaken.

Thy Lord has decreed that ye shall not serve other than Him; and kindness to one's parents, whether one or both of them reach old age with thee; and say not to them, "'Fie!'" and do not grumble at them, but speak to them a generous speech. [25] And lower to them the wing of humility out of compassion, and say, "'O Lord! have compassion on them as they brought me up when I was little!'"

Your Lord knows best what is in your souls if ye be righteous, and, verily, He is forgiving unto those who come back penitent.

And give thy kinsman his due and the poor and the son of the road; and waste not wastefully, for the wasteful were ever the devil's brothers; and the devil is ever ungrateful to his Lord.

[30] But if thou dost turn away from them to seek after mercy from thy Lord, which thou hopest for, then speak to them an easy speech.

Make not thy hand fettered to thy neck, nor yet spread it out quite open, lest thou shouldst have to sit down blamed and straitened in means. Verily, thy Lord spreads out provision to whomsoever He will or He doles it out. Verily, He is ever well aware of and sees His servants.

And slay not your children for fear of poverty; we will provide for them; beware! for to slay them is ever a great sin!

And draw not near to fornication; verily, it is ever an abomination, and evil is the way thereof.

[35] And slay not the soul that God has forbidden you, except for just cause; for he who is slain unjustly we have given his next of kin authority; yet let him not exceed in slaying; verily, he is ever helped.

And draw not near to the wealth of the orphan, save to improve it, until he reaches the age of puberty, and fulfil your compacts; verily, a compact is ever enquired of.

And give full measure when ye measure out, and weigh with a right balance; that is better and a fairer determination.

And do not pursue that of which thou hast no knowledge; verily, the hearing, the sight, and the heart, all of these shall be enquired of.

And walk not on the earth proudly; verily, thou canst not cleave the earth, and thou shalt not reach the mountains in height.

[40] All this is ever evil in the sight of your Lord and abhorred.

The Bhagavad Gita*

Chapter I

Arguna said:

Seeing these kinsmen, O Krishna! standing here desirous to engage in battle, my limbs droop down; my mouth is quite dried up; a tremor comes on my body; and my hairs stand on end; the Gândîva bow slips from my hand; my

*Bhagavadgita. Translated by Kashinath TrimbakTelang in *Sacred Books of the East*, edited by Max Müller (Oxford: Clarendon Press, 1882).

skin burns intensely. I am unable, too, to stand up; my mind whirls round, as it were; O Kesava! I see adverse omens; and I do not perceive any good to accrue after killing my kinsmen in the battle. I do not wish for victory, O Krishna! nor sovereignty, nor pleasures: what is sovereignty to us, O Govinda! what enjoyments, and even life? Even those, for whose sake we desire sovereignty, enjoyments, and pleasures, are standing here for battle, abandoning life and wealth—preceptors, fathers, sons as well as grandfathers, maternal uncles, fathers-in-law, grandsons, brothers-in-law, as also other relatives. These I do not wish to kill, though they kill me, O destroyer of Madhu! even for the sake of sovereignty over the three worlds, how much less then for this earth alone? What joy shall be ours, O Ganârdana! after killing Dhritarâshtra's sons? Killing these felons we shall only incur sin. Therefore it is not proper for us to kill our own kinsmen, the sons of Dhritarâshtra. For how, O Mâdhava! shall we be happy after killing our own relatives? Although having their consciences corrupted by avarice, they do not see the evils flowing from the extinction of a family, and the sin in treachery to friends, still, O Ganârdana! should not we, who do see the evils flowing from the extinction of a family, learn to refrain from that sin? On the extinction of a family, the eternal rites of families are destroyed. Those rites being destroyed, impiety predominates over the whole family. In consequence of the predominance of impiety, O Krishna! the women of the family become corrupt; and the women becoming corrupt, O descendant of Vrishni! intermingling of castes results; that intermingling necessarily leads the family and the destroyers of the family to hell; for when the ceremonies of offering the balls of food and water to them fail, their ancestors fall down to hell. By these transgressions of the destroyers of families, which occasion interminglings of castes, the eternal rites of castes and rites, of families are subverted. And O Ganârdana! we have heard that men whose family-rites are subverted, must necessarily live in hell. Alas! we are engaged in committing a heinous sin, seeing that we are making efforts for killing our own kinsmen out of greed of the pleasures of sovereignty. If the sons of Dhritarâshtra, weapon in hand, should kill me in battle, me weaponless and not defending myself, that would be better for me.

Sañgaya said:

Having spoken thus, Arguna cast aside his bow together with the arrows, on the battle-field, and sat down in his chariot, with a mind agitated by grief.

Chapter II

Sañgaya said:

To him, who was thus overcome with pity, and dejected, and whose eyes were full of tears and turbid, the destroyer of Madhu spoke these words.

The Deity said:

How comes it that this delusion, O Arguna! which is discarded by the good, which excludes from heaven, and occasions infamy, has overtaken you in this place of peril? Be not effeminate, O son of Prithâ! it is not worthy of you. Cast off this base weakness of heart, and arise, O terror of your foes!

Arguna said:

How, O destroyer of Madhu! shall I encounter with arrows in the battle Bhîshma and Drona—both, O destroyer of enemies! entitled to reverence? Not killing my preceptors—men of great glory—it is better to live even on alms in this world. But killing them, though they are avaricious of worldly goods, I should only enjoy blood-tainted enjoyments. Nor do we know which of the two is better for us—whether that we should vanquish them, or that they should vanquish us. Even those, whom having killed, we do not wish to live—even those sons of Dhritarâshtra stand arrayed against us. With a heart contaminated by the taint of helplessness, with a mind confounded about my duty, I ask you. Tell me what is assuredly good for me. I am your disciple; instruct me, who have thrown myself on your indulgence. For I do not perceive what is to dispel that grief which will dry up my organs after I shall have obtained a prosperous kingdom on earth without a foe, or even the sovereignty of the gods.

Sañgaya said:

Having spoken thus to Hrishîkesa, O terror of your foes! Gudâkesa said to Govinda, 'I shall not engage in battle;' and verily remained silent. To him thus desponding between the two armies, O descendant of Bharata! Hrishîkesa spoke these words with a slight smile.

The Deity said:

You have grieved for those who deserve no grief, and you talk words of wisdom. Learned men grieve not for the living nor the dead. Never did I not exist, nor you, nor these rulers of men; nor will any one of us ever hereafter cease to be. As, in this body, infancy and youth and old age come to the embodied self, so does the acquisition of another body; a sensible man is not deceived about that The contacts of the senses, O son of Kuntî! which produce cold and heat, pleasure and pain, are not permanent, they are ever coming and going. Bear them, O descendant of Bharata! For, O chief of men! that sensible man whom they afflict not (pain and pleasure being alike to him), he merits immortality. There is no existence for that which is unreal; there is no non-existence for that which is real. And the correct conclusion about both is perceived by those who perceive the truth. Know that to be indestructible which pervades all this; the destruction of that inexhaustible principle none can bring about. These bodies appertaining to the embodied self which is eternal, indestructible, and indefinable, are said to be perishable; therefore do engage in battle, O descendant of Bharata! He who thinks it to be the killer and he who thinks it to be killed, both know nothing. It kills not, is not killed. It is not born, nor does it ever die, nor, having existed, does it exist no more. Unborn, everlasting, unchangeable, and primeval, it is not killed when the body is killed. O son of Prithâ! how can that man who knows it thus to be indestructible, everlasting, unborn, and inexhaustible, how and whom can he kill, whom can he cause to be killed? As a man, casting off old clothes, puts on others and new ones, so the embodied self casting off old bodies, goes to others and new ones. Weapons do not divide it into pieces; fire does not burn it, waters do not moisten it; the wind does not dry it up. It is not divisible; it is not combustible; it is not to be moistened; it is not to be dried up. It is everlasting, all-pervading, stable, firm, and eternal. It is said to be unperceived, to be unthinkable, to be unchangeable. Therefore knowing it to be such, you ought not to grieve, But even if you think that it is constantly born, and constantly dies, still, O you of mighty arms! you ought not to grieve thus. For to one that is born, death is certain; and to one that dies, birth is certain. Therefore about this unavoidable thing, you ought not to grieve. The source of things, O descendant of Bharata! is unperceived; their middle state is perceived; and their end again is unperceived. What occasion is there for any lamentation regarding them? One looks upon it as a wonder; another similarly speaks of it as a wonder; another too hears of it as a wonder; and even after having heard of it, no one does really know it. This embodied self, O descendant of Bharata! within every one's body is ever indestructible. Therefore you ought not to grieve for any being. Having regard to your own duty also, you ought not to falter, for there is nothing better for a Kshatriya than a righteous battle. Happy those Kshatriyas, O son of Prithâ! who can find such a battle to fight—come of itself—an open door to heaven! But if you will not fight this righteous battle, then you will have abandoned your own duty and your fame, and you will incur sin. All beings, too, will tell of your everlasting infamy; and to one who has been honoured, infamy is a greater evil than death. Warriors who are masters of great cars will think that you abstained from the battle through fear, and having been highly thought of by them, you will fall down to littleness. Your enemies, too, decrying your power, will speak much about you that should not be spoken. And what, indeed, more lamentable than that? Killed, you will obtain heaven; victorious, you will enjoy the earth. Therefore arise, O son of Kuntî! resolved to engage in battle. Looking alike on pleasure and pain, on gain and loss, on victory and defeat, then prepare for battle, and thus you will not incur sin. The knowledge here declared to you is that relating to the Sânkhya,. Now hear that relating to the Yoga. Possessed of this knowledge, O son of Prithâ! you will cast off the bonds of action. In this path to final emancipation nothing that is commenced becomes abortive; no obstacles exist; and even a little of this form of piety protects one from great danger. There is here, O descendant of Kuru! but one state of mind consisting in firm understanding. But the states of mind of those who have no firm understanding are many-branched and endless. The state of mind consisting in firm understanding regarding steady contemplation does not belong to those, O son of Prithâ! who are strongly attached to worldly pleasures and power, and whose minds are drawn away by that flowery talk which is full of (ordinances of) specific acts for the attainment of those pleasures and that power, and which promises birth as the fruit of acts—that flowery talk which those unwise ones utter, who are enamoured of Vedic words, who say there is nothing else, who are full of desires, and whose goal is heaven. The Vedas merely relate to the effects of the three qualities; do you, O Arguna! rise above those effects of the three qualities, and be free from the pairs of opposites, always preserve courage, be free from anxiety for new acquisitions or protection of old acquisitions, and be self-controlled. To the instructed Brâhmana, there is in all the Vedas as much utility as in a reservoir of water into which waters flow from all sides. Your business is with action alone; not by any means with fruit. Let not the fruit of action be your motive to action. Let not your attachment be fixed on inaction. Having recourse to devotion, O Dhanañgaya! perform actions, casting off all attachment, and being equable in success or ill-success; such equability is called devotion. Action, O Dhanañgaya! is far inferior to the devotion of the mind. In that devotion seek shelter. Wretched are those whose motive (to action) is the fruit of action. He who has obtained devotion in this world casts off both merit and sin. Therefore apply yourself to devotion; devotion in all actions is wisdom. The wise who have obtained devotion cast off the fruit of action; and released from the shackles of repeated births, repair to that seat where there is no unhappiness. When your mind shall have crossed beyond the taint of delusion, then will you become indifferent to all that you have heard or will heard. When your mind, confounded by what you have heard, will stand firm and steady in contemplation, then will you acquire devotion.

Arguna said:

What are the characteristics, O Kesava! of one whose mind is steady, and who is intent on contemplation? How should one of steady mind speak, how sit, how move?

The Deity said:

When a man, O son of Prithâ! abandons all the desires of his heart, and is pleased in his self only and by his self, he is then called one of steady mind. He whose heart is not agitated in the midst of calamities, who has no longing for pleasures, and from whom the feelings of affection, fear, and wrath have departed, is called a sage of steady mind. His mind is steady, who, being without attachments anywhere, feels no exultation and no aversion on encountering the various agreeable and disagreeable things of this world. A man's mind is steady, when he withdraws his senses from all objects of sense, as the tortoise withdraws its limbs from all sides. Objects of sense draw back from a person who is abstinent; not so the taste for those objects. But even the taste departs from him, when he has seen the Supreme. The boisterous senses, O son of Kuntî! carry away by force the mind even of a wise man, who exerts himself for final emancipation. Restraining them all, a man should remain engaged in devotion, making me his only resort. For his mind is steady whose senses are under his control. The man who ponders over objects of sense forms an attachment to them; from that attachment is produced desire; and from desire anger is produced; from anger results want of discrimination; from want of discrimination, confusion of the memory; from confusion of the memory, loss of reason; and in consequence of loss of reason. he is utterly ruined. But the self-restrained man who moves among objects with senses under the control of his own self, and free from affection and aversion, obtains tranquillity. When there is tranquillity, all his miseries are destroyed, for the mind of him whose heart is tranquil soon becomes steady. He who is not self-restrained has no steadiness of mind; nor has he who is not self-restrained perseverance in the pursuit of self-knowledge; there is no tranquillity for him who does not persevere in the pursuit of self-knowledge; and whence can there be happiness for one who is not tranquil? For the heart which follows the rambling senses leads away his judgment, as the wind leads a boat astray upon the waters. Therefore, O you of mighty arms! his mind is steady whose senses are restrained on all sides from objects of sense. The self-restrained man is awake, when it is night for all beings; and when all beings are awake, that is the night of the right-seeing sage. He into whom all objects of desire enter, as waters enter the ocean, which, though replenished, still keeps its position unmoved,—he only obtains tranquillity; not he who desires those objects of desire. The man who, casting off all desires, lives free from attachments, who is free from egoism, and from the feeling that this or that is mine, obtains tranquillity. This, O son of Prithâ! is the Brahmic state; attaining to this, one is never deluded; and remaining in it in one's last moments, one attains brahma-nirvâna, the Brahmic bliss.

God and the Basis of Morality*

Kai Nielsen

I

Consider the fundamental religious beliefs common to the Judeo-Christian-Islamic traditions. If, as it seems likely, they cannot be proven to be true, can they be reasonably believed to be true because they can in some other way be justified? What I want to know is whether it is more reasonable to hold fundamental religious beliefs, such as there is a God and that we shall survive the death of our present bodies, than not to hold them. (I have discussed such general questions in Nielsen, 1971a, 1971b, 1973a and 1982a.)

Part of that probing, the whole of which is surely complicated and many faceted, will be the burden of this essay. Here I shall put questions of immortality and bodily resurrection aside and only consider what is indeed even more central to Judaism and Christianity, namely belief in God. It is—rightly or wrongly—widely believed now that no proof can be given of God's existence and that it is not even the case that we can give evidence or grounds for the claim that it is probable that God exists. Indeed, the very notion of trying to do any of these things is frequently thought to be a confusion based on a misconception of the realities of Jewish and Christian belief. (There are forceful statements of this in MacIntyre, 1957 and 1959.) But it is also sometimes thought that such apologetic moves are entirely unnecessary, for, scandal to the intellect or not, a reasonable, morally concerned human being will accept God humbly on faith, for, without that faith and the belief in God which it entails, morality, human integrity, and the basis of our self-respect will be undermined and life will be revealed as an utterly useless passion. We must believe in God to make sense of our lives and to find a moral Archimedean point. Whatever intellectual impediments we have to belief in God, such a religious belief is morally necessary. Without it we can hardly have a rooted moral belief-system and without that, as social theorists such as Durkheim and Bell have stressed, we cannot have a stable, well-ordered society. I am not suggesting that the claim is, or should be, that we can "will to believe" but I am asserting that the apologetic claim is that without belief in the God characteristic of the Judeo-Christian-Islamic tradition reasonable people should conclude that a moral community is impossible and that life is indeed meaningless.

---

*Kai Nielsen, "God and the Basis of Morality" in *The Journal of Religious Ethics* 10, no. 2 (Fall 1982): 335–50. Reprinted with permission.

I shall argue that such an apologetic claim has not been sustained. There are in my judgment fundamental unresolved questions about the foundations of morality, and attempts, such as those of Mill, Kant, Sidgwick, and Rawls, to lay out a systematic moral philosophy to assess our moral practices and social institutions have not been remarkable for their success (Nielsen, 1982b, 1982c). But such difficulties notwithstanding, there is no good ground for claiming that only through belief in God can we attain a sufficient moral anchorage to make sense of our tangled lives. I shall argue that there is some moral understanding that is *logically independent* of belief in God and is necessary even to be able to understand the concept of God and that, God or no God, some actions can be appreciated to be desirable and some as through and through evil and despicable. It is not true that if God is dead nothing matters. Belief in God cannot be justified, shown to be something we must just accept, if we are to be through and through reasonable, because it is a necessary foundation for the moral life. That, I shall argue, is just not so.

II

Let us first ask: "Is something good because God wills or commands it or does God command it because it is good?" If we say God commands it *because* it is good, this implies that something can be good independently of God. This is so because "God commands it because it is good" implies that God apprehends it to be good or takes it to be good or in some way knows it to be good and then tells us to do it. But if God does this, then it is at least *logically* possible for us to come to see or in some way know or come to appreciate that it is good without God's telling us to do it or informing us that it is good. Moreover, on this alternative, its goodness does not depend on its being willed by God or even on there being a God.

The points made above need explanation and justification. In making those remarks, I am giving to understand that good is not a creation of God but rather that something is good is something which is itself apprehended by God or known by God. (If all that talk seems too "cognitive" a way to speak of moral notions, we can alternatively speak of God's appreciating something to be good.) If this is so, it is in some way there to be apprehended or known or appreciated and thus it is at least *logically* possible for us to apprehend it or know it or appreciate it without knowing anything of God. Furthermore, since God himself apprehends it to be good and since it doesn't, on this alternative, become good simply because he wills it or commands it, there can be this goodness even in a godless world. Translated into the concrete, this means that, at the very least, it could be correct to assert that even in a world without God, killing little children is evil and caring for them is good.

Someone might grant that there is this logical (conceptual) independence of morality from religion, but still argue that, given man's corrupt and vicious nature in his fallen state, he, as a matter of fact, needs God's help to understand what is good, to know what he ought to do and to quite categorically bind himself to striving to act as morality requires.

Though there is indeed extensive corruption in the palace of justice, such a response is still confused. With or without a belief in God, we can recognize such corruption. In some concrete situations at least, we understand perfectly well what is good, what we ought to do, and what morality requires of us. Moreover, the corruption religious apologists have noted does not lie here. The corruption comes not principally in our knowledge or understanding but in our "weakness of will." We find it in our inability to do what in a cool hour, we acknowledge to be good—"the good I would do that I do not." Religion, for some people at any rate, may be of value in putting their *hearts* into virtue, but that religion is necessary for some in this way does not show us how it can provide us with a knowledge of good and evil or an ultimate criterion for making such judgments (Toulmin, 1950: 202–225). It does not provide us, even if we are believers, with an ultimate standard of goodness.

Suppose we say instead—as Emil Brunner (1947) or C. E Henry (1957), for example, surely would—that an action or attitude is right or good simply because God *wills* it or *commands* it. Its goodness arises from Divine *fiat*. God makes something good simply by commanding it.

Can *anything* be good or become good simply by being commanded or willed? Can a fiat, command, or ban *create* goodness or moral obligation? I do not think so. To see that it cannot, consider first some ordinary, mundane examples of ordering or commanding. Suppose I tell my students in a class I am teaching, "You must get a looseleaf notebook for this class." My commanding it, my telling my class they must do it, does not *eo ipso* make it something they *ought* to do or even make doing it good, though it might make it a prudent thing for them to do. But, whether or not it is prudent for them to do it, given my position of authority *vis-à-vis* them, it is, if there are no reasons for it, a perfectly arbitrary injunction on my part and not some thing that could correctly be said to be good.

Suppose, to use another example, a mother says to her college-age daughter, "It's not a good thing to go to school dressed like that." Her telling her daughter that does not *eo ipso* make her daughter's manner of dress a bad thing. For her mother to be right here, she must be able to give reasons for her judgment that her daughter ought not to dress like that.

More generally speaking, the following are all perfectly intelligible:

X wills y but should I do it?
X commands it but is it good?

X told me to do it, but all the same I ought not to do it.
X proclaimed it but all the same what he proclaimed is evil.

(3) and (4) are not contradictions and (1) and (2) are not senseless, self-answering questions like "Is a wife a married woman?" This clearly indicates that the moral concepts "'should,'" "'good,'" and "'ought'" are not identified with the willing of something, the commanding or the proclaiming of something, or even with simply telling someone to do something. Even if moral utterances characteristically tell us to do something, not all "tellings to" are moral utterances. Among other things, "moral tellings to" are "tellings to" which, typically at least, must be supportable by *reasons*. This, however, is not true for simple commands or imperatives. In short, as a mere inspection of usage reveals, moral utterances are not identifiable with commands or anything of that order.

To this it will surely be replied: "It is true that these moral concepts cannot be identified with just any old command, but it is their being *Divine* commands which makes all the difference. It is *God's* willing it, *God's* telling us to do it, that makes it good" (Falk, 1956: 123–131).

It is indeed true, for the believer at least, that it is *God's* commanding it or God's willing it which makes all the difference. This is so because the believer assumes and indeed fervently believes that God is good. But how, it should be asked, does the believer know that God is good, except by what is in the end his own quite fallible moral judgment or, if you will, appreciation or perception, that God is good? We must, to know that God is good, see that his acts, his revelation, his commands, are good. It is through the majesty and the goodness of his revelation, the depth and extent of his love, as revealed in the Scriptures, that we come to understand that God is good, that—so the claim goes—God is in reality the ultimate criterion for all our moral actions and attitudes.

It could, of course, be denied that *all* the commands, all the attitudes, exhibited in the Bible are of the highest moral quality. The behavior of Lot's daughters and the damnation of unbelievers are cases in point. But let us assume that the moral insights revealed in our scriptures are of the very highest and that through his acts God reveals his goodness to us. But here we have in effect conceded the critical point put by the secularist. We can see from the very argumentation here that we must quite unavoidably use our own moral insight to decide that God's acts are good. We finally, and quite unavoidably, to come to any conclusion here, must judge for ourselves the moral quality of the alleged revelation; or, if you will, it is finally by what is no doubt fallible human insight that we must judge that what *purports* to be revelation is indeed revelation. We cannot avoid using our own moral understanding, corruptible and deceitful though it be, if we are ever to know that God is good. Fallible or not, our own moral understanding and judgment here is the *logically* prior thing.

The believer might indeed concede that if we start to inquire into, to deliberate about, the goodness of God, we cannot but end up saying what I have just said. But my mistake, he could argue, is in ever starting this line of inquiry in the first place. Who is man to inquire into, to question, the goodness of God? Who is he to ask whether God should be obeyed? That is utter blasphemy and folly. No *genuine believer* thinks for one moment he can question God's goodness or the bindingness of God's will. That God is good, that indeed God is the Perfect Good, is a *given* for the believer. "God is good" or "God is the perfect Good" are, in the technical jargon of philosophy, analytic. Given the believer's usage, it makes no sense to ask if what God commands is good or if God is good. Any being who was not good could not properly be called "God," where what we are talking about is the God of the Judeo-Christian tradition. Similarly, we could not properly call anything that was not perfectly good God. A person who seriously queried "Should I do what God ordains?" could not possibly be a believer. Indeed Jews and Christians do not mean by "He should do x," "God ordains x"; and "One should do what God ordains" is not equivalent to "What God ordains God ordains"; but not all tautologies, or analytic propositions, are statements of identity. It is not only blasphemy, it is, as well, logically speaking *senseless to question* the goodness of God.

Whence then, one might ask, the ancient problem of evil? But let us, for the occasion, assume, what it is at least reasonable to assume, namely that in some way "God is good" and "God is the Perfect Good" are analytic or "truths of reason." Even if this is so, it still remains true—though now it is a little less easy to see this—that we can only come to know that anything is good or evil through our own moral insight.

Let us see how this is so. First it is important to see that "God is good" is not an identity statement, e.g., "God" is not equivalent to "good." "God spoke to Moses" makes sense. "Good spoke to Moses" is not even English. "The steak is good" and "Knowles's speech in Parliament was good" are both standard English sentences but if "God" replaces "good" as the last word in these sentences we have gibberish. But, as I have just said, not all tautologies are statements of identity. "Wives are women," "Triangles are three-sided" are not statements of identity, but they are clear cases of analytic propositions. It is at least reasonable to argue "God is good" has the same status, but, if it does, we still must independently understand what is meant by "good" and thus the criterion of goodness remains *independent* of God.

As we could not apply the predicate "women" to wives, if we did not first understand what women are, and the predicate "three-sided" to triangles if we did not understand what it was for something to be three-sided, so we could not apply the predicate "good" to God unless we already understood what it meant to say that something was good and unless we had some criterion of goodness.

Furthermore, we can and do meaningfully apply the predicate "good" to many things and attitudes that can be understood by a person who knows nothing of God. Even in a godless world, to relieve suffering would still be good.

But is not "God is the Perfect Good" an identity statement? Do not "God" and "the Perfect Good" refer to and/or mean the same thing? The meaning of both of these terms is so very indefinite that it is hard to be sure, but it is plain enough that a believer cannot seriously question the truth of "God is the Perfect Good" and still remain a Christian or Jewish believer. But granting that, we still must have a criterion for goodness that is independent of religion, that is, independent of a belief in God, for clearly we could not judge anything to be *perfectly* good unless we could judge that it was good, and we have already seen that our criterion for goodness must be at least logically independent of God.

Someone still might say: Something must have gone wrong somewhere. No believer thinks he can question or presume to *judge* God. A devoutly religious person simply must use God as his *ultimate criterion* for moral behavior. (Brown, 1963: 235–244; and 1966–67: 269–276. But in response see Nielsen, 1971a: 243–257.) If God wills it, he, as a "knight of faith," must do it!

Surely this is *in a way* so, but it is perfectly compatible with everything I have so far said. "God" by *definition* is "a being worthy of worship," "wholly good," "a being upon whom we are completely dependent." These phrases partially define the God of Judaism and Christianity. This being so, it makes no sense at all to speak of *judging* God or deciding that God is good or worthy of worship. But the crucial point here is this: before we can make any judgments at all that any conceivable being, force, Ground of Being, transcendental reality, Person or whatever could be *worthy* of worship, could be properly called "good," let alone "the Perfect Good," we must have a logically prior understanding of goodness (Nielsen, 1964). That we could call anything, or any foundation of anything, "God," presupposes we have a moral understanding and the ability to discern what would be *worthy* of worship or perfectly good. Morality does not presuppose religion; religion presupposes morality. Feuerbach was at least partially right: our very concept of God seems, in an essential part at least, a logical product of our moral categories. (For contemporary statements of this see Braithwaite, 1964 and Hare, 1973. See in critical response Nielsen, 1981a.)

It is the failure to keep firmly in mind many of the distinctions that I have drawn above, some of which I also drew years ago in *Mind*, which makes it possible for D. Z. Phillips (1970: 223–233) to continue to claim that "nothing could be further from the truth" than to claim that "moral judgment is necessarily prior to religious assent" (Nielsen, 1961: 175–186). It is not a question of "submitting God to moral judgment" but of the recognition that even to speak of a being or Being as being God is already to have come to understand that that being is superlatively worthy of worship. This means that the person must have decided—using his own sense of good and evil—that there is some being who is worthy of worship and is properly called "God" and thus is to be unconditionally obeyed. What Phillips fails to appreciate is that this very movement of thought and judgment shows that moral judgment is logically prior to religious assent. There is in short no recognition that some thing is worthy of worship without first recognizing that it is good.

It is worth noting that Phillips does nothing in his "God and Ought" (1970: 223–233) to show, against the standard objections, how for believers, or for anyone else, "'good' means 'whatever God wills'." A person with certain moral commitments—commitments about the worth of family relationships and the institution of the family—will pass from "He is my Father" to "I must not leave him destitute." But, as criticisms of Searle's attempted derivation of an ought from an is in effect show, the institutional facts appealed to are not themselves normatively neutral: they already embody certain moral commitments (Jaggar, 1974; Nielsen, 1978; Mackie, 1977). Similarly a religious person will automatically go from "God wills it" to "I should do it," but he can do this only because he has already come to accept certain moral views in coming to believe *in* God. But that those distinctively religious normative views have not been enshrined, as logical or conceptual truths built into a language common to believer and nonbeliever alike, is shown in the fact that both believers and skeptics alike can intelligibly ask, as even Phillips admits, "Ought God's will be obeyed?".

Phillips also remarks that to "understand what it *means* to believe in God is to understand why God must be obeyed" (1970: 223–233). But this is plainly false, for one can very well understand what it is to believe in God and still not believe in God because one does not believe that there is, or perhaps even could be, anything *worthy* of worship, though, if one does believe in God and does not just believe that there is an all powerful and all knowing being who created the world from nothing—one will also conclude that God must be obeyed. To believe in God is to accept an internal connection between the will of God and what one ought to do, but that is only possible for someone who comes to believe that there actually is a being *worthy* of worship who is to be called "God," i.e., believes that this is to be his proper honorific title. Yet that very recognition, i.e., that there can be and indeed is a being worthy of worship, requires in a way that Phillips utterly misses, a moral judgment which is not logically dependent on any religious or theological understanding at all (1970: 223–233).

In *sum* then we can say this: a radically Reformationist ethic, divorcing itself from natural moral law conceptions, breaks down because something's being commanded cannot *eo ipso* make something good. Some Jews and Christians mistakenly think it can because they take God to be good and to be a being who always wills what is good. And it is probably true that "God is good" has the status of a tautology or analyticity in Christian thought; still "God is good" is not a statement of identity and we must first understand what "good" means (including what criteria it has) before we can employ with understanding "God is good" and "God is Perfectly Good." Moreover, we must be able to judge ourselves, concerning *any command* whatever, whether it ought to be obeyed; and we must use, whether we like it or not, our own moral insight and wisdom, defective though it undoubtedly is, to judge of anything whatsoever whether it is good. And if we are to avow such propositions at all, we cannot escape this for judgments about the Perfect Good. Indeed, with all our confusions and inadequacies, it is we human beings who finally must judge whether anything could *possibly* be so perfectly good or *worthy* of worship. If this be arrogance or Promethean hubris, it is inescapable, for such conceptual links are built into the logic of our language about God. We cannot base our morality on our conception of God. Rather our very ability to have the Jewish-Christian concept of God presupposes a reasonably sophisticated and independent moral understanding on our part. Brunner and Divine Command theorists like him have the whole *matter* topsy-turvy.[1]

III

Suppose someone argues that it is a matter of *faith* with him that what God commands is what he ought to do; it is a matter of *faith* with him that God's willing it is his ultimate criterion for something's being good. He might say, "I see the force of your argument, but for me it remains a straight matter of faith that there can be no goodness without God. I do not *know* that this is so; I cannot give *grounds* for believing that this is so; I simply humbly accept it on faith that something is good simply because God says that it is. I have no independent moral criterion."

My answer to such a fideist—to fix him with a label—is that in the very way he reasons, in his very talk of God as a being *worthy* of worship, he shows, his protestations to the contrary notwithstanding, that he has such an independent criterion. He shows in his very behavior, including his linguistic behavior, that something being willed or commanded does not *eo ipso* make it good or make it something that he ought to do, but that its being willed by a being *he takes* to be superlatively *worthy* of worship does make it some thing he, morally speaking, must do. But we should also note that it is by his own reflective decisions, by his own honest avowals, that he takes some being or, if you will, some x to be so *worthy* of worship, and thus he shows, in his very behavior, including his linguistic behavior, though not in his talk *about* his behavior, that he does not even take anything to be properly called "God" unless he has already made a moral judgment about that being. He says that he takes God as his ultimate criterion for good on faith, but his actions, including, of course, his everyday linguistic behavior and not just his talk about talk, speak louder than his words, and he shows by them that even his God is in part a product of his moral awareness. Only if he had such a moral awareness could he use the word "God," as a Jew or a Christian uses it. So that his protestations notwithstanding, he clearly has a criterion for good and evil that is *logically independent* of his belief in God. His talk of faith does not and cannot at all alter that.

If the fideist replies: "Look, I take it on faith that your argument here or any such skeptical argument is wrong. I'll not trust you or any philosopher or even *my* own reason against *my* faith. I take my stand here on faith and I won't listen to anyone." If he takes his stand here, we must shift our argument. Whether he will listen or not, we can indeed point out that in so acting, he is acting like a blind, fanatical irrationalist—a man suffering from the systematic false consciousness of a *total* ideology.

Suppose he replies: "So what? Then I am an irrationalist!" We can then point out to him the painful consequences to himself and others of his irrationalism. We can point out to him that, even if, for some reason, he is right in claiming that one ought to accept a religious morality, he is mistaken in accepting it on such irrational grounds. The consequences of irrationalism are such that anything goes, and this, if really lived, would be disastrous for him and others. If he says, "So what; I do not even care about that," then it seems to me that, if we were to continue to reason with him, we would now have to, perhaps like a psychoanalytic sleuth, question his *motives* for responding in such a way. He can no longer have any reasons for his claims; we can only reasonably inquire into what *makes* him take this absurd stance.

There is another objection that I need briefly to consider. Someone might say: "I'm not so sure about all these fancy semantical arguments of yours. I confess I do not know exactly what to say to them, but one thing is certain, if there is a God, then he is the author, the creator, and the sustainer of every thing. He created everything other than himself. Nothing else could exist without God and in this fundamental way morality and everything else is totally dependent on God. Without God there could be nothing to which moral principles or moral claims could be applied. Thus, in one important respect, morality, logic, and everything else are dependent on God."

I first would like to argue that there is a strict sense in which this claim of the religionist is not so. When we talk about what is morally good or morally right, we are not talking about what, except incidentally, is the case but about what ought to be the case or about what ought to exist. Even if there was nothing at all, that is, if there were no objects, processes, relations, or sentient creatures, it would still be correct to say that *if* there were sentient creatures, then a world in which there was less pain, suffering, degradation, and exploitation than there is in the present world would be a better world than a world such as ours. The truth of this is quite independent of the *actual* existence of either the world or of anything existing at all, though indeed we would have to have some *idea* of what it would be like for there to be sentient life and thus a world to understand such talk. Though no one could announce this truth if there were no people, and there would be no actual "we" or actual understanding of such talk, it still would be true that if there were such a country and it had a parliament, then it would be wrong to do certain things in it. It would be wrong to pass a law which allowed the exploitation of children or the torture of the innocent. To talk about what exists is one thing; to talk about what is good or about what ought to exist is another. God, let us assume, could, and indeed did, create the world, but he could not—logically could not—create moral values. Existence is one thing; value is another (Nielsen, 1978). And it is no contravention of God's omnipotence to point out that he cannot do what is *logically* impossible.

If all this talk of what ought to be as being something independent of what is, is stuff of a too heady nature for you, consider this supplementary argument against the theist's reply. To assert that nothing would be good or bad, right or wrong, if nothing existed, is not to deny that we can come to understand, without reference to God, that it is wrong to exploit underdeveloped countries and that religious tolerance is a good thing. The religious moralist has not shown that such exploitation would not be wrong and that such tolerance would not be good even if the atheist were right and God did not exist. But, if his position is to be made out, the religious apologist must show that in a godless world morality and moral values would be impossible. He must show that in such a world nothing could be good or bad or right or wrong. If there is no reason to believe that torturing little children would cease to be bad in a godless world, we have no reason to believe that, in any important sense, morality is dependent on religion. But God or no God, religion or no religion, it is still wrong to inflict pain on helpless infants when so inflicting pain on them is without any rational point (Ewing, 1957: 49).

IV

There is a further stage in the dialectic of the argument about religion and ethics that I want now to consider. I have shown that in a purely logical sense moral notions cannot simply rest on the doctrinal cosmic claims of religion. In fact quite the reverse is the case, namely that only if a human being has a concept of good and evil which is not religiously dependent can he even have the Jewish-Christian-Islamic conception of Deity. In this very fundamental sense, it is not morality that rests on religion but religion on morality. Note that this argument could be made out, even if we grant the theist his meta-physical claims about what there is. That is to say, the claims I have hitherto made are quite independent of skeptical arguments about the reliability or even the coherence of claims to the effect that God exists.

Some defenders of the faith will grant that there is indeed such a fundamental independence of ethical belief from religious belief, though very few would accept my last argument about the dependence of religious belief on human moral understanding. But what is important to see here is that they could accept at least part of my basic claim and still argue that to develop a *fully human and adequate normative* ethic one must make it a God-centered ethic (Hick, 1959: 494–516). (For a criticism of such views see Nielsen, 1973.) Here in the arguments, for and against, the intellectual reliability of religious claims will become relevant.

The claim that such a religious moralist wishes to make is that only with a God-centered morality could we get a morality that would be adequate, that would go beyond the relativities and formalisms of a nonreligious ethic. Only a God-centered and perhaps only a Christ-centered morality could meet our deepest and most persistent moral demands. People have certain desires and needs; they experience loneliness and despair; they create certain "images of excellence;" they seek happiness and love. If the human animal was not like this, if man were not this searching, anxiety-ridden creature with a thirst for happiness and with strong desires and aversions, there would be no good and evil, no morality at all. In short, our moralities are relative to our human natures. And given the human nature that we in fact have, we cannot be satisfied with any purely secular ethic. Nothing "the world" can give us will finally satisfy us. We thirst for a father who will protect us—who will not let life be just one damn thing after another until we die and rot; we long for a God who can offer us the promise of a blissful everlasting life with him. We need to love and obey such a father. Unless we can convincingly picture to ourselves that we are creatures of such a loving sovereign, our deepest moral hopes will be frustrated.

No purely secular ethic can—or indeed should—offer such a hope, a hope that is perhaps built on an illusion, but still a hope that is worth, the believer will claim, the full risk of faith. Whatever the rationality of such a faith, our very human nature, some Christian moralists maintain, makes us long for such assurances. Without it our lives will be without significance, without moral sense; morality finds its *psychologically realistic foundation* in certain human purposes. And given human beings with their nostalgia for the absolute, human life without God will be devoid of all purpose or at least devoid of everything but trivial purposes. Thus without a belief in God, there could be no humanly satisfying morality. Secular humanism in any of its many varieties is in reality inhuman.

It is true that a secular morality can offer no hope for a blissful immortality or a bodily resurrection to a "new life," and it is also true that secular morality does not provide for a protecting, loving father or some over-arching purpose *to* life. But we have to balance this off against the fact that these religious concepts are myths—sources of illusion and self-deception. We human beings are helpless, utterly dependent creatures for years and years. Because of this long period of infancy, there develops in us a deep psychological need for an all protecting father; we thirst for such security, but there is not the slightest reason to think that there is *such* security. Moreover, that people have feelings of dependence does not mean that there is something on which they can depend. That we have such needs most certainly does not give us any reason at all to think that there is such a super-mundane prop for our feelings of dependence.

Furthermore, and more importantly, if there is no such architectonic purpose *to* life, as our religions claim, this does not at all mean that there is no purpose *in* life—that there is no way of living that is ultimately satisfying and significant. It indeed appears to be true that all small purposes, if pursued too relentlessly and exclusively, leave us with a sense of emptiness. Even Mozart quartets listened to endlessly become boring, but a varied life lived with verve and with a variety of conscious aims can survive the destruction of Valhalla. That there is no purpose *to* life does not imply that there is no purpose *in* life. Human beings may not have a function and if this is so, then, unlike a tape recorder or a pencil or even a kind of homunculus, we do not have a purpose. There is nothing we are made for. But even so, we can and do have purposes in the sense that we have aims, goals, and things we find worth seeking and admiring. There are indeed things we prize and admire; the achievement of these things and the realization of our aims and desires, including those we are most deeply committed to, give moral significance to our lives (Baier, 1981; Nielsen, 1981b). We do not need a God to *give* meaning to our lives by making us for his sovereign purpose and perhaps thereby robbing us of our freedom. We, by our deliberate acts and commitments, can give meaning to our own lives. Here man has that "dreadful freedom" that makes possible his human dignity; freedom will indeed bring him anxiety, but he will then be the *rider* and not the *ridden* and, by being able to choose, seek out and sometimes realize those things he most deeply prizes and admires, his life will take on a significance (Berlin, 1969). A life lived without purpose is indeed a most dreadful life—a life in which we might have what the existentialists rather pedantically call the experience of nothingness. But we do not need God or the gods to give purpose to our lives or to give the lie to this claim about nothingness. And we can grow into a fallibilism without a nostalgia for the absolute.

There are believers who would resist some of this and who would respond that these purely human purposes, forged in freedom and anguish, are not sufficient to meet our deepest moral needs. Beyond that, they argue, man needs very much to see himself as a creature with a purpose in a divinely ordered universe. He needs to find some *cosmic* significance for his ideals and commitments; he wants and needs the protection and certainty of having a function. This certainty, as the Grand Inquisitor realized, is even more desirable than his freedom. He wants and needs to live and be guided by the utterly sovereign will of God.

If, after wrestling through the kind of philosophical considerations I have been concerned to set forth, a religious moralist still really wants this and would continue to want it after repeated careful reflection, after all the consequences of his view and the alternatives had been placed vividly before him, after logical confusions had been dispelled, and after he had taken the matter to heart, his secularist interlocutor may find that with him he is finally caught in some ultimate disagreement in attitude.[2] Even this is far from certain, however, for it is not at all clear that there are certain determinate places in such dubious battles where argument and the giving of reasons just must come to an end and we must instead resort to persuasion or some other nonrational methods if we are to resolve our fundamental disagreements (Stevenson, 1944: Chapters VIII, IX and XIII; Stevenson, 1963: Chapter IV; Stevenson, 1966: 197–217).[3] But even if we finally do end up in such "pure disagreements in attitude," before we get there, there is a good bit that can be said. How could his purposes really be *his* own purposes, if he were a creature made to serve God's sovereign purpose and to live under the sovereign will of God? In such a circumstance would his ends be something he had deliberately chosen or would they simply be something that he could not help realizing? Moreover, is it really compatible with human dignity to be *made for* something? We should reflect here that we cannot without insulting people ask what they are for. Finally, is it not *infantile* to go on looking for some father, some order, some absolute, that will lift all the burden of *decision* from us? (Evans, 1973) Children follow rules blindly, but do we want to be children all our lives? Is it really *hubris* or arrogance or sin on our part to wish for a life where we make our own decisions, where we follow the rules we do because we see the *point* of them and where we need not crucify our intellects by believing in some transcendent purpose whose very intelligibility is seriously in question? Perhaps by saying this I am only exhibiting my own *hubris*, my own corruption of soul, but I cannot believe that to ask this question is to exhibit such arrogance.

Notes

1. In reviewing my *Ethics Without God*, Robert A. Oakes claims that "God is good" is both analytic and substantive, whatever that could mean. Moreover, he believes that "X is good" follows from "God wills X." "God's will," he tells us, "can be *criterial* of moral goodness without being constitutive of it." God's will "is to be taken as criterial of moral goodness precisely because 'a perfectly good being' is part of what is meant by 'God'." But this utterly fails to meet my argument that to even be able intelligibly to assert that there is a *perfectly* good being, we must have a logically prior criterion of what it is for something to be good. Thus, God's will cannot be our ultimate or most basic criterion of goodness. We must not only understand how to use "good" before

we can understand how to use "God"; we must have some logically prior criterion of goodness or we could not know that there is a God, i.e., a perfectly good being or a being worthy of worship or even understand what it is to make such a claim. It is not a dogma, or even a mistake, to claim that analytic propositions are nonsubstantive. There are no logically necessary genuine *existential* propositions, though there are propositions of a "There is" form which are logically necessary, e.g., "There is an infinite number of natural numbers," but, as Stuart Brown among others has shown against Norman Malcolm, there are very good grounds for believing that none of these statements are both existential and logically necessary (see Stuart Brown, 1973: 33–40; and Robert A. Oakes, 1975: 275). I should add that Oakes's account also misses the force of my arguments about appeals to God's will as being criterial of moral goodness (Nielsen, 1971a: 251–253).

2. That there is still a lot of room for argument here is brought out by Findlay (1963: Chapters IV, VI, IX and XV; and Findlay, 1957: 97–114).

3. Even if as thoroughly as Alasdair MacIntyre we reject the "emotivism" of the "enlightenment project," we do not have a more objective basis for our moral claims if we follow MacIntyre's positive program (MacIntyre, 1980 and 1981).

References

Baier, Kurt

1981 "The Meaning of Life." Pp. 156–172 in E. D. Klemke (ed.), *The Meaning of Life*. New York: Oxford University Press.

Berlin, Isaiah

1969 *Four Essays on Liberty*. New York: Oxford University Press.

Braithwaite, R. B.

1964 "An Empiricist's view of the nature of religious belief." Pp. 198–201 in John Hick (ed.), *The Existence of God*. New York: Macmillan.

Brown, Patterson

1963 "Religious morality." *Mind* 72 (April): 235–244.

1966 "God and the good." *Religious Studies* 2/2 (April): 269–276.

Brown, Stuart

1973 *Proof and the Existence of God*. London: The Open University Press.

Brunner, Emil

1947 *The Divine Imperative*. Trans. O. Wyon. Philadelphia: Westminister Press.

Evans, Donald

1973 "Does religious faith conflict with moral freedom?" Pp. 305–342 in Gene Outka and John P. Reeder, Jr. (eds.), *Religion and Morality*. Garden City, NY: Anchor Books.

Ewing, A. C.

1957 "The Autonomy of ethics." Pp. 62–83 in I. T. Ramsey (ed.), *Prospects for Metaphysics*. London: George Allen and Unwin.

Falk, W. D.

1956 "Moral perplexity." *Ethics* 66 (January): 123–131.

Findlay, J. N.
1957 "The Structure of the kingdom of ends." *Proceedings of the British Academy* 43: 97–114.
1963 *Language, Mind and Value*. London: George Allen and Unwin.

Hare, R. N.
1973 "The Simple believer." Pp. 294–304 in Gene Outka and John P. Reeder, Jr.. (eds.), *Religion and Morality*. Garden City, NY: Anchor Books.

Henry, E. H.
1957 *Christian Personal Ethics*. Grand Rapids, MI: William B. Eardmans.

Hick, John
1959 "Belief and life: the fundamental nature of the Christian ethic." *Encounter* 20/4 (January): 494–516.

Jaggar, Alison
1974 "It does not matter whether we can derive 'ought' from 'is'." *Canadian Journal of Philosophy* 3/3 (March): 373–379.

MacIntyre, Alasdair
1957 "The Logical status of religious belief." Pp. 169–205 in Ronald Hepburn, Alasdair MacIntyre, and Stephen Toulmin (eds.), *Metaphysical Beliefs*. London: S.C.M. Press.
1959 *Difficulties in Christian Belief*. London: S.C.M. Press.
1980 "A Crisis in moral philosophy: why is the search for the foundations of ethics so frustrating?" Pp. 18–35 in H. T. Engelhardt, Jr. and Daniel Callahan (eds.), *Knowing and Valuing*. Volume IV, *The Foundations of Ethics and Its Relationship to Science*. Hastings-on-Hudson, NY: The Hastings Center.
1981 *After Virtue*. Notre Dame, IN: University of Notre Dame Press.

Mackie, John
1977 *Ethics: Inventing Right and Wrong*. Harmondsworth, Middlesex, England: Penguin Books.

Nielsen, Kai
1961 "Some remarks on the independence of morality from religion." *Mind* 70 (April): 175–186.
1964 "God and the good: does morality need religion?" *Theology Today* 211 (April): 47–58.
1971a *Reason and Practice*. New York: Harper and Row.
1971b *Contemporary Critiques of Religion*. New York: Herder and Herder.
1973a *Skepticism*. New York: St. Martins Press.
1973b *Ethics Without God*. London: Pemberton Books.
1978 "Why there is a problem about ethics." *Danish Yearbook of Philosophy* 15: 68–96.
1981a "Christian empiricism." *The Journal of Religion* 61/2 (April): 146–167.
1981b "Linguistic philosophy and the meaning of life." Pp. 175–192 in E. D. Klemke (ed.), *The Meaning of Life*. New York: Oxford University Press.

1982a *An Introduction to the Philosophy of Religion*. London: The Macmillan Press Ltd.

1982b "On needing a moral theory." *Metaphilosophy*, forthcoming.

1982c "Grounding rights and a method of reflective equilibrium." *Inquiry*, forthcoming.

Oakes, Robert A.

1975 "Review of *Ethics without God*." *Philosophy and Phenomenological Research* 361 (December): 273–276.

Phillips, D. Z.

1970 *Faith and Philosophical Enquiry*. London: Routledge and Kegan Paul.

Stevenson, C. L.

1944 *Ethics and Language*. New Haven: Yale University Press.

1963 *Facts and Values*. New Haven: Yale University Press.

1973 "Ethical Fallibility." Pp. 197–217 in Richard T. De George (ed.), *Ethics and Society*. Garden City, NY: Anchor Books.

Toulmin, Stephen

1950 *An Examination of the Place of Reason in Ethics*. Cambridge, England: Cambridge University Press.

Commands for Grown-ups*

Richard J. Mouw

> In what, then Lord, does true perfection stand?
>
> It stands in a man offering all his heart wholly to God, not seeking himself or his own will, either in great things or in small, in time or in eternity, but abiding always unchanged and always yielding to God equal thanks for things pleasing and displeasing.

Thus Thomas à Kempis.[1] But the sentiments he expresses in these sentences could just as easily come from other Christian writers in other times and places: from, say, Catherine of Siena or John of Damascus or John Knox or Catherine Booth. And those hosts of Christians who agree with Thomas that human beings are at their best when they are surrendering to the will of God in all things can also claim solid biblical support for their conviction. The whole of our human duty, says the writer of Ecclesiastes, can be summarized in these words: "Fear God and keep his commandments" (Ecclesiastes 12: 13), an emphasis that is repeated in the Pauline call for human creatures to yield themselves completely to God as ones "who have been brought from death to life" (Romans 6: 13).

---

*From Richard Mouw, *The God Who Commands*, pp 6–21. © 1990 by the University of Notre Dame. Reprinted with permission.

As Christians have traditionally viewed things, a posture of obedience to God's revealed will is foundational to moral well-being, indeed to human well-being as such. For those who assume such a posture it is unthinkable that people might legitimately struggle with a moral issue for any length of time without asking, "What is it that the Lord requires?" Since there is a God who has provided guidance for the living of human life, obedience to divine directives is essential for human flourishing.

And yet, as Peter Geach has observed: "In modern ethical treatises we find hardly any mention of God; and the idea that if there really is a God, his commandments might be morally relevant is wont to be dismissed by a short and simple argument."[2] The argument that Geach has in mind is a contemporary appropriation of Plato's well-known discussion in the *Euthyphro*. But it seems clear that such a line of argument, if it is used at all, merely serves as an optional tool to be appealed to when convenient by those who are actually committed to the outlook that John Courtney Murray called "postulatory atheism"[3]; often the moral irrelevance of divine directives is simply accepted as a postulate of modernity.

Many thinkers today take it for granted that anyone who looks to divine commandments for moral direction fails to understand, in a very basic way, the proper requirements of moral decision making. Indeed, the belief that there is something fundamentally wrong with people who submit to moral directives "imposed" upon them from "above" seems capable of uniting proponents of rather diverse philosophical perspectives: Marxists, Freudians, existentialists, scientific humanists, New Age religionists, and "go-with-the-flow" romanticists.

There are even self-styled Christian thinkers who are willing to join this consensus. For example, Graeme de Graff once offered this candid observation, in the course of developing what he took to be a defense of Christian morality: "There is no room in morality for commands, whether they are the father's, the schoolmaster's, or the priest's. There is still no room for them when they are God's commands."[4]

Anyone who is familiar with recent theological trends will be able to think of various reasons why a contemporary Christian thinker might dismiss the notion that God issues commands that we must obey. Some Christians manage to avoid references to divine commands by denying the view of revelation that was presupposed in the more traditional Christian perspective. Others seem to hold that, whatever revelations might have occurred in the past, the directives recorded in the Bible are not binding for us today.

There are complex issues at stake in such discussions. These sorts of deviations from the tradition concern us here only insofar as they serve as evidence that some Christians share the modern conviction that there is something wrong with basing a morality, to say nothing of a whole way of life, on submission to God's directives. It is this conviction that I am concerned to understand and evaluate in this discussion.

Biblical Imperatives

My own commitment, in dealing with issues of religious authority, is to the kind of *sola scriptura* emphasis that was a prominent feature of the Protestant Reformation, and is still dear to the hearts of many conservative Protestants. But I want in no way to imply that a belief in the moral relevance of divine commands is the exclusive property of people who spell out the issues of authority in a strong bibliocentric manner. For example, some Christians—especially some Anglicans and Roman Catholics—understand "natural law" in such a way that when someone makes moral decisions with reference to natural law that person is obeying divine commands. Others hold that submission to the *magisterium* of a specific ecclesiastical body counts as obedience to divine directives. Others assume that individual Christians, even those who are not members of ecclesiastical hierarchies, can receive specific and extrabiblical commands from God, such as "Quit smoking!" or "Get out of New Haven!" Still others hold that the will of God can be discerned by examining our natural inclinations or by heeding the dictates of conscience.

None of these is, strictly speaking, incompatible with a *sola scriptura* emphasis. One could hold, for example, that the Bible itself commands us to conform to natural law, or to submit to the church's teachings, or to consult our consciences. Or one could simply view these alternative sources as necessary supplements to, or glosses on, biblical revelation. The view which I am attempting to elucidate here, while formulated in terms that signal my own *sola scriptura* orientation, is not meant to rule out the propriety of appeals to these other sources. Rather, I am assuming a perspective from which the Bible is viewed as a clarifier of these other modes, as the authoritative source against which deliverances from these other sources must be tested.

I should also make it clear that I will be assuming in this discussion that the Bible offers detailed moral guidance to us. On the view that I mean to be elucidating, the good life must be pursued with serious and sustained attention to the rich message of the Scriptures. This is no trivial matter to mention. There have been Christian ethicists in recent years who contend that there is only one divine commandment that is morally relevant, namely, the command to love God and neighbor. That seemed to be Joseph Fletcher's contention when he described himself, in *Situation Ethics*, as "rejecting all 'revealed' norms but the one command—to love God in the neighbor."[5]

If the command to love is the only biblical command which has normative relevance to moral decision making, then much of the substance of Christian ethics can be established without reference to the Scriptures. But if the Bible does offer other commands and considerations which bear on our decision making, then the task will be one of finding correlations between biblical revelation and moral issues at many different points.

It is interesting, though, that when Fletcher explained his grounds for his mono-imperativism, his arguments were not so much directed against the moral relevance of other divine commands as they were against their "absoluteness." To hold, however, that there is a plurality of divine commands which are morally relevant and binding is not to commit oneself to the view that each of these commands is indefeasible. It may well be that there is only one indefeasible command, the so-called "law of love"—such that in any situation in which the course of action prescribed by the law of love is one's duty, it is one's actual duty, and that only the law of love has this property. But this does not rule out the possibility that there are other divine commandments which prescribe courses of action which are at least one's *prima facie* duties to perform in those situations in which the commands in question are morally relevant.

Not that *all* the commandments which are found in the Bible are morally relevant for us today. As Lewis Smedes puts it, they do not all "tell us what God wants us to do."[6] For example, God commanded Abraham to leave Ur of the Chaldees, and Jonah was told by the Lord to preach in Nineveh; it would be silly to suppose that it is a part of our contemporary Christian duty to obey these commands, or even to think of them as included in our functioning moral repertoire.

I do not mean to promote, then, a fascination with all of those biblical sentences that are in the imperative mood. In fact, my references to "commands" here should be taken as a kind of shorthand that I am using to refer to a somewhat broader pattern of divine address. The Bible is much more than a compendium of imperatives; the sacred writings contain historical narratives, prayers, sagas, songs, parables, letters, complaints, pleadings, visions, and so on. The moral relevance of the divine commandments found in the Scriptures can only be understood by viewing them in their interrelatedness with these other types of writings. The history, songs, predictions, and so on, of the Bible serve to sketch out the character of the biblical God; from this diversity of materials we learn what God's creating and redeeming purposes are, what sorts of persons and actions the Lord approves of, and so on. Divine commands must be evaluated and interpreted in this larger context.

Furthermore, we would actually miss some of the divine imperatives which the Bible transmits to us if we only attended to grammatical imperatives. For example, nowhere in the New Testament is there a literal command to the original followers of Jesus to stop discriminating against the Samaritans. But the New Testament record has Jesus telling stories and engaging in activities which make it very clear that he is directing his disciples to change their attitudes toward Samaritans. Thus it is accurate to say that Jesus "commanded" his disciples to love the Samaritans, even though the words (or their Greek or Aramaic equivalents) "Stop discriminating against Samaritans" never appear in the Bible.

When the writer of Ecclesiastes concludes, then, that our whole duty consists in obeying God's commandments, we must not understand him to be instructing us to attend only to divine utterances which have a specific grammatical form. He is telling us, rather, that we must conform to whatever God requires of us, to all that the Creator instructs us to do—whether that guidance is transmitted through parables, accounts of divine dealings with nations and individuals, or sentences which embody commands.

"Infantile" Obedience?

Why is the posture of obedience to divine directives such an affront to so many contemporary thinkers? Why is it that people want to insist that there can be "no room" (remembering de Graff's words) in morality for commands, even when they are commands that come from God?

Patrick Nowell-Smith put the objection very bluntly in an article he wrote for the *Rationalist Annual* in the early 1960s. The Christian posture, he said, is "infantile"; it possesses the "characteristics of deontology, heteronomy, and realism which are proper and indeed necessary in the development of a child, but not proper to an adult."[7] Unfortunately, Nowell-Smith does not offer much by way of an argument to support this negative assessment of the Christian position. But he does refer us to Piaget's work in the area of moral development—indeed, Nowell-Smith's use of the terms "deontology," "heteronomy," and "realism," is an obvious borrowing from Piaget.

Since Nowell-Smith does not elaborate at length on how he sees the relationship between his own claim that Christian morality is "infantile" and Piaget's studies of moral development, it is necessary to try to reconstruct the argument which he might have in mind. Piaget distinguishes, in his book *The Moral Judgment of the Child*, several stages in the moral development of children. For our present purposes we can refer to two major stages. At an early point in the life of the child, moral decision making follows what Piaget calls a "heteronomous" pattern—which is what Nowell-Smith apparently has in mind when he uses the same term. According to Piaget, this stage is dominated by a "primitive consciousness of duty" during which "duty is nothing more than the acceptance of commands received from without.[8] In the process of maturing however, this stage is replaced by one of "autonomy," in which the rigid sense of duty gives way to a "morality of goodness." Rather than uncritically accepting externally imposed commands, the autonomous person asks *why* the commands ought to be obeyed; the maturing child begins to reflect on the *point* of the moral rules and practices to which submission is demanded. In short, at the autonomous stage the child begins "to appeal to his reason in order to bring unity into the moral material."[9]

It is not difficult to get some idea of what Nowell-Smith has in mind when he refers to these distinctions formulated by Piaget. Nowell-Smith is suggesting that the Christian believer, in submitting to commands which come from "without" or "above," is very much like the child who unquestioningly obeys the command of a parent. But this "heteronomous" posture is one which ought to be outgrown in a properly maturing human being. Thus, it seems, Christians are victims of an arrested moral development. They are "frozen" at the heteronomous stage of moral growth.

But we must push the argument a little further. If we are going to rely on Piaget's analysis to cast aspersions on Christian posture, then we must ask: What would things have been like if the religious believer had developed properly? Here Piaget's description of a normal transition from the heteronomous stage to the autonomous one is helpful:

> It seems to us an undeniable fact that in the course of the child's mental development, unilateral respect or the respect felt by the small for the great plays an essential part: it is what makes the child accept all the commands transmitted to him by his parents and is thus the great factor of continuity between different generations. But it seems to us no less undeniable. . . that as the child grows in years the nature of his respect changes. In so far as individuals decide questions on an equal footing—no matter whether subjectively or objectively—the pressure they exercise upon each other becomes collateral.[10]

For Piaget, then, the normal transition from heteronomy to autonomy takes place when the child experiences a change of attitude toward the commanding parent: the more the child comes to see the parent as an individual similar to herself—in Piaget's words, when "the respect felt by the small for the great" diminishes, or when the parent is seen as one who decides matters on an "equal footing" to that of the child—the less the child will be inclined toward an unquestioning submission to the commands of the parent. And, to take the case a step further, a person who has never come to view adults as near-equals or equals, someone who always views the commanding adult as separated from herself by the gulf which separates the small from the great—such a person might be thought of as being arrested, or frozen, at the heteronomous stage. She views a specific commander as very different from herself, when in fact she ought to view the commander as possessing relevant similarities, characteristics which permit the commandee to think through her own moral decisions.

Once we state Piaget's case in this way, however—and I have attempted to stay as close as I can to what I think are Piaget's own intentions—it is difficult to see how it bears directly on Nowell-Smith's charge that obedience to divine commands is an "infantile" posture. At the very least we need some transferral of what Piaget says about the child-parent relationship to the kind of relationship which Christians see as holding between themselves and God.

Suppose we try to make that transferral. We might state the case as follows: a human being is arrested at the heteronomous stage, with respect to the relationship between humans and God, when she fails to come to view God as an equal, or near equal, with respect to moral decision making. In order for Nowell-Smith's account to work, then, he must argue that there should come a time when the Christian begins to see God as someone who operates on an "equal footing" with human beings; the "respect felt by the small for the great" must disappear from the relationship between God and adult humans.

But once we put the matter in this way, it hardly seems worthy of serious consideration. Someone might want to argue, of course, that there simply *is* no deity; this might be one way of supporting the claim that we ought not to think of God as greater than ourselves in the area of moral decision making. Short of that kind of argument, however, it would seem quite unreasonable to expect Christian believers to treat God as an equal when, according to the best accounts of what the deity is like, God is obviously *superior* to any human being.

For any pattern of moral decision making to be considered mature, it should presumably be characterized by a willingness to act in the light of the facts as one views them. And the fact is that Christianity views God as being much greater—infinitely greater—than human beings. On such a view of things, a refusal to recognize God's moral greatness would not only be self-deceptive, it would also be, in its own way, a kind of "infantile" discourtesy.

Let me be very clear about exactly what I am arguing in my response to Nowell-Smith. He appeals to Piaget in order to portray Christian morality as "infantile." I have replied by showing that this is an inaccurate use of Piaget's developmental scheme. Now it may also be the case that there are defects in Piaget's own account of moral development. Certainly Kohlberg and others have taken the study of such things well beyond Piaget in some important respects.[11] Nonetheless, however the assessment of the details of such developmental schemes might go, it seems to me very unlikely that those schemes could cast legitimate doubt on the propriety of adopting an attitude of awe before the divine Sovereign.

"Prehuman" Submission?

We must not assume, though, that we can put this line of criticism completely to rest merely by showing that the appeal to developmental theory is less than convincing. There are thinkers who insist that the posture of obedience is associated with an inadequate moral consciousness, without resting their claims on empirical studies in psychology.

Consider, for example, the way in which Erich Fromm presents the biblical story of Adam's fall into sin:

> Acting against God's orders means freeing himself from coercion, emerging from the unconscious existence of prehuman life to the level of man. Acting against the command of authority, committing a sin, is in its positive human aspect the first act of freedom, that is, the first *human* act. In the myth the sin in its formal aspect is the eating of the tree of knowledge. The act of disobedience as an act of freedom is the beginning of reason.[12]

There is no reference here to the ways in which individual human beings pass through the stages of moral development. Fromm simply characterizes the posture of obedience to the divine will as a state of affairs that is intrinsically bad.

Fromm offers this analysis in a context where he is explaining two options which are open to human beings in their attempts to relate to physical and social reality.[13] The first is the pattern of "submission": this is the "prehuman" pattern wherein individuals submit to some external authority, thereby sacrificing their own individuality. The second pattern is one where the individual engages in a "spontaneous relationship to man and nature" in such a way that individuality is kept intact.

Obedience to divine commands, is, for Fromm, an instance of the first pattern. But it is interesting to note how he describes the second, and for him preferable, pattern: it promotes "the integration and strength of the total personality" and is "subject to the very limits that exist for the growth of the self."[14]

Why couldn't a Christian, when faced with the choice between sacrificing her individuality and seeking the "integration and strength of the total personality," actually choose the second pattern as Fromm describes it? To insist that she could not make that choice is to assume that it is necessary for Christians to embrace the "despotic" model of the God-human relationship which Fromm wants to link to obedience to the divine will.

We must, however, challenge this assumption. There is no reason why Christians cannot agree with Fromm when he advocates that we human beings involve ourselves in the kind of "growth process" that encourages integrated personhood. Having sided with him in this, though, we will also want to underscore Fromm's own insistence that this growth process is "subject to [certain] limits." The rub comes, of course, when we ask: What limits are *proper* to the pattern of human growth? From what *source* do we come to know what these limits are? In what sorts of *activities* does the "total personality" gain its "strength"?

Fromm's case here is very similar to that of Karl Marx, who tells us that "in religion the spontaneous activity of the human imagination, of the human brain and the human heart, operates independently of the individual—that is, operates on him as an alien, divine or diabolical activity"—resulting in "the loss of his self."[15] For Marx any authority relationship seems to be one in which one person "possesses" another, with the result that the commandee becomes the "property" of the commander.

The Christian can respond to this kind of charge by insisting that obedience to divine commands is best understood as another way of engaging in the "spontaneous" patterns of relationship which Fromm cherishes; it is another way of avoiding the "loss of self" which Marx fears. But it should also be admitted that this line of response will not work if we assume some of the views which Christians themselves have offered as explanations of the relationship between God and human beings. For example, consider the explanation offered by Peter Geach:

> I shall be told by [some] philosophers that since I am saying not: It is your supreme moral duty to obey God, but simply: It is insane to set about defying an Almighty God, my attitude is plain power-worship. So it is: but it is worship of the Supreme power, and as such is wholly different from, and does not carry with it, a cringing attitude towards earthly powers. An earthly potentate does not compete with God, even unsuccessfully: he may threaten all manner of afflictions, but only from God's hands can any affliction actually come upon us.[16]

Geach's contention here is that we ought to submit to the will of God because God has the power to destroy us if we do not—and that, furthermore, the divine Sovereign will exercise that power. This is a very Hobbesian account of the relationship between God and human creatures. We submit to God's power out of a fear of being destroyed by that power. The appeal here is not so much to a sense of the fittingness of that submission as it is to an awareness of what is in our self-interest.

As stated, this view seems to be similar to what Fromm calls the "prehuman" pattern of "submission." And if that were the only alternative, we might well reject it. It may be in some sense "insane" to defy supreme power, but it does not seem to be *ipso facto* immoral. We are not inclined, for example, to despise someone who resists the will of a perverse human despot, even though he knows with near certainty that he will be killed for his resistance. Such stubbornness may be "insanity," but it is of a rather admirable sort. Taken as a response to Fromm and Marx, then, Geach's defense of the Christian posture does not seem to be adequate.

Indeed, to focus briefly on the Genesis account to which Fromm explicitly refers, it would seem that the despotic model of the relationship between God and humans—which both Fromm and Geach seem to accept—is not the one which the Genesis writer means to present in a favorable light. Rather, despotism is the revisionist view which the serpent—with obvious success—propagates to Eve. Throughout the Scriptures the commandments of God are viewed as the guidelines offered by a loving Creator who desires the well-being of created reality. The serpent in Genesis, however, challenges this assumption. Has God said that disobeying his commands will lead to death? he asks Eve. Well, then, God is deceiving you—"you shall not surely die." Eat from the tree and "you shall be as gods" (Gen. 3: 4–5).

This revisionist theology involves what I have called elsewhere "two serpentine falsehoods."[17] First, the decision to eat the fruit was based on a shift from viewing God as a loving Creator to that of a deceptive despot. Second, the subsequent attempt on the part of the first human beings to become their own gods was based on the assumption that they must conform to the despotic model of deity: each human being attempted to become the kind of despotic ruler which the serpent characterized God as being.

If this analysis of the serpent's revisionist theology in the Genesis account is accepted, then we can understand the importance of being very clear about what view of God is being employed when objections are lodged against the Christian posture of obedience to God's commands. If God is a despot, then to say that I belong to God is, as Marx argues, to reduce myself to mere "property." But if God is instead a loving Creator who wants us to experience the divine shalom, then to belong to God is to realize new dimensions of selfhood. And this is what is at stake when the Apostle speaks of "bondage" and "liberty" in a manner that, from the perspective of Fromm's kind of secularism, has things reversed. For on the biblical view a life dedicated to the proving of one's allegedly sovereign mastery over others is a life of fearful bondage, while the ability to obey when that is the proper response, to engage in selfless service when this is required of us, to recognize authority and expertise when that is evident—that is, from a biblical perspective, liberation.

One final observation about Fromm's account. He uses the terms "freedom" and "reason"—matters which he greatly values—as if they refer to features which are the exclusive properties of a humanistic perspective. The Christian ought not to concede this. The loving Creator of the Scriptures desires that human beings freely submit to revealed directives, without coercing them into a grudging obedience. Furthermore, if the Christian's basis for submitting to divine authority is related to the assessment of the credentials of the one who issues authoritative commands, then this too involves a kind of rational evaluation.

Beyond Heteronomy

In assessing Nowell-Smith's objection to the Christian moral posture, I allowed his characterization of Christianity as "heteronomous" to stand unchallenged. For apologetic purposes this seems to me to be quite acceptable. If the posture of obedience to divine commands is indeed a heteronomous one, then heteronomy deserves a better reputation than it is often accorded. It might even be necessary to speak of certain heteronomies as mature ones—especially those which view the God-human relationship as a covenantal partnership that is characterized by trust, mutual respect, responsible obedience, and a free acceptance of obligation.

But it is probably wiser to follow the lead of those thinkers who have insisted that neither the heteronomous nor the autonomous is adequate for characterizing a healthy relationship to God. Paul Tillich, as is well known, preferred to think of the Christian pattern as one of "theonomy."[18] The same choice was advocated by the Dutch theologian Herman Bavinck, in the lectures he gave on his tour of North America during the 1908–1909 academic year. The Christian's delight in the Law of the Lord, Bavinck argued, is "the ultimate fulfillment" of the deepest intentions and hopes of "autonomous morality." The autonomous pursuit of

> the true, and the good, and the beautiful . . . can only come to perfection when the absolute good is at the same time the almighty, divine will, which not only prescribes the good in the moral law, but also works it effectually in man himself. The heteronomy of law and the autonomy of man are reconciled only by this theonomy.[19]

Viewed from "inside" the Christian life, it can seem quite inappropriate to describe a Christian's relationship to God simply as one where a human being receives commands from an "external other." In both the Old and New Testaments there is a clear sense of direction toward an "internalization" of the moral life of the believer. The Law at Sinai may have been handed down on tablets of stone from the heavens above; but it was not long before those who had received that Law were talking about a word of guidance that was to be written in their own hearts—a sense of inner-directedness that culminates in the New Testament teaching concerning the indwelling of the Holy Spirit. From such a perspective, it may be difficult to identify one's own pattern of obedience as that of submitting to commands which are "handed down" from "above."

Similarly, a purely heteronomous account of Christian morality does not capture the intimacy of relationship between Commander and commandee in the Christian life. The God who commands is the same one who has, in the person of Jesus, entered into a human frame of reference. The Creator became Redeemer, stooping to become like one of us. When God commands, he does so with an intimate knowledge of our condition, having suffered in the same ways that we suffer.

We in turn receive divine guidance as persons who are in the process of internalizing the spirit of Jesus, as temples of the divine Comforter. The intimacy here between God and ourselves is, to be sure, not one of metaphysical merger; rather, it is an interpersona intimacy—not a unity of undifferentiated being but an increasing merger of purposes in the context of covenantal mutuality. For this kind of relationship "heteronomy" is too formal and lifeless to serve as a proper label in accounting for the facts of the case.

It is very necessary to emphasize all of this lest the arguments offered here be used to endorse heteronomy-as-such. If the defense of obedience to divine commands is formulated in too simple terms, the arguments for obeying God might be extended into arguments for obeying moral "experts" in general.

This suggests that attention must be directed toward the unique status of divine authority. I believe that God possesses the absolute authority to tell us what to do. At the same time I have no desire to expand my case into a more general defense of moral hierarchism. I am convinced that it is on occasion reasonable to submit to commands whose rationale we do not fully grasp, and the relationship between human beings and the God of the Bible satisfies, I am also convinced, the required conditions for such obedience. But I would not want to encourage analogous claims on behalf of obedience to political dictators and religious gurus.

Each case or relationship must be considered on its own merits. Whether a given individual possesses the authority to command our obedience is a matter which must be decided by examining the credentials of the would-be commander. In this regard it is important to note that the God of Scriptures regularly offers credentials for our examination. The God who issues the "Thou shalts" of Exodus 20 is the one who prefaces those directives with the reminder that we have been delivered from the house of bondage. And the one who, in the New Testament, tells us to keep his commandments, does so on the basis of the fact that when we were yet sinners he died for us. The God who commands in the Scriptures is the one who offers the broken chariots of the Egyptians and the nail-scarred hands of the divine Son as a vindication of the right to tell us what to do. This should make us sensitive to the need to examine the credentials of others who claim the authority to be moral commanders.

It is not merely for apologetic purposes, therefore, that we insist that it is possible for Christians to pursue obedience to divine commands in a reasonable fashion. The appeal to reasonableness is also important for the maintenance of a healthy and sensible Christianity. Indeed, such an emphasis, in the final analysis, may have more of a chance of bearing fruit within the Christian community than outside of it. It is not likely that the kind of case I have laid out thus far will convince most unbelievers that obedience to divine commands is a "healthy" way to order one's life. The most we can hope for is that people will see that some of the arguments used against the Christian posture are less than compelling.

A morality based on obedience to divine commands cannot be attacked without also challenging a complex of beliefs with which it is intimately associated. To criticize such a morality on psychological grounds is to enter into a discussion of issues which go far beyond the facts of psychological development. Appeals to "maturity"' or "freedom" or "rationality" open up legitimate questions about the larger theoretical frameworks in which those terms can be understood. Ultimately, one is led to issues relating to the human condition, the existence and nature of the deity, and the proper locus of moral authority.

And those questions are very much worth discussing. Even if a Christian thinker should decide that we need not spend much time defending the basic assumptions of our way of viewing things against the present-day cultured despisers of the faith, we would still have much to talk about among ourselves on these basic issues.

I can imagine, for example, Christians who would have strong sympathies with what I have said so far, but who might nonetheless be a bit nervous about pushing too hard on some of these themes. They would have no difficulty admitting that Christianity is characterized by a willingness to conform to God's will for human living, but they would be somewhat uncomfortable with an ethic that places a strong and explicit emphasis on the notion of obeying divine directives.

For one thing, they might worry about the understanding of human agency that such an emphasis could promote. Doesn't a pattern of thinking that refers without embarrassment to a commandee-Commander relationship run the risk of individualism? Isn't there a strong hint here of a naked self standing alone before God? And isn't this a bad thing to promulgate?

What about the picture of God that is strongly suggested by the language I have been using in this chapter? Doesn't it smack, and more than a little, of hierarchism? Isn't the image of a moral Commander—in spite of my efforts in this discussion to "soften" the picture—something that we would do well to abandon? In times when Christians are being asked to recognize the inhumanity that has attended "patriarchy" and the creation of "dependency" relations, would it not be better to formulate the Christian case in very different terms than those which I have been employing?

And what about the "tone" of the moral life as I have been depicting it? Isn't there something quietistic—even compulsively introspective—about a way of life that stresses obedience to God's will? Can't this understanding of the patterns of Christian morality promote—as in some strands of Puritanism—a brooding, sullen spirit of withdrawal?

These are important questions. I sense a special obligation to deal with them, since I have much sympathy for viewpoints and emphases that are sometimes labeled "individualistic," "hierarchical," and "quietistic."

Notes

1. Thomas à Kempis, *The Imitation of Christ*, ed. with an Introduction by Harold C. Gardiner (Garden City, N.Y.: Doubleday & Co., Image Books, 1955), 143.

2. Peter Geach, *God and the Soul*, Studies in Ethics and the Philosophy of Religion (New York: Schocken Books, 1969), 117.

3. John Courtney Murray, *The Problem of God: Yesterday and Today*, St. Thomas More Lectures (New Haven: Yale University Press, 1964), 105–106.

4. Graeme de Graff, "God and Morality," in *Christian Ethics and Contemporary Philosophy*, ed. Ian T. Ramsey (New York: Macmillan, 1966), 34.

5. Joseph Fletcher, *Situation Ethics: The New Morality* (Philadelphia: Westminster Press, 1966), 26.

6. Lewis B. Smedes, *Mere Morality: What God Expects from Ordinary People* (Grand Rapids, Mich.: Eerdmans, 1983), 5.

7. Patrick H. Nowell-Smith, "Morality: Religious and Secular," reprinted in *Christian Ethics and Contemporary Philosophy*, ed. Ramsey, 103.

8. Jean Piaget, *The Moral Judgment of the Child*, trans. Marjorie Gabain (New York: Free Press, 1965), 106.

9. Ibid.

10. Ibid., 107.

11. For a concise account of Kohlberg's scheme, see Lawrence Kohlberg, "stages of Moral Development as a Basis for Moral Education," in *Moral Education: Interdisciplinary Approaches*, eds., Beck, Crittenden, and Sullivan (Toronto: University of Toronto Press, 1971).

12. Erich Fromm, *Escape from Freedom* (New York: Avon Books, Discus Edition, 1941), 50.

13. Ibid., 45–46.

14. Ibid., 46.

15. Karl Marx, *Economic and Philosophic Manuscripts of 1844*, ed. with an Introduction by Dirk J. Struik, trans. Martin Milligan (New York: International Publishers, 1964), 111.

16. Geach, *God and Soul*, 127.

17. See my *Politics and the Biblical Drama* (Grand Rapids, Mich.: Eerdmans, 1976), 39–41.

18. Paul Tillich, *Systematic Theology*, 3 vols. (Chicago: University of Chicago Press, 1951–63), 1 (1951): 92–96; see also 3 (1963): 264–282.

19. Herman Bavinck, *The Philosophy of Revelation* (Longman, Green & Co., 1909; repr., Grand Rapids, Mich.: Baker Book House, 1979), 262–263.

Declaration Toward a Global Ethic*

Parliament of the World's Religions, 4 September 1993, Chicago, U.S.A.

The Principles of a Global Ethic

Our world is experiencing a *fundamental crisis*: A crisis in global economy, global ecology, and global politics. The lack of a grand vision, the tangle of unresolved problems, political paralysis, mediocre political leadership with little insight or foresight, and in general too little sense for the commonweal are seen everywhere: Too many old answers to new challenges.

Hundreds of millions of human beings on our planet increasingly suffer from unemployment, poverty, hunger, and the destruction of their families. Hope for a lasting peace among nations slips away from us. There are tensions between the sexes and generations. Children die, kill, and are killed. More and more countries are shaken by corruption in politics and business. It is increasingly difficult to live together peacefully in our cities because of social, racial, and ethnic conflicts, the abuse of drugs, organized crime, and even anarchy. Even neighbors often live in fear of one another. Our planet continues to be ruthlessly plundered. A collapse of the ecosystem threatens us.

Time and again we see leaders and members of *religions* incite aggression, fanaticism, hate, and xenophobia—even inspire and legitimize violent and bloody conflicts. Religion often is misused for purely power-political goals, including war. We are filled with disgust. We condemn these blights and declare that they need not be. An ethic already exists within the religious teachings of the world which can counter the global distress. Of course this ethic provides no direct solution for all the immense problems of the world, but it does supply the moral foundation for a better individual and global order: A vision which can lead women and men away from despair, and society away from chaos. We are persons who have committed ourselves to the precepts and practices of the world's religions. We confirm that there is already a consensus among the religions which can be the basis for a global ethic—a minimal *fundamental consensus* concerning binding *values*, irrevocable *standards*, and *fundamental moral attitudes*.

I. No new global order without a new global ethic!

We women and men of various religions and regions of Earth therefore address all people, religious and non-religious. We wish to express the following convictions which we hold in common:

- We all have a *responsibility for a better global order*.
- Our involvement for the sake of human rights, freedom, justice, peace, and the preservation of Earth is absolutely necessary.
- Our different religious and cultural traditions must not prevent our common involvement in opposing all forms of inhumanity and working for greater humaneness.
- The principles expressed in this Global Ethic can be affirmed by all persons with ethical convictions, whether religiously grounded or not.
- As *religious and spiritual persons* we base our lives on an Ultimate Reality, and draw spiritual power and hope there from, in trust, in prayer or meditation, in word or silence. We have a special responsibility for the welfare of all humanity and care for the planet Earth. We do not consider ourselves better than other women and men, but we trust that the ancient wisdom of our religions can point the way for the future.

After two world wars and the end of the cold war, the collapse of fascism and Nazism, the shaking to the foundations of communism and colonialism, humanity has entered a new phase of its history. Today we possess sufficient economic, cultural, and spiritual resources to introduce a better global order. But old and new *ethnic, national, social, economic, and religious tensions* threaten the peaceful building of a better world. We have experienced greater technological progress than ever before, yet we see that world-wide poverty, hunger, death of children, unemployment, misery, and the destruction of nature have not diminished but rather have increased. Many peoples are threatened with economic ruin, social disarray, political marginalization, ecological catastrophe, and national collapse.

In such a dramatic global situation humanity needs a *vision of peoples living peacefully together*, of ethnic and ethical groupings and of religions sharing responsibility for the care of Earth. A vision rests on hopes, goals, ideals, standards. But all over the world these have slipped from our hands. Yet we are convinced that, despite their frequent abuses and failures, it is the communities of faith who bear a responsibility to demonstrate that such hopes, ideals, and standards can be guarded, grounded, and lived. This is especially true in the modern state. Guarantees of freedom of conscience and religion are necessary but they do not substitute for binding values, convictions, and norms which are valid for all humans regardless of their social origin, sex, skin color, language, or religion.

We are convinced of the fundamental unity of the human family on Earth. We recall the 1948 Universal Declaration of Parliament of the Worlds Religions Human Rights of the United Nations. What it formally proclaimed on the level of *rights* we wish to confirm and deepen here from the perspective of an *ethic*: The full realization of the intrinsic dignity of the human person, the inalienable freedom and equality in principle of all humans, and the necessary solidarity and interdependence of all humans with each other. On the basis of personal experiences and the burdensome history of our planet we have learned

- that a better global order cannot be created or enforced by laws, prescriptions, and conventions alone; that the realization of peace, justice, and the protection of Earth depends on the insight and readiness of men and women to act justly;
- that action in favor of rights and freedoms presumes a consciousness of responsibility and duty, and that therefore both the minds and hearts of women and men must be addressed;
- that rights without morality cannot long endure, and that *there will be no better global order without a global ethic.*

By a *global ethic* we do not mean a *global ideology or a single unified religion* beyond all existing religions, and certainly not the domination of one religion over all others. By a global ethic we mean *a fundamental consensus on binding values, irrevocable standards, and personal attitudes*. Without such a fundamental consensus on an ethic, sooner or later every community will be threatened by chaos or dictatorship, and individuals will despair.

II. A fundamental demand: Every human being must be treated humanely

We are all fallible, imperfect men and women with limitations and defects. We know the reality of evil. Precisely because of this, we feel compelled for the sake of global welfare to express what the fundamental elements of a global ethic should be—for individuals as well as for communities and organizations, for states as well as for the religions themselves. We trust that our often millennia-old religious and ethical traditions provide an *ethic* which is *convincing and practicable for all women and men of good will*, religious and nonreligious.

At the same time we know that our various religious and ethical traditions often offer very different bases for what is helpful and what is unhelpful for men and women, what is right and what is wrong, what is good and what is evil. We do not wish to gloss over or ignore the serious differences among the individual religions. However, they should not hinder us from proclaiming publicly those things which *we already hold in common* and which we jointly affirm, each on the basis of our own religious or ethical grounds.

We know that religions cannot solve the environmental, economic, political; and social problems of Earth. However they can provide what obviously cannot be attained by economic plans, political programs, or legal regulations alone: A *change* in the inner orientation, the whole *mentality*, *the 'hearts' of people*, and a conversion from a false path to a new orientation for life. Humankind urgently needs social and ecological reforms, but it needs *spiritual renewal* just as urgently. As religious or spiritual persons we commit ourselves to this task. The spiritual powers of the religions can offer a fundamental sense of trust, a ground of meaning, ultimate standards, and a spiritual home. Of course religions are credible only when they eliminate those conflicts which spring from the religions themselves, dismantling mutual arrogance, mistrust, prejudice, and even hostile images, and thus demonstrate respect for the traditions, holy places, feasts, and rituals of people who believe differently.

Now as before, *women and men are treated inhumanely* all over the world. They are robbed of their opportunities and their freedom; their human rights are trampled underfoot; their dignity is disregarded. But might does not make right! In the face of all inhumanity our religious and ethical convictions demand that *every human being must be treated humanely!*

This means that every human being without distinction of age, sex, race, skin color, physical or mental ability, language, religion, political view, or national or social origin possesses an inalienable and *untouchable dignity*, and everyone, the individual as well as the state, is therefore obliged to honor this dignity and protect it. Humans must always be the subjects of rights, must be ends, never mere means, never objects of commercialization and industrialization in economics, politics and media, in research institutes, and industrial corporations. No one stands 'above good and evil'—no human being, no social class, no influential interest group, no cartel, no police apparatus, no army, and no state. On the contrary: Possessed of reason and conscience, every human is obliged to behave in a genuinely human fashion, *to do good and avoid evil*!

It is the intention of this Global Ethic to clarify what this means. In it we wish to recall irrevocable, unconditional ethical norms. These should not be bonds and chains, but helps and supports for people to find and realize once again their lives' direction, values, orientations, and meaning.

There is a principle which is found and has persisted in many religious and ethical traditions of humankind for thousands of years: *What you do not wish done to your self do not do to others*. Or in positive terms: *What you wish done to yourself do to others!* This should be the irrevocable, unconditional norm for all areas of life, for families and communities, for races, nations, and religions.

Every form of egoism should be rejected: All selfishness, whether individual or collective, whether in the form of class thinking, racism, nationalism, or sexism. We condemn these because they prevent humans from being authentically human. Self-determination and self-realization are thoroughly legitimate so long as they are not separated from human self-responsibility and global responsibility, that is, from responsibility for fellow humans and for the planet Earth.

This principle implies very concrete standards to which we humans should hold firm. From it arise *four broad, ancient guidelines* for human behavior which are found in most of the religions of the world.

III. Irrevocable directives

1. Commitment to a culture of non-violence and respect for life Numberless women and men of all regions and religions strive to lead lives not determined by egoism but by commitment to their fellow humans and to the world around them. Nevertheless, all over the world we find endless hatred, envy, jealousy, and violence, not only between individuals but also between social and ethnic groups, between classes, races, nations, and religions. The use of violence, drug trafficking and organized crime, often equipped with new technical possibilities, has reached global proportions. Many places still are ruled by terror "from above"; dictators oppress their own people, and institutional violence is widespread. Even in some countries where laws exist to protect individual freedoms, prisoners are tortured, men and women are mutilated, hostages are killed.

A. In the great ancient religious and ethical traditions of humankind we find the directive: *You shall not kill*! Or in positive terms: *Have respect for life!* Let us reflect anew on the consequences of this ancient directive: All people have a right to life, safety, and the free development of personality insofar as they do not injure the rights of others. No one has the right physically or psychically to torture, injure, much less kill, any other human being. And no people, no state, no race, no religion has the right to hate, to discriminate against, to 'cleanse', to exile, much less to liquidate a 'foreign' minority which is different in behavior or holds different beliefs.

B. Of course, wherever there are humans there will be conflicts. Such conflicts, however, should be resolved without violence within a framework of justice. This is true for states as well as for individuals. Persons who hold political power must work within the framework of a just order and commit themselves to the most non-violent, peaceful solutions possible. And they should work for this within an international order of peace which itself has need of protection and defense against perpetrators of violence. Armament is a mistaken path; disarmament is the commandment of the times. Let no one be deceived: There is no survival for humanity without global peace!

C. Young people must learn at home and in school that violence may not be a means of settling differences with others. Only thus can a *culture of non-violence* be created.

D. A human person is infinitely precious and must be unconditionally protected. But likewise the *lives of animals and plants* which inhabit this planet with us deserve protection, preservation, and care. Limitless exploitation of the natural foundations of life, ruthless destruction of the biosphere, and militarization of the cosmos are all outrages. As human beings we have a special responsibility—especially with a view to future generations—for Earth and the cosmos, for the air, water, and soil. *We are all intertwined together* in this cosmos and we are all dependent on each other. Each one of us depends on the welfare of all. Therefore the dominance of humanity over nature and the cosmos must not be encouraged. Instead we must cultivate living in harmony with nature and the cosmos.

E. To be authentically human in the spirit of our great religious and ethical traditions means that in public as well as in private life we must be concerned for others and ready to help. We must never be ruthless and brutal. Every people, every race, every religion must show tolerance and respect—indeed high appreciation—for every other. Minorities need protection and support, whether they be racial, ethnic, or religious.

2. Commitment to a culture of solidarity and a just economic order Numberless men and women of all regions and religions strive to live their lives in solidarity with one another and to work for authentic fulfillment of their vocations. Nevertheless, all over the world we find endless hunger, deficiency, and need. Not only individuals, but especially unjust institutions and structures are responsible for these tragedies. Millions of people are without work; millions are exploited by poor wages, forced to the edges of society, with their possibilities for the future destroyed. In many lands the gap between the poor and the rich, between the powerful and the powerless is immense. We live in a world in which totalitarian state socialism as well as unbridled capitalism have hollowed out and destroyed many ethical and spiritual values. A materialistic mentality breeds greed for unlimited profit and a grasping for endless plunder. These demands claim more and more of the community's resources without obliging the individual to contribute more. The cancerous social evil of corruption thrives in the developing countries and in the developed countries alike.

A. In the great ancient religious and ethical traditions of humankind we find the directive: You shall not steal! Or in positive terms: Deal honestly and fairly! Let us reflect anew on the consequences of this ancient directive: No one has the right to rob or dispossess in any way whatsoever any other person or the commonweal. Further, no one has the right to use her or his possessions without concern for the needs of society and Earth.

B. Where extreme poverty reigns, helplessness and despair spread, and theft occurs again and again for the sake of survival. Where power and wealth are accumulated ruthlessly, feelings of envy, resentment, and deadly hatred and rebellion inevitably well up in the disadvantaged and marginalized. This leads to a vicious circle of violence and counter-violence. Let no one be deceived: There is no global peace without global justice!

C. Young people must learn at home and in school that property, limited though it may be, carries with it an obligation, and that its uses should at the same time serve the common good. Only thus can a *just economic order* be built up.

D. If the plight of the poorest billions of humans on this planet, particularly women and children, is to be improved, the world economy must be structured more justly. Individual good deeds, and assistance projects, indispensable though they be, are insufficient. The participation of all states and the authority of international organizations are needed to build just economic institutions.

A solution which can be supported by all sides must be sought for the debt crisis and the poverty of the dissolving second world, and even more the third world. Of course conflicts of interest are unavoidable. In the developed countries, a distinction must be made between necessary and limitless consumption, between socially beneficial and non-beneficial uses of property, between justified and unjustified uses of natural resources, and between a profit-only and a socially beneficial and ecologically oriented market economy. Even the developing nations must search their national consciences.

Wherever those ruling threaten to repress those ruled, wherever institutions threaten persons, and wherever might oppresses right, we are obligated to resist—whenever possible non-violently.

E. To be authentically human in the spirit of our great religious and ethical traditions means the following:

- We must utilize economic and political power for *service to humanity* instead of misusing it in ruthless battles for domination. We must develop a spirit of compassion with those who suffer, with special care for the children, the aged, the poor, the disabled, the refugees, and the lonely.
- We must cultivate *mutual respect* and consideration, so as to reach a reasonable balance of interests, instead of thinking only of unlimited power and unavoidable competitive struggles.
- We must value a sense *of moderation and modesty* instead of an unquenchable greed for money, prestige, and consumption. In greed humans lose their 'souls', their freedom, their composure, their inner peace, and thus that which makes them human.

3. *Commitment to a culture of tolerance and a life of truthfulness* Numberless women and men of all regions and religions strive to lead lives of honesty and truthfulness. Nevertheless, all over the world we find endless lies, and deceit, swindling and hypocrisy, ideology and demagoguery:

- Politicians and businesspeople who use lies as a means to success;
- Mass media which spread ideological propaganda instead of accurate reporting, misinformation instead of information, cynical commercial interest instead of loyalty to the truth;
- Scientists and researchers who give themselves over to morally questionable ideological or political programs or to economic interest groups, or who justify research which violates fundamental ethical values;
- Representatives of religions who dismiss other religions as of little value and who preach fanaticism and intolerance instead of respect and understanding.

A. In the great ancient religious and ethical traditions of humankind we find the directive: *You shall not lie!* Or in positive terms: *Speak and act truthfully!* Let us reflect anew on the consequences of this ancient directive: No woman or man, no institution, no state or church or religious community has the right to speak lies to other humans.

B. This is especially true

- for those who work in the *mass media*, to whom we entrust the freedom to report for the sake of truth and to whom we thus grant the office of guardian. They do not stand above morality but have the obligation to respect human dignity, human rights, and fundamental values. They are duty-bound to objectivity, fairness, and the preservation of human dignity. They have no right to intrude into individuals' private spheres, to manipulate public opinion, or to distort reality;
- for *artists, writers, and scientists*, to whom we entrust artistic and academic freedom. They are not exempt from general ethical standards and must serve the truth;
- for the leaders of countries, *politicians*, and *political parties*, to whom we entrust our own freedoms. When they lie in the faces of their people, when they manipulate the truth, or when they are guilty of venality or ruthlessness in domestic or foreign affairs, they forsake their credibility and deserve to lose their offices and their voters. Conversely, public opinion should support those politicians who dare to speak the truth to the people at all times;
- finally, for *representatives of religion*. When they stir up prejudice, hatred, and enmity towards those of different belief, or even incite or legitimize religious wars, they deserve the condemnation of humankind and the loss of their adherents. Let no one be deceived: There is no global justice without truthfulness and humaneness!

C. Young people must learn at home and in school to think, speak, and act truthfully. They have a right to information and education to be able to make the decisions that will form their lives, Without an ethical formation they will hardly be able to distinguish the important from the unimportant. In the daily flood of information, ethical standards will help them discern when opinions are portrayed as facts, interests veiled, tendencies exaggerated, and facts twisted.

D. To be authentically human in the spirit of our great religious and ethical traditions means the following:

- We must not confuse freedom with arbitrariness or pluralism with indifference to truth.
- We must *cultivate truthfulness* in all our relationships instead of dishonesty, dissembling, and opportunism.
- We must *constantly seek truth* and incorruptible sincerity instead of spreading ideological or partisan half-truths.

- We must courageously *serve the truth* and we must remain *constant* and *trustworthy*, instead of yielding to opportunistic accommodation to life.

4. Commitment to a culture of equal rights and partnership between men and women Numberless men and women of all regions and religions strive to live their lives in a spirit of partnership and responsible action in the areas of love, sexuality, and family. Nevertheless, all over the world there are condemnable forms of patriarchy, domination of one sex over the other, exploitation of women, sexual misuse of children, and forced prostitution. Too frequently, social inequities force women and even children into prostitution as a means of survival—particularly in less developed countries.

A. In the great ancient religious and ethical traditions of humankind we find the directive: *You shall not commit sexual immorality!* Or in positive terms: *Respect and love one another!* Let us reflect anew on the consequences of this ancient directive: No one has the right to degrade others to mere sex objects, to lead them into or hold them in sexual dependency.

B. We condemn sexual exploitation and sexual discrimination as one of the worst forms of human degradation. We have the duty to resist wherever the domination of one sex over the other is preached—even in the name of religious conviction; wherever sexual exploitation is tolerated, wherever prostitution is fostered or children are misused. Let no one be deceived: There is no authentic humaneness without a living together in partnership!

C. Young people must learn at home and in school that sexuality is not a negative, destructive, or exploitative force, but creative and affirmative. Sexuality as a life-affirming shaper of community can only be effective when partners accept the responsibilities of caring for one another's happiness.

D. The relationship between women and men should be characterized not by patronizing behavior or exploitation, but by love, partnership, and trustworthiness. Human fulfillment is not identical with sexual pleasure. Sexuality should express and reinforce a loving relationship lived by equal partners.

Some religious traditions know the ideal of a voluntary renunciation of the full use of sexuality. Voluntary renunciation also can be an expression of identity and meaningful fulfillment.

E. The social institution of marriage, despite all its cultural and religious variety, is characterized by love, loyalty, and permanence. It aims at and should guarantee security and mutual support to husband, wife, and child. It should secure the rights of all family members. All lands and cultures should develop economic and social relationships which will enable marriage and family life worthy of human beings, especially for older people. Children have a right of access to education. Parents should not exploit children, nor children parents. Their relationships should reflect mutual respect, appreciation, and concern.

F. To be authentically human in the spirit of our great religious and ethical traditions means the following:

- We need mutual respect, *partnership*, and understanding, instead of patriarchal domination and degradation, which are expressions of violence and engender counter-violence.
- We need mutual concern, tolerance, readiness for reconciliation, and *love*, instead of any form of possessive lust or sexual misuse. Only what has already been experienced in personal and familial relationships can be practiced on the level of nations and religions.

IV. A Transformation of Consciousness

Historical experience demonstrates the following: Earth cannot be changed for the better unless we achieve a transformation in the consciousness of individuals and in public life. The possibilities for transformation have already been glimpsed in areas such as war and peace, economy, and ecology, where in recent decades fundamental changes have taken place. This transformation must also be achieved in the area of ethics and values! Every individual has intrinsic dignity and inalienable rights, and each also has an inescapable responsibility for what she or he does and does not do. All our decisions and deeds, even our omissions and failures, have consequences.

Keeping this sense of responsibility alive, deepening it and passing it on to future generations, is the special task of religions. We are realistic about what we have achieved in this consensus, and so we urge that the following be observed:

1. A universal consensus on *many disputed ethical questions* (from bio- and sexual ethics through mass media and scientific ethics to economic and political ethics) will be difficult to attain. Nevertheless, even for many controversial questions, suitable solutions should be attainable in the spirit of the fundamental principles we have jointly developed here.
2. In many areas of life a new consciousness of ethical responsibility has already arisen. Therefore we would be pleased if as many professions as possible, such as those of physicians, scientists, businesspeople, journalists, and politicians, would develop up-to-date codes of ethics which would provide specific guidelines for the vexing questions of these particular professions.
3. Above all, we urge the *various communities of faith* to formulate their very *specific ethics*: What does each faith tradition have to say, for example, about the meaning of life and death, the enduring of suffering and the forgiveness of guilt, about selfless sacrifice and the necessity of renunciation,

about compassion and joy? These will deepen, and make more specific, the already discernible global ethic.

In conclusion, we appeal to all the inhabitants of this planet. Earth cannot be changed for the better unless the consciousness of individuals is changed. We pledge to work for such transformation in individual and collective consciousness, for the awakening of our spiritual powers through reflection, meditation, prayer, or positive thinking, for a *conversion of the heart*. Together we can move mountains! Without a willingness to take risks and a readiness to sacrifice there can be no fundamental change in our situation! Therefore we commit ourselves to a common global ethic, to better mutual understanding, as well as to socially beneficial, peace-fostering, and Earth-friendly ways of life.

We invite all men and women, whether religious or not, to do the same!

Study Questions

1. The Sermon on the Mount presents a lofty ethical vision based on selflessness and unconditional love for others. Some Christians have claimed that human sinfulness, rooted in selfishness or pride, makes it impossible for us to live up to these teachings without God's grace. Do you think Jesus's ethical teachings are too difficult for human beings to live up to without divine help? Should the person who does not believe in God regard these teachings as reasonable or unreasonable? Explain.

2. While Paul declares love to be a higher virtue than faith and hope, traditional Christian teaching maintains that faith in God is required for the spiritual virtues of hope and love. Do you think one needs to believe in God in order to be genuinely loving? Why or why not? Consider how Kai Nielsen would respond to this question.

3. As the Bhagavad Gita opens, Arjuna finds himself in a moral dilemma arising from a conflict of duties. What is Arjuna's dilemma? Do you think that we each have duties specific to our social roles or caste? Are there sometimes conflicts between the duties of our personal, social, family or religious life? Krishna resolves Arjuna's moral dilemma by telling him to act with detachment. Why does Krishna consider acting with detachment to be virtuous? Can you think of any instances when acting in this manner would be less than virtuous?

4. Divine command theorists are faced with the following difficulty. If ethical principles are dependent on God's will, then morality seems to be arbitrary. But if ethical principles are not dependent on God's will, then God's will is not completely free or sovereign since it is subject to an independent standard of right and wrong. Some philosophers have tried to resolve this difficulty by identifying values like goodness or justice with God's being. On this view, God *is* goodness-itself and justice-itself, so these ethical standards or values do not exist independently of God. Does the idea that God *is* goodness-itself resolve the problem? Explain.

5. The philosopher Immanuel Kant (see chapter 6) claimed that mature moral agents must have *autonomy* with regard to ethics, that is, must obey ethical principles that derive from our own ethical reasoning rather than simply obeying principles imposed from another (*heteronomy*). Since divine command theory maintains that ethical principles derive from the mind and will of God, it conforms to what Kant would regard as heteronomous, and therefore, morally immature. How does Richard Mouw respond to the charge that divine command theory is morally immature? Do you find his defense convincing?

6. The "Declaration Toward a Global Ethic" purports that there are basic, universal ethical principles, derived from the world's religions, that all people can agree on. Do you agree with this claim? Does this statement undermine the view that religious moralities are relative? Must one be religious to accept the ethical principles put forth in this statement? How might an atheist respond to it?

For Further Reading

Adams, Robert. *Finite and Infinite Goods: A Framework for Ethics*. New York: Oxford University Press, 2002.

Boulton, Wayne G., Thomas D. Kennedy, and Allen Verhey, eds. *From Christ to the World: Introductory Readings in Christian Ethics*. Grand Rapids, MI: Eerdmans, 1994.

Dorff, Elliot N., and Louis E. Newman, eds. *Contemporary Jewish Ethics and Morality*. New York: Oxford University Press, 1995.

Helm, Paul, ed. *Divine Commands and Morality*. Oxford: Oxford University Press, 1981.

Küng, Hans. *A Global Ethic for Global Politics and Economics*. New York: Oxford University Press, 1998.

MacIntyre, Alasdair, and Paul Ricoeur. *The Religious Significance of Atheism*. New York: Columbia University Press, 1969.

Nasr, S. H. *Ideals and Realities of Islam*. Revised ed. Chicago: Kazi Publications, 2000.

Perrett, Roy W. *Hindu Ethics: A Philosophical Study*. Honolulu: University of Hawaii Press, 1998.

CHAPTER THREE

Moral Relativism

Perhaps you have had the opportunity to travel in a foreign country. If so, you will have noticed that things are done differently there than what you were used to at home. People may drive on a different side of the road, eat foods that people at home would find distasteful and stand closer or further away when talking than you are used to doing. We tend to think that these are matters of convention—differing cultural choices that add to the diversity and interest in the world, but not matters on which we think *we* are *right* and *they* are *wrong*.

But what if we find upon visiting another country that cripples are expected to beg on the streets for food? Or that if a husband beats his wife severely in public, people think it is "none of their business" and pass by without intervening or calling the police? Or that when the military is running short of recruits it kidnaps teenage boys and forces them to become soldiers? We might think that these practices are not just *different* but that they are *wrong*.

Often too, we may talk with visitors to our own country who cannot pass off the cultural differences they observe as mere matters of custom. They find out that our elderly are routinely put into "rest homes" where families seldom visit and where they spend many hours lying in bed or sitting while being ignored by the busy staff. They find out that four-person or three-person (or even two-person) families live in houses that look like hotels to them, with room after room barely in use, while they see many people sleeping on the street. They find that we throw tons of good food away while others go hungry. They sadly shake their heads in puzzled wonder at the indifference and waste. They think that our practices are not just different but *wrong*.

Moral relativism is the philosophical position that *all* value judgments—moral evaluations as well as personal preferences, or matters of etiquette and taste—are equally matters of convention. Right and wrong are always relative to particular groups or cultures; there is no truth to the matter of whether one culture's ethical views are better or worse than another's.

Our increasingly global society brings the issue of cross-cultural moral evaluations before us daily. Yet this important philosophical issue is not new. The ancient Greek historian Herodotus raised the question of how different cultures evaluate each other. A group of teachers in classical Greece called Sophists maintained that "man is the measure of all things," in other words, that there was no way of adjudicating among conflicting social conventions. Philosophers such as Socrates, Plato and Aristotle disagreed. In the thousands of years since then, philosophers and others have been debating whether or not some form of moral relativism is true and whether or not there are moral principles that apply to all cultures and times.

One thing that has changed in the last two hundred years is the rise of the social sciences, along with the professional organizations that represent them. Social scientists, especially anthropologists, have been committed to observing varieties of human behavior and societies while remaining objective and impartial. Yet, as the 1947 Statement on Human Rights from the *American Anthropologist* makes clear, professional groups of social scientists have recognized the tension between respect for diverse cultures and the intuition that there are basic human rights that should be recognized in every culture. The statement clearly advocates cultural relativism (the view that there are in fact vast differences among the systems of morality endorsed within cultures). But as we will see in other essays contained in this section, cultural relativism (a descriptive view about the patterns of evaluations are made) does not necessarily entail *moral relativism* (a philosophical view about the validity or status of those evaluations). The statement thus goes on to wrestle with the important question: "Is the notion of universal human rights itself just a culturally-conditioned belief—a product of Western individualism—or do such rights apply to everyone irrespective of their culture?" Note how this document attempts to distinguish, with varying degrees of accuracy and success, scientific and normative questions, as well as what it assumes about the relationships between them.

The essays by philosophers Gilbert Harman and Louis Pojman represent the range of opinion among philosophers concerning moral relativism. Harman argues that a particular form of moral relativism is both true and defensible, while Pojman thinks that much of the appeal of moral relativism rests on confusions of one sort or another.

Gilbert Harman asserts that moral reasoning is a kind of practical reasoning and, as such, aims at internal coherence, stability and maximizing the needs and desires of people who live within communities. Different cultures develop differing moral codes that have varying degrees of these features. Harman calls ethical evaluations that use the terms right, wrong, ought or ought not, "inner judgments." Making such an inner judgment as "It is wrong to stand by and watch a man beat a woman, even if she is his wife" is to claim that (1) the person you are making a judgment about *has a reason to do something* and (2) that the person making the judgment and the audience of the judgment *endorse these reasons*. Inner judgments are, if Harman is right, relative to certain cultures or subcultures—those who recognize and endorse certain particular reasons for acting or refraining from action. For someone who does not recognize those reasons, the judgment that his or her actions are wrong will be false.

Notice Harman does not think that his form of moral relativism rules out moral reform. This is because the internal inconsistencies and incoherencies within a moral code may be used to argue for resolving those inconsistencies in the direction of what external evaluators would recognize as a better moral code. Note also that even though outsiders may not be able to say that actions by those in another culture or subculture are wrong, they will be able to correctly label them as bad, or even evil. But notice, finally, that Harman's view goes so far as to endorse what Pojman calls subjectivism. After reading both articles, it would be appropriate for you to decide whether you believe Pojman's reasons for thinking that subjectivism makes no sense are devastating to Harman's view or whether Harman could successfully rebut them.

Louis Pojman thinks that many people believe in moral relativism either because they think it follows logically from cultural relativism or because they think that the only alternative to moral relativism is an implausible form of moral absolutism. As we have already noted, cultural relativism (which Pojman also calls the *diversity thesis*) is the uncontroversial view that cultures do differ remarkably from one another in their ethical views and moral codes. Pojman tries to show that it is fallacious to infer from this that morality is dependent on group or individual opinion (what Pojman calls the *dependency thesis*). He goes on to detail what he considers to be a number of serious philosophical problems with moral relativism. Pojman argues that a modest, nonreligious form of moral objectivism is true. In reading his essay, note the contrast that he draws between objectivism (the view that there are some moral principles that all people and cultures should recognize) and moral absolutism (the view that there are some moral principles that cannot be overridden no matter what the circumstances). Pojman's version of moral objectivism is indebted to the views of W. D. Ross (an excerpt from Ross is contained in the section on Ethics of Duty on page 234). Pojman lists principles that he claims are part of a universal core morality. Decide for yourself whether you think that these principles should be embraced by all cultures, no matter how much their customs, histories and circumstances may vary.

Loretta Kopelman's essay brings us from the abstract philosophical debate between relativists and objectivists to a very particular current controversy about the practice of excising parts of the genitals of young girls. Male circumcision, while not universal, is a relatively common medical procedure in modern Western cultures. Some African and Arabian cultures view what critics call "female genital mutilation" as analogous to male circumcision and even call it female circumcision. Those in favor of female circumcision argue that it has religious and cultural significance for groups that practice it and that it is valued both by women and men in those cultures. Kopelman cites critics of the practice that are members of these very cultures, as well as considerable medical evidence that the practice is damaging and dangerous. As you read her article it might be interesting to ask yourself whether the danger and damage is an easily remedied by-product of the way the practice is currently done (picture what the effects of male circumcision might be like if done with sharp rocks or kitchen knives instead of with sterilized instruments in a hospital). Yet scarring and infection do not seem to be the biggest issues here. At bottom what needs to be decided is whether something so basic to being human as the capacity for sexual pleasure can permissibly be taken from someone even if she does not value it or believe in it or values it far less than following the customs of her culture.

Statement on Human Rights*

Submitted to the Commission on Human Rights, United Nations, by the Executive Board, American Anthropological Association

The problem faced by the Commission on Human Rights of the United Nations in preparing its Declaration on the Rights of Man must be approached from two points of view. The first, in terms of which the Declaration is ordinarily conceived, concerns the respect for the personality of the individual as such, and his right to its fullest development as a member of his society. In a world order, however, respect for the cultures of differing human groups is equally important.

These are two facets of the same problem, since it is a truism that groups are composed of individuals, and human beings do not function outside the societies of which they form a part. The problem is thus to formulate a statement of hu-

*Reproduced by permission of the American Anthropological Association from *American Anthropologist* 49, no. 4 (1947): 539–43. Not for sale or further reproduction.

man rights that will do more than just phrase respect for the individual as an individual. It must also take into full account the individual as a member of the social group of which he is a part, whose sanctioned modes of life shape his behavior, and with whose fate his own is thus inextricably bound.

Because of the great numbers of societies that are in intimate contact in the modern world, and because of the diversity of their ways of life, the primary task confronting those who would draw up a Declaration on the Rights of Man is thus, in essence, to resolve the following problem: How can the proposed Declaration be applicable to all human beings, and not be a statement of rights conceived only in terms of the values prevalent in the countries of Western Europe and America?

Before we can cope with this problem, it will be necessary for us to outline some of the findings of the sciences that deal with the study of human culture, that must be taken into account if the Declaration is to be in accord with the present state of knowledge about man and his modes of life.

If we begin, as we must, with the individual, we find that from the moment of his birth not only his behavior, but his very thought, his hopes, aspirations, the moral values which direct his action and justify and give meaning to his life in his own eyes and those of his fellows, are shaped by the body of custom of the group of which he becomes a member. The process by means of which this is accomplished is so subtle, and its effects are so far-reaching, that only after considerable training are we conscious of it. Yet if the essence of the Declaration is to be, as it must, a statement in which the right of the individual to develop his personality to the fullest is to be stressed, then this must be based on a recognition of the fact that the personality of the individual can develop only in terms of the culture of his society.

Over the past fifty years, the many ways in which man resolves the problems of subsistence, of social living, of political regulation of group life, of reaching accord with the Universe and satisfying his aesthetic drives has been widely documented by the researches of anthropologists among peoples living in all parts of the world. All peoples do achieve these ends. No two of them, however, do so in exactly the same way, and some of them employ means that differ, often strikingly, from one another.

Yet here a dilemma arises. Because of the social setting of the learning process, the individual cannot but be convinced that his own way of life is the most desirable one. Conversely, and despite changes originating from within and without his culture that he recognizes as worthy of adoption, it becomes equally patent to him that, in the main, other ways than his own, to the degree they differ from it, are less desirable than those to which he is accustomed. Hence valuations arise, that in themselves receive the sanction of accepted belief.

The degree to which such evaluations eventuate in action depends on the basic sanctions in the thought of a people. In the main, people are willing to live and let live, exhibiting a tolerance for behavior of another group different than their own, especially where there is no conflict in the subsistence field. In the history of Western Europe and America, however, economic expansion, control of armaments, and an evangelical religious tradition have translated the recognition of cultural differences into a summons to action. This has been emphasized by philosophical systems that have stressed absolutes in the realm of values and ends. Definitions of freedom, concepts of the nature of human rights, and the like, have thus been narrowly drawn. Alternatives have been decried, and suppressed where controls have been established over non-European peoples. The hard core of *similarities* between cultures has consistently been overlooked.

The consequences of this point of view have been disastrous for mankind. Doctrines of the "white man's burden" have been employed to implement economic exploitation and to deny the right to control their own affairs to millions of peoples over the world, where the expansion of Europe and America has not meant the literal extermination of whole populations. Rationalized in terms of ascribing cultural inferiority to these peoples, or in conceptions of their backwardness in development of their '"primitive mentality," that justified their being held in the tutelage of their superiors, the history of the expansion of the western world has been marked by demoralization of human personality and the disintegration of human rights among the peoples over whom hegemony has been established.

The values of the ways of life of these peoples have been consistently misunderstood and decried. Religious beliefs that for untold ages have carried conviction, and permitted adjustment to the Universe have been attacked as superstitious, immoral, untrue. And, since power carries its own conviction, this has furthered the process of demoralization begun by economic exploitation and the loss of political autonomy. The white man's burden, the civilizing mission, have been heavy indeed. But their weight has not been borne by those who, frequently in all honesty, have journeyed to the far places of the world to uplift those regarded by them as inferior.

We thus come to the first proposition that the study of human psychology and culture dictates as essential in drawing up a Bill of Human Rights in terms of existing knowledge:

1. The individual realizes his personality through his culture, hence respect for individual differences entails a respect for cultural differences.

There can be no individual freedom, that is, when the group with which the individual identifies himself is not free. There can be no full development of the individual personality as long as the individual is told, by men who have the power to enforce their commands, that the way of life of his group is inferior to that of those who wield the power.

This is more than an academic question, as becomes evident if one looks about him at the world as it exists today. Peoples who on first contact with European and American might were awed and partially convinced of the superior ways of their rulers have, through two wars and a depression, come to re-examine the new and the old. Professions of love of democracy, of devotion to freedom have come with something less than conviction to those who are themselves denied the right to lead their lives as seems proper to them. The religious dogmas of those who profess equality and practice discrimination, who stress the virtue of humility and are themselves arrogant in insistence on their beliefs have little meaning for peoples whose devotion to other faiths makes these inconsistencies as clear as the desert landscape at high noon. Small wonder that these peoples, denied the right to live in terms of their own cultures, are discovering new values in old beliefs they had been led to question.

No consideration of human rights can be adequate without taking into account the related problem of human capacity. Man, biologically, is one. *Homo sapiens* is a single species, no matter how individuals may differ in their aptitudes, their abilities, their interests. It is established that any normal individual can learn any part of any culture other than his own, provided only he is afforded the opportunity to do so. That cultures differ in degree of complexity, of richness of content, is due to historic forces, not biological ones. All existing ways of life meet the test of survival. Of those cultures that have disappeared, it must be remembered that their number includes some that were great, powerful, and complex as well as others that were modest, content with the *status quo*, and simple. Thus we reach a second principle:

> 2. *Respect for differences between cultures is validated by the scientific fact that no technique of qualitatively evaluating cultures has been discovered.*

This principle leads us to a further one, namely that the aims that guide the life of every people are self-evident in their significance to that people. It is the principle that emphasizes the universals in human conduct rather than the absolutes that the culture of Western Europe and America stresses. It recognizes that the eternal verities only seem so because we have been taught to regard them as such; that every people, whether it expresses them or not, lives in devotion to verities whose eternal nature is as real to them as are those of Euroamerican culture to Euroamericans. Briefly stated, this third principle that must be introduced into our consideration is the following:

3. Standards and values are relative to the culture from which they derive so that any attempt to formulate postulates that grow out of the beliefs or moral codes of one culture must to that extent detract from the applicability of any Declaration of Human Rights to mankind as a whole.

Ideas of right and wrong, good and evil, are found in all societies, though they differ in their expression among different peoples. What is held to be a human right in one society may be regarded as anti-social by another people, or by the same people in a different period of their history. The saint of one epoch would at a later time be confined as a man not fitted to cope with reality. Even the nature of the physical world, the colors we see, the sounds we hear, are conditioned by the language we speak, which is part of the culture into which we are born.

The problem of drawing up a Declaration of Human Rights was relatively simple in the Eighteenth Century, because it was not a matter of human rights, but of the rights of men within the framework of the sanctions laid by a single society. Even then, so noble a document as the American Declaration of Independence, or the American Bill of Rights, could be written by men who themselves were slave-owners, in a country where chattel slavery was a part of the recognized social order. The revolutionary character of the slogan "Liberty, Equality, Fraternity" was never more apparent than in the struggles to implement it by extending it to the French slave-owning colonies.

Today the problem is complicated by the fact that the Declaration must be of world-wide applicability. It must embrace and recognize the validity of many different ways of life. It will not be convincing to the Indonesian, the African, the Indian, the Chinese, if it lies on the same plane as like documents of an earlier period. The rights of Man in the Twentieth Century cannot be circumscribed by the standards of any single culture, or be dictated by the aspirations of any single people. Such a document will lead to frustration, not realization of the personalities of vast numbers of human beings.

Such persons, living in terms of values not envisaged by a limited Declaration, will thus be excluded from the freedom of full participation in the only right and proper way of life that can be known to them, the institutions, sanctions and goals that make up the culture of their particular society.

Even where political systems exist that deny citizens the right of participation in their government, or seek to conquer weaker peoples, underlying cultural values may be called on to bring the peoples of such states to a realization of the consequences of the acts of their governments, and thus enforce a brake upon discrimination and conquest. For the political system of a people is only a small part of their total culture.

World-wide standards of freedom and justice, based on the principle that man is free only when he lives as his society defines freedom, that his rights are those he recognizes as a member of his society, must be basic. Conversely, an effective world-order cannot be devised except insofar as it permits the free play of personality of the members of its constituent social units, and draws strength from the enrichment to be derived from the interplay of varying personalities.

The world-wide acclaim accorded the Atlantic Charter, before its restricted applicability was announced, is evidence of the fact that freedom is understood and sought after by peoples having the most diverse cultures. Only when a statement of the right of men to live in terms of their own traditions is incorporated into the proposed Declaration, then, can the next step of defining the rights and duties of human groups as regards each other be set upon the firm foundation of the present-day scientific knowledge of Man.

June 24, 1947

The Case Against Ethical Relativsm*

Louis Pojman

"Who's to Judge What's Right or Wrong?"

> Like many people, I have always been instinctively a moral relativist. As far back as I can remember . . . it has always seemed to be obvious that the dictates of morality arise from some sort of convention or understanding among people, that different people arrive at different understandings, and that there are no basic moral demands that apply to everyone. This seemed so obvious to me I assumed it was everyone's instinctive view, or at least everyone who gave the matter any thought in this day and age.[1] (Gilbert Harman)

> Ethical relativism is the doctrine that the moral rightness and wrongness of actions vary from society to society and that there are not absolute universal moral standards on all men at all times. Accordingly, it holds that whether or not it is right for an individual to act in a certain way depends on or is relative to the society to which he belongs.[2] (John Ladd)

Gilbert Harman's intuitions about the self-evidence of ethical relativism contrasts strikingly with Plato's or Kant's equal certainty about the truth of objectivism, the doctrine that universally valid or true ethical principles exist.[3] "Two things fill the soul with ever new and increasing wonder and reverence the

---

*From Louis Pojman, *Ethical Theory*, Fifth Edition.

oftener and more fervently reflection ponders on it: the starry heavens above and the moral law within," wrote Kant. On the basis of polls taken in my ethics and introduction to philosophy classes over the past several years, Harman's views may signal a shift in contemporary society's moral understanding. The polls show a 2–1 ratio in favor of moral relativism over moral absolutism, with less than 5 percent of the respondents recognizing that a third position between these two polar opposites might exist. Of course, I'm not suggesting that all of these students had a clear understanding of what relativism entails, for many who said that they were relativists also contended in the same polls that abortion except to save the mother's life is always wrong, that capital punishment is always wrong, or that suicide is never morally permissible.

Among my university colleagues, a growing number also seem to embrace moral relativism. Recently, one of my nonphilosopher colleagues voted to turn down a doctoral dissertation proposal because the student assumed an objectivist position in ethics. (Ironically, I found in this same colleague's work rhetorical treatment of individual liberty that raised it to the level of a non-negotiable absolute.) But irony and inconsistency aside, many relativists are aware of the tension between their own subjective positions and their metatheory that entails relativism. I confess that I too am tempted by the allurements of this view and find some forms of it plausible and worthy of serious examination. However, I also find it deeply troubling.

In this essay, I will examine the central notions of ethical relativism and look at the implications that seem to follow from it. Then I will present the outline of a very modest objectivism, one that takes into account many of the insights of relativism and yet stands as a viable option to it.

1. An Analysis of Relativism

Let us examine the theses contained in John Ladd's succinct statement on ethical (conventional) relativism that appears at the beginning of this essay. If we analyze it, we derive the following argument:

1. Moral rightness and wrongness of actions vary from society to society, so there are no universal, moral standards held by all societies.
2. Whether or not it is right for individuals to act in a certain way depends on (or is relative to) the society to which they belong.
3. Therefore, there are no absolute or objective moral standards that apply to all people everywhere.

1. The first thesis, which may be called the *diversity thesis*, is simply a description that acknowledges the fact that moral rules differ from society to society. Eskimos allow their elderly to die by starvation, whereas we believe that this is

morally wrong. The Spartans of ancient Greece and the Dobu of New Guinea believe(d) that stealing is morally right, but we believe it is wrong. A tribe in East Africa once threw deformed infants to the hippopotamuses, but we abhor infanticide. Ruth Benedict describes a tribe in Melanesia that views cooperation and kindness as vices, whereas we see them as virtues. Sexual practices vary over time and place. Some cultures permit homosexual behavior, while others condemn it. Some cultures practice polygamy, while others view it as immoral. Some cultures accept cannibalism, while the very idea revolts us. Cultural relativism is well documented, and "custom is the king o'er all." There may or may not be moral principles held in common by every society, but if there are any, they seem to be few, at best. Certainly, it would be very difficult to derive any single "true" morality by observing various societies' moral standards. Nevertheless, as Hume pointed out long ago, the fact that different cultures have different practices no more refutes ethical objectivism than the fact that water flows in different directions in different places refutes the law of gravity. A further premise is needed.

2. The second thesis, the *dependency thesis*, asserts that individual acts are right or wrong depending on the nature of the society from which they emanate. Morality does not occur in a vacuum, and what is considered morally right or wrong must be seen in a context that depends on the goals, wants, beliefs, history, and environment of the society in question. As William G. Sumner says,

> We learn the morals as unconsciously as we learn to walk and hear and breathe, and [we] never know any reason why the [morals] are what they are. The justification of them is that when we wake to consciousness of life we find them facts which already hold us in the bonds of tradition, custom, and habit.[4]

Trying to see things from an independent, noncultural point of view would be like taking out our eyes in order to examine their contours and qualities. There is no "innocent eye." We are simply culturally determined beings.

We could, of course, distinguish between a weak and strong thesis of dependency, for the nonrelativist can accept a certain degree of relativity in the way moral principles are *applied*, in various cultures, depending on beliefs, history, and environment. For example, Asians show respect by covering the head and uncovering the feet, whereas Westerners do the opposite. Both sides adhere to a principle of respect but apply it differently. But the ethical relativist must maintain a stronger thesis, one that insists that the moral principles themselves are products of the cultures and may vary from society to society. The ethical relativist contends that even beyond environmental factors and differences in beliefs, a fundamental disagreement exists among societies.

In a sense we all live in radically different worlds. But the relativist wants to go further and maintain that there is something conventional about *any* morality, so that every morality really depends on a level of social acceptance. Not only do various societies adhere to different moral systems, but the very same society could (and often does) change its moral views over place and time. For example, the majority of people in the southern United States now view slavery as immoral, whereas one hundred and forty years ago they did not. Our society's views on divorce, sexuality, abortion, and assisted suicide have changed somewhat as well—and they are still changing.

3. The conclusion that there are no absolute or objective moral standards binding on all people follows from the first two propositions. Combining cultural relativism (*the diversity thesis*) with the *dependency thesis* yields ethical relativism in its classic form. If there are different moral principles from culture to culture and if all morality is rooted in culture, then it follows that there are no universal moral principles that are valid (or true) for all cultures and peoples at all times.

2. *Subjectivism*

Some people think that this conclusion is still too tame, and they maintain that morality is not dependent on the society but rather on the individual. As my students sometimes maintain, "Morality is in the eye of the beholder." They treat morality like taste or aesthetic judgments, person relative. This form of moral subjectivism has the sorry consequence that it makes morality a very useless concept, for, on its premises, little or no interpersonal criticism or judgment is logically possible. Suppose that you are repulsed by observing John torturing a child. You cannot condemn him if one of his principles is "torture little children for the fun of it." The only basis for judging him wrong might be that he was a hypocrite who condemned others for torturing, but suppose that another of his principles is that hypocrisy is morally permissible (for him), so that we cannot condemn him for condemning others for doing what he does.

On the basis of subjectivism Adolf Hitler and serial murderer Ted Bundy could be considered as moral as Gandhi, as long as each lived by his own standards, whatever those might be. Witness the following paraphrase of a tape-recorded conversation between Ted Bundy and one of his victims in which Bundy justifies his murder:

> Then I learned that all moral judgments are "value judgments," that all value judgments are subjective, and that none can be proved to be either "right" or "wrong." I even read somewhere that the Chief Justice of the United States had written that the American Constitution expressed nothing more than collective value judgments. Believe it or not, I figured out for myself—what apparently the Chief Justice couldn't figure out for himself—that if the rationality of one value judgment was zero, multiplying it by millions would not make it one whit

> more rational. Nor is there any "reason" to obey the law for anyone, like myself, who has the boldness and daring—the strength of character—to throw off its shackles. . . . I discovered that to become truly free, truly unfettered, I had to become truly uninhibited. And I quickly discovered that the greatest obstacle to my freedom, the greatest block and limitation to it, consists in the insupportable "value judgment" that I was bound to respect the rights of others. I asked myself, who were these "others"? Other human beings, with human rights? Why is it more wrong to kill a human animal than any other animal, a pig or a sheep or a steer? Is your life more to you than a hog's life to a hog? Why should I be willing to sacrifice my pleasure more for the one than for the other? Surely, you would not, in this age of scientific enlightenment, declare that God or nature has marked some pleasures as "moral" or "good" and others as "immoral" or "bad"? In any case, let me assure you, my dear young lady, that there is absolutely no comparison between the pleasure I might take in eating ham and the pleasure I anticipate in raping and murdering you. That is the honest conclusion to which my education has led me—after the most conscientious examination of my spontaneous and uninhibited self.[5]

Notions of good and bad, or right and wrong, cease to have interpersonal evaluative meaning. We might be revulsed by the views of Ted Bundy, but that is just a matter of taste. A student might not like it when her teacher gives her an F on a test paper, while he gives another student an A for a similar paper, but there is no way to criticize him for injustice, because justice is not one of his chosen principles.

Absurd consequences follow from subjectivism. If it is correct, then morality reduces to aesthetic tastes about which there can be neither argument nor interpersonal judgment. Although many students say they espouse subjectivism, there is evidence that it conflicts with other of their moral views. They typically condemn Hitler as an evil man for his genocidal policies. A contradiction seems to exist between subjectivism and the very concept of morality, which it is supposed to characterize, for morality has to do with *proper* resolution of interpersonal conflict and the amelioration of the human predicament. Whatever else it does, morality has a minimal aim of preventing a Hobbesian state of nature, wherein life is "solitary, nasty, poor, brutish and short." But if so, subjectivism is no help at all, for it rests neither on social agreement of principle (as the conventionalist maintains) nor on an objectively independent set of norms that bind all people for the common good. If there were only one person on earth, there would be no occasion for morality because there wouldn't be any interpersonal conflicts to resolve or others whose suffering he or she would have a duty to ameliorate. Subjectivism implicitly assumes something of this solipsism, an atomism in which isolated individuals make up separate universes.

Radical individualistic ethical relativism is incoherent. If so, it follows that the only plausible view of ethical relativism must be one that grounds morality in the group or culture. This form is called *conventionalism*.

3. Conventionalism

Conventional Ethical Relativism, the view that there are no objective moral principles but that all valid moral principles are justified (or are made true) by virtue of their cultural acceptance, recognizes the social nature of morality. That is precisely its power and virtue. It does not seem subject to the same absurd consequences that plague Subjectivism. Recognizing the importance of our social environment in generating customs and beliefs, many people suppose that ethical relativism is the correct metaethical theory. Furthermore, they are drawn to it for its liberal philosophical stance. It seems to be an enlightened response to the sin of ethnocentricity, and it seems to entail or strongly imply an attitude of tolerance toward other cultures. As anthropologist Ruth Benedict says in recognizing ethical relativity "We shall arrive at a more realistic social faith, accepting as grounds of hope and as new bases for tolerance the coexisting and equally valid patterns of life which mankind has created for itself from the raw materials of existence."[6] The most famous of those holding this position is anthropologist Melville Herskovits, who argues even more explicitly than Benedict that ethical relativism entails intercultural tolerance.

1. If Morality is relative to its culture, then there is no independent basis for criticizing the morality of any other culture but one's own.
2. If there is no independent way of criticizing any other Culture, we ought to be *tolerant* of the moralities of other cultures.
3. Morality is relative to its culture. Therefore,
4. We ought to be tolerant of the moralities of other cultures.[7]

Tolerance is certainly a virtue, but is this a good argument for it? I think not. If morality simply is relative to each culture, then if the culture in question does not have a principle of tolerance, its members have no obligation to be tolerant. Herskovits seems to be treating the *principle of tolerance* as the one exception to his relativism. He seems to be treating it as an absolute moral principle. But from a relativistic point of view there is no more reason to be tolerant than to be intolerant and neither stance is objectively morally better than the other.

Not only do relativists fail to offer a basis for criticizing those who are intolerant, but they cannot rationally criticize anyone who espouses what they might regard as a heinous principle. If, as seems to be the case, valid criticism supposes an objective or impartial standard, relativists cannot morally criticize anyone outside their own culture. Adolf Hitler's genocidal actions, as long as they are culturally accepted, are as morally legitimate as Mother Teresa's works of mercy. If Conventional Relativism is accepted, racism, genocide of unpopular minorities, oppression of the poor, slavery, and even the advocacy of war for its own sake are as equally moral as their opposites. And if a subculture decided that starting a nuclear war was somehow morally acceptable, we could not morally criticize these people. Any actual morality, whatever its content, is as valid as every other, and more valid than ideal moralities—since the latter aren't adhered to by any culture.

There are other disturbing consequences of ethical relativism. It seems to entail that reformers are always (morally) wrong since they go against the tide of cultural standards. William Wilberforce was wrong in the eighteenth century to oppose slavery, the British were immoral in opposing *suttee* in India (the burning of widows, which is now illegal in India). The Early Christians were wrong in refusing to serve in the Roman army or bow down to Caesar, since the majority in the Roman Empire believed that these two acts were moral duties. In fact, Jesus himself was immoral in breaking the law of his day by healing on the Sabbath day and by advocating the principles of the Sermon on the Mount, since it is clear that few in his time (or in ours) accepted them.

Yet we normally feel just the opposite, that the reformer is a courageous innovator who is right, who has the truth, against the mindless majority. Sometimes the individual must stand alone with the truth, risking social censure and persecution. As Dr. Stockman says in Ibsen's *Enemy of the People*, after he loses the battle to declare his town's profitable, but polluted, tourist spa unsanitary, "The most dangerous enemy of the truth and freedom among us—is the compact majority. Yes, the damned, compact and liberal majority. The majority has *might*—unfortunately—but *right* it is not. Right—are I and a few others." Yet if relativism is correct, the opposite is necessarily the case. Truth is with the crowd and error with the individual.

Similarly, Conventional Ethical Relativism entails disturbing judgments about the law. Our normal view is that we have a prima facie duty to obey the law, because law, in general, promotes the human good. According to most objective systems, this obligation is not absolute but relative to the particular law's relation to a wider moral order. Civil disobedience is warranted in some cases where the law seems to be in serious conflict with morality. However, if moral relativism is true, then neither law nor civil disobedience has a firm foundation. On the one hand, from the side of the society at large, civil disobedience will be morally wrong, as long as the majority culture agrees with the law in question. On the other hand, if you belong to the relevant subculture that doesn't recognize the particular law in question (because it is unjust from your point of view), disobedience will be morally mandated. The Ku Klux Klan, which believes that Jews, Catholics, and blacks are evil or undeserving of high regard, are, given conventionalism, morally permitted or required to break the laws that protect these endangered groups. Why should I obey a law that my group doesn't recognize as valid?

To sum up, unless we have an independent moral basis for law, it is hard to see why we have any general duty to obey it; and unless we recognize the priority of a universal moral law, we have' no firm basis to justify our acts of civil disobedience against "unjust laws." Both the validity of law and morally motivated disobedience of unjust laws are annulled in favor of a power struggle.

There is an even more basic problem with the notion that morality is dependent on cultural acceptance for its validity. The problem is that the notion of a *culture* or *society* is notoriously difficult to define. This is especially so in a pluralistic society like our own where the notion seems to be vague with unclear boundary lines. One person may belong to several societies (subcultures) with different value emphases and arrangements of principles. A person may belong to the nation as a single society with certain values of patriotism, honor, courage, laws (including some that are controversial but have majority acceptance, such as the current law on abortion). But he or she may also belong to a church that opposes some of the laws of the State. He may also be an integral member of a socially mixed community where different principles hold sway, and he may belong to clubs and a family where still other rules are adhered to. Relativism would seem to tell us that where he is a member of societies with conflicting moralities he must be judged both wrong and not-wrong whatever he does. For example, if Mary is a U.S. citizen and a member of the Roman Catholic church, she is wrong (qua Catholic) if she chooses to have an abortion and not-wrong (qua citizen of the United States) if she acts against the teaching of the church on abortion. As a member of a racist university fraternity, KKK, John has no obligation to treat his fellow black student as an equal, but as a member of the university community itself (where the principle of equal rights is accepted) he does have the obligation; but as a member of the surrounding community (which may reject the principle of equal rights) he again has no such obligation; but then again as a member of the nation at large (which accepts the principle) he is obligated to treat his fellow with respect. What is the morally right thing for John to do? The question no longer makes much sense in this moral Babel. It has lost its action-guiding function.

Perhaps the relativist would adhere to a principle that says that in such cases the individual may choose which group to belong to as primary. If Mary chooses to have an abortion, she is choosing to belong to the general society relative to that principle. And John must likewise choose among groups. The trouble with this option is that it seems to lead back to counterintuitive results. If Murder Mike of Murder, Incorporated, feels like killing bank manager Ortcutt and wants to feel good about it, he identifies with the Murder,

Incorporated society rather than the general public morality. Does this justify the killing? In fact, couldn't one justify anything simply by forming a small subculture that approved of it? Ted Bundy would be morally pure in raping and killing innocents simply by virtue of forming a little coterie. How large must the group be in order to be a legitimate subculture or society? Does it need ten or fifteen people? How about just three? Come to think about it, why can't my burglary partner and I found our own society with a morality of its own? Of course, if my partner dies, I could still claim that I was acting from an originally social set of norms. But why can't I dispense with the interpersonal agreements altogether and invent my own morality—since morality, on this view, is only an invention anyway? Conventionalist Relativism seems to reduce to Subjectivism. And Subjectivism leads, as we have seen, to moral solipsism, to the demise of morality altogether.

Should one object that this is an instance of the *Slippery Slope Fallacy*,[8] let that person give an alternative analysis of what constitutes a viable social basis for generating valid (or true) moral principles. Perhaps we might agree (for the sake of argument, at least) that the very nature of morality entails two people making an agreement. This move saves the conventionalist from moral solipsism, but it still permits almost any principle at all to count as moral. And what's more, those principles can be thrown out and their contraries substituted for them as the need arises. If two or three people decide that they will make cheating on exams morally acceptable for themselves, via forming a fraternity *Cheaters Anonymous* at their university, then cheating becomes moral. Why not? Why not rape, as well?

However, I don't think you can stop the move from conventionalism to subjectivism. The essential force of the validity of the chosen moral principle is that it is dependent on *choice*. The conventionalist holds that it is the choice of the group, but why should I accept the group's silly choice, when my own is better (for me)? Why should anyone give such august authority to a culture of society? If this is all morality comes to, why not reject it altogether—even though one might want to adhere to its directives when others are looking in order to escape sanctions?

4. A *Critique of Ethical Relativism*

However, while we may fear the demise of morality, as we have known it, this in itself may not be a good reason for rejecting relativism—that is, for judging it false. Alas, truth may not always be edifying. But the consequences of this position are sufficiently alarming to prompt us to look carefully for some weakness in the relativist's argument. So let us examine the premises and conclusion listed at the beginning of this essay as the three theses of relativism.

1. *The diversity thesis.* What is considered morally right and wrong varies from society to society, so that there are no moral principles accepted by all societies.
2. *The dependency thesis.* All moral principles derive their validity from cultural acceptance.
3. *Ethical relativism.* Therefore, there are no universally valid moral principles, objective standards that apply to all people everywhere and at all times.

Does any one of these seem problematic? Let us consider the first thesis, the diversity thesis, which we have also called Cultural Relativism. Perhaps there is not as much diversity as anthropologists like Sumner and Benedict suppose. One can also see great similarities between the moral codes of various cultures. E. O. Wilson has identified more than a score of common features[9] and before him Clyde Kluckhohn has noted some significant common ground.

> Every culture has a concept of murder, distinguishing this from execution, killing in war, and other "justifiable homicides." The notions of incest and other regulations upon sexual behavior, the prohibitions upon untruth under defined circumstances, of restitution and reciprocity, of mutual obligations between parents and children—these and many other moral concepts are altogether universal.[10]

Colin Turnbull's description of the sadistic, semidisplaced, disintegrating Ik in Northern Uganda supports the view that a people without principles of kindness, loyalty, and cooperation will degenerate into a Hobbesian state of nature. But he has also produced evidence that underneath the surface of this dying society, there is a deeper moral code from a time when the tribe flourished, which occasionally surfaces and shows its nobler face.

On the other hand, there is enormous cultural diversity and many societies have radically different moral codes. Cultural relativism seems to be a fact, but, even if it is, it does not by itself establish the truth of ethical relativism. Cultural diversity in itself is neutral between theories. For the objectivist could concede complete cultural relativism, but still defend a form of universalism; for he or she could argue that some cultures simply lack correct moral principles.[11]

On the other hand, a denial of complete cultural relativism (i.e., an admission of some universal principles) does not disprove ethical relativism. For even if we did find one or more universal principles, this would not prove that they had any objective status. We could still *imagine* a culture that was an exception to the rule and be unable to criticize it. So the first premise doesn't by itself imply ethical relativism and its denial doesn't disprove ethical relativism.

We turn to the crucial second thesis, the dependency thesis. Morality does not occur in a vacuum, but rather what is considered morally right or wrong must be seen in a context, depending on the goals, wants, beliefs, history, and environment of the society in question. We distinguished a *weak* and a *strong* thesis of dependency. The weak thesis says that the application of principles depends on the particular cultural predicament, whereas the strong thesis affirms that the principles themselves depend on that predicament. The nonrelativist can accept a certain relativity in the way moral principles are *applied in* various cultures, depending on beliefs, history, and environment. For example, a raw environment with scarce natural resources may justify the Eskimos' brand of euthanasia to the objectivist, who in another environment would consistently reject that practice. The members of a tribe in the Sudan throw their deformed children into the river because of their belief that such infants *belong* to the hippopotamus, the god of the river. We believe that they have a false belief about this, but the point is that the same principles of respect for property and respect for human life are operative in these contrary practices. They differ with us only in belief, not in substantive moral principle. This is an illustration of how nonmoral beliefs (e.g., deformed children belong to the hippopotamus) when applied to common moral principles (e.g., give to each his due) generate different actions in different cultures. In our own culture the difference in the nonmoral belief about the status of a fetus generates opposite moral prescriptions. The major difference between pro-choicers and pro-lifers is not whether we should kill persons but whether fetuses are really persons. It is a debate about the facts of the matter, not the principle of killing innocent persons.

So the fact that moral principles are weakly dependent doesn't show that ethical relativism is valid. In spite of this weak dependency on non-moral factors, there could still be a set of general moral norms applicable to all cultures and even recognized in most, which are disregarded at a culture's own expense.

What the relativist needs is a strong thesis of dependency, that somehow all principles are essentially cultural inventions. But why should we choose to view morality this way? Is there anything to recommend the strong thesis over the weak thesis of dependency? The relativist may argue that in fact we don't have an obvious impartial standard from which to judge. "Who's to say which culture is right and which is wrong?" But this seems to be dubious. We can reason and perform thought experiments in order to make a case for one system over another. We may not be able to *know* with certainty that our moral beliefs are closer to the truth than those of another culture or those of others within our own culture, but we may be *justified* in believing that they are. If we can be closer to the truth regarding factual or scientific matters, why can't we be closer to the truth on moral matters? Why can't a culture simply be confused or wrong about its moral perceptions? Why can't we say that the society like the Ik which sees nothing wrong with enjoying watching its own children fall into fires is less moral in that regard than the culture that cherishes children and grants them protection and equal rights? To take such a stand is not to commit the fallacy of ethnocentricism, for we are seeking to derive principles through critical reason, not simply uncritical acceptance of one's own mores.

Many relativists embrace relativism as a default position. Objectivism makes no sense to them. I think this is Ladd and Harman's position, as the latter's quotation at the beginning of this article seems to indicate. Objectivism has insuperable problems, so the answer must be relativism. . . .

5. *The Case for Moral Objectivism*

If nonrelativists are to make their case, they will have to offer a better explanation of cultural diversity and why we should nevertheless adhere to moral objectivism. One way of doing this is to appeal to a divine law and human sin that causes deviation from that law. Although I think that human greed, selfishness, pride, self-deception, and other maladies have a great deal to do with moral differences and that religion may lend great support to morality, I don't think that a religious justification is necessary for the validity of moral principles. In any case, in this section I shall outline a modest nonreligious objectivism, first, by appealing to our intuitions and, second, by giving a naturalist account of morality that transcends individual cultures.

First, I must make it clear that I am distinguishing Moral *Absolutism* from Moral *Objectivism*. The absolutist believes that there are nonoverridable moral principles that ought never to be violated. Kant's system, or one version of it, is a good example of this. One ought never break a promise, no matter what. Act utilitarianism also seems absolutist, for the principle: do that act that has the most promise of yielding the most utility, is nonoverridable. An objectivist need not posit any nonoverridable principles, at least not in unqualified general form, and so need not be an absolutist. As Renford Bambrough put it,

> To suggest that there is a *right* answer to a moral problem is at once to be accused of or credited with a belief in moral absolutes. But it is no more necessary to believe in moral absolutes in order to believe in moral objectivity than it is to believe in the existence of absolute space or absolute time in order to believe in the objectivity of temporal and spatial relations and of judgements about them.[12]

On the Objectivist's account moral principles are what William Ross refers to as *prima facie* principles, valid rules of action that should generally be adhered to, but that may be overridden by another moral principle in cases of moral conflict. For example, while a principle of justice may generally outweigh a principle of benevolence, there are times when enormous good could be done by sacrificing a small amount of justice, so that an objectivist would be inclined to act according to the principle of benevolence. There may be some absolute or nonoverridable principles, but there need not be any or many for objectivism to be true.[13]

If we can establish or show that it is reasonable to believe that there is at least one objective moral principle that is binding on all people everywhere in some ideal sense, we shall have shown that relativism is probably false and that a limited objectivism is true. Actually, I believe that there are many qualified general ethical principles that are binding on all rational beings, but one will suffice to refute relativism. The principle I've chosen is the following:

A. It is morally wrong to torture people for the fun of it.

I claim that this principle is binding on all rational agents, so that if some agent, S, rejects A, we should not let that affect our intuition that A is a true principle but rather try to explain S's behavior as perverse, ignorant, or irrational instead. For example, suppose Adolf Hitler doesn't accept A. Should that affect our confidence in the truth of A? Is it not more reasonable to infer that Adolf is morally deficient, morally blind, ignorant, or irrational than to suppose that his noncompliance is evidence against the truth of A?

Suppose further that there is a tribe of Hitlerites somewhere who enjoy torturing people. The whole culture accepts torturing others for the fun of it. Suppose that Gandhi or Mother Teresa tried unsuccessfully to convince them that they should stop torturing people altogether, and they responded by torturing the reformers. Should this affect our confidence in A? Would it not be more reasonable to look for some explanation of Hitlerite behavior? For example, we might hypothesize that this tribe lacked a developed sense of sympathetic imagination necessary for the moral life. Or we might theorize that this tribe was on a lower evolutionary level than most Homo sapiens. Or we might simply conclude that the tribe was closer to a Hobbesian state of nature than most societies, and as such probably would not survive. But we need not know the correct answer as to why the tribe was in such bad shape in order to maintain our confidence in A as a moral principle. If A is a basic or core belief for us, we will be more likely to doubt the Hitlerites' sanity or ability to think morally than to doubt the validity of A.

We can perhaps produce other candidates for membership in our minimally basic objective moral set. For example:

1. Do not kill innocent people.
2. Do not cause unnecessary pain or suffering.
3. Do not cheat or steal.

4. Keep your promises and honor your contracts.
5. Do not deprive another person of his or her freedom.
6. Do justice, treating equals equally and unequals unequally.
7. Tell the truth.
8. Help other people, at least when the cost to oneself is minimal.
9. Reciprocate (show gratitude for services rendered).
10. Obey just laws.

These ten principles are examples of the *core morality*, principles necessary for the good life. They are not arbitrary, for we can give reasons why they are necessary to social cohesion and human flourishing. Principles like the Golden Rule, not killing innocent people, treating equals equally, truth-telling, promise-keeping, and the like are central to the fluid progression of social interaction which ethics is about (at least minimal morality is, even though there may be more to morality than simply these kinds of concerns). For example, language itself depends on a general and implicit commitment to the principle of truth-telling. Accuracy of expression is a primitive form of truthfulness. Hence, every time we use words correctly we are telling the truth. Without this behavior, language wouldn't be possible. Likewise, without the recognition of a rule of promise-keeping, contracts are of no avail and cooperation is less likely to occur. And without the protection of life and liberty, we could not secure our other goals.

A moral code or theory would be adequate if it contained a requisite set of these objective principles or the core morality, but there could be more than one adequate moral code or theory that contained different rankings of these principles and other principles consistent with *core morality*. That is, there may be a certain relativity to secondary principles (whether to opt for monogamy rather than polygamy, whether to include a principle of high altruism in the set of moral duties, whether to allocate more resources to medical care than to environmental concerns, whether to institute a law to drive on the left side of the road or the right side of the road, and so forth), but in every morality a certain core will remain, though applied somewhat differently because of differences in environment, belief, tradition, and the like.

The core moral rules are analogous to the set of vitamins necessary for a healthy diet. We need an adequate amount of each vitamin—some humans more of one than another—but in prescribing a nutritional diet we don't have to set forth recipes, specific foods, place settings, or culinary habits. Gourmets will meet the requirements differently than ascetics and vegetarians, but the basic nutrients may be had by all without rigid regimentation or an absolute set of recipes.

Stated more positively, an objectivist who bases his or her moral system on a common human nature with common needs and desires might argue for objectivism somewhat in this manner:

1. Human nature is relatively similar in essential respects, having a common set of needs and interests.
2. Moral principles are functions of human needs and interests, instituted by reason in order to promote the most significant interests and needs of rational beings (and perhaps others).
3. Some moral principles will promote human interests and meet human needs better than others.
4. Those principles that will meet essential needs and promote the most significant interests of humans in optimal ways can be said to be objectively valid moral principles.
5. Therefore, since there is a common human nature, there is an objectively valid set of moral principles, applicable to all humanity.

This argument assumes that there is a common human nature. In a sense, I accept a *strong dependency thesis*—morality *depends* on human nature and the needs and interests of humans in general, but not on any specific cultural choice. There is only one large human framework to which moral principles are relative.[14] I have considered the evidence for this claim (toward the end of Section 4), but the relativist may object. I cannot defend it any further in this paper, but suppose we content ourselves with a less controversial first premise, stating that some principles will tend to promote the most significant interests of persons. The revised argument would go like this:

1. Objectively valid moral principles are those adherence to which meets the needs and promotes the most significant interests of persons.
2. Some principles are such that adherence to them meets the needs and promotes the most significant interests of persons.
3. Therefore, there are some objectively valid moral principles.

Either argument would satisfy objectivism, but the former makes it clearer that it is our common human nature that generates the common principles.[15] However, as I mentioned, some philosophers might not like to be tied down to the concept of a common human nature, in which case the second version of the argument may be used. It has the advantage that even if it turned out that we did have somewhat different natures or that other creatures in the universe had somewhat different natures, some of the basic moral principles would still survive.

If this argument succeeds, there are ideal moralities (and not simply adequate ones). Of course, there could still be more than one ideal morality, which presumably an ideal observer would choose under optimal conditions. The ideal observer may conclude that out of an infinite set of moralities two, three, or more combinations would tie for first place. One would expect that these would be similar, but there is every reason to believe that all of these would contain the set of core principles.

Of course, we don't know what an ideal observer would choose, but we can imagine that the conditions under which such an observer would choose would be conditions of maximal knowledge about the consequences of action-types and impartiality, second-order qualities that ensure that agents have the best chance of making the best decisions. If this is so, then the more we learn to judge impartially and the more we know about possible forms of life, the better chance we have to approximate an ideal moral system. And if there is the possibility of approximating ideal moral systems with an objective core and other objective components, then ethical relativism is certainly false. We can confidently dismiss it as an aberration and get on with the job of working out better moral systems.

Let me make the same point by appealing to your intuitions in another way. Imagine that you have been miraculously transported to the dark kingdom of hell, and there you get a glimpse of the sufferings of the damned. What is their punishment? Well, they have eternal back itches, which ebb and flow constantly. But they cannot scratch their backs, for their arms are paralyzed in a frontal position, so they writhe with itchiness throughout eternity. But just as you are beginning to feel the itch in your own back, you are suddenly transported to heaven. What do you see in the kingdom of the blessed? Well, you see people with eternal back itches, who cannot scratch their own backs. But they are all smiling instead of writhing. Why? Because everyone has his or her arms stretched out to scratch someone else's back, and, so arranged in one big circle, a hell is turned into a heaven of ecstasy.

If we can imagine some states of affairs or cultures that are better than others in a way that depends on human action, we can ask what are those character traits that make them so. In our story people in heaven, but not in hell, cooperate for the amelioration of suffering and the production of pleasure. These are very primitive goods, not sufficient for a full-blown morality, but they give us a hint as to the objectivity of morality. Moral goodness has something to do with the ameliorating of suffering, the resolution of conflict, and the promotion of human flourishing. If our heaven is really better than the eternal itchiness of hell, then whatever makes it so is constitutively related to moral rightness.

6. An Explanation of the Attraction of Ethical Relativism

Why, then, is there such a strong inclination toward ethical relativism? I think that there are four reasons, which haven't been adequately emphasized. One is that the options are usually presented as though absolutism and relativism are the only alternatives, so conventionalism wins out against an implausible competitor. At the beginning of this paper I referred to a student questionnaire that I have been giving for twenty years. It reads as follows: "Are there any ethical absolutes, moral duties binding on all persons at all times, or are moral duties relative to culture? Is there any alternative to these two positions?" Less than 5 percent suggest a third position and very few of them identify objectivism. Granted, it takes a little philosophical sophistication to make the crucial distinctions, and it is precisely for lack of this sophistication or reflection that relativism has procured its enormous prestige. But, as Ross and others have shown and as I have argued in this chapter, one can have an objective morality without being absolutist.

The second reason for an inclination toward ethical relativism is the confusion of moral objectivism with moral realism. A realist is a person who holds that moral values have independent existence, if only as emergent properties. The anti-realist claims that they do not have independent existence. But objectivism is compatible with either of these views. All it calls for is deep inter-subjective agreement among humans due to a common nature and common goals and needs.

An example of a philosopher who confuses objectivity with realism is the late J. L. Mackie, who rejects objectivism because there are no good arguments for the independent existence of moral values. But he admits, however, that there is a great deal of intersubjectivity in ethics. "There could be agreement in valuing even if valuing is just something people do, even if this activity is not further validated. Subjective agreement would give intersubjective values, but intersubjectivity is not objectivity."[16] But Mackie fails to note that there are two kinds of intersubjectivity, and that one of them gives all that the objectivist wants for a moral theory. Consider the following situations of intersubjective agreement:

Set A

A1. All the children in first grade at School S would agree that playing in the mud is preferable to learning arithmetic.

A2. All the youths in the district would rather take drugs than go to school.

A3. All the people in Jonestown, British Guiana agree that Rev. Jones is a prophet from God and love him dearly.

A4. Almost all the people in community C voted for George W. Bush.

Set B

B1. All the thirsty desire water to quench their thirst.

B2. All humans (and animals) prefer pleasure to pain.

B3. Almost all people agree that living in society is more satisfying than living alone as hermits.

The naturalist contrasts these two sets of intersubjective agreements and says that the first set is accidental, not part of what it means to be a person, whereas the agreements in the second set are basic to being a person, basic to our nature. Agreement on the essence of morality, the core set, is the kind of intersubjective agreement more like the second kind, not the first. It is part of the essence of a human in community, part of what it means to flourish as a person, to agree and adhere to the moral code.

The third reason is that our recent sensitivity to cultural relativism and the evils of ethnocentricism, which have plagued the relations of Europeans and Americans with those of other cultures, has made us conscious of the frailty of many aspects of our moral repertoire, so that there is a tendency to wonder "Who's to judge what's really right or wrong?" However, the move from a reasonable cultural relativism, which rightly causes us to rethink our moral systems, to an ethical relativism, which causes us to give up the heart of morality altogether, is an instance of the fallacy of confusing factual or descriptive statements with normative ones. Cultural relativism doesn't entail ethical relativism. The very reason that we are against ethnocentricism constitutes the same basis for our being for an objective moral system: that impartial reason draws us to it.

We may well agree that cultures differ and that we ought to be cautious in condemning what we don't understand, but this in no way need imply that there are not better and worse ways of living. We can understand and excuse, to some degree at least, those who differ from our best notions of morality, without abdicating the notion that cultures without principles of justice or promise-keeping or protection of the innocent are morally poorer for these omissions.

A fourth reason that has driven some to moral nihilism and others to relativism is the decline of religion in Western society. As one of Dostoevsky's characters has said, "If God is dead, all things are permitted." The person who has lost religious faith feels a deep vacuum and understandably confuses it with a moral vacuum or, he or she finally resigns to a form of secular conventionalism. Such people reason that if there is no God to guarantee the validity of the moral order, there must not be a universal moral order. There is just radical cultural diversity and death at the end. But even if there turns out to be no God and no immortality, we still will want to live happy, meaningful lives during our four-score years on earth. If this is true, then it matters by which principles we live and those that win out in the test of time will be objectively valid principles.

In conclusion, I have argued (1) that Cultural Relativism (the fact that there are cultural differences regarding moral principles) does not entail Ethical Relativism (the thesis that there are no objectively valid universal moral principles);

(2) that the Dependency Thesis (that morality derives its legitimacy from individual cultural acceptance) is mistaken; and (3) that there are universal moral principles based on a common human nature and a need to solve conflicts of interest and flourish.

So "Who's to judge what's right or wrong?" We are. We are to do so on the basis of the best reasoning we can bring forth, and with sympathy and understanding.[17]

Notes

1. Gilbert Harman, "Is There a Single True Morality?" in *Morality, Reason and Truth*, ed. David Copp and David Zimmerman (Rowman and Allanheld, 1984).

2. John Ladd, *Ethical Relativism* (Wadsworth, 1973).

3. Lest I be misunderstood, in this essay I will generally be speaking about the validity, rather than the truth of moral principles. Validity holds that they are proper guides to action, whereas truth presupposes something more. It presupposes Moral Realism, the theory that moral principles have special ontological status. Although this may be true, not all objectivists agree. R. M. Hare, for instance, argues that moral principles, while valid, do not have truth value. They are like imperatives that have practical application but cannot be said to be true. Also, I am mainly concerned with the status of *principles*, not theories themselves. There may be a plurality of valid moral theories, all containing the same objective principles. I am grateful to Edward Sherline for drawing this distinction to my attention.

4. William G. Sumner, *Folkways* (Ginn & Co., 1906), p. 76.

5. This is a paraphrased and rewritten statement of Ted Bundy by Harry V. Jaffa, *Homosexuality and the Natural Law* (Claremont, CA: The Claremont Institute of the Study of Statesmanship and Political Philosophy, 1990), pp. 3–4.

6. Ruth Benedict, *Patterns of Culture* (New American Library, 1934), p. 257.

7. Melville Herskovits, *Cultural Relativism* (Random House, 1972).

8. This is the fallacy of objecting to a proposition on the erroneous grounds that, if accepted, it will lead to a chain of states of affairs that are absurd or unacceptable.

9. E. O. Wilson, *On Human Nature* (Bantam Books, 1979), pp. 22–23.

10. Clyde Kluckhohn, "Ethical Relativity: Sic et Non," *Journal of Philosophy* 52 (1955).

11. Colin Turnbull, *The Mountain People* (Simon & Schuster, 1972).

12. Renford Bambrough, *Moral Skepticism and Moral Knowledge* (Routledge and Kegan Paul, 1979), p. 33.

13. William Ross, *The Right and the Good* (Oxford University Press, 1931), p. 18f.

14. In his essay, "Moral Relativism" in *Moral Relativism and Moral Objectivity* (Blackwell, 1996) by Gilbert Harman and Judith Jarvis Thomson, Harman defines moral relativism as the claim that "There is no single true morality. There are many different moral frameworks, none of which is more correct than the others" (p. 5). I hold that morality has a function of serving the needs and interests of human beings, so that some frameworks do this better than others. Essentially, all adequate theories will contain the principles I have identified in this essay.

15. I owe the reformulation of the argument to Bruce Russell. Edward Sherline has objected (correspondence) that assuming a common human nature in the first argument begs the question against the relativist. You may be the judge

16. J. L. Mackie, *Ethics: Inventing Right and Wrong* (Penguin, 1977), p. 22.

17. Bruce Russell, Morton Winston, Edward Sherline, and an anonymous reviewer made important criticisms on earlier versions of this article, resulting in this revision.

Moral Relativism Defended*

Gilbert Harman

My thesis is that morality arises when a group of people reach an implicit agreement or come to a tacit understanding about their relations with one another. Part of what I mean by this is that moral judgments—or, rather, an important class of them—make sense only in relation to and with reference to one or another such agreement or understanding. This is vague, and I shall try to make it more precise in what follows. But it should be clear that I intend to argue for a version of what has been called moral relativism.

In doing so, I am taking sides in an ancient controversy. Many people have supposed that the sort of view which I am going to defend is obviously correct—indeed, that it is the only sort of account that could make sense of the phenomenon of morality. At the same time there have also been many who have supposed that moral relativism is confused, incoherent, and even immoral, at the very least obviously wrong.

Most arguments against relativism make use of a strategy of dissuasive definition; they define moral relativism as an inconsistent thesis. For example, they define it as the assertion that (*a*) there are no universal moral principles and (*b*) one ought to act in accordance with the principles of one's own group, where this latter principle, (*b*), is supposed to be a universal moral principle.[1] It is easy enough to show that this version of moral relativism will not do, but that is no reason to think that a defender of moral relativism cannot find a better definition.

My moral relativism is a soberly logical thesis—a thesis about logical form, if you like. Just as the judgment that something is large makes sense only in relation to one or another comparison class, so too, I will argue, the judgment that it is wrong of someone to do something makes sense only in relation to an agreement or understanding. A dog may be large in relation

---

*Gilbert Harman, "Moral Relativism Defended" in *The Philosophical Review* 84, no. 1 (Jan. 1975): 3–22.

to Chihuahuas but not large in relation to dogs in general. Similarly, I will argue, an action may be wrong in relation to one agreement but not in relation to another. Just as it makes no sense to ask whether a dog is large, period, apart from any relation to a comparison class, so too, I will argue, it makes no sense to ask whether an action is wrong, period, apart from any relation to an agreement.

There is an agreement, in the relevant sense, if each of a number of people intends to adhere to some schedule, plan, or set of principles, intending to do this on the understanding that the others similarly intend. The agreement or understanding need not be conscious or explicit; and I will not here try to say what distinguishes moral agreements from, for example, conventions of the road or conventions of etiquette, since these distinctions will not be important as regards the purely logical thesis that I will be defending.

Although I want to say that certain moral judgments are made in relation to an agreement, I do not want to say this about all moral judgments. Perhaps it is true that all moral judgments are made in relation to an agreement; nevertheless, that is not what I will be arguing. For I want to say that there is a way in which certain moral judgments are relative to an agreement but other moral judgments are not. My relativism is a thesis only about what I will call "inner judgments," such as the judgment that someone ought or ought not to have acted in a certain way or the judgment that it was right or wrong of him to have done so. My relativism is not meant to apply, for example, to the judgment that someone is evil or the judgment that a given institution is unjust.

In particular, I am not denying (nor am I asserting) that some moralities are "objectively" better than others or that there are objective standards for assessing moralities. My thesis is a soberly logical thesis about logical form.

I. Inner Judgments

We make inner judgments about a person only if we suppose that he is capable of being motivated by the relevant moral considerations. We make other sorts of judgment about those who we suppose are not susceptible of such motivation. Inner judgments include judgments in which we say that someone should or ought to have done something or that someone was right or wrong to have done something. Inner judgments do not include judgments in which we call someone (literally) a savage or say that someone is (literally) inhuman, evil, a betrayer, a traitor, or an enemy.

Consider this example. Intelligent beings from outer space land on Earth, beings without the slightest concern for human life and happiness. That a certain course of action on their part might injure one of us means nothing to them; that fact by itself gives them no reason to avoid the action. In such a case it would be odd to say that nevertheless the beings ought to avoid injuring us or that it would be wrong for them to attack us. Of course we will want to resist them if they do such things and we will make negative judgments about them; but we will judge that they are dreadful enemies to be repelled and even destroyed, not that they should not act as they do.

Similarly, if we learn that a band of cannibals has captured and eaten the sole survivor of a shipwreck, we will speak of the primitive morality of the cannibals and may call them savages, but we will not say that they ought not to have eaten their captive.

Again, suppose that a contented employee of Murder, Incorporated was raised as a child to honor and respect members of the "family" but to have nothing but contempt for the rest of society. His current assignment, let us suppose, is to kill a certain bank manager, Bernard J. Ortcutt. Since Ortcutt is not a member of the "family," the employee in question has no compunction about carrying out his assignment. In particular, if we were to try to convince him that he should not kill Ortcutt, our argument would merely amuse him. We would not provide him with the slightest reason to desist unless we were to point to practical difficulties, such as the likelihood of his getting caught. Now, in this case it would be a misuse of language to say of him that he ought not to kill Ortcutt or that it would be wrong of him to do so, since that would imply that our own moral considerations carry some weight with him, which they do not. Instead we can only judge that he is a criminal, someone to be hunted down by the police, an enemy of peace-loving citizens, and so forth.

It is true that we can make certain judgments about him using the word "ought." For example, investigators who have been tipped off by an informer and who are waiting for the assassin to appear at the bank can use the "ought" of expectation to say, "He ought to arrive soon," meaning that on the basis of their information one would expect him to arrive soon. And, in thinking over how the assassin might carry out his assignment, we can use the "ought" of rationality to say that he ought to go in by the rear door, meaning that it would be more rational for him to do that than to go in by the front door. In neither of these cases is the moral "ought" in question.

There is another use of "ought" which is normative and in a sense moral but which is distinct from what I am calling the moral "ought." This is the use which occurs when we say that something ought or ought not to be the case. It ought not to be the case that members of Murder, Incorporated go around killing people; in other words, it is a terrible thing that they do so.[2] The same thought can perhaps be expressed as "They ought not to go around killing people," meaning that it ought not to be the case that they do, not that they are wrong to do what they do. The normative "ought to be" is used to assess a situation; the moral "ought to do" is used to describe a relation between an agent and a type of act that he might perform or has performed.

The sentence "They ought not to go around killing people" is therefore multiply ambiguous. It can mean that one would not expect them to do so (the "ought" of expectation), that it is not in their interest to do so (the "ought" of rationality), that it is a bad thing that they do so (the normative "ought to be"), or that they are wrong to do so (the moral "ought to do"). For the most part I am here concerned only with the last of these interpretations.

The word "should" behaves very much like "ought to." There is a "should" of expectation ("They should be here soon"), a "should" of rationality ("He should go in by the back door"), a normative "should be" ("They shouldn't go around killing people like that"), and the moral "should do" ("You should keep that promise"). I am of course concerned mainly with the last sense of "should."

"Right" and "wrong" also have multiple uses; I will not try to say what all of them are. But I do want to distinguish using the word "wrong" to say that a particular situation or action is wrong from using the word to say that it is wrong *of someone* to do something. In the former case, the word "wrong" is used to assess an act or situation. In the latter case it is used to describe a relation between an agent and an act. Only the latter sort of judgment is an inner judgment. Although we would not say concerning the contented employee of Murder, Incorporated mentioned earlier that it was wrong *of him* to kill Ortcutt, we could say that *his action* was wrong and we could say that it is wrong that there is so much killing.

To take another example, it sounds odd to say that Hitler should not have ordered the extermination of the Jews, that it was wrong of him to have done so. That sounds somehow "too weak" a thing to say. Instead we want to say that Hitler was an evil man. Yet we can properly say, "Hitler ought not to have ordered the extermination of the Jews," if what we mean is that it ought never to have happened; and we can say without oddity that what Hitler did was wrong. Oddity attends only the inner judgment that Hitler was wrong to have acted in that way. That is what sounds "too weak."

It is worth noting that the inner judgments sound too weak not because of the enormity of what Hitler did but because we suppose that in acting as he did he shows that he could not have been susceptible to the moral considerations on the basis of which we make our judgment. He is in the relevant sense beyond the pale and we therefore cannot make inner judgments about him. To see that this is so, consider, say, Stalin, another mass-murderer. We can perhaps imagine someone taking a sympathetic view of Stalin. In such a view, Stalin realized that the course he was going to pursue would mean the murder of millions of people and he dreaded such a prospect; however, the alternative seemed to offer an even greater disaster—so, reluctantly and with great anguish, he went ahead. In relation to such a view of Stalin, inner judgments about Stalin are not as odd as similar judgments about Hitler. For we might easily continue the story by saying that, despite what he hoped to gain, Stalin should not have undertaken the course he did, that it was wrong of him to have done so. What makes inner judgments about Hitler odd, "too weak," is not that the acts judged seem too terrible for the words used but rather that the agent judged seems beyond the pale—in other words beyond the motivational reach of the relevant moral considerations.

Of course, I do not want to deny that for various reasons a speaker might pretend that an agent is or is not susceptible to certain moral considerations. For example, a speaker may for rhetorical or political reasons wish to suggest that someone is beyond the pale, that he should not be listened to, that he can be treated as an enemy. On the other hand, a speaker may pretend that someone is susceptible to certain moral considerations in an effort to make that person or others susceptible to those considerations. Inner judgments about one's children sometimes have this function. So do inner judgments made in political speeches that aim at restoring a lapsed sense of morality in government.

II. The Logical Form of Inner Judgments

Inner judgments have two important characteristics. First, they imply that the agent has reasons to do something. Second, the speaker in some sense endorses these reasons and supposes that the audience also endorses them. Other moral judgments about an agent, on the other hand, do not have such implications; they do not imply that the agent has reasons for acting that are endorsed by the speaker.

If someone *S* says that A (morally) ought to do *D*, *S* implies that A has reasons to do *D* and *S* endorses those reasons—whereas if *S* says that *B* was evil in what *B* did, *S* does not imply that the reasons *S* would endorse for not doing what *B* did were reasons for *B* not to do that thing; in fact, *S* implies that they were not reasons for *B*.

Let us examine this more closely. If *S* says that (morally) A ought to do *D*, *S* implies that A has reasons to do *D* which *S* endorses. I shall assume that such reasons would have to have their source in goals, desires, or intentions that *S* takes A to have and that *S* approves of A's having because *S* shares those goals, desires, or intentions. So, if *S* says that (morally) A ought to do *D*, there are certain motivational attitudes M which *S* assumes are shared by *S*, A, and *S*'s audience.

Now, in supposing that reasons for action must have their source in goals, desires, or intentions, I am assuming something like an Aristotelian or Humean account of these matters, as opposed, for example, to a Kantian approach which sees a possible source of motivation in reason itself.[3] I must defer a full-scale discussion of the issue to another occasion. Here I simply assume that the Kantian approach is wrong. In particular, I assume that there might be no reasons at all for a being from outer space to avoid harm to us; that, for Hitler, there might have been no reason at all not to order the extermination of the Jews; that the contented employee of Murder, Incorporated might have no reason at all not to kill Ortcutt; that the cannibals might have no reason not to eat their captive. In other words, I assume that the possession of rationality is not sufficient to provide a source for relevant reasons, that certain desires, goals, or intentions are also necessary. Those who accept this assumption will, I think, find that they distinguish inner moral judgments from other moral judgments in the way that I have indicated.

Ultimately, I want to argue that the shared motivational attitudes M are intentions to keep an agreement (supposing that others similarly intend). For I want to argue that inner moral judgments are made relative to such an agreement. That is, I want to argue that, when *S* makes the inner judgment that *A* ought to do *D*, *S* assumes that *A* intends to act in accordance with an agreement which *S* and *S*'s audience also intend to observe. In other words, I want to argue that the source of the reasons for doing *D* which *S* ascribes to *A* is *A*'s sincere intention to observe a certain agreement. I have not yet argued for the stronger thesis, however. I have argued only that *S* makes his judgment relative to some motivational attitudes M which *S* assumes are shared by *S*, *A*, and *S*'s audience.

Formulating this as a logical thesis, I want to treat the moral "ought" as a four-place predicate (or "operator"), "Ought (*A*, *D*, C, M)," which relates an agent *A*, a type of act *D*, considerations C, and motivating attitudes M. The relativity to considerations C can be brought out by considering what are sometimes called statements of prima-facie obligation, "Considering that you promised, you ought to go to the board meeting, but considering that you are the sole surviving relative, you ought to go to the funeral; all things considered, it is not clear what you ought to do."[4] The claim that there is *this* relativity, to considerations, is not, of course, what makes my thesis a version of moral relativism, since any theory must acknowledge relativity to considerations. The relativity to considerations does, however, provide a model for a coherent interpretation of moral relativism as a similar kind of relativity.

It is not as easy to exhibit the relativity to motivating attitudes as it is to exhibit the relativity to considerations, since normally a speaker who makes a moral "ought" judgment intends the relevant motivating attitudes to be ones that the speaker shares with the agent and the audience, and normally it will be obvious what attitudes these are. But sometimes a speaker does invoke different attitudes by invoking a morality the speaker does not share. Someone may say, for example, "As a Christian, you ought to turn the other cheek; I, however, propose to strike back." A spy who has been found out by a friend might say,

"As a citizen, you ought to turn me in, but I hope that you will not." In these and similar cases a speaker makes a moral "ought" judgment that is explicitly relative to motivating attitudes that the speaker does not share.

In order to be somewhat more precise, then, my thesis is this. "Ought (A, *D*, C, M)" means roughly that, given that A has motivating attitudes M and given C, *D* is the course of action for A that is supported by the best reasons. In judgments using this sense of "ought," C and M are often not explicitly mentioned but are indicated by the context of utterance. Normally, when that happens, C will be "all things considered" and M will be attitudes that are shared by the speaker and audience.

I mentioned that inner judgments have two characteristics. First, they imply that the agent has reasons to do something that are capable of motivating the agent. Second, the speaker endorses those reasons and supposes that the audience does too. Now, any "Ought (A, *D*, C, M)" judgment has the first of these characteristics, but as we have just seen a judgment of this sort will not necessarily have the second characteristic if made with explicit reference to motivating attitudes not shared by the speaker. If reference is made either implicitly or explicitly (for example, through the use of the adverb "morally") to attitudes that are shared by the speaker and audience, the resulting judgment has both characteristics and is an inner judgment. If reference is made to attitudes that are not shared by the speaker, the resulting judgment is not an inner judgment and does not represent a full-fledged moral judgment on the part of the speaker. In such a case we have an example of what has been called an inverted-commas use of "ought."[5]

III. Moral Bargaining

I have argued that moral "ought" judgments are relational, "Ought (A, *D*, C, M)," where M represents certain motivating attitudes. I now want to argue that the attitudes M derive from an agreement. That is, they are intentions to adhere to a particular agreement on the understanding that others also intend to do so. Really, it might be better for me to say that I put this forward as a hypothesis, since I cannot pretend to be able to prove that it is true. I will argue, however, that this hypothesis accounts for an otherwise puzzling aspect of our moral views that, as far as I know, there is no other way to account for.

I will use the word "intention" in a somewhat extended sense to cover certain dispositions or habits. Someone may habitually act in accordance with the relevant understanding and therefore may be disposed to act in that way without having any more or less conscious intention. In such a case it may sound odd to say that he *intends* to act in accordance with the moral understanding. Nevertheless, for present purposes I will count that as his having the relevant intention in a dispositional sense.

I now want to consider the following puzzle about our moral views, a puzzle that has figured in recent philosophical discussion of issues such as abortion. It has been observed that most of us assign greater weight to the duty not to harm others than to the duty to help others. For example, most of us believe that a doctor ought not to save five of his patients who would otherwise die by cutting up a sixth patient and distributing his healthy organs where needed to the others, even though we do think that the doctor has a duty to try to help as many of his patients as he can. For we also think that he has a stronger duty to try not to harm any of his patients (or anyone else) even if by so doing he could help five others.[6]

This aspect of our moral views can seem very puzzling, especially if one supposes that moral feelings derive from sympathy and concern for others. But the hypothesis that morality derives from an agreement among people of varying powers and resources provides a plausible explanation. The rich, the poor, the strong, and the weak would all benefit if all were to try to avoid harming one another. So everyone could agree to that arrangement. But the rich and the strong would not benefit from an arrangement whereby everyone would try to do as much as possible to help those in need. The poor and weak would get all of the benefit of this latter arrangement. Since the rich and the strong could foresee that they would be required to do most of the helping and that they would receive little in return, they would be reluctant to agree to a strong principle of mutual aid. A compromise would be likely and a weaker principle would probably be accepted. In other words, although everyone could agree to a strong principle concerning the avoidance of harm, it would not be true that everyone would favor an equally strong principle of mutual aid. It is likely that only a weaker principle of the latter sort would gain general acceptance. So the hypothesis that morality derives from an understanding among people of different powers and resources can explain (and, according to me, does explain) why in our morality avoiding harm to others is taken to be more important than helping those who need help.

By the way, I am here only trying to *explain* an aspect of our moral views. I am not therefore *endorsing* that aspect. And I defer until later a relativistic account of the way in which aspects of our moral view can be criticized "from within."

Now we need not suppose that the agreement or understanding in question is explicit. It is enough if various members of society knowingly reach an agreement in intentions—each intending to act in certain ways on the understanding that the others have similar intentions. Such an implicit agreement is reached through a process of mutual adjustment and implicit bargaining.

Indeed, it is essential to the proposed explanation of this aspect of our moral views to suppose that the relevant moral understanding is thus the result of bargaining. It is necessary to suppose that, in order to further our interests, we form certain conditional intentions, hoping that others will do the same. The others, who have different interests, will form somewhat different conditional intentions. After implicit bargaining, some sort of compromise is reached.

Seeing morality in this way as a compromise based on implicit bargaining helps to explain why our morality takes it to be worse to harm someone than to refuse to help someone. The explanation requires that we view our morality as an implicit agreement about what to do. This sort of explanation could not be given if we were to suppose, say, that our morality represented an agreement only about the facts (naturalism). Nor is it enough simply to suppose that our morality represents an agreement in attitude, if we forget that such agreement can be reached, not only by way of such principles as are mentioned, for example, in Hare's "logic of imperatives,"[7] but also through bargaining. According to Hare, to accept a general moral principle is to intend to do something.[8] If we add to his theory that the relevant intentions can be reached through implicit bargaining, the resulting theory begins to look like the one that I am defending.

Many aspects of our moral views can be given a utilitarian explanation. We could account for these aspects, using the logical analysis I presented in the previous section of this paper, by supposing that the relevant "ought" judgments presuppose shared attitudes of sympathy and benevolence. We can equally well explain them by supposing that considerations of utility have influenced our implicit agreements, so that the appeal is to a shared intention to adhere to those agreements. Any aspect of morality that is susceptible of a utilitarian explanation can also be explained by an implicit agreement, but not conversely. There are aspects of our moral views that seem to be explicable only in the second way, on the assumption that morality derives from an agreement. One example, already cited, is the distinction we make between harming and not helping. Another is our feeling that each person has an inalienable right of self-defense and self-preservation. Philosophers have not been able to come up with a really satisfactory utilitarian justification of such a right, but it is easily intelligible on our present hypothesis, as Hobbes observed many years ago. You cannot, except in very special circumstances, rationally form the intention not to try to preserve your life if it should ever be threatened, say, by society or the state, since you know that you cannot now control what you would do in such a situation. No matter what you now decided to do, when the time came, you would ignore your prior decision and try to save your life. Since you cannot now intend to do something later which you now know that you would not do, you cannot now intend to keep an agreement not to preserve your life if it is threatened by others in your society.[9] This concludes the positive side of my argument that what I have called inner moral judgments are made in relation to an implicit agreement. I now want to argue that this theory avoids difficulties traditionally associated with implicit agreement theories of morality.

IV. Objections and Replies

One traditional difficulty for implicit agreement theories concerns what motivates us to do what we have agreed to do. It will, obviously, not be enough to say that we have implicitly agreed to keep agreements, since the issue would then be why we keep that agreement. And this suggests an objection to implicit agreement theories. But the apparent force of the objection derives entirely from taking an agreement to be a kind of ritual. To agree in the relevant sense is not just to say something; it is to intend to do something—namely, to intend to carry out one's part of the agreement on the condition that others do their parts. If we agree in this sense to do something, we intend to do it and intending to do it is already to be motivated to do it. So there is no problem as to why we are motivated to keep our agreements in this sense.

We do believe that in general you ought not to pretend to agree in this sense in order to trick someone else into agreeing. But that suggests no objection to the present view. All that it indicates is that our moral understanding contains or implies an agreement to be open and honest with others. If it is supposed that this leaves a problem about someone who has not accepted our agreement—"What reason does he have not to pretend to accept our agreement so that he can then trick others into agreeing to various things?"—the answer is that such a person may or may not have such a reason. If someone does not already accept something of our morality it may or may not be possible to find reasons why he should.

A second traditional objection to implicit agreement theories is that there is not a perfect correlation between what is generally believed to be morally right and what actually is morally right. Not everything generally agreed on is right and sometimes courses of action are right that would not be generally agreed to be right. But this is no objection to my thesis. My thesis is not that the implicit agreement from which a morality derives is an agreement in moral judgment; the thesis is rather that moral judgments make reference to and are made in relation to an agreement in intentions. Given that a group of people have agreed in this sense, there can still be disputes as to what the agreement implies for various situations. In my view, many moral disputes are of this sort. They presuppose a basic agreement and they concern what implications that agreement has for particular cases.

There can also be various things wrong with the agreement that a group of people reach, even from the point of view of that agreement, just as there can be defects in an individual's plan of action even from the point of view of that plan. Given what is known about the situation, a plan or agreement can in various ways be inconsistent, incoherent, or self-defeating. In my view, certain moral disputes are concerned with internal defects of the basic moral understanding of a group, and what changes should be made from the perspective of that understanding itself. This is another way in which moral disputes make sense with reference to and in relation to an underlying agreement.

Another objection to implicit agreement theories is that not all agreements are morally binding—for example, those made under compulsion or from a position of unfair disadvantage, which may seem to indicate that there are moral principles prior to those that derive from an implicit agreement. But, again, the force of the objection derives from an equivocation concerning what an agreement is. The principle that compelled agreements do not obligate concerns agreement in the sense of a certain sort of ritual indicating that one agrees. My thesis concerns a kind of agreement in intentions. The principle about compelled agreements is part of, or is implied by, our agreement in intentions. According to me it is only with reference to some such agreement in intentions that a principle of this sort makes sense.

Now it may be true our moral agreement in intentions also implies that it is wrong to compel people who are in a greatly inferior position to accept an agreement in intentions that they would not otherwise accept, and it may even be true that there is in our society at least one class of people in an inferior position who have been compelled thus to settle for accepting a basic moral understanding, aspects of which they would not have accepted had they not been in such an inferior position. In that case there would be an incoherence in our basic moral understanding and various suggestions might be made concerning the ways in which this understanding should be modified. But this moral critique of the understanding can proceed from that understanding itself rather than from "prior" moral principles.

In order to fix ideas, let us consider a society in which there is a well-established and long-standing tradition of hereditary slavery. Let us suppose that everyone accepts this institution, including the slaves. Everyone treats it as in the nature of things that there should be such slavery. Furthermore, let us suppose that there are also aspects of the basic moral agreement which speak against slavery. That is, these aspects together with certain facts about the situation imply that people should not own slaves and that slaves have no obligation to acquiesce in their condition. In such a case, the moral understanding would be defective, although its defectiveness would presumably be hidden in one or another manner, perhaps by means of a myth that slaves are physically and mentally subhuman in a way that makes appropriate the sort of treatment elsewhere reserved for beasts of burden. If this myth were to be exposed, the members of the society would then be faced with an obvious incoherence in their basic moral agreement and might come eventually to modify their agreement so as to eliminate its acceptance of slavery.

In such a case, even relative to the old agreement it might be true that slave owners ought to free their slaves, that slaves need not obey their masters, and that people ought to work to eliminate slavery. For the course supported by the best reasons, given that one starts out with the intention of adhering to a particular agreement, may be that one should stop intending to adhere to certain aspects of that agreement and should try to get others to do the same.

We can also (perhaps but see below) envision a second society with hereditary slavery whose agreement has no aspects that speak against slavery. In that case, even if the facts of the situation were fully appreciated, no incoherence would appear in the basic moral understanding of the society and it would not be true in relation to that understanding that slave owners ought to free their slaves, that slaves need not obey their masters, and so forth. There might nevertheless come a time when there were reasons of a different sort to modify the basic understanding, either because of an external threat from societies opposed to slavery or because of an internal threat of rebellion by the slaves.

Now it is easier for us to make what I have called inner moral judgments about slave owners in the first society than in the second. For we can with reference to members of the first society invoke principles that they share with us and, with reference to those principles, we can say of them that they ought not to have kept slaves and that they were immoral to have done so. This sort of inner judgment becomes increasingly inappropriate, however, the more distant they are from us and the less easy it is for us to think of our moral understanding as continuous with and perhaps a later development of theirs. Furthermore, it seems appropriate to make only non-inner judgments of the slave owners in the second society. We can say that the second society is unfair and unjust, that the slavery that exists is wrong, that it ought not to exist. But it would be inappropriate in this case to say that it was morally wrong of the slave owners to own slaves. The relevant aspects of our moral understanding, which we would invoke in moral judgments about them, are not aspects of the moral understanding that exists in the second society. (I will come back to the question of slavery below.)

Let me turn now to another objection to implicit agreement theories, an objection which challenges the idea that there is an agreement of the relevant sort. For, if we have agreed, when did we do it? Does anyone really remember having agreed? How did we indicate our agreement? What about those who do not want to agree? How do they indicate that they do not agree and what are the consequences of their not agreeing? Reflection on these and similar questions can make the hypothesis of implicit agreement seem too weak a basis on which to found morality.

But once again there is equivocation about agreements. The objection treats the thesis as the claim that morality is based on some sort of ritual rather than an agreement in intentions. But, as I have said, there is an agreement in the relevant sense when each of a number of people has an intention on the assumption that others have the same intention. In this sense of "agreement," there is no given moment at which one agrees, since one continues to agree in this sense as long as one continues to have the relevant intentions. Someone refuses to agree to the extent that he or she does not share these intentions. Those who do not agree are outside the agreement; in extreme cases they are outlaws or enemies. It does not follow, however, that there are no constraints on how those who agree may act toward those who do not, since for various reasons the agreement itself may contain provisions for dealing with outlaws and enemies.

This brings me to one last objection, which derives from the difficulty people have in trying to give an explicit and systematic account of their moral views. If one actually agrees to something, why is it so hard to say what one has agreed? In response I can say only that many understandings appear to be of this sort. It is often possible to recognize what is in accordance with the understanding and what would violate it without being able to specify the understanding in any general way. Consider, for example, the understanding that exists among the members of a team of acrobats or a symphony orchestra.

Another reason why it is so difficult to give a precise and systematic specification of any actual moral understanding is that such an understanding will not in general be constituted by absolute rules but will take a vaguer form, specifying goals and areas of responsibility. For example, the agreement may indicate that one is to show respect for others by trying where possible to avoid actions that will harm them or interfere with what they are doing; it may indicate the duties and responsibilities of various members of the family, who is to be responsible for bringing up the children, and so forth. Often what will be important will be not so much exactly what actions are done as how willing participants are to do their parts and what attitudes they have—for example, whether they give sufficient weight to the interests of others.

The vague nature of moral understandings is to some extent alleviated in practice. One learns what can and cannot be done in various situations. Expectations are adjusted to other expectations. But moral disputes arise nonetheless. Such disputes may concern what the basic moral agreement implies for particular situations; and, if so, that can happen either because of disputes over the facts or because of a difference in basic understanding. Moral disputes may also arise concerning whether or not changes should be made in the basic agreement. Racial and sexual issues seem often to be of this second sort; but there is no clear line between the two kinds of dispute. When the implications of an agreement for a particular situation are considered, one possible outcome is that it becomes clear that the agreement should be modified.

Moral reasoning is a form of practical reasoning. One begins with certain beliefs and intentions, including intentions that are part of one's acceptance of the moral understanding in a given group. In reasoning, one modifies one's intentions, often by forming new intentions, sometimes by giving up old ones, so that one's plans become more rational and coherent—or, rather, one seeks to make all of one's attitudes coherent with each other.

The relevant sort of coherence is not simply consistency. It is something very like the explanatory coherence which is so important in theoretical reasoning. Coherence involves generality and lack of arbitrariness. Consider our feelings about cruelty to animals. Obviously these do not derive from an agreement that has been reached with animals. Instead it is a matter of coherence. There is a prima-facie arbitrariness and lack of generality in a plan that involves avoiding cruelty to people but not to animals.

On the other hand, coherence in this sense is not the only relevant factor in practical reasoning. Another is conservatism or inertia. A third is an interest in satisfying basic desires or needs. One tries to make the least change that will best satisfy one's desires while maximizing the overall coherence of one's attitudes. Coherence by itself is not an overwhelming force. That is why our attitudes towards animals are weak and wavering, allowing us to use them in ways we would not use people.

Consider again the second hereditary slave society mentioned above. This society was to be one in which no aspects of the moral understanding shared by the masters spoke against slavery. In fact that is unlikely, since there is some arbitrariness in the idea that people are to be treated in different ways depending on whether they are born slave or free. Coherence of attitude will no doubt speak at least a little against the system of slavery. The point is that the factors of conservatism and desire might speak more strongly in favor of the status quo, so that, all things considered, the slave owners might have no reason to change their understanding.

One thing that distinguishes slaves from animals is that slaves can organize and threaten revolt, whereas animals cannot. Slaves can see to it that both coherence and desire oppose conservatism, so that it becomes rational for the slave owners to arrive at a new, broader, more coherent understanding, one which includes the slaves.

It should be noted that coherence of attitude provides a constant pressure to widen the consensus and eliminate arbitrary distinctions. In this connection it is useful to recall ancient attitudes toward foreigners, and the ways people used to think about "savages," "natives," and "Indians." Also, recall that infanticide used to be considered as acceptable as we consider abortion to be. There has been a change here in our moral attitudes, prompted, I suggest, largely by considerations of coherence of attitude.

Finally, I would like to say a few brief words about the limiting case of group morality, when the group has only one member; then, as it were, a person comes to an understanding with himself. In my view, a person can make inner judgments in relation to such an individual morality only about himself. A familiar form of pacifism is of this sort. Certain pacifists judge that it would be wrong of them to participate in killing, although they are not willing to make a similar judgment about others. Observe that such a pacifist is unwilling only to make *inner* moral judgments about others. Although he is unwilling to judge that those who do participate are wrong to do so, he is perfectly willing to say that it is a bad thing that they participate. There are of course many other examples of individual morality in this sense, when a person imposes standards on himself that he does not apply to others. The existence of such examples is further confirmation of the relativist thesis that I have presented.

My conclusion is that relativism can be formulated as an intelligible thesis, the thesis that morality derives from an implicit agreement and that moral judgments are in a logical sense made in relation to such an agreement. Such a theory helps to explain otherwise puzzling aspects of our own moral views, in particular why we think that it is more important to avoid harm to others than to help others. The theory is also partially confirmed by what is, as far as I can tell, a previously unnoticed distinction between inner and non-inner moral judgments. Furthermore, traditional objections to implicit agreement theories can be met.[10]

Notes

1. Bernard Williams, *Morality: An Introduction to Ethics* (New York, 1972), pp. 20–21; Marcus Singer, *Generalization in Ethics* (New York, 1961), p. 332.

2. Thomas Nagel has observed that often, when we use the evaluative "ought to be" to say that something ought to be the case, we imply that someone ought to do something or ought to have done something about it. To take his example, we would not say that a certain hurricane ought not to have killed fifty people just on the ground that it was a terrible thing that the hurricane did so; but we might say this if we had in mind that the deaths from the hurricane would not have occurred except for the absence of safety or evacuation procedures which the authorities ought to have provided.

3. For the latter approach, see Thomas Nagel, *The Possibility of Altruism* (Oxford, 1970).

4. See Donald Davidson, "Weakness of Will," in Joel Feinberg (ed.), *Moral Concepts* (Oxford, 1969).

5. R. M. Hare, *The Language of Morals* (Oxford, 1952), pp. 164–168.

6. Philippa Foot, "Abortion and the Doctrine of Double Effect," in James Rachels (ed.), *Moral Problems* (New York, 1971).

7. R. M. Hare, *op. cit.* and *Freedom and Reason* (Oxford, 1963).

8. *The Language of Morals*, pp. 18–20, 168–169.

9. Cf. Thomas Hobbes, *Leviathan* (Oxford, 1957, *inter alia*), Pt. I, Ch. 14, "Of the First and Second Natural Laws, And of Contracts."

10. Many people have given me good advice about the subjects discussed in this paper, which derives from a larger study of practical reasoning and morality. I am particularly indebted to Donald Davidson, Stephen Schiffer, William Alston, Frederick Schick, Thomas Nagel, Walter Kaufmann, Peter Singer, Robert Audi, and the editors of the *Philosophical Review*.

Female Circumcision/Genital Mutilation and Ethical Relativism*

Loretta M. Kopelman

In northern Africa and southern Arabia many girls undergo ritual surgery involving removal of parts of their external genitalia; the surgery is often accompanied by ceremonies intended to honor and welcome the girls into their communities. About 80 million living women have had this surgery, and an additional 4 or 5 million girls undergo it each year (Kouba and Muasher 1985; Ntiri 1993). Usually performed between infancy and puberty, these ancient practices are supposed to promote chastity, religion, group identity, cleanliness, health, family values, and marriage goals. This tradition is prevalent and deeply embedded in many countries, including Ethiopia, the Sudan, Somalia, Sierra Leone, Kenya, Tanzania, Central African Republic, Chad, Gambia, Liberia, Mali, Senegal, Eritrea, Ivory Coast, Upper Volta, Mauritania, Nigeria, Mozambique, Botswana, Lesotho, and Egypt (Abdalla 1982; Ntiri 1993; Calder et al. 1993; Rushwan 1990; El Dareer 1982; Koso-Thomas 1987). Modified versions of the surgeries are also performed in Southern Yemen and Musqat-Oman (Abdalla 1982). Tragically, the usual ways of performing these surgeries deny women sexual orgasms, cause significant morbidity or mortality among women and children, and strain the overburdened health care systems in these developing countries. Some refer to these practices as female circumcision, but those wishing to stop them increasingly use the description female genital mutilation.

Impassioned cultural clashes erupt when people from societies practicing female circumcision/genital mutilation settle in other parts of the world and bring these rites with them. It is practiced, for example, by Muslim groups in

*Loretta M. Kopelman, "Female Circumcision/Genital Mutilation and Ethical Relativism," *Second Opinion* 20, no. 2 (October 1994): 55–71. Reprinted by permission of the Park Ridge Center.

the Philippines, Malaysia, Pakistan, Indonesia, Europe, and North America (Kluge 1993; Thompson 1989; Abdalla 1982; Koso-Thomas 1987). Parents may use traditional practitioners or seek medical facilities to reduce the morbidity or mortality of this genital surgery. Some doctors and nurses perform the procedures for large fees or because they are concerned about the unhygienic techniques that traditional practitioners may use. In the United Kingdom, where about 2,000 girls undergo the surgery annually, it is classified as child abuse (Thompson 1989). Other countries have also classified it as child abuse, including Canada and France (Kluge 1993).

Many international agencies like UNICEF, the International Federation of Gynecology and Obstetrics, and the World Health Organization (WHO) openly condemn and try to stop the practices of female genital mutilation (WHO 1992; Rushwan 1990). Such national groups as the American Medical Association (AMA 1991) have also denounced these rituals. Women's groups from around the world protest these practices and the lack of notice they receive. (A common reaction to the attention given to the Bobbitt case, where an abused wife cut off her husband's penis, was, "Why was there a media circus over one man's penis while the excision of the genitalia of millions of girls annually receives almost no attention?")

Most women in cultures practicing female circumcision/genital mutilation, when interviewed by investigators from their culture, state that they do not believe that such practices deprive them of anything important (Koso-Thomas 1987). They do not think that women can have orgasms or that sex can be directly pleasing to women but assume that their pleasure comes only from knowing they contribute to their husbands' enjoyment (El Dareer 1982; Abdalla 1982). Some critics argue that women who hold such beliefs cannot be understood to be making an informed choice; they thus condemn this custom as a form of oppression (Sherwin 1992; Walker 1992).

International discussion, criticisms, and condemnation of female circumcision/genital mutilation help activists who struggle to change these rites that are thoroughly entrenched in their own cultures (El Dareer 1982; Ntiri 1993; Kouba and Muasher 1985; Koso-Thomas 1987; Abdalla 1982). Not surprisingly, people who want to continue these practices resent such criticisms, seeing them as assaults upon their deeply embedded and popular cultural traditions.

Underlying intercultural disputes is often a basic moral controversy: Does praise or criticism from outside a culture or society have any moral authority within it? That is, do the moral judgments from one culture have any relevance to judgments about what is right or wrong within another culture? According to some versions of ethical relativism, to say that something is right means that it is approved of in the speaker's culture; to say that something is wrong means that it is disapproved. If this is correct, there is no rational basis for establishing across cultures that one set of culturally established moral values is right and the other wrong. The right action is one that is approved by the person's society or culture, and the wrong action is one that is disapproved by the person's society or culture; there are moral truths, but they are determined by the norms of the society. On this view, then, the cultural approval of female circumcision/genital mutilation means that the practice is right; disapproval means that it is wrong.

In contrast to such versions of ethical relativism, other traditions hold that to say something is morally right means that the claim can be defended with reasons in a certain way. Saying that something is approved (such as slavery) does not settle whether it is right, because something can be wrong even when it is approved by most people in a culture. Moral judgments do not describe what is approved but prescribe what ought to be approved; if worthy of being called moral or ethical judgments, they must be defensible with reasons that are consistent and empirically defensible. As we shall find, advocates of the practice of female circumcision/genital mutilation do not say, "We approve of these rituals, and that is the end of the matter." Rather, they try to defend the practice as useful in promoting many important goals. In fact, however, the practice is inconsistent with important goals and values of the cultures in which it is practiced. We find that we can evaluate some of the reasons given for performing these rituals and that despite our cultural differences about what to value and how to act, we share many methods of discovery, evaluation, and explanation. These enable us sometimes correctly to judge other cultures, and they us. Moral judgments can be evaluated at least in terms of their consistency and their relation to stable evidence, like medical or scientific findings. By this means certain moral claims can be challenged, even where we have different cultural values, and the practice of female circumcision/genital mutilation shown to be wrong. Thus, both intercultural and intracultural discussions, criticisms, and condemnation of female genital mutilation as well as support for activists seeking to stop the practice can have moral authority, or so I argue.

After considering some of the health hazards of female circumcision/genital mutilation, I review the version of ethical relativism that denies moral authority to cross-cultural moral judgments. By examining the cultural reasons used to justify female circumcision/genital mutilation, I want to show that many aspects of this discussion are open to cross-cultural evaluation and understanding and hence that this version of ethical relativism fails. After discussing some anticipated objections, I conclude that these relativists have a heavy burden of proof to show why we cannot make intercultural judgments that have moral force concerning female genital mutilation, just as we do concerning such things as oppression, intolerance, exploitation, waste, aggression, and torture or imprisonment of dissidents.

Types of Surgery and Their Health Consequences

Female circumcision/genital mutilation takes three forms. Type 1 circumcision involves pricking or removing the clitoral hood, or prepuce. This is the least mutilating type and should not preclude sexual orgasms in later life, unlike other forms. When this surgery is performed on infants and small children, however, it may be difficult to avoid removal of additional tissue, because infants' genitalia are small, and the tools commonly used are pins, scissors, razors, and knives. In the southern Arabian countries of Southern Yemen and Musqat-Oman, Type 1 circumcision is commonly practiced.[1] In African countries, however, Type 1 circumcision is often not regarded as a genuine circumcision (Koso-Thomas 1987; Abdalla 1982). Only about 3 percent of the women in one east African survey had this type of circumcision (El Dareer 1982), and none in another (Ntiri 1993) where all the women surveyed had been circumcised.

Type 2, or intermediary, circumcision involves removal of the clitoris and most or all of the labia minora. In Type 3 circumcision, or infibulation, the clitoris, labia minora, and parts of the labia majora are removed. The gaping wound to the vulva is stitched tightly closed, leaving a tiny opening so that the woman can pass urine and menstrual flow. (Type 3 is also known as Pharaonic circumcision, suggesting that it has been done since the time of the pharaohs [Abdalla 1982].) In some African countries most young girls between infancy and 10 years of age have Type 3 circumcision (Abdalla 1982; Ntiri 1993; Calder et al. 1993). Traditional practitioners often use sharpened or hot stones, razors, or knives, frequently without anesthesia or antibiotics (Rushwan 1990; Abdalla 1982; El Dareer 1982). In many communities thorns are used to stitch the wound closed, and a twig is inserted to keep an opening. The girl's legs may be bound for a month or more while the scar heals (Abdalla 1982; El Dareer 1982).[2]

Types 2 and 3, both of which preclude orgasms, are the most popular forms. More than three-quarters of the girls in the Sudan, Somalia, Ethiopia, and other north African and southern Arabian countries undergo Type 2 or Type 3 circumcision, with many of the others circumcised by Type 1 (El Dareer 1982; Ntiri 1993; Calder et al. 1993; Koso-Thomas 1987; Ogiamien 1988). One survey by Sudanese physician Asma El Dareer (1982) shows that over 98 percent of Sudanese women have had this ritual surgery, 12 percent with Type 2 and 83 percent with Type 3. A 1993 study of 859 Somali women finds that all were circumcised, 98 percent with Type 3 and 2 percent with Type 2; on 70 percent of them, the surgery was done with a machete (Ntiri 1993).

Medical science is divided over whether the practice of male circumcision has any benefits (see American Academy of Pediatrics 1989 and Alibhai 1993 for discussion of the pros and cons). In contrast, female circumcision/genital mutilation has no benefits and is harmful in many ways, with both short- and long-term complications documented in a series of studies from Nigeria (Ozumba 1992), the Sudan (El Dareer 1982), Sierra Leone (Koso-Thomas 1987), and Somalia (Abdalla 1982; Ntiri 1993; Dirie and Lindmark 1992).

Almost all girls experience immediate pain following the surgery (Rushwan 1990; El Dareer 1982). El Dareer found other immediate consequences, including bleeding, infection, and shock correlating with the type of circumcision: Type 1, 8.1 percent; Type 2, 24.1 percent; and Type 3, 25.6 percent. Bleeding occurred in all forms of circumcision, accounting for 21.3 percent of the immediate medical problems in El Dareer's survey. She writes, "Hemorrhage can be either primary, from injuries to arteries or veins, or secondary, as a result of infection" (1982:33). Infections are frequent because the surgical conditions are often unhygienic (Rushwan 1990; El Dareer 1982). The inability to pass urine was common, constituting 21.65 percent of the immediate complications (El Dareer 1982). El Dareer found 32.2 percent of the women surveyed had long-term problems, with 24.54 percent suffering urinary tract infections and 23.8 percent suffering chronic pelvic infection. The published studies by investigators from the regions where these rituals are practiced uniformly find that women expressed similar complaints and had similar complications from female circumcision/genital mutilation: at the site of the surgery, scarring can make penetration difficult and intercourse painful; cysts may form, requiring surgical repairs; a variety of menstrual problems arise if the opening left is too small to allow adequate drainage; fistulas or tears in the bowel or urinary tract are common, causing incontinence, which in turn leads to social as well as medical problems; maternal-fetal complications and prolonged and obstructed labor are also well-established consequences (Kouba and Muasher 1985; Rushwan 1990; El Dareer 1982; Koso-Thomas 1987; Abdalla 1982; Ozumba 1992; Ntiri 1993; Dirie and Lindmark 1992; Ogiamien 1988; Thompson 1989). El Dareer (1982: iii–iv) writes, "The result almost invariably causes immediate and long-term medical complications, especially at childbirth. Consummation of marriage is always a difficult experience for both partners, and marital problems often result. Psychological disturbances in girls due to circumcision are not uncommon." The operation can also be fatal because of shock, tetanus, and septicemia (Rushwan 1990).

Ethical Relativism

Female circumcision/genital mutilation serves as a test case for some versions of ethical relativism because the practice has widespread approval within the cultures where it is practiced and widespread disapproval outside those cultures. Relativism, however, means different things to different "academic cultures." Indeed one of the most striking things about the term relativism is that it is used in so many different ways, spanning the banal to the highly controversial. In the *Encyclopedia of Philosophy*, Richard D. Brandt (1967:75) writes, "Contemporary philosophers generally apply the term [ethical relativism] to some position they disagree with or consider absurd, seldom to their own views; social scientists, however, often classify themselves as relativists." Philosophers and those in religious studies often distinguish two ways to understand relativism: one is controversial, and the other is not (Brandt 1967; Sober 1991). The noncontroversial, descriptive version, often called descriptive relativism, is the view that people from different cultures do act differently and have distinct norms. Social scientists often work as descriptive relativists: they try to understand cultural differences and look for any underlying similarities. Those studying or criticizing female circumcision/genital mutilation, of course, recognize that we do act differently and have different values. But descriptions about how or in what way we are different do not entail statements about how we ought to act.

The controversial position, called ethical relativism, is that an action is right if it is approved in a person's culture and wrong if it is disapproved. Another version of this controversial view is that to say something is right means it has cultural approval; to say something is wrong means it has cultural disapproval. According to this view, which some call cultural relativism (Holmes 1993), there is no way to evaluate moral claims across cultures; positions taken by international groups like the World Health Organization merely express a cluster of particular societal opinions and have no moral standing in other cultures. On this view it is incoherent to claim that something is wrong in a culture yet approved, or right yet disapproved; people can express moral judgments about things done in their own or other cultures, but they are expressing only their cultural point of view, not one that has moral authority in another culture.

Many social scientists and (despite what Brandt says) some philosophers defend ethical relativism. For example, philosopher Bernard Williams (1985) argues that moral knowledge is inherited by people within particular cultural traditions and has objectivity only within those cultures. Anthropologists Faye Ginsberg (1991) and Nancy Scheper-Hughes (1991) point out that ethical relativism has held an important place in anthropology despite the uncomfortable consequence that acceptance of that position means that practices like female circumcision are right within the cultures where they are approved. Anthropologists by their own admission, however, do not use the terms cultural relativism or ethical relativism consistently (Shweder 1990).

Often relativism is presented as the only alternative to clearly implausible views such as absolutism or cultural imperialism; sometimes it is used to stress the obvious points that different rankings and interpretations of moral values or rules by different groups may be justifiable, or employed to highlight the indisputable influence of culture on moral development, reasoning, norms, and decisions. It may also be used to show that decisions about what we ought to do depend on the situation—for example, that it may not be wrong to lie in some cases. These points are not in dispute herein or even controversial, so my comments do not apply to these versions of relativism.

Nor do the criticisms offered herein necessarily challenge relativists who agree that cross-cultural moral judgments sometimes have moral force. Generally they wish to accent the role of culture in shaping our moral judgments, showing why it is dangerous to impose external cultural judgments hastily or stressing that there is often a link between established moral systems and oppression. For example, moral philosopher Susan Sherwin maintains that "normative conclusions reached by traditional theorists generally support the mechanism of oppression; for example, by promoting subservience among women" and concludes, "Feminist moral relativism remains absolutist on the question of the moral wrong of oppression but is relativist on other moral matters" (1992:58, 75). She uses this form of relativism to argue that female circumcision is wrong.

In contrast, the distinctive feature of the version of ethical relativism criticized herein is its defense of the skeptical position that one can never make a sound cross-cultural moral judgment, that is, one that has moral force outside one's culture.[3] This version of ethical relativism is false if people from one culture can sometimes make judgments that have moral authority about actions in another society. Its defenders regard their view to be the consequence of a proper understanding of the limits of knowledge (Williams 1985; Ginsberg 1991; Shweder 1990). Many attacks, however, have been made on the skepticism underlying such ethical relativism (Bambrough 1979; Hampshire 1989), and my remarks are in this tradition.

I would begin by observing that we seem to share methods of discovery, evaluation, negotiation, and explanation that can be used to help assess moral judgments. For example, we agree how to evaluate methods and research in science, engineering, and medicine, and on how to translate, debate, deliberate, criticize, negotiate, and use technology. To do these things, however, we must first have agreed to some extent on how to distinguish good and bad methods and research in science, engineering, and medicine, and what constitutes a good or bad translation, debate, deliberation, criticism, negotiation, or use of technology. These shared methods can be used to help evaluate moral judgments from one culture to another in a way that sometimes has moral authority. An example of a belief that could be evaluated by stable medical evidence is the assertion by people in some regions that the infant's "death could result if, during delivery, the baby's head touches the clitoris" (Koso-Thomas 1987:10). In addition, some moral claims can be evaluated in terms of their coherence. It seems incompatible to promote maternal-fetal health as a good and also to advocate avoidable practices known to cause serious perinatal and neonatal infections.

We need not rank values similarly with people in another culture, or our own, to have coherent discussions about their consistency, consequences, or factual presuppositions. That is, even if some moral or ethical (I use these terms interchangeably) judgments express unique cultural norms, they may still be morally evaluated by another culture on the basis of their logical consistency and their coherence with stable and cross-culturally accepted empirical information. In addition, we seem to share some moral values, goals, and judgments such as those about the evils of unnecessary suffering and lost opportunities, the need for food and shelter, the duty to help children, and the goods of promoting public health and personal well-being (Hampshire 1989). Let us consider, therefore, the reasons given by men and women who practice female circumcision/genital mutilation in their communities. The information presented herein is based upon studies done by investigators who come from these cultures, some of whom had this ritual surgery as children (El Dareer is one such investigator). We can examine whether these reasons allow people from other cultures any way of entering the debate based upon such considerations as consistency or stable medical findings.

Reasons Given for Female Circumcision/Genital Mutilation

According to four independent series of studies conducted by investigators from countries where female circumcision is widely practiced (El Dareer 1982; Ntiri 1993; Koso-Thomas 1987; Abdalla 1982), the primary reasons given for performing this ritual surgery are that it (1) meets a religious requirement, (2) preserves group identity, (3) helps to maintain cleanliness and health, (4) preserves virginity and family honor and prevents immorality, and (5) furthers marriage goals including greater sexual pleasure for men.

El Dareer conducted her studies in the Sudan, Dr. Olayinka Koso-Thomas in and around Sierra Leone, and Raquiya Haji Dualeh Abdalla and Daphne Williams Ntiri in Somalia. They argue that the reasons for continuing this practice in their respective countries float on a sea of false beliefs, beliefs that thrive because of a lack of education and open discussion about reproduction and sexuality. Insofar as intercultural methods for evaluating factual and logical statements exist, people from other cultures should at least be able to understand these inconsistencies or mistaken factual beliefs and use them as a basis for making some judgments having intercultural moral authority.

First, according to these studies the main reason given for performing female circumcision/genital mutilation is that it is regarded as a religious requirement. Most of the people practicing this ritual are Muslims, but it is not a practice required by the Koran (El Dareer 1982; Ntiri 1993). El Dareer writes: "Circumcision of women is not explicitly enjoined in the Koran, but there are two implicit sayings of the Prophet Mohammed: 'Circumcision is an ordinance in men and an embellishment in women' and, reportedly Mohammed said to Om Attiya, a woman who circumcised girls in El Medina, 'Do not go deep. It is more illuminating to the face and more enjoyable to the husband.' Another version says, 'Reduce but do not destroy. This is enjoyable to the woman and preferable to the man.' But there is nothing in the Koran to suggest that the Prophet commanded that women be circumcised. He advised that it was important to both sexes that very little should be taken" (1992:72). Female circumcision/genital mutilation, moreover, is not practiced in the spiritual center of Islam, Saudi Arabia (Calder et al. 1993). Another reason for questioning this as a Muslim practice is that clitoridectomy and infibulation predate Islam, going back to the time of the pharaohs (Abdalla 1982; El Dareer 1992).

Second, many argue that the practice helps to preserve group identity. When Christian colonialists in Kenya introduced laws opposing the practice of female circumcision in the 1930s, African leader Kenyatta expressed a view still popular today: "This operation is still regarded as the very essence of an institution which has enormous educational, social, moral and religious implications, quite apart from the operation itself. For the present, it is impossible for a member of the [Kikuyu] tribe to imagine an initiation without clitoridectomy . . . the abolition of IRUA [the ritual operation] will destroy the tribal symbol which identifies the age group and prevent the Kikuyu from perpetuating that spirit of collectivism and national solidarity which they have been able to maintain from time immemorial" (Scheper-Hughes 1991:27). In addition, the practice is of social and economic importance to older women who are paid for performing the rituals (El Dareer 1982; Koso-Thomas 1987; Abdalla 1982; Ginsberg 1991).

Drs. Koso-Thomas, El Dareer, and Abdalla agree that people in these countries support female circumcision as a good practice, but only because they do not understand that it is a leading cause of sickness or even death for girls, mothers, and infants, and a major cause of infertility, infection, and maternal-fetal and marital complications. They conclude that these facts are not confronted because these societies do not speak openly of such matters. Abdalla writes,

"There is no longer any reason, given the present state of progress in science, to tolerate confusion and ignorance about reproduction and women's sexuality" (1982:2). Female circumcision/genital mutilation is intended to honor women as male circumcision honors men, and members of cultures where the surgery is practiced are shocked by the analogy of clitoridectomy to removal of the penis (El Dareer 1982).

Third, the belief that the practice advances health and hygiene is incompatible with stable data from surveys done in these cultures, where female circumcision/genital mutilation has been linked to mortality or morbidity such as shock, infertility, infections, incontinence, maternal-fetal complications, and protracted labor. The tiny hole generally left for blood and urine to pass is a constant source of infection (El Dareer 1982; Koso-Thomas 1987; Abdalla 1982; Calder et al. 1993; Ntiri 1993). Koso-Thomas writes, "As for cleanliness, the presence of these scars prevents urine and menstrual flow escaping by the normal channels. This may lead to acute retention of urine and menstrual flow, and to a condition known as hematocolpos, which is highly detrimental to the health of the girl or woman concerned and causes odors more offensive than any that can occur through the natural secretions" (Koso-Thomas 1987:10). Investigators completing a recent study wrote: "The risk of medical complications after female circumcision is very high as revealed by the present study [of 290 Somali women, conducted in the capital of Mogadishu]. Complications which cause the death of the young girls must be a common occurrence especially in the rural areas. . . . Dribbling urine incontinence, painful menstruations, hematocolpos and painful intercourse are facts that Somali women have to live with—facts that strongly motivate attempts to change the practice of female circumcision" (Dirie and Lindmark 1992: 482).

Fourth, investigators found that circumcision is thought necessary in these cultures to preserve virginity and family honor and to prevent immorality. Type 3 circumcision is used to keep women from having sexual intercourse before marriage and conceiving illegitimate children. In addition, many believe that Types 2 and 3 circumcision must be done because uncircumcised women have excessive and uncontrollable sexual drives. El Dareer, however, believes that this view is not consistently held—that women in the Sudan are respected and that Sudanese men would be shocked to apply this sometimes-held cultural view to members of their own families. This reason also seems incompatible with the general view, which investigators found was held by both men and women in these cultures, that sex cannot be pleasant for women (El Dareer 1982; Koso-Thomas 1987; Abdalla 1982). In addition, female circumcision/genital mutilation offers no foolproof way to promote chastity and can even lead to promiscuity because it does not diminish desire or libido even where it makes orgasms impossible (El Dareer 1982). Some women continually seek experiences with new sexual partners because they are left unsatisfied in their sexual encounters (Koso-Thomas 1987). Moreover, some pretend to be virgins by getting stitched up tightly again (El Dareer 1982).

Fifth, interviewers found that people practicing female circumcision/genital mutilation believe that it furthers marriage goals, including greater sexual pleasure for men. To survive economically, women in these cultures must marry, and they will not be acceptable marriage partners unless they have undergone this ritual surgery (Abdalla 1982; Ntiri 1993). It is a curse, for example, to say that someone is the child of an uncircumcised woman (Koso-Thomas 1987). The widely held belief that infibulation enhances women's beauty and men's sexual pleasure makes it difficult for women who wish to marry to resist this practice (Koso-Thomas 1987; El Dareer 1992). Some men from these cultures, however, report that they enjoy sex more with uncircumcised women (Koso-Thomas 1987). Furthermore, female circumcision/genital mutilation is inconsistent with the established goals of some of these cultures because it is a leading cause of disability and contributes to the high mortality rate among mothers, fetuses, and children. Far from promoting the goals of marriage, it causes difficulty in consummating marriage, infertility, prolonged and obstructed labor, and morbidity and mortality.

Criticisms of Ethical Relativism

Examination of the debate concerning female circumcision suggests several conclusions about the extent to which people from outside a culture can understand or contribute to moral debates within it in a way that has moral force. First, the fact that a culture's moral and religious views are often intertwined with beliefs that are open to rational and empirical evaluation can be a basis of cross-cultural examination and intercultural moral criticism (Bambrough 1979). Beliefs that the practice enhances fertility and promotes health, that women cannot have orgasms, and that allowing the baby's head to touch the clitoris during delivery causes death to the baby are incompatible with stable medical data (Koso-Thomas 1987). Thus an opening is allowed for genuine cross-cultural discussion or criticism of the practice.

Some claims about female circumcision/genital mutilation, however, are not as easily open to cross-cultural understanding. For example, cultures practicing the Type 3 surgery, infibulation, believe that it makes women more beautiful. For those who are not from these cultures, this belief is difficult to understand, especially when surveys show that many women in these cultures, when interviewed, attribute to infibulation their keloid scars, urine retention, pelvic infections, puerperal sepsis, and obstetrical problems (Ntiri 1993; Abdalla 1982). Koso-Thomas writes: "None of the reasons put forward in favor of circumcision have any real scientific or logical basis. It is surprising that aesthetics and the maintenance of cleanliness are advanced as grounds for female circumcision. The scars could hardly be thought of as contributing to beauty. The hardened scar and stump usually seen where the clitoris should be, or in the case of the infibulated vulva, taut skin with an ugly long scar down the middle, present a horrifying picture" (Koso-Thomas 1987:10). Thus not everyone in these cultures believes that these rituals enhance beauty; some find such claims difficult to understand.

Second, the debate over female circumcision/genital mutilation illustrates another difficulty for defenders of this version of ethical relativism concerning the problem of differentiating cultures. People who brought the practice of female circumcision/genital mutilation with them when they moved to another nation still claim to be a distinct cultural group. Some who moved to Britain, for example, resent the interference in their culture represented by laws that condemn the practice as child abuse (Thompson 1989). If ethical relativists are to appeal to cultural approval in making the final determination of what is good or bad, right or wrong, they must tell us how to distinguish one culture from another.

How exactly do we count or separate cultures? A society is not a nation-state, because some social groups have distinctive identities within nations. If we do not define societies as nations, however, how do we distinguish among cultural groups, for example, well enough to say that an action is child abuse in one culture but not in another? Subcultures in nations typically overlap and have many variations. Even if we could count cultural groups well enough to say exactly how to distinguish one culture from another, how and when would this be relevant? How big or old or vital must a culture, subculture, group, or cult be in order to be recognized as a society whose moral distinctions are self-contained and self-justifying?

A related problem is that there can be passionate disagreement, ambivalence, or rapid changes within a culture or group over what is approved or disapproved. According to ethical relativism, where there is significant disagreement within a culture there is no way to determine what is right or wrong. But what disagreement is significant?

Third, despite some clear disagreement such as that over the rightness of female circumcision/genital mutilation, people from different parts of the world share common goals like the desirability of promoting people's health, happiness, opportunities, and cooperation, and the wisdom of stopping war, pollution, oppression, torture, and exploitation. These common goals make us a world community, and using shared methods of reasoning and evaluation, we can discuss how they are understood or how well they are implemented in different parts of our world community. We can use these shared goals to assess whether female circumcision/genital mutilation is more like respect or oppression, more like enhancement or diminishment of opportunities, or more like pleasure or torture. Another way to express this is to say that we should recognize universal human rights or be respectful of each other as persons capable of reasoned discourse.

Fourth, this version of ethical relativism, if consistently held, leads to the abhorrent conclusion that we cannot make intercultural judgments with moral force about societies that start wars, practice torture, or exploit and oppress other groups; as long as these activities are approved in the society that does them, they are allegedly right. Yet the world community believed that it was making a cross-cultural judgment with moral force when it criticized the Communist Chinese government for crushing a pro-democracy student protest rally, the South Africans for upholding apartheid, the Soviets for using psychiatry to suppress dissent, and the Bosnian Serbs for carrying out the siege of Sarajevo.

And the judgment was expressed without anyone's ascertaining whether the respective actions had wide-spread approval in those countries. In each case, representatives from the criticized society usually said something like, "You don't understand why this is morally justified in our culture even if it would not be in your society." If ethical relativism were convincing, these responses ought to be as well.

Relativists who want to defend sound social cross-cultural and moral judgments about the value of freedom and human rights in other cultures seem to have two choices. On the one hand, if they agree that some cross-cultural norms have moral authority, they should also agree that some intercultural judgments about female circumcision/genital mutilation may have moral authority. Some relativists take this route (see, for example, Sherwin 1992), thereby abandoning the version of ethical relativism being criticized herein. On the other hand, if they defend this version of ethical relativism yet make cross-cultural moral judgments about the importance of values like tolerance, group benefit, and the survival of cultures, they will have to admit to an inconsistency in their arguments. For example, anthropologist Scheper-Hughes (1991) advocates tolerance of other cultural value systems; she fails to see that she is saying that tolerance between cultures is right and that this is a cross-cultural moral judgment using a moral norm (tolerance). Similarly, relativists who say it is wrong to eliminate rituals that give meaning to other cultures are also inconsistent in making a judgment that presumes to have genuine cross-cultural moral authority.

The burden of proof, then, is upon defenders of this version of ethical relativism to show why we cannot do something we think we sometimes do very well, namely, engage in intercultural moral discussion, cooperation, or criticism and give support to people whose welfare or rights are in jeopardy in other cultures. In addition, defenders of ethical relativism need to explain how we can justify the actions of international professional societies that take moral stands in adopting policy. For example, international groups may take moral stands that advocate fighting pandemics, stopping wars, halting oppression, promoting health education, or eliminating poverty, and they seem to have moral authority in some cases. Some might respond that our professional groups are themselves cultures of a sort. But this response raises the already discussed problem of how to individuate a culture or society.

Objections

Some standard rejoinders are made to criticism of relativism, but they leave untouched the arguments against the particular version of ethical relativism discussed herein. First, some defenders argue that cross-cultural moral judgments perpetuate the evils of absolutism, cultural dogmatism, or cultural imperialism. People rarely admit to such transgressions, often enlisting medicine, religion, science, or the "pure light of reason" to arrive at an allegedly impartial, disinterested, and justified conclusion that they should "enlighten" and "educate" the "natives," "savages," or "infidels." Anthropologist Scheper-Hughes writes, "I don't 'like' the idea of clitoridectomy any better than any other woman I know. But I like even less the western 'voices of reason' [imposing their views]" (1991:27). Scheper-Hughes and others suggest that, in arguing that we can make moral judgments across cultures, we are thereby claiming a particular culture knows best and has the right to impose its allegedly superior knowledge on other cultures.

Claiming that we can sometimes judge another culture in a way that has moral force, however, does not entail that one culture is always right, that absolutism is legitimate, or that we can impose our beliefs on others. Relativists sometimes respond that even if this is not a strict logical consequence, it is a practical result. Sherwin writes, "Many social scientists have endorsed versions of relativism precisely out of their sense that the alternative promotes cultural dominance. They may be making a philosophical error in drawing that conclusion, but I do not think that they are making an empirical one" (1992:63–64).

The version of ethical relativism we have been considering, however, does not avoid cultural imperialism. To say that an act is right, on this view, means that it has cultural approval, including acts of war, oppression, enslavement, aggression, exploitation, racism, or torture. On this view, the disapproval of other cultures is irrelevant in determining whether these acts are right or wrong; accordingly, the disapproval of people in other cultures, even victims of war, oppression, enslavement, aggression, exploitation, racism, or torture, does not count in deciding what is right or wrong except in their own culture. This view thus leads to abhorrent conclusions. It entails not only the affirmation that female circumcision/genital mutilation is right in cultures where it is approved but the affirmation that anything with wide social approval is right, including slavery, war, discrimination, oppression, racism, and torture. If defenders of the version of ethical relativism criticized herein are consistent, they will dismiss any objections by people in other cultures as merely an expression of their own cultural preferences, having no moral standing whatsoever in the society that is engaging in the acts in question.

Defenders of ethical relativism must explain why we should adopt a view leading to such abhorrent conclusions. They may respond that cultures sometimes overlap and hence that the victims' protests within or between cultures ought to count. But this response raises two further difficulties for defenders of ethical relativism. First, it is inconsistent if it means that the views of people in other cultures have moral standing and oppressors ought to consider the views of victims. Such judgments are inconsistent with this version of ethical relativism because they are cross-cultural judgments with moral authority. The second difficulty with this defense, also discussed above, is that it raises the problem of how we differentiate a culture or society.

Second, some defenders of ethical relativism argue that we cannot know enough about another culture to make any cross-cultural moral judgments. We cannot really understand another society well enough to criticize it, they claim, because our feelings, concepts, or ways of reasoning are too different; our so-called ordinary moral views about what is permissible are determined by our upbringing and environments to such a degree that they cannot be transferred to other cultures. There are two ways to understand this objection (Sober 1991). The first is that nothing counts as understanding another culture except being raised in it. If that is what is meant, then the objection is valid in a trivial way. But it does not address the important issue of whether we can comprehend well enough to make relevant moral distinctions or engage in critical ethical discussions about the universal human right to be free of oppression.

The second, and nontrivial, way to understand this objection is that we cannot understand another society well enough to justify claiming to know what is right or wrong in that society or even to raise moral questions about what enhances or diminishes life, promotes opportunities, and so on. Overwhelming data, however, suggest that we think we can do this very well. Travelers to other countries often quickly understand that approved practices in their own country are widely condemned elsewhere, sometimes for good reasons. For example, they learn that the U.S. population consumes a disproportionate amount of the world's resources, a fact readily noticed and condemned by citizens in other cultures. We ordinarily view international criticism and international responses concerning human rights violations, aggression, torture, and exploitation as important ways to show that we care about the rights and welfare of other people, and in some cases these responses have moral authority.

People who deny the possibility of genuine cross-cultural moral judgments must account for why we think we can and should make them, or why we sometimes agree more with people from other cultures than with our own relatives and neighbors about the moral assessments of aggression, oppression, capital punishment, abortion, euthanasia, rights to health care, and so on. International meetings, moreover, seem to employ genuinely cross-cultural moral judgments when they seek to distinguish good from bad uses of technology, promote better environmental or health policies, and so on.

Third, some defenders of ethical relativism object that eliminating important rituals from a culture risks destroying the society. They insist that these cultures cannot survive if they change such a central practice as female circumcision (Scheper-Hughes 1991). This counterargument, however, is not decisive. Slavery, oppression, and exploitation are also necessary to some ways of life, yet few would defend these actions in order to preserve a society. Others reply to this objection by questioning the assumption that these cultures can survive only by continuing clitoridectomy or infibulation (El Dareer 1982). These cultures, they argue, are more likely to be transformed by war, famine, disease, urbanization, and industrialization than by the cessation of this ancient ritual surgery. A further argument is that if slavery, oppression, and exploitation are wrong whether or not there are group benefits, then a decision to eliminate female circumcision/genital mutilation should not depend on a process of weighing its benefits to the group. It is also incoherent or inconsistent to hold that group benefit is so important that other cultures should not interfere with local practices. For this view elevates group benefit as an overriding cross-cultural value, something that these ethical relativists claim cannot be justified. If there are no cross-cultural values about what is wrong or right, a defender of ethical relativism cannot consistently say such things as "One culture ought not interfere with others," "We ought to be tolerant," "Every culture is equally valuable," or "It is wrong to interfere with another culture."

Comment

We have sufficient reason, therefore, to conclude that these rituals of female circumcision/genital mutilation are wrong. For me to say they are wrong does not mean that they are disapproved by most people in my culture but wrong for reasons similar to those given by activists within these cultures who are working to stop these practices. They are wrong because the usual forms of the surgery deny women orgasms and because they cause medical complications and even death.

Notes

The author wishes to thank Robert Holmes, Suzanne Poirier, Sandy Pittman, Barbara Hofmaier, Richard McCarty, and Holly Mathews for their help in reviewing this manuscript.

1. According to Abdalla (1982:16), in these regions the unusual practice is followed of putting "salt into the vagina after childbirth . . . [because this] induces the narrowing of the vagina . . . to restore the vagina to its former shape and size and make intercourse more pleasurable for the husband."

2. Some authors cite incidences of a very rare operation they call Type 4, or introcision, where the vaginal opening is enlarged by tearing it downward, cutting the perineum (see, for example, Rushwan 1990). It is practiced in Mali and sometimes in Senegal and northern Nigeria (Kouba and Muasher 1985).

References

Abdalla, Raquiya H. D. 1982. *Sisters in Affliction: Circumcision and Infibulation of Women in Africa*. London: Zed Press.

Alibhai, Shabbir M. H. 1993. "Male and Female Circumcision in Canada" (letter to the editor). *Canadian Medical Association Journal* 149, no. 1 (1 July): 16–17.

American Academy of Pediatrics. 1989. "Report of the Task Force on Circumcision." *Pediatrics* 84, no. 2 (August): 388–91. (Published erratum appears in *Pediatrics* 84, no. 5 [November 1989]: 761.)

American Medical Association. 1991. "Surgical Modification of Female Genitalia." House of Delegates Amended Resolution 13 (June).

Bambrough, Renford. 1979. *Moral Skepticism and Moral Knowledge*. London: Routledge and Kegan Paul.

Brandt, Richard D. 1967. *Encyclopedia of Philosophy*, s.v. "ethical relativism."

Calder, Barbara L., Yvonne M. Brown, and Donna I. Rac. 1993. "Female Circumcision/Genital Mutilation: Culturally Sensitive Care." *Health Care for Women International* 14, no. 3 (May-June): 227–38.

Dirie, M. A., and G. Lindmark. 1992. "The Risk of Medical Complication after Female Circumcision." *East African Medical Journal* 69, no. 9 (September): 479–82.

El Dareer, Asma. 1982. *Woman, Why Do You Weep? Circumcision and Its Consequences*. London: Zed Press.

Fourcroy, Jean L. 1983. "L'Eternal Couteau: Review of Female Circumcision." *Urology* 22, no. 4 (October): 458–61.

Ginsberg, Faye. 1991. "What Do Women Want?: Feminist Anthropology Confronts Clitoridectomy." *Medical Anthropology Quarterly* 5, no. 1 (March): 17–19.

Hampshire, Stuart. 1989. *Innocence and Experience*. Cambridge, Mass.: Harvard University Press.

Holmes, Robert L. 1993. *Basic Moral Philosophy*. Belmont, Calif.: Wadsworth Publishing.

Kluge, Eike-Henner. 1993. "Female Circumcision: When Medical Ethics Confronts Cultural Values" (editorial). *Canadian Medical Association Journal* 148, no. 2 (15 January): 288–89.

Koso-Thomas, Olayinka. 1987. *The Circumcision of Women*. London: Zed Press.

Kouba, Leonard J., and Judith Muasher. 1985. "Female Circumcision in Africa: An Overview." *African Studies Review* 28, no. 1 (March): 95–109.

Ntiri, Daphne Williams. 1993. "Circumcision and Health among Rural Women of Southern Somalia as Part of a Family Life Survey." *Health Care for Women International* 14, no. 3 (May-June): 215–16.

Ogiamien, T. B. E. 1988. "A Legal Framework to Eradicate Female Circumcision." *Medicine, Science and the Law* 28, no. 2 (April): 115–19.

Ozumba, B. C. 1992. "Acquired Gynetresia in Eastern Nigeria." *International Journal of Gynaecology and Obstetrics* 37, no. 2: 105–9.

Ruminjo, J. 1992. "Circumcision in Women." *East African Medical Journal* 69, no. 2 (September): 477–78.

Rushwan, Hamid. 1990. "Female Circumcision." *World Health*, April–May, 24–25.

Scheper-Hughes, Nancy. 1991. "Virgin Territory: The Male Discovery of the Clitoris." *Medical Anthropology Quarterly* 5, no. 1 (March): 25–28.

Sherwin, Susan. 1992. *No Longer Patient: Feminist Ethics and Health Care*. Philadelphia: Temple University Press.

Shweder, Richard. 1990. "Ethical Relativism: Is There a Defensible Version?" *Ethos* 18:205–18.

Sober, Elliott. 1991. *Core Questions in Philosophy*. New York: Macmillan.

Thompson, June. 1989. "Torture by Tradition." *Nursing Times* 85, no. 15: 17–18.

Walker, Alice. 1992. *Possessing the Secret of Joy*. New York: Harcourt Brace Jovanovich.

Williams, Bernard. 1985. *Ethics and the Limits of Philosophy*. Cambridge, Mass.: Harvard University Press.

World Health Organization. 1992. *International Journal of Gynaecology and Obstetrics* 37, no. 2: 149.

Study Questions

1. Note that the Statement on Human Rights from the *American Anthropologist* asserts that people are free only when they live as their society defines freedom. Some people live in societies where, for members of poor families that have no other alternative, freedom is defined as obeying the person to whom your parents sold you in order to have food to feed yourself and your siblings. Is freedom relative to cultures? Do all people have the right not to be slaves or is such a right relative to cultures? Discuss.

2. Discuss how Gilbert Harman and Louis Pojman would evaluate the example in question 1. What reasons would they give for their differing ethical evaluations of the example?

3. The essays in this section attempt to show how important it is to distinguish clearly several concepts that are easily confused with one another. On the

basis of your reading, clearly explain in your own words what cultural relativism (which Pojman also calls the *diversity thesis*), moral/ethical relativism and moral subjectivism are and how they differ from one another. Do the same with moral absolutism and moral objectivism.

4. Do you think that there is a set of general ethical principles that apply to all cultures? If so, how much can those principles vary in their application to differing cultures? After formulating your answer, consider some of the objections to a view like yours that you have encountered in the reading in this section. How would you reply to those objections?

5. Loretta Kopelman argues that female circumcision (which she would view as female genital mutilation) is morally wrong even in cultures and subcultures where it is endorsed and seen as important for social cohesion. Summarize what you take to be her most important line of argument in your own words. Do you agree with her argument(s)? Why or why not?

6. What kind of objections might Gilbert Harman make in response to Kopelman's argument(s)? How similar are the principles that she applies to this controversy to Pojman's universal principles of core morality?

For Further Reading

Benedict, Ruth. *Patterns of Culture*. Boston: Houghton Mifflin, 1934.

Cook, Rebecca J., Bernard M. Dickens, and Mahmoud F. Fathalla. *Reproductive Health and Human Rights: Integrating Medicine, Ethics and Law*. New York: Oxford University Press, 2003.

Midgley, Mary. *Can't We Make Moral Judgements?* New York: Palgrave Macmillan, 1993.

Moody-Adams, M. M. *Fieldwork in Familiar Places: Morality, Culture, and Philosophy*. Cambridge, MA: Harvard University Press, 1997.

Moser, P. K., and T. L. Carson, eds. *Moral Relativism: A Reader*. New York: Oxford University Press, 2001.

Wong, D. B. *Moral Relativity*. Berkeley: University of California Press, 1984.

CHAPTER FOUR

Natural Law Theory

"Always let your conscience be your guide." In offering this advice to Pinocchio, Jiminy Cricket is stating a key aspect of natural law theory, which maintains that people have an inherent or natural "moral compass" or sense of right and wrong. While natural law theorists have differed over the extent to which this inner moral sense or "conscience" is innate or acquired, they are united by the view that morality need not depend on divine revelation. According to natural law theory, human beings are capable of knowing the basic principles of morality through their own natural reason. To be sure, some natural law theorists, such as St. Thomas Aquinas, believe that this inner sense of right and wrong nonetheless is "written on our hearts" (as Paul says in his letter to the Romans in the Bible) by God. But what makes Aquinas a natural law theorist is his belief that human reason unaided by divine revelation is capable of knowing the basic requirements of morality. All natural law theorists share this belief, although not all share Aquinas's views concerning the theological foundations of the natural law.

Natural law theory has a long history. We see it, for example, in the philosophy of the Stoics (see the selection from Epictetus on page 442), who take their cue from the age-old notion that the moral law derives from the law of nature, that there is a cosmic justice that governs both the natural and moral realms. This conception of the natural law can be found in such ideas as *ma'at* in ancient Egypt or *rta* in ancient India or *dike* in ancient Greece. These ideas denote that there is an objective and universal order of things and that human action must correspond to and help maintain this order. On this view, human reason can discover the nature of right and wrong from an understanding of the nature of things, in particular, the nature of human beings. For natural law theory, there is no fact/

value distinction; moral facts derive from natural facts. Contrary to David Hume (see chapter 7), natural law theorists maintain we can derive "ought" from "is."

Modern natural law theorists emphasize the way practical rationality is guided by fundamental principles of right and wrong that are self-evident to reason. These principles are knowable by all persons, and, as such, are universally binding and inviolable. The political notion of natural (or inalienable) rights derives from this conception of natural law, for such natural rights are grounded not in local customs or contingent "positive" laws, but rather universal principles of reason. As such, they are the same for everyone and cannot be violated or over-ridden by particular, contingent human laws. When Thomas Jefferson writes in the *Declaration of Independence*, "We hold such truths to be self-evident, that all men are created equal, that they are endowed by their Creator with certain inalienable Rights, that among these are Life, Liberty, and the pursuit of Happiness," he is expressing a view of natural rights first articulated by the seventeenth-century English philosopher John Locke, rooted in natural law theory.

The selection that follows from the *Summa Theologiae* of St. Thomas Aquinas captures many of the key features of natural law theory. For Aquinas, natural law refers primarily to our participation by reason in the "eternal law," that is, God's rational ordering of the universe. The first principle of the natural law serves as the basic principle of practical reason and states that self-evident truth that "good is to be done and promoted and evil avoided." Human reason receives guidance regarding what is, in fact, good to pursue from our natural inclinations, since God inclines us naturally to pursue that which is good for us. The basic goods to be pursued include (1) self-preservation and that which promotes life and prevents its destruction, (2) sexual procreation and the rearing and education of children and (3) knowledge of God and living in society.

While it is not suggested that this is an exhaustive list of the basic goods to be pursued, natural law theorists maintain that there is an absolute prohibition against violating these fundamental precepts of the natural law. In this sense, natural law theory is often regarded as a form of moral absolutism. Other absolute moral precepts may also be derived from them, such as prohibitions against the killing of innocent persons or the doing of unnecessary harm to another (they violate the promotion of life, etc.), as well as lying and theft (they violate the pursuit of truth and living in society), among others.

Aquinas's natural law theory has been very influential in the area of sexual morality, especially within, but not limited to, the Roman Catholic Church. For example, the second precept of the natural law leads to a prohibition against sexual intercourse outside of marriage on the grounds that the children that result from such unions are compromised with regard to child-rearing. In addition, Aquinas makes use of the Aristotelian notion of a "natural end," that is, the idea that things, processes and actions have some *telos* or goal toward which they tend provided there is no impediment. The natural end of the eye is to see;

the natural end of eating is the digestion of food. Aquinas's natural law theory assumes that it is wrong to frustrate natural ends. Since sexual relations have as their natural end the procreation of children, sexual practices such as sodomy are deemed unnatural and, hence, immoral. Abortions are considered immoral since they violate the principle of promoting life and also undermine the natural goal of a pregnancy, namely, the birth of a child. The use of birth control is also prohibited for similar reasons, as are acts of euthanasia.

The selection from Alan Donagan offers some explanation of the basic teachings of Aquinas's natural law theory and defends it against the criticism that it commits the fallacy of deriving ethical truths from non-ethical ones and that it is too theologically rooted to be helpful to contemporary analytic philosophers. For Donagan, Aquinas's natural law theory, like Kant's ethical theory (see chapter 6), is primarily about the moral demands of practical reason. He rejects, therefore, the view that an act is wrong on the basis of the frustration of natural ends. Such reasoning will not work, for example, to show that lying is wrong since one cannot maintain that all speech acts must tend toward the truth as their end. Little white lies do not, but they communicate nonetheless. Instead, Donagan thinks Aquinas's natural law theory can be recast along Kantian lines, based on the self-evident principle that persons must be treated as ends in themselves and never as a means only, a principle he thinks is implicit in Aquinas's thought. Lying would then be considered morally wrong because it is treating another person as a means to an end. Since it is evil to do so, and since the first precept of the natural law maintains that evil is to be avoided, lying is morally wrong. In this way, specific moral precepts of the natural law are derived from Kantian considerations rather than the outdated teleology of natural ends.

Even if one leaves behind the notion of natural ends, it is still the case that actions may be defined in terms of the agent's goals and intentions. For Aquinas, all human actions proceed freely from the will toward a goal or end apprehended by reason. A necessary, but not sufficient, condition of good moral acts is that the agent performs them in order to bring about a good end. But what about cases where an action aims at a good end that is achieved only through what is, according to natural law, evil? For example, in order to preserve my life (a basic good according to natural law), I must kill my attacker. Since killing violates the basic good of life, I seemingly violated the natural law at the same time I was obeying it. The "principle of double effect" has been developed by natural law theorists to resolve such dilemmas. In brief, the principle states that, in the attempt to bring about a good end, it is morally permissible that a foreseen yet unintended evil result. The unintended evil is the second side effect ("double" effect) of the intended good end of the action. In the case of self-defense, the intended good end of the stranglehold on my attacker is my self-preservation, even though I realize that my act will likely kill my attacker. Since the death of my attacker is a foreseen, though *unintended*, consequence of my act of self-defense, it is morally permissible.

The principle of double effect is often invoked in discussions of the morality of war and in cases of medical ethics. The selection that follows from Joseph M. Boyle Jr. provides a thorough account of this controversial ethical principle. Boyle treats the principle of double effect as a principle of justification of actions that would otherwise be morally impermissible if done intentionally. Boyle pays special attention to two features of the principle of double effect: (1) there is a clear distinction between what in an act is intended and what is consented to or accepted as a side effect and (2) the good that results is proportionally greater than the evil side effect.

The selection from Philippa Foot contains an examination of the doctrine of double effect in the context of its application to the issue of abortion. Like Boyle, Foot thinks that the principle of double effect focuses on the distinction between a direct intention and a side effect, which she calls an oblique or indirect intention. Double effect permits bringing about by indirect intention (as a side effect) what one is not morally justified in bringing about by direct intention. As such, the principle has been used to justify the abortion of a fetus in some cases but not in others. A pregnant woman's cancerous uterus can be removed to save her life even though it has the foreseen but indirectly intended result of the death of the fetus. On the other hand, the principle has also been used to establish that it is illicit to abort a fetus in a case where a prolonged and difficult labor will result in the death of the mother, if that would involve crushing the skull of the fetus, because then the death of the fetus would be directly intended. Foot finds that the first sort of case is permissible but the second sort of case is not. She sees this as evidence that the doctrine of double effect should be rejected. Foot thinks the distinction between negative duties and positive duties is much more helpful in clarifying and justifying our moral intuitions about such cases. For Foot, the negative duty to refrain from killing is stronger than the positive duty to save a life. She makes her point using such fanciful examples as the fat man stuck in the cave preventing others from getting out and the runaway train that could either go down one track and kill one person or the other and kill five persons. (This example has come to be known as "the Trolley Problem." See the selection from Judith Jarvis Thomson on page 240.)

Foot's application of the principle of double effect to the issue of abortion yields different results depending on the particulars of the case. But she denies an absolute prohibition against abortion (the Catholic Church's position) to save the life of the mother in the case where the fetus would die anyway. As with the other ethical theories encountered in this book, it is not always easy to arrive at straightforward answers to the difficult moral decisions that face us. But these theories help us see more clearly what is at issue and what kinds of considerations we must make in order to make thoughtful moral judgments.

*Summa Theologica**

St. Thomas Aquinas

Part II of the First Part, Question XCIV: Of the Natural Law (In Six Articles)

We must now consider the natural law; concerning which there are six points of inquiry: (1) What is the natural law? (2) What are the precepts of the natural law? (3) Whether all acts of virtue are prescribed by the natural law? (4) Whether the natural law is the same in all? (5) Whether it is changeable? (6) Whether it can be abolished from the heart of man?

Whether the natural law is a habit?

Objection 1: It would seem that the natural law is a habit. Because, as the Philosopher says (Ethic. ii, 5), "there are three things in the soul: power, habit, and passion." But the natural law is not one of the soul's powers: nor is it one of the passions; as we may see by going through them one by one. Therefore the natural law is a habit.

Objection 2: Further, Basil [*Damascene, De Fide Orth. iv, 22] says that the conscience or "synderesis is the law of our mind"; which can only apply to the natural law. But the "synderesis" is a habit, as was shown in the FP, Q[79], A[12]. Therefore the natural law is a habit.

Objection 3: Further, the natural law abides in man always, as will be shown further on (A[6]). But man's reason, which the law regards, does not always think about the natural law. Therefore the natural law is not an act, but a habit.

On the contrary, Augustine says (De Bono Conjug. xxi) that "a habit is that whereby something is done when necessary." But such is not the natural law: since it is in infants and in the damned who cannot act by it. Therefore the natural law is not a habit.

I answer that, A thing may be called a habit in two ways. First, properly and essentially: and thus the natural law is not a habit. For it has been stated above (Q[90], A[1], ad 2) that the natural law is something appointed by reason, just as a proposition is a work of reason. Now that which a man does is not the same as that whereby he does it: for he makes a becoming speech by the habit of grammar. Since then a habit is that by which we act, a law cannot be a habit properly and essentially.

Secondly, the term habit may be applied to that which we hold by a habit: thus faith may mean that which we hold by faith. And accordingly, since the

*From Thomas Aquinas, *Summa Theologica*. Translated by Fathers of the English Dominican Province (London: Burns Oates & Washbourne, 1915).

precepts of the natural law are sometimes considered by reason actually, while sometimes they are in the reason only habitually, in this way the natural law may be called a habit. Thus, in speculative matters, the indemonstrable principles are not the habit itself whereby we hold those principles, but are the principles the habit of which we possess.

Reply to Objection 1: The Philosopher proposes there to discover the genus of virtue; and since it is evident that virtue is a principle of action, he mentions only those things which are principles of human acts, viz. powers, habits and passions. But there are other things in the soul besides these three: there are acts; thus "to will" is in the one that wills; again, things known are in the knower; moreover its own natural properties are in the soul, such as immortality and the like.

Reply to Objection 2: "Synderesis" is said to be the law of our mind, because it is a habit containing the precepts of the natural law, which are the first principles of human actions.

Reply to Objection 3: This argument proves that the natural law is held habitually; and this is granted.

To the argument advanced in the contrary sense we reply that sometimes a man is unable to make use of that which is in him habitually, on account of some impediment: thus, on account of sleep, a man is unable to use the habit of science. In like manner, through the deficiency of his age, a child cannot use the habit of understanding of principles, or the natural law, which is in him habitually.

Whether the natural law contains several precepts, or only one?

Objection 1: It would seem that the natural law contains, not several precepts, but one only. For law is a kind of precept, as stated above (Q[92], A[2]). If therefore there were many precepts of the natural law, it would follow that there are also many natural laws.

Objection 2: Further, the natural law is consequent to human nature. But human nature, as a whole, is one; though, as to its parts, it is manifold. Therefore, either there is but one precept of the law of nature, on account of the unity of nature as a whole; or there are many, by reason of the number of parts of human nature. The result would be that even things relating to the inclination of the concupiscible faculty belong to the natural law.

Objection 3: Further, law is something pertaining to reason, as stated above (Q[90], A[1]). Now reason is but one in man. Therefore there is only one precept of the natural law.

On the contrary, The precepts of the natural law in man stand in relation to practical matters, as the first principles to matters of demonstration. But there are several first indemonstrable principles. Therefore there are also several precepts of the natural law.

I answer that, As stated above (Q[91], A[3]), the precepts of the natural law are to the practical reason, what the first principles of demonstrations are to the speculative reason; because both are self-evident principles. Now a thing is said to be self-evident in two ways: first, in itself; secondly, in relation to us. Any proposition is said to be self-evident in itself, if its predicate is contained in the notion of the subject: although, to one who knows not the definition of the subject, it happens that such a proposition is not self-evident. For instance, this proposition, "Man is a rational being," is, in its very nature, self-evident, since who says "man," says "a rational being": and yet to one who knows not what a man is, this proposition is not self-evident. Hence it is that, as Boethius says (De Hebdom.), certain axioms or propositions are universally self-evident to all; and such are those propositions whose terms are known to all, as, "Every whole is greater than its part," and, "Things equal to one and the same are equal to one another." But some propositions are self-evident only to the wise, who understand the meaning of the terms of such propositions: thus to one who understands that an angel is not a body, it is self-evident that an angel is not circumscriptively in a place: but this is not evident to the unlearned, for they cannot grasp it.

Now a certain order is to be found in those things that are apprehended universally. For that which, before aught else, falls under apprehension, is "being," the notion of which is included in all things whatsoever a man apprehends. Wherefore the first indemonstrable principle is that "the same thing cannot be affirmed and denied at the same time," which is based on the notion of "being" and "not-being": and on this principle all others are based, as is stated in Metaph. iv, text. 9. Now as "being" is the first thing that falls under the apprehension simply, so "good" is the first thing that falls under the apprehension of the practical reason, which is directed to action: since every agent acts for an end under the aspect of good. Consequently the first principle of practical reason is one founded on the notion of good, viz. that "good is that which all things seek after." Hence this is the first precept of law, that "good is to be done and pursued, and evil is to be avoided." All other precepts of the natural law are based upon this: so that whatever the practical reason naturally apprehends as man's good (or evil) belongs to the precepts of the natural law as something to be done or avoided.

Since, however, good has the nature of an end, and evil, the nature of a contrary, hence it is that all those things to which man has a natural inclination, are naturally apprehended by reason as being good, and consequently as objects of pursuit, and their contraries as evil, and objects of avoidance. Wherefore according to the order of natural inclinations, is the order of the precepts of the natural law. Because in man there is first of all an inclination to good in accordance with the nature which he has in common with all substances: inasmuch as every substance seeks the preservation of its own being, according to its nature: and by reason of this inclination, whatever is a means of preserving human life, and of warding off its obstacles, belongs to the natural law. Secondly, there is in man an inclination to things that pertain to him more specially, according to that nature which he has in common with other animals: and in virtue of this inclination, those things are said to belong to the natural law, "which nature has taught to all animals" [*Pandect. Just. I, tit. i], such as sexual intercourse, education of offspring and so forth. Thirdly, there is in man an inclination to good, according to the nature of his reason, which nature is proper to him: thus man has a natural inclination to know the truth about God, and to live in society: and in this respect, whatever pertains to this inclination belongs to the natural law; for instance, to shun ignorance, to avoid offending those among whom one has to live, and other such things regarding the above inclination.

Reply to Objection 1: All these precepts of the law of nature have the character of one natural law, inasmuch as they flow from one first precept.

Reply to Objection 2: All the inclinations of any parts whatsoever of human nature, e.g. of the concupiscible and irascible parts, in so far as they are ruled by reason, belong to the natural law, and are reduced to one first precept, as stated above: so that the precepts of the natural law are many in themselves, but are based on one common foundation.

Reply to Objection 3: Although reason is one in itself, yet it directs all things regarding man; so that whatever can be ruled by reason, is contained under the law of reason.

Whether all acts of virtue are prescribed by the natural law?
Objection 1: It would seem that not all acts of virtue are prescribed by the natural law. Because, as stated above (Q[90], A[2]) it is essential to a law that it be ordained to the common good. But some acts of virtue are ordained to the private good of the individual, as is evident especially in regards to acts of temperance. Therefore not all acts of virtue are the subject of natural law.

Objection 2: Further, every sin is opposed to some virtuous act. If therefore all acts of virtue are prescribed by the natural law, it seems to follow that all sins are against nature: whereas this applies to certain special sins.

Objection 3: Further, those things which are according to nature are common to all. But acts of virtue are not common to all: since a thing is virtuous in one, and vicious in another. Therefore not all acts of virtue are prescribed by the natural law.

On the contrary, Damascene says (De Fide Orth. iii, 4) that "virtues are natural." Therefore virtuous acts also are a subject of the natural law.

I answer that, We may speak of virtuous acts in two ways: first, under the aspect of virtuous; secondly, as such and such acts considered in their proper species. If then we speak of acts of virtue, considered as virtuous, thus all virtuous acts belong to the natural law. For it has been stated (A[2]) that to the natural law belongs everything to which a man is inclined according to his nature. Now each thing is inclined naturally to an operation that is suitable to it according to its form: thus fire is inclined to give heat. Wherefore, since the rational soul is the proper form of man, there is in every man a natural inclination to act according to reason: and this is to act according to virtue. Consequently, considered thus, all acts of virtue are prescribed by the natural law: since each one's reason naturally dictates to him to act virtuously. But if we speak of virtuous acts, considered in themselves, i.e. in their proper species, thus not all virtuous acts are prescribed by the natural law: for many things are done virtuously, to which nature does not incline at first; but which, through the inquiry of reason, have been found by men to be conducive to well-living.

Reply to Objection 1: Temperance is about the natural concupiscences of food, drink and sexual matters, which are indeed ordained to the natural common good, just as other matters of law are ordained to the moral common good.

Reply to Objection 2: By human nature we may mean either that which is proper to man—and in this sense all sins, as being against reason, are also against nature, as Damascene states (De Fide Orth. ii, 30): or we may mean that nature which is common to man and other animals; and in this sense, certain special sins are said to be against nature; thus contrary to sexual intercourse, which is natural to all animals, is unisexual lust, which has received the special name of the unnatural crime.

Reply to Objection 3: This argument considers acts in themselves. For it is owing to the various conditions of men, that certain acts are virtuous for some, as being proportionate and becoming to them, while they are vicious for others, as being out of proportion to them.

Whether the natural law is the same in all men?
Objection 1: It would seem that the natural law is not the same in all. For it is stated in the Decretals (Dist. i) that "the natural law is that which is contained in the Law and the Gospel." But this is not common to all men; because, as it is written (Rom. 10:16), "all do not obey the gospel." Therefore the natural law is not the same in all men.

Objection 2: Further, "Things which are according to the law are said to be just," as stated in Ethic. v̇. But it is stated in the same book that nothing is so universally just as not to be subject to change in regard to some men. Therefore even the natural law is not the same in all men.

Objection 3: Further, as stated above (AA[2],3), to the natural law belongs everything to which a man is inclined according to his nature. Now different men are naturally inclined to different things; some to the desire of pleasures, others to the desire of honors, and other men to other things. Therefore there is not one natural law for all.

On the contrary, Isidore says (Etym. v, 4): "The natural law is common to all nations."

I answer that, As stated above (AA[2],3), to the natural law belongs those things to which a man is inclined naturally: and among these it is proper to man to be inclined to act according to reason. Now the process of reason is from the common to the proper, as stated in Phys. i. The speculative reason, however, is differently situated in this matter, from the practical reason. For, since the speculative reason is busied chiefly with the necessary things, which cannot be otherwise than they are, its proper conclusions, like the universal principles, contain the truth without fail. The practical reason, on the other hand, is busied with contingent matters, about which human actions are concerned: and consequently, although there is necessity in the general principles, the more we descend to matters of detail, the more frequently we encounter defects. Accordingly then in speculative matters truth is the same in all men, both as to principles and as to conclusions: although the truth is not known to all as regards the conclusions, but only as regards the principles which are called common notions. But in matters of action, truth or practical rectitude is not the same for all, as to matters of detail, but only as to the general principles: and where there is the same rectitude in matters of detail, it is not equally known to all.

It is therefore evident that, as regards the general principles whether of speculative or of practical reason, truth or rectitude is the same for all, and is equally known by all. As to the proper conclusions of the speculative reason, the truth is the same for all, but is not equally known to all: thus it is true for all that the three angles of a triangle are together equal to two right angles, although it is not known to all. But as to the proper conclusions of the practical reason, neither is the truth or rectitude the same for all, nor, where it is the same, is it equally known by all. Thus it is right and true for all to act according to reason: and from this principle it follows as a proper conclusion, that goods entrusted to another should be restored to their owner. Now this is true for the majority of cases: but it may happen in a particular case that it would be injurious, and therefore unreasonable, to restore goods held in trust; for instance, if they are claimed for the purpose of fighting against one's country. And this principle will be found to fail the more, according as we descend further into detail, e.g. if one were to say that goods held in trust should be restored with such and such a guarantee, or in such and such a way; because the greater the number of conditions added, the greater the number of ways in which the principle may fail, so that it be not right to restore or not to restore.

Consequently we must say that the natural law, as to general principles, is the same for all, both as to rectitude and as to knowledge. But as to certain matters of detail, which are conclusions, as it were, of those general principles, it is the same for all in the majority of cases, both as to rectitude and as to knowledge; and yet in some few cases it may fail, both as to rectitude, by reason of certain obstacles (just as natures subject to generation and corruption fail in some few cases on account of some obstacle), and as to knowledge, since in some the reason is perverted by passion, or evil habit, or an evil disposition of nature; thus formerly, theft, although it is expressly contrary to the natural law, was not considered wrong among the Germans, as Julius Caesar relates (De Bello Gall. vi).

Reply to Objection 1: The meaning of the sentence quoted is not that whatever is contained in the Law and the Gospel belongs to the natural law, since they contain many things that are above nature; but that whatever belongs to the natural law is fully contained in them. Wherefore Gratian, after saying that "the natural law is what is contained in the Law and the Gospel," adds at once, by way of example, "by which everyone is commanded to do to others as he would be done by."

Reply to Objection 2: The saying of the Philosopher is to be understood of things that are naturally just, not as general principles, but as conclusions drawn from them, having rectitude in the majority of cases, but failing in a few.

Reply to Objection 3: As, in man, reason rules and commands the other powers, so all the natural inclinations belonging to the other powers must needs be directed according to reason. Wherefore it is universally right for all men, that all their inclinations should be directed according to reason.

Whether the natural law can be changed?

Objection 1: It would seem that the natural law can be changed. Because on Ecclus. 17:9, "He gave them instructions, and the law of life," the gloss says: "He wished the law of the letter to be written, in order to correct the law of nature." But that which is corrected is changed. Therefore the natural law can be changed.

Objection 2: Further, the slaying of the innocent, adultery, and theft are against the natural law. But we find these things changed by God: as when God commanded Abraham to slay his innocent son (Gn. 22:2); and when he ordered the Jews to borrow and purloin the vessels of the Egyptians (Ex. 12:35); and when He commanded Osee to take to himself "a wife of fornications" (Osee 1:2). Therefore the natural law can be changed.

Objection 3: Further, Isidore says (Etym. 5:4) that "the possession of all things in common, and universal freedom, are matters of natural law." But these things are seen to be changed by human laws. Therefore it seems that the natural law is subject to change.

On the contrary, It is said in the Decretals (Dist. v): "The natural law dates from the creation of the rational creature. It does not vary according to time, but remains unchangeable."

I answer that, A change in the natural law may be understood in two ways. First, by way of addition. In this sense nothing hinders the natural law from being changed: since many things for the benefit of human life have been added over and above the natural law, both by the Divine law and by human laws.

Secondly, a change in the natural law may be understood by way of subtraction, so that what previously was according to the natural law, ceases to be so. In this sense, the natural law is altogether unchangeable in its first principles: but in its secondary principles, which, as we have said (A[4]), are certain detailed proximate conclusions drawn from the first principles, the natural law is not changed so that what it prescribes be not right in most cases. But it may be changed in some particular cases of rare occurrence, through some special causes hindering the observance of such precepts, as stated above (A[4]).

Reply to Objection 1: The written law is said to be given for the correction of the natural law, either because it supplies what was wanting to the natural law; or because the natural law was perverted in the hearts of some men, as to certain matters, so that they esteemed those things good which are naturally evil; which perversion stood in need of correction.

Reply to Objection 2: All men alike, both guilty and innocent, die the death of nature: which death of nature is inflicted by the power of God on account of original sin, according to 1 Kings 2:6: "The Lord killeth and maketh alive." Consequently, by the command of God, death can be inflicted on any man, guilty or innocent, without any injustice whatever. In like manner adultery is intercourse with another's wife; who is allotted to him by the law emanating from God. Consequently intercourse with any woman, by the command of God, is neither adultery nor fornication. The same applies to theft, which is the taking of another's property. For whatever is taken by the command of God, to Whom all things belong, is not taken against the will of its owner, whereas it is in this that theft consists. Nor is it only in human things, that whatever is commanded by God is right; but also in natural things, whatever is done by God, is, in some way, natural, as stated in the FP, Q[105], A[6], ad 1.

Reply to Objection 3: A thing is said to belong to the natural law in two ways. First, because nature inclines thereto: e.g. that one should not do harm to another. Secondly, because nature did not bring in the contrary: thus we might say that for man to be naked is of the natural law, because nature did not give him clothes, but art invented them. In this sense, "the possession of all things in common and universal freedom" are said to be of the natural law, because, to wit, the distinction of possessions and slavery were not brought in by nature, but devised by human reason for the benefit of human life. Accordingly the law of nature was not changed in this respect, except by addition.

Whether the law of nature can be abolished from the heart of man?

Objection 1: It would seem that the natural law can be abolished from the heart of man. Because on Rom. 2:14, "When the Gentiles who have not the law," etc. a gloss says that "the law of righteousness, which sin had blotted out, is graven on the heart of man when he is restored by grace." But the law of righteousness is the law of nature. Therefore the law of nature can be blotted out.

Objection 2: Further, the law of grace is more efficacious than the law of nature. But the law of grace is blotted out by sin. Much more therefore can the law of nature be blotted out.

Objection 3: Further, that which is established by law is made just. But many things are enacted by men, which are contrary to the law of nature. Therefore the law of nature can be abolished from the heart of man.

On the contrary, Augustine says (Confess. ii): "Thy law is written in the hearts of men, which iniquity itself effaces not." But the law which is written in men's hearts is the natural law. Therefore the natural law cannot be blotted out.

I answer that, As stated above (AA[4],5), there belong to the natural law, first, certain most general precepts, that are known to all; and secondly, certain secondary and more detailed precepts, which are, as it were, conclusions following closely from first principles. As to those general principles, the natural law, in the abstract, can nowise be blotted out from men's hearts. But it is blotted out in the case of a particular action, in so far as reason is hindered from applying the general principle to a particular point of practice, on account of concupiscence or some other passion, as stated above (Q[77], A[2]). But as to the other, i.e. the secondary precepts, the natural law can be blotted out from the human heart, either by evil persuasions, just as in speculative matters errors occur in respect of necessary conclusions; or by vicious customs and corrupt habits, as among some men, theft, and even unnatural vices, as the Apostle states (Rom. i), were not esteemed sinful.

Reply to Objection 1: Sin blots out the law of nature in particular cases, not universally, except perchance in regard to the secondary precepts of the natural law, in the way stated above.

Reply to Objection 2: Although grace is more efficacious than nature, yet nature is more essential to man, and therefore more enduring.

Reply to Objection 3: This argument is true of the secondary precepts of the natural law, against which some legislators have framed certain enactments which are unjust.

The Scholastic Theory of Moral Law in the Modern World*

Alan Donagan

Although no more than one religion can be true, it is now generally accepted that there may be honest mistakes about whether a given religion is the true one. Yet neither scholastic philosophers nor most plain men have yet been brought to agree that there may be honest fundamental mistakes about morality. Differences about morality are socially divisive and dangerous, because many plain men consider it to be the duty of the state to enforce morality by legislation, if it can do so without infringing its citizens' moral rights. I remember that the church in which I was brought up as a child in Australia provoked great hostility by supporting legislation to close all liquor bars, in order to make it difficult to commit what it held to be the grave sin of drinking alcohol. Since there were, then as now, more drinkers than would-be divorcers, that hostility was much

*Alan Donagan, "The Scholastic Theory of Moral Law in the Modern World" in *Proceedings of the American Catholic Philosophical Association* 40 (1966): 30–40. Used by permission of publisher.

greater than what has been aroused toward the Catholic Church in New York by the opposition of some Catholics to changes in the divorce laws. Since such examples are familiar to all of us, I need not argue that the philosophical question: "How can what belongs to common morality be distinguished from what belongs to the way of life of a particular religion?' is a timely one.

That question is also appropriate for discussion in a meeting the theme of which is scholasticism in the modern world. For the distinction drawn by St. Thomas between those precepts of the divine law (the revealed positive law of God) which are also precepts of the natural law (the law of reason "where by each one knows, and is conscious of, what is good and what is evil'[1]) and those which are not, not only is the foundation of scholastic theory on the subject, but also, I shall argue, may prove to be common ground between scholastic and non-scholastic philosophers.

§1. The Natural Law and Contemporary Analytic Philosophy

The non-scholastic philosophers I shall have in mind throughout this paper are those working in the tradition variously labelled 'analytic', or 'linguistic', or even 'empiricist'. I shall not define it, beyond saying that it is the tradition now dominant in non-Catholic professional philosophy in North America, the British Commonwealth, and northwestern Europe except for France and Germany. The reason why I have this sort of non-scholastic philosophy in mind, and not existential philosophy, which is dominant in France, Germany, and southwestern Europe, and strongly represented in other countries, is that existential philosophy concerns itself with the nature of authentic moral choice, rather than with the question of the rightness or wrongness of what is chosen. To it, the theory of the natural law is at best an irrelevancy and at worst bad faith. In analytic philosophy, on the other hand, no question is more anxiously debated than how the rightness or wrongness of an act can be established.

My first thesis, then, is that the scholastic theory of natural law may have (and in some quarters is beginning to have) an important influence in contemporary analytic ethical theory.

There are two reasons for dismissing this thesis as a fantastic absurdity. I shall therefore begin by attempting to dispose of them. The first is derived from a cardinal doctrine of analytic ethical theory, the second from an equally cardinal doctrine of scholasticism.

The vast majority of analytic philosophers would accept the doctrine of the autonomy of ethics as fundamental. Following Professor A. N. Prior, that doctrine may be formulated as follows: 'the claim to deduce ethical propositions from ones which are admitted to be non-ethical'[2] is fallacious. It is true that this doctrine has recently been questioned[3]; but I do not think that it has been shaken. If the scholastic theory of natural law should imply that ethics is not autonomous, it could have no serious influence on analytic ethical theory.

Yet St. Thomas himself appears to imply it, by deriving the first precept of the natural law, *bonum est faciendum et prosequendum, et malum vitandum*, from a non-ethical statement about the nature of good, *bonum est quod omnia appetunt*.[4]

Fortunately for my thesis, what St. Thomas said need not be interpreted as denying the autonomy of ethics. He certainly did not mean that we all ought to do and promote whatever we in fact seek; for he admitted that many of us seek what is evil. His statement that *good is that which all things seek* must be understood as meaning good is that which all things *by nature* seek; and, since man is a rational animal, applied to man it means that human good is that which all men seek *by virtue of their nature as rational animals*. Evildoers choose to do and to promote what is opposed to what they seek by virtue of their rational nature; they affront their own reason. Now I do not think that any analytic philosopher would deny that the words '*quod omnia appetunt*', so understood, express an ethical concept. The objection to my thesis from the analytic side therefore fails: the scholastic theory of natural law is not incompatible with, the autonomy of ethics, or at least is not obviously so.

The objection from the scholastic side goes deeper. The scholastic philosophers were theologians too, and every great scholastic system is Christian: that is, its purely philosophical part is presented as not merely incomplete and incompletable by philosophy alone, but as finding its completion in revealed theology. It is, therefore, legitimate to doubt whether the theory of natural law is intelligible to philosophy alone. Partly for this reason, Miss G. E. M. Anscombe has expressed the view that the scholastic theory of moral law is theological in essence, and that the part of scholastic moral theory that is philosophical is the Aristotelian theory of the cardinal virtues.[5] And it cannot be denied that St. Thomas defines natural law theologically: having explained that a rational creature is subject to divine providence in a higher way than a brute, in that it partakes of the divine reason, he lays it down that 'such participation at the eternal law in a rational creature is called natural law'.[6] The eternal law, being 'the very Idea of the government of things existing in God the ruler of the universe',[7] is studied by theology rather than by philosophy.

Yet from the fact that St. Thomas, in a theological work, defines natural law theologically, it follows neither that it cannot be defined philosophically, nor that a philosophical definition would be incomplete, as according to St. Thomas, any account of the natural end of man the neglected divine revelation would be incomplete. Although this is not stated in terms by St. Thomas, it is implied by his assertion that 'all men know . . . the common principles of the natural law'.[8] It is also presupposed in his derivations of the various precepts of the natural law, in none of which does he make any appeal to revealed theology. Nor does he explicitly draw upon natural theology, except in deriving precepts having to do with divine worship.

At this point, St. Thomas can be instructively contrasted with Kant. In an excellent Thomist textbook of Ethics I found the following:

> The distinctive thing about the rationally free agent is not, as Kant thought, that he is a law unto himself. Man is not the ultimate source or principle of the moral law. Rather, human reason is subject to the laws of reality, which come from the divine reason.

These remarks exhibit a misunderstanding precisely opposite to the misunderstanding that St. Thomas has no strictly philosophical conception of natural law. Kant defines the moral law philosophically. After defining an objective principle as 'valid for every rational being',[9] he goes on to say that if there is to be a moral law for men, i.e. a categorical imperative, 'it must be such that from the idea of something which is necessarily an end for everyone because it is an *end in itself*, it forms an *objective* principle of the will'.[10] I take it to be patent that Kant is not saying that a rational being is a law unto himself: such a being must indeed determine for himself what the law is, but he must do so according to *objective* principles. And those objective principles are valid for every rational being because they have an objective foundation in 'something which is necessarily an end for everyone because it is an end in itself'.

Writing as a philosopher, Kant defined the moral law without reference to God. Yet he held, as a theologian, that the moral law is derived from the divine reason. In the *Groundwork* he was at pains to point out that the divine will cannot be said to be subject to the objective principles of the moral law as to imperatives, because it is 'already of itself necessarily in harmony with [them]'.[11]

Kant and St. Thomas differ about what the fundamental principles of the moral law are, although not as much as many believe; but I have yet to be convinced that they differ in any significant way about the relation between what St. Thomas would call the 'natural law' and what he would call the 'eternal law'. From the point of view of moral philosophy, the natural law is a set of precepts the binding force of which can be ascertained by human reason; from the point of view of theology, it is that part of what God eternally and rationally wills that can be grasped by human reason as binding upon human beings (Kant would say, upon all rational beings). Just as in theology Kant can agree with St. Thomas that the moral law is a participation of the eternal law in a rational creature, so in moral philosophy St. Thomas can agree with Kant that in determining what the precepts of the natural law are, theological considerations are out of place.

On this point, what holds of Kant also holds of contemporary analytic philosophy.

§2. Scholastic Derivations of the Precepts of the Natural Law

My first thesis was that non-scholastic philosophers have much to learn from what scholastic philosophers have accomplished in the theory of natural law. If you ask me why they have not already learned more from it than they have, I will at once acknowledge that prejudice and ignorance are part of the explanation. But I do not believe that they are the whole of it. My second thesis is that, despite what has been accomplished, no adequate scholastic *philosophy* of natural law has yet been elaborated. That, too, must enter into any satisfactory explanation of why non-scholastic philosophers have neglected the scholastic achievement. It should also be mentioned in any explanation of why explicit natural law arguments are rarely found convincing by non-Catholics.

I shall try to establish my second thesis by examining St. Thomas's derivation of a precept of the natural law that is not very controversial: the precept that lying (*mendacium*) is evil and to be avoided. St. Thomas defines a lie as speech contrary to the speaker's mind,[12] and he holds lying so defined to be prohibited by the natural law for the following reason:

> . . . since words are naturally signs of thoughts, it is unnatural and wrong for anyone by speech to signify something he does not have in his mind (*Summa Theologiae*, II-II, 110, 3).

This argument plainly presupposes an unstated principle, namely, that if an activity has a natural end, then voluntarily to engage in that activity in such a way as to prevent the attainment of its end is unnatural and wrong. Both this presupposition, and St. Thomas's explicit premiss, that the natural end of speech is to signify what the speaker thinks, may be questioned.

What is meant by the 'natural end' of a process? The concept is Aristotelian, and it is too fundamental to be usefully defined. Natural processes go on of themselves, as natural substances come into being from other natural substances, without the help of any artificer. Living things, the best specimens of natural substances, are generated, grow, and decay in characteristic ways. It is usual to speak and think of them as tending to grow to maturity, and as resisting decay. In general, Aristotle would say of such things that their natural end is to achieve the state of maturity characteristic of their species. Similarly, of the parts of a thing which has a natural end, Aristotle would say that their natural end is to contribute to the efficient functioning of the whole: thus, the natural end of an eye is to enable its possessor to see. The same also holds of processes that go on in natural things: if they contribute to the efficient functioning of the thing in which they occur, as most of them do, then their natural end is to make that contribution. It makes no difference whether those processes are voluntary or involuntary. Thus the natural end of the involuntary process of breathing is (on Aristotelian principles, although Aristotle did not know it) to convey oxygen to the blood, and to expel carbon dioxide from the lungs; and the natural end of the voluntary process of eating is to convey food to the digestive organs.

It cannot be too strongly insisted upon that Aristotle neither personifies nature nor endows it with *conscious* purpose. Conscious purposes are found in nature, in intelligent beings; but most natural ends or purposes are not conscious. Art imitates nature, but nature is not an artificer.[13] '[T]hose things are natural which, by a continuous movement originated from an internal principle, arrive at some completion: the same completion is not reached from every principle; nor any chance completion; but always the tendency in each is towards the same end, if there is no impediment.'[14]

That natural things and natural processes, in Aristotle's sense, can be found I will not question. However, the use in ethics to which Aristotle and St. Thomas put the concept of a natural end presupposes more than that. Above all, it presupposes that it is wrong to frustrate nature. This presupposition must, of course, be qualified. When a cow eats grass, it prevents that grass from completing its natural growth; and when a man slaughters and eats or sells the flesh of a cow, he prevents that cow from completing its natural growth. Hence, St. Thomas lays it down that the sub-rational part of nature is for the use of the rational part.[15] This, if I understand it correctly, is an ethical and not a physical principle. From the point of view of physics, the flesh of cattle is no more naturally food for man than is the blood of man food for mosquitoes. But, although he allows man's right to use non-rational natural things for his own purposes, St. Thomas denies that he may voluntarily engage in any natural activity, if he does so in such a way as to prevent that activity from arriving at its natural end. If you voluntarily engage in eating, you must not increase your capacity to eat by resorting, as some Romans did, to the vomitorium; for that would prevent the activity of eating from arriving at its natural end of digestion.

A second presupposition, which has important moral consequences, is that natural things and processes have only one end, or have one that is pre-eminent Aristotle seems to have thought this obvious. 'Nature', he declared in the *Politics*, 'is not niggardly, like the smith who fashions the Delphian knife for many uses; she makes each thing for a single use'.[16] Eating both nourishes and gives pleasure; but Aristotle would consider it obvious that the pre-eminent natural end of eating is nourishment, not pleasure.

We are now in a position to decide upon the validity or otherwise of St. Thomas's demonstration that lying is wrong. In my opinion, neither its premiss, that the natural end of speech is to express what is in the speaker's mind, nor its presupposition, that it is wrong voluntarily to engage in a natural activity and to prevent that activity from arriving at its natural end, is evident upon reflection. Let me take each in turn.

It is simply not true that speech is related to its alleged end of expressing what is in the speaker's mind in the way in which eating is related to nourishment, or the eye to seeing. Eating that is not completed by digestion has been interfered with in some way; and an eye that cannot see in suitable conditions is either defective or damaged. But, from the point of view of natural science, a lying speech act is not, *per se*, either defective or interfered with. If speech acts have a natural end, in Aristotle's sense, it is to express whatever thought the speaker chooses to express.

It is, indeed, possible to argue that veracity must be the norm for speech acts. As Professor J. M. Cameron has observed in his Terry Lectures, 'Lying could not be the norm for purely logical reasons, since the point of telling a lie is that it should be taken to be the truth and this could not happen unless truth-telling were the norm'.[17] But it does not follow that the natural end of a speech act is to conform to that norm; for a thing tends towards its natural end provided there is no impediment, and a lying speech act does not in the least tend towards truth. Nor, conceding that veracity is the norm for speech, does it appear to follow that every speech act ought to conform to that norm. If people wish to communicate by speech, then logically they must normally tell the truth—but not always. And this logical necessity does not appear to me to be a moral obligation. It holds for liars and truth-tellers alike.

St. Thomas's presupposition that it is wrong voluntarily to engage in any natural activity in such a way as to prevent it from arriving at its natural end, is equally vulnerable. If St. Thomas considers that rational beings have the right to interfere with and even destroy sub-rational natural things for their own purposes, why should he think it wrong *per se* for them to interfere, for their own purposes, with the natural activities in which they engage? I am aware that, in asking this, I shall appear to some to be frivolous and wanting in natural piety. But any philosopher who wishes to argue as St. Thomas does should take account of the fact that I am by no means alone. In the sagacious and lucid introduction to his translation of the third and fourth books of Aristotle's *Politics*, Richard Robinson has stated my objection more sharply than I:

> Once we have explicitly asked ourselves why we should do anything just because nature does it, or why we should aid nature in her purposes, we see that there is no reason why we should. Let nature look to her own purposes, if she has any. *We* will look to *ours*.[18]

§3. Strengths and Weaknesses in the Scholastic Theory of Natural Law

It does not follow from the objections I have urged against St. Thomas's discussion of lying that his theory of the natural law is false. St. Thomas's definition of the natural law, and his statement of its first precept, neither of which I desire to question, are logically separable from his derivation of further precepts from the first precept. Indeed, I make bold to say that one reason why the scholastic theory has had less influence outside Catholic circles than it merits, is that it is assumed to be a seamless unity, and that little is known of it but arguments like

St. Thomas's against lying. It is widely believed that if you reject such arguments (that against artificial contraception is, of course, the best known) then you must deny that there is a natural law: that is, you must abandon the conception of the moral law as a matter of human reason.

If my objections to St. Thomas's discussion of lying are just, then St. Thomas was mistaken in looking to Aristotelian natural philosophy for a way of specifying the goods we are bidden by natural law to seek, and the evils we are bidden to avoid. However, nothing in his definition of natural law obliged him to make that mistake. Nor did anything in Aristotle's *Ethics* do so.

I am inclined to conjecture that he was led to make it by his belief in creation: accepting Aristotle's views about natural teleology, and believing that the natural world was created by God, it may have seemed reasonable to treat the ends of natural things and processes not only as divinely appointed, but as divinely sanctioned. Yet, as we have seen, St. Thomas himself invoked the doctrine of the subordination of the weaker and less perfect in nature to the stronger and more perfect,[19] to justify man's interference with *some* natural processes.

I do not wish to give the impression that the only part of the scholastic theory of the natural law that I think strong is its foundation, or that I wish to level the edifice erected by the scholastics on that foundation. Although I have no time to examine it now, the treatment of specific moral questions in scholastic philosophy is every whit as important as its treatment of first principles. Indeed, if one looks for exact and detailed inquiry into the more notorious moral difficulties, there is almost nowhere to go in contemporary philosophy except to the writings of the neo-scholastics.

§4. Prospect

My final thesis is that if the weakness in the scholastic theory of natural law I believe myself to have detected is to be corrected, then the philosophical problem of how to derive specific moral precepts from the first precept of the natural law must be approached afresh, and without theological preconceptions. In the few minutes remaining to me, I venture to suggest a possible way of doing so.

St. Thomas's recognition of subordination in nature, and his doctrine that 'man is the end of the whole order of generation',[20] suggests that he might have accepted Kant's principle that 'man, and in general every rational being, exists as an end in himself, not merely as a means for arbitrary use by this or that will'.[21]" The principle is, in my opinion, self-evident. It must not be interpreted as implying that man is not ordered towards anything higher, as St. Thomas held that he is ordered to God, but rather as implying that if he is so ordered, it must be in a way consistent with his nature as an end. This is, of course, amply acknowledged in Christian theology.

Kant's principle, which I take to be implicit in the work of St. Thomas, furnishes a way of specifying good and evil. Let me sketch how it might be applied to the case of lying. According to it, any act by the nature of which a rational being is used *merely* as a means is evil; and hence, by the first precept of the natural law, is to be avoided. But, in ordinary conditions of free communication, to tell another something that you do not believe is to use him merely as a means. By arrogating to yourself the right to misinform him merely because for some reason you so choose, you treat him merely as a means to your ends. Hence in ordinary conditions of free communication, lying to others is unconditionally prohibited.

In conditions of violence, as for example in the classic case of a would-be murderer who demands with threats to be told in which direction somebody he is pursuing has made off, the situation is otherwise. By employing or threatening violence, the questioner has already treated the person questioned merely as a means. He has no right to be told anything, and the person questioned is entitled to protect himself, and the pursued quarry, by a lie. (It is a question whether the word 'lie' should be used in such a case. Perhaps the qualification 'in conditions of free communication' should be added to St. Thomas's definition.)

In the cases I have considered, our principle yields results that conform to common-sense, and to the moral tradition generally, although in the latter case, under the influence of St. Thomas's argument, scholastic philosophers are apt either to be absurdly rigorous, or to explain away the justified lie by postulating improbable speech conventions (e.g. the so-called 'broad mental reservation'). But there are innumerable difficult cases.

For example, what is it permissible to do when you are obliged to keep a secret, and find yourself in a situation, probably by your own fault, in which you will reveal the secret whether you answer a question truthfully or refuse to answer it? Any principle by which such cases are other than difficult might be dismissed on that ground alone. I submit that Kant's principle both exhibits their difficulty, and yet contains resources for dealing with them. It is instructive, armed with that principle, to work through the moral cases in a good manual of casuistry.

Lest I should appear to be recommending the absorption of scholastic moral philosophy into Kantianism, may I repeat that I am pleading for a fresh and purely philosophical approach to the problem of deriving the specific moral precepts of the natural law, and that one of my reasons for suggesting that Kant's principle might be invoked in such derivations was that I took it to be implicit in St. Thomas's thought. I should be interested in exploring other suggestions. And, far from desiring that scholastic moral philosophy be absorbed in Kantianism, I hope that the influence of scholasticism may help us to free what is true in Kant's moral philosophy, which is a great deal, from the eccentric moral opinions Kant fallaciously drew from his principles.

My ultimate hope is even more ambitious. That the scholastic theory of natural law has an important contribution to make to any rational theory of morality is beyond question. But a thoroughly reconsidered and purely philosophical theory of natural law could do even more. It could provide the foundation of that rational moral consensus which is the necessary cement of a pluralist society.

Notes

1. Gloss on *Romans* ii, 14, quoted by St. Thomas, *Summa Theologiae*, I-II, 91, 2.
2. A. N. Prior, *Logic and the Basis of Ethics* (Oxford: Oxford Univ. Press, 1949), p. 95.
3. E.g. by John Searle, "How to Derive 'Ought' from 'Is'," *Philosophical Review*, LXXIII (1964), 43–58; Max Black, 'The Gap Between 'Is' and 'Should'," Ibid., 165–81.
4. *Summa Theologiae*, I-II, 94, 2.
5. Modern Moral Philosophy,' *Philosophy*, XXXIII (1958), 1–19. In Miss Anscombe's position, I can find no place for natural law; she makes all law positive i.e. either divine or human.
6. *Summa Theologiae*, I-II, 91, 2.
7. '[I]psa ratio gubernation is rerum in Deo sicut in principe universita existens' (*Summa Theologiae*, I-II, 91, 1).
8. *Summa Theologiae*, I-II, 93, 2.
9. *The Moral Law, or Kant's Groundwork of the Metaphysic of Morals*, tr. H. J. Paton (London 1948), p. 88 (2nd German edn., p. 51n.).
10. Ibid., p. 96 (2nd German edn., p. 66).
11. Ibid., p. 81 (2nd German edn., p. 39)
12. This is far more satisfactory than St. Augustine's 'a false statement uttered with intent to deceive', for reasons explained by St. Thomas (*Summa Theologiae*, II-II, 110, 1 *ad* 1, 3). Yet variants of St. Augustine's definition still turn up in contemporary analytic philosophy. E.g. C. D. Broad, *Five Types of Ethical Theory* (London: 1930), p. 209.
13. Aristotle, *Physics*, II, 199 b 25–31.
14. Aristotle, *Physics* (tr. R. P. Hardie and R. K. Gaye) n, 199 b 15–19.
15. St Thomas Aquinas, *Summa contra Gentiles*, III, 22, [8].
16. Aristotle, *Politics* (tr. Benjamin Jowett) I, 1252 b 1–5.
17. J. M. Cameron, *Images of Authority* (New Haven: 1966), p. 27. Professor Cameron does not use this premiss in the way I object to. He argues only that mendacity could not count as a moral *virtue*.
18. *Aristotle's* Politics *Books III and IV*, tr. with Introduction and Comments by Richard Robinson (Oxford: 1962). p. xxiii.
19. ". . . quaedam etiam perfectiora et virtuosiora ex quibusdam imperfectioribus et infirmioribus [nutrimentum habent]" (*Summa contra Gentiles*, III, 22, [8]).
20. *Summa contra Gentiles*, III, 22, [7].
21. *The Moral Law, or Kant's Groundwork of the Metaphysic of Morals*, tr. H. J. Paton (London: 1948), p. 95 (2nd German edn., p. 64).

Toward Understanding the Principle of Double Effect*

Joseph M. Boyle Jr.

The Principle of Double Effect (hereafter PDE) has long been a mainstay of Catholic moral thinking.[1] In recent years, however, the use and discussion of this doctrine have not been limited to Catholics or to theologians.[2] The PDE, or propositions closely related to it, have come up for considerable discussion by English-speaking philosophers.[3]

In spite of this discussion, however, the PDE remains something of a mystery. As I hope to show, its purpose, its essential claims, and its presuppositions are not adequately understood. This lack of understanding is due both to the difficulties and ambiguities in traditional formulations of the PDE and to the fact that its central conceptions are either foreign or contrary to much of contemporary ethics and action theory.[4]

The purpose of this paper, therefore, is to state plainly the propositions involved in the PDE and at least some of the propositions concerning intention, action, and moral responsibility which must be true if some version of the PDE is to be defensible and morally relevant. I will not seek to defend or criticize these propositions here. My aim is to state them clearly and thus to make possible a more intelligent and more decisive discussion of the PDE.

The classic modern formulation of the PDE is presented in J. P. Gury's widely used and often revised manual, *Compendium theologiae moralis*: "It is licit to posit a cause which is either good or indifferent from which there follows a twofold effect, one good, the other evil, if a proportionately grave reason is present, and if the end of the agent is honorable—that is, if he does not intend the evil effect."[5] In a clarification of this statement Gury makes it clear that the PDE contains four conditions, all of which together are required for the type of act in question to be licit: (1) the agent's end must be morally acceptable (*honestus*), (2) the cause must be good or at least indifferent, (3) the good effect must be immediate, and (4) there must be a grave reason for positing the cause.[6]

The determination of what constitutes a grave reason is a matter of normative ethics which I will not consider here; moreover it is sufficiently clear that a grave reason is required to bring about an evil state of affairs—one which it would presumably not be licit to bring about except under these conditions.[7] The sense of 'immediate' in the third condition seems to be that the evil effect may not be a means to the good effect. This is suggested by Gury's remark that, if the good came about through the evil effect (*mediante pravo effectu*), good would be sought through evil, and this can never be moral.[8] Thus this condition allows that the evil effect should follow from the good effect, or that the evil

---

*Joseph M. Boyle Jr., "Toward Understanding the Principle of Double Effect" in *Ethics* 90 (July 1980): 527–38.

effect and the good effect should follow independently from the cause, but not that the good effect should follow from the evil effect.

The second condition—that it must be morally permissible to posit the cause—suggests that the cause which brings about both effects can be morally evaluated independently of either of its effects. Thus we may take the first condition to refer to a human undertaking, the executing of a choice, which can be the subject of moral evaluation independent of the good and evil effects which are brought about. The application of these four conditions to many cases has been widely controverted. But several clear examples show how it is intended to work. The killing of noncombatants in a justified military action is one example used by Gury: the action may be justified—even if it is foreseen that some noncombatants will certainly be killed—if killing them is not a means of achieving one's military objective, since in this case undertaking the action may be presumed to be in itself good, the bringing about of the deaths is not intended, and there is a grave reason for the action. Gury says that the death of the innocents follows *per accidens*, and is not intended but only permitted.

The justification of killing in self-defense is another frequently used but more controversial application of the PDE. According to Saint Thomas, one intends only one's self-defense, the aggressor's death being outside the agent's intention—an effect of one's defensive act and not a means to one's defense.[9]

Discussion of the application of the PDE to cases like this is beyond the scope of this paper. Such a discussion presupposes that the PDE is intelligible. A first step in understanding the PDE is the determination of what it is meant to do. Is it meant to show that certain acts which, except under these conditions, would be morally impermissible, are, if its conditions are met, morally justified? Or is the PDE meant to be a principle of excuse—that is, a principle which lessens the imputability of a bad act?[10]

The Catholic moralists who developed this doctrine are none too clear on this point. Gury, for example, in stating the PDE, formulates it as a set of conditions for the licitness or permissibility of a certain action. But Gury in other places and other authors in this tradition write in such a way as to suggest that the PDE is a principle of excuse. They say, in effect, that the unintended consequences of one's acts are not imputable to the agent, or they suggest that the imputability is diminished or somehow indirect.[11] This interpretation is reinforced by the fact that most of these authors deal with the PDE in their treatments of the various kinds of voluntary acts and because of the importance of intention in the PDE.

I believe, however, that the PDE should be understood as a principle of *justification*, and that the tradition, even if it is unclear on this point, is most coherently understood in this way.[12] There are two reasons for thinking this. First, the unintended evil effect, the bringing about of which is rendered licit by the PDE, is clearly imputable to the agent: he knowingly and willingly brings it about. The scholastics often say that it is permitted or consented to; one could more clearly say in modern English that it is *accepted*. But permitting, consenting to, and so on, are volitional acts, or at least volitional dispositions, even if they are not volitional in the paradigmatic sense of intentional actions.[13] There might be a difference in the mode of responsibility one has for what one intends to bring about from that which one has for what one does not intend but willingly accepts. In both cases there might be degrees of imputability, but there is no necessary difference in degree between the two types of willing. What one intends and what one permits are both voluntarily brought about, and thus *both* are imputable. If what one permits were not voluntarily brought about, and thus ascribable to the agent, the fourth condition of the PDE would have no use. This condition states a requirement for the permissibility of permitting certain effects which one may not intend to bring about.

My second reason is a historical consideration. Aquinas's view of human action and intention forms the background for the distinctions upon which the PDE is based. The moralists who articulate and use the PDE often refer explicitly to his analysis of killing in self-defense, and some of the ancestors of the PDE are the sixteenth- and seventeenth-century commentaries on Aquinas's theory of action.[14] This is not to say, of course, that modern proponents of the PDE either consistently or clearheadedly develop his action theory.

According to Aquinas, an act is, morally speaking, the kind of act it is in virtue of what is intended.[15] In other words, Aquinas believes that actions are at least in part defined by the intention with which the agent performs them; intention is an act of volition, and it is necessarily the case that one intend whatever functions as an end or goal in one's actions;[16] one must intend not only the more distant and ulterior goals but also the immediate aim one has in undertaking an action. Thus one must intend what Aquinas calls the *formal object* of one's act.[17] In more contemporary language, an action is undertaking to bring about a certain state of affairs. This state of affairs is intrinsic or essential to the act and is necessarily intended.[18]

If this understanding of action is applied to the conditions of the PDE, it becomes clear that the first condition is invoked to determine the moral kind of the act which is at issue. In the first condition it is required that the agent's end be morally acceptable. The end referred to here might be either the immediate object of the act—the state of affairs the bringing about of which defines the act—or it might be a more remote end. In either case, it is among the things one must intend in acting.[19] Moreover, as Gury explicitly states, this condition is meant to exclude the agent's intending the evil effect. If the good effect is intended and the evil effect is not intended, the act will be, morally speaking, a good act. It will be specified by the good effect as a morally good act.

The act-defining character of intention is also relevant for understanding the third condition. If the evil effect is brought about as a means to the good effect, then the evil effect must be intended, and the bringing about of the instrumental state of affairs is morally impermissible. The bad effect is intended if it is chosen as a means because it becomes something which the agent is committed to realizing. The bringing about of this instrumental state of affairs is a morally impermissible act because this state of affairs—the bad effect—determines the moral character of the undertaking. Thus, the third condition is implied by the first condition and the definition of a "means." This condition does not assume, therefore, that the causal sequence of the effects is itself morally significant, as is often supposed.[20] In most cases in which one chooses a certain means, it is because of one's beliefs about the causal consequences of what one chooses as a means that one chooses it, but what is morally significant about such a choice is the intention and action involved in executing it.[21]

The first condition and the third, therefore, are attempts to determine exactly what one's act is in situations where the causal initiative involved in one's undertaking brings about both good and evil states of affairs. Together with the fourth condition, these conditions constitute a basis for the *justification* of actions having evil effects: such actions are not themselves evil in kind and there is grave reason for performing them.

The foregoing attempt to explain the PDE as a principle of justification by reference to Aquinas's theory of action can also accommodate the second condition of the PDE—namely, that initiating the causal sequence must be morally permissible independently of its good and bad effects. If this "positing of the cause" can be determined to be impermissible independently of the evil effect at issue, or of some other evil end, then one is not justified in initiating the causal sequence.

To the extent that this condition suggests that it is possible to determine the morality of initiating the causal sequence without reference to *any* effect, then it is inconsistent with Aquinas's view of action. But to that extent it is also confused: cause and effect are correlative, and "positing a cause" can be immoral only because it brings about *some* effect which it is impermissible to bring about.

This way of understanding the second condition has the effect of rendering it, strictly speaking, superfluous. If an act is not permissible, then the doing of that act would involve the intention of what is evil, and this is prohibited by the first condition.

By this point my attempt to treat the PDE as a principle of justification may appear to be radically revisionist. The second condition is rendered superfluous, and the third is implied by the first together with the definition of a means.

The redundancy of the traditional formulations of the PDE, however, is understandable if one considers the casuistical purpose for which the PDE was meant to be used and the distinctions the scholastics were accustomed to make. Following Aquinas, the scholastics held that the moral character of an act was determined by the end, the object of the act, and the circumstances in which the act was performed.[22] Thus, the first condition could be taken to exclude acts done for an immoral purpose; the second to exclude acts which are intrinsically immoral—that is, whose object it is impermissible to bring about; and the third to exclude immoral means to good ends—an exclusion which is not always covered by the second condition.

More concretely, the first condition would exclude, for example, giving someone money in order to get him drunk; the second, making oneself drunk in order to give someone a lesson in the value of sobriety; and the third, giving someone money in order to get him drunk in order to teach him a lesson. In the first case, the "positing of the cause" is permissible and there is no evil means to a good end, but the aim is evil. In the second case, the aim is good but the cause posited—getting oneself drunk—is evil. In the third case, the final end of the action is good, as is the positing of the cause, but an intermediate means is evil—namely, getting the person drunk.

The PDE, then, can be understood as a principle of justification. In its briefest form it can be stated in the following way: it is morally permissible to undertake an action when one knows that the undertaking will bring about at least one state of affairs such that, if this state of affairs were intrinsic to the action undertaken, the action would be rendered morally impermissible, if and only if (1) the state of affairs is not intrinsic to the action undertaken—that is, it is not intended—and (2) there is a serious reason for undertaking the action.

This formulation, however, gives rise to further questions. In particular, it gives rise to questions about the distinctions made by the PDE and about the moral significance of these distinctions.

First, the PDE as explained here forces one to draw in an odd way the distinction between the objective considerations about the rightness or wrongness of behavior and the subjective considerations relevant to evaluating the moral quality of the agent. One might expect that the question of rightness or wrongness is a question about behavior and its consequences, whereas questions about the goodness or badness of the agent would consider such things as the agent's motives and intentions as well as factors related to the imputability of his act. The PDE as explained here, however, requires one to regard the question of rightness or wrongness not simply as a question about behavior but also as a question about actions which contain intentions as an essential part.

Second, the PDE requires the moral significance of a distinction which, according to many, cannot even be drawn. Many modern philosophers regard the difference between what is intended and what is foreseen and "permitted," but not intended, as a merely verbal difference.[23] Moreover, it is certainly not clear what significance this difference has—supposing it can be drawn—for purposes of the moral evaluation of acts. Even if one admits that acts are defined by the agent's intentions and distinguished from foreseen consequences which are merely "permitted," one might wonder why it is that an agent's acts have a moral significance which is different from—and more decisive than—the moral significance of the foreseen consequences of what he does. It is important to recognize that the PDE does not require that the foreseen consequences of acts be in no way relevant to determining the rightness or wrongness of the agent's concrete behavior; they are relevant, but only in a subsidiary way. Thus, if the action is itself morally permissible, and if there is a serious reason for undertaking it, then it may be done morally no matter what the foreseen consequences may be.

The answers to these questions are based on a factor which has been completely overlooked in discussions of the PDE[24]—namely, the view of voluntariness and responsibility which the PDE presupposes. An account of this view goes something like the following:[25] There are many different types of voluntary acts; in fact, the notion of "voluntariness" is an equivocal one. There is, however, an order in these senses such that one could say with the medievals that voluntariness is an "analogous" notion, or, in more current language, that there are family resemblances between the various senses of "voluntary."

In this ordered set of meanings of "voluntary" one is paradigmatic—namely, that sense in which it is said of an act which is the execution of deliberate, free choice. In this case, the elements which all voluntary acts have in one way or another are preeminently present;[26] no human act is so clearly or properly self-initiated as is an action which executes a free choice. A free choice is a choice in which all the causal factors other than the agent's choosing are not sufficient to bring about the choice.[27] Moreover, in a deliberate choice one knows what one is doing; one considers and reflects upon the options and their various attractions.

By contrast, actions which are voluntary in any other sense of the word involve some diminishing of one or both of these components. Nondeliberate acts—for example, actions done out of passion or fear or under duress—will lack the cognitional component involved in deliberate choices. Similarly, habitual acts, automatic reactions, and the actions of children and of those who are not *compos mentis* are in various ways not self-initiated as free choices are; they are self-initiating but the self is not in control.

Human behavior which carries out deliberate free choices, therefore, is voluntary in the strongest sense of the term.[28] Thus it is not surprising that such behavior is often regarded as the primary subject of moral evaluation.

Such behavior can be understood in the following way: In deliberating one considers various incompatible practical proposals—one's bringing about state of affairs *P* or one's bringing about state of affairs *Q* (where *P* includes non-*Q* and *Q* non-*P*). Choice is one's selection of one's bringing about *P* rather than *Q* or *Q* rather than *P*. The behavior consequent upon a choice is the undertaking to bring about *P* or to bring about *Q*. In other words, the agent acts with the intention of bringing about *P* or with the intention of bringing about *Q*.

Thus, one who, after considering several practical proposals and freely selecting one of them, executes his choice by undertaking to bring about the state of affairs proposed is performing a paradigmatically voluntary act. This performance is, according to this view of voluntariness, a doing of the type that is either right or wrong.

But how is this performance to be understood? Should the performance be understood in a formal way—as simply bringing about the state of affairs which it was undertaken to bring about? Or should this performance be taken as a kind of individual, a concrete event with many causal connections which bring about many states of affairs? It seems to me that the controverted ontological question of whether actions are individuals of some sort or the bringing about of certain abstract states of affairs can be set aside for present purposes. If an action is a concretum, then it will be truly described by a number of propositions. The question relevant here, should such an ontological view be accepted, would be under which of the descriptions the act should be morally evaluated in the first instance.

The proponent of the PDE would hold that the performance should be understood formally, since the performance is—insofar as it is the type of voluntary act defined above—the execution of a choice, and the choice is the commitment to bring about a certain definite state of affairs.

In other words, while an agent's performance involves a causal initiative that can have many foreseeable consequences, it is not the performance as a willing causal initiative, together with some set of the effects of that initiative, which is primarily voluntary or the primary subject of moral evaluation.[29] A causal initiative—or at least the willful refraining from such an initiative—is part of the notion of a voluntary act in this paradigmatic sense. But it is part of the act only insofar as it executes the choice and not as a concrete event with an indefinite set of effects.

This is not to say, of course, that the bringing about of the foreseen effects of one's performances is not voluntary. It is, but not in the way in which the executions of choices—regarded just as such—are voluntary. The foreseen consequences of one's potential performances are no doubt a part of what is considered in the deliberation leading to choices. But they are included in this deliberative process in a unique way. Frequently, they do not appear to be of any practical consequence to the person deliberating, and sometimes they are seen to interfere with the achievement of either the state of affairs one is considering bringing about or some further goal with respect to which this state of affairs is taken to be instrumental. In other words, the foreseen consequences of one's bringing about an intended state of affairs are often considered in deliberating, but not as reasons for the action—rather, they are sometimes conditions in spite of which one acts. It is not for the sake of such conditions that one selects an option; it is not these effects to which one is committed in acting.

If this is correct, the agent in acting has a fundamentally different attitude toward what he intends and toward what he foresees and consents to or accepts but does not intend. The agent who acts with the intention of bringing about a certain state of affairs makes that state of affairs his goal; he sees it as worthwhile or as instrumentally valuable and commits himself to bringing it about. Clearly, what is thus regarded as valuable is not all that one foresees will come about by his initiative. For example, pain involved in undergoing surgery is not regarded as valuable by the patient. He would avoid it if he could.

The agent's attitude toward such consequences as this is entirely different from his attitude toward what he intends. These consequences need not be seen as good or as desirable; there is no commitment to bring them about; in many cases the agent would avoid them if he could. They are not a part of what one chooses to bring about.

This account of voluntary action provides the basis for answering the questions listed above. Given this account of voluntary action, the distinction between factors relevant to determining the rightness of actions and factors relevant to assessing the moral qualities of agents are properly drawn where the PDE requires. The primary object of the moral evaluation of the act is the bringing about of the state of affairs which the agent is committed to realizing. This action includes and is defined by the agent's intention. Moreover, this way of drawing the distinction between factors relevant to determining the imputability of the act and factors relevant to characterizing the act to be evaluated allows for the obvious excusing factors. It allows for questions about whether the agent knows the moral character of his undertaking and questions about whether the agent's choice is free. It does imply, however, that an action will be regarded as if it were a voluntary act even if in fact it is not imputable, because it is only as the execution of a choice that behavior can be characterized as morally significant. Thus, for example, if an omission or piece of habitual behavior is regarded as morally wrong, it is because that omission or piece of behavior would be wrong if it embodied the execution of a deliberate choice.

The second question is also resolved by this account of voluntary action; the distinction between what is intended and what is consented to is intelligible in terms of this account. A morally significant act is the execution of a choice. What one chooses is not an indeterminate set of foreseeable results of one's performance but the bringing about of a definite state of affairs regarded as worthwhile or valuable. Thus there is a basis for the distinction between what is intended and what is not intended but consented to, or between actions defined by the state of affairs intended and the consequences of actions defined by what is not intended but consented to.

Moreover, this account of voluntary action shows why the distinction between what is intended and what is foreseen and accepted but not intended is taken to be morally relevant. Since it is one's choices and their execution which are primarily voluntary, it is these which are the primary object of moral evaluation. The states of affairs intended in such acts are what the agent, as it were, sets his or her heart on. It is the commitment to these states of affairs which is the basis upon which a person forms his character and makes himself a certain kind of person. Moreover, if moral demands are regarded as unconditional demands upon one's free choice,[30] then it is by choosing and committing oneself to some such states of affairs that one acts morally or immorally. In other words, if moral demands are demands upon one's free choice and if free choice is the adopting of a proposal that one bring about a certain state of affairs regarded as valuable or worthwhile, then what moral normativeness primarily bears upon—as far as behavior goes—is human action in the sense defined here.

This account of the view of voluntary action presupposed by the PDE also throws light on the connection between the PDE and the so-called absolutism of traditional Catholic ethics. By "absolutism" I mean the view that there are exceptionless moral proscriptions.

First of all, absolutism is not required by the PDE. The PDE does not explain how one is to come to the normative judgments presupposed by the first three conditions and enjoined by the fourth. The first three conditions, if met, are sufficient to characterize the act in question as a good type of act. But they do not explain how acts of that type are judged to be morally good. Likewise, these conditions require that the "evil effect" would be a bad kind of act if any of the first three is not met, and that there must be a grave reason for accepting such an act, but they do not specify what makes an immoral act immoral. This judgment might well be made on the basis of the view that such an act is proscribed by a general exceptionless proscription, but it need not be so based. Any normative theory which allows that there are kinds of acts which are good and bad could be consistent with the PDE and could make use of the PDE.

Furthermore, the PDE is not required by all forms of absolutism. An absolutist system such as Kant's, for example, does not make use of the PDE, and it is possible to use principles other than the PDE to resolve cases of moral perplexity.[31] Moreover, an absolutist might limit his exceptionless proscriptions so that cases dealt with by the PDE are either clearly prohibited or clearly allowed by the relevant rule.

But there is a vital connection between the PDE and the form of "absolutism" with which it is usually associated. This form of absolutism does not depend on a set of intuited or commanded absolutes, or a set of absolutes based on generalizations from particular cases, but on moral rules which direct one to respect basic human goods or values. Specifically moral precepts mandate that these basic goods be promoted whenever possible and that they not be attacked or acted against. This leads to moral norms—including absolute proscriptions—of a very general sort. For example, human life is taken to be a basic human good. The proscription of killing, therefore, will be quite general.[32] Moreover, these goods are the basis for deliberation and choice. They are pursued—in the morally relevant way—by voluntary acts and especially by acts executing free choices. The demand that we respect all the human goods—and especially that we not act against them—is a demand on our free choice.

This normative view does require the PDE, but *not* simply because it is absolutist. This connection is not a matter of straightforward implication. The normative theory in question does imply a part of the theory of human agency presupposed by the PDE. Thus they both imply the same thing. The necessity of the connection between this normative theory and the PDE is established by the facts that (1) the actual world is such that the realization of most human choices is by way of causal initiatives which bring about many states of affairs other than that state of affairs which the agent intends to realize through his performance, and (2) some of these states of affairs are contrary to one or more basic goods. These facts require that one committed to a normative theory demanding respect for a set of basic goods hold the PDE. Otherwise respecting the goods becomes an impossibility, since any performance can—and many performances do—bring about what is contrary to one or more basic goods.

To sum up: the PDE is a coherent doctrine of justification. But it continues to be misunderstood because the theory of agency which it presupposes is ignored. If this view of human agency is false, then the PDE must be abandoned; but if this theory of agency is true, and if the normative theory which makes use of the PDE can be defended, then the PDE is a long way toward vindication.

Notes

The work for this paper was begun while on a College Teachers in Residence Fellowship of the National Endowment for the Humanities. I have profited from discussing the issues taken up here with R. M. Chisholm and Alan Donagan. I thank Germain Grisez for help on several drafts of this paper.

1. See Joseph Mangan, S.J., "An Historical Analysis of the Principle of Double Effect," *Theological Studies* 10 (1949): 41–61; J. Ghoos, "L'Acte a double effet: Etude de theologie positive," *Ephemerides theologicae Louvaniensis* 27 (1951): 30–52; and F. J. Connell, in *The New Catholic Encyclopedia*, s.v. "Principle of Double Effect."

2. E.g., Paul Ramsey, the eminent Methodist theologian, makes extensive use of the PDE; see his *War and the Christian Conscience* (Durham, N.C.: Duke University Press, 1961). For a nontheologian, see G. E. M. Anscombe, "War and Murder," in *War and Morality*, ed. R. Wasserstrom (Belmont, Calif.: Wadsworth Publishing Co., 1970), pp. 50–51.

3. See, e.g., Philippa Foot, "Abortion and the Doctrine of Double Effect," in *Moral Problems*, ed. J. Rachels (New York: Harper & Row, 1971), pp. 28–41; Jonathan Bennett, "Whatever the Consequences," *Analysis* 26 (1966): 83–102 and the ensuing discussion; Alan Donagan, *The Theory of Morality* (Chicago: University of Chicago Press, 1977), pp. 122–27, 157–64.

4. See Germain Grisez, "Toward a Consistent Natural Law Ethics of Killing," *American Journal of Jurisprudence* 15 (1970): 73–79, for a critique of certain aspects of traditional formulations.

5. J. P. Gury, S.J. (revised by A. Ballerini, S.J.), *Compendium theologiae moralis*, 2d ed. (Rome and Turin, 1869), p.

6. The translation from the Latin is mine. Mangan, pp. 60–61, provides a translation from the fifth German edition of Gury's entire treatment of the PDE. 6. Gury, p. 8.

7. This condition can, but need not, be understood in a consequentialist way. It can be understood as requiring that relevant obligations other than those bearing on the directness or indirectness of the bringing about of the evil effect be considered.

8. Gury, p. 8.

9. S.T. II-II,64,7.

10. See J. L. Austin, "A Plea for Excuses," in *Philosophical Papers*, ed. J. O. Urmson and G.J. Warnock, 2d ed. (London: Oxford University Press, 1970), pp. 175–77, for an explanation of the difference between justification and excuse.

11. See, e.g., Arthurus Vermeersch, S.J., *Theologiae moralis: Principia, responsa, consilia* (Rome: Gregorian University Press, 1922), 1:118. Vermeersch, one of the most important Catholic moralists in the early decades of [the twentieth] century, states the PDE as follows: "Effectus malus qui actionem sequi permittitur, *non imputatur*, si diversa est efficientia immediate, et permissio ratione proportionate gravi excusatur" (emphasis mine).

12. See William Conway, "The Act of Two Effects," *Irish Theological Quarterly* 18 (1951): 127–29.

13. See R. G. Frey, "Some Aspects to the Doctrine of Double Effect," *Canadian Journal of Philosophy* 5 (1975): 265.

14. See John of St. Thomas, *Cursus theologicus, tome 6: De bonitate et malitia actuum humanorum*, disputatio 11 (Paris, 1885); and Salmanticenses, *Cursus theologicus*, tome 7, tractatus 13, disputatio 10, dubium 6 (Paris, 1877).

15. S.T. II-II,64,7: "Morales autem actus recipiunt speciem secundum id quod intenditur, . . ." See also S.T. I-II,72,1.

16. S.T. I-II,12,1; *De Veritate* 22,14. For a discussion of these and other relevant texts, see my "Aquinas on *Praeter Intentionem*," *Thomist* 42 (1978): 649–65.

17. S.T. I-II,20,4;I-II,72,3, ad 2;I-II,73,1.

18. See G. H. von Wright, *Norm and Action: A Logical Inquiry* (New York: Humanities Press, 1963), pp. 39–41; *The Varieties of Goodness* (New York: Humanities Press, 1963), pp. 39–41, 123–25.

19. Gury, p. 7.

20. E.g., by Frey, pp. 261, 280–81.

21. See Grisez, pp. 87–89, for a critique of traditional formulations of the PDE on this point.

22. S.T. I-II,18,2,3,4.

23. See Henry Sidgwick, *Methods of Ethics*, 7th ed. (New York: Dover Publications, 1966), p. 202; R. M. Chisholm, "The Structure of Intention, "*Journal of Philosophy* 67 (1970): 636; for a response and reference to other literature, see Joseph M. Boyle, Jr., and

Thomas D. Sullivan, "The Diffusiveness of Intention Principle: A Counter-Example," *Philosophical Studies* 31(1977): 357–60.

24. For example, by R. A. Duff, "Absolute Principles and Double Effect," *Analysis* 36 (1976): 68–80.

25. The following paragraphs are inspired by *S.T.* I-II,6–21.

26. The notion of "voluntary act" supposed is Aristotle's; see *Nichomachean Ethics* 3.1 109b30–111b3, and esp. 1111a22–23: "The voluntary would seem to be that of which the moving principle is in the agent himself, he being aware of the particular circumstances of the action."

27. Joseph M. Boyle, Jr., Germain Grisez, and Olaf Tollefsen, *Free Choice: A Self-referential Argument* (Notre Dame, Ind.: University of Notre Dame Press, 1976), pp. 11–23.

28. See *S.T.* I-I I,6,1: "Whence when a human being most fully [*maxime*] knows the end of his act and moves himself, then is his act most fully [*maxime*] voluntary."

29. See Donagan, pp. 37–52, 112–22, for a contrary view.

30. See Boyle et al., pp. 164–66, for an exposition of this view of moral norms.

31. See Donagan, pp. 149–56.

32. See ibid., pp. 60–65; and Grisez.

The Problem of Abortion and the Doctrine of the Double Effect*

Philippa Foot

One of the reasons why most of us feel puzzled about the problem of abortion is that we want, and do not want, to allow to the unborn child the rights that belong to adults and children. When we think of a baby about to be born it seems absurd to think that the next few minutes or even hours could make so radical a difference to its status; yet as we go back in the life of the foetus we are more and more reluctant to say that this is a human being and must be treated as such. No doubt this is the deepest source of our dilemma, but it is not the only one. For we are also confused about the general question of what we may and may not do where the interests of human beings conflict. We have strong intuitions about certain cases; saying, for instance, that it is all right to raise the level of education in our country, though statistics allow us to predict that a rise in the suicide rate will follow, while it is not all right to kill the feeble-minded to aid cancer research. It is not easy, however, to see the principles involved, and one way of throwing light on the abortion issue will be by setting up parallels involving adults or children once born. So we will be able to isolate the "equal rights" issue, and should be able to make some advance.

*From *The Oxford Review*, no. 5, 1967.

I shall not, of course, discuss all the principles that may be used in deciding what to do where the interests or rights of human beings conflict. What I want to do is to look at one particular theory, known as the "doctrine of the double effect" which is invoked by Catholics in support of their views on abortion but supposed by them to apply elsewhere. As used in the abortion argument this doctrine has often seemed to non-Catholics to be a piece of complete sophistry. In the last number of the *Oxford Review* it was given short shrift by Professor Hart.[1] And yet this principle has seemed to some non-Catholics as well as to Catholics to stand as the only defense against decisions on other issues that are quite unacceptable. It will help us in our difficulty about abortion if this conflict can be resolved.

The doctrine of the double effect is based on a distinction between what a man foresees as a result of his voluntary action and what, in the strict sense, he intends. He intends in the strictest sense both those things that he aims at as ends and those that he aims at as means to his ends. The latter may be regretted in themselves but nevertheless desired for the sake of the end, as we may intend to keep dangerous lunatics confined for the sake of our safety. By contrast a man is said not strictly, or directly, to intend the foreseen consequences of his voluntary actions where these are neither the end at which he is aiming nor the means to this end. Whether the word "intention" should be applied in both cases is not of course what matters: Bentham spoke of "oblique intention", contrasting it with the "direct intention" of ends and means, and we may as well follow his terminology. Everyone must recognize that some such distinction can be made, though it may be made in a number of different ways, and it is the distinction that is crucial to the doctrine of the double effect. The words "double effect" refer to the two effects that an action may produce: the one aimed at, and the one foreseen but in no way desired. By "the doctrine of the double effect" I mean the thesis that it is sometimes permissible to bring about by oblique intention what one may not directly intend. Thus the distinction is held to be relevant to moral decision in certain difficult cases. It is said for instance that the operation of hysterectomy involves the death of the foetus as the foreseen but not strictly or directly intended consequence of the surgeon's act, while other operations kill the child and count as the direct intention of taking an innocent life, a distinction that has evoked particularly bitter reactions on the part of non-Catholics. If you are permitted to bring about the death of the child, what does it matter how it is done? The doctrine of the double effect is also used to show why in another case, where a woman in labour will die unless a craniotomy operation is performed, the intervention is not to be condoned. There, it is said, we may not operate but must let the mother die. We foresee her death but do not directly intend it, whereas to crush the skull of the child would count as direct intention of its death.[2]

This last application of the doctrine has been queried by Professor Hart on the ground that the child's death is not strictly a means to saving the mother's life and should logically be treated as an unwanted but foreseen consequence by those who make use of the distinction between direct and oblique intention. To interpret the doctrine in this way is perfectly reasonable given the language that has been used; it would, however, make nonsense of it from the beginning. A certain event may be desired under one of its descriptions, unwanted under another, but we cannot treat these as two different events, one of which is aimed at and the other not. And even if it be argued that there are here two different events—the crushing of the child's skull and its death—the two are obviously much too close for an application of the doctrine of the double effect. To see how odd it would be to apply the principle like this we may consider the story, well known to philosophers, of the fat man stuck in the mouth of the cave. A party of potholers have imprudently allowed the fat man to lead them as they make their way out of the cave, and he gets stuck, trapping the others behind him. Obviously the right thing to do is to sit down and wait until the fat man grows thin; but philosophers have arranged that floodwaters should be rising within the cave. Luckily (luckily?) the trapped party have with them a stick of dynamite with which they can blast the fat man out of the mouth of the cave. Either they use the dynamite or they drown. In one version the fat man, whose head is *in* the cave, will drown with them; in the other he will be rescued in due course.[3] Problem: may they use the dynamite or not? Later we will find parallels to this example. Here it is introduced for light relief and because it will serve to show how ridiculous one version of the doctrine of the double effect would be. For suppose that the trapped explorers were to argue that the death of the fat man might be taken as a merely foreseen consequence of the act of blowing him up. ("We didn't want to kill him . . . only to blow him into small pieces" or even ". . . only to blast him out of the mouth of the cave.") I believe that those who use the doctrine of the double effect would rightly reject such a suggestion, though they will, of course, have considerable difficulty in explaining where the line is to be drawn. What is to be the criterion of "closeness" if we say that anything very close to what we are literally aiming at counts as if part of our aim?

Let us leave this difficulty aside and return to the arguments for and against the doctrine, supposing it to be formulated in the way considered most effective by its supporters, and ourselves bypassing the trouble by taking what must on any reasonable definition be clear cases of "direct" or "oblique" intention.

The first point that should be made clear, in fairness to the theory, is that no one is suggesting that it does not matter what you bring about as long as you merely foresee and do not strictly intend the evil that follows. We might think, for instance, of the (actual) case of wicked merchants selling, for cooking, oil they knew to be poisonous and thereby killing a number of innocent people, comparing and contrasting it with that of some unemployed gravediggers, desperate for custom, who got hold of this same oil and sold it (or perhaps *they* secretly gave it away) in order to create orders for graves. They strictly (directly) intend the deaths they cause, while the merchants could say that it was not part of their *plan* that anyone should die. In morality, as in law, the merchants, like the gravediggers, would be considered as murderers; nor are the supporters of the doctrine of the double-effect bound to say that there is the least difference between them in respect of moral turpitude. What they are committed to is the thesis that *sometimes* it makes a difference to the permissibility of an action involving harm to others that this harm, although foreseen, is not part of the agent's direct intention. An end such as earning one's living is clearly not such as to justify *either* the direct or oblique intention of the death of innocent people, but in certain cases one is justified in bringing about knowingly what one could not directly intend.

It is now time to say why this doctrine should be taken seriously in spite of the fact that it sounds rather odd, that there are difficulties about the distinction on which it depends, and that it seemed to yield one sophistical conclusion when applied to the problem of abortion. The reason for its appeal is that its opponents have often *seemed* to be committed to quite indefensible views. Thus the controversy has raged around examples such as the following. Suppose that a judge or magistrate is faced with rioters demanding that a culprit be found for a certain crime and threatening otherwise to take their own bloody revenge on a particular section of the community. The real culprit being unknown, the judge sees himself as able to prevent the bloodshed only by framing some innocent person and having him executed. Beside this example is placed another in which a pilot whose aeroplane is about to crash is deciding whether to steer from a more to a less inhabited area. To make the parallel as close as possible it may rather be supposed that he is the driver of a runaway tram which he can only steer from one narrow track on to another; five men are working on one track and one man on the other; anyone on the track he enters is bound to be killed. In the case of the riots the mob have five hostages, so that in both the exchange is supposed to be one man's life for the lives of five. The question is why we should say, without hesitation, that the driver should steer for the less occupied track, while most of us would be appalled at the idea that the innocent man could be framed. It may be suggested that the special feature of the latter case is that it involves the corruption of justice, and this is, of course, very important indeed. But if we remove that special feature, supposing that some private individual is to kill an innocent person and pass him off as the criminal we still find ourselves horrified by the idea. The doctrine of double effect offers us a way out of the difficulty, insisting that it is one thing to steer towards someone foreseeing that you will kill him and another to aim at his death as part of your plan. Moreover there is one very important element of good in what is here insisted. In real life it would hardly ever be certain that the man on the narrow track would be killed. Perhaps he might find a foothold on the side of the tunnel and cling on as the vehicle hurtled by. The driver of the tram does *not* then leap off and brain him with a crowbar. The judge, however, needs the death of the innocent man for his (good) purposes. If the victim proves hard to hang he must see to it that he dies another way. To choose to execute him is to choose that this evil *shall come about*, and this must therefore count as a *certainty* in weighing up the good and evil involved. The distinction between direct and oblique intention is crucial here, and is of great importance in an uncertain world. Nevertheless this is no way to defend the doctrine of the double effect. For the question is whether the difference between aiming at something and obliquely intending it is *in itself* relevant to moral decisions; not whether it is important when correlated with a difference of certainty in the balance of good and evil. Moreover we are particularly interested in the application of the doctrine of the double effect to the question of abortion, and no one can deny that in medicine there are sometimes certainties so complete that it would be a mere quibble to speak of the "probable outcome" of this course of action or that. It is not, therefore, with a merely philosophical interest that we should put aside the uncertainty and scrutinize the examples to test the doctrine of the double effect. Why can we not argue from the case of the steering driver to that of the judge?

Another pair of examples poses a similar problem. We are about to give to a patient who needs it to save his life a massive dose of a certain drug in short supply. There arrive, however, five other patients each of whom could be saved by one-fifth of that dose. We say with regret that we cannot spare our whole supply of the drug for a single patient, just as we should say that we could not spare the whole resources of a ward for one dangerously ill individual when ambulances arrive bringing in the victims of a multiple crash. We feel bound to let one man die rather than many if that is our only choice. Why then do we not feel justified in killing people in the interests of cancer research or to obtain, let us say, spare parts for grafting on to those who need them? We can suppose, similarly, that several dangerously ill people can be saved only if we kill a certain individual and make a serum from his dead body. (These examples are not over fanciful considering present controversies about prolonging the life of mortally ill patients whose eyes or kidneys are to be used for others.) Why cannot we argue from the case of the scarce drug to that of the body needed for medical purposes? Once again the doctrine of the double effect comes up with an explanation. In one kind of case but not the other we aim at the death of the innocent man.

A further argument suggests that if the doctrine of the double effect is rejected this has the consequence of putting us hopelessly in the power of bad men. Suppose for example that some tyrant should threaten to torture five men if we ourselves would not torture one. Would it be our duty to do so, supposing we believed him, because this would be no different from choosing to rescue five men from his torturers rather than one? If so anyone who wants us to do something we think wrong has only to threaten that otherwise he himself will do something we think worse. A mad murderer, known to keep his promises, could thus make it our duty to kill some innocent citizen to prevent him from killing two. From this conclusion we are again rescued by the doctrine of the double effect. If we refuse, we foresee that the greater number will be killed but we do not intend it: it is he who intends (that is strictly or directly intends) the death of innocent persons; we do not.

At one time I thought that these arguments in favour of the doctrine of the double effect were conclusive, but I now believe that the conflict should be solved in another way. The clue that we should follow is that the strength of the doctrine seems to lie in the distinction it makes between what we *do* (equated with direct intention) and what we allow (thought of as obliquely intended). Indeed it is interesting that the disputants tend to argue about whether we are to be held responsible for what we allow as we are for what we do.[4] Yet it is not obvious that this is what they should be discussing, since the distinction between what one does and what one allows to happen is not the same as that between direct and oblique intention. To see this one has only to consider that it is possible *deliberately* to allow something to happen, aiming at it either for its own sake or as part of one's plan for obtaining some thing else. So one person might want another person dead, and deliberately allow him to die. And again one may be said to do things that one does not aim at, as the steering driver would kill the man on the track. Moreover there is a large class of things said to be brought about rather than either done or allowed, and either kind of intention is possible. So it is possible to *bring about* a man's death by getting him to go to sea in a leaky boat, and the intention of his death may be either direct or oblique.

Whatever it may, or may not, have to do with the doctrine of the double effect, the idea of *allowing* is worth looking into in this context. I shall leave aside the special case of giving permission, which involves the idea of authority, and consider the two main divisions into which cases of allowing seem to fall. There is firstly the allowing which is forbearing to prevent. For this we need a sequence thought of as somehow already in train, and something that the agent could do to intervene. (The agent must be able to intervene, but does not do so.) So, for instance, he could warn someone, but *allows* him to walk into a trap. He could feed an animal but *allows* it to die for lack of food. He could stop a leaking tap but *allows* the water to go on flowing. This is the case of allowing with which we shall be concerned, but the other should be mentioned. It is the kind of allowing which is roughly equivalent to *enabling*; the root idea being the removal of some obstacle which is, as it were, holding back a train of events. So someone may remove a plug and *allow* water to flow; open a door and *allow* an animal to get out; or give someone money and *allow* him to get back on his feet.

The first kind of allowing requires an omission, but there is no other general correlation between omission and allowing, commission and bringing about or doing. An actor who fails to turn up for a performance will generally spoil it rather than allow it to be spoiled. I mention the distinction between omission and commission only to set it aside.

Thinking of the first kind of allowing (forbearing to prevent), we should ask whether there is any difference, from the moral point of view, between what one does or causes and what one merely allows. It seems clear that on occasions one is just as bad as the other, as is recognized in both morality and law. A man may murder his child or his aged relatives, by allowing them to die of starvation as well as by giving poison; he may also be convicted of murder on either account. In another case we would, however, make a distinction. Most of us allow people to die of starvation in India and Africa, and there is surely something wrong with us that we do; it would be nonsense, however, to pretend that it is only in law that we make a distinction between allowing people in the underdeveloped countries to die of starvation and sending them poisoned food. There is worked into our moral system a distinction between what we owe people in the form of aid and what we owe them in the way of non-interference. Salmond, in his *Jurisprudence*, expressed as follows the distinction between the two.

> A positive right corresponds to a positive duty, and is a right that he on whom the duty lies shall do some positive act on behalf of the person entitled. A negative right corresponds to a negative duty, and is a right that the person bound shall refrain from some act which would operate to the prejudice of the person entitled. The former is a right to be positively benefited; the latter is merely a right not to be harmed.[5]

As a general account of rights and duties this is defective, since not all are so closely connected with benefit and harm. Nevertheless for our purposes it will do well. Let us speak of negative duties when thinking of the obligation to refrain from such things as killing or robbing, and of the positive duty, e.g., to look after children or aged parents. It will be useful, however, to extend the notion of positive duty beyond the range of things that are strictly called duties, bringing acts of charity under this heading. These are owed only in a rather loose sense, and some acts of charity could hardly be said to be *owed* at all, so I am not following ordinary usage at this point.

Let us now see whether the distinction of negative and positive duties explains why we see differently the action of the steering driver and that of the judge, of the doctors who withhold the scarce drug and those who obtain a body for medical purposes, of those who choose to rescue the five men rather than one man from torture and those who are ready to torture the one man themselves in order to save five. In each case we have a conflict of duties, but what kind of duties are they? Are we, in each case, weighing positive duties against positive, negative against negative, or one against the other? Is the duty to refrain from injury, or rather to bring aid?

The steering driver faces a conflict of negative duties, since it is his duty to avoid injuring five men and also his duty to avoid injuring one. In the circumstances he is not able to avoid both, and it seems clear that he should do the least injury he can. The judge, however, is weighing the duty of not inflicting injury against the duty of bringing aid. He wants to rescue the innocent people threatened with death but can do so only by inflicting injury himself. Since one does not *in general* have the same duty to help people as to refrain from injuring them, it is not possible to argue to a conclusion about what he should do from the steering driver case. It is interesting that, even where the strictest duty of positive aid exists, this still does not weigh as if a negative duty were involved. It is not, for instance, permissible to commit a murder to bring one's starving children food. If the choice is between inflicting injury on one or many there seems only one rational course of action; if the choice is between aid to some at the cost of injury to others, and refusing to inflict the injury to bring the aid, the whole matter is open to dispute. So it is not inconsistent of us to think that the driver must steer for the road on which only one man stands while the judge (or his equivalent) may not kill the innocent person in order to stop the riots. Let us now consider the second pair of examples, which concern the scarce drug on the one hand and on the other the body needed to save lives. Once again we find a difference based on the distinction between the duty to avoid injury and the duty to provide aid. Where one man needs a massive dose of the drug and we withhold it from him in order to save five men, we are weighing aid against aid. But if we consider killing a man in order to use his body to save others, we are thinking of doing him injury to bring others aid. In an interesting variant of the model, we may suppose that instead of killing someone we deliberately let him die. (Perhaps he is a beggar to whom we are thinking of giving food, but then we say "No, they need bodies for medical research.") Here it does seem relevant that in allowing him to die we are aiming at his death, but presumably we are inclined to see this as a violation of negative rather than positive duty. If this is right, we see why we are unable in either case to argue to a conclusion from the case of the scarce drug.

In the examples involving the torturing of one man or five men, the principle seems to be the same as for the last pair. If we are bringing aid (rescuing people about to be tortured by the tyrant), we must obviously rescue the larger rather than the smaller group. It does not follow, however, that we would be justified in inflicting the injury, or getting a third person to do so, in order to save the five. We may therefore refuse to be forced into acting by the threats of bad men. To refrain from inflicting injury ourselves is a stricter duty than to prevent other people from inflicting injury, which is not to say that the other is not a very strict duty indeed.

So far the conclusions are the same as those at which we might arrive following the doctrine of the double effect, but in others they will be different, and the advantage seems to be all on the side of the alternative. Suppose, for instance, that there are five patients in a hospital whose lives could be saved by the manufacture of a certain gas, but that this inevitably releases lethal fumes into the room of another patient whom for some reason we are unable to move. His death, being of no use to us, is clearly a side effect, and not directly intended. Why then is the case different from that of the scarce drug, if the point about that is that we foresaw but did not strictly intend the death of the single patient? Yet it surely is different. The relatives of the gassed patient would presumably be successful if they sued the hospital and the whole story came out. We may find it particularly revolting that someone should be *used* as in the case where he is killed or allowed to die in the interest of medical research, and the fact of *using* may even determine what we would decide to do in some cases, but the principle seems unimportant compared with our reluctance to bring such injury for the sake of giving aid.

My conclusion is that the distinction between direct and oblique intention plays only a quite subsidiary role in determining what we say in these cases, while the distinction between avoiding injury and bringing aid is very important indeed. I have not, of course, argued that there are no other principles. For instance it clearly makes a difference whether our positive duty is a strict duty or rather an act of charity: feeding our own children or feeding those in faraway countries. It may also make a difference whether the person about to suffer is one thought of as uninvolved in the threatened disaster, and whether it is his presence that constitutes the threat to the others. In many cases we find it very hard to know what to say, and I have not been arguing for any general conclusion such as that we may never, whatever the balance of good and evil, I bring injury to one for the sake of aid to others, even when this injury amounts to death. I have only tried to show that even if we reject the doctrine of the double effect we are not forced to the conclusion that the size of the evil must always be our guide.

Let us now return to the problem of abortion, carrying out our plan of finding parallels involving adults or children rather than the unborn. We must say something about the different cases in which abortion might be considered on medical grounds.

First of all there is the situation in which nothing that can be done will save the life of child and mother, but where the life of the mother can be saved by killing the child. This is parallel to the case of the fat man in the mouth of the cave who is bound to be drowned with the others if nothing is done. Given the certainty of the outcome, as it was postulated, there is no serious conflict of interests here, since the fat man will perish in either case, and it is reasonable that the action that will save someone should be done. It is a great objection to those who argue that the direct intention of the death of an innocent person is never justifiable that the edict will apply even in this case. The Catholic doctrine on abortion must here conflict with that of most reasonable men. Moreover we would be justified in performing the operation whatever the method used, and it is neither a necessary nor a good justification of the special case of hysterectomy that the child's death is not directly intended, being rather a foreseen consequence of what is done. What difference could it make as to how the death is brought about?

Secondly we have the case in which it is possible to perform an operation which will save the mother and kill the child or kill the mother and save the child. This is parallel to the famous case of the shipwrecked mariners who believed that they must throw someone overboard if their boat was not to founder in a storm, and to the other famous case of the two sailors, Dudley and Stephens, who killed and ate the cabin boy when adrift on the sea without food. Here again there is no conflict of interests so far as the decision to act is concerned; only in deciding whom to save. Once again it would be reasonable to act, though one would respect someone who held back from the appalling action either because he preferred to perish rather than do such a thing or because he held on past the limits of reasonable hope. In real life the certainties postulated by philosophers hardly ever exist, and Dudley and Stephens were rescued not long after their ghastly meal. Nevertheless if the certainty were absolute, as it might be in the abortion case, it would seem better to save one than none. Probably we should decide in favour of the mother when weighing her life against that of the unborn child, but it is interesting that, a few years later, we might easily decide it the other way.

The worst dilemma comes in the third kind of example where to save the mother we must kill the child, say by crushing its skull, while if nothing is done the mother will perish but the child can be safely delivered after her death. Here the doctrine of the double effect has been invoked to show that we may not intervene, since the child's death would be directly intended while the mother's would not. On a strict parallel with cases not involving the unborn we might find the conclusion correct though the reason given was wrong. Suppose, for instance, that in later life the presence of a child was certain to bring death to the mother. We would surely not think ourselves justified in ridding her of it by a process that involved its death. For in general we do not think that we can kill one innocent person to rescue another, quite apart from the special care that we feel is due to children once they have prudently got themselves born. What we would be prepared to do when a great many people were involved is another matter, and this is probably the key to one quite common view of abortion on the part of those who take quite seriously the rights of the unborn child. They probably feel that if *enough* people are involved one must be sacrificed, and they think of the mother's life against the unborn child's life as if it were many against one. But of course many people do not view it like this at all, having no inclination to accord to the foetus or unborn child anything like ordinary human status in the matter of rights. I have not been arguing for or against these points of view but only trying to discern some of the currents that are pulling us back and forth. The levity of the examples is not meant to offend.

Notes

1. H. L. A. Hart, 'Intention and Punishment', *Oxford Review*, Number 4, Hilary 1967. I owe much to this article and to a conversation with Professor Hart, though I do not know whether he will approve of what follows.

2. For discussions of the Catholic doctrine on abortion see Glanville Williams, *The Sanctity of Life and the Criminal Law* (New York, 1957); also N. St. John Stevas, *The Right to Life* (London, 1963).

3. It was Professor Hart who drew my attention to this distinction.

4. See, e.g., J. Bennett, 'Whatever the Consequences', *Analysis*, January 1966, and G. E. M. Anscombe's reply in *Analysis*, June 1966. See also Miss Anscombe's 'Modern Moral Philosophy' in *Philosophy*, January 1958.

5. Salmond, *Jurisprudence*, 11th edition, p. 283.

Study Questions

1. According to Aquinas, "grace does not destroy but perfects nature" (*Summa Theologica*, quest. 1, art. 8, ad. 2). This means that, for Aquinas, in the area of ethics, divine revelation does not replace human reason but adds to it. In light of this claim, explain Aquinas's understanding of natural law. Is it possible for one to believe in both divine command theory and natural law theory? Explain your answer.

2. As a form of moral absolutism, natural law theory stands in stark contrast to moral relativism. In your view, does natural law theory present a refutation of moral relativism? How might a moral relativist respond to natural law theory?

3. Many philosophers since the Enlightenment have endorsed a fact/value distinction, maintaining, with David Hume, that one cannot derive an "ought" from an "is." Natural law theory denies the fact/value distinction. Which position on this matter do you find yourself in agreement with and why?

4. Donagan believes natural law theory does not need the notion of natural ends. Do you think Donagan's interpretation of natural law theory is right? Traditional natural law theorists have applied the principle that natural ends ought not to be frustrated to the area of sexual morality, with resulting prohibitions against birth control and homosexuality, among others. Does Donagan's interpretation of natural law lead to different results in the area of sexual morality?

5. Explain the principle of double effect in terms of the intended and unintended consequences of an act. Do you find this distinction to be helpful in sorting out cases where we have conflicting moral duties? Some critics of this principle worry that it might be used to render almost any action morally permissible. Do you agree with this charge? Explain your answer.

6. Comment on Foot's treatment of the issue of abortion in terms of the principle of double effect. Do you find the examples she uses, and her assessment of them, help to clarify the moral complexity of this issue? Could you think of other examples that might help one's moral evaluation of this issue? Explain.

For Further Reading

Finnis, John. *Natural Law and Natural Rights*. Oxford: Oxford University Press, 1980.

George, Robert P. *Natural Law Theory: Contemporary Essays*. New York: Oxford University Press, 1992.

Lisska, Anthony. *Aquinas's Theory of Natural Law: An Analytic Reconstruction*. Oxford: Oxford University Press, 1996.

Murphy, Mark C. *Natural Law and Practical Rationality*. Cambridge: Cambridge University Press, 2001.

Noonan, John T., Jr., "An Almost Absolute Value in History." In *The Morality of Abortion: Legal and Historical Perspectives*. Ed. John T. Noonan, Jr. Cambridge, MA: Harvard University Press, 1970: 51–59.

Thomson, Judith Jarvis. "A Defense of Abortion." *Philosophy and Public Affairs* 1 (1971): 47–66.

Woodward, P. A., ed. *The Doctrine of Double Effect: Philosophers Debate a Controversial Moral Principle*. Notre Dame, IN: University of Notre Dame Press, 2001.

Yolton, John. "Locke on the Law of Nature." *Philosophical Review* 67 (1958): 477–98.

CHAPTER FIVE

Utilitarianism

Utilitarianism has a long history, dating back to the views of Epicurus in ancient Greece. Epicurus's central thought was that pain was the only ultimate evil and pleasure the only ultimate good. Anything other than pleasure that is good derives its goodness from being a cause of pleasure or a means of avoiding pain. Epicurus's view is often called Hedonism (from the Greek term for pleasure), but notice that Epicurus is not a hedonist as the term is commonly used. In ordinary parlance, a hedonist is someone who cares only about his or her *own* pleasure. Philosophers call such people egoists. Epicurus, in contrast to egoism, is urging his readers to consider the pleasures and pains for *everyone affected by their actions*. This was the seed of the doctrine dubbed utilitarianism and elaborated by an eighteenth-century British philosopher named Jeremy Bentham. Bentham had advocated a "utilitarian calculus" for weighing various pains and pleasures, which he thought could be used to determine which among the available alternative actions in any given situation was morally required. The nineteenth-century philosopher John Stuart Mill, who was the son of a close friend of Bentham, is the most famous proponent of utilitarianism.

Bentham and Mill, who were also active in social reform, championed the idea that any ethical duties that we have must be based on the outcomes of our actions. The main principle of ethics, on this view, is "Always act so that you maximize the pleasure and minimize the pain of all those affected by your actions." This principle is called the principle of utility or the greatest happiness principle. Utilitarians do not dispute that we have, for example, duties to feed our children or duties to keep promises. However, they think that the foundation of these duties lie in the fact that parental obligations and promise-keeping decrease suffering and contribute to human well-being. Moreover, they hold that "hard cases" where duties conflict need to be settled by appeal to the principle of utility. If I have promised to meet someone for lunch at a particular time but pass someone in need of immediate assistance, keeping my promise out of a sense of duty would be an ethical mistake. This is because failure to help would have worse consequences than breaking a lunch date.

There are various complex questions that are disputed concerning the details of utilitarianism. Views on how best to settle these issues give rise to different types of utilitarianism. For example, Bentham is what is called an "act utilitarian" while Mill is usually interpreted as defending "rule utilitarianism." Act utilitarians (sometimes called "direct utilitarians") hold that we should weigh the pleasure and pain following every particular action in order to determine what the right action is. Act utilitarians value what they take to be this view's clarity and obviousness. What ethically serious person could possibly desire creating more pain than pleasure for those affected by his or her actions? What possible reason could there be for following a supposed ethical rule if in a particular case that would cause more suffering than happiness? Twentieth-century act utilitarian J. J. C. Smart accused those opposed to his view of "irrational rule worship."

Yet several problems have been noted with act utilitarianism. Each action has a vast number of potential consequences. How can I possibly foresee all the consequences of my actions and have time to weigh them before I act? Additionally, I would seem to have to know a lot about the psychological consequences of my actions on others and be able to weigh the intensity and duration of other people's pleasure and pain. How can I know this? As you will see in the selection from his book *Utilitarianism* that follows, John Stuart Mill's answer to this question was that *collective human experience* answers these questions and the wisdom of experience is the foundation of ethical rules like "Keep your promises" and "Don't lie." It is only in exceptional cases, when these rules seem to lead in divergent directions, that we need to go behind the rules and directly appeal to calculations of utility. As you will see in reading the selection from Mill, he was convinced that this shift from focusing on acts to focusing on rules solved many of the objections that had been raised to earlier forms of utilitarianism.

The selection in this chapter by twentieth-century philosopher Bernard Williams raises an objection to utilitarianism that Mill did not anticipate or address. Williams presents two specific situations that he thinks raise problems for utilitarianism, one of which concerns a person named Jim who appears to be able to save the lives of ten Indians by killing one of them. "Jim and the Indians" has become a minor classic, and is one of the most discussed attempted counterexample to utilitarian thought. Williams thinks that his two stories show that utilitarianism cannot make sense of personal integrity and the need for people to have defining commitments to plans and projects that should not need to be sacrificed to maximizing pleasure and minimizing pain.

Williams also makes the important observation that happiness (which he calls a second-order good) cannot be conceived of apart from the assumption that people already have plans and projects that are defined independently from the maximization of happiness (he calls these first-order goods). Williams's point seems to be this: Suppose that you want to make your parents, or your friends, or your significant other happy. You can only do this if they already care about something (in your parents' case perhaps that would be that their children succeed in college; in your friend's case it might be improving his or her athletic abilities). We derive pleasure from getting what we care about; people who cared about nothing could not aim at happiness because they don't value anything from which they could derive pleasure or joy. Some of our first-order plans and projects will be trivial but others will be fundamental to what makes life worthwhile for us. It is these fundamental projects that Williams thinks utilitarianism inappropriately asks us sometimes to sacrifice in order to maximize the happiness of others. To ask a person to jettison a fundamental commitment for the sake of morality would be not just unreasonable but incoherent, for it would be asking him to sacrifice his integrity.

Because of its focus on the outcomes of our actions, utilitarianism is sometimes called consequentialism. Brad Hooker's essay "Rule-Consequentialism" advocates a structural improvement that he argues will keep outcome-focused ethical theories from falling prey to the traditional objections to rule utilitarianism. One such objection is that utilitarianism would require us to make supererogatory sacrifices. "Supererogatory" means acting in a way that is above and beyond our duty. Requiring the supererogatory would not only make an ethical system unattractive, it would seem to make it incoherent by making a duty of what is *beyond* duty. Hooker's recommended rule consequentialism maintains that we need to evaluate moral rules as they function in *systems*, rather than in isolation from one another, and we need to pay attention to the consequences of *everyone* adopting the same rules. According to Hooker, rule consequentialism requires us to give only as much of our surplus income to the needy as would be required to meet their needs *if the rule about giving applied to and was followed by everyone*. Pay careful attention to Hooker's case for thinking that this solves the problem of consequentialism's purported excessive demands.

Hooker's rule consequentialism strives to bring outcome-based ethics into closer conformity with our ordinary, common sense intuitions about ethical requirements. In contrast, Peter Singer's "The Singer Solution to World Poverty" says that if common sense holds that we have no obligation to give money that we use to buy unnecessary luxuries to people who will starve if we do not give, then so much the worse for our commonsense intuitions. Singer gives several vivid examples to persuade us of morality's requirement to prevent great harm if we can do so without sacrificing something of comparable moral importance. He thinks that this claim is much more cogent than our sense that we have a right to luxuries if we can afford them. After all, this latter claim may be something we believe because of selfishness rather than because of intuitive ethical insight.

Utilitarianism has been widely influential, especially since the eighteenth century. It has been especially appealing to those who seek a religiously neutral way of forging social policy in situations where there are competing interests. Yet utilitarianism has also been hotly debated. Objectors have focused both on instances where it appears that utilitarianism would endorse violating important duties to others and to ourselves. Objectors have also accused utilitarianism of making us sacrifice too much to aiding others in pursuing their plans and projects, leaving us too little room to pursue other things we care about besides morality. Weigh the evidence presented in these selections carefully as you decide for yourself whether some form of utilitarianism is a better ethical theory than its alternatives.

*Utilitarianism**

John Stuart Mill

Chapter II. What Utilitarianism Is

The creed which accepts as the foundation of morals, Utility, or the Greatest Happiness Principle, holds that actions are right in proportion as they tend to promote happiness, wrong as they tend to produce the reverse of happiness. By happiness is intended pleasure, and the absence of pain; by unhappiness, pain, and the privation of pleasure. To give a clear view of the moral standard set up by the theory, much more requires to be said; in particular, what things it includes in the ideas of pain and pleasure; and to what extent this is left an open question. But these supplementary explanations do not affect the theory of life on which this theory of morality is grounded—namely, that pleasure, and freedom from pain, are the only things desirable as ends; and that all desirable things (which are as numerous in the utilitarian as in any other scheme) are desirable either for the pleasure inherent in themselves, or as means to the promotion of pleasure and the prevention of pain.

Now, such a theory of life excites in many minds, and among them in some of the most estimable in feeling and purpose, inveterate dislike. To suppose that

*From John Stuart Mill, *Utilitarianism* (1863).

life has (as they express it) no higher end than pleasure—no better and nobler object of desire and pursuit—they designate as utterly mean and groveling; as a doctrine worthy only of swine, to whom the followers of Epicurus were, at a very early period, contemptuously likened; and modern holders of the doctrine are occasionally made the subject of equally polite comparisons by its German, French, and English assailants.

When thus attacked, the Epicureans have always answered, that it is not they, but their accusers, who represent human nature in a degrading light; since the accusation supposes human beings to be capable of no pleasures except those of which swine are capable. If this supposition were true, the charge could not be gainsaid, but would then be no longer an imputation; for if the sources of pleasure were precisely the same to human beings and to swine, the rule of life which is good enough for the one would be good enough for the other. The comparison of the Epicurean life to that of beasts is felt as degrading, precisely because a beast's pleasures do not satisfy a human being's conceptions of happiness. Human beings have faculties more elevated than the animal appetites, and when once made conscious of them, do not regard anything as happiness which does not include their gratification. I do not, indeed, consider the Epicureans to have been by any means faultless in drawing out their scheme of consequences from the utilitarian principle. To do this in any sufficient manner, many Stoic, as well as Christian elements require to be included. But there is no known Epicurean theory of life which does not assign to the pleasures of the intellect, of the feelings and imagination, and of the moral sentiments, a much higher value as pleasures than to those of mere sensation. It must be admitted, however, that utilitarian writers in general have placed the superiority of mental over bodily pleasures chiefly in the greater permanency, safety, uncostliness, etc., of the former—that is, in their circumstantial advantages rather than in their intrinsic nature. And on all these points utilitarians have fully proved their case; but they might have taken the other, and, as it may be called, higher ground, with entire consistency. It is quite compatible with the principle of utility to recognise the fact, that some kinds of pleasure are more desirable and more valuable than others. It would be absurd that while, in estimating all other things, quality is considered as well as quantity, the estimation of pleasures should be supposed to depend on quantity alone.

If I am asked what I mean by difference of quality in pleasures, or what makes one pleasure more valuable than another, merely as a pleasure, except its being greater in amount, there is but one possible answer. Of two pleasures, if there be one to which all or almost all who have experience of both give a decided preference, irrespective of any feeling of moral obligation to prefer it, that is the more desirable pleasure. If one of the two is, by those who are competently acquainted with both, placed so far above the other that they prefer it, even though knowing it to be attended with a greater amount of discontent, and would not resign it for any quantity of the other pleasure which their nature is capable of, we are justified in ascribing to the preferred enjoyment a superiority in quality, so far outweighing quantity as to render it, in comparison, of small account.

Now it is an unquestionable fact that those who are equally acquainted with, and equally capable of appreciating and enjoying, both, do give a most marked preference to the manner of existence which employs their higher faculties. Few human creatures would consent to be changed into any of the lower animals, for a promise of the fullest allowance of a beast's pleasures; no intelligent human being would consent to be a fool, no instructed person would be an ignoramus, no person of feeling and conscience would be selfish and base, even though they should be persuaded that the fool, the dunce, or the rascal is better satisfied with his lot than they are with theirs. They would not resign what they possess more than he for the most complete satisfaction of all the desires which they have in common with him. If they ever fancy they would, it is only in cases of unhappiness so extreme, that to escape from it they would exchange their lot for almost any other, however undesirable in their own eyes. A being of higher faculties requires more to make him happy, is capable probably of more acute suffering, and certainly accessible to it at more points, than one of an inferior type; but in spite of these liabilities, he can never really wish to sink into what he feels to be a lower grade of existence. We may give what explanation we please of this unwillingness; we may attribute it to pride, a name which is given indiscriminately to some of the most and to some of the least estimable feelings of which mankind are capable: we may refer it to the love of liberty and personal independence, an appeal to which was with the Stoics one of the most effective means for the inculcation of it; to the love of power, or to the love of excitement, both of which do really enter into and contribute to it: but its most appropriate appellation is a sense of dignity, which all human beings possess in one form or other, and in some, though by no means in exact, proportion to their higher faculties, and which is so essential a part of the happiness of those in whom it is strong, that nothing which conflicts with it could be, otherwise than momentarily, an object of desire to them.

Whoever supposes that this preference takes place at a sacrifice of happiness—that the superior being, in anything like equal circumstances, is not happier than the inferior—confounds the two very different ideas, of happiness, and content. It is indisputable that the being whose capacities of enjoyment are low, has the greatest chance of having them fully satisfied; and a highly endowed being will always feel that any happiness which he can look for, as the world is constituted, is imperfect. But he can learn to bear its imperfections, if they are at all bearable; and they will not make him envy the being who is indeed unconscious of the imperfections, but only because he feels not at all the good which those imperfections qualify. It is better to be a human being dissatisfied than a pig satisfied; better to be Socrates dissatisfied than a fool satisfied. And if the fool, or the pig, are of a different opinion, it is because they only know their own side of the question. The other party to the comparison knows both sides.

It may be objected that many who are capable of the higher pleasures, occasionally, under the influence of temptation, postpone them to the lower. But this is quite compatible with a full appreciation of the intrinsic superiority of the higher. Men often, from infirmity of character, make their election for the nearer good, though they know it to be the less valuable; and this no less when the choice is between two bodily pleasures, than when it is between bodily and mental. They pursue sensual indulgences to the injury of health, though perfectly aware that health is the greater good.

It may be further objected, that many who begin with youthful enthusiasm for everything noble, as they advance in years sink into indolence and selfishness. But I do not believe that those who undergo this very common change, voluntarily choose the lower description of pleasures in preference to the higher. I believe that before they devote themselves exclusively to the one, they have already become incapable of the other. Capacity for the nobler feelings is in most natures a very tender plant, easily killed, not only by hostile influences, but by mere want of sustenance; and in the majority of young persons it speedily dies away if the occupations to which their position in life has devoted them, and the society into which it has thrown them, are not favourable to keeping that higher capacity in exercise. Men lose their high aspirations as they lose their intellectual tastes, because they have not time or opportunity for indulging them; and they addict themselves to inferior pleasures, not because they deliberately prefer them, but because they are either the only ones to which they have access, or the only ones which they are any longer capable of enjoying. It may be questioned whether any one who has remained equally susceptible to both classes of pleasures, ever knowingly and calmly preferred the lower; though many, in all ages, have broken down in an ineffectual attempt to combine both.

From this verdict of the only competent judges, I apprehend there can be no appeal. On a question which is the best worth having of two pleasures, or which of two modes of existence is the most grateful to the feelings, apart from its moral attributes and from its consequences, the judgment of those who are qualified by knowledge of both, or, if they differ, that of the majority among them, must be admitted as final. And there needs be the less hesitation to accept this judgment respecting the quality of pleasures, since there is no other tribunal to be referred to even on the question of quantity. What means are there of determining which is the acutest of two pains, or the intensest of two pleasurable sensations, except the general suffrage of those who are familiar with both? Neither pains nor pleasures are homogeneous, and pain is always heterogeneous with pleasure.

What is there to decide whether a particular pleasure is worth purchasing at the cost of a particular pain, except the feelings and judgment of the experienced? When, therefore, those feelings and judgment declare the pleasures derived from the higher faculties to be preferable in kind, apart from the question of intensity, to those of which the animal nature, disjoined from the higher faculties, is susceptible, they are entitled on this subject to the same regard.

I have dwelt on this point, as being a necessary part of a perfectly just conception of Utility or Happiness, considered as the directive rule of human conduct. But it is by no means an indispensable condition to the acceptance of the utilitarian standard; for that standard is not the agent's own greatest happiness, but the greatest amount of happiness altogether; and if it may possibly be doubted whether a noble character is always the happier for its nobleness, there can be no doubt that it makes other people happier, and that the world in general is immensely a gainer by it. Utilitarianism, therefore, could only attain its end by the general cultivation of nobleness of character, even if each individual were only benefited by the nobleness of others, and his own, so far as happiness is concerned, were a sheer deduction from the benefit. But the bare enunciation of such an absurdity as this last, renders refutation superfluous.

According to the Greatest Happiness Principle, as above explained, the ultimate end, with reference to and for the sake of which all other things are desirable (whether we are considering our own good or that of other people), is an existence exempt as far as possible from pain, and as rich as possible in enjoyments, both in point of quantity and quality; the test of quality, and the rule for measuring it against quantity, being the preference felt by those who in their opportunities of experience, to which must be added their habits of self-consciousness and self-observation, are best furnished with the means of comparison. This, being, according to the utilitarian opinion, the end of human action, is necessarily also the standard of morality; which may accordingly be defined, the rules and precepts for human conduct, by the observance of which an existence such as has been described might be, to the greatest extent possible, secured to all mankind; and not to them only, but, so far as the nature of things admits, to the whole sentient creation . . .

. . . All the grand sources, in short, of human suffering are in a great degree, many of them almost entirely, conquerable by human care and effort; and though their removal is grievously slow—though a long succession of generations will perish in the breach before the conquest is completed, and this world becomes all that, if will and knowledge were not wanting, it might easily be made—yet every mind sufficiently intelligent and generous to bear a part, however small and unconspicuous, in the endeavour, will draw a noble enjoyment from the contest itself, which he would not for any bribe in the form of selfish indulgence consent to be without.

And this leads to the true estimation of what is said by the objectors concerning the possibility, and the obligation, of learning to do without happiness. Unquestionably it is possible to do without happiness; it is done involuntarily by nineteen-twentieths of mankind, even in those parts of our present world which are least deep in barbarism; and it often has to be done voluntarily by the hero or the martyr, for the sake of something which he prizes more than his individual happiness. But this something, what is it, unless the happiness of others or some of the requisites of happiness? It is noble to be capable of resigning entirely one's own portion of happiness, or chances of it: but, after all, this self-sacrifice must be for some end; it is not its own end; and if we are told that its end is not happiness, but virtue, which is better than happiness, I ask, would the sacrifice be made if the hero or martyr did not believe that it would earn for others immunity from similar sacrifices? Would it be made if he thought that his renunciation of happiness for himself would produce no fruit for any of his fellow creatures, but to make their lot like his, and place them also in the condition of persons who have renounced happiness? All honour to those who can abnegate for themselves the personal enjoyment of life, when by such renunciation they contribute worthily to increase the amount of happiness in the world; but he who does it, or professes to do it, for any other purpose, is no more deserving of admiration than the ascetic mounted on his pillar. He may be an inspiriting proof of what men can do, but assuredly not an example of what they should.

Though it is only in a very imperfect state of the world's arrangements that any one can best serve the happiness of others by the absolute sacrifice of his own, yet so long as the world is in that imperfect state, I fully acknowledge that the readiness to make such a sacrifice is the highest virtue which can be found in man. I will add, that in this condition the world, paradoxical as the assertion may be, the conscious ability to do without happiness gives the best prospect of realising, such happiness as is attainable. For nothing except that consciousness can raise a person above the chances of life, by making him feel that, let fate and fortune do their worst, they have not power to subdue him: which, once felt, frees him from excess of anxiety concerning the evils of life, and enables him, like many a Stoic in the worst times of the Roman Empire, to cultivate in tranquillity the sources of satisfaction accessible to him, without concerning himself about the uncertainty of their duration, any more than about their inevitable end.

Meanwhile, let utilitarians never cease to claim the morality of self-devotion as a possession which belongs by as good a right to them, as either to the Stoic or to the Transcendentalist. The utilitarian morality does recognise in human beings the power of sacrificing their own greatest good for the good of others. It only refuses to admit that the sacrifice is itself a good. A sacrifice which does not increase, or tend to increase, the sum total of happiness, it considers as wasted. The only self-renunciation which it applauds, is devotion to the happiness, or to some of the means of happiness, of others; either of mankind collectively, or of individuals within the limits imposed by the collective interests of mankind.

I must again repeat, what the assailants of utilitarianism seldom have the justice to acknowledge, that the happiness which forms the utilitarian standard of what is right in conduct, is not the agent's own happiness, but that of all concerned. As between his own happiness and that of others, utilitarianism requires him to be as strictly impartial as a disinterested and benevolent spectator. In the golden rule of Jesus of Nazareth, we read the complete spirit of the ethics of utility. To do as you would be done by, and to love your neighbour as yourself, constitute the ideal perfection of utilitarian morality. As the means of making the nearest approach to this ideal, utility would enjoin, first, that laws and social arrangements should place the happiness, or (as speaking practically it may be called) the interest, of every individual, as nearly as possible in harmony with the interest of the whole; and secondly, that education and opinion, which have so vast a power over human character, should so use that power as to establish in the mind of every individual an indissoluble association between his own happiness and the good of the whole; especially between his own happiness and the practice of such modes of conduct, negative and positive, as regard for the universal happiness prescribes; so that not only he may be unable to conceive the possibility of happiness to himself, consistently with conduct opposed to the general good, but also that a direct impulse to promote the general good may be in every individual one of the habitual motives of action, and the sentiments connected therewith may fill a large and prominent place in every human being's sentient existence. If the impugners of the utilitarian morality represented it to their own minds in this its true character, I know not what recommendation possessed by any other morality they could possibly affirm to be wanting to it; what more beautiful or more exalted developments of human nature any other ethical system can be supposed to foster, or what springs of action, not accessible to the utilitarian, such systems rely on for giving effect to their mandates.

The objectors to utilitarianism cannot always be charged with representing it in a discreditable light. On the contrary, those among them who entertain anything like a just idea of its disinterested character, sometimes find fault with its standard as being too high for humanity. They say it is exacting too much to require that people shall always act from the inducement of promoting the general interests of society. But this is to mistake the very meaning of a standard of morals, and confound the rule of action with the motive of it. It is the business of ethics to tell us what are our duties, or by what test we may know them; but no system of ethics requires that the sole motive of all we do shall be a feeling of duty; on the contrary, ninety-nine hundredths of all our actions are done from other motives, and rightly so done, if the rule of duty does not condemn them. It is the more unjust to utilitarianism that this particular misapprehension should be made a ground of objection to it, inasmuch as utilitarian moralists have gone beyond almost all others in affirming that the motive has nothing to do with the morality of the action, though much with the worth of the agent. He who saves a fellow creature from drowning does what is morally right, whether his motive be duty, or the hope of being paid for his trouble; he who betrays the friend that trusts him, is guilty of a crime, even if his object be to serve another friend to whom he is under greater obligations. But to speak only of actions done from the motive of duty, and in direct obedience to principle: it is a misapprehension of the utilitarian mode of thought, to conceive it as implying that people should fix their minds upon so wide a generality as the world, or society at large. The great majority of good actions are intended not for the benefit of the world, but for that of individuals, of which the good of the world is made up; and the thoughts of the most virtuous man need not on these occasions travel beyond the particular persons concerned, except so far as is necessary to assure himself that in benefiting them he is not violating the rights, that is, the legitimate and authorised expectations, of any one else. The multiplication of happiness is, according to the utilitarian ethics, the object of virtue: the occasions on which any person (except one in a thousand) has it in his power to do this on an extended scale, in other words to be a public benefactor, are but exceptional; and on these occasions alone is he called on to consider public utility; in every other case, private utility, the interest or happiness of some few persons, is all he has to attend to. Those alone the influence of whose actions extends to society in general, need concern themselves habitually about so large an object. In the case of abstinences indeed—of things which people forbear to do from moral considerations, though the consequences in the particular case might be beneficial—it would be unworthy of an intelligent agent not to be consciously aware that the action is of a class which, if practised generally, would be generally injurious, and that this is the ground of the obligation to abstain from it. The amount of regard for the public interest implied in this recognition, is no greater than is demanded by every system of morals, for they all enjoin to abstain from whatever is manifestly pernicious to society.

A Critique of Utilitarianism*

Bernard Williams

Let us look more concretely at two examples, to see what utilitarianism might say about them, what we might say about utilitarianism and, most importantly

*From J. J. C. Smart and Bernard Williams, *Utilitarianism: For and Against*, pp. 96–117.

of all, what would be implied by certain ways of thinking about the situations. The examples are inevitably schematized, and they are open to the objection that they beg as many questions as they illuminate. There are two ways in particular in which examples in moral philosophy tend to beg important questions. One is that, as presented, they arbitrarily cut off and restrict the range of alternative courses of action—this objection might particularly be made against the first of my two examples. The second is that they inevitably present one with the situation as a going concern, and cut off questions about how the agent got into it, and correspondingly about moral considerations which might flow from that: this objection might perhaps specially arise with regard to the second of my two situations. These difficulties, however, just have to be accepted, and if anyone finds these examples cripplingly defective in this sort of respect, then he must in his own thought rework them in richer and less question-begging form. If he feels that no presentation of any imagined situation can ever be other than misleading in morality, and that there can never be any substitute for the concrete experienced complexity of actual moral situations, then this discussion, with him, must certainly grind to a halt: but then one may legitimately wonder whether every discussion with him about conduct will not grind to a halt, including any discussion about the actual situations, since discussion about how one would think and feel about situations somewhat different from the actual (that is to say, situations to that extent imaginary) plays an important role in discussion of the actual.

(1) George, who has just taken his Ph.D. in chemistry, finds it extremely difficult to get a job. He is not very robust in health, which cuts down the number of jobs he might be able to do satisfactorily. His wife has to go out to work to keep them, which itself causes a great deal of strain, since they have small children and there are severe problems about looking after them. The results of all this, especially on the children, are damaging. An older chemist, who knows about this situation, says that he can get George a decently paid job in a certain laboratory, which pursues research into chemical and biological warfare. George says that he cannot accept this, since he is opposed to chemical and biological warfare. The older man replies that he is not too keen on it himself, come to that, but after all George's refusal is not going to make the job or the laboratory go away; what is more, he happens to know that if George refuses the job, it will certainly go to a contemporary of George's who is not inhibited by any such scruples and is likely if appointed to push along the research with greater zeal than George would. Indeed, it is not merely concern for George and his family, but (to speak frankly and in confidence) some alarm about this other man's excess of zeal, which has led the older man to offer to use his influence to get George the job. . . . George's wife, to whom he is deeply attached, has views (the details of which need not concern us)

from which it follows that at least there is nothing particularly wrong with research into CBW. What should he do?

(2) Jim finds himself in the central square of a small South American town. Tied up against the wall are a row of twenty Indians, most terrified, a few defiant, in front of them several armed men in uniform. A heavy man in a sweat-stained khaki shirt turns out to be the captain in charge and, after a good deal of questioning of Jim which establishes that he got there by accident while on a botanical expedition, explains that the Indians are a random group of the inhabitants who, after recent acts of protest against the government, are just about to be killed to remind other possible protestors of the advantages of not protesting. However, since Jim is an honoured visitor from another land, the captain is happy to offer him a guest's privilege of killing one of the Indians himself. If Jim accepts, then as a special mark of the occasion, the other Indians will be let off. Of course, if Jim refuses, then there is no special occasion, and Pedro here will do what he was about to do when Jim arrived, and kill them all. Jim, with some desperate recollection of schoolboy fiction, wonders whether if he got hold of a gun, he could hold the captain, Pedro and the rest of the soldiers to threat, but it is quite clear from the setup that nothing of that kind is going to work: any attempt at that sort of thing will mean that all the Indians will be killed, and himself. The men against the wall, and the other villagers, understand the situation, and are obviously begging him to accept. What should he do?

To these dilemmas, it seems to me that utilitarianism replies, in the first case, that George should accept the job, and in the second, that Jim should kill the Indian. Not only does utilitarianism give these answers but, if the situations are essentially as described and there are no further special factors, it regards them, it seems to me, as *obviously* the right answers. But many of us would certainly wonder whether, in (1), that could possibly be the right answer at all; and in the case of (2), even one who came to think that perhaps that was the answer, might well wonder whether it was obviously the answer. Nor is it just a question of the rightness or obviousness of these answers. It is also a question of what sort of considerations come into finding the answer. A feature of utilitarianism is that it cuts out a kind of consideration which for some others makes a difference to what they feel about such cases: a consideration involving the idea, as we might first and very simply put it, that each of us is specially responsible for what *he* does, rather than for what other, people do. This is an idea closely connected with the value of integrity. It is often suspected that utilitarianism, at least in its direct forms, makes integrity as a value more or less unintelligible. I shall try to show that this suspicion is correct. Of course, even if that is correct, it would not necessarily follow that we should reject utilitarianism; perhaps, as utilitarians sometimes suggest, we should just forget about integrity, in favour of such things as a concern for the general good. However, if I am right, we cannot merely do that, since the reason why utilitarianism cannot understand integrity is that it cannot coherently describe the relations between a man's projects and his actions.

What projects does a utilitarian agent have? As a utilitarian, he has the general project of bringing about maximally desirable outcomes; how he is to do this at any given moment is a question of what causal levers, so to speak, are at that moment within reach. The desirable outcomes, however, do not just consist of agents carrying out *that* project; there must be other more basic or lower-order projects which he and other agents have, and the desirable outcomes are going to consist, in part, of the maximally harmonious realization of those projects ('in part', because one component of a utilitarianly desirable outcome may be the occurrence of agreeable experiences which are not the satisfaction of anybody's projects). Unless there were first-order projects, the general utilitarian project would have nothing to work on, and would be vacuous. What do the more basic or lower-order projects comprise? Many will be the obvious kinds of desires for things for oneself, one's family, one's friends, including basic necessities of life, and in more relaxed circumstances, objects of taste. Or there may be pursuits and interests of an intellectual, cultural or creative character. I introduce those as a separate class not because the objects of them lie in a separate class, and provide—as some utilitarians, in their churchy way, are fond of saying—"higher" pleasures. I introduce them separately because the agent's identification with them may be of a different order. It does not have to be: cultural and aesthetic interests just belong, for many, along with any other taste; but some people's commitment to these kinds of interests just is at once more thoroughgoing and serious than their pursuit of various objects of taste, while it is more individual and permeated with character than the desire for the necessities of life.

Beyond these, someone may have projects connected with his support of some cause: Zionism, for instance, or the abolition of chemical and biological warfare. Or there may be projects which flow from some more general disposition towards human conduct and character, such as a hatred of injustice, or of cruelty, or of killing.

It may be said that this last sort of disposition and its associated project do not count as (logically) 'lower-order' relative to the higher-order project of maximizing desirable outcomes; rather, it may be said, it is itself a 'higher-order' project. The vital question is not, however, how it is to be classified, but whether it and similar projects are to count among the projects whose satisfaction is to be included in the maximizing sum, and, correspondingly, as contributing to the agent's happiness. If the utilitarian says 'no' to that, then he is almost certainly committed to a version of utilitarianism as absurdly superficial and shallow as Benthamite versions have often been accused of being. For this project will be discounted, presumably, on the ground that it involves, in the specification of its object, the mention of other people's happiness or interests: thus it is the kind of project which (unlike the pursuit of food for myself) presupposes a reference to other people's projects. But that criterion would eliminate any desire at all which was not blankly and in the most straightforward sense egoistic.[1] Thus we should be reduced to frankly egoistic first-order projects, and—for all essential purposes—the one second-order utilitarian project of maximally satisfying first-order projects. Utilitarianism has a tendency to slide in this direction, and to leave a vast hole in the range of human desires, between egoistic inclinations and necessities at one end, and impersonally benevolent happiness-management at the other. But the utilitarianism which has to leave this hole is the most primitive form, which offers a quite rudimentary account of desire. Modern versions of the theory are supposed to be neutral with regard to what sorts of things make people happy or what their projects are. Utilitarianism would do well then to acknowledge the evident fact that among the things that make people happy is not only making other people happy, but being taken up or involved in any of a vast range of projects, or—if we waive the evangelical and moralizing associations of the word—commitments. One can be committed to such things as a person, a cause, an institution, a career, one's own genius, or the pursuit of danger.

Now none of these is itself the *pursuit of happiness*: by an exceedingly ancient platitude, it is not at all clear that there could be anything which was just that, or at least anything that had the slightest chance of being successful. Happiness, rather, requires being involved in, or at least content with, something else.[2] It is not impossible for utilitarianism to accept that point: it does not have to be saddled with a naïve and absurd philosophy of mind about the relation between desire and happiness. What it does have to say is that if such commitments are worthwhile, then pursuing the projects that flow from them, and realizing some of those projects, will make the person for whom they are worthwhile, happy. It may be that to claim that is still wrong: it may well be that a commitment can make sense to a man (can make sense of his life) without his supposing that it will make him *happy*.[3] But that is not the present point; let us grant to utilitarianism that all worthwhile human projects must conduce, one way or another, to happiness. The point is that even if that is true, it does not follow, nor could it possibly be true, that those projects are themselves projects of pursuing happiness. One has to believe in or at least want, or quite minimally, be content with, other things, for there to be anywhere that happiness can come from.

Utilitarianism, then, should be willing to agree that its general aim of maximizing happiness does not imply that what everyone is doing is just pursuing happiness. On the contrary, people have to be pursuing other things. What those other things may be, utilitarianism, sticking to its professed empirical stance, should be prepared just to find out. No doubt some possible projects it will want to discourage, on the grounds that their being pursued involves a negative balance of happiness to others: though even there, the unblinking accountant's eye of the strict utilitarian will have something to put in the positive column, the satisfactions of the destructive agent. Beyond that, there will be a vast variety of generally beneficent or at least harmless projects; and some no doubt, will take the form not just of tastes or fancies, but of what I have called 'commitments'. It may even be that the utilitarian researcher will find that many of those with commitments, who have really identified themselves with objects outside themselves, who are thoroughly involved with other persons, or institutions, or activities or causes, are actually happier than those whose projects and wants are not like that. If so, that is an important piece of utilitarian empirical lore.

When I say 'happier' here, I have in mind the sort of consideration which any utilitarian would be committed to accepting: as for instance that such people are less likely to have a break-down or commit suicide. Of course that is not all that is actually involved, but the point in this argument is to use to the maximum degree utilitarian notions, in order to locate a breaking point in utilitarian thought.

Let us now go back to the agent as utilitarian, and his higher-order project of maximizing desirable outcomes. At this level, he is committed only to that: what the outcome will actually consist of will depend entirely on the facts, on what persons with what projects and what potential satisfactions there are within calculable reach of the causal levers near which he finds himself. His own substantial projects and commitments come into it, but only as one lot among others—they potentially provide one set of satisfactions among those which he may be able to assist from where he happens to be. He is the agent of the satisfaction system who happens to be at a particular point at a particular time: in Jim's case, our man in South America. His own decisions as a utilitarian agent are a function of all the satisfactions which he can affect from where he is: and this means that the projects of others, to an indeterminately great extent, determine his decision.

This may be so either positively or negatively, It will be so positively if agents within the causal field of his decision have projects which are at any rate harmless, and so should be assisted. It will equally be so, but negatively, if there is an agent within the causal field whose projects are harmful, and have to be frustrated to maximize desirable outcomes. So it is with Jim and the soldier Pedro. On the utilitarian view, the undesirable projects of other people as much determine, in this negative way, one's decisions as the desirable ones do positively: if those people were not there, or had different projects, the causal nexus would be different, and it is the actual state of the causal nexus which determines the decision. The determination to an indefinite degree of my decisions by other people's projects is just another aspect of my unlimited responsibility to act for the best in a causal framework formed to a considerable extent by their projects.

The decision so determined is, for utilitarianism, the right decision. But what if it conflicts with some project of mine? This, the utilitarian will say, has already been dealt with: the satisfaction to you of fulfilling your project, and any satisfactions to others of your so doing, have already been through the calculating device and have been found inadequate. Now in the case of many sorts of projects, that is a perfectly reasonable sort of answer. But in the case of projects of the sort I have called 'commitments', those with which one is more deeply and extensively involved and identified, this cannot just by itself be an adequate answer, and there may be no adequate answer at all. For, to take the extreme sort of case, how can a man, as a utilitarian agent, come to regard as one satisfaction among others, and a dispensable one, a project or attitude round which he has built his life, just because someone else's projects have so structured the causal scene that that is how the utilitarian sum comes out?

The point here is not, as utilitarians may hasten to say, that if the project or attitude is that central to his life, then to abandon it will be very disagreeable to him and great loss of utility will be involved. The point is that he is identified with his actions as flowing from projects and attitudes which in some cases he takes seriously at the deepest level, as what his life is about (or, in some case, this section of his life—seriousness is not necessarily the same as persistence). It is absurd to demand of such a man, when the sums come in from the utility network which the projects of others have in part determined, that he should just step aside from his own project and decision and acknowledge the decision which utilitarian calculation requires. It is to alienate him in a real sense from his actions and the source of his action in his own convictions. It is to make him into a channel between the input of everyone's projects, including his own, and an output of optimific decision; but his is to neglect the extent to which *his* actions and *his* decision have to be seen as the actions and decision which flow from the projects and attitudes with which he is most closely identified. It is thus, in the most literal sense, an attack on his integrity.[4]

These sorts of considerations do not in themselves give solutions to practical dilemmas such as those provided by our examples; but I hope they help to provide other ways of thinking about them. In fact, it is not hard to see that in George's case, viewed from this perspective, the utilitarian solution would be wrong. Jim's case is different, and harder. But if (as I suppose) the utilitarian is probably right in this case, that is not to be found out just by asking the utilitarian's questions. Discussions of it—and I am not going to try to carry it further here—will have to take seriously the distinction between my killing someone, and its coming about because of what I do that someone else kills them; a distinction based, not so much on the distinction between action and inaction, as on the distinction between my projects and someone else's projects. At least it will have to start by taking that seriously, as utilitarianism does not; but then it will have to build out from there by asking why that distinction seems to have less, or a different, force in this case than it has in George's. One question here would be how far one's powerful objection to killing people just is, in fact, an application of a powerful objection to their being killed. Another dimension of that is the issue of how much it matters that the people at risk are actual, and there, as opposed to hypothetical, or future, or merely elsewhere.[5]

Notes

1. On the subject of egoistic and non-egoistic desires, see 'Egoism and altruism', in *Problems of the Self* (Cambridge University Press, London, 1973).

2. This does not imply that there is no such thing as the project of pursuing pleasure. Some writers who have correctly resisted the view that all desires are desires for pleasure, have given an account of pleasure so thoroughly adverbial as to leave it quite unclear how there could be a distinctively hedonist way of life at all. Some room has to be left for that, though there are important difficulties both in defining it and living it. Thus (particularly in the case of the very rich) it often has highly ritual aspects, apparently part of a strategy to counter boredom.

3. For some remarks on this possibility, see *Morality*, section on 'What is morality about?'

4. Interestingly related to these notions is the Socratic idea that courage is a virtue particularly connected with keeping a clear sense of what one regards as most important. They also centrally raise questions about the value of pride. Humility, as something beyond the real demand of correct self-appraisal, was specially a Christian virtue because it involved subservience to God. In a secular context it can only represent subservience to other men and their projects.

5. For a more general discussion of this issue see Charles Fried, *An Anatomy of Values* (Harvard University Press, Cambridge, Mass., 1970), Part Three.

Rule-Consequentialism*

Brad Hooker

Suppose that accepting rules is a matter of having certain desires and dispositions. Now consider the theory that an act is morally right if and only if it is called for by the set of desires and dispositions the having of which by everyone

*Brad Hooker, "Rule-Consequentialism" Mind 99, no. 393 (Jan. 1990): 67–77.

would result in at least as good consequences judged impartially as any other.[1] For lack of a better name, we might call this theory *disposition/rule-consequentialism*, or just *rule-consequentialism* for short. Two crucial features of this theory should be noted. One is that it assesses the rightness and wrongness of any particular act, not directly in terms of its consequences, but indirectly in terms of a set of desires, dispositions, and rules, which is then assessed in terms of the consequences of everyone's having that set.[2] The other is that it assesses the rightness of any given act, not in terms of the desires, dispositions, and rules which are such that the agent's having them would bring about the best overall consequences, but rather in terms of the desires, dispositions, and rules which are such that everyone's having them would bring about the best overall consequences.[3] Let me refer to the set of desires, dispositions, and rules which are such that everyone's having them would bring about the best overall consequences as the *optimific* set.

To those who are attracted to consequentialism but want a moral theory that accords with at least most of our intuitions, rule-consequentialism should have considerable initial appeal. In section I of this paper I try to bring out the attractions of rule-consequentialism by showing how it can be formulated so as to be safe from the main objections to other consequentialist theories. Yet, even if the best version of rule-consequentialism is immune to the objections that plague other consequentialist theories, rule-consequentialism has difficulties of its own—one of the most serious of which is the so-called partial compliance objection.[4] In section II I consider how rule-consequentialists might reply to the partial compliance objection. Then, in section III I explore the question of whether rule-consequentialists can avoid the partial compliance objection without opening up their theory to the objection that it makes unreasonably severe demands on individuals.

I

One of the most popular objections to utilitarianism is that interpersonal comparisons of utility are impossible. I assume any plausible version of rule-consequentialism will have a utilitarian component, and will therefore need an answer to the objection about interpersonal comparisons. But for the purposes of this paper I shall simply assume that some acceptable way of making interpersonal comparisons *is* possible.[5]

Another prominent objection to act-utilitarianism is that it does not allow that fairness or equality in the distribution of benefits and burdens can be morally required even when a less fair or less egalitarian distribution would provide greater net welfare.[6] But it is possible to accommodate this objection without abandoning even *act*-consequentialism. For it might be held that, while the right act is still just whatever one will bring about the best outcome, outcomes are to be ranked in terms of not only how much well-being they contain but also how equally or fairly it is distributed.[7]

A prominent objection to standard kinds of act-consequentialism is that they give no direct weight to deontological, agent-relative considerations: standard kinds of act-consequentialism hold that it is morally right to harm people, or to ignore one's special obligations to those with whom one has some special connection, when such acts would bring about even slightly more good overall.[8] Many people confidently believe that it is morally wrong to commit murder, to torture someone for information, to frame the innocent, to steal, to break one's promises, to fail to give special weight to the interests of those with whom one has some special connection, and so on, *even when doing one of these things would produce somewhat better consequences judged impartially*. But here, too, much can be said in defense of act-consequentialism.[9] Defenders of the theory usually start by pointing out that the kinds of act in question very rarely produce the best available outcome. They add that human limitations and biases are such that we are not accurate calculators of the expected consequences—for everyone—of our alternatives. That is, we frequently do not have the needed information, time, or the capacity to weight benefits and harms impartially (for example, most of us are biased in such a way that we tend to underestimate the harm to others of acts that would benefit us). For these reasons, a sophisticated act-consequentialism would prescribe that we inculcate and maintain in ourselves and others *both* firm dispositions not to commit some kinds of acts *and* dispositions to disapprove of others who do commit them. Indeed, given our psychological limitations, act-consequentialism may favor our moral dispositions' running so deep that we could not bring ourselves to do the kinds of act in question even in the rare cases in which they *would* bring about the best consequences impartially calculated. Such might be the dispositions—of those sets that are psychologically possible—which are such that one's having them would produce the most good. But all this notwithstanding, *act*-consequentialists insist that *right* acts are those which would result in the most overall good (even if morally good people could not bring themselves to perform some of these acts). And in making this claim act-consequentialism conflicts sharply with the deontological convictions I mentioned.[10]

Rule-consequentialism, however, does not make that problematic claim. Rule-consequentialiam claims instead that individual acts of murder, torture, promise-breaking, and so on, can be wrong even when those particular acts bring about better consequences than any alternative acts would have. For rule-consequentialism makes the rightness and wrongness of particular acts, not a matter of the consequences of those individual acts, but rather a matter of conformity with that set of fairly general rules whose acceptance by (more or less) everyone would have the best consequences.[11] And, this acceptance of fairly general rules forbidding murder, torture, promise-breaking, and so on, would clearly have better consequences than everyone's accepting fairly general rules permitting such acts. (This point could just as easily be put in terms of dispositions rather than rules.)

Consider now one more objection to act-utilitarianism—that it is unreasonably demanding, construing as duties what one would have thought were supererogatory self-sacrifices.[12] To fully appreciate this objection we need to keep in mind the following three things: (1) money and other material goods usually have diminishing marginal utility; (2) each dollar can buy vastly more food in, for example, Ethiopia than it can in a 'First-World' country; and (3) other relatively well-off people will not give much. We must thus accept that it would be utility-maximizing, and thus optimific according to most versions of act-consequentialism, if I gave away most of my material goods to the appropriate charities. I must, of course, take into account the effects of my present actions on my future capacity to give. In the light of that consideration, I should keep whatever proportion of my income and possessions is necessary for me to continue earning so that I can maximize the amount I can give over the course of my whole life.[13] But, presumably, what I am allowed to keep for myself is still very little. And many of us may on reflection think that it would be *morally unreasonable* to demand this level of self-sacrifice for the sake of others.[14] This thought is not inconsistent with the realization that morality can from time to time require significant self-sacrifice for the sake of others; nor does it oppose the claim that giving most of what one has to the needy is both permissible and extremely praiseworthy. But most of us are quite confident that such self-sacrifice is supererogatory—that is, not something morality *requires* of us.

I admit that there is something unsavory about objecting to a moral theory because of the severity of its requirements. One might be tempted to think that the demandingness objection will appeal to people whose self-interest is clouding their moral judgment, that it will appeal to people who have a lot to lose from a strong requirement to aid others.[15] But it would be unfair to dismiss the objection on such grounds—to do so would be to find the objection 'guilty by association'. Furthermore, even after we acknowledge that the demandingness objection may appeal to some disreputable characters, the objection retains considerable force.

I have been discussing the act-utilitarian requirement to keep making sacrifices for others until further sacrifices would result in less overall welfare in the long run. Consider now an alternative and less demanding principle of aid. This principle is that we are required to come to the aid of others as long as the benefit to them is very great in comparison to the sacrifice to us.[16] Even this less demanding principle makes heavy demands on those of us with spare money: most of us would have to sacrifice most of our welfare in helping others before we reached the point at which the sacrifice to us would no longer be very much smaller than the benefits produced for them.[17] And it might well be thought that a requirement that one sacrifice *most* of one's own welfare for the sake of strangers whose suffering is not one's fault is unreasonably demanding, particularly when most others in a position to help are not doing so.

Indeed, one of the notable initial attractions of rule-consequentialism is that it—unlike both act-consequentialism and the more modest principle of aid just mentioned—calls for an amount of self-sacrifice that is not unreasonable.[18] If each relatively well-off person contributed some relatively small percentage of his or her income to famine relief; there would be enough to feed the world. Perhaps ten percent from each of the well-off would be enough. Though giving that much may seem difficult enough for most of us, the demand that we do so does not seem unreasonable. Rule-consequentialism therefore seems to escape the demandingness objection. If so, it is acquitted of all of the main charges against act-utilitarianism.

I do not mean to suggest that there are not other powerful reasons for finding rule-consequentialism the most appealing form of consequentialism. One might well think that reflection on the nature of morality suggests that it must serve as a public system of principles to which we can appeal to justify our behavior to one another, and that rule-consequentialism does, but act-consequentialism does not, do justice to this insight.[19] Or one might well think that rule-consequentialism does justice to the importance of the common question 'what if everyone did that?' in a way that act-consequentialism cannot. I also do not mean to suggest that the only way of reacting to the excessive demands of act-consequentialism is to join up with the rule-consequentialists.[20] But those are matters I do not want to explore here.

II

What is the partial compliance objection to rule-consequentialism? It is that following the moral code that would be optimal in a world in which everyone accepted it can be (in Brandt's words) 'counterproductive or useless' in the real world where there is actually only partial social acceptance of that code.[21] To use an example Brandt cites, suppose that what would produce optimal results would be for everyone to act in a race-blind way. But suppose also that you are surrounded by people with fierce racial prejudices. It is easy to imagine that your acting in a race-blind way in front of these rabid racists would have very bad consequences.

On the simplest rule-consequentialist view, the best set of rules, desires, and dispositions is whatever set is such that, if absolutely everyone accepted those rules and had those desires and dispositions, the results would be better than if absolutely everyone accepted other rules and had other desires and dispositions. But then how can it make sense to object that some dispositions which would produce the most good if *everyone* had them would be counter-productive or useless in situations where *not everyone* had them? It is clearly illogical to imagine both that everyone accepts a certain code of rules or has a certain set of dispositions and that at the same time some do not accept that code and do not have those dispositions. Brandt provides a neat solution to this problem: he defines the optimal moral code as the one that would result in the most good if it were accepted by 'all except those whose agreement is precluded by a description of some moral-problem situations'.[22]

But there remain problems with how to interpret the partial compliance objection to rule-consequentialism. Consider three possibilities:

1. The objection might be that you might sometimes be required by the rules whose currency would produce the most good to do something that, because others are not complying, would produce *slightly* worse consequences viewed impartially.
2. Or the objection might be that you might sometimes be required by the rules to do something that, because others are not complying, would be *harmful or inconvenient to you and beneficial to the very people who are not complying.*
3. Or the objection might be that you might sometimes be required by these rules to do something that, because others are not complying, would produce *very much* worse consequences viewed impartially.

The first of these interpretations can, I think, be dismissed. The claim that one should follow certain rules even when breaking them would produce slightly more good does not seem counter-intuitive (except to hard-line act-consequentialists).[23]

So consider now the second interpretation of the objection—that, sometimes, because others are not complying, my following simple rules would be both harmful to me and beneficial to the very people who are not complying. The idea that the simple rules provide the criterion of rightness and wrongness for such cases does offend against our sentiments about fairness.[24] But it is pretty obvious how rule-consequentialists can defuse this objection: they can agree it is not wrong to refuse to follow certain rules in one's dealings with those who do not reciprocate. The moral rules that would produce the most good in our partial compliance world would have provisions written into them designed to give incentives to those who are possible beneficiaries of our rule-following to do their part in following the rules. Such provisions would permit us to ignore the ordinarily appropriate rules when we are dealing with those who refuse to follow those rules.

The third interpretation of the objection seems the most powerful. Rule-consequentialism is less than credible if it claims one is required always to follow certain rules, even when not following these rules would prevent *very much* worse consequences for others. (Since from now on I shall ignore the first two ways of construing the partial compliance objection, I shall henceforth refer to the objection construed in the third way as simply the partial compliance objection.) Now, can rule-consequentialists provide a convincing reply to the objection?

Brandt articulates what would seem to be the natural reply for the rule-consequentialist to make. He suggests that rule-consequentialism would prescribe our having a set of moral motivations consisting of

1. the standing motivations corresponding to the usual simple moral rules (that is, a standing desire to treat others fairly, another standing desire not to hurt others, another not to steal, another not to break one's promises, another not to lie, and so on),
2. a standing desire to prevent great harm, and
3. a standing desire to promote the wider acceptance of the optimific rules.[25]

Rule-consequentialists would presumably say that an act is morally wrong if it is one that this set of motivations would oppose. We might summarize this reply to the partial compliance objection as follows: by including in their favoured code a particularly strong requirement that one prevent great harm, rule-consequentialists can escape having to maintain that it is morally right to stick to the (normally optimific) rules in those situations in which our doing so would result in very much worse consequences. (For the purposes of the rest of this paper, however, we can focus on (1) and (2) above and ignore (3). This is so because in at least many situations the desire to prevent great harm would not need the help of the desire to promote wider acceptance of the optimific rules in order to prevail in a battle with the motivations corresponding to the simple rules. And those are the cases I shall be focusing on.)

III

Unfortunately, relying on a strong principle of preventing harm in order to deal with the partial compliance problem threatens to make rule-consequentialism excessively demanding. Suppose that, of the various possible rules about coming to others' aid, the rule whose acceptance by absolutely everyone relatively well off would produce the most good requires one to donate a tenth of one's income to famine relief. Suppose that this is what I have just done. Knowing that most others in a position to donate are not complying with that requirement, I am now trying to decide whether I must donate more. There are still people dying who would be saved if I gave more. My doing so would thus prevent serious harm to others. Given these conditions, Brandt's proposal would require me to give more of my income. And even if I give another tenth, there would be other people whom I would save by giving more. So yet again serious harm would be avoided if I kept giving. In fact, I would have to make myself quite badly off before I myself would be so poor that the further sacrifices I could make would be too little to save others in desperate need from great harm. And so the code in question seems to require self-sacrifices up to that point. But to require self-sacrifices all the way up to this point seems unreasonably demanding, especially when others in a position to help are not doing their share.[26]

So my argument might be put like this. The partial compliance objection to rule-utilitarianism is extremely important—after all, we live in a partial compliance world. Rule-consequentialism can be rescued from the partial compliance objection by bringing in a strong requirement that one prevent great harm. But this move seems to pull rule-consequentialism out of the mouth of one objection only to throw it into the mouth of another.

What might rule-consequentialists say in reply? They might try to claim that the optimific set of rules and dispositions *would permit* me to depart from a given rule in order to prevent great harm, but *would not require* me to do so. This reply might sound good when we think about the famine relief cases, but we can see it cannot be right when we think about the other partial compliance cases, the cases in which the agent's own welfare is not in play. To give an intuitively acceptable answer for the cases in which the agent's own welfare is not in play, rule-consequentialists must say that the optimific code requires the agent not to do what would result in great harm. And it would seem that the most natural way for rule consequentialists to accomplish this is to maintain that we should obey the code of rules that would be optimific if everyone complied with it, except when our following that code would result in great harm because of others' non-compliance, and that in those cases we should do what would prevent that harm. But, as I have explained, this answer will make rule consequentialism terribly demanding in the famine relief cases.

Here is a more promising reply that rule-consequentialists might try. Rule-consequentialists favour the code of rules whose currency would produce the most good. One of the factors counted in the cost-benefit assessment of any proposed code is what we might call its maintenance costs, that is, the costs of sustaining people's commitment to it and of teaching it to the young. Furthermore, many rule-consequentialists (Brandt among them) hold that wrong acts are those forbidden by that moral code whose general currency among human beings *with their natural biases and limitations* would produce the best consequences.[27] And, given natural human selfishness, etc., it might well be true that an *extremely* demanding morality could be successfully taught to, and sustained in, people *only at great cost.*[28] Therefore, the currency of a somewhat less demanding morality might have better consequences, all things considered. That is, the moral code whose currency would result in the greatest good overall might be less demanding than we would have thought if we had forgotten about maintenance costs.

The question now is: even after we take maintenance costs into account, would the optimific set of rules nevertheless be unreasonably demanding? It is hard to be sure. Part of the reason for this is that our sense of what counts as being unreasonably demanding is somewhat vague (though determinate enough to license the charges of excessive demandingness made earlier in this paper). But equally important is that we are uncertain which rule of the alternative possible ones about coming to the aid of others is such that its acceptance by everyone (except those whose acceptance is precluded by the description of the problem situation in question) would produce the most good. In other words, we do not know how demanding the optimific rule about coming to the aid of others would be.[29] Just where the line is between reasonable and unreasonable demandingness and just how demanding the optimific rule would be are questions that require further work. But at least we can throw down the gauntlet, challenging rule-consequentialists to show that the rule about coming to the aid of others which is such that its general acceptance would produce better consequences on the whole than the general acceptance of any alternative would not be in conflict with our *fairly confident* convictions about what is above and beyond the call of duty.[30]

Notes

This paper is much better than it would otherwise have been because of written comments on earlier drafts from Penelope Mackie, Mark Overvold, Peter Vallentyne, Anthony Ellis, Mark Nelson, and Richard Brandt. I am extremely grateful to these people, and to Alan Fuchs, James Griffin, R. M. Hare, Roger Crisp, David Dyzenhaus, Cheryl Misak, Eldon Soifer, Howard Robinson, Madison Powers, and Greg Trianosky for helpful discussions about the ideas in the paper. Remaining defects, however, are my responsibility.

1. I do not want to make any controversial assumptions about what desires and dispositions human beings are capable of having. I do not want to enter here into debates about how 'plastic' human nature has been up to now; nor do we need to take up questions about whether trying to 'improve' human nature via genetic engineering would be advisable.

2. So rule-consequentialism is a kind of *indirect* consequentialism. It is a mistake to think that indirect consequentialism assesses not acts but only the rightness and wrongness of other things such as motives, standing dispositions, rules, and social practices.

Indirect consequentialism does assess acts as well (see B. Williams, 'A Critique of Utilitarianism', in J. J. C. Smart and B. Williams, *Utilitarianism: For and Against*, Cambridge, Cambridge University Press, 1973, p. 121).

3. See R. M. Adam's distinction between 'Individualistic motive utilitarianism' and 'Universalistic motive utilitarianism' ('Motive Utilitarianism', *Journal of Philosophy*, 1976, p.480) and D. Parfit's distinction between 'Individual Consequentialism' and 'Collective Consequentialism', *Reasons and Persons*, Oxford, Clarendon Press, 1984, pp. 30–1. There might seem to be something fishy about the claim that the right act is whatever one would be called for by the desires, dispositions, and rules which are such that, if *every last person* had them, the best consequences would result. I shall return to this.

4. Indeed, R. Brandt—long one of the pre-eminent rule-consequentialists—admits that this problem is the most important of the problems peculiar to the indirect form of consequentialism. See his 'Fairness to Indirect Optimific Theories in Ethics', *Ethics*, 1988, pp. 341–60.

5. As consequentialists have long pointed out, it had better be, if we are to be able to conform even with a common-sense duty of beneficence, such as W. D. Ross's (on which see Ross, *The Right and the Good*, Oxford, Clarendon Press, 1930, ch. 2). For a recent defence of interpersonal comparisons of utility, see J. Griffin, *Well-being: Its Meaning, Measurement and Moral Importance*, Oxford, Clarendon Press, 1986, Part Two.

6. For an account of the main intuitive objections to act-utilitarianism, see S. Scheffler's 'Introduction' to his collection *Consequentialisim and its Critics*, Oxford, Oxford University Press, 1988, pp. 1–13, esp. pp. 2–4.

7. See, for example, T. M. Scanlon, 'Rights, Goals, and Fairness', in *Public and Private Morality*, ed. S. Hampshire, Cambridge, Cambridge University Press, 1978, pp. 93–111, especially sect. 2. This paper is reprinted in Scheffler's collection *Consequentialism and its Critics*. See also Scheffler, *The Rejection of Consequentialism*, Oxford, Clarendon Press, 1982, pp. 26–34, 70–9 and Parfit, *Reasons and Persons*, p. 26.

8. Of course, Scheffler himself advances a powerful attack on the idea that deontological considerations should figure in the most basic, or first, principles of morality (*Rejection of Consequentialism*, ch. 4).

9. Prominent among those associated with the defence I am about to summarize are H. Sidgwick, *The Methods of Ethics*, 7th ed, London, Macmillan, 1907, bk. IV, ch. III; R. M. Hare, *Moral Thinking*, Oxford, Clarendon Press, 1981, pp. 35–52, 130–59; Parfit, *Reasons and Persons*, pp. 27–8; and P. Railton, 'Alienation, Consequenrialism, and Morality', *Philosophy and Public Affairs*, 1984, pp. 134–71, esp. pp. 153–4, 157–9 (Railton's paper is also reprinted in Scheffler's collection).

10. See Conrad Johnson, 'The Authority of the Moral Agent', in *Consequentialism and its Critics*, ed. Scheffier, p. 264.

11. The rules in question must of course be 'fairly general' because rule-consequentialism collapses into extensional equivalence with act-consequentialism if the rules are allowed to be infinitely specific. Brandt mentions this problem ('Indirect Optimific Theories', p. 347). The question of just how universal the acceptance of the moral code must be is one I return to below.

12. This objection is discussed in many places. Sidgwick acknowledges that utilitarianism 'seems to require a more *comprehensive and unceasing* subordination of self-interest to the common good' than common-sense morality does (*Methods of Ethics*, p. 87, italics added). See also ibid., pp. 492, 499. Other discussions of this objection include: K. Baier, *The Moral Point of View*, Ithaca, Cornell University Press, 1958, pp. 203–4; Scheffler, 'Introduction' to *Consequentialism and its Critics*, pp. 3–4; G. Harman, *The Nature of Morality*, New York, Oxford University Press, 1977, p. 157–62; F. Feldman, *Introductory Ethics*, Englewood Cliffs, Prentice-Hall, 1978; R. Brandt, *A Theory of the Good and the Right*, Oxford, Clarendon Press, 1979, p. 276; J. Hospera, *Human Conduct: Problems of Ethics*, 2nd edn, New York, Harcourt Brace Jovanovich, 1982, pp. 162–5; D. Brock, 'Utilitarianism and Aiding Others', in *The Limits of Utilitarianism*, ed. H. Miller and W. Williams, Minneapolis, University of Minnesota Press, 1982; Thomas Carson, 'Utilitarianism and World Poverty', in Miller and Williams; Parfit, *Reasons and Persons*, pp. 30–1; and B. Williams, *Ethics and the Limits of Philosophy*, Cambridge, Mass., Harvard University Press, 1985, p. 77. And consider the following passage from Railton, a *defender* of *act*-consequentialism:

> [J]ust *how* demanding or disruptive it [act-consequentialism] would be for an individual is a function—as it arguably should be—of how bad the state of the world is, how others typically act, what institutions exist, and how much that individual is capable of doing. If wealth were more equitably distributed, if political systems were less repressive and more responsive to the needs of their citizens, and if people were more generally prepared to accept certain responsibilities, then individuals' everyday lives would not have to be constantly disrupted for the sake of the good (p. 161).

So act-consequentialism holds that in the real world, where wealth is not equitably distributed, where political systems are repressive and unresponsive to the needs of their citizens, and where most others are not more generally prepared to accept certain responsibilities, most of your acts will not be morally right unless your everyday life *is* constantly disrupted for the sake of the good? And one of the main ways in which act-consequentialism can become not constantly disruptive is for a much wider group of people to make sacrifices for the sake of those in need?

13. See P. Singer, *Practical Ethics*, Cambridge, Cambridge University Press, 1979, p. 163.

14. Scheffler and T. Nagel usefully set out a number of different ways moral theorists might respond to a very demanding moral conception (Scheffler, 'Morality's Demands and their Limits', *Journal of Philosophy*, 1986, pp. 531–7; Nagel, *The View from Nowhere*, New York, Oxford University Press, 1986, ch. X; but cf. Griffin, *Well-Being*, pp. 127–62, 195–206, 246–51, 302–7; Railton, pp. 169–70 n.42; and D. Brink, 'Utilitarian Morality and the Personal Point of View', *Journal of Philosophy*, 1986, pp. 432–8). Particularly important is the following contrast. When confronted with an account of morality which pictures it as extremely demanding, some of us would respond by rejecting that account of morality's content. Another response is to accept that account of its content but then limit morality's rational authority. Though there are other possible responses as well, the idea I am drawing on in this paper is that any account of the content of

morality which makes it constantly and relentlessly demanding is ultimately mistaken. The purpose of the second half of this note is to acknowledge that not everyone will find that idea seductive.

15. See Carson, 'Utilitarianism and World Poverty', p. 243.

16. A principle Sidgwick thinks is part of 'common-sense morality' and even, 'broadly speaking, unquestionable' (*Methods*, p. 348–9; see also pp. 253, 261).

17. This claim is similar to one of the central points of J. Fishkin's tightly argued *Limits of Obligation*, New Haven, Yale University Press1982, a book with profound implications. See also Nagel's observation that given existing world circumstances not just act-utilitarianism but any morality with a substantial impersonal component will make voracious demands (*View from Nowhere*, p. 192).

18. See Parfit, *Reasons and Persons*, p. 31. Cf. Singer, *Practical Ethics*, ch. 8, esp. pp. 180–1; and Fishkin, *Limits of Obligation*, pp. 162–3.

19. The literature on the 'publicity condition' is voluminous. For a sampling, see Sidgwick, *Methods*, pp. 489–90: K. Baier, *Moral Point of View*, p. 198; A. Donagan, 'Is There a Credible Form of Utilitarianism?' in *Contemporary Utilitarianism*, ed. M. Bayles, Garden City, NY, Doubleday & Co., 1968, pp. 187–202, p. 194 J. Rawls, *A Theory of Justice*, Cambridge, Mass., Harvard University Press, 1971, pp. 130 n. 5, 133, 181, 582; J. Hospers, *Human Conduct, Problems of Ethics*, New York, Harcourt Brace Jovanovich, Inc., 1972, pp. 314–15; Brandt, *Theory of the Good and the Right*, pp. 173–4, and 'Indirect Optimific Theories', p. 348; Parfit, *Reasons and Persons*, sect. 17; Williams, *Ethics and the Limits of Philosophy*, pp. 101–2, 108–9.

20. A different response is Scheffler's advocacy of an agent-relative prerogative to give one's own projects and commitments somewhat greater weight than those of others. See his *Rejection of Consequentialism*. Scheffler's theory is not yet fully worked out, but the difficulties with it (on which see S. Kagan, 'Does Consequentialism Demand Too Much? Recent Work on the Limits of Obligation', *Philosophy and Public Affairs*, 1984, pp. 239–54, esp. p. 251) are serious enough to keep us from dropping work on rule-consequentialism. Another interesting idea is that *act*-consequentialism turns out not to be unreasonably demanding once we take into consideration the point that every criterion of right and wrong must be sensitive to a requirement of psychological realism, i.e., act-consequentialism cannot demand more self-sacrifice than human nature can deliver. I am grateful to James Griffin for this suggestion, but I do not have room to explore it here.

21. Brandt, 'Fairness to Indirect Optimific Theories in Ethics', p. 357. See also his *Theory of the Good and the Right*, pp. 297–9, and his 'Problems of Contemporary Utilitarianism: Real and Alleged', in *Ethical Theory in the Last Quarter of the Twentieth Century*, ed. N. E. Bowie, Indianapolis, Hackett Publishing Co., 1983, pp. 99–102. I should mention that I will usually follow common practice in contrasting full and partial *compliance*. But, since the best versions of rule-consequentialism (including Brandt's) are concerned with *acceptance*-utility rather than *compliance*-utility, this terminology will be less than perfectly accurate. The distinction between acceptance-utility and compliance-utility is important because the consequences of everyone's accepting some code (and being motivated accordingly) may involve more than the consequences of their acts of

compliance with that code. (On this, see Williams, 'Critique of Utilitarianism', pp. 119–30; Adams, 'Motive Utilitarianism', pp. 467–81, p. 470; S. Blackburn, 'Errors and the Phenomenology of Value', in *Morality and Objectivity, A Tribute to J. L. Mackie*, ed. T. Honderich, London, Routledge and Kegan Paul, 1985, p. 21 n. 12.)

22. 'Fairness to Indirect Optimific Theories in Ethics', p. 342; see also p. 358.

23. See the famous discussion in Ross, *Right and the Good*, pp. 34–5. The claim made in my text must not be misconstrued as a reply to the following common objection against rule-consequentialism: given that rule-consequentialism says the point of following moral rules is to optimize, its refusal to permit us to break the rules when doing so would be optimific makes the theory internally incoherent. I do not have room here to go into detail about this well-worn objection, which Brandt does take up in 'Fairness to Indirect Optimific Theories' on pp. 353–7, and to which I believe that there are persuasive indirect consequentialist replies. But I am grateful to Anthony Ellis for pointing out that I need to distinguish the idea I discuss in the text from this objection.

24. For a recent attempt to deal with fairness by someone sympathetic to utilitarianism, see Griffin, *Well-being*, ch. X.

25. Actually this is not exactly what Brandt presents. He says that his proposal would lead us to think that in the example from South Africa in which the agent is being watched by rabid racists 'the requirement to treat people equally now may be weaker than the prohibition on causing great harm, but the requirement to do what one can to improve matters will be stronger than simple capitulation to the rules subscribed to by the majority' ('Indirect Optimific Theories', p. 359). This is confusing because it suggests that the optimal moral code would include an intrinsic motivation to capitulate to the rules subscribed to by the majority—which must be a mistake. To be sure, we might accept the idea that attempts at moral reform may be most successful if they try to build on, rather than completely overturn, existing rules. (On this idea, see Sidgwick, *Methods of Ethics*, pp. 467–71, 473–6, 480–4; Griffin, *Well-being*, pp. 206, 302; Brandt, *Theory of the Good and the Right*, p. 290, and 'Indirect Optimific Theories', pp. 350, 356–7.) But to accept that attempts at moral reform may be most successful if they try to build on existing rules is not to accept the idea that people should be motivated to capitulate to whatever moral rules the majority accepts.

26. For the suggestion that rule-utilitarianism will, under not far-fetched conditions, describe as *duties* acts which surely are merely *supererogaory*, see Donagan, 'Is There a Credible Form of Utilitarianism?' pp. 194–6.

27. See 'Indirect Optimific Theories', pp. 346–7, 349–50; and 'Problems of Contemporary Utilitarianism', p. 98. See also J. L. Mackie's remark that in devising a moral code 'we are to take men as they are and moral laws as they might be' (*Ethics: Inventing Right and Wrong*, Harmondsworth, Penguin Books, 1977, p. 133).

28. If at all! As Brandt observes in his book, 'What these rules [of obligation] may require is limited by the strain of self-interest in everyone, and [by] the specific desires and aversions bound to develop in nearly everyone . . .' (p. 287).

29. As Brandt concedes, 'the optimific indirect theory does run into complications when we try to work out the details in any realistic way' ('Indirect Optimific Theories', p. 360).

30. Cf. J. Arthur, 'Equality, Entitlements, and the Distribution of Income', in *Applying Ethics*, ed. J. Olen and V. Barry, Belmont, CA, Wadsworth Inc., 1989, pp. 362–72.

Brandt's *Theory of the Good and the Right* contains a powerful and celebrated attack on the idea that we should judge moral theories by how much they agree with our intuitions (see op. cit., ch. I sect. 3). But see also N. Daniels, 'Can Cognitive Psychotherapy Reconcile Reason and Desire?', *Ethics*, 1983, pp. 772–85, esp. pp. 778–81. My own opinion is that, while we must heed Sidgwick's warning that 'it cannot be denied that any strong sentiment, however purely subjective, is apt to transform itself into the semblance of an intuition' (*Methods*, p. 339) considered judgements might nevertheless play a legitimate role in the testing of moral theories.

The Singer Solution to World Poverty*

Peter Singer

In the Brazilian film *Central Station*, Dora is a retired schoolteacher who makes ends meet by sitting at the station writing letters for illiterate people. Suddenly she has an opportunity to pocket $1,000. All she has to do is persuade a homeless 9-year-old boy to follow her to an address she has been given. (She is told he will be adopted by wealthy foreigners.) She delivers the boy, gets the money, spends some of it on a television set and settles down to enjoy her new acquisition. Her neighbor spoils the fun, however, by telling her that the boy was too old to be adopted—he will be killed and his organs sold for transplantation. Perhaps Dora knew this all along, but after her neighbor's plain speaking, she spends a troubled night. In the morning Dora resolves to take the boy back.

Suppose Dora had told her neighbor that it is a tough world, other people have nice new TV's too, and if selling the kid is the only way she can get one, well, he was only a street kid. She would then have become, in the eyes of the audience, a monster. She redeems herself only by being prepared to bear considerable risks to save the boy.

At the end of the movie, in cinemas in the affluent nations of the world, people who would have been quick to condemn Dora if she had not rescued the boy go home to places far more comfortable than her apartment. In fact, the average family in the United States spends almost one-third of its income on things that are no more necessary to them than Dora's new TV was to her. Going out to nice restaurants, buying new clothes because the old ones are no longer stylish, vacationing at beach resorts—so much of our income is spent on things not essential to the preservation of our lives and health. Donated to

---

*Peter Singer, "The Singer Solution to World Poverty," *The New York Times Magazine*, September 5, 1999, pp. 60–63. Reprinted by permission of the author.

one of a number of charitable agencies, that money could mean the difference between life and death for children in need.

All of which raises a question: In the end, what is the ethical distinction between a Brazilian who sells a homeless child to organ peddlers and an American who already has a TV and upgrades to a better one—knowing that the money could be donated to an organization that would use it to save the lives of kids in need?

Of course, there are several differences between the two situations that could support different moral judgments about them. For one thing, to be able to consign a child to death when he is standing right in front of you takes a chilling kind of heartlessness; it is much easier to ignore an appeal for money to help children you will never meet. Yet for a utilitarian philosopher like myself—that is, one who judges whether acts are right or wrong by their consequences—if the upshot of the American's failure to donate the money is that one more kid dies on the streets of a Brazilian city, then it is, in some sense, just as bad as selling the kid to the organ peddlers. But one doesn't need to embrace my utilitarian ethic to see that, at the very least, there is a troubling incongruity in being so quick to condemn Dora for taking the child to the organ peddlers while, at the same time, not regarding the American consumer's behavior as raising a serious moral issue.

In his 1996 book, "Living High and Letting Die," the New York University philosopher Peter Unger presented an ingenious series of imaginary examples designed to probe our intuitions about whether it is wrong to live well without giving substantial amounts of money to help people who are hungry, malnourished or dying from easily treatable illnesses like diarrhea. Here's my paraphrase of one of these examples:

Bob is close to retirement. He has invested most of his savings in a very rare and valuable old car, a Bugatti, which he has not been able to insure. The Bugatti is his pride and joy. In addition to the pleasure he gets from driving and caring for his car, Bob knows that its rising market value means that he will always be able to sell it and live comfortably after retirement. One day when Bob is out for a drive, he parks the Bugatti near the end of a railway siding and goes for a walk up the track. As he does so, he sees that a runaway train, with no one aboard, is running down the railway track. Looking farther down the track, he sees the small figure of a child very likely to be killed by the runaway train. He can't stop the train and the child is too far away to warn of the danger, but he can throw a switch that will divert the train down the siding where his Bugatti is parked. Then nobody will be killed—but the train will destroy his Bugatti. Thinking of his joy in owning the car and the financial security it represents, Bob decides not to throw the switch. The child is killed. For many years to come, Bob enjoys owning his Bugatti and the financial security it represents.

Bob's conduct, most of us will immediately respond, was gravely wrong. Unger agrees. But then he reminds us that we, too, have opportunities to save the lives of children. We can give to organizations like Unicef or Oxfam America. How much would we have to give one of these organizations to have a high probability of saving the life of a child threatened by easily preventable diseases? (I do not believe that children are more worth saving than adults, but since no one can argue that children have brought their poverty on themselves, focusing on them simplifies the issues.) Unger called up some experts and used the information they provided to offer some plausible estimates that include the cost of raising money, administrative expenses and the cost of delivering aid where it is most needed. By his calculation, $200 in donations would help a sickly 2-year-old transform into a healthy 6-year-old—offering safe passage through childhood's most dangerous years. To show how practical philosophical argument can be, Unger even tells his readers that they can easily donate funds by using their credit card and calling one of these toll-free numbers: (800) 367-5437 for Unicef; (800) 693-2687 for Oxfam America.

Now you, too, have the information you need to save a child's life. How should you judge yourself if you don't do it? Think again about Bob and his Bugatti. Unlike Dora, Bob did not have to look into the eyes of the child he was sacrificing for his own material comfort. The child was a complete stranger to him and too far away to relate to in an intimate, personal way. Unlike Dora, too, he did not mislead the child or initiate the chain of events imperiling him. In all these respects, Bob's situation resembles that of people able but unwilling to donate to overseas aid and differs from Dora's situation.

If you still think that it was very wrong of Bob not to throw the switch that would have diverted the train and saved the child's life, then it is hard to see how you could deny that it is also very wrong not to send money to one of the organizations listed above. Unless, that is, there is some morally important difference between the two situations that I have overlooked.

Is it the practical uncertainties about whether aid will really reach the people who need it? Nobody who knows the world of overseas aid can doubt that such uncertainties exist. But Unger's figure of $200 to save a child's life was reached after he had made conservative assumptions about the proportion of the money donated that will actually reach its target.

One genuine difference between Bob and those who can afford to donate to overseas aid organizations but don't is that only Bob can save the child on the tracks, whereas there are hundreds of millions of people who can give $200 to overseas aid organizations. The problem is that most of them aren't doing it. Does this mean that it is all right for you not to do it?

Suppose that there were more owners of priceless vintage cars—Carol, Dave, Emma, Fred and so on, down to Ziggy—all in exactly the same situation as Bob, with their own siding and their own switch, all sacrificing the child in order to preserve their own cherished car. Would that make it all right for Bob to do the same? To answer this question affirmatively is to endorse follow-the-crowd ethics—the kind of ethics that led many Germans to look away when the Nazi atrocities were being committed. We do not excuse them because others were behaving no better.

We seem to lack a sound basis for drawing a clear moral line between Bob's situation and that of any reader of this article with $200 to spare who does not donate it to an overseas aid agency. These readers seem to be acting at least as badly as Bob was acting when he chose to let the runaway train hurtle toward the unsuspecting child. In the light of this conclusion, I trust that many readers will reach for the phone and donate that $200. Perhaps you should do it before reading further.

Now that you have distinguished yourself morally from people who put their vintage cars ahead of a child's life, how about treating yourself and your partner to dinner at your favorite restaurant? But wait. The money you will spend at the restaurant could also help save the lives of children overseas! True, you weren't planning to blow $200 tonight, but if you were to give up dining out just for one month, you would easily save that amount. And what is one month's dining out, compared to a child's life? There's the rub. Since there are a lot of desperately needy children in the world, there will always be another child whose life you could save for another $200. Are you therefore obliged to keep giving until you have nothing left? At what point can you stop?

Hypothetical examples can easily become farcical. Consider Bob. How far past losing the Bugatti should he go? Imagine that Bob had got his foot stuck in the track of the siding, and if he diverted the train, then before it rammed the car it would also amputate his big toe. Should he still throw the switch? What if it would amputate his foot? His entire leg?

As absurd as the Bugatti scenario gets when pushed to extremes, the point it raises is a serious one: only when the sacrifices become very significant indeed would most people be prepared to say that Bob does nothing wrong when he decides not to throw the switch. Of course, most people could be wrong; we can't decide moral issues by taking opinion polls. But consider for yourself the level of sacrifice that you would demand of Bob, and then think about how much money you would have to give away in order to make a sacrifice that is roughly equal to that. It's almost certainly much, much more than $200. For most middle-class Americans, it could easily be more like $200,000.

Isn't it counterproductive to ask people to do so much? Don't we run the risk that many will shrug their shoulders and say that morality, so conceived, is fine for saints but not for them? I accept that we are unlikely to see, in the near or even medium-term future, a world in which it is normal for wealthy Americans to give the bulk of their wealth to strangers. When it comes to praising or blaming people for what they do, we tend to use a standard that is relative to some conception of normal behavior. Comfortably off Americans who give, say, 10 percent of their income to overseas aid organizations are so far ahead of most of their equally comfortable fellow citizens that I wouldn't go out of my way to chastise them for not doing more. Nevertheless, they should be doing much more, and they are in no position to criticize Bob for failing to make the much greater sacrifice of his Bugatti.

At this point various objections may crop up. Someone may say: "If every citizen living in the affluent nations contributed his or her share I wouldn't have to make such a drastic sacrifice, because long before such levels were reached, the resources would have been there to save the lives of all those children dying from lack of food or medical care. So why should I give more than my fair share?" Another, related, objection is that the Government ought to increase its overseas aid allocations, since that would spread the burden more equitably across all taxpayers.

Yet the question of how much we ought to give is a matter to be decided in the real world—and that, sadly, is a world in which we know that most people do not, and in the immediate future will not, give substantial amounts to overseas aid agencies. We know, too, that at least in the next year, the United States Government is not going to meet even the very modest United Nations–recommended target of 0.7 percent of gross national product; at the moment it lags far below that, at 0.09 percent, not even half of Japan's 0.22 percent or a tenth of Denmark's 0.97 percent. Thus, we know that the money we can give beyond that theoretical "fair share" is still going to save lives that would otherwise be lost. While the idea that no one need do more than his or her fair share is a powerful one, should it prevail if we know that others are not doing their fair share and that children will die preventable deaths unless we do more than our fair share? That would be taking fairness too far.

Thus, this ground for limiting how much we ought to give also fails. In the world as it is now, I can see no escape from the conclusion that each one of us with wealth surplus to his or her essential needs should be giving most of it to help people suffering from poverty so dire as to be life-threatening. That's right: I'm saying that you shouldn't buy that new car, take that cruise, redecorate the house or get that pricey new suit. After all, a $1,000 suit could save five children's lives.

So how does my philosophy break down in dollars and cents? An American household with an income of $50,000 spends around $30,000 annually on necessities, according to the Conference Board, a nonprofit economic research organization. Therefore, for a household bringing in $50,000 a year, donations to help the world's poor should be as close as possible to $20,000. The $30,000 required for necessities holds for higher incomes as well. So a household making $100,000 could cut a yearly check for $70,000. Again, the formula is simple: whatever money you're spending on luxuries, not necessities, should be given away.

Now, evolutionary psychologists tell us that human nature just isn't sufficiently altruistic to make it plausible that many people will sacrifice so much for strangers. On the facts of human nature, they might be right, but they would be wrong to draw a moral conclusion from those facts. If it is the case that we ought to do things that, predictably, most of us won't do, then let's face that fact head-on. Then, if we value the life of a child more than going to fancy restaurants, the next time we dine out we will know that we could have done something better with our money. If that makes living a morally decent life extremely arduous, well, then that is the way things are. If we don't do it, then we should at least know that we are failing to live a morally decent life—not because it is good to wallow in guilt but because knowing where we should be going is the first step toward heading in that direction.

When Bob first grasped the dilemma that faced him as he stood by that railway switch, he must have thought how extraordinarily unlucky he was to be placed in a situation in which he must choose between the life of an innocent child and the sacrifice of most of his savings. But he was not unlucky at all. We are all in that situation.

Study Questions

1. What is the principle of utility? Why is the "greatest happiness principle" (the title that John Stuart Mill gives this principle) an apt alternative name? Utilitarianism is sometimes confused with egoism—the view that each person should do whatever makes that person most happy. Clearly explain the difference between utilitarianism and egoism.

2. Explain the difference between act utilitarianism (direct utilitarianism), Mill's version of rule utilitarianism and Brad Hooker's rule consequentialism. Which of these versions of outcome-oriented ethical theory do you find most plausible? Explain.

3. Peter Singer is sometimes interpreted as being an act utilitarian. On the basis of your reading of his essay in this section, discuss whether or not you think this interpretation is correct.

4. Briefly retell Bernard Williams's story about Jim and the Indians in your own words. What do you think Jim is ethically required to do in this case? Justify your answer. What does your answer show about your stance toward various forms of utilitarianism?

5. Explain in your own words why Williams thinks that utilitarianism is incompatible with personal integrity. Do you think that Brad Hooker's rule consequentialism leaves room for preserving personal integrity? Discuss.

6. When is self-sacrifice required, according to various forms of utilitarianism? What would be the utilitarian evaluation of Mother Teresa? Should a person who prefers watching TV in their spare time to working in a soup kitchen or reading to the blind spend any time doing volunteer work? Explain how Mill, Hooker and Singer would each answer this question.

For Further Reading

Bentham, Jeremy. *An Introduction to the Principles of Morals and Legislation*. Garden City, NY: Doubleday, 1961.

Gorovitz, Samuel, ed. *Utilitarianism: Text with Critical Essays*. Indianapolis: Bobbs-Merrill, 1971.

Hare, R. M. *Moral Thinking: Its Levels, Method, and Point*. Oxford: Oxford University Press, 1981.

Lyons, David. *Forms and Limits of Utilitarianism*. Oxford: Clarendon Press, 1965.

Scheffler, Samuel. *Consequentialism and Its Critics*. Oxford: Oxford University Press, 1988.

Sen, Amartya, and Bernard Williams, eds. *Utilitarianism and Beyond*. Cambridge: Cambridge University Press, 1982.

Sidgwick, Henry. *The Methods of Ethics*. 7th ed. London: Macmillan, 1907.

Singer, Peter. *Practical Ethics*. 2nd ed. Cambridge: Cambridge University Press, 1993.

Smart, J. J. C. "Extreme and Restricted Utilitarianism." *The Philosophical Quarterly* 6 (1956): 344–54.

Unger, Peter. *Living High and Letting Die: Our Illusion of Ignorance*. New York: Oxford University Press, 1996.

CHAPTER SIX

Ethics of Duty

Duty-oriented ethical views focus on evaluations of actions based on obligations a person has to act in certain ways or to refrain from acting in other ways. Intuitively, we think that some roles carry particular duties. A parent, for example, has obligations of support and nurture to his or her children. A parent who has food but who withholds the food from his or her child is falling short of a particular duty of parenthood. We also have ways of binding ourselves to particular future obligations. For example, in general, I do not have an obligation to give money to any particular charity, but if I promise to contribute $100 to Habitat for Humanity, then by promising I have created a duty to contribute.

There seem to be certain important duties that we have to all people, no matter what our other relationships are to them. Duties of this kind that are relatively uncontroversial are duties not to wantonly kill or harm others. Many people also think that we have duties to help those who are in desperate need, especially if we can do so with little cost to ourselves. Calling 911 when we see someone being attacked outside our window would be an example of such a duty of beneficence.

The eighteenth-century philosopher Immanuel Kant has had enormous influence on the ethics of duty. Kant is at once one of the most important and one of the most difficult philosophers of all time. His mature work as a philosopher is aimed at preserving the autonomy and validity of morality in light of the growing (and deserved) authority of Newtonian science. Kant saw human beings as having two very different aspects. Human beings, like all physical beings, are subject to the laws of physics—laws that Kant thought were deterministic. These laws determine our actions to the extent that they are explicable by such sciences as biology and psychology. But human beings are also free; we have the ability, given by reason, to be self-governing. We can choose our own ends and goals, and can conclude that even though our biology or psychology is pulling in one direction that our dignity as human beings necessitates acting otherwise. Yet Kant thought that even in freedom, humans are subject to law—the law that Kant called the "categorical imperative": "Act always in such a way that you could will the maxim of your action to be a universal law." When Kant talks about the respect for law that must always be the incentive of ethical action, he means this moral law, not the particular legal codes that happen to be in force in any given time and place.

The focus of Kant's approach is on the claim that human nature, as such, demands ethical respect. Respect for humanity sets limits on what we can do—even in cases where acting in a particular way would bring about many good things. Another memorable version of Kant's categorical imperative is "Always act in accord with maxims (policies of actions) that treat humanity, whether in yourself or another, as an end in itself and never as a mere means." When I threaten someone with bodily harm in order to get him to give me his money, I am using him as a means to becoming richer. I ignore that he may be prevented from pursuing projects that he values because I have taken money he may need. I treat him and his projects as if they have no value. Notice in the selection from Kant's *Fundamental Principles of the Metaphysic of Morals* that he claims that two basic kinds of duties follow from the categorical imperative—negative duties (for example, duties *not* to deceive, assault or mock people) and positive duties (for example, duties to help others, especially if they are in great need). Notice also that we have duties to ourselves (to cultivate our talents and character) and duties to others (to promote their happiness).

Contemporary Kantian Marcia W. Baron clarifies Kant's ethical views and attempts to show how they contrast favorably with consequentialist views (for a discussion of consequentialism, see chapter 5 on utilitarianism). She underscores and explains Kant's claim that we have a duty to make others happy but not to make them ethical. While we have a strict duty to develop ourselves morally, we should not engage in paternalism (that is the project of presuming to know more about what another person's ends should be than the person himself or herself). Anti-paternalism is an important aspect of respecting people's autonomy.

Baron thinks that contrasting views on *maximization* are among the most important differences between Kantians and consequentialists, such as utilitarians. For Kantians, our duty to make others happy is an *imperfect* or *open-ended* duty. As long as I am not indifferent to the happiness of others, I am free to pick and choose (within limits) whom to help and whose happiness matters most to me. I have no duty to choose actions that will cause the most happiness for the most people. Moreover, the cultivation of my own talents and the pursuit of my own ends (even when those ends do not maximize overall happiness) are duties to myself that are as weighty as my imperfect duties to others. Our *perfect* or *strict* duties are almost all duties to *refrain* from damaging actions. As long as I care about being an ethical person, am not actively harming others and am respecting their autonomy, I have enormous latitude in living my life in pursuit of my own freely chosen ends.

Kantianism is not the only form of the ethics of duty. W. D. Ross, who was an early twentieth-century British philosopher, developed a view (often called ethical intuitionism) that he contrasted both with Kantianism and utilitarianism. Unlike Kant, Ross maintained that there are no strict or perfect or exceptionless duties. Unlike utilitarians, Ross thought we should often act in ways that do not maximize the happiness of everyone affected. In order to determine what ethics requires of us we must weigh all of the morally relevant characteristics of our actions—which may point toward a variety of divergent courses of action. Ross calls these morally relevant characteristics *prima facie duties*. His list of examples of such duties includes duties of fidelity, reparations, gratitude, justice, beneficence and self-improvement, as well as the duty to refrain from harm. In any given situation, we must ascertain what *prima facie* duties we have and "weigh" them to see which is strongest in order to determine what our ethical duty *sans phrase* (our duty without qualification or our duty all things considered) is.

Judith Jarvis Thomson was a twentieth-century American philosopher who became justly famous for her ability to invent thought-provoking examples that raise ethical puzzles or illumine subtle ethical distinctions. Her essay in this section presents numerous scenarios to test our intuitions about whether and when there is an ethically important distinction between killing a person and letting a person die. She uses highly imaginative examples to undercut a claim that is often made within the ethics of duty—that negative duties not to harm are more stringent than positive duties to help. As you ponder her examples, ask yourself what Kant and Baron and Ross would be likely to conclude in each case. Most importantly, ask yourself what you think ethics requires.

*Fundamental Principles of the Metaphysic of Morals**

Immanuel Kant

First Section: Transition from the Common Rational Knowledge of Morality to the Philosophical

Nothing can possibly be conceived in the world, or even out of it, which can be called good, without qualification, except a Good Will. Intelligence, wit, judgement, and the other *talents* of the mind, however they may be named, or courage, resolution, perseverance, as qualities of temperament, are undoubtedly good and desirable in many respects; but these gifts of nature may also become extremely bad and mischievous if the will which is to make use of them, and which, therefore, constitutes what is called *character*, is not good. It is the same with the *gifts of fortune*. Power, riches, honour, even health, and the general well-being and contentment with one's condition which is called *happiness*, inspire pride, and often presumption, if there is not a good will to correct the influence of these on the mind, and with this also to rectify the whole principle of acting and adapt it to its end. The sight of a being who is not adorned with a single feature of a pure and good will, enjoying unbroken prosperity, can never give pleasure to an impartial rational spectator. Thus a good will appears to constitute the indispensable condition even of being worthy of happiness. There are even some qualities which are of service to this good will itself and may facilitate its action, yet which have no intrinsic unconditional value, but always presuppose a good will, and this qualifies the esteem that we justly have for them and does not permit us to regard them as absolutely good. Moderation in the affections and passions, self-control, and calm deliberation are not only good in many respects, but even seem to constitute part of the intrinsic worth of the person; but they are far from deserving to be called good without qualification, although they have been so unconditionally praised by the ancients. For without the principles of a good will, they may become extremely bad, and the coolness of a villain not only makes him far more dangerous, but also directly makes him more abominable in our eyes than he would have been without it. A good will is good not because of what it performs or effects, not by its aptness for the attainment of some proposed end, but simply by virtue of the volition; that is, it is good in itself, and considered by itself is to be esteemed much higher than all

---

*From Immanuel Kant, *The Metaphysics of Morals*, Part II. Translated by T. K. Abbott in *Kant's Critique of Practical Reason and Other Works on The Theory of Ethics* (London: Longmans, Green and Co., 1873).

that can be brought about by it in favour of any inclination, nay even of the sum total of all inclinations. Even if it should happen that, owing to special disfavour of fortune, or the niggardly provision of a step-motherly nature, this will should wholly lack power to accomplish its purpose, if with its greatest efforts it should yet achieve nothing, and there should remain only the good will (not, to be sure, a mere wish, but the summoning of all means in our power), then, like a jewel, it would still shine by its own light, as a thing which has its whole value in itself. Its usefulness or fruitfulness can neither add nor take away anything from this value. It would be, as it were, only the setting to enable us to handle it the more conveniently in common commerce, or to attract to it the attention of those who are not yet connoisseurs, but not to recommend it to true connoisseurs, or to determine its value. There is, however, something so strange in this idea of the absolute value of the mere will, in which no account is taken of its utility, that notwithstanding the thorough assent of even common reason to the idea, yet a suspicion must arise that it may perhaps really be the product of mere high-flown fancy, and that we may have misunderstood the purpose of nature in assigning reason as the governor of our will. Therefore we will examine this idea from this point of view. In the physical constitution of an organized being, that is, a being adapted suitably to the purposes of life, we assume it as a fundamental principle that no organ for any purpose will be found but what is also the fittest and best adapted for that purpose. Now in a being which has reason and a will, if the proper object of nature were its *conservation*, its *welfare*, in a word, its *happiness*, then nature would have hit upon a very bad arrangement in selecting the reason of the creature to carry out this purpose. For all the actions which the creature has to perform with a view to this purpose, and the whole rule of its conduct, would be far more surely prescribed to it by instinct, and that end would have been attained thereby much more certainly than it ever can be by reason. Should reason have been communicated to this favoured creature over and above, it must only have served it to contemplate the happy constitution of its nature, to admire it, to congratulate itself thereon, and to feel thankful for it to the beneficent cause, but not that it should subject its desires to that weak and delusive guidance and meddle bunglingly with the purpose of nature. In a word, nature would have taken care that reason should not break forth into *practical exercise*, nor have the presumption, with its weak insight, to think out for itself the plan of happiness, and of the means of attaining it. Nature would not only have taken on herself the choice of the ends, but also of the means, and with wise foresight would have entrusted both to instinct. And, in fact, we find that the more a cultivated reason applies itself with deliberate purpose to the enjoyment of life and happiness, so much the more does the man fail of true satisfaction. And from this circumstance there arises in many, if they are candid enough to confess it, a certain degree of *misology*, that is, hatred of reason, especially in the case of those who are most experienced in the use of it, because after calculating all the advantages they derive, I do not say from the invention of all the arts of common luxury, but even from the sciences (which seem to them to be after all only a luxury of the understanding), they find that they have, in fact, only brought more trouble on their shoulders, rather than gained in happiness; and they end by envying, rather than despising, the more common stamp of men who keep closer to the guidance of mere instinct and do not allow their reason much influence on their conduct. And this we must admit, that the judgement of those who would very much lower the lofty eulogies of the advantages which reason gives us in regard to the happiness and satisfaction of life, or who would even reduce them below zero, is by no means morose or ungrateful to the goodness with which the world is governed, but that there lies at the root of these judgements the idea that our existence has a different and far nobler end, for which, and not for happiness, reason is properly intended, and which must, therefore, be regarded as the supreme condition to which the private ends of man must, for the most part, be postponed. For as reason is not competent to guide the will with certainty in regard to its objects and the satisfaction of all our wants (which it to some extent even multiplies), this being an end to which an implanted instinct would have led with much greater certainty; and since, nevertheless, reason is imparted to us as a practical faculty, i.e., as one which is to have influence on the *will*, therefore, admitting that nature generally in the distribution of her capacities has adapted the means to the end, its true destination must be to produce a *will*, not merely good as a *means* to something else, but *good in itself*, for which reason was absolutely necessary. This will then, though not indeed the sole and complete good, must be the supreme good and the condition of every other, even of the desire of happiness. Under these circumstances, there is nothing inconsistent with the wisdom of nature in the fact that the cultivation of the reason, which is requisite for the first and unconditional purpose, does in many ways interfere, at least in this life, with the attainment of the second, which is always conditional, namely, happiness. Nay, it may even reduce it to nothing, without nature thereby failing of her purpose. For reason recognizes the establishment of a good will as its highest practical destination, and in attaining this purpose is capable only of a satisfaction of its own proper kind, namely that from the attainment of an end, which end again is determined by reason only, notwithstanding that this may involve many a disappointment to the ends of inclination. We have then to develop the notion of a will which deserves to be highly esteemed for itself and is good without a view to anything further, a notion which exists already in the sound natural understanding, requiring rather to be cleared up than to be taught, and which in estimating the value of our actions always takes the first place and constitutes the condition of all the rest. In order to do this, we will take the notion of duty, which includes that of a good will, although implying certain subjective restrictions and hindrances. These, however, far from concealing it, or rendering it unrecognizable, rather bring it out by contrast and make it shine forth so much the brighter. I omit here all actions which are already recognized as inconsistent with duty, although they may be useful for this or that purpose, for with these the question whether they are done *from duty* cannot arise at all, since they even conflict with it. I also set aside those actions which really conform to duty, but to which men have *no* direct *inclination*, performing them because they are impelled thereto by some other inclination. For in this case we can readily distinguish whether the action which agrees with duty is done *from duty*, or from a selfish view. It is much harder to make this distinction when the action accords with duty and the subject has besides a *direct* inclination to it. For example, it is always a matter of duty that a dealer should not overcharge an inexperienced purchaser; and wherever there is much commerce the prudent tradesman does not overcharge, but keeps a fixed price for everyone, so that a child buys of him as well as any other. Men are thus *honestly* served; but this is not enough to make us believe that the tradesman has so acted from duty and from principles of honesty: his own advantage required it; it is out of the question in this case to suppose that he might besides have a direct inclination in favour of the buyers, so that, as it were, from love he should give no advantage to one over another. Accordingly the action was done neither from duty nor from direct inclination, but merely with a selfish view. On the other hand, it is a duty to maintain one's life; and, in addition, everyone has also a direct inclination to do so. But on this account the anxious care which most men take for it has no intrinsic worth, and their maxim has no moral import. They preserve their life *as duty requires*, no doubt, but not *because duty requires*. On the other hand, if adversity and hopeless sorrow have completely taken away the relish for life; if the unfortunate one, strong in mind, indignant at his fate rather than desponding or dejected, wishes for death, and yet preserves his life without loving it—not from inclination or fear, but from duty—then his maxim has a moral worth. To be beneficent when we can is a duty; and besides this, there are many minds so sympathetically constituted that, without any other motive of vanity or self-interest, they find a pleasure in spreading joy around them and can take delight in the satisfaction of others so far as it is their own work. But I maintain that in such a case an action of this kind, however proper, however amiable it may be, has nevertheless no true moral worth, but is on a level with other inclinations, *e.g.*, the inclination to honour, which, if it is happily directed to that which is in fact of public utility and accordant with duty and consequently honourable, deserves praise and encouragement, but not esteem. For the maxim lacks the moral import, namely, that such actions be done *from duty*, not from inclination. Put the case that the mind of that philanthropist were clouded by sorrow of his own, extinguishing all sympathy with the lot of others, and that, while he still has the power to benefit others in distress, he is not touched by their trouble because he is absorbed with his own; and now suppose that he tears himself out of this dead insensibility, and performs the action without any inclination to it, but simply from duty, then first has his action its genuine moral worth. Further still; if nature has put little sympathy in the heart of this or that man; if he, supposed to be an upright man, is by temperament cold and indifferent to the sufferings of others, perhaps because in respect of his own he is provided with the special gift of patience and fortitude and supposes, or even requires, that others should have the same—and such a man would certainly not be the meanest product of nature—but if nature had not specially framed him for a philanthropist, would he not still find in himself a source from whence to give himself a far higher worth than that of a good-natured temperament could be? Unquestionably. It is just in this that the moral worth of the character is brought out which is incomparably the highest of all, namely, that he is beneficent, not from inclination, but from duty. To secure one's own happiness is a duty, at least indirectly; for discontent with one's condition, under a pressure of many anxieties and amidst unsatisfied wants, might easily become a great *temptation to transgression of duty*. But here again, without looking to duty, all men have already the strongest and most intimate inclination to happiness, because it is just in this idea that all inclinations are combined in one total. But the precept of happiness is often of such a sort that it greatly interferes with some inclinations, and yet a man cannot form any definite and certain conception of the sum of satisfaction of all of them which is called happiness. It is not then to be wondered at that a single inclination, definite both as to what it promises and as to the time within which it can be gratified, is often able to overcome such a fluctuating idea, and that a gouty patient, for instance, can choose to enjoy what he likes, and to suffer what he may, since, according to his calculation, on this occasion at least, he has not sacrificed the enjoyment of the present moment to a possibly mistaken expectation of a happiness which is supposed to be found in health. But even in this case, if the general desire for happiness did not influence his will, and supposing that in his particular case health was not a necessary element in this calculation, there yet remains in this, as in all other cases, this law, namely, that he should promote his happiness not from inclination but from duty, and by this would his conduct first acquire true moral worth. It is in this manner, undoubtedly, that we are to understand those passages of Scripture also in which we are commanded to love our neighbour, even our enemy. For love, as an affection, cannot be commanded, but beneficence for duty's sake may; even though we are not impelled to it by any inclination—nay, are even repelled by a natural and unconquerable aversion. This is *practical* love and not *pathological*—a love which is seated in the will, and not in the propensions of sense—in principles of action and not of tender sympathy; and it is this love alone which can be commanded. The second proposition is: That an action done from duty derives its moral worth, *not from the purpose* which is to be attained by it, but from the maxim by which it is determined, and therefore does not depend on the realization of the object of the action, but merely on the *principle of volition* by which the action has taken place, without regard to any object of desire. It is clear from what precedes that the purposes which we may have in view in our actions, or their effects regarded as ends and springs of the will, cannot give to actions any unconditional or moral worth. In what, then, can their worth lie, if it is not to consist in the will and in reference to its expected effect? It cannot lie anywhere but in the *principle of the will* without regard to the ends which can be attained by the action. For the will stands between its *a priori* principle, which is formal, and its *a posteriori* spring, which is material, as between two roads, and as it must be determined by something, it follows that it must be determined by the formal principle of volition when an action is done from duty, in which case every material principle has been withdrawn from it. The third proposition, which is a consequence of the two preceding, I would express thus: *Duty is the necessity of acting from respect for the law*. I may have *inclination* for an object as the effect of my proposed action, but I cannot have *respect* for it, just for this reason, that it is an effect and not an energy of will. Similarly I cannot have respect for inclination, whether my own or another's; I can at most, if my own, approve it; if another's, sometimes even love it; *i.e.*, look on it as favourable to my own interest. It is only what is connected with my will as a principle, by no means as an effect—what does not subserve my inclination, but overpowers it, or at least in case of choice excludes it from its calculation—in other words, simply the law of itself, which can be an object of respect, and hence a command. Now an action done from duty must wholly exclude the influence of inclination and with it every object of the will, so that nothing remains which can determine the will except objectively the *law*, and subjectively *pure respect* for this practical law, and consequently the maxim[1] that I should follow this law even to the thwarting of all my inclinations. Thus the moral worth of an action does not lie in the effect expected from it, nor in any principle of action which requires to borrow its motive from this expected effect. For all these effects—agreeableness of one's condition and even the promotion of the happiness of others—could have been also brought about by other causes, so that for this there would have been no need of the will of a rational being; whereas it is in this alone that the supreme and unconditional good can be found. The pre-eminent good which we call moral can therefore consist in nothing else than *the conception of law* in itself, *which certainly is only possible in a rational being*, in so far as this conception, and not the expected effect, determines the will. This is a good which is already present in the person who acts accordingly, and we have not to wait for it to appear first in the result.[2] But what sort of law can that be, the conception of which must determine the will, even without paying any regard to the effect expected from it, in order that this will may be called good absolutely and without qualification? As I have deprived the will of every impulse which could arise to it from obedience to any law, there remains nothing but the universal conformity of its actions to law in general, which alone is to serve the will as a principle, *i.e.*, I am never to act otherwise than so *that I could also will that my maxim should become a universal law*. Here, now, it is the simple conformity to law in general, without assuming any particular law applicable to certain actions, that serves the will as its principle and must so serve it, if duty is not to be a vain delusion and a chimerical notion. The common reason of men in its practical judgements perfectly coincides with this and always has in view the principle here suggested. Let the question be, for example: May I when in distress make a promise with the intention not to keep it? I readily distinguish here between the two significations which the question may have: Whether it is prudent, or whether it is right, to make a false promise? The former may undoubtedly often be the case. I see clearly indeed that it is not enough to extricate myself from a present difficulty by means of this subterfuge, but it must be well considered whether there may not hereafter spring from this lie much greater inconvenience than that from which I now free myself, and as, with all my supposed cunning, the consequences cannot be so easily foreseen but that credit once lost may be much more injurious to me than any mischief which I seek to avoid at present, it should be considered whether it would not be more *prudent* to act herein according to a universal maxim and to make it a habit to promise nothing except with the intention of keeping it. But it is soon clear to me that such a maxim will still only be based on the fear of consequences. Now it is a wholly different thing to be truthful from duty and to be so from apprehension of injurious consequences. In the first case, the very notion of the action already implies a law for me; in the second case, I must first look about elsewhere to see what results may be combined with it which would affect myself. For to deviate from the principle of duty is beyond all doubt wicked; but to be unfaithful to my maxim of prudence may often be very advantageous to me, although to abide by it is certainly safer. The shortest way, however, and an unerring one, to discover the answer to this question whether a lying promise is consistent with duty, is to ask myself, "Should I be content that my maxim (to extricate myself from difficulty by a false promise) should hold good as a universal law, for myself as well as for others? And should I be able to say to myself, "Every one may make a deceitful promise when he finds himself in a difficulty from which he cannot otherwise extricate himself?" Then I presently become aware that while I can will the lie, I can by no means will that lying should be a universal law. For with such a law there would be no promises at all, since it would be in vain to allege my intention in regard to my future actions to those who would not believe this allegation, or if they over hastily did so would pay me back in my own coin. Hence my maxim, as soon as it should be made a universal law, would necessarily destroy itself . . .

Second Section: Transition from Popular Moral Philosophy to the Metaphysic of Morals

. . . Everything in nature works according to laws. Rational beings alone have the faculty of acting according *to the conception* of laws, that is according to principles, *i.e.*, have a *will*. Since the deduction of actions from principles requires *reason*, the will is nothing but practical reason. If reason infallibly determines the will, then the actions of such a being which are recognised as objectively necessary are subjectively necessary also, i.e., the will is a faculty to choose *that only* which reason independent of inclination recognises as practically necessary, *i.e.*, as good. But if reason of itself does not sufficiently determine the will, if the latter is subject also to subjective conditions (particular impulses) which do not always coincide with the objective conditions; in a word, if the will does not *in itself* completely accord with reason (which is actually the case with men), then the actions which objectively are recognised as necessary are subjectively contingent, and the determination of such a will according to objective laws is *obligation*, that is to say, the relation of the objective laws to a will that is not thoroughly good is conceived as the determination of the will of a rational being by principles of reason, but which the will from its nature does not of necessity follow. The conception of an objective principle, in so far as it is obligatory for a will, is called a command (of reason), and the formula of the command is called an imperative. All imperatives are expressed by the word *ought* [or *shall*], and thereby indicate the relation of an objective law of reason to a will, which from its subjective constitution is not necessarily determined by it (an obligation). They say that something would be good to do or to forbear, but they say it to a will which does not always do a thing because it is conceived to be good to do it. That is practically *good*, however, which determines the will by means of the conceptions of reason, and consequently not from subjective causes, but objectively, that is on principles which are valid for every rational being as such. It is distinguished from the *pleasant*, as that which influences the will only by means of sensation from merely subjective causes, valid only for the sense of this or that one, and not as a principle of reason, which holds for every one.[3] A perfectly good will would therefore be equally subject to objective laws (viz., laws of good), but could not be conceived as *obliged* thereby to act lawfully, because of itself from its subjective constitution it can only be determined by the conception of good. Therefore no imperatives hold for the Divine will, or in general for a *holy* will; *ought* is here out of place, because the volition is already of itself necessarily in unison with the law. Therefore imperatives are only formulae to express the relation of objective laws of all volition to the subjective imperfection of the will of this or that rational being, *e.g.*, the human will. Now all *imperatives* command either *hypothetically* or *categorically*. The former represent the practical necessity of a possible action as means to something else that is willed (or at least which one might possibly will). The categorical imperative would be that which represented an action as necessary of itself without reference to another end, *i.e.*, as objectively necessary. Since every practical law represents a possible action as good and, on this account, for a subject who is practically determinable by reason, necessary, all imperatives are formulae determining an action which is necessary according to the principle of a will good in some respects. If now the action is good only as a means to something else, then the imperative is *hypothetical*; if it is conceived as good *in itself* and consequently as being necessarily the principle of a will which of itself conforms to reason, then it is *categorical*. . . . When I conceive a hypothetical imperative, in general I do not know beforehand what it will contain until I am given the condition. But when I conceive a categorical imperative, I know at once what it contains. For as the imperative contains besides the law only the necessity that the maxims[4] shall conform to this law, while the law contains no conditions restricting it, there remains nothing but the general statement that the maxim of the action should conform to a universal law, and it is this conformity alone that the imperative properly represents as necessary. There is therefore but one categorical imperative, namely, this: *Act only on that maxim whereby thou canst at the same time will that it should become a universal law*. Now if all imperatives of duty can be deduced from this one imperative as from their principle, then, although it should remain undecided what is called duty is not merely a vain notion, yet at least we shall be able to show what we understand by it and what this notion means. Since the universality of the law according to which effects are produced constitutes what is properly called nature in the most general sense (as to form), that is the existence of things so far as it is determined by general laws, the imperative of duty may be expressed thus: *Act as if the maxim of thy action were to become by thy will a universal law of nature*. We will now enumerate a few duties, adopting the usual division of them into duties to ourselves and ourselves and to others, and into perfect and imperfect duties. 1. A man reduced to despair by a series of misfortunes feels wearied of life, but is still so far in possession of his reason that he can ask himself whether it would not be contrary to his duty to himself to take his own life. Now he inquires whether the maxim of his action could become a universal law of nature. His maxim is: "From self-love I adopt it as a principle to shorten my life when its longer duration is likely to bring more evil than satisfaction." It is asked then simply whether this principle founded on self-love can become a universal law of nature. Now we see at once that a system of nature of which it should be a law to destroy life by means of the very feeling whose special nature it is to impel to the improvement of life would contradict itself and, therefore, could not exist as a system of nature; hence that maxim cannot possibly exist as a universal law of nature and, consequently, would be wholly inconsistent with the supreme principle of all duty. 2. Another finds himself forced by necessity to borrow money. He knows that he will not be able to repay it, but sees also that nothing will be lent to him unless he promises stoutly to repay it in a definite time. He desires to make this promise, but he has still so much conscience as to ask himself: "Is it not unlawful and inconsistent with duty to get out of a difficulty in this way?" Suppose however that he resolves to do so: then the maxim of his action would be expressed thus: "When I think myself in want of money, I will borrow money and promise to repay it, although I know that I never can do so." Now this principle of self-love or of one's own advantage may perhaps be consistent with my whole future welfare; but the question now is, "Is it right?" I change then the suggestion of self-love into a universal law, and state the question thus: "How would it be if my maxim were a universal law?" Then I see at once that it could never hold as a universal law of nature, but would necessarily contradict itself. For supposing it to be a universal law that everyone when he thinks himself in a difficulty should be able to promise whatever he pleases, with the purpose of not keeping his promise, the promise itself would become impossible, as well as the end that one might have in view in it, since no one would consider that anything was promised to him, but would ridicule all such statements as vain pretences. 3. A third finds in himself a talent which with the help of some culture might make him a useful man in many respects. But he finds himself in comfortable circumstances and prefers to indulge in pleasure rather than to take pains in enlarging and improving his happy natural capacities. He asks, however, whether his maxim of neglect of his natural gifts, besides agreeing with his inclination to indulgence, agrees also with what is called duty. He sees then that a system of nature could indeed subsist with such a universal law although men (like the South Sea islanders) should let their talents rest and resolve to devote their lives merely to idleness, amusement, and propagation of their species—in a word, to enjoyment; but he cannot possibly will that this should be a universal law of nature, or be implanted in us as such by a natural instinct. For, as a rational being, he necessarily wills that his faculties be developed, since they serve him and have been given him, for all sorts of possible purposes. 4. A fourth, who is in prosperity, while he sees that others have to contend with great wretchedness and that he could help them, thinks: "What concern is it of mine? Let everyone be as happy as Heaven pleases, or as he can make himself; I will take nothing from him nor even envy him, only I do not wish to contribute anything to his welfare or to his assistance in distress!"

Now no doubt if such a mode of thinking were a universal law, the human race might very well subsist and doubtless even better than in a state in which everyone talks of sympathy and good-will, or even takes care occasionally to put it into practice, but, on the other side, also cheats when he can, betrays the rights of men, or otherwise violates them. But although it is possible that a universal law of nature might exist in accordance with that maxim, it is impossible to will that such a principle should have the universal validity of a law of nature. For a will which resolved this would contradict itself, inasmuch as many cases might occur in which one would have need of the love and sympathy of others, and in which, by such a law of nature, sprung from his own will, he would deprive himself of all hope of the aid he desires.

. . . The will is conceived as a faculty of determining oneself to action *in accordance with the conception of certain laws*. And such a faculty can be found only in rational beings. Now that which serves the will as the objective ground of its self-determination is the *end*, and, if this is assigned by reason alone, it must hold for all rational beings. On the other hand, that which merely contains the ground of possibility of the action of which the effect is the end, this is called the *means* . . . The ends which a rational being proposes to himself at pleasure as effects of his actions (material ends) are all only relative, for it is only their relation to the particular desires of the subject that gives them their worth, which therefore cannot furnish principles universal and necessary for all rational beings and for every volition, that is to say practical laws. Hence all these relative ends can give rise only to hypothetical imperatives. Supposing, however, that there were something *whose existence* has *in itself* an absolute worth, something which, being *an end in itself*, could be a source of definite laws; then in this and this alone would lie the source of a possible categorical imperative, *i.e.*, a practical law. Now I say: man and generally any rational being *exists* as an end in himself, *not merely as a means* to be arbitrarily used by this or that will, but in all his actions, whether they concern himself or other rational beings, must be always regarded at the same time as an end. All objects of the inclinations have only a conditional worth, for if the inclinations and the wants founded on them did not exist, then their object would be without value. But the inclinations, themselves being sources of want, are so far from having an absolute worth for which they should be desired that on the contrary it must be the universal wish of every rational being to be wholly free from them. Thus the worth of any object which is *to be acquired* by our action is always conditional. Beings whose existence depends not on our will but on nature's, have nevertheless, if they are irrational beings, only a relative value as means, and are therefore called *things*; rational beings, on the contrary, are called *persons*, because their very nature points them out as ends in themselves, that is as something which must not be used merely as means, and so far therefore restricts freedom of action (and is an object of respect). These, therefore, are not merely subjective ends whose existence has a worth *for us* as an effect of our action, but *objective ends*, that is, things whose existence is an end in itself; an end moreover for which no other can be substituted, which they should subserve *merely* as means, for otherwise nothing whatever would possess *absolute worth*; but if all worth were conditioned and therefore contingent, then there would be no supreme practical principle of reason whatever. If then there is a supreme practical principle or, in respect of the human will, a categorical imperative, it must be one which, being drawn from the conception of that which is necessarily an end for everyone because it is *an end in itself*, constitutes an *objective* principle of will, and can therefore serve as a universal practical law. The foundation of this principle is: *rational nature exists as an end in itself*. Man necessarily conceives his own existence as being so; so far then this is a subjective principle of human actions. But every other rational being regards its existence similarly, just on the same rational principle that holds for me: so that it is at the same time an objective principle, from which as a supreme practical law all laws of the will must be capable of being deduced. Accordingly the practical imperative will be as follows: *So act as to treat humanity, whether in thine own person or in that of any other, in every case as an end withal, never as means only*.

. . . Looking back now on all previous attempts to discover the principle of morality, we need not wonder why they all failed. It was seen that man was bound to laws by duty, but it was not observed that the laws to which he is subject are *only those of his own giving*, though at the same time they are *universal*, and that he is only bound to act in conformity with his own will; a will, however, which is designed by nature to give universal laws. For when one has conceived man only as subject to a law (no matter what), then this law required some interest, either by way of attraction or constraint, since it did not originate as a law from *his own* will, but this will was according to a law obliged by *something else* to act in a certain manner. Now by this necessary consequence all the labour spent in finding a supreme principle of *duty* was irrevocably lost. For men never elicited duty, but only a necessity of acting from a certain interest. Whether this interest was private or otherwise, in any case the imperative must be conditional and could not by any means be capable of being a moral command. I will therefore call this the principle of *Autonomy* of the will, in contrast with every other which I accordingly reckon as *Heteronomy*. The conception of the will of every rational being as one which must consider itself as giving in all the maxims of its will universal laws, so as to judge itself and its actions from this point of view—this conception leads to another which depends on it and is very fruitful, namely that of *a kingdom of ends*. By a *kingdom* I understand the union of different rational beings in a system by common laws. Now since it is by laws that ends are determined as regards their universal validity, hence, if we abstract from the personal differences of rational beings and likewise from all the content of their private ends, we shall be able to conceive all ends combined in a systematic whole (including both rational beings as ends in themselves, and also the special ends which each may propose to himself), that is to say, we can conceive a kingdom of ends, which on the preceding principles is possible. For all rational beings come under the *law* that each of them must treat itself and all others *never merely as means*, but in every case *at the same time as ends in themselves*. Hence results a systematic union of rational being by common objective laws, *i.e.*, a kingdom which may be called a kingdom of ends, since what these laws have in view is just the relation of these beings to one another as ends and means. It is certainly only an ideal.

Notes

1. A maxim is the subjective principle of volition. The objective principle (i.e., that which would also serve subjectively as a practical principle to all rational beings if reason had full power over the faculty of desire) is the practical law.

2. It might be here objected to me that I take refuge behind the word respect in an obscure feeling, instead of giving a distinct solution of the question by a concept of the reason. But although respect is a feeling, it is not a feeling received through influence, but is self-wrought by a rational concept, and, therefore, is specifically distinct from all feelings of the former kind, which may be referred either to inclination or fear. What I recognise immediately as a law for me, I recognise with respect. This merely signifies the consciousness that my will is subordinate to a law, without the intervention of other influences on my sense. The immediate determination of the will by the law, and the consciousness of this, is called respect, so that this is regarded as an effect of the law on the subject, and not as the cause of it. Respect is properly the conception of a worth which thwarts my self-love. Accordingly it is something which is considered neither as an object of inclination nor of fear, although it has something analogous to both. The object of respect is the law only, and that the law which we impose on ourselves and yet recognise as necessary in itself. As a law, we are subjected to it without consulting self-love; as imposed by us on ourselves, it is a result of our will. In the former aspect it has an analogy to fear, in the latter to inclination. Respect for a person is properly only respect for the law (of honesty, etc.) of which he gives us an example. Since we also look on the improvement of our talents as a duty, we consider that we see in a person of talents, as it were, the example of a law (viz., to become like him in this by exercise), and this constitutes our respect. All so-called moral interest consists simply in respect for the law.

3. The dependence of the desires on sensations is called inclination, and this accordingly always indicates a want. The dependence of a contingently determinable will on principles of reason is called an interest. This therefore, is found only in the case of a dependent will which does not always of itself conform to reason; in the Divine will we cannot conceive any interest. But the human will can also take an interest in a thing without therefore acting from interest. The former signifies the practical interest in the

action, the latter the pathological in the object of the action. The former indicates only dependence of the will on principles of reason in themselves; the second, dependence on principles of reason for the sake of inclination, reason supplying only the practical rules how the requirement of the inclination may be satisfied. In the first case the action interests me; in the second the object of the action (because it is pleasant to me). We have seen in the first section that in an action done from duty we must look not to the interest in the object, but only to that in the action itself, and in its rational principle (viz., the law).

4. A MAXIM is a subjective principle of action, and must be distinguished from the objective principle, namely, practical law. The former contains the practical rule set by reason according to the conditions of the subject (often its ignorance or its inclinations), so that it is the principle on which the subject acts; but the law is the objective principle valid for every rational being, and is the principle on which it ought to act that is an imperative.

Kantian Ethics*

Marcia Baron

Within Kantian ethics, the reason why certain principles are to be adhered to is, in a word, humanity. We are to respect humanity as an end in itself. In a famous passage Kant proclaims that "man, and in general every rational being, *exists* as an end in himself, *not merely as a means* for arbitrary use by this or that will: he must in all his actions, whether they are directed to himself or to other rational beings, always be viewed *at the same time as an end*" (G 428).[1] It is crucial here that "end" doesn't mean "goal." The end must be conceived "not as an end to be produced, *but as a self-existent* end" (G 437). (See Wood 1995.)

What, more precisely, is it that we are to respect? And what does this respect entail? We are to respect humanity or rational nature. (Kant generally uses these two words interchangeably, since humans are, if not the only rational beings, the only ones we know about.) More specifically, it is our capacity to set ends—any ends whatsoever—for ourselves. This capacity allows an individual to resolve to swim for at least thirty minutes daily, or to adhere to a particular moral principle; it makes it possible to refuse to do something, no matter how tempting it is, if we judge it to be wrong. On a Kantian view, we are not governed by our impulses. There are some people who may seem to be, but what is really happening is that they are choosing to act impulsively. If I claim "I just couldn't help myself; I was overcome by desire," what I claim is, on a Kantian

*From Marcia W. Baron, Phillip Pettit, Michael Slote, *Three Methods of Ethics: A Debate*, pp. 10–20.

view, not strictly speaking true. What has really happened is that I've let desire determine how I'll act. That we can say "No" to any impulse or desire is brought out dramatically in the following passage in Kant's *Critique of Practical Reason*:

> Suppose that someone says his lust is irresistible when the desired object and opportunity are present. Ask him whether he would not control his passion if, in front of the house where he has this opportunity, a gallows were erected on which he would be hanged immediately after gratifying his lust. We do not have to guess very long what his answer would be. But ask him whether he thinks it would be possible for him to overcome his love of life, however great it may be, if his sovereign threatened him with the same sudden death unless he made a false deposition against an honorable man whom the ruler wished to destroy under a plausible pretext. Whether he would or not he perhaps will not venture to say; but that it would be possible for him he would certainly admit without hesitation. He judges, therefore, that he can do something because he knows that he ought, and he recognizes that he is free—a fact which, without the moral law, would have remained unknown to him. (*PrR* 30)[2]

Respecting persons means respecting them as rational agents, as beings who set ends for themselves, beings who act on reasons. ("Everything in nature works in accordance with laws. Only a rational being has the power to act *in accordance with his idea* of laws—that is, in accordance with principles" (G 412).) We are to respect humanity in ourselves and in others and respect it both positively and negatively. Respecting it negatively means recognizing that various types of action are wrong: deceiving, manipulating, assaulting (except in certain instances, such as self-defense), mocking, and so on. Respecting it positively does not mean treating it as a goal—there is no duty to try to create more of it—but placing a positive value on it and acting accordingly. To place a positive value on it is to have as ends one's own perfection and the happiness of others. Having these ends entails that one is to develop one's talents and seek to improve oneself morally and promote others' happiness, but there is no requirement that one do all of this as much as possible.

Before discussing these ends and duties in greater detail, let us—partly by way of summary, partly in anticipation of things to come—go over the contrasts between consequentialism and Kantian ethics. Consequentialism differs from Kantian ethics in the role it allows for side-constraints, and since different consequentialisms allow different roles for side-constraints, some consequentialisms differ more from Kantian ethics than do others. Kantian ethics is much closer to rule-consequentialism than to act-consequentialism. Rule-consequentialists can recognize side-constraints: if binding oneself to a particular side-constraint promotes better consequences than not binding oneself to it, then it is obligatory to bind oneself to it. But side-constraints are only justifiable, on a consequentialist view, if adhering to them promotes the best consequences, and this of course is not the Kantian view.

Related to this difference are two others. First, consequentialism is concerned to produce some good; this is not a central concern of Kantian ethics.[3] Second, consequentialists typically are concerned to maximize. If it is good to help others, it is best to help others as much as one possibly can. Kantian ethics has very little concern with maximizing. This will become clearer shortly, as we explore the Kantian notions of obligatory ends and imperfect duties.

Obligatory Ends

The notion of an obligatory end may seem odd to contemporary ears. We are used to hearing of obligatory actions, but obligatory ends? The idea, which plays a central role in Kant's ethics but tends to be neglected in the classroom, is that we are morally required to have certain ends. We are obligated to act accordingly, but the duty to act in certain ways is secondary, and is based on our duty to have certain ends. The ends that we are obligated to have are the happiness of others and our own perfection. We are to promote others' happiness and improve ourselves. Promoting others' happiness means helping them to realize their ends. Self-improvement has two dimensions: developing one's talents and improving oneself morally.

Others' Happiness

"Promoting others' happiness" can be thought of in either of two ways: promoting what we, who seek to help, take the other person's happiness to be; or promoting what the other person takes her happiness to consist in. With some qualification, the second option is the one that Kant takes. The duty to promote others' happiness is the duty to help them to realize their ends.

But, a critical reader will ask, surely I am not to aid the embezzler in figuring out the surest way to embezzle without being caught! Surely I am not to aid the stalker by learning, and then disclosing to him, the daily routine of the woman he is stalking. Indeed Kant does build in a qualification: we are to promote only their permissible ends. In helping others, we are of course not to aid and abet crime, or even less serious vice. We are not to "give a lazy fellow soft cushions so that he [can] pass his life away in sweet idleness," nor "see to it that a drunkard is never short of wine and whatever else he needs to get drunk" (MM 481). Furthermore, Kant does not require (or even recommend) that we help others to achieve their permissible ends without regard to which ones we think most worthwhile. What is ruled out is ignoring their ends and imposing on them what we think their ends should be. In seeking to help them, we seek to promote their (permissible) ends; but we may choose to help to promote those which we think are most worthwhile. "It is for them to decide what they count as belonging to their happiness; but it is open to me to refuse them many things that *they* think will make them happy but that I do not, as long as they have no right to demand them from me as what is theirs" (MM 388). So, the duty to promote others' happiness leaves room for discretion but does not leave room for heavy-handed paternalism. It doesn't allow for deciding that while his ends are *w*, *x*, *y*, and *z*, really he should care much more for *a*, and so I'll seek to promote his happiness by providing him with, or promoting as if it were his end, *a*.

In Kant's insistence that it is others' ends that (with the qualifications noted) define how we are to understand what it is that we are to promote, we see his opposition to paternalism. This is a reflection of his emphasis on autonomy, a value that is also evident in the following asymmetry: we are to promote our own moral perfection, but not that of others. Why is this? Why aren't we to promote human perfection in general? Why aren't we to seek to perfect others as well as ourselves? The basic idea is that it is not our business to try to transform or even reform other people. One's relation to oneself is special: we are responsible for our own conduct (and to some extent, our characters), not for that of others.

Three comments are in order. First, we are of course talking about adults here. Parents bear some responsibility for the conduct of their children, and certainly have an obligation to help them to be and become good people. Second, while we are not to seek to perfect others, helping them to perfect themselves is a different matter. Recognizing that friends may be able to help each other to become more virtuous, Kant says that "it is . . . a duty for one of the friends to point out the other's faults to him" (MM 470). This is, he says, "a duty of love" (MM 470). Pointing out a friend's faults, we hope, helps him to improve himself. Furthermore, we should bear in mind that our conduct (whether or not intentionally) may facilitate or pose obstacles to their self-improvement. And so in addition to having a duty to point out our friend's faults to him, we should take care not to facilitate vice by, for example, keeping the drunkard supplied with wine.[4]

Third, it would be a mistake to think that the point about responsibility—that we are responsible for our own conduct but not that of others—carries over to responsibility for the *fate* of others. Each individual bears a special responsibility for his or her character and conduct, but we "share fate." We have a duty to promote others' happiness; there is no notion that their problems are theirs, not for us to be concerned with. "Minding one's own business" means not trying to manage others' characters or decide for them what their ends should be; it does not mean ignoring them when they are suffering. We are very much obligated to try to alleviate suffering.[5]

Self-Improvement

It might be thought that the duty to improve ourselves—or, as Kant often puts it, to perfect ourselves—would allow us to improve ourselves in any way we like, with no further specification. In fact, it splits into two parts, one of which has more latitude than the other. The part that is quite open-ended is the duty to develop our talents. But whatever talents we choose to develop, we are also required to perfect ourselves morally. In his brief discussions of this duty, Kant spells it out in terms of moral motivation: it is a duty to make "the thought of duty for its own sake . . . the sufficient incentive of every action conforming to duty" (MM 393; see also 387). In other words, it is a duty to see to it that duty is a sufficient incentive for us. Elsewhere, however, he offers a lengthy discussion of qualities that we are to cultivate in ourselves—most notably, sympathetic feeling—and of other qualities that he says are vices. This provides yet more content to the duty to improve ourselves. Envy, ingratitude, and malice are vices, as are contempt, arrogance, and servility.[6] And there are vices that fall under these headings; one form of malice—the sweetest, Kant says—is the desire for revenge. Part of moral self-improvement would thus be ridding oneself as much as possible of vices such as envy and the desire for revenge, detecting in oneself tendencies in those directions and attempting to check them. The duty to improve oneself morally will clearly involve considerable self-scrutiny. So it's not surprising to find Kant saying that the first command of all duties to oneself is "*know* (scrutinize, fathom) *yourself*" (MM 441).

Further details about the obligatory end of self-improvement will emerge in the course of the next section, as we examine the latitude inherent in imperfect duties. I turn now to two features of obligatory ends that are particularly important. The first is the fact that there are two and neither trumps the other. The second concerns the nature of the duties that they generate, more specifically, the fact that they involve considerable latitude. I'll address these in reverse order.

Imperfect Duties

The duties generated by the obligatory ends are imperfect duties. These are duties to help others and to develop one's talents. Exactly what one does—whom one helps, how and how often—is not specified. This is not a gap in Kant's ethics; this is the way it is supposed to be. The imperfect duties leave a lot of latitude. We do not have a duty to help others as much as we possibly can and whenever we can; we do not have a duty to do as much good for others as is possible for us. Likewise, we do not have a duty to develop all of our talents as much as we can, nor to pick one or two talents and develop them maximally. How we go about helping others and developing our talents is left open.

Imperfect duties contrast, not surprisingly, with perfect duties. (The labels, which have a history that predates Kant, are misleading; there is nothing "imperfect" in the usual sense about imperfect duties.) Perfect duties are reasonably clear-cut. Though they sometimes leave us latitude as to how we discharge them (if I owe you $20, I can discharge my duty by paying by mail or in person, today or tomorrow, by cash or by check) they don't leave us anything like the latitude entailed by the imperfect duties. I shall have little to say about them. It is the imperfect duties that give Kant's ethics a distinctive flavor.

There are, to be sure, limits to how we may go about helping others and developing our talents. Some of these are imposed by the perfect duties: I may not help my friends by cheating others, or help the needy by robbing the wealthy.[7] The limits that are harder to spell out are those entailed by the obligatory ends. If I decide to help others only when it will be rewarded, this indicates that I have not really adopted the end of others' happiness. It indicates that I regard their happiness as worth promoting only when I can reap some benefit from doing so. So it will not do to have the following sort of attitude: "I want to be moral, and to be moral I have to help people sometimes, since helping others is obligatory. I might as well do this in a way that will best promote my own interests, so I'll help people only when the fact that I'm helping is amply noticed and appreciated. This way, I can kill two birds with one stone: I can meet the moral requirement of helping others and enhance my reputation." The person with this attitude has not really embraced the end of others' happiness. He is just trying to meet a requirement. He is thinking of ethics as if it were simply a set of rules to follow. But for Kant, there is far more to ethics than that. One has to care, not just act a certain way.

There are limits to how we may go about helping others and developing our talents, but there is latitude, as well. We are not required to help others at every opportunity, and there needn't always be a compelling reason for not helping (such as that one is exhausted and needs to rest if one is to be able to go on helping others in the future). At the same time, there are instances where a failure to help would indicate that the agent has not really embraced the end of others' happiness. Suppose, for example, Joe is taking a stroll and sees someone grab his chest and collapse. There is no one else around and there is a telephone within easy reach. It would be inexcusable not to dial the emergency number to get help for the unfortunate man. "I do care about the welfare of others, but this is not my way of helping; I contribute money to charity and help my friends fix their cars, and I am great at lending an ear to a friend who wants to tell me his woes, but in instances like this, where someone I don't know is in trouble, I keep my distance" would be unconvincing. Joe could not be said, on a Kantian view, really to care about the welfare of others. He may well care about the happiness of certain others and be prepared to try to further it, and he may also like the idea of helping those he doesn't know now and then, when it suits him, but he doesn't regard the needs of others as making a normative claim on him. He doesn't accept Kant's position that "the maxim of common interest, of beneficence towards those in need, is a universal duty of people, just because they are to be considered fellow humans, that is, rational beings with needs, united by nature in one dwelling place so that they can help one another" (MM 453, translation altered).

It is clear from the example of Joe that the latitude in Kant's imperfect duties does not extend so far as to allow us to help only those near and dear to us, and neglect to help everyone else. ("To *do good* to others insofar as we can is a duty, whether one loves them or not" {MM 402; "other men" replaced by "others"}.) But are we then required to help others without regard to our personal ties to them? Must we select whom to help without any regard to our history with them, how well we know them, and the like? No. I have a duty of non-indifference towards others; the needs of others make a claim on me even if they are strangers to me. But it is part of the latitude in the duty to promote others' happiness that I don't have to help everyone equally, or help without regard to my personal ties to certain others.

So how much latitude is there in imperfect duties? This cannot be spelled out very exactly. The most we can say is that one's maxim must be consistent with, and indeed must reflect, a genuine commitment to the obligatory end.[8] A maxim of helping only when it is convenient, or only when it seems likely to reap some reward, does not. Indeed, it suggests that the agent is trying to qualify in a very superficial way as moral: trying to meet the letter of morality but not the spirit. (On a Kantian view this makes no sense; one can't count as moral unless one is genuinely committed to acting morally and being moral.)

A word about the use of "maxim" here. To say that we have a duty to embrace the happiness of others and our own perfection is equivalent to saying that it is obligatory to have among one's maxims, "Promote the happiness of others" and "Perfect thyself." A maxim is basically a personal policy, a principle that guides one's conduct. We shall have more to say about maxims later.

The notion of embracing an end and acting accordingly is rather different from the understanding of promoting an end that we find in consequentialism. The idea is that we care about the end and act accordingly; we take it very seriously, and both honor it and seek to further it. But this cannot be cashed out as seeking to bring about a state of affairs in which there is as much as possible of the end in question. While it is very common among consequentialists to speak as if what matters most is bringing about certain states of affairs, it is alien to Kantian ethics. And as has been noted, the idea of maximizing plays a key role in consequentialism (though there are some consequentialists who see it as inessential to their theory) but virtually no role in Kantian ethics. This is evident from the latitude involved in the imperfect duties. They require us to embrace the obligatory ends and act accordingly, but do not require that we do as much as possible to help others and perfect ourselves.

Now it might be thought that even though the obligatory ends do not require that we maximize, Kant would nonetheless hold that the more we do by way of helping others and perfecting ourselves, the better we are. Although Kant's writings are not unambiguous on this point, this seems not to be his view.[9] And this brings me to the second feature of imperfect duties that I want to highlight.

Two Obligatory Ends

A very common view, both within academic moral philosophy and outside of it, is that the people who are ethically most admirable are those who are most committed to improving the welfare of others. Except among those who are too troubled by her opposition to abortion and contraception to overlook it, Mother Teresa is regularly cited as a moral exemplar: about as good a person as one finds. And thus one might expect that Kant ranks promoting others' happiness higher than perfecting oneself. But in fact this is not the case. Neither obligatory end is ranked higher than the other. This, conjoined with the latitude accorded the imperfect duties, has an interesting implication: it precludes a unitary conception of moral excellence. Moral excellence comes in considerable variety, on a Kantian view. Although there is room for some ranking, there isn't the clear "best" that we find on views which see ethics as strictly other-directed and regard altruism as the most important virtue.

The importance of the pluralistic conception of moral excellence entailed by Kant's ethics is evident in the fact that it prevents his theory from some pitfalls that have received a lot of attention in contemporary moral philosophy.

The first pitfall is what might be called the "excessive demands" problem. Morality, as understood on some moral theories, is said to make excessive demands on people, in particular, to require us to give up our pet projects and possibly even what gives our lives meaning. To the extent that this problem has a foothold, it is a problem for theories that ask us, as consequentialist theories often do, to maximize the good. If the good to be maximized is a general good, such as human happiness, rather than a personal good, such as one's own happiness, the injunction to maximize happiness may leave little room for pursuing one's own project. The entomologist who is fascinated by the habits of a certain type of insect and devotes much of her time to studying it probably is not maximizing the general happiness. Her research skills could be put to a more humanitarian use. Yet do we want to say that she is acting immorally in pursuing her research in entomology? Or even that her choice of career shows a lack of virtue? Presumably not, and this suggests that the conception of morality in theories which require us to maximize human happiness may be faulty.

Kantian ethics is not open to this charge. We are not morally required to maximize human happiness, but only to take it very seriously, see it as making a normative claim on us, and seek (in some ways or other) to promote it. There are many ways in which a commitment to promote the welfare of others may be expressed. The entomologist is not deficient for having allowed her fascination with bugs to shape her career choice rather than selecting a line of work solely on the basis of what would best promote human welfare. Kant's ethics allows us to pursue our own projects provided that we abide by the perfect duties and the principles of imperfect duty.

Notes

1. In citing Kant's works, I use the abbreviations and translations given below. All references except *Lectures on Ethics* are to *Kants gesammelte Schriften (KGS), herausgegeben von der Deutschen* (formerly *Königlichen Preussischen*) *Akademie der Wissenschaften*, 29 volumes (Berlin: Walter de Gruyter (and predecessors), 1902). Where the translations used do not provide the page number of the German text, I also provide the page number of the translation. *Lectures on Ethics*, it should be noted, is a compilation of notes from Kant's students (carefully checked against other students' notes). Page references are to the English translation. Occasionally I have altered the translations, but I always alert the reader that I am doing so. Most alterations concern the translation of *Mensch* as "man." Since *Mensch* in German is gender-neutral while "man" in English is not, I have in some instances altered the translations of *Mensch* so as to make clear that there is no reason to assume that only men are intended.

A *Anthropologie in pragmatischer Hinsicht* (*KGS*, vol. 7). *Anthropology from a Pragmatic Point of View*, trans. Mary J. Gregor, The Hague: Nijhoff, 1974.

G *Grundlegung zur Metaphysik der Sitten* (*KGS*, vol. 4). *Groundwork of the Metaphyusics of Morals* trans. H. J. Paton, New York: Harper & Row, 1964.

LE *Eine Vorlesung über Ethik*, ed. Paul Menzer, Berlin: Rolf Heise, 1924. *Lectures on Ethics*, trans. Louis Infield, Indianapolis, Ind.: Hackett, 1981.

MM *Die Metaphysik der Sitten* (*KGS*, vol. 6). *The Metaphysics of Morals*, trans. Mary J. Gregor, Cambridge: Cambridge University Press, 1991.

PrR *Kritik der praktischen Vernunft* (*KGS*, vol. 5). *Critique of Practical Reason*, trans. Lewis White Beck, Indianapolis, Ind.: Bobbs-Merrill, 1956.

R *Die Religion innerhalb der Grenzen der blossen Vermunft* (*KGS*, vol. 6). *Religion within the Limits of Reason Alone*, trans. Theodore M. Greene and Hoyt H. Hudson, New York: Harper & Row, 1960.

WE "Was Ist Erklärung?" (*KGS*, vol. 8). "An answer to the question: What is enlightenment?" in *Perpetual Peace and Other Essays on Politics, History, and Morals*, trans. Ted Humphrey, Indianapolis, Ind.: Hackett, 1983.

2. I should note that many Kantians accept both the idea of respecting humanity as an end in itself and the construal of humanity as the power to set ends for ourselves but do not accept the conception of freedom implicit in the above quote. There is, moreover, considerable disagreement as to how Kant's theory of freedom is to be understood. See Allison 1990 and Wood 1984 for differing views on Kant on freedom. For a very helpful discussion of humanity see Hill 1992, ch. 2.

3. Occasionally one encounters the mistaken view that there is no concern at all in Kant's ethics to seek to bring about certain goods. That this is mistaken is evident from (among other things) the duties to promote others' happiness and to develop one's talents, discussed below.

4. For extensive discussion of both responsibility and friendship in the context of Kant's ethics, see Korsgaard 1996a, ch. 7.

5. Why we have a duty only to promote others' happiness, not our own, is somewhat more mysterious. Kant's view is not entirely clear, and insofar as it is clear, many contemporary Kantians, myself included, find it unconvincing. Kant says that we have no duty to promote our own happiness because we seek it anyway, and we only have a duty to those things which we have some temptation to neglect. Yet at G 399 he recognizes the temptation to neglect one's own happiness, and indicates that a person so tempted might nonetheless further his happiness from duty. The duty he says, is indirect; it is a duty to assure one's own happiness because "discontent with one's state, in a press of cares and amidst unsatisfied wants, might easily become a great *temptation to the transgression of duty*" (G399). Cf. MM 387–8, where he says that while this might seem to ground a duty to promote one's own happiness, in fact the end in this case "is not the subject's happiness but his morality." He adds that "to seek prosperity for its own sake is not directly a duty, but indirectly it can well be a duty, that of warding off poverty insofar as this is a great temptation to vice. But then it is not my happiness but the preservation of my moral integrity that is my end and also my duty."

6. Kant classifies the first three under the heading of duties of love to others. They are "vices of hatred for others" (MM 458). Contempt and arrogance violate the "duties of respect for others" (465). (In both quotes I substitute "others" for "other men.") But though these vices are classified under a different heading, they clearly are at the same time qualities the rooting out (or moderating) of which would constitute self-improvement. This is one of many instances in which the duty to promote others' happiness and the duty to perfect oneself converge.

7. The wealthy, however, would do well not to have too strong a sense of entitlement to their riches. His staunch defense of property rights notwithstanding, Kant suggests that for the wealthy, helping the needy should not be strictly a matter of charity; it may be required by justice.

> Having the means to practice such beneficence as depends on the goods of fortune is, for the most part, a result of certain men being favored through the injustice of the government, which introduces an inequality of wealth that makes others need their beneficence. Under such circumstances, does a rich man's help to the needy, on which he so readily prides himself as something meritorious, really deserve to be called beneficence at all? (MM 454).

8. For those who would like more detail, ch. 3 of my *Kantian Ethics Almost Without Apology* might be helpful. I argue there that some imperfect duties admit of more latitude, in Kant's scheme, than do others. The duty to perfect ourselves morally involves the least latitude.

9. A passage that suggests that it *is* his view is MM 390.

What Makes Right Acts Right?*

W. D. Ross

When a plain man fulfils a promise because he thinks he ought to do so, it seems clear that he does so with no thought of its total consequences, still less with any opinion that these are likely to be the best possible. He thinks in fact much more of the past than of the future. What makes him think it right to act in a certain way is the fact that he has promised to do so—that and, usually, nothing more. That his act will produce the best possible consequences is not his reason for calling it right. What lends colour to the theory we are examining, then, is not the actions (which form probably a great majority of our actions) in which some such reflection as 'I have promised' is the only reason we give ourselves for thinking a certain action right, but the exceptional cases in which the consequences of fulfilling a promise (for instance) would be so disastrous to others that we judge it right not to do so. It must of course be admitted that such cases exist. If I have promised to meet a friend at a particular time for some trivial purpose, I should certainly think myself justified in breaking my engagement if by doing so I could prevent a serious accident or bring relief to the victims of one. And the supporters of the view we are examining hold that my thinking so is due to my thinking that I shall bring more good into existence by the one action than by the other. A different account may, however, be given of the matter, an account which will, I believe, show itself to be the true one. It may be said that besides the duty of fulfilling promises I have and recognize a duty of relieving distress,[1] and that when I think it right to do the latter at the cost of not doing the former, it is not because I think I shall produce more good thereby but because I think it the duty which is in the circumstances more of a duty. This account surely corresponds much more closely with what we really think in such a situation. If, so far as I can see, I could bring equal amounts of good into being by fulfilling my promise and by helping some one to whom I had made no promise, I should not hesitate to regard the former as my duty. Yet on the view that what is right is right because it is productive of the most good I should not so regard it.

There are two theories, each in its way simple, that offer a solution of such cases of conscience. One is the view of Kant, that there are certain duties of perfect obligation, such as those of fulfilling promises, of paying debts, of telling the truth, which admit of no exception whatever in favour of duties of imperfect

---

obligation, such as that of relieving distress. The other is the view of, for instance, Professor Moore and Dr. Rashdall, that there is only the duty of producing good, and that all 'conflicts of duties' should be resolved by asking 'by which action will most good be produced?' But it is more important that our theory fit the facts than that it be simple, and the account we have given above corresponds (it seems to me) better than either of the simpler theories with what we really think, viz. that normally promise-keeping, for example, should come before benevolence, but that when and only when the good to be produced by the benevolent act is very great and the promise comparatively trivial, the act of benevolence becomes our duty.

In fact the theory of 'ideal utilitarianism', if I may for brevity refer so to the theory of Professor Moore, seems to simplify unduly our relations to our fellows. It says, in effect, that the only morally significant relation in which my neighbours stand to me is that of being possible beneficiaries by my action.[2] They do stand in this relation to me, and this relation is morally significant. But they may also stand to me in the relation of promisee to promiser, of creditor to debtor, of wife to husband, of child to parent, of friend to friend, or fellow countryman to fellow countryman, and the like; and each of these relations is the foundation of a *prima facie* duty, which is more or less incumbent on me according to the circumstances of the case. When I am in a situation, as perhaps I always am, in which more than one *of* these *prima facie* duties is incumbent on me, what I have to do is to study the situation as fully as I can until I form the considered opinion (it is never more) that in the circumstances one of them is more incumbent than any other; then I am bound to think that to do this *prima facie* duty is my duty *sans phrase* in the situation.

I suggest '*prima facie* duty' or 'conditional duty' as a brief way of referring to the characteristic (quite distinct from that of being a duty proper) which an act has, in virtue of being of a certain kind (e.g. the keeping of a promise), of being an act which would be a duty proper if it were not at the same time of another kind which is morally significant. Whether an act is a duty proper or actual duty depends on *all* the morally significant kinds it is an instance of. The phrase '*prima facie* duty' must be apologized for, since (1) it suggests that what we are speaking of is a certain kind of duty, whereas it is in fact not a duty, but something related in a special way to duty. Strictly speaking, we want not a phrase in which duty is qualified by an adjective, but a separate noun. (2) '*Prima*' *facie* suggests that one is speaking only of an appearance which a moral situation presents at first sight, and which may turn out to be illusory; whereas what I am speaking of is an objective fact involved in the nature of the situation, or more strictly in an element of its nature, though not, as duty proper does, arising from its *whole* nature. I can, however, think of no term which fully meets the case.

There is nothing arbitrary about these *prima facie* duties. Each rests on a definite circumstance which cannot seriously be held to be without moral significance. Of *prima facie* duties I suggest, without claiming completeness or finality for it, the following division.[3]

(1) Some duties rest on previous acts of my own. These duties seem to include two kinds, (*a*) those resting on a promise or what may fairly be called an implicit promise, such as the implicit undertaking not to tell lies which seems to be implied in the act of entering into conversation (at any rate by civilized men), or of writing books that purport to be history and not fiction. These may be called the duties of fidelity. (*b*) Those resting on a previous wrongful act. These may be called the duties of reparation. (2) Some rest on previous acts of other men, i.e. services done by them to me. These may be loosely described as the duties of gratitude. (3) Some rest on the fact or possibility of a distribution of pleasure or happiness (or of the means there to) which is not in accordance with the merit of the persons concerned; in such cases there arises a duty to upset or prevent such a distribution. These are the duties of justice. (4) Some rest on the mere fact that there are other beings in the world whose condition we can make better in respect of virtue, or of intelligence, or of pleasure. These are the duties of beneficence. (5) Some rest on the fact that we can improve our own condition in respect of virtue or of intelligence. These are the duties of self-improvement. (6) I think that we should distinguish from (4) the duties that may be summed up under the title of 'not injuring others'. No doubt to injure others is incidentally to fail to do them good; but it seems to me clear that non-maleficence is apprehended as a duty distinct from that of beneficence, and as a duty of a more stringent character. It will be noticed that this alone among the types of duty has been stated in a negative way. An attempt might no doubt be made to state this duty, like the others, in a positive way. It might be said that it is really the duty to prevent ourselves from acting either from an inclination to harm others or from an inclination to seek our own pleasure, in doing which we should incidentally harm them. But on reflection it seems clear that the primary duty here is the duty not to harm others, this being a duty whether or not we have an inclination that if followed would lead to our harming them; and that when we have such an inclination the primary duty not to harm others gives rise to a consequential duty to resist the inclination. The recognition of this duty of non-maleficence is the first step on the way to the recognition of the duty of beneficence; and that accounts for the prominence of the commands 'thou shalt not kill', 'thou shalt not commit adultery', 'thou shalt not steal', 'thou shalt not bear false witness', in so early a code as the Decalogue. But even when we have come to recognize the duty of beneficence, it appears to me that the duty of non-maleficence is recognized as a distinct one, and as *prima facie* more binding. We should not in general consider it justifiable to kill

one person in order to keep another alive, or to steal from one in order to give alms to another.

The essential defect of the 'ideal utilitarian' theory is that it ignores, or at least does not do full justice to, the highly personal character of duty. If the only duty is to produce the maximum of good, the question who is to have the good—whether it is myself, or my benefactor, or a person to whom I have made a promise to confer that good on him, or a mere fellow man to whom I stand in no such special relation—should make no difference to my having a duty to produce that good. But we are all in fact sure that it makes a vast difference.

One or two other comments must be made on this provisional list of the divisions of duty. (1) The nomenclature is not strictly correct. For by 'fidelity' or 'gratitude' we mean, strictly, certain states of motivation; and, as I have urged, it is not our duty to have certain motives, but to do certain acts. By 'fidelity', for instance, is meant, strictly, the disposition to fulfil promises and implicit promises *because we have made them*. We have no general word to cover the actual fulfilment of promises and implicit promises *irrespective of motive*; and I use 'fidelity', loosely but perhaps conveniently, to fill this gap. So too I use 'gratitude' for the returning of services, irrespective of motive. The term 'justice' is not so much confined, in ordinary usage, to a certain state of motivation, for we should often talk of a man as acting justly even when we did not think his motive was the wish to do what was just simply for the sake of doing so. Less apology is therefore needed for our use of 'justice' in this sense. And I have used the word 'beneficence' rather than 'benevolence', in order to emphasize the fact that it is our duty to do certain things, and not to do them from certain motives.

(2) If the objection be made, that this catalogue of the main types of duty is an unsystematic one resting on no logical principle, it may be replied, first, that it makes no claim to being ultimate. It is a *prima facie* classification of the duties which reflection on our moral convictions seems actually to reveal. And if these convictions are, as I would claim that they are, of the nature of knowledge, and if I have not misstated them, the list will be a list of authentic conditional duties, correct as far as it goes though not necessarily complete. The list *of goods* put forward by the rival theory is reached by exactly the same method—the only sound one in the circumstances—viz, that of direct reflection on what we really think. Loyalty to the facts is worth more than a symmetrical architectonic or a hastily reached simplicity. If further reflection discovers a perfect logical basis for this or for a better classification, so much the better.

An attempt may be made to arrange in a more systematic way the main types of duty which we have indicated. In the first place it seems self-evident that if there are things that are, intrinsically good, it is *prima facie* a duty to bring them into existence rather than not to do so, and to bring as much of them into existence as possible. There are three main things that are intrinsically good—virtue, knowledge, and, with certain limitations, pleasure. And since a given virtuous disposition, for instance, is equally good whether it is realized in myself or in another, it seems to be my duty to bring it into existence whether in myself or in another. So too with a given piece of knowledge.

If these contentions are right, what we have called the duty of beneficence and the duty of self-improvement rest on the same ground. No different principles of duty are involved in the two cases. If we feel a special responsibility for improving our own character rather than that of others, it is not because a special principle is involved, but because we are aware that the one is more under our control than the other. It was on this ground that Kant expressed the practical law of duty in the form 'seek to make yourself good and other people happy'. He was so persuaded of the internality of virtue that he regarded any attempt by one person to produce virtue in another as bound to produce, at most, only a counterfeit of virtue, the doing of externally right acts not from the true principle of virtuous action but out of regard to another person. It must be admitted that one man cannot compel another to be virtuous; compulsory virtue would just not be virtue. But experience clearly shows that Kant overshoots the mark when he contends that one man cannot do anything to *promote* virtue in another, to bring such influences to bear upon him that his own response to them is more likely to be virtuous than his response to other influences would have been. And our duty to do this is not different in kind from our duty to improve our own characters.

It is equally clear, and clear at an earlier stage of moral development, that if there are things that are bad in themselves we ought, *prima facie*, not to bring them upon others; and on this fact rests the duty of non-maleficence.

The duty of justice is particularly complicated, and the word is used to cover things which are really very different—things such as the payment of debts, the reparation of injuries done by oneself to another, and the bringing about of a distribution of happiness between other people in proportion to merit. I use the word to denote only the last of these three.

But besides this general obligation, there are special obligations. These may arise, in the first place, incidentally, from acts which were not essentially meant to create such an obligation, but which nevertheless create it. From the nature of the case such acts may be of two kinds—the infliction of injuries on others, and the acceptance of benefits from them. It seems clear that these put us under a special obligation to other men, and that only these acts can do so incidentally. From these arise the twin duties of reparation and gratitude.

And finally there are special obligations arising from acts the very intention of which, when they were done, was to put us under such an obligation. The name for such acts is 'promises'; the name is wide enough if we are willing to include under it implicit promises, i.e. modes of behaviour in which without explicit verbal promise we intentionally create an expectation that we can be counted on to behave in a certain way in the interest of another person.

These seem to be, in principle, all the ways in which *prima facie* duties arise. In actual experience they are compounded together in highly complex ways.

It is necessary to say something by way of clearing up the relation between *prima facie* duties and the actual or absolute duty to do one particular act in particular circumstances. If, as almost all moralists except Kant are agreed, and as most plain men think, it is sometimes right to tell a lie or to break a promise, it must be maintained that there is a difference between *prima facie* duty and actual or absolute duty. When we think ourselves justified in breaking, and indeed morally obliged to break, a promise in order to relieve some one's distress, we do not for a moment cease to recognize *a prima facie* duty to keep our promise, and this leads us to feel, not indeed shame or repentance, but certainly compunction, for behaving as we do; we recognize, further, that it is our duty to make up somehow to the promisee for the breaking of the promise. We have to distinguish from the characteristic of being our duty that of tending to be our duty. Any act that we do contains various elements in virtue of which it falls under various categories. In virtue of being the breaking of a promise, for instance, it tends to be wrong; in virtue of being an instance of relieving distress it tends to be right. Tendency to be one's duty may be called a parti-resultant attribute, i.e. one which belongs to an act in virtue of some one component in its nature. *Being* one's duty is a toti-resultant attribute, one which belongs to an act in virtue of its whole nature and of nothing less than this. This distinction between parti-resultant and toti-resultant attributes is one which we shall meet in another context also.

Notes

1. These are not strictly speaking duties, but things that tend to be our duty, or *prima facie* duties.

2. Some will think it, apart from other considerations, a sufficient refutation of this view to point out that I also stand in that relation to myself, so that for this view the distinction of oneself from others is morally insignificant.

3. I should make it plain at this stage that I am *assuming* the correctness of some of our main convictions as to *prima facie* duties, or, more strictly, am claiming that we *know* them to be true. To me it seems as self-evident as anything could be, that to make a promise, for instance, is to create a moral claim on us in someone else. Many readers will perhaps say that they do *not* know this to be true. If so, I certainly cannot prove it to them; I can only ask them to reflect again, in the hope that they will ultimately agree that they also know it to be true. The main moral convictions of the plain man seem to me to be, not opinions which it is for philosophy to prove or disprove, but knowledge from the start; and in my own case I seem to find little difficulty in distinguishing these essential convictions from other moral convictions which also have, which are merely

fallible opinions based on an imperfect study of the working for good or evil of certain institutions or types of action.

Killing, Letting Die, and the Trolley Problem*

Judith Jarvis Thomson

1. Morally speaking it may matter a great deal how a death comes about whether from natural causes, or at the hands of another, for example. Does it matter whether a man was killed or only let die? A great many people think it does: they think that killing is worse than letting die. And they draw conclusions from this for abortion, euthanasia, and the distribution of scarce medical resources. Others think it doesn't, and they think this shown by what we see when we construct a pair of cases which are so far as possible in all other respects alike, except that in the one case the agent kills, in the other he only lets die. So, for example, imagine that

(1) Alfred hates his wife and wants her dead. He puts cleaning fluid in her coffee thereby killing her,

and that

(2) Bert hates his wife and wants her dead. She puts cleaning fluid in her coffee (being muddled, thinking it's cream). Bert happens to have the antidote to cleaning fluid, but he does not give it to her; he lets her die.[1]

Alfred kills his wife out of a desire for her death; Bert lets his wife die out of a desire for her death. But what Bert does is surely every bit as bad as what Alfred does. So killing isn't worse than letting die.

But I am now inclined to think that this argument is a bad one. Compare the following argument for the thesis that cutting off a man's head is no worse than punching a man in the nose. "Alfrieda knows that if she cuts off Alfred's head he will die, and, wanting him to die, cuts it off; Bertha knows that if she punches Bert in the nose he will die—Bert is in a peculiar physical condition—and, wanting him to die, punches him in the nose. But what Bertha does is surely every bit as bad as what Alfrieda does. So cutting off a man's head isn't worse than punching a man in the nose." It's not easy to say just exactly what goes wrong in this argument, because it's not clear what we mean when we say, as we do, such things as that cutting off a man's head is worse than punching a man in the nose. The argument brings out that we don't mean by it anything which entails that for every pair of acts, actual or possible, one of which is a nose-punching,

*Judith J. Thompson, "Killing, Letting Die and the Trolley Problem," *The Monist* 59, no. 1 (1976): 204–17. Reprinted by permission of publisher.

the other of which is a head-cutting-off, but which are so far as possible in all other respects alike, the second is worse than the first. Or at least the argument brings out that we can't mean anything which entails this by "Cutting off a man's head is worse than punching a man in the nose" if we want to go on taking it for true. Choice is presumably in question, and the language which comes most readily is perhaps this: if you can cut off a man's head or punch him in the nose, then if he's in normal condition—and if other things are equal—you had better not choose cutting off his head. But there is no need to go into any of this for present purposes. Whatever precisely we do mean by "Cutting off a man's head is worse than punching a man in the nose," it surely (a) is not disconfirmed by the cases of Alfrieda and Bertha, and (b) is confirmed by the fact that if you can now either cut off my head, or punch me in the nose, you had better not choose cutting off my head. This latter is a fact. I don't say that you had better choose punching me in the nose: best would be to do neither. Nor do I say it couldn't have been the case that it would be permissible to choose cutting off my head. But things being as they are, you had better not choose it.

I'm not going to hazard a guess as to what precisely people mean by saying "Killing is worse than letting die." I think the argument of the first paragraph brings out that they can't mean by it anything which entails that for every pair of acts, actual or possible, one of which is a letting die, the other of which is killing, but which are so far as possible in all other respects alike, the second is worse than the first—i.e., they can't if they want to go on taking it for true. I think here too that choice is in question, and that what they mean by it is something which is not disconfirmed by the cases of Alfred and Bert. And it isn't what they mean by it confirmed by the fact—isn't it a fact?—that in the following case, Charles must not kill, that he must instead let die:

(3) Charles is a great transplant surgeon. One of his patients needs a new heart, but is of a relatively rare blood-type. By chance, Charles learns of a healthy specimen with that very blood-type. Charles can take the healthy specimen's heart, killing him, and install it in his patient, saving him. Or he can refrain from taking the healthy specimen's heart, letting his patient die.

I should imagine that most people would agree that Charles must not choose to take out the one man's heart to save the other: he must let his patient die.

And isn't what they mean by it further confirmed by the fact—isn't it a fact?—that in the following case, David must not kill, that he must instead let die:

(4) David is a great transplant surgeon. Five of his patients need new parts—one needs a heart, the others need, respectively, liver, stomach, spleen, and spinal cord—but all are of the same, relatively rare, blood-type. By chance, David learns of a healthy specimen with that very blood-type. David can take the healthy specimen's parts, killing him, and install them in his patients,

saving them. Or he can refrain from taking the healthy specimen's parts, letting his patients die.

If David may not even choose to cut up one where *five* will thereby be saved surely what people who say "Killing is worse than letting die" mean by it must be right!

On the other hand, there is a lovely, nasty difficulty which confronts us at this point. Philippa Foot says[2]—and seems right to say—that it is permissible for Edward, in the following case, to kill:

(5) Edward is the driver of a trolley, whose brakes have just failed. On the track ahead of him are five people; the banks are so steep that they will not be able to get off the track in time. The track has a spur leading off to the right, and Edward can turn the trolley onto it. Unfortunately there is one person on the right-hand track. Edward can turn the trolley, killing the one; or he can refrain from turning the trolley, killing the five.

If what people who say "Killing is worse than letting die" mean by it is true, how is it that Edward may choose to turn that trolley?

Killing and letting die apart, in fact, it's a lovely, nasty difficulty: why is it that Edward may turn that trolley to save his five, but David may not cut up his healthy specimen to save his five? I like to call this the trolley problem, in honor of Mrs. Foot's example.

Mrs. Foot's own solution to the trolley problem is this. We must accept that our 'negative duties', such as the duty to refrain from killing, are more stringent than our 'positive duties', such as the duty to save lives. If David does nothing, he violates a positive duty to save five lives; if he cuts up the healthy specimen, he violates a negative duty to refrain from killing one. Now the negative duty to refrain from killing one is not merely more stringent than the positive duty to save one, it is more stringent even than the positive duty to save five. So of course Charles may not cut up his one to save one; and David may not cut up his one even to save five. But Edward's case is different. For if Edward 'does nothing', he doesn't do nothing; he kills the five on the track ahead, for he drives right into them with his trolley. Whichever Edward does, turn or not turn, he kills. There is, for Edward, then, not a conflict between a positive duty to save five and a negative duty to refrain from killing one; there is, for Edward, a conflict between a negative duty to refrain from killing five and a negative duty to refrain from killing one. But this is no real conflict: a negative duty to refrain from killing five is surely more stringent than a negative duty to refrain from killing one. So Edward may, indeed must, turn the trolley.

Now I am inclined to think that Mrs. Foot is mistaken about why Edward may turn his trolley, but David may not cut up his healthy specimen. I say only that Edward "may" turn his trolley, and not that he must: my intuition tells me that it is not required that he turn it, but only that it is permissible for him to do so. But this isn't important now: it is, at any rate, permissible for him to do so. Why? Compare (5) with

(6) Frank is a passenger on a trolley whose driver has just shouted that the trolley's brakes have failed, and who then died of the shock. On the track ahead are five people; the banks are so steep that they will not be able to get off the track in time. The track has a spur leading off to the right, and Frank can turn the trolley onto it. Unfortunately there is one person on the right-hand track. Frank can turn the trolley, killing the one; or he can refrain from turning the trolley, letting the five die.

If Frank turns his trolley, he plainly kills his one, just as if Edward turns his trolley, he kills his one: anyone who turns a trolley onto a man presumably kills him. Mrs. Foot thinks that if Edward does nothing, he kills his five, and I agree with this: if a driver of a trolley drives it full speed into five people, he kills them, even if he only drives it into them because his brakes have failed. But it seems to me that if Frank does nothing, he kills no one. He at worst lets the trolley kill the five; he does not himself kill them, but only lets them die.

But then by Mrs. Foot's principles, the conflict for Frank is between the negative duty to refrain from killing one, and the positive duty to save five, just as it was for David. On her view, the former duty is the more stringent: its being more stringent was supposed to explain why David could not cut up his healthy specimen. So by her principles, Frank may no more turn that trolley than David may cut up his healthy specimen. Yet I take it that anyone who thinks Edward may turn his trolley will also think that Frank may turn his. Certainly the fact that Edward is driver, and Frank only passenger could not explain so large a difference.

So we stand in need, still, of a solution: why can Edward and Frank turn their trolleys, whereas David cannot cut up his healthy specimen? One's intuitions are, I think, fairly sharp on these matters. Suppose, for a further example, that

(7) George is on a footbridge over the trolley tracks. He knows trolleys, and can see that the one approaching the bridge is out of control. On the track back of the bridge there are five people; the banks are so steep that they will not be able to get off the track in time. George knows that the only way to stop an out-of-control trolley is to drop a very heavy weight into its path. But the only available, sufficiently heavy weight is a fat man, also watching the trolley from the footbridge. George can shove the fat man onto the track in the path of the trolley, killing the fat man; or he can refrain from doing this, letting the five die.

Presumably George may not shove the fat man into the path of the trolley; he must let the five die. Why may Edward and Frank turn their trolleys to save their fives, whereas George must let his five die? George's shoving the fat man into the path of the trolley seems to be very like David's cutting up his healthy specimen. But what is the relevant likeness?

Further examples come from all sides. Compare, for example, the following two cases:

(8) Harry is President, and has just been told that the Russians have launched an atom bomb towards New York. The only way in which the bomb can be prevented from reaching New York is by deflecting it; but the only deflection-path available will take the bomb onto Worcester. Harry can do nothing, letting all of New York die; or he can press a button, deflecting the bomb, killing all of Worcester.

(9) Irving is President, and has just been told that the Russians have launched an atom bomb towards New York. The only way in which the bomb can be prevented from reaching New York is by dropping one of our own atom bombs on Worcester: the blast of the American bomb will pulverize the Russian bomb. Irving can do nothing, letting all of New York die; or he can press a button, which launches an American bomb onto Worcester, killing all of Worcester.

Most people, I think, would feel that Harry may act in (8): he may deflect the Russian bomb from its New York path onto Worcester, in order to minimize the damage it does. (Notice that if Harry doesn't deflect that bomb, he kills no one—just as Frank kills no one if he doesn't turn his trolley.) But I think most people would feel that Irving may not drop an American bomb onto Worcester: a President simply may not launch an atomic attack on one of his own cities, even to save a larger one from a similar attack.

Why? I think it is the same problem.

2. Perhaps the most striking difference between the cases I mentioned in which the agent may act, and the cases I mentioned in which he may not, is this: in the former what is in question is deflecting a threat from a larger group onto a smaller group, in the latter what is in question is bringing a different threat to bear on the smaller group. But it is not easy to see why this should matter so crucially. I think it does, and have a suggestion as to why, but it is no more than a suggestion.

I think we may be helped if we turn from evils to goods. Suppose there are six men who are dying. Five are standing in one clump on the beach, one is standing further along. Floating in on the tide is a marvelous pebble, the Health-Pebble, I'll call it: it cures what ails you. The one needs for cure the whole Health-Pebble; each of the five needs only a fifth of it. Now in fact that Health-Pebble is drifting towards the one, so that if nothing is done to alter its course, the one will get it. We happen to be swimming nearby, and are in a position to deflect it towards the five. Is it permissible for us to do this? It seems to me that it is permissible for us to deflect the Health-Pebble if and only if the one has no more claim on it than any of the five does.

What could make it be the case that the one has more claim on it than any of the five does? One thing that I think *doesn't* is the fact that the one pebble is headed for the one, and that he will get it if we do nothing. There is no Principle of Moral Inertia: there is no prima facie duty to refrain from interfering with existing states of affairs just because they are existing states of affairs. A burglar whose burgling we interfere with cannot say that since, but for our interference, he would have got the goods, he had a claim on them; it is not as if we weigh the burglar's claim on the goods against the owner's claim on them, and find the owner's claim weightier, and therefore interfere—the burglar has no claim on the goods to be weighed.

Well, the Health-Pebble might actually belong to the one. (It fell off his boat.) Or it might belong to us, and we had promised it to the one. If either of these is the case, the one has a claim on it in the sense of a right to it. If the one alone owns it, or if we have promised it only to the one, then he plainly has more claim on it than any of the five do; and we may not deflect it away from him.

But I mean to be using the word "claim" more loosely. So, for example, suppose that the five are villains who had intentionally caused the one's fatal illness, hoping he would die. (Then they became ill themselves.) It doesn't seem to me obvious that a history like this gives the one a *right* to that pebble; yet it does seem obvious that in some sense it gives the one a claim on it—anyway, more of a claim on it than any of the five has. Certainly anyway one feels that if it comes to a choice between them and him, he ought to get it. Again, suppose the six had played pebble-roulette: they had seen the pebble floating in, and agreed to flip a coin for positions on the beach and take their chances. And now the pebble is floating in towards the one. It doesn't seem to me that a history like this gives the one a *right* to that pebble; yet it does seem obvious that in some sense it gives him a claim on it, anyway, more claim on it than any of the five has. (While the fact that a pebble is floating towards one does not give him more claim on it, the compound fact that a pebble is floating towards him and that there was a background of pebble-roulette does, I think, give him more claim. If two groups have agreed to take what comes, and have acted in good faith in accordance with that agreement, I think we cannot intervene.)

I leave it open just precisely what sorts of things might give the one more claim on that Health-Pebble than any of the five has. What seems clear enough, however, is this: if the one has no more claim on it than any of the five has, we may deflect it away from him and towards the five. If the one has no more claim on it than any of the five has, it is permissible for us to deflect it in order to bring about that it saves more lives than it would do if we did not act.

Now that Health-Pebble is a good to those dying men on the beach: if they get to eat it, they live. The trolley is an evil to the living men on the tracks: if they get run down by it, they die. And deflecting the Health-Pebble away from one and towards five is like deflecting the trolley away from five and towards one. For if the pebble is deflected, one life is lost and five are saved; and if the trolley is deflected, so also is one life lost and five saved. The analogy suggests a thesis: that Edward (or Frank) may deflect his trolley if and only if the one has no more claim against the trolley than any of the five has—i.e., that under these circumstances he may deflect it in order to bring about that it takes fewer lives than it would do if he did not.

But while it was at least relatively clear what sorts of things might give the one more of a claim *on* the Health-Pebble, it is less clear what could give the one more of a claim *against* a trolley. Nevertheless there are examples in which it is clear enough that the one has more of a claim against the trolley than any of the five does. Suppose that

(i) The five on the track ahead are regular track workmen, repairing the track—they have been warned of the dangers of their job, and are paid specially high salaries to compensate. The right-hand track is a dead end, unused in ten years. The Mayor, representing the City, has set out picnic tables on it, and invited the convalescents at the nearby City Hospital to have lunch there, guaranteeing them safety from trolleys. The one on the right-hand track is a convalescent having his lunch there; it would never have occurred to him to have his lunch there but for the Mayor's invitation and guarantee of safety. And Edward (Frank) is the Mayor.

The situation if (i) is true is very like the situation if we own the Health-Pebble which is floating in on the tide, and have promised it to the one. If we have promised the Health-Pebble to the one and not to the five, the one has more claim on it than any of the five does, and we therefore may not deflect it away from him; if Edward (Frank) has promised that no trolley shall run down the one, and has not made this promise to the five, the one has more claim to not be run down by it—than any of the five does, and Edward therefore may not deflect it onto him.

So in fact I cheated: it isn't permissible for Edward and Frank to turn their trolleys in *every* possible instance of (5) and (6). Why did it seem as if it would be? The cases were underdescribed, and what you supplied as filler was that the six on the tracks are on a par: that there was nothing further true of any of them which had a bearing on the question whether or not it was permissible to turn the trolleys. In particular, then, you were assuming that it was not the case that the one had more claim against the trolleys than any of any of the five did.

Compare, by contrast, the situation if

(ii) All six on the tracks are regular track workmen, repairing the tracks. As they do every day, they drew straws for their assignments for the day. The one who is on the right-hand track just happened to draw the straw tagged "Right-hand track."

Or if

(iii) All six are innocent people whom villains have tied to the trolley tracks, five on one track, one on the other.

If (ii) or (iii) is true, all six are on a par in the relevant respect: the one has no more claim against the trolley than any of the five has and so the trolley may be turned.

Again, consider the situation if

(iv) The five on the track ahead are regular track workmen, repairing the track. The one on the right-hand track is a schoolboy, collecting pebbles on the track. He knows he doesn't belong there: he climbed the fence to get onto the track, ignoring all warning signs, thinking "Who could find it in his heart to turn a trolley onto a schoolboy?"

At the risk of seeming hardhearted about schoolboys, I have to say I think that if (iv) is true, the trolley not only may be, but must be turned. So it seems to me arguable that if—as I take to be the case if (iv) is true—the five have more case against the trolley than the one does, the trolley not only may be, but must be turned. But for present purposes what counts is only what makes it permissible to turn it where it is permissible to turn it.

President Harry's case, (8), is of course like the cases of Edward and Frank. Harry also deflects something which will harm away from a larger group onto a smaller group. And my proposal is that he may do this because (as we may presume) the Worcesters have no more claim against a Russian bomb than the New Yorkers do.

The situation could have been different. Suppose an avalanche is descending towards a large city. It is possible to deflect it onto a small one. May we? Not if the following is the case. Large City is in avalanche country—the risk of an avalanche is very high there. The founders of Large City were warned of this risk when they built there, and all settlers in it were warned of it before settling there. But lots and lots of people did accept the risk and settle there, because of the beauty of the countryside and the money to be made there. Small City, however, is not in avalanche country—it's flat for miles around; and settlers in Small City settled for a less lovely city, and less money precisely because they did not wish to run the risk of being overrun by an avalanche. Here it seems plain we may not deflect that avalanche onto Small City to save Large City: the Small Cityers have more claim against it than the Large Cityers do. And it could have been the case that New York was settled in the teeth of Russian-bomb-risk.

The fact that it is permissible for President Harry in (8) to deflect that atom bomb onto Worcester brings out something of interest. Mrs. Foot has asked us to suppose "that some tyrant should threaten to torture five men if we ourselves would not torture one." She then asked: "Would it be our duty to do so, supposing we believed him. . .?" Surely not, she implies: for if so anyone who wants us to do something we think wrong has only to threaten that otherwise he himself will do something we think worse. A mad murderer, known to keep his promises, could thus make it our duty to kill some innocent citizen to prevent him from killing two."[3] Mrs. Foot is surely right. But it would be unfair to Mrs. Foot to summarize her point in this way: we must not do a villain's dirty work for him. And wrong, in any case, for suppose the Russians don't really care about New York. The city they really want to destroy is Worcester. But for some reason they can only aim their bomb at New York, which they do in the hope that President Harry will himself deflect it onto Worcester. It seems to me it makes no difference what their aim is: whether they want Worcester or not, Harry can still deflect the bomb onto Worcester. But in doing so, he does the villains' dirty work for them: for if he deflects their bomb, he kills Worcester for them.

Similarly, it doesn't matter whether or not the villains in (iii) want the one on the right-hand track dead: Edward and Frank can all the same turn their trolleys onto him. That a villain wants a group dead gives them no more claim against a bomb or a trolley than these in the other group have.

Mrs. Foot's examples in the passages I quoted are of villains who have not yet launched their threat against anyone, but only threaten to: they have not yet set in train any sequence of events—e.g., by launching a bomb, or by starting a trolley down a track—such that if we don't act, a group will be harmed. The villains have as yet only *said* they would set such a sequence of events in train. I don't object to our acting on the ground of uncertainties: one may, as Mrs. Foot supposes, be perfectly certain that a villain will do exactly what he says he will do. There are two things that make it impermissible to act in this kind of case. In the first place, there are straightforward utilitarian objections to doing so: the last thing we need is to give further villains reason to think they will succeed if they too say such things.[4] But this doesn't take us very far, for as I said, we may deflect an already launched threat away from one group and onto another, and we don't want further villains thinking they'll succeed if they only manage to get such a sequence of events set in train. So the second point is more important: in such cases, to act is *not* to deflect a threat away from one group and onto another, but instead to bring a different threat to bear on the other group. It is to these cases we should now turn.

3. Edward and Frank may turn their trolleys if and only if the one has no more claim against the trolleys than any of the five do. Why is it impermissible for David to cut up his healthy specimen?

I think the Health-Pebble helps here. I said earlier that we might suppose that the one actually owns the Health-Pebble which is floating in on the tide. (It fell off his boat.) And I said that in that case, he has more claim on it than any of the five has, so that we may not deflect it away from him and towards the five. Let's suppose that deflecting isn't in question any more: the pebble has already floated in, and the one has it. Let's suppose he's already put it in his mouth. Or that he's already swallowed it. We certainly may not cut him open to get it out—even if it's not yet digested, and can still be used to save five. Analogously, David may not cut up his healthy specimen to give his parts to five. One doesn't come to own one's parts in the way in which one comes to own a pebble, or a car, or one's grandfather's desk, but a man's parts are his all the same. And therefore that healthy specimen has more claim on those parts than any of the five has—just as if the one owns the Health-Pebble, he has more claim on it than any of the five do.

I do not, and did not, mean to say that we may *never* take from one what belongs to him to give to five. Perhaps there are situations in which we may even take from one something that he needs for life itself in order to give to five. Suppose, for example, that that healthy specimen had caused the five to catch the ailments because of which they need new parts—he deliberately did this in hope the five would die. No doubt a legal code which permitted a surgeon to transplant in situations such as this would be open to abuses, and bad for that reason; but it seems to me it would not be unjust.

So perhaps we can bring David's case in line with Edward's and Frank's, and put the matter like this: David may cut up his healthy specimen and give his parts to the five if and only if the healthy specimen has no more claim on his parts than any of the five do. This leaves it open that in some instances of (4), David may act.

But I am inclined to think there is more to be said of David's case than this. I suggested earlier that if George, in (7), shoves the fat man into the path of the trolley, he does something very like what David does if David cuts up his healthy specimen. Yet George wouldn't be taking anything away from the one in order to give it to the five. George would be 'taking' the fat man's life of course; but what this means is only that George would be killing the fat man, and Edward and Frank kill someone too. And similarly for Irving in (9): if he bombs Worcester, he doesn't take anything away from the Worcesters in order to give it to the New Yorkers.

Moreover, consider the following variant on David's case:

(4') Donald is a great diagnostician. Five of his patients are dying. By chance Donald learns of a healthy specimen such that if Donald cuts him into bits, a peculiar physiological process will be initiated in the five, curing them. Donald can cut his healthy specimen up into bits, killing him, thereby saving his patients. Or he can refrain from doing this, letting his patients die.

In (4'), Donald does not need to give anything which belongs to his healthy specimen to his five; unlike David, he need only cut his healthy specimen up into bits, which can then be thrown out. Yet presumably in whatever circumstances David may not act, Donald may not act either.

So something else is involved in George's, Irving's, and Donald's cases than I drew attention to in David's; and perhaps this other thing is present in David's too.

Suppose that in the original story, where the pebble is floating in on the tide, we are for some reason unable to deflect the pebble away from the one and towards the five. All we can do, if we want the five to get it instead of the one, is to shove the one away, off the beach, out of reach of where the pebble will land; or all we can do is to drop a bomb on the one; or all we can do is cut the one up into bits.

I suppose that there might be circumstances in which it would permissible for us to do one or another of these things to the one—even in circumstances which include that the one owns the pebble. Perhaps it would be permissible to do them if the one had caused the five to catch the ailments because of which they need the pebble, and did this deliberately, in hope the five would die. The important point, however, is this. The fact that the one has no more claim on the pebble than any of the five do does make it permissible for us to deflect the pebble away from the one and towards the five; it does not make it permissible for us to shove the one away, bomb him, or cut him to bits in order to bring about that the five get it.

Why? Here is a good, up for distribution, a Health-Pebble. If we do nothing, one will get it, and five will not; so one will live and five will die. It strikes us that it would be better for five to live and one die than for one to live and five die, and therefore that a better distribution of the good would be for the five to get it, and the one not to. If the one has no more claim on the good than any of the five has, he cannot complain if we do something to *it* in order to bring about that it is better distributed; but he can complain if we do something to *him* in order to bring about that it is better distributed.

If there is a pretty shell on the beach and it is unowned, I cannot complain if you pocket it to give to another person who would get more pleasure from it than I would. But I can complain if you shove me aside so as to be able to pocket it to give to another person who would get more pleasure from it than I would. It's unowned; so you can do to it whatever would be necessary to bring about a better distribution of it. But a *person* is not something unowned, to be knocked about in order to bring about a better distribution of something else.

Here is something bad, up for distribution, a speeding trolley. If nothing is done, five will get it, and one will not; so five will die and one will live. It strikes us that it would be better for five to live and one die than for one to live and five die, and therefore that a better distribution of the bad thing would be for the one to get it, and the five not to. If the one has no more claim against the bad thing than any of the five has, he cannot complain if we do something to *it* in order to bring about that it is better distributed: i.e., it is permissible for Edward and Frank to turn their trolleys. But even if the one has no more claim against the bad thing than any of the five has, he can complain if we do something to *him* in order to bring about that the bad thing is better distributed: i.e., it is not permissible for George to shove his fat man off the bridge into the path of the trolley.

It is true that if Edward and Frank turn their trolleys, they don't merely turn their trolleys: they turn their trolleys onto the one, they run down and thereby kill him. And if you turn a trolley onto a man, if you run him down and thereby kill him, you certainly do something to *him*. (I don't know whether or not it should be said that if you deflect a Health-Pebble away from one who needs it for life, and would get it if you didn't act, you have killed him; perhaps it would be said that you didn't kill him, but only caused his death. It doesn't matter: even if you only caused his death, you certainly did something to him.) So haven't their ones as much ground for complaint as George's fat man? No, for Edward's (Frank's) turning his trolley onto the one, his running the one down and thereby killing him, isn't something he does to the one to bring about that the trolley is better distributed. The trolley's being better distributed *is* its getting onto the one, it *is* running the one down and thereby killing him; and Edward doesn't turn his trolley onto the one, he doesn't run the one down and thereby kill him, in order to bring this about—what he does to bring it about is to turn his trolley. You don't bring about that a thing melts or breaks by melting or breaking it; you bring about that it melts or breaks by (as it might be) putting it on the stove or hitting it with a brick. Similarly, you don't bring about that a thing gets to a man by getting it to him; you bring about that it gets to him by (as it might be) deflecting it, turning it, throwing it—whatever it is you do, by the doing of which you will have got it to the man.

By contrast, George, if he acts, does something to the fat man (shoves him off the bridge into the path of the trolley) to bring about the better distribution of the trolley, viz., that the one (the fat man) gets it instead of the five.

A good bit more would have to be said about the distinction I appeal here if my suggestion is to go through. In part we are hampered by the lack of a theory of action, which should explain, in particular, what it is to bring something about by doing something. But perhaps the intuition is something to take off from: that what matters in these cases in which a threat is to be distributed is whether the agent distributes it by doing something to it, or whether he distributes it by doing something to a person.

The difference between Harry's case and Irving's is, I think, the same. Harry, if he acts, does something to the Russian bomb (deflect it), in order to bring about that it is better distributed: the few Worcesters get it instead of the many New Yorkers. Irving, however, does something to the Worcesters (drops one of our own bombs on them) in order to bring about that the Russian bomb is better distributed: instead of the many New Yorkers getting it, nobody does. Hence the fact that the Worcesters have no more claim against the Russian bomb than the New Yorkers do makes it permissible for Harry to act; but not for Irving to.

If we can speak of making a better distribution of an ailment, we can say of Donald too that if he acts, he does something to his healthy specimen (cut him up into bits) in order to bring about a better distribution of the ailments threatening his five patients: instead of the five patients getting killed by them, nobody is.

And then the special nastiness in David, if he acts, lies in this: in the first place, he gives to five what belongs to the one (viz., bodily parts), *and* in the second place, in order to bring about a better distribution of the ailments threatening his five—i.e., in order to bring about that instead of the five patients getting killed by them, nobody is—he does something to the one (viz., cuts him up).

4. Is killing worse than letting die? I suppose that what those who say it is have in mind may well be true. But this is because I suspect that they do not have in mind anything which is disconfirmed by the fact that there are pairs of acts containing a killing and a letting die in which the first is no worse than the second (e.g,, the pair containing Alfred's and Bert's) *and* also do not have in mind anything which is disconfirmed by the fact that there are cases in which an agent may kill instead of letting die (e.g., Frank's and Harry's). What I suspect they have in mind is something which is confirmed by certain cases in which an agent may not kill instead of letting die (e.g., David's and Donald's). So as I say, I think they may be right. More generally, I suspect that Mrs. Foot and others may be right to say that negative duties are more than positive duties. But we shan't be able to decide until we get clearer what these things come to. I think it's no special worry for them, however. For example, I take it most people think that cutting a man's head off is worse than punching a man in the nose, and I think we aren't any clearer about what this means than they are about their theses. The larger question is a question for all of us.

Meanwhile, however, the thesis that killing is worse than letting die cannot be used in any simple, mechanical way in order to yield conclusions about abortion, euthanasia, and the distribution of scarce medical resources. The cases have to be looked at individually. If nothing else comes out of the preceding discussion, it may anyway serve as a reminder of this: that there are circumstances in which—even if it is true that killing is worse than letting die—one may choose to kill instead of letting die.

Notes

1. Cf. Judith Jarvis Thomson, "Rights and Deaths," *Philosophy and Public Affairs* (Winter 1973), sec. 3. Cf. also Michael Tooley, "Abortion and Infanticide," *Philosophy and*

Public Affairs (Fall 1972), sec. 5, and James Rachels, "Active and Passive Euthanasia," *New England Journal of Medicine*. January 9, 1975.

2. In her very rich article, "Abortion and the Doctrine of the Double Effect," *Oxford Review* 5, (1967). Most of my examples are more or less long-winded expansions of hers. See also G. E. M. Anscombe's brief reply, "Who Is Wronged?" in the same issue of the *Oxford Review*.

3. Foot, "Abortion and the Doctrine," p. 10.

4. Cf. D. H. Hodgson, *Consequences of Utilitarianism: A Study in Normative Ethics & Legal Theory* (New York: Oxford University Press, 1967), pp. 77ff.

Study Questions

1. Explain Kant's distinction between "acting from duty" and "acting according to duty." Of the two, which kind of action is morally right and why? In general, do you agree with Kant that the morality of an action is determined by the motive behind the act and not the consequences of the act? Discuss.

2. Kant understands morality in terms of duty to the moral law, and moral duties are always understood to be matters of constraint, that is, of pulling ourselves back from what we are inclined to do but should not, or toward what we are obliged to do but would rather not. Do you agree with this conception of morality? Why or why not?

3. Why does Kant think that all people are worthy of respect? Notice that he thinks that even vicious and wicked people need to be respected. Do you agree? Why or why not?

4. In light of Kant's "supreme principle of morality," the categorical imperative, explain the difference between perfect duties and imperfect duties. Give some examples of each type of duty from the Kant selection, from the Baron selection and from your own application of the concepts.

5. Explain, in your own words, the difference between Kantianism and W. D. Ross's view (called ethical intuitionism). Give an example where the two views would come to divergent ethical conclusions. What strengths do you see in each of these views? What weaknesses? Which of these views comes closest to your own way of thinking about ethics? Discuss.

6. Explain, in your own words, what Judith Jarvis Thomson calls the "trolley problem." Explain what she argues that these sorts of trolley problems show. Do

you think that Thomson's view is closer to Kantianism, ethical intuitionism or utilitarianism? Discuss.

For Further Reading

Herman, Barbara. *The Practice of Moral Judgment*. Cambridge, MA: Harvard University Press, 1993.

Hill, Thomas E., Jr. *Dignity and Practical Reason in Kant's Moral Theory*. Ithaca, NY: Cornell University Press, 1992.

Kamm, Frances Myrna. "Harming Some to Save Others." *Philosophical Studies* 57 (1989): 227–60.

Korsgaard, Christine M. *Creating the Kingdom of Ends*. Cambridge: Cambridge University Press, 1996.

McNaughton, David. "An Unconnected Heap of Duties?" *Philosophical Quarterly* 46 (1996): 433–47.

Nell (O'Neill), Onora. *Acting on Principle: An Essay on Kantian Ethics*. New York: Columbia University Press, 1975.

Paton, H. J. *The Categorical Imperative*. Philadelphia: University of Pennsylvania Press, 1971.

Rawls, John. *A Theory of Justice*. Cambridge, MA: Harvard University Press, 1971.

Wolff, Robert Paul, ed. *Foundations of the Metaphysics of Morals: Text and Critical Essays*. New York: Bobbs-Merrill, 1969.

CHAPTER SEVEN

Virtue Ethics

Contemporary ethical theory has undergone a significant shift in recent years. After a long period of neglect, virtue ethics has received renewed attention from philosophers and reclaimed its historic place alongside other approaches to ethical theory. Virtue ethics focuses on the qualities or traits of human beings that render us excellent or good as human beings. Virtue ethics is primarily an ethics of *being* rather than an ethics of *doing*. It is concerned more with traits of good character than rules for right action, maintaining that right action is determined by good character.

The notion of "virtue" or *arête* (human excellence) arises early on in Western philosophy, after its introduction in the epic poetry of Homer. Homer's conception of *arête*, with its connection to Ares, the Greek god of war, extols the personal qualities of the effective warrior, emphasizing such virtues as cleverness and physical courage. Greek philosophers, theorizing centuries later, conceived of virtue in less militaristic ways. For Plato, wisdom rather than martial skill is seen as the master virtue. Although courage remains a principal or "cardinal" virtue, along with temperance and justice, wisdom guides these personal qualities that all persons, whether citizens, soldiers or politicians, require to lead lives aimed at both individual and social flourishing. (We will encounter Plato's ethical theory in chapter 9.) It is Plato's student Aristotle (384–322 B.C.E.) who provides the most systematic account of virtue in ancient Greek philosophy, and the selections from his *Nicomachean Ethics* that follow are representative of classical virtue theory.

Aristotle portrays ethics as a practical science whose aim is the achievement of happiness (*eudaimonia*), the highest good of human life. Virtues are those qualities of the soul that both lead to, and are constitutive of, the happy or flourishing human life. Aristotle thought that reason set humans apart from other animals; thus for human beings to flourish, they must live in accordance with reason. For Aristotle, virtues are those stable dispositions or habits that enable us to think, feel and act in accordance with reason. Aristotle's discussion of virtue includes a distinction between virtues of the mind, or intellectual virtues, and virtues of character, or moral virtues. Intellectual virtues are cultivated by teaching and learning. Moral virtues are formed by repeatedly acting in the right way. The moral virtues achieve their task when they dispose the soul to desire, and choose, the mean between extremes. While it might be difficult at first to mold our desires to right reason, it can become second nature to us through gradual habituation, as choosing wisely and acting rightly becomes easy and pleasurable. We have developed moral character.

Virtue ethics can also be found in non-Western philosophical traditions. The ethical teachings of Confucius, or Konzi, (551–479 B.C.E.), the most important philosophical figure in Chinese and all Far-Eastern cultures, are primarily concerned with issues of character development. Confucius was the founder and leading figure of the philosophical School of Literati or Scholars. Teaching during a period in Chinese history characterized by incessant warfare, Confucius sought to bring peace and order to society. In the selections from the *Analects* (*Lunyu*) that follow, we see that Confucian philosophy is mainly concerned with the perfection of society through the perfection of human beings. This requires a process of moral self-cultivation, whereby persons are molded and refined, through education and enculturation, into virtuous individuals modeled after the sages and kings of old. Confucian training in moral character is designed to produce a *junzi*, a superior person, a term that has its origins in the feudal system of ancient China for a member of the aristocratic class, literally, a "son of the ruler." In general, the *junzi* is courteous, proper, broad-minded, diligent, kind, respectful of tradition and others, sincere and calm and seeks to "enlarge" or aid others. As such, the *junzi* is contrasted with the small or petty person, who only seeks his or her own profit or self-interest.

The highest virtue for Confucius is *ren*, which means "benevolence" or "human-heartedness," but can also mean "love" or "kindness" or simply "virtue." The virtuous person also possesses a sense of righteousness expressed primarily through the qualities of conscientiousness regarding the welfare of others and altruism, whereby one does not do to others what one does not want done to oneself. For Confucius, moral self-cultivation begins at home, as reverence and respect for one's parents extends to all elders and all family members and eventually, all persons in society. It is also aided by the arts of peace, such as music, poetry and calligraphy, among others, which helps one develop self-discipline while instilling a sense of harmony and an appreciation for proper, ritualized action. The virtuous person or *junzi* serves as an example for others to follow; indeed, for Confucius, the flourishing of society requires that its political leaders be persons of virtue, who lead by moral example rather than by power or force.

To return our attention to Western culture, with the rise of the Enlightenment, evaluations of actions outcome-based (consequentialist) or duty-based (deontological) ethical theories come to dominate modern moral philosophy to the exclusion of virtue ethics. Eighteenth-century Scottish philosopher David Hume, whose perspective stands in what is often called the British sentimentalist tradition, is an important exception. He is among those who thought that morality is based more in human *feeling* than in human *reason*. Hume thought that reason always concerns what *is*—matters of fact or of logic that concern the nature of reality. Facts and logic, Hume thought, were inert—they cannot, in and of themselves, move us or motivate us to action. In contrast, morality always concerns *the way things ought to be* and gives us motivation for either acting in ways that bring about certain outcomes or refraining from action from a desire to avoid certain outcomes. Morality, he concluded, must be rooted in some fundamental emotion shared by all persons. Hume calls this emotion "the sentiment of humanity"—our tendency to be pleased by what pleases others and pained by what others find painful.

The following selection from *An Enquiry Concerning the Principles of Morals* summarizes Hume's account of humanity and how the various virtues and vices stem from this emotional source. Some characteristics are pleasing to human beings in general because they are useful; others are immediately agreeable—they just are the kind of thing that delights all human beings. These categories of the useful and the immediately agreeable are further subdivided into characteristics that are useful or agreeable to *oneself* and characteristics that are useful or agreeable to *others*.

There is perhaps no one more responsible for the renewed attention amongst philosophers to the once-neglected notion of virtue than Alasdair MacIntyre. In *After Virtue*, published in 1981, MacIntyre unleashed a stunning critique of both modern morality and its intellectual expression, modern moral philosophy. In their attempt to find rational justification for universal principles of morality, MacIntyre claims, modern moral philosophers became bogged down in endless debates about the rules that ground moral action and ignored such traditional moral matters as the nature of the good life and the personal qualities that make one a good human being—the virtues. For MacIntyre, the "Enlightenment Project" is characterized by the attempt to rise above any particular, historical tradition of moral ideals or practices in order to latch on to a set of ahistorical, universal moral principles justified by pure reason alone. What had to be discarded in this attempt at establishing neutral moral principles with which all rational agents could agree was an allegiance to a particular moral community or tradition and a shared conception of what it was to satisfy the end or aim (*telos*) of human life. As a result, notions of the human good and the particular traits of character needed to achieve life's ultimate end or highest good—the virtues—were also abandoned.

MacIntyre advocates a return to the Aristotelian tradition of the virtues to right the wrong turn made by modern moral philosophy, but in doing so he wishes to eschew Aristotle's "metaphysical biology." In presenting his own version of virtue ethics, MacIntyre focuses on personal qualities that enable human beings to achieve goods internal to practices rather than external to such practices. An example of a good internal to practice would be patient health in the practice of medicine, whereas goods external to the practice of medicine would be money or fame. A good physician would have qualities that enabled her to achieve patient health, not money or fame, even if these external goods are acquired as well. Virtues would then also require a community that sets the standards of excellence for practices that achieve the ends or goods of the practice in question, as well as a narrative conception of the self that is set within the larger story of a community or tradition. MacIntyre's "communitarian" conception of the virtues has led some to criticize his perspective as too relativistic to serve as an alternative to the types of ethical theories MacIntyre hopes virtue ethics will replace.

Our final selection in this chapter is an applied example of virtue ethics. In "Ideals of Human Excellence and Preserving Natural Environments," Thomas Hill Jr. argues that reasons against destroying the natural world drawn from standard moral theories—plant's rights, the sacredness of the Earth, the intrinsic value of life, etcetera—fail to be persuasive to many who are simply not concerned by such acts of destruction. He suggests that instead of trying to show that acts of destruction against nature are wrong, we focus instead on the character of the person who acts to destroy nature, and ask "What sort of person would do this on purpose?" For Hill, the kind of indifference displayed by those who are unconcerned by the destruction of nature might easily reflect other moral qualities such as ignorance or self-importance in that it is a failure to understand or appreciate one's place in nature. Since many would regard such ignorance or self-importance as vices opposed to desirable personal qualities or virtues such as humility or gratitude or sensitivity to others, many would then have good reason to treat the natural world with love and respect rather than indifference to its destruction.

*Nicomachean Ethics**

Aristotle

Book I

1

Every art and every inquiry, and similarly every action and pursuit, is thought to aim at some good; and for this reason the good has rightly been declared to be that at which all things aim. But a certain difference is found among ends; some are activities, others are products apart from the activities that produce them. Where there are ends apart from the actions, it is the nature of the products to be better than the activities. Now, as there are many actions, arts, and sciences, their ends also are many; the end of the medical art is health, that of shipbuilding a vessel, that of strategy victory, that of economics wealth. But where such arts fall under a single capacity—as bridle-making and the other arts concerned with the equipment of horses fall under the art of riding, and this and every military action under strategy, in the same way other arts fall under yet others—in all of these the ends of the master arts are to be preferred to all the subordinate ends; for it is for the sake of the former that the latter are pursued. It makes no difference whether the activities themselves are the ends of the actions, or something else apart from the activities, as in the case of the sciences just mentioned.

2

If, then, there is some end of the things we do, which we desire for its own sake (everything else being desired for the sake of this), and if we do not choose everything for the sake of something else (for at that rate the process would go on to infinity, so that our desire would be empty and vain), clearly this must be the good and the chief good. Will not the knowledge of it, then, have a great influence on life? Shall we not, like archers who have a mark to aim at, be more likely to hit upon what is right? If so, we must try, in outline at least, to determine what it is, and of which of the sciences or capacities it is the object. It would seem to belong to the most authoritative art and that which is most truly the master art. And politics appears to be of this nature; for it is this that ordains which of the sciences should be studied in a state, and which each class of citizens should learn and up to what point they should learn them; and we see even the most highly esteemed of capacities to

*From *The Works of Aristotle*, translated by W. D. Ross (Oxford University Press, 1915).

fall under this, e.g. strategy, economics, rhetoric; now, since politics uses the rest of the sciences, and since, again, it legislates as to what we are to do and what we are to abstain from, the end of this science must include those of the others, so that this end must be the good for man. For even if the end is the same for a single man and for a state, that of the state seems at all events something greater and more complete whether to attain or to preserve; though it is worth while to attain the end merely for one man, it is finer and more godlike to attain it for a nation or for city-states. These, then, are the ends at which our inquiry aims, since it is political science, in one sense of that term.

3

Our discussion will be adequate if it has as much clearness as the subject-matter admits of, for precision is not to be sought for alike in all discussions, any more than in all the products of the crafts. Now fine and just actions, which political science investigates, admit of much variety and fluctuation of opinion, so that they may be thought to exist only by convention, and not by nature. And goods also give rise to a similar fluctuation because they bring harm to many people; for before now men have been undone by reason of their wealth, and others by reason of their courage. We must be content, then, in speaking of such subjects and with such premisses to indicate the truth roughly and in outline, and in speaking about things which are only for the most part true and with premisses of the same kind to reach conclusions that are no better. In the same spirit, therefore, should each type of statement be received; for it is the mark of an educated man to look for precision in each class of things just so far as the nature of the subject admits; it is evidently equally foolish to accept probable reasoning from a mathematician and to demand from a rhetorician scientific proofs.

Now each man judges well the things he knows, and of these he is a good judge. And so the man who has been educated in a subject is a good judge of that subject, and the man who has received an all-round education is a good judge in general. Hence a young man is not a proper hearer of lectures on political science; for he is inexperienced in the actions that occur in life, but its discussions start from these and are about these; and, further, since he tends to follow his passions, his study will be vain and unprofitable, because the end aimed at is not knowledge but action. And it makes no difference whether he is young in years or youthful in character; the defect does not depend on time, but on his living, and pursuing each successive object, as passion directs. For to such persons, as to the incontinent, knowledge brings no profit; but to those who desire and act in accordance with a rational principle knowledge about such matters will be of great benefit.

These remarks about the student, the sort of treatment to be expected, and the purpose of the inquiry, may be taken as our preface.

4

Let us resume our inquiry and state, in view of the fact that all knowledge and every pursuit aims at some good, what it is that we say political science aims at and what is the highest of all goods achievable by action. Verbally there is very general agreement; for both the general run of men and people of superior refinement say that it is happiness, and identify living well and doing well with being happy; but with regard to what happiness is they differ, and the many do not give the same account as the wise. For the former think it is some plain and obvious thing, like pleasure, wealth, or honour; they differ, however, from one another—and often even the same man identifies it with different things, with health when he is ill, with wealth when he is poor; but, conscious of their ignorance, they admire those who proclaim some great ideal that is above their comprehension. Now some thought that apart from these many goods there is another which is self-subsistent and causes the goodness of all these as well. To examine all the opinions that have been held were perhaps somewhat fruitless; enough to examine those that are most prevalent or that seem to be arguable.

Let us not fail to notice, however, that there is a difference between arguments from and those to the first principles. For Plato, too, was right in raising this question and asking, as he used to do, 'are we on the way from or to the first principles?' There is a difference, as there is in a race-course between the course from the judges to the turning-point and the way back. For, while we must begin with what is known, things are objects of knowledge in two senses—some to us, some without qualification. Presumably, then, we must begin with things known to us. Hence any one who is to listen intelligently to lectures about what is noble and just, and generally, about the subjects of political science must have been brought up in good habits. For the fact is the starting-point, and if this is sufficiently plain to him, he will not at the start need the reason as well; and the man who has been well brought up has or can easily get starting-points. And as for him who neither has nor can get them, let him hear the words of Hesiod:

> Far best is he who knows all things himself;
> Good, he that hearkens when men counsel right;
> But he who neither knows, nor lays to heart
> Another's wisdom, is a useless wight.

5

Let us, however, resume our discussion from the point at which we digressed. To judge from the lives that men lead, most men, and men of the most vulgar type, seem (not without some ground) to identify the good, or happiness, with pleasure; which is the reason why they love the life of enjoyment. For there are, we may say, three prominent types of life—that just mentioned, the political, and thirdly the contemplative life. Now the mass of mankind are evidently quite slavish in their tastes, preferring a life suitable to beasts, but they get some ground for their view from the fact that many of those in high places share the tastes of Sardanapallus. A consideration of the prominent types of life shows that people of superior refinement and of active disposition identify happiness with honour; for this is, roughly speaking, the end of the political life. But it seems too superficial to be what we are looking for, since it is thought to depend on those who bestow honour rather than on him who receives it, but the good we divine to be something proper to a man and not easily taken from him. Further, men seem to pursue honour in order that they may be assured of their goodness; at least it is by men of practical wisdom that they seek to be honoured, and among those who know them, and on the ground of their virtue; clearly, then, according to them, at any rate, virtue is better. And perhaps one might even suppose this to be, rather than honour, the end of the political life. But even this appears somewhat incomplete; for possession of virtue seems actually compatible with being asleep, or with lifelong inactivity, and, further, with the greatest sufferings and misfortunes; but a man who was living so no one would call happy, unless he were maintaining a thesis at all costs. But enough of this; for the subject has been sufficiently treated even in the current discussions. Third comes the contemplative life, which we shall consider later.

The life of money-making is one undertaken under compulsion, and wealth is evidently not the good we are seeking; for it is merely useful and for the sake of something else. And so one might rather take the aforenamed objects to be ends; for they are loved for themselves. But it is evident that not even these are ends; yet many arguments have been thrown away in support of them. Let us leave this subject, then.

6

We had perhaps better consider the universal good and discuss thoroughly what is meant by it, although such an inquiry is made an uphill one by the fact that the Forms have been introduced by friends of our own. Yet it would perhaps be thought to be better, indeed to be our duty, for the sake of maintaining the truth even to destroy what touches us closely, especially as we are philosophers or lovers of wisdom; for, while both are dear, piety requires us to honour truth above our friends.

The men who introduced this doctrine did not posit Ideas of classes within which they recognized priority and posteriority (which is the reason why they did not maintain the existence of an Idea embracing all numbers); but the term 'good' is used both in the category of substance and in that of quality and in that of relation, and that which is per se, i.e. substance, is prior in nature to the relative (for the latter is like an offshoot and accident of being); so that there could not be a common Idea set over all these goods. Further, since 'good' has as many senses as 'being' (for it is predicated both in the category of substance, as of God and of reason, and in quality, i.e. of the virtues, and in quantity, i.e. of that which is moderate, and in relation, i.e. of the useful, and in time, i.e. of the right opportunity, and in place, i.e. of the right locality and the like), clearly it cannot be something universally present in all cases and single; for then it could not have been predicated in all the categories but in one only. Further, since of the things answering to one Idea there is one science, there would have been one science of all the goods; but as it is there are many sciences even of the things that fall under one category, e.g. of opportunity, for opportunity in war is studied by strategics and in disease by medicine, and the moderate in food is studied by medicine and in exercise by the science of gymnastics. And one might ask the question, what in the world they mean by 'a thing itself', is (as is the case) in 'man himself' and in a particular man the account of man is one and the same. For in so far as they are man, they will in no respect differ; and if this is so, neither will 'good itself' and particular goods, in so far as they are good. But again it will not be good any the more for being eternal, since that which lasts long is no whiter than that which perishes in a day. The Pythagoreans seem to give a more plausible account of the good, when they place the one in the column of goods; and it is they that Speusippus seems to have followed.

But let us discuss these matters elsewhere; an objection to what we have said, however, may be discerned in the fact that the Platonists have not been speaking about all goods, and that the goods that are pursued and loved for themselves are called good by reference to a single Form, while those which tend to produce or to preserve these somehow or to prevent their contraries are called so by reference to these, and in a secondary sense. Clearly, then, goods must be spoken of in two ways, and some must be good in themselves, the others by reason of these. Let us separate, then, things good in themselves from things useful, and consider whether the former are called good by reference to a single Idea. What sort of goods would one call good in themselves? Is it those that are pursued even when isolated from others, such as intelligence, sight, and certain pleasures and honours? Certainly, if we pursue these also for the sake of something else, yet one would place them among things good in themselves. Or is nothing other than the Idea of good good in itself? In that case the Form will be empty. But if the things we have named are also things good in themselves, the account of the good will have to appear as something identical in them all, as that of whiteness is identical in snow and in white lead. But of honour, wisdom, and pleasure, just in respect of their goodness, the accounts are distinct and diverse. The good, therefore, is not some common element answering to one Idea.

But what then do we mean by the good? It is surely not like the things that only chance to have the same name. Are goods one, then, by being derived from one good or by all contributing to one good, or are they rather one by analogy? Certainly as sight is in the body, so is reason in the soul, and so on in other cases. But perhaps these subjects had better be dismissed for the present; for perfect precision about them would be more appropriate to another branch of philosophy. And similarly with regard to the Idea; even if there is some one good which is universally predicable of goods or is capable of separate and independent existence, clearly it could not be achieved or attained by man; but we are now seeking something attainable. Perhaps, however, some one might think it worthwhile to recognize this with a view to the goods that are attainable and achievable; for having this as a sort of pattern we shall know better the goods that are good for us, and if we know them shall attain them. This argument has some plausibility, but seems to clash with the procedure of the sciences; for all of these, though they aim at some good and seek to supply the deficiency of it, leave on one side the knowledge of the good. Yet that all the exponents of the arts should be ignorant of, and should not even seek, so great an aid is not probable. It is hard, too, to see how a weaver or a carpenter will be benefited in regard to his own craft by knowing this 'good itself', or how the man who has viewed the Idea itself will be a better doctor or general thereby. For a doctor seems not even to study health in this way, but the health of man, or perhaps rather the health of a particular man; it is individuals that he is healing. But enough of these topics.

7

Let us again return to the good we are seeking, and ask what it can be. It seems different in different actions and arts; it is different in medicine, in strategy, and in the other arts likewise. What then is the good of each? Surely that for whose sake everything else is done. In medicine this is health, in strategy victory, in architecture a house, in any other sphere something else, and in every action and pursuit the end; for it is for the sake of this that all men do whatever else they do. Therefore, if there is an end for all that we do, this will be the good achievable by action, and if there are more than one, these will be the goods achievable by action.

So the argument has by a different course reached the same point; but we must try to state this even more clearly. Since there are evidently more than one end, and we choose some of these (e.g. wealth, flutes, and in general instruments) for the sake of something else, clearly not all ends are final ends; but the chief good is evidently something final. Therefore, if there is only one final end, this will be what we are seeking, and if there are more than one, the most final of these will be what we are seeking. Now we call that which is in itself worthy of pursuit more final than that which is worthy of pursuit for the sake of something else, and that which is never desirable for the sake of something else more final than the things that are desirable both in themselves and for the sake of that other thing, and therefore we call final without qualification that which is always desirable in itself and never for the sake of something else.

Now such a thing happiness, above all else, is held to be; for this we choose always for self and never for the sake of something else, but honour, pleasure, reason, and every virtue we choose indeed for themselves (for if nothing resulted from them we should still choose each of them), but we choose them also for the sake of happiness, judging that by means of them we shall be happy. Happiness, on the other hand, no one chooses for the sake of these, nor, in general, for anything other than itself.

From the point of view of self-sufficiency the same result seems to follow; for the final good is thought to be self-sufficient. Now by self-sufficient we do not mean that which is sufficient for a man by himself, for one who lives a solitary life, but also for parents, children, wife, and in general for his friends and fellow citizens, since man is born for citizenship. But some limit must be set to this; for if we extend our requirement to ancestors and descendants and friends' friends we are in for an infinite series. Let us examine this question, however, on another occasion; the self-sufficient we now define as that which when isolated makes life desirable and lacking in nothing; and such we think happiness to be; and further we think it most desirable of all things, without being counted as one good thing among others—if it were so counted it would clearly be made more desirable by the addition of even the least of goods; for that which is added becomes an excess of goods, and of goods the greater is always more desirable. Happiness, then, is something final and self-sufficient, and is the end of action.

Presumably, however, to say that happiness is the chief good seems a platitude, and a clearer account of what it is still desired. This might perhaps be given, if we could first ascertain the function of man. For just as for a flute-player, a sculptor, or an artist, and, in general, for all things that have a function or activity, the good and the 'well' is thought to reside in the function, so would it seem to be for man, if he has a function. Have the carpenter, then, and the tanner certain functions or activities, and has man none? Is he born without a function? Or as eye, hand, foot, and in general each of the parts evidently has a function, may one lay it down that man similarly has a function apart from all these? What then can this be? Life seems to be common even to plants, but we are seeking what is peculiar to man. Let us exclude, therefore, the life of nutrition and growth. Next there would be a life of perception, but it also seems to be common even to the horse, the ox, and every animal. There remains, then, an active life of the element that has a rational principle; of this, one part has such a principle in the sense of being obedient to one, the other in the sense of possessing one and exercising thought. And, as 'life of the rational element' also has two meanings, we must state that life in the sense of activity is what we mean; for this seems to be the more proper sense of the term. Now if the function of man is an activity of soul which follows or implies a rational principle, and if we say 'so-and-so' and 'a good so-and-so' have a function which is the same in kind, e.g. a lyre, and a good lyre-player, and so without qualification in all cases, eminence in respect of goodness being added to the name of the function (for the function of a lyre-player is to play the lyre, and that of a good lyre-player is to do so well): if this is the case, and we state the function of man to be a certain kind of life, and this to be an activity or actions of the soul implying a rational principle, and the function of a good man to be the good and noble performance of these, and if any action is well performed when it is performed in accordance with the appropriate excellence: if this is the case, human good turns out to be activity of soul in accordance with virtue, and if there are more than one virtue, in accordance with the best and most complete.

But we must add 'in a complete life.' For one swallow does not make a summer, nor does one day; and so too one day, or a short time, does not make a man blessed and happy.

Let this serve as an outline of the good; for we must presumably first sketch it roughly, and then later fill in the details. But it would seem that any one is capable of carrying on and articulating what has once been well outlined, and that time is a good discoverer or partner in such a work; to which facts the advances of the arts are due; for any one can add what is lacking. And we must also remember what has been said before, and not look for precision in all things alike, but in each class of things such precision as accords with the subject-matter, and so much as is appropriate to the inquiry. For a carpenter and a geometer investigate the right angle in different ways; the former does so in so far as the right angle is useful for his work, while the latter inquires what it is or what sort of thing it is; for he is a spectator of the truth. We must act in the same way, then, in all other matters as well, that our main task may not be subordinated to minor questions. Nor must we demand the cause in all matters alike; it is enough in some cases that the fact be well established, as in the case of the first principles; the fact is the primary thing or first principle. Now of first principles we see some by induction, some by perception, some by a certain habituation, and others too in other ways. But each set of principles we must try to investigate in the natural way, and we must take pains to state them definitely, since they have a great influence on what follows. For the beginning is thought to be more than half of the whole, and many of the questions we ask are cleared up by it.

8

We must consider it, however, in the light not only of our conclusion and our premisses, but also of what is commonly said about it; for with a true view all the data harmonize, but with a false one the facts soon clash. Now goods have been divided into three classes, and some are described as external, others as relating to soul or to body; we call those that relate to soul most properly and truly goods, and psychical actions and activities we class as relating to soul. Therefore our account must be sound, at least according to this view, which is an old one and agreed on by philosophers. It is correct also in that we identify the end with certain actions and activities; for thus it falls among goods of the soul and not among external goods. Another belief which harmonizes with our account is that the happy man lives well and does well; for we have practically defined happiness as a sort of good life and good action. The characteristics that are looked for in happiness seem also, all of them, to belong to what we have defined happiness as being. For some identify happiness with virtue, some with practical wisdom, others with a kind of philosophic wisdom, others with these, or one of these, accompanied by pleasure or not without pleasure; while others include also external prosperity. Now some of these views have been held by many men and men of old, others by a few eminent persons; and it is not probable that either of these should be entirely mistaken, but rather that they should be right in at least some one respect or even in most respects.

With those who identify happiness with virtue or some one virtue our account is in harmony; for to virtue belongs virtuous activity. But it makes, perhaps, no small difference whether we place the chief good in possession or in use, in state of mind or in activity. For the state of mind may exist without producing any good result, as in a man who is asleep or in some other way quite inactive, but the activity cannot; for one who has the activity will of necessity be acting, and acting well. And as in the Olympic Games it is not the most beautiful and the strongest that are crowned but those who compete (for it is some of these that are victorious), so those who act win, and rightly win, the noble and good things in life.

Their life is also in itself pleasant. For pleasure is a state of soul, and to each man that which he is said to be a lover of is pleasant; e.g. not only is a horse pleasant to the lover of horses, and a spectacle to the lover of sights, but also in the same way just acts are pleasant to the lover of justice and in general virtuous acts to the lover of virtue. Now for most men their pleasures are in conflict with one another because these are not by nature pleasant, but the lovers of what is noble find pleasant the things that are by nature pleasant; and virtuous actions are such, so that these are pleasant for such men as well as in their own nature. Their life, therefore, has no further need of pleasure as a sort of adventitious charm, but has its pleasure in itself. For, besides what we have said, the man who does not rejoice in noble actions is not even good; since no one would call a man just who did not enjoy acting justly, nor any man liberal who did not enjoy liberal actions; and similarly in all other cases. If this is so, virtuous actions must be in themselves pleasant. But they are also good and noble, and have each of these attributes in the highest degree, since the good man judges well about these attributes; his judgement is such as we have described. Happiness then is the best, noblest, and most pleasant thing in the world, and these attributes are not severed as in the inscription at Delos

> Most noble is that which is justest, and best is health;
> But pleasantest is it to win what we love.

For all these properties belong to the best activities; and these, or one—the best—of these, we identify with happiness.

Yet evidently, as we said, it needs the external goods as well; for it is impossible, or not easy, to do noble acts without the proper equipment. In many actions we use friends and riches and political power as instruments; and there are some things the lack of which takes the lustre from happiness, as good birth, goodly children, beauty; for the man who is very ugly in appearance or ill-born or solitary and childless is not very likely to be happy, and perhaps a man would be still less likely if he had thoroughly bad children or friends or had lost good children or friends by death. As we said, then, happiness seems to need this sort of prosperity in addition; for which reason some identify happiness with good fortune, though others identify it with virtue.

9

For this reason also the question is asked, whether happiness is to be acquired by learning or by habituation or some other sort of training, or comes in virtue of some divine providence or again by chance. Now if there is any gift of the gods to men, it is reasonable that happiness should be god-given, and most surely god-given of all human things inasmuch as it is the best. But this question would perhaps be more appropriate to another inquiry; happiness seems, however, even if it is not god-sent but comes as a result of virtue and some process of learning or training, to be among the most godlike things; for that which is the prize and end of virtue seems to be the best thing in the world, and something godlike and blessed.

It will also on this view be very generally shared; for all who are not maimed as regards their potentiality for virtue may win it by a certain kind of study and care. But if it is better to be happy thus than by chance, it is reasonable that the facts should be so, since everything that depends on the action of nature is by nature as good as it can be, and similarly everything that depends on art or any rational cause, and especially if it depends on the best of all causes. To entrust to chance what is greatest and most noble would be a very defective arrangement.

The answer to the question we are asking is plain also from the definition of happiness; for it has been said to be a virtuous activity of soul, of a certain kind. Of the remaining goods, some must necessarily pre-exist as conditions of happiness, and others are naturally co-operative and useful as instruments. And this will be found to agree with what we said at the outset; for we stated the end of political science to be the best end, and political science spends most of its pains on making the citizens to be of a certain character, viz. good and capable of noble acts.

It is natural, then, that we call neither ox nor horse nor any other of the animals happy; for none of them is capable of sharing in such activity. For this reason also a boy is not happy; for he is not yet capable of such acts, owing to his age; and boys who are called happy are being congratulated by reason of the hopes we have for them. For there is required, as we said, not only complete virtue but also a complete life, since many changes occur in life, and all manner of chances, and the most prosperous may fall into great misfortunes in old age, as is told of Priam in the Trojan Cycle; and one who has experienced such chances and has ended wretchedly no one calls happy.

10

Must no one at all, then, be called happy while he lives; must we, as Solon says, see the end? Even if we are to lay down this doctrine, is it also the case that a man is happy when he is dead? Or is not this quite absurd, especially for us who say that happiness is an activity? But if we do not call the dead man happy, and if Solon does not mean this, but that one can then safely call a man blessed as being at last beyond evils and misfortunes, this also affords matter for discussion; for both evil and good are thought to exist for a dead man, as much as for one who is alive but not aware of them; e.g. honours and dishonours and the good or bad fortunes of children and in general of descendants. And this also presents a problem; for though a man has lived happily up to old age and has had a death worthy of his life, many reverses may befall his descendants—some of them may be good and attain the life they deserve, while with others the opposite may be the case; and clearly too the degrees of relationship between them and their ancestors may vary indefinitely. It would be odd, then, if the dead man were to share in these changes and become at one time happy, at another wretched; while it would also be odd if the fortunes of the descendants did not for some time have some effect on the happiness of their ancestors.

But we must return to our first difficulty; for perhaps by a consideration of it our present problem might be solved. Now if we must see the end and only then call a man happy, not as being happy but as having been so before, surely this is a paradox, that when he is happy the attribute that belongs to him is not to be truly predicated of him because we do not wish to call living men happy, on account of the changes that may befall them, and because we have assumed happiness to be something permanent and by no means easily changed, while a single man may suffer many turns of fortune's wheel. For clearly if we were to keep pace with his fortunes, we should often call the same man happy and again wretched, making the happy man out to be chameleon and insecurely based. Or is this keeping pace with his fortunes quite wrong? Success or failure in life does not depend on these, but human life, as we said, needs these as mere additions, while virtuous activities or their opposites are what constitute happiness or the reverse.

The question we have now discussed confirms our definition. For no function of man has so much permanence as virtuous activities (these are thought to be more durable even than knowledge of the sciences), and of these themselves the most valuable are more durable because those who are happy spend their life most readily and most continuously in these; for this seems to be the reason why we do not forget them. The attribute in question, then, will belong to the happy man, and he will be happy throughout his life; for always, or by preference to everything else, he will be engaged in virtuous action and contemplation, and he will bear the chances of life most nobly and altogether decorously, if he is 'truly good' and 'foursquare beyond reproach'.

Now many events happen by chance, and events differing in importance; small pieces of good fortune or of its opposite clearly do not weigh down the scales of life one way or the other, but a multitude of great events if they turn out well will make life happier (for not only are they themselves such as to add beauty to life, but the way a man deals with them may be noble and good), while if they turn out ill they crush and maim happiness; for they both bring pain with them and hinder many activities. Yet even in these nobility shines through, when a man bears with resignation many great misfortunes, not through insensibility to pain but through nobility and greatness of soul.

If activities are, as we said, what gives life its character, no happy man can become miserable; for he will never do the acts that are hateful and mean. For the man who is truly good and wise, we think, bears all the chances in life becomingly and always makes the best of circumstances, as a good general makes the best military use of the army at his command and a good shoemaker makes the best shoes out of the hides that are given him; and so with all other craftsmen. And if this is the case, the happy man can never become miserable; though he will not reach blessedness, if he meet with fortunes like those of Priam.

Nor, again, is he many-coloured and changeable; for neither will he be moved from his happy state easily or by any ordinary misadventures, but only by many great ones, nor, if he has had many great misadventures, will he recover his happiness in a short time, but if at all, only in a long and complete one in which he has attained many splendid successes.

When then should we not say that he is happy who is active in accordance with complete virtue and is sufficiently equipped with external goods, not for some chance period but throughout a complete life? Or must we add 'and who is destined to live thus and die as befits his life'? Certainly the future is obscure to us, while happiness, we claim, is an end and something in every way final. If so, we shall call happy those among living men in whom these conditions are, and are to be, fulfilled—but happy men. So much for these questions.

11

That the fortunes of descendants and of all a man's friends should not affect his happiness at all seems a very unfriendly doctrine, and one opposed to the opinions men hold; but since the events that happen are numerous and admit of all sorts of difference, and some come more near to us and others less so, it seems a long—nay, an infinite—task to discuss each in detail; a general outline will perhaps suffice. If, then, as some of a man's own misadventures have a certain weight and influence on life while others are, as it were, lighter, so too there are differences among the misadventures of our friends taken as a whole, and it makes a difference whether the various suffering befall the living or the dead (much more even than whether lawless and terrible deeds are presupposed in a tragedy or done on the stage), this difference also must be taken into account; or rather, perhaps, the fact that doubt is felt whether the dead share in any good or evil. For it seems, from these considerations, that even if anything whether good or evil penetrates to them, it must be something weak and negligible, either in itself or for them, or if not, at least it must be such in degree and kind as not to make happy those who are not happy nor to take away their blessedness from those who are. The good or bad fortunes of friends, then, seem to have some effects on the dead, but effects of such a kind and degree as neither to make the happy unhappy nor to produce any other change of the kind.

12

These questions having been definitely answered, let us consider whether happiness is among the things that are praised or rather among the things that are prized; for clearly it is not to be placed among potentialities. Everything that is praised seems to be praised because it is of a certain kind and is related somehow to something else; for we praise the just or brave man and in general both the good man and virtue itself because of the actions and functions involved, and we praise the strong man, the good runner, and so on, because he is of a certain kind and is related in a certain way to something good and important. This is clear also from the praises of the gods; for it seems absurd that the gods should be referred to our standard, but this is done because praise involves a reference, to something else. But if praise is for things such as we have described, clearly what applies to the best things is not praise, but something greater and better, as is indeed obvious; for what we do to the gods and the most godlike of men is to call them blessed and happy. And so too with good things; no one praises happiness as he does justice, but rather calls it blessed, as being something more divine and better.

Eudoxus also seems to have been right in his method of advocating the supremacy of pleasure; he thought that the fact that, though a good, it is not praised indicated it to be better than the things that are praised, and that this is what God and the good are; for by reference to these all other things are judged. Praise is appropriate to virtue, for as a result of virtue men tend to do noble deeds, but encomia are bestowed on acts, whether of the body or of the soul. But perhaps nicety in these matters is more proper to those who have made a study of encomia; to us it is clear from what has been said that happiness is among the things that are prized and perfect. It seems to be so also from the fact that it is a first principle; for it is for the sake of this that we all do all that we do, and the first principle and cause of goods is, we claim, something prized and divine.

13

Since happiness is an activity of soul in accordance with perfect virtue, we must consider the nature of virtue; for perhaps we shall thus see better the nature of happiness. The true student of politics, too, is thought to have studied virtue above all things; for he wishes to make his fellow citizens good and obedient to the laws. As an example of this we have the lawgivers of the Cretans and the Spartans, and any others of the kind that there may have been. And if this inquiry belongs to political science, clearly the pursuit of it will be in accordance with our original plan. But clearly the virtue we must study is human virtue; for the good we were seeking was human good and the happiness human happiness. By human virtue we mean not that of the body but that of the soul; and happiness also we call an activity of soul. But if this is so, clearly the student of politics must know somehow the facts about soul, as the man who is to heal the eyes or the body as a whole must know about the eyes or the body; and all the more since politics is more prized and better than medicine; but even among doctors the best educated spend much labour on acquiring knowledge of the body. The student of politics, then, must study the soul, and must study it with these objects in view, and do so just to the extent which is sufficient for the questions we are discussing; for further precision is perhaps something more laborious than our purposes require.

Some things are said about it, adequately enough, even in the discussions outside our school, and we must use these; e.g. that one element in the soul is irrational and one has a rational principle. Whether these are separated as the parts of the body or of anything divisible are, or are distinct by definition but by nature inseparable, like convex and concave in the circumference of a circle, does not affect the present question.

Of the irrational element one division seems to be widely distributed, and vegetative in its nature, I mean that which causes nutrition and growth; for it is this kind of power of the soul that one must assign to all nurslings and to embryos, and this same power to fullgrown creatures; this is more reasonable than to assign some different power to them. Now the excellence of this seems to be common to all species and not specifically human; for this part or faculty seems to function most in sleep, while goodness and badness are least manifest in sleep (whence comes the saying that the happy are not better off than the wretched for half their lives; and this happens naturally enough, since sleep is an inactivity of the soul in that respect in which it is called good or bad), unless perhaps to a small extent some of the movements actually penetrate to the soul, and in this respect the dreams of good men are better than those of ordinary people. Enough of this subject, however; let us leave the nutritive faculty alone, since it has by its nature no share in human excellence.

There seems to be also another irrational element in the soul—one which in a sense, however, shares in a rational principle. For we praise the rational principle of the continent man and of the incontinent, and the part of their soul that has such a principle, since it urges them aright and towards the best objects; but there is found in them also another element naturally opposed to the rational principle, which fights against and resists that principle. For exactly as paralysed limbs when we intend to move them to the right turn on the contrary to the left, so is it with the soul; the impulses of incontinent people move in contrary directions. But while in the body we see that which moves astray, in the soul we do not. No doubt, however, we must none the less suppose that in the soul too there is something contrary to the rational principle, resisting and opposing it. In what sense it is distinct from the other elements does not concern us. Now even this seems to have a share in a rational principle, as we said; at any rate in the continent man it obeys the rational principle and presumably in the temperate and brave man it is still more obedient; for in him it speaks, on all matters, with the same voice as the rational principle.

Therefore the irrational element also appears to be two-fold. For the vegetative element in no way shares in a rational principle, but the appetitive and in general the desiring element in a sense shares in it, in so far as it listens to and obeys it; this is the sense in which we speak of 'taking account' of one's father or one's friends, not that in which we speak of 'accounting for' a mathematical property. That the irrational element is in some sense persuaded by a rational principle is indicated also by the giving of advice and by all reproof and exhortation. And if this element also must be said to have a rational principle, that which has a rational principle (as well as that which has not) will be twofold, one subdivision having it in the strict sense and in itself, and the other having a tendency to obey as one does one's father.

Virtue too is distinguished into kinds in accordance with this difference; for we say that some of the virtues are intellectual and others moral, philosophic wisdom and understanding and practical wisdom being intellectual, liberality and temperance moral. For in speaking about a man's character we do not say that he is wise or has understanding but that he is good-tempered or temperate; yet we praise the wise man also with respect to his state of mind; and of states of mind we call those which merit praise virtues.

Book II

1

Virtue, then, being of two kinds, intellectual and moral, intellectual virtue in the main owes both its birth and its growth to teaching (for which reason it requires experience and time), while moral virtue comes about as a result of habit, whence also its name (ethike) is one that is formed by a slight variation from the word ethos (habit). From this it is also plain that none of the moral virtues arises in us by nature; for nothing that exists by nature can form a habit contrary to its nature. For instance the stone which by nature moves downwards cannot be habituated to move upwards, not even if one tries to train it by throwing it up ten thousand times; nor can fire be habituated to move downwards, nor can anything else that by nature behaves in one way be trained to behave in another. Neither by nature, then, nor contrary to nature do the virtues arise in us; rather we are adapted by nature to receive them, and are made perfect by habit.

Again, of all the things that come to us by nature we first acquire the potentiality and later exhibit the activity (this is plain in the case of the senses; for it was not by often seeing or often hearing that we got these senses, but on the contrary we had them before we used them, and did not come to have them by using them); but the virtues we get by first exercising them, as also happens in the case of the arts as well. For the things we have to learn before we can do them, we learn by doing them, e.g. men become builders by building and lyre-players by playing the lyre; so too we become just by doing just acts, temperate by doing temperate acts, brave by doing brave acts.

This is confirmed by what happens in states; for legislators make the citizens good by forming habits in them, and this is the wish of every legislator, and those who do not effect it miss their mark, and it is in this that a good constitution differs from a bad one.

Again, it is from the same causes and by the same means that every virtue is both produced and destroyed, and similarly every art; for it is from playing the lyre that both good and bad lyre-players are produced. And the corresponding statement is true of builders and of all the rest; men will be good or bad builders as a result of building well or badly. For if this were not so, there would have been no need of a teacher, but all men would have been born good or bad at their craft. This, then, is the case with the virtues also; by doing the acts that we do in our transactions with other men we become just or unjust, and by doing the acts that we do in the presence of danger, and being habituated to feel fear or confidence, we become brave or cowardly. The same is true of appetites and feelings of anger; some men become temperate and good-tempered, others self-indulgent and irascible, by behaving in one way or the other in the appropriate circumstances. Thus, in one word, states of character arise out of like activities. This is why the activities we exhibit must be of a certain kind; it is because the states of character correspond to the differences between these. It makes no small difference, then, whether we form habits of one kind or of another from our very youth; it makes a very great difference, or rather all the difference.

2

Since, then, the present inquiry does not aim at theoretical knowledge like the others (for we are inquiring not in order to know what virtue is, but in order to become good, since otherwise our inquiry would have been of no use), we must examine the nature of actions, namely how we ought to do them; for these determine also the nature of the states of character that are produced, as we have said. Now, that we must act according to the right rule is a common principle and must be assumed—it will be discussed later, i.e. both what the right rule is, and how it is related to the other virtues. But this must be agreed upon beforehand, that the whole account of matters of conduct must be given in outline and not precisely, as we said at the very beginning that the accounts we demand must be in accordance with the subject-matter; matters concerned with conduct and questions of what is good for us have no fixity, any more than matters of health. The general account being of this nature, the account of particular cases is yet more lacking in exactness; for they do not fall under any art or precept but the agents themselves must in each case consider what is appropriate to the occasion, as happens also in the art of medicine or of navigation.

But though our present account is of this nature we must give what help we can. First, then, let us consider this, that it is the nature of such things to be destroyed by defect and excess, as we see in the case of strength and of health (for to gain light on things imperceptible we must use the evidence of sensible things); both excessive and defective exercise destroys the strength, and similarly drink or food which is above or below a certain amount destroys the health, while that which is proportionate both produces and increases and preserves it. So too is it, then, in the case of temperance and courage and the other virtues.

For the man who flies from and fears everything and does not stand his ground against anything becomes a coward, and the man who fears nothing at all but goes to meet every danger becomes rash; and similarly the man who indulges in every pleasure and abstains from none becomes self-indulgent, while the man who shuns every pleasure, as boors do, becomes in a way insensible; temperance and courage, then, are destroyed by excess and defect, and preserved by the mean.

But not only are the sources and causes of their origination and growth the same as those of their destruction, but also the sphere of their actualization will be the same; for this is also true of the things which are more evident to sense, e.g. of strength; it is produced by taking much food and undergoing much exertion, and it is the strong man that will be most able to do these things. So too is it with the virtues; by abstaining from pleasures we become temperate, and it is when we have become so that we are most able to abstain from them; and similarly too in the case of courage; for by being habituated to despise things that are terrible and to stand our ground against them we become brave, and it is when we have become so that we shall be most able to stand our ground against them.

3

We must take as a sign of states of character the pleasure or pain that ensues on acts; for the man who abstains from bodily pleasures and delights in this very fact is temperate, while the man who is annoyed at it is self-indulgent, and he who stands his ground against things that are terrible and delights in this or at least is not pained is brave, while the man who is pained is a coward. For moral excellence is concerned with pleasures and pains; it is on account of the pleasure that we do bad things, and on account of the pain that we abstain from noble ones. Hence we ought to have been brought up in a particular way from our very youth, as Plato says, so as both to delight in and to be pained by the things that we ought; for this is the right education.

Again, if the virtues are concerned with actions and passions, and every passion and every action is accompanied by pleasure and pain, for this reason also virtue will be concerned with pleasures and pains. This is indicated also by the fact that punishment is inflicted by these means; for it is a kind of cure, and it is the nature of cures to be effected by contraries.

Again, as we said but lately, every state of soul has a nature relative to and concerned with the kind of things by which it tends to be made worse or better; but it is by reason of pleasures and pains that men become bad, by pursuing and avoiding these—either the pleasures and pains they ought not or when they ought not or as they ought not, or by going wrong in one of the other similar ways that may be distinguished. Hence men even define the virtues as certain states of impassivity and rest; not well, however, because they speak absolutely, and do not say 'as one ought' and 'as one ought not' and 'when one ought or ought not', and the other things that may be added. We assume, then, that this kind of excellence tends to do what is best with regard to pleasures and pains, and vice does the contrary.

The following facts also may show us that virtue and vice are concerned with these same things. There being three objects of choice and three of avoidance, the noble, the advantageous, the pleasant, and their contraries, the base, the injurious, the painful, about all of these the good man tends to go right and the bad man to go wrong, and especially about pleasure; for this is common to the animals, and also it accompanies all objects of choice; for even the noble and the advantageous appear pleasant.

Again, it has grown up with us all from our infancy; this is why it is difficult to rub off this passion, engrained as it is in our life. And we measure even our actions, some of us more and others less, by the rule of pleasure and pain. For this reason, then, our whole inquiry must be about these; for to feel delight and pain rightly or wrongly has no small effect on our actions.

Again, it is harder to fight with pleasure than with anger, to use Heraclitus' phrase, but both art and virtue are always concerned with what is harder; for even the good is better when it is harder. Therefore for this reason also the whole concern both of virtue and of political science is with pleasures and pains; for the man who uses these well will be good, he who uses them badly bad.

That virtue, then, is concerned with pleasures and pains, and that by the acts from which it arises it is both increased and, if they are done differently, destroyed, and that the acts from which it arose are those in which it actualizes itself—let this be taken as said.

4

The question might be asked, what we mean by saying that we must become just by doing just acts, and temperate by doing temperate acts; for if men do just and temperate acts, they are already just and temperate, exactly as, if they do what is in accordance with the laws of grammar and of music, they are grammarians and musicians.

Or is this not true even of the arts? It is possible to do something that is in accordance with the laws of grammar, either by chance or at the suggestion of another. A man will be a grammarian, then, only when he has both done something grammatical and done it grammatically; and this means doing it in accordance with the grammatical knowledge in himself.

Again, the case of the arts and that of the virtues are not similar; for the products of the arts have their goodness in themselves, so that it is enough that they should have a certain character, but if the acts that are in accordance with the virtues have themselves a certain character it does not follow that they are done justly or temperately. The agent also must be in a certain condition when he does them; in the first place he must have knowledge, secondly he must choose the acts, and choose them for their own sakes, and thirdly his action must proceed from a firm and unchangeable character. These are not reckoned in as conditions of the possession of the arts, except the bare knowledge; but as a condition of the possession of the virtues knowledge has little or no weight, while the other conditions count not for a little but for everything, i.e. the very conditions which result from often doing just and temperate acts.

Actions, then, are called just and temperate when they are such as the just or the temperate man would do; but it is not the man who does these that is just and temperate, but the man who also does them as just and temperate men do them. It is well said, then, that it is by doing just acts that the just man is produced, and by doing temperate acts the temperate man; without doing these no one would have even a prospect of becoming good.

But most people do not do these, but take refuge in theory and think they are being philosophers and will become good in this way, behaving somewhat like patients who listen attentively to their doctors, but do none of the things they are ordered to do. As the latter will not be made well in body by such a course of treatment, the former will not be made well in soul by such a course of philosophy.

5

Next we must consider what virtue is. Since things that are found in the soul are of three kinds—passions, faculties, states of character, virtue must be one of these. By passions I mean appetite, anger, fear, confidence, envy, joy, friendly feeling, hatred, longing, emulation, pity, and in general the feelings that are accompanied by pleasure or pain; by faculties the things in virtue of which we are said to be capable of feeling these, e.g. of becoming angry or being pained or feeling pity; by states of character the things in virtue of which we stand well or badly with reference to the passions, e.g. with reference to anger we stand badly if we feel it violently or too weakly, and well if we feel it moderately; and similarly with reference to the other passions.

Now neither the virtues nor the vices are passions, because we are not called good or bad on the ground of our passions, but are so called on the ground of our virtues and our vices, and because we are neither praised nor blamed for our passions (for the man who feels fear or anger is not praised, nor is the man who simply feels anger blamed, but the man who feels it in a certain way), but for our virtues and our vices we are praised or blamed.

Again, we feel anger and fear without choice, but the virtues are modes of choice or involve choice. Further, in respect of the passions we are said to be moved, but in respect of the virtues and the vices we are said not to be moved but to be disposed in a particular way.

For these reasons also they are not faculties; for we are neither called good nor bad, nor praised nor blamed, for the simple capacity of feeling the passions; again, we have the faculties by nature, but we are not made good or bad by nature; we have spoken of this before. If, then, the virtues are neither passions nor faculties, all that remains is that they should be states of character.

Thus we have stated what virtue is in respect of its genus.

6

We must, however, not only describe virtue as a state of character, but also say what sort of state it is. We may remark, then, that every virtue or excellence both brings into good condition the thing of which it is the excellence and makes the work of that thing be done well; e.g. the excellence of the eye makes both the eye and its work good; for it is by the excellence of the eye that we see well. Similarly the excellence of the horse makes a horse both good in itself and good at running and at carrying its rider and at awaiting the attack of the enemy. Therefore, if this is true in every case, the virtue of man also will be the state of character which makes a man good and which makes him do his own work well.

How this is to happen we have stated already, but it will be made plain also by the following consideration of the specific nature of virtue. In everything that is continuous and divisible it is possible to take more, less, or an equal amount, and that either in terms of the thing itself or relatively to us; and the equal is an intermediate between excess and defect. By the intermediate in the object I mean that which is equidistant from each of the extremes, which is one and the same for all men; by the intermediate relatively to us that which is neither too much nor too little—and this is not one, nor the same for all. For instance, if ten is many and two is few, six is the intermediate, taken in terms of the object; for it exceeds and is exceeded by an equal amount; this is intermediate according to arithmetical proportion. But the intermediate relatively to us is not to be taken so; if ten pounds are too much for a particular person to eat and two too little, it does not follow that the trainer will order six pounds; for this also is perhaps too much for the person who is to take it, or too little—too little for Milo, too much for the beginner in athletic exercises. The same is true of running and wrestling. Thus a master of any art avoids excess and defect, but seeks the intermediate and chooses this—the intermediate not in the object but relatively to us.

If it is thus, then, that every art does its work well—by looking to the intermediate and judging its works by this standard (so that we often say of good works of art that it is not possible either to take away or to add anything, implying that excess and defect destroy the goodness of works of art, while the mean preserves it; and good artists, as we say, look to this in their work), and if, further, virtue is more exact and better than any art, as nature also is, then virtue must have the quality of aiming at the intermediate. I mean moral virtue; for it is this that is concerned with passions and actions, and in these there is excess, defect, and the intermediate. For instance, both fear and confidence and appetite and anger and pity and in general pleasure and pain may be felt both too much and too little, and in both cases not well; but to feel them at the right times, with reference to the right objects, towards the right people, with the right motive, and in the right way, is what is both intermediate and best, and this is characteristic of virtue. Similarly with regard to actions also there is excess, defect, and the intermediate. Now virtue is concerned with passions and actions, in which excess is a form of failure, and so is defect, while the intermediate is praised and is a form of success; and being praised and being successful are both characteristics of virtue. Therefore virtue is a kind of mean, since, as we have seen, it aims at what is intermediate.

Again, it is possible to fail in many ways (for evil belongs to the class of the unlimited, as the Pythagoreans conjectured, and good to that of the limited), while to succeed is possible only in one way (for which reason also one is easy and the other difficult—to miss the mark easy, to hit it difficult); for these reasons also, then, excess and defect are characteristic of vice, and the mean of virtue.

For men are good in but one way, but bad in many.

Virtue, then, is a state of character concerned with choice, lying in a mean, i.e. the mean relative to us, this being determined by a rational principle, and by that principle by which the man of practical wisdom would determine it. Now it is a mean between two vices, that which depends on excess and that which depends on defect; and again it is a mean because the vices respectively fall short of or exceed what is right in both passions and actions, while virtue both finds and chooses that which is intermediate. Hence in respect of its substance and the definition which states its essence virtue is a mean, with regard to what is best and right an extreme.

But not every action nor every passion admits of a mean; for some have names that already imply badness, e.g. spite, shamelessness, envy, and in the case of actions adultery, theft, murder; for all of these and suchlike things imply by their names that they are themselves bad, and not the excesses or deficiencies of them. It is not possible, then, ever to be right with regard to them; one must always be wrong. Nor does goodness or badness with regard to such things depend on committing adultery with the right woman, at the right time, and in the right way, but simply to do any of them is to go wrong. It would be equally absurd, then, to expect that in unjust, cowardly, and voluptuous action there should be a mean, an excess, and a deficiency; for at that rate there would be a mean of excess and of deficiency, an excess of excess, and a deficiency of deficiency. But as there is no excess and deficiency of temperance and courage because what is intermediate is in a sense an extreme, so too of the actions we have mentioned there is no mean nor any excess and deficiency, but however they are done they are wrong; for in general there is neither a mean of excess and deficiency, nor excess and deficiency of a mean.

7

We must, however, not only make this general statement, but also apply it to the individual facts. For among statements about conduct those which are general apply more widely, but those which are particular are more genuine, since conduct has to do with individual cases, and our statements must harmonize with the facts in these cases. We may take these cases from our table. With regard to feelings of fear and confidence courage is the mean; of the people who exceed, he who exceeds in fearlessness has no name (many of the states have no name), while the man who exceeds in confidence is rash, and he who exceeds in fear and falls short in confidence is a coward. With regard to pleasures and pains—not all of them, and not so much with regard to the pains—the mean is temperance, the excess self-indulgence. Persons deficient with regard to the pleasures are not often found; hence such persons also have received no name. But let us call them 'insensible'.

With regard to giving and taking of money the mean is liberality, the excess and the defect prodigality and meanness. In these actions people exceed and fall short in contrary ways; the prodigal exceeds in spending and falls short in taking, while the mean man exceeds in taking and falls short in spending. (At present we are giving a mere outline or summary, and are satisfied with this; later these states will be more exactly determined.) With regard to money there are also other dispositions—a mean, magnificence (for the magnificent man differs from the liberal man; the former deals with large sums, the latter with small ones), an excess, tastelessness and vulgarity, and a deficiency, niggardliness; these differ from the states opposed to liberality, and the mode of their difference will be stated later. With regard to honour and dishonour the mean is proper pride, the excess is known as a sort of 'empty vanity', and the deficiency is undue humility; and as we said liberality was related to magnificence, differing from it by dealing with small sums, so there is a state similarly related to proper pride, being concerned with small honours while that is concerned with great. For it is possible to desire honour as one ought, and more than one ought, and less, and the man who exceeds in his desires is called ambitious, the man who falls short unambitious, while the intermediate person has no name. The dispositions also are nameless, except that that of the ambitious man is called ambition. Hence the people who are at the extremes lay claim to the middle place; and we ourselves sometimes call the intermediate person ambitious and sometimes unambitious, and sometimes praise the ambitious man and sometimes the unambitious. The reason of our doing this will be stated in what follows; but now let us speak of the remaining states according to the method which has been indicated.

With regard to anger also there is an excess, a deficiency, and a mean. Although they can scarcely be said to have names, yet since we call the intermediate person good-tempered let us call the mean good temper; of the persons at the extremes let the one who exceeds be called irascible, and his vice irascibility, and the man who falls short an inirascible sort of person, and the deficiency inirascibility.

There are also three other means, which have a certain likeness to one another, but differ from one another: for they are all concerned with intercourse in words and actions, but differ in that one is concerned with truth in this sphere, the other two with pleasantness; and of this one kind is exhibited in giving amusement, the other in all the circumstances of life. We must therefore speak of these too, that we may the better see that in all things the mean is praiseworthy, and the extremes neither praiseworthy nor right, but worthy of blame. Now most of these states also have no names, but we must try, as in the other cases, to invent names ourselves so that we may be clear and easy to follow. With regard to truth, then, the intermediate is a truthful sort of person and the mean may be called truthfulness, while the pretence which exaggerates is boastfulness and the person characterized by it a boaster, and that which understates is mock modesty and the person characterized by it mock-modest. With regard to pleasantness in the giving of amusement the intermediate person is ready-witted and the disposition ready wit, the excess is buffoonery and the person characterized by it a buffoon, while the man who falls short is a sort of boor and his state is boorishness. With regard to the remaining kind of pleasantness, that which is exhibited in life in general, the man who is pleasant in the right way is friendly and the mean is friendliness, while the man who exceeds is an obsequious person if he has no end in view, a flatterer if he is aiming at his own advantage, and the man who falls short and is unpleasant in all circumstances is a quarrelsome and surly sort of person.

There are also means in the passions and concerned with the passions; since shame is not a virtue, and yet praise is extended to the modest man. For even in these matters one man is said to be intermediate, and another to exceed, as for instance the bashful man who is ashamed of everything; while he who falls short or is not ashamed of anything at all is shameless, and the intermediate person is modest. Righteous indignation is a mean between envy and spite, and these states are concerned with the pain and pleasure that are felt at the fortunes of our neighbours; the man who is characterized by righteous indignation is pained at undeserved good fortune, the envious man, going beyond him, is pained at all good fortune, and the spiteful man falls so far short of being pained that he even rejoices. But these states there will be an opportunity of describing elsewhere; with regard to justice, since it has not one simple meaning, we shall, after describing the other states, distinguish its two kinds and say how each of them is a mean; and similarly we shall treat also of the rational virtues.

8

There are three kinds of disposition, then, two of them vices, involving excess and deficiency respectively, and one a virtue, viz. the mean, and all are in a sense opposed to all; for the extreme states are contrary both to the intermediate state and to each other, and the intermediate to the extremes; as the equal is greater relatively to the less, less relatively to the greater, so the middle states are excessive relatively to the deficiencies, deficient relatively to the excesses, both in passions and in actions. For the brave man appears rash relatively to the coward, and cowardly relatively to the rash man; and similarly the temperate man appears self-indulgent relatively to the insensible man, insensible relatively to the self-indulgent, and the liberal man prodigal relatively to the mean man, mean relatively to the prodigal. Hence also the people at the extremes push the intermediate man each over to the other, and the brave man is called rash by the coward, cowardly by the rash man, and correspondingly in the other cases.

These states being thus opposed to one another, the greatest contrariety is that of the extremes to each other, rather than to the intermediate; for these are further from each other than from the intermediate, as the great is further from the small and the small from the great than both are from the equal. Again, to the intermediate some extremes show a certain likeness, as that of rashness to courage and that of prodigality to liberality; but the extremes show the greatest unlikeness to each other; now contraries are defined as the things that are furthest from each other, so that things that are further apart are more contrary.

To the mean in some cases the deficiency, in some the excess is more opposed; e.g. it is not rashness, which is an excess, but cowardice, which is a deficiency, that is more opposed to courage, and not insensibility, which is a deficiency, but self-indulgence, which is an excess, that is more opposed to temperance. This happens from two reasons, one being drawn from the thing itself; for because one extreme is nearer and liker to the intermediate, we oppose not this but rather its contrary to the intermediate. E.g. since rashness is thought liker and nearer to courage, and cowardice more unlike, we oppose rather the latter to courage; for things that are further from the intermediate are thought more contrary to it. This, then, is one cause, drawn from the thing itself; another is drawn from ourselves; for the things to which we ourselves more naturally tend seem more contrary to the intermediate. For instance, we ourselves tend more naturally to pleasures, and hence are more easily carried away towards self-indulgence than towards propriety. We describe as contrary to the mean, then, rather the directions in which we more often go to great lengths; and therefore self-indulgence, which is an excess, is the more contrary to temperance.

9

That moral virtue is a mean, then, and in what sense it is so, and that it is a mean between two vices, the one involving excess, the other deficiency, and that it is such because its character is to aim at what is intermediate in passions and in actions, has been sufficiently stated. Hence also it is no easy task to be good. For in everything it is no easy task to find the middle, e.g. to find the middle of a circle is not for every one but for him who knows; so, too, any one can get angry—that is easy—or give or spend money; but to do this to the right person, to the right extent, at the right time, with the right motive, and in the right way, that is not for every one, nor is it easy; wherefore goodness is both rare and laudable and noble.

Hence he who aims at the intermediate must first depart from what is the more contrary to it, as Calypso advises

> Hold the ship out beyond that surf and spray.

For of the extremes one is more erroneous, one less so; therefore, since to hit the mean is hard in the extreme, we must as a second best, as people say, take the least of the evils; and this will be done best in the way we describe. But we must consider the things towards which we ourselves also are easily carried away; for some of us tend to one thing, some to another; and this will be recognizable from the pleasure and the pain we feel. We must drag ourselves away to the contrary extreme; for we shall get into the intermediate state by drawing well away from error, as people do in straightening sticks that are bent.

Now in everything the pleasant or pleasure is most to be guarded against; for we do not judge it impartially. We ought, then, to feel towards pleasure as the elders of the people felt towards Helen, and in all circumstances repeat their saying; for if we dismiss pleasure thus we are less likely to go astray. It is by doing this, then, (to sum the matter up) that we shall best be able to hit the mean.

But this is no doubt difficult, and especially in individual cases; for it is not easy to determine both how and with whom and on what provocation and how long one should be angry; for we too sometimes praise those who fall short and call them good-tempered, but sometimes we praise those who get angry and call them manly. The man, however, who deviates little from goodness is not blamed, whether he do so in the direction of the more or of the less, but only the man who deviates more widely; for he does not fail to be noticed. But up to what point and to what extent a man must deviate before he becomes blameworthy it is not easy to determine by reasoning, any more than anything else that is perceived by the senses; such things depend on particular facts, and the decision rests with perception. So much, then, is plain, that the intermediate state is in all things to be praised, but that we must incline sometimes towards the excess, sometimes towards the deficiency; for so shall we most easily hit the mean and what is right.

*Analects**

Confucius

1

1. The Master said, "Is it not pleasant to learn with a constant perseverance and application?

"Is it not delightful to have friends coming from distant quarters?

"Is he not a man of complete virtue, who feels no discomposure though men may take no note of him?"

2. The philosopher Yu said, "They are few who, being filial and fraternal, are fond of offending against their superiors. There have been none, who, not liking to offend against their superiors, have been fond of stirring up confusion.

"The superior man bends his attention to what is radical. That being established, all practical courses naturally grow up. Filial piety and fraternal submission,—are they not the root of all benevolent actions?"

The Master said, "Fine words and an insinuating appearance are seldom associated with true virtue."

6. The Master said, "A youth, when at home, should be filial, and, abroad, respectful to his elders. He should be earnest and truthful. He should overflow in love to all, and cultivate the friendship of the good. When he has time and opportunity, after the performance of these things, he should employ them in polite studies."

7. Tsze-hsia said, "If a man withdraws his mind from the love of beauty, and applies it as sincerely to the love of the virtuous; if, in serving his parents, he can exert his utmost strength; if, in serving his prince, he can devote his life; if, in his intercourse with his friends, his words are sincere:—although men say that he has not learned, I will certainly say that he has."

8. The Master said, "If the scholar be not grave, he will not call forth any veneration, and his learning will not be solid.

---

*From *The Confucian Analects*, translated by James Legge in *Sacred Books of the East*, edited by Max Müller (Oxford: Clarendon Press, 1893).

"Hold faithfulness and sincerity as first principles.

"Have no friends not equal to yourself.

"When you have faults, do not fear to abandon them."

9. The philosopher Tsang said, "Let there be a careful attention to perform the funeral rites to parents, and let them be followed when long gone with the ceremonies of sacrifice;—then the virtue of the people will resume its proper excellence."

10. Tsze-ch'in asked Tsze-kung saying, "When our master comes to any country, he does not fail to learn all about its government. Does he ask his information? or is it given to him?"

Tsze-kung said, "Our master is benign, upright, courteous, temperate, and complaisant and thus he gets his information. The master's mode of asking information,—is it not different from that of other men?"

11. The Master said, "While a man's father is alive, look at the bent of his will; when his father is dead, look at his conduct. If for three years he does not alter from the way of his father, he may be called filial."

12. The philosopher Yu said, "In practicing the rules of propriety, a natural ease is to be prized. In the ways prescribed by the ancient kings, this is the excellent quality, and in things small and great we follow them.

"Yet it is not to be observed in all cases. If one, knowing how such ease should be prized, manifests it, without regulating it by the rules of propriety, this likewise is not to be done."

13. The philosopher Yu said, "When agreements are made according to what is right, what is spoken can be made good. When respect is shown according to what is proper, one keeps far from shame and disgrace. When the parties upon whom a man leans are proper persons to be intimate with, he can make them his guides and masters."

14. The Master said, "He who aims to be a man of complete virtue in his food does not seek to gratify his appetite, nor in his dwelling place does he seek the appliances of ease; he is earnest in what he is doing, and careful in his speech; he frequents the company of men of principle that he may be rectified:—such a person may be said indeed to love to learn."

2

1. The Master said, "He who exercises government by means of his virtue may be compared to the north polar star, which keeps its place and all the stars turn towards it."

2. The Master said, "In the Book of Poetry are three hundred pieces, but the design of them all may be embraced in one sentence 'Having no depraved thoughts.'"

3. The Master said, "If the people be led by laws, and uniformity sought to be given them by punishments, they will try to avoid the punishment, but have no sense of shame.

"If they be led by virtue, and uniformity sought to be given them by the rules of propriety, they will have the sense of shame, and moreover will become good."

4. The Master said, "At fifteen, I had my mind bent on learning.

"At thirty, I stood firm.

"At forty, I had no doubts.

"At fifty, I knew the decrees of Heaven.

"At sixty, my ear was an obedient organ for the reception of truth.

"At seventy, I could follow what my heart desired, without transgressing what was right."

4

2. The Master said, "Those who are without virtue cannot abide long either in a condition of poverty and hardship, or in a condition of enjoyment. The virtuous rest in virtue; the wise desire virtue."

3. The Master said, "It is only the truly virtuous man, who can love, or who can hate, others."

4. The Master said, "If the will be set on virtue, there will be no practice of wickedness."

8. The Master said, "If a man in the morning hear the right way, he may die in the evening without regret."

11. The Master said, "The superior man, in the world, does not set his mind either for anything, or against anything; what is right he will follow."

12. The Master said, "The superior man thinks of virtue; the small man thinks of comfort. The superior man thinks of the sanctions of law; the small man thinks of favors which he may receive."

13. The Master said: "He who acts with a constant view to his own advantage will be much murmured against."

15. The Master said, "Shan, my doctrine is that of an all-pervading unity."

The disciple Tsang replied, "Yes."

The Master went out, and the other disciples asked, saying, "What do his words mean?"

Tsang said, "The doctrine of our master is to be true to the principles—of our nature and the benevolent exercise of them to others,—this and nothing more."

16. The Master said, "The mind of the superior man is conversant with righteousness; the mind of the mean man is conversant with gain."

17. The Master said, "When we see men of worth, we should think of equaling them; when we see men of a contrary character, we should turn inwards and examine ourselves."

18. The Master said, "In serving his parents, a son may remonstrate with them, but gently; when he sees that they do not incline to follow his advice, he shows an increased degree of reverence, but does not abandon his purpose; and should they punish him, he does not allow himself to murmur."

19. The Master said, "While his parents are alive, the son may not go abroad to a distance. If he does go abroad, he must have a fixed place to which he goes."

20. The Master said, "If the son for three years does not alter from the way of his father, he may be called filial."

24. The Master said, "The superior man wishes to be slow in his speech and earnest in his conduct."

25. The Master said, "Virtue is not left to stand alone. He who practices it will have neighbors."

5

16. The Master said of Tsze-ch'an that he had four of the characteristics of a superior man—in his conduct of himself, he was humble; in serving his superior, he was respectful; in nourishing the people, he was kind; in ordering the people, he was just."

6

29. The Master said, "Perfect is the virtue which is according to the Constant Mean! Rare for a long time has been its practice among the people."

7

1. The Master said, "A transmitter and not a maker, believing in and loving the ancients, I venture to compare myself with our old P'ang."

3. The Master said, "The leaving virtue without proper cultivation; the not thoroughly discussing what is learned; not being able to move towards righteousness of which a knowledge is gained; and not being able to change what is not good:—these are the things which occasion me solicitude."

6. The Master said, "Let the will be set on the path of duty.

"Let every attainment in what is good be firmly grasped.

"Let perfect virtue be accorded with.

"Let relaxation and enjoyment be found in the polite arts."

20. The Master said, "I am not one who was born in the possession of knowledge; I am one who is fond of antiquity, and earnest in seeking it there."

21. The subjects on which the Master did not talk, were—extraordinary things, feats of strength, disorder, and spiritual beings.

22. The Master said, "When I walk along with two others, they may serve me as my teachers. I will select their good qualities and follow them, their bad qualities and avoid them."

23. The Master said, "Heaven produced the virtue that is in me. Hwan T'ui—what can he do to me?"

25. There were four things which the Master taught,—letters, ethics, devotion of soul, and truthfulness.

26. The Master said, "A sage it is not mine to see; could I see a man of real talent and virtue, that would satisfy me."

The Master said, "A good man it is not mine to see; could I see a man possessed of constancy, that would satisfy me.

"Having not and yet affecting to have, empty and yet affecting to be full, straitened and yet affecting to be at ease:—it is difficult with such characteristics to have constancy."

37. The Master said, "The superior man is satisfied and composed; the mean man is always full of distress."

38. The Master was mild, and yet dignified; majestic, and yet not fierce; respectful, and yet easy.

8

2. The Master said, "Respectfulness, without the rules of propriety, becomes laborious bustle; carefulness, without the rules of propriety, becomes timidity; boldness, without the rules of propriety, becomes insubordination; straightforwardness, without the rules of propriety, becomes rudeness.

"When those who are in high stations perform well all their duties to their relations, the people are aroused to virtue. When old friends are not neglected by them, the people are preserved from meanness."

11

12. Chi Lu asked about serving the spirits of the dead. The Master said, "While you are not able to serve men, how can you serve their spirits?"

Chi Lu added, "I venture to ask about death?" He was answered, "While you do not know life, how can you know about death?"

12

1. Yen Yuan asked about perfect virtue.

The Master said, "To subdue one's self and return to propriety, is perfect virtue. If a man can for one day subdue himself and return to propriety, an under heaven will ascribe perfect virtue to him. Is the practice of perfect virtue from a man himself, or is it from others?"

Yen Yuan said, "I beg to ask the steps of that process."

The Master replied, "Look not at what is contrary to propriety; listen not to what is contrary to propriety; speak not what is contrary to propriety; make no movement which is contrary to propriety."

Yen Yuan then said, "Though I am deficient in intelligence and vigor, I will make it my business to practice this lesson."

2. Chung-kung asked about perfect virtue.

The Master said, "It is, when you go abroad, to behave to every one as if you were receiving a great guest; to employ the people as if you were assisting at a great sacrifice; not to do to others as you would not wish done to yourself; to have no murmuring against you in the country, and none in the family."

Chung-kung said, "Though I am deficient in intelligence and vigor, I will make it my business to practice this lesson."

3. Sze-ma Niu asked about perfect virtue.

The Master said, "The man of perfect virtue is cautious and slow in his speech."

"Cautious and slow in his speech!" said Niu;—"is this what is meant by perfect virtue?"

The Master said, "When a man feels the difficulty of doing, can he be other than cautious and slow in speaking?"

4. Sze-ma Niu asked about the superior man.

The Master said, "The superior man has neither anxiety nor fear."

"Being without anxiety or fear!" said Nui; "does this constitute what we call the superior man?"

The Master said, "When internal examination discovers nothing wrong, what is there to be anxious about, what is there to fear?"

16. The Master said, "The superior man seeks to perfect the admirable qualities of men, and does not seek to perfect their bad qualities. The mean man does the opposite of this."

24. Tsze-kung asked, saying, "What do you say of a man who is loved by all the people of his neighborhood?"

The Master replied, "We may not for that accord our approval of him."

"And what do you say of him who is hated by all the people of his neighborhood?"

The Master said, "We may not for that conclude that he is bad. It is better than either of these cases that the good in the neighborhood love him, and the bad hate him."

25. The Master said, "The superior man is easy to serve and difficult to please. If you try to please him in any way which is not accordant with right,

he will not be pleased. But in his employment of men, he uses them according to their capacity. The mean man is difficult to serve, and easy to please. If you try to please him, though it be in a way which is not accordant with right, he may be pleased. But in his employment of men, he wishes them to be equal to everything."

26. The Master said, "The superior man has a dignified ease without pride. The mean man has pride without a dignified ease."

27. The Master said, "The firm, the enduring, the simple, and the modest are near to virtue."

15

21. The Master said, "What the superior man seeks, is in himself. What the mean man seeks, is in others."

22. The Master said, "The superior man is dignified, but does not wrangle. He is sociable, but not a partisan."

23. The Master said, "The superior man does not promote a man simply on account of his words, nor does he put aside good words because of the man."

24. Tsze-kung asked, saying, "Is there one word which may serve as a rule of practice for all one's life?"

The Master said, "Is not RECIPROCITY such a word? What you do not want done to yourself, do not do to others."

16

8. Confucius said, "There are three things of which the superior man stands in awe. He stands in awe of the ordinances of Heaven. He stands in awe of great men. He stands in awe of the words of sages.

"The mean man does not know the ordinances of Heaven, and consequently does not stand in awe of them. He is disrespectful to great men. He makes sport of the words of sages."

9. Confucius said, "Those who are born with the possession of knowledge are the highest class of men. Those who learn, and so readily get possession of knowledge, are the next. Those who are dull and stupid, and yet compass the learning, are another class next to these. As to those who are dull and stupid and yet do not learn;—they are the lowest of the people."

10. Confucius said, "The superior man has nine things which are subjects with him of thoughtful consideration. In regard to the use of his eyes, he is anxious to see clearly. In regard to the use of his ears, he is anxious to hear distinctly. In regard to his countenance, he is anxious that it should be benign. In regard to his demeanor, he is anxious that it should be respectful. In regard to his speech, he is anxious that it should be sincere. In regard to his doing of business, he is anxious that it should be reverently careful. In regard to what he

doubts about, he is anxious to question others. When he is angry, he thinks of the difficulties his anger may involve him in. When he sees gain to be got, he thinks of righteousness."

*An Enquiry Concerning the Principles of Morals**

David Hume

Section IX: Conclusion

Part I

. . . [A]s every quality which is useful or agreeable to ourselves or others is, in common life, allowed to be a part of personal merit; so no other will ever be received, where men judge of things by their natural, unprejudiced reason, without the delusive glosses of superstition and false religion. Celibacy, fasting, penance, mortification, self-denial, humility, silence, solitude, and the whole train of monkish virtues; for what reason are they everywhere rejected by men of sense, but because they serve to no manner of purpose; neither advance a man's fortune in the world, nor render him a more valuable member of society; neither qualify him for the entertainment of company, nor increase his power of self-enjoyment? We observe, on the contrary, that they cross all these desirable ends; stupify the understanding and harden the heart, obscure the fancy and sour the temper. We justly, therefore, transfer them to the opposite column, and place them in the catalogue of vices; nor has any superstition force sufficient among men of the world, to pervert entirely these natural sentiments. A gloomy, hair-brained enthusiast, after his death, may have a place in the calendar; but will scarcely ever be admitted, when alive, into intimacy and society, except by those who are as delirious and dismal as himself.

. . . Avarice, ambition, vanity, and all passions vulgarly, though improperly, comprised under the denomination of *self-love*, are here excluded from our theory concerning the origin of morals, not because they are too weak, but because they have not a proper direction for that purpose. The notion of morals implies some sentiment common to all mankind, which recommends the same object to general approbation, and makes every man, or most men, agree in the same opinion or decision concerning it. It also implies some sentiment, so universal and comprehensive as to extend to all mankind, and render the actions and conduct, even of the persons the most remote, an object of applause or censure, according as they agree or disagree with that rule of right which is established. These two requisite circumstances belong alone to the

*From David Hume, *An Enquiry Concerning the Principles of Morals* (1777).

sentiment of humanity here insisted on. The other passions produce in every breast, many strong sentiments of desire and aversion, affection and hatred; but these neither are felt so much in common, nor are so comprehensive, as to be the foundation of any general system and established theory of blame or approbation.

When a man denominates another his *enemy*, his *rival*, his *antagonist*, his *adversary*, he is understood to speak the language of self-love, and to express sentiments, peculiar to himself, and arising from his particular circumstances and situation. But when he bestows on any man the epithets of *vicious* or *odious* or *depraved*, he then speaks another language, and expresses sentiments, in which he expects all his audience are to concur with him. He must here, therefore, depart from his private and particular situation, and must choose a point of view, common to him with others; he must move some universal principle of the human frame, and touch a string to which all mankind have an accord and symphony. If he mean, therefore, to express that this man possesses qualities, whose tendency is pernicious to society, he has chosen this common point of view, and has touched the principle of humanity, in which every man, in some degree, concurs. While the human heart is compounded of the same elements as at present, it will never be wholly indifferent to public good, nor entirely unaffected with the tendency of characters and manners. And though this affection of humanity may not generally be esteemed so strong as vanity or ambition, yet, being common to all men, it can alone be the foundation of morals, or of any general system of blame or praise. One man's ambition is not another's ambition, nor will the same event or object satisfy both; but the humanity of one man is the humanity of every one, and the same object touches this passion in all human creatures.

But the sentiments, which arise from humanity, are not only the same in all human creatures, and produce the same approbation or censure; but they also comprehend all human creatures; nor is there any one whose conduct or character is not, by their means, an object to every one of censure or approbation. On the contrary, those other passions, commonly denominated selfish, both produce different sentiments in each individual, according to his particular situation; and also contemplate the greater part of mankind with the utmost indifference and unconcern. Whoever has a high regard and esteem for me flatters my vanity; whoever expresses contempt mortifies and displeases me; but as my name is known but to a small part of mankind, there are few who come within the sphere of this passion, or excite, on its account, either my affection or disgust. But if you represent a tyrannical, insolent, or barbarous behaviour, in any country or in any age of the world, I soon carry my eye to the pernicious tendency of such a conduct, and feel the sentiment of repugnance and displeasure towards it. No character can be so remote as to be, in this light, wholly indifferent to me. What is beneficial to society or to the person himself must still be preferred. And every quality or action, of every human being, must, by this means, be ranked under some class or denomination, expressive of general censure or applause.

What more, therefore, can we ask to distinguish the sentiments, dependent on humanity, from those connected with any other passion, or to satisfy us, why the former are the origin of morals, not the latter? Whatever conduct gains my approbation, by touching my humanity, procures also the applause of all mankind, by affecting the same principle in them; but what serves my avarice or ambition pleases these passions in me alone, and affects not the avarice and ambition of the rest of mankind. There is no circumstance of conduct in any man, provided it have a beneficial tendency, that is not agreeable to my humanity, however remote the person; but every man, so far removed as neither to cross nor serve my avarice and ambition, is regarded as wholly indifferent by those passions. The distinction, therefore, between these species of sentiment being so great and evident, language must soon be moulded upon it, and must invent a peculiar set of terms, in order to express those universal sentiments of censure or approbation, which arise from humanity, or from views of general usefulness and its contrary. Virtue and Vice become then known; morals are recognized; certain general ideas are framed of human conduct and behaviour; such measures are expected from men in such situations. This action is determined to be conformable to our abstract rule; that other, contrary. And by such universal principles are the particular sentiments of self-love frequently controlled and limited.

. . . [T]hese principles, we must remark, are social and universal; they form, in a manner, the *party* of humankind against vice or disorder, its common enemy. And as the benevolent concern for others is diffused, in a greater or less degree, over all men, and is the same in all, it occurs more frequently in discourse, is cherished by society and conversation, and the blame and approbation, consequent on it, are thereby roused from that lethargy into which they are probably lulled, in solitary and uncultivated nature. Other passions, though perhaps originally stronger, yet being selfish and private, are often overpowered by its force, and yield the dominion of our breast to those social and public principles.

Another spring of our constitution, that brings a great addition of force to moral sentiments, is the love of fame; which rules, with such uncontrolled authority, in all generous minds, and is often the grand object of all their designs and undertakings. By our continual and earnest pursuit of a character, a name, a reputation in the world, we bring our own deportment and conduct frequently in review, and consider how they appear in the eyes of those who approach and regard us. This constant habit of surveying ourselves, as it were, in reflection, keeps alive all the sentiments of right and wrong, and begets, in noble natures, a certain reverence for themselves as well as others, which is the surest guardian of every virtue. The animal conveniencies and pleasures sink gradually in their value; while every inward beauty and moral grace is studiously acquired, and the mind is accomplished in every perfection, which can adorn or embellish a rational creature.

Here is the most perfect morality with which we are acquainted: here is displayed the force of many sympathies. Our moral sentiment is itself a feeling chiefly of that nature, and our regard to a character with others seems to arise only from a care of preserving a character with ourselves; and in order to attain this end, we find it necessary to prop our tottering judgement on the correspondent approbation of mankind.

. . . [E]very quality of the mind, which is *useful* or *agreeable* to the *person himself* or to *others*, communicates a pleasure to the spectator, engages his esteem, and is admitted under the honourable denomination of virtue or merit. Are not justice, fidelity, honour, veracity, allegiance, chastity, esteemed solely on account of their tendency to promote the good of society? Is not that tendency inseparable from humanity, benevolence, lenity, generosity, gratitude, moderation, tenderness, friendship, and all the other social virtues? Can it possibly be doubted that industry, discretion, frugality, secrecy, order, perseverance, forethought, judgement, and this whole class of virtues and accomplishments, of which many pages would not contain the catalogue; can it be doubted, I say, that the tendency of these qualities to promote the interest and happiness of their possessor, is the sole foundation of their merit? Who can dispute that a mind, which supports a perpetual serenity and cheerfulness, a noble dignity and undaunted spirit, a tender affection and good-will to all around; as it has more enjoyment within itself, is also a more animating and rejoicing spectacle, than if dejected with melancholy, tormented with anxiety, irritated with rage, or sunk into the most abject baseness and degeneracy? And as to the qualities, immediately *agreeable* to *others*, they speak sufficiently for themselves; and he must be unhappy, indeed, either in his own temper, or in his situation and company, who has never perceived the charms of a facetious wit or flowing affability, of a delicate modesty or decent genteelness of address and manner.

Part II

Having explained the moral *approbation* attending merit or virtue, there remains nothing but briefly to consider our interested *obligation* to it, and to inquire whether every man, who has any regard to his own happiness and welfare, will not best find his account in the practice of every moral duty. If this can be clearly ascertained from the foregoing theory, we shall have the satisfaction to reflect, that we have advanced principles, which not only, it is hoped, will stand the test of reasoning and inquiry, but may contribute to the amendment of men's lives, and their improvement in morality and social virtue. And though the philosophical truth of any proposition by no means depends on its tendency to promote the interests of society; yet a man has but a bad grace, who delivers a theory, however true, which, he must confess, leads to a practice dangerous and pernicious. Why rake into those corners of nature which spread a nuisance all around? Why dig up the pestilence from the pit in which it is buried? The ingenuity of your researches may be admired, but your systems will be detested; and mankind will agree, if they cannot refute them, to sink them, at least, in eternal silence and oblivion. Truths which are pernicious to society, if any such there be, will yield to errors which are salutary and *advantageous*.

But what philosophical truths can be more advantageous to society, than those here delivered, which represent virtue in all her genuine and most engaging charms, and makes us approach her with ease, familiarity, and affection? The dismal dress falls off, with which many divines, and some philosophers, have covered her; and nothing appears but gentleness, humanity, beneficence, affability; nay, even at proper intervals, play, frolic, and gaiety. She talks not of useless austerities and rigours, suffering and self-denial. She declares that her sole purpose is to make her votaries and all mankind, during every instant of their existence, if possible, cheerful and happy; nor does she ever willingly part with any pleasure but in hopes of ample compensation in some other period of their lives. The sole trouble which she demands, is that of just calculation, and a steady preference of the greater happiness. And if any austere pretenders approach her, enemies to joy and pleasure, she either rejects them as hypocrites and deceivers; or, if she admit them in her train, they are ranked, however, among the least favoured of her votaries.

And, indeed, to drop all figurative expression, what hopes can we ever have of engaging mankind to a practice which we confess full of austerity and rigour? Or what theory of morals can ever serve any useful purpose, unless it can show, by a particular detail, that all the duties which it recommends, are also the true interest of each individual? The peculiar advantage of the foregoing system seems to be, that it furnishes proper mediums for that purpose.

That the virtues which are immediately *useful* or *agreeable* to the person possessed of them, are desirable in a view to self-interest, it would surely be superfluous to prove. Moralists, indeed, may spare themselves all the pains which they often take in recommending these duties. To what purpose collect arguments to evince that temperance is advantageous, and the excesses of pleasure hurtful, when it appears that these excesses are only denominated such, because they are hurtful; and that, if the unlimited use of strong liquors, for instance, no more impaired health or the faculties of mind and body than the use of air or water, it would not be a whit more vicious or blameable?

It seems equally superfluous to prove, that the *companionable* virtues of good manners and wit, decency and genteelness, are more desirable than the contrary qualities. Vanity alone, without any other consideration, is a sufficient motive to make us wish for the possession of these accomplishments. No man was ever willingly deficient in this particular. All our failures here proceed from bad education, want of capacity, or a perverse and unpliable disposition. Would you have your company coveted, admired, followed; rather than hated, despised, avoided? Can any one seriously deliberate in the case? As no enjoyment is sincere, without some reference to company and society; so no society can be agreeable, or even tolerable, where a man feels his presence unwelcome, and discovers all around him symptoms of disgust and aversion.

. . . Now if life, without passion, must be altogether insipid and tiresome; let a man suppose that he has full power of modelling his own disposition, and let him deliberate what appetite or desire he would choose for the foundation of his happiness and enjoyment. Every affection, he would observe, when gratified by success, gives a satisfaction proportioned to its force and violence; but besides this advantage, common to all, the immediate feeling of benevolence and friendship, humanity and kindness, is sweet, smooth, tender, and agreeable, independent of all fortune and accidents. These virtues are besides attended with a pleasing consciousness or remembrance, and keep us in humour with ourselves as well as others; while we retain the agreeable reflection of having done our part towards mankind and society. And though all men show a jealousy of our success in the pursuits of avarice and ambition; yet are we almost sure of their good-will and good wishes, so long as we persevere in the paths of virtue, and employ ourselves in the execution of generous plans and purposes. What other passion is there where we shall find so many advantages united; an agreeable sentiment, a pleasing consciousness, a good reputation? But of these truths, we may observe, men are, of themselves, pretty much convinced; nor are they deficient in their duty to society, because they would not wish to be generous, friendly, and humane; but because they do not feel themselves such.

Treating vice with the greatest candour, and making it all possible concessions, we must acknowledge that there is not, in any instance, the smallest pretext for giving it the preference above virtue, with a view of self-interest; except, perhaps, in the case of justice, where a man, taking things in a certain light, may often seem to be a loser by his integrity. And though it is allowed that, without a regard to property, no society could subsist; yet according to the imperfect way in which human affairs are conducted, a sensible knave, in particular incidents, may think that an act of iniquity or infidelity will make a considerable addition to his fortune, without causing any considerable breach in the social union and confederacy. That *honesty is the best policy*, may be a good general rule, but is liable to many exceptions; and he, it may perhaps be thought, conducts himself with most wisdom, who observes the general rule, and takes advantage of all the exceptions. I must confess that, if a man think that this reasoning much requires an answer, it would be a little difficult to find any which will to him appear satisfactory and convincing. If his heart rebel not against such pernicious maxims, if he feel no reluctance to the thoughts of villainy or baseness, he has indeed lost a considerable motive to virtue; and we may expect that this practice will be answerable to his speculation. But in all ingenuous natures, the antipathy to treachery and roguery is too strong to be counter-balanced by any views of profit or pecuniary advantage. Inward peace of mind, consciousness of integrity, a satisfactory review of our own conduct; these are circumstances, very requisite to happiness, and will be cherished and cultivated by every honest man, who feels the importance of them.

Such a one has, besides, the frequent satisfaction of seeing knaves, with all their pretended cunning and abilities, betrayed by their own maxims; and while they purpose to cheat with moderation and secrecy, a tempting incident occurs, nature is frail, and they give into the snare; whence they can never extricate themselves, without a total loss of reputation, and the forfeiture of all future trust and confidence with mankind.

But were they ever so secret and successful, the honest man, if he has any tincture of philosophy, or even common observation and reflection, will discover that they themselves are, in the end, the greatest dupes, and have sacrificed the invaluable enjoyment of a character, with themselves at least, for the acquisition of worthless toys and gewgaws. How little is requisite to supply the *necessities* of nature? And in a view to *pleasure*, what comparison between the unbought satisfaction of conversation, society, study, even health and the common beauties of nature, but above all the peaceful reflection on one's own conduct; what comparison, I say, between these and the feverish, empty amusements of luxury and expense? These natural pleasures, indeed, are really without price; both because they are below all price in their attainment, and above it in their enjoyment.

The Nature of the Virtues*

Alasdair MacIntyre

One response to the history which I have narrated so far might well be to suggest that even within the relatively coherent tradition of thought which I have

*From Alasdair MacIntyre, *After Virtue: A Study in Moral Theory*, Third Edition, pp. 181–203. Copyright © 1981, 1984, 2007 by Alasdair MacIntyre. Published by the University of Notre Dame Press. Reprinted with permission.

sketched there are just too many different and incompatible conceptions of a virtue for there to be any real unity to the concept or indeed to the history. Homer, Sophocles, Aristotle, the New Testament and medieval thinkers differ from each other in too many ways. They offer us different and incompatible lists of the virtues; they give a different rank order of importance to different virtues; and they have different and incompatible theories of the virtues. If we were to consider later Western writers on the virtues, the list of differences and incompatibilities would be enlarged still further; and if we extended our enquiry to Japanese, say, or American Indian cultures, the differences would become greater still. It would be all too easy to conclude that there are a number of rival and alternative conceptions of the virtues, but, even within the tradition which I have been delineating, no single core conception.

The case for such a conclusion could not be better constructed than by beginning from a consideration of the very different lists of items which different authors in different times and places have included in their catalogues of virtues. Some of these catalogues—Homer's, Aristotle's and the New Testament's—I have already noticed at greater or lesser length. Let me at the risk of some repetition recall some of their key features and then introduce for further comparison the catalogues of two later Western writers, Benjamin Franklin and Jane Austen.

The first example is that of Homer. At least some of the items in a Homeric list of the *aretai* would clearly not be counted by most of us nowadays as virtues at all, physical strength being the most obvious example. To this it might be replied that perhaps we ought not to translate the word *aretê* in Homer by our word 'virtue', but instead by our word 'excellence'; and perhaps, if we were so to translate it, the apparently surprising difference between Homer and ourselves would at first sight have been removed. For we could allow without any kind of oddity that the possession of physical strength is the possession of an excellence. But in fact we would not have removed, but instead would merely have relocated, the difference between Homer and ourselves. For we would now seem to be saying that Homer's concept of an *aretê*, an excellence, is one thing and that our concept of a virtue is quite another since a particular quality can be an excellence in Homer's eyes, but not a virtue in ours and *vice versa*.

But of course it is not that Homer's list of virtues differs only from our own; it also notably differs from Aristotle's. And Aristotle's of course also differs from our own. For one thing, as I noticed earlier, some Greek virtue-words are not easily translated into English or rather out of Greek. Moreover consider the importance of friendship as a virtue in Aristotle's list—how different from us! Or the place of *phronêsis*—how different from Homer and from us! The mind receives from Aristotle the kind of tribute which the body receives from Homer. But it is not just the case that the difference between Aristotle and Homer lies in the inclusion of some items and the omission of others in their respective catalogues. It turns out also in the way in which those catalogues are ordered, in which items are ranked as relatively central to human excellence and which marginal.

Moreover the relationship of virtues to the social order has changed. For Homer the paradigm of human excellence is the warrior; for Aristotle it is the Athenian gentleman. Indeed according to Aristotle certain virtues are only available to those of great riches and of high social status; there are virtues which are unavailable to the poor man, even if he is a free man. And those virtues are on Aristotle's view ones central to human life; magnanimity—and once again, any translation of *megalopsuchia* is unsatisfactory—and munificence are not just virtues, but important virtues within the Aristotelian scheme.

At once it is impossible to delay the remark that the most striking contrast with Aristotle's catalogue is to be found neither in Homer's nor in our own, but in the New Testament's. For the New Testament not only praises virtues of which Aristotle knows nothing—faith, hope and love—and says nothing about virtues such as *phronêsis* which are crucial for Aristotle, but it praises at least one quality as a virtue which Aristotle seems to count as one of the vices relative to magnanimity, namely humility. Moreover since the New Testament quite clearly sees the rich as destined for the pains of Hell, it is clear that the key virtues cannot be available to them; yet they *are* available to slaves. And the New Testament of course differs from both Homer and Aristotle not only in the items included in its catalogue, but once again in its rank ordering of the virtues.

Turn now to compare all three lists of virtues considered so far—the Homeric, the Aristotelian, and the New Testament's—with two much later lists, one which can be compiled from Jane Austen's novels and the other which Benjamin Franklin constructed for himself. Two features stand out in Jane Austen's list. The first is the importance that she allots to the virtue which she calls 'constancy', a virtue about which I shall say more in a later chapter. In some ways constancy plays a role in Jane Austen analogous to that of *phronêsis* in Aristotle; it is a virtue the possession of which is a prerequisite for the possession of other virtues. The second is the fact that what Aristotle treats as the virtue of agreeableness (a virtue for which he says there is no name) she treats as only the simulacrum of a genuine virtue—the genuine virtue in question is the one she calls amiability. For the man who practices agreeableness does so from considerations of honor and expediency, according to Aristotle; whereas Jane Austen thought it possible and necessary for the possessor of that virtue to have a certain real affection for people as such. (It matters here that Jane Austen is a Christian.) Remember that Aristotle himself had treated military courage as a simulacrum of true courage. Thus we find here yet another type of disagreement over the virtues; namely, one as to which human qualities are genuine virtues and which mere simulacra.

In Benjamin Franklin's list we find almost all the types of difference from at least one of the catalogues we have considered and one more. Franklin includes virtues which are new to our consideration such as cleanliness, silence and industry; he clearly considers the drive to acquire itself a part of virtue, whereas for most ancient Greeks this is the vice of *pleonexia;* he treats some virtues which earlier ages had considered minor as major; but he also redefines some familiar virtues. In the list of thirteen virtues which Franklin compiled as part of his system of private moral accounting, he elucidates each virtue by citing a maxim obedience to which *is* the virtue in question. In the case of chastity the maxim is 'Rarely use venery but for health or offspring—never to dullness, weakness or the injury of your own or another's peace or reputation'. This is clearly not what earlier writers had meant by 'chastity'.

We have therefore accumulated a startling number of differences and incompatibilities in the five stated and implied accounts of the virtues. So the question which I raised at the outset becomes more urgent. If different writers in different times and places, but all within the history of Western culture, include such different sets and types of items in their lists, what grounds have we for supposing that they do indeed aspire to list items of one and the same kind, that there is any shared concept at all? A second kind of consideration reinforces the presumption of a negative answer to this question. It is not just that each of these five writers lists different and differing kinds of items; it is also that each of these lists embodies, is the expression of a different theory about what a virtue is.

In the Homeric poems a virtue is a quality the manifestation of which enables someone to do exactly what their well-defined social role requires. The primary role is that of the warrior king and that Homer lists those virtues which he does becomes intelligible at once when we recognize that the key virtues therefore must be those which enable a man to excel in combat and in the games. It follows that we cannot identify the Homeric virtues until we have first identified the key social roles in Homeric society and the requirements of each of them. The concept of *what anyone filling such-and-such a role ought to do* is prior to the concept of a virtue; the latter concept has application only via the former.

On Aristotle's account matters are very different. Even though some virtues are available only to certain types of people, nonetheless virtues attach not to men as inhabiting social roles, but to man as such. It is the *telos* of man as a species which determines what human qualities are virtues. We need to remember however that although Aristotle treats the acquisition and exercise of the virtues as means to an end, the relationship of means to end is internal and not external. I call a means internal to a given end when the end cannot be adequately characterized independently of a characterization of the means. So it is with the virtues and the *telos* which is the good life for man on Aristotle's account. The exercise of the virtues is itself a crucial component of the good life for man. This distinction between internal and external means to an end is not drawn by Aristotle himself in the *Nicomachean Ethics*, as I noticed earlier, but it is an essential distinction to be drawn if we are to understand what Aristotle intended. The distinction *is* drawn explicitly by Aquinas in the course of his defence of St. Augustine's definition of a virtue, and it is clear that Aquinas understood that in drawing it he was maintaining an Aristotelian point of view.

The New Testament's account of the virtues, even if it differs as much as it does in content from Aristotle's—Aristotle would certainly not have admired Jesus Christ and he would have been horrified by St Paul—does have the same logical and conceptual structure as Aristotle's account. A virtue is, as with Aristotle, a quality the exercise of which leads to the achievement of the human *telos*. *The* good for man is of course a supernatural and not only a natural good, but supernature redeems and completes nature. Moreover the relationship of virtues as means to the end which is human incorporation in the divine kingdom of the age to come is internal and not external, just as it is in Aristotle. It is of course this parallelism which allows Aquinas to synthesize Aristotle and the New Testament. A key feature of this parallelism is the way in which the concept of *the good life for man* is prior to the concept of a virtue in just the way in which on the Homeric account the concept of a social role was prior. Once again it is the way in which the former concept is applied which determines how the latter is to be applied. In both cases the concept of a virtue is a secondary concept.

The intent of Jane Austen's theory of the virtues is of another kind. C.S. Lewis has rightly emphasized how profoundly Christian her moral vision is and Gilbert Ryle has equally rightly emphasized her inheritance from Shaftesbury and from Aristotle. In fact her views combine elements from Homer as well, since she is concerned with social roles in a way that neither the New Testament nor Aristotle are. She is therefore important for the way in which she finds it possible to combine what are at first sight disparate theoretical accounts of the virtues. But for the moment any attempt to assess the significance of Jane Austen's synthesis must be delayed. Instead we must notice the quite different style of theory articulated in Benjamin Franklin's account of the virtues.

Franklin's account, like Aristotle's, is teleological; but unlike Aristotle's, it is utilitarian. According to Franklin in his *Autobiography* the virtues are means to an end, but he envisages the means-ends relationship as external rather than internal. The end to which the cultivation of the virtues ministers is happiness, but happiness understood as success, prosperity in Philadelphia and ultimately in heaven. The virtues are to be useful and Franklin's account continuously stresses utility as a criterion in individual cases: 'Make no expence but to do good to others or yourself; i.e. waste nothing', 'Speak not but what may benefit others or yourself. Avoid trifling conversation' and, as we have already seen, 'Rarely use venery but for health or offspring . . .'. When Franklin was in Paris he was horrified by Parisian architecture: 'Marble, porcelain and gilt are squandered without utility.'

We thus have at least three very different conceptions of a virtue to confront: a virtue is a quality which enables an individual to discharge his or her social role (Homer); a virtue is a quality which enables an individual to move towards the achievement of the specifically human *telos*, whether natural or supernatural (Aristotle, the New Testament and Aquinas); a virtue is a quality which has utility in achieving earthly and heavenly success (Franklin). Are we to take these as three different rival accounts of the same thing? Or are they instead accounts of three different things? Perhaps the moral structures in archaic Greece, in fourth-century Greece, and in eighteenth-century Pennsylvania were so different from each other that we should treat them as embodying quite different concepts, whose difference is initially disguised from us by the historical accident of an inherited vocabulary which misleads us by linguistic resemblance long after conceptual identity and similarity have failed. Our initial question has come back to us with redoubled force.

Yet although I have dwelt upon the *prima facie* case for holding that the differences and incompatibilities between different accounts at least suggest that there is no single, central, core conception of the virtues which might make a claim for universal allegiance, I ought also to point out that each of the five moral accounts which I have sketched so summarily does embody just such a claim. It is indeed just this feature of those accounts that makes them of more than sociological or antiquarian interest. Every one of these accounts claims not only theoretical, but also an institutional hegemony. For Odysseus the Cyclopes stand condemned because they lack agriculture, an *agora* and *themis*. For Aristotle the barbarians stand condemned because they lack the *polis* and are therefore incapable of politics. For New Testament Christians there is no salvation outside the apostolic church. And we know that Benjamin Franklin found the virtues more at home in Philadelphia than in Paris and that for Jane Austen the touchstone of the virtues is a certain kind of marriage and indeed a certain kind of naval officer (that is, a certain kind of *English* naval officer).

The question can therefore now be posed directly: are we or are we not able to disentangle from these rival and various claims a unitary core concept of the virtues of which we can give a more compelling account than any of the other accounts so far? I am going to argue that we can in fact discover such a core concept and that it turns out to provide the tradition of which I have written the history with its conceptual unity. It will indeed enable us to distinguish in a clear way those beliefs about the virtues which genuinely belong to the tradition from those which do not. Unsurprisingly perhaps it is a complex concept, different parts of which derive from different stages in the development of the tradition. Thus the concept itself in some sense embodies the history of which it is the outcome.

One of the features of the concept of a virtue which has emerged with some clarity from the argument so far is that it always requires for its application the acceptance for some prior account of certain features of social and moral life in terms of which it has to be defined and explained. So in the Homeric account the concept of a virtue is secondary to that of *a social role*, in Aristotle's account it is secondary to that of *the good life for man* conceived as the *telos* of human action and in Franklin's much later account it is secondary to that of utility. What is it in the account which, I am about to give which provides in a similar way the necessary background against which the concept of a virtue has to be made intelligible? It is in answering this question that the complex, historical, multi-layered character of the core concept of virtue becomes clear. For there are no less than three stages in the logical development of the concept which have to be identified in order, if the core conception of a virtue is to be understood, and each of these stages has its own conceptual background. The first stage requires a background account of what I shall call a practice, the second an account of what I have already characterized as the narrative order of a single human life and the third an account a good deal fuller than I have given up to now of what constitutes a moral tradition. Each later stage presupposes the earlier, but not *vice versa*. Each earlier stage is both modified by and reinterpreted in the light of, but also provides an essential constituent of each later stage. The progress in the development of the concept is closely related to, although it does not recapitulate in any straightforward way, the history of the tradition of which it forms the core.

In the Homeric account of the virtues—and in heroic societies more generally—the exercise of a virtue exhibits qualities which are required for sustaining a social role and for exhibiting excellence in some well-marked area of social practice: to excel is to excel at war or in the games, as Achilles does, in sustaining a household, as Penelope does, in giving counsel in the assembly, as Nestor does, in the telling of a tale, as Homer himself does. When Aristotle speaks of excellence in human activity, he sometimes though not always, refers to some well-defined type of human practice: flute-playing, or war, or geometry. I am going to suggest that this notion of a particular type of practice as providing the arena in which the virtues are exhibited and in terms of which they are to receive their primary, if incomplete, definition is crucial to the whole enterprise of identifying a core concept of the virtues. I hasten to add two *caveats* however.

The first is to point out that my argument will not in any way imply that virtues are *only* exercised in the course of what I am calling practices. The second is to warn that I shall be using the word 'practice' in a specially defined way which does not completely agree with current ordinary usage, including my own previous use of that word. What am I going to mean by it?

By a 'practice' I am going to mean any coherent and complex form of socially established cooperative human activity through which goods internal to that form of activity are realized in the course of trying to achieve those standards of excellence which are appropriate to, and partially definitive of, that form of activity, with the result that human powers to achieve excellence, and human conceptions of the ends and goods involved, are systematically extended. Tic-tac-toe is not an example of a practice in this sense, nor is throwing a football with skill; but the game of football is, and so is chess. Bricklaying is not a practice; architecture is. Planting turnips is not a practice; farming is. So are the enquiries of physics, chemistry and biology, and so is the work of the historian, and so are painting and music. In the ancient and medieval worlds the creation and sustaining of human communities—of households, cities, nations—is generally taken to be a practice in the sense in which I have defined it. Thus the range of practices is wide: arts, sciences, games, politics in the Aristotelian sense, the making and sustaining of family life, all fall under the concept. But the question of the precise range of practices is not at this stage of the first importance. Instead let me explain some of the key terms involved in my definition, beginning with the notion of goods internal to a practice.

Consider the example of a highly intelligent seven-year-old child whom I wish to teach to play chess, although the child has no particular desire to learn the game. The child does however have a very strong desire for candy and little chance of obtaining it. I therefore tell the child that if the child will play chess with me once a week I will give the child 50 cents worth of candy; moreover I tell the child that I will always play in such a way that it will be difficult, but not impossible, for the child to win and that, if the child wins, the child will receive an extra 50 cents worth of candy. Thus motivated the child plays and plays to win. Notice however that, so long as it is the candy alone which provides the child with a good reason for playing chess, the child has no reason not to cheat and every reason to cheat, provided he or she can do so successfully. But, so we may hope, there will come a time when the child will find in those goods specific to chess, in the achievement of a certain highly particular kind of analytical skill, strategic imagination and competitive intensity, a new set of reasons, reasons now not just for winning on a particular occasion, but for trying to excel in whatever way the game of chess demands. Now if the child cheats, he or she will be defeating not me, but himself or herself.

There are thus two kinds of good possibly to be gained by playing chess. On the one hand there are those goods externally and contingently attached to chess-playing and to other practices by the accidents of social circumstance—in the case of the imaginary child candy, in the case of real adults such goods as prestige, status and money. There are always alternative ways for achieving such goods, and their achievement is never to be had *only* by engaging in some particular kind of practice. On the other hand there are the goods internal to the practice of chess which cannot be had in any way but by playing chess or some other game of that specific kind. We call them internal for two reasons: first, as I have already suggested, because we can only specify them in terms of chess or some other game of that specific kind and by means of examples from such games (otherwise the meagerness of our vocabulary for speaking of such goods forces us into such devices as my own resort to writing of 'a certain highly particular kind of'); and secondly because they can only be identified and recognized by the experience of participating in the practice in question. Those who lack the relevant experience are incompetent thereby as judges of internal goods.

This is clearly the case with all the major examples of practices: consider for example—even if briefly and inadequately—the practice of portrait painting as it developed in Western Europe from the late middle ages to the eighteenth century. The successful portrait painter is able to achieve many goods which are in the sense just defined external to the practice of portrait painting—fame, wealth, social status, even a measure of power and influence at courts upon occasion. But those external goods are not to be confused with the goods which are internal to the practice. The internal goods are those which result from an extended attempt to show how Wittgenstein's dictum 'The human body is the best picture of the human soul' (*Investigations*, p. 178e) might be made to become true by teaching us 'to regard . . . the picture on our wall as the object itself (the men, landscape and so on) depicted there' (p. 205e) in a quite new way. What is misleading about Wittgenstein's dictum as it stands is its neglect of the truth in George Orwell's thesis 'At fifty everyone has the face he deserves'. What painters from Giotto to Rembrandt learnt to show was how the face at any age may be revealed as the face that the subject of a portrait deserves.

Originally in medieval paintings of the saints the face was an icon; the question of a resemblance between the depicted face of Christ or St. Peter and the face that Jesus or Peter actually possessed at some particular age did not even arise. The antithesis to this iconography was the relative naturalism of certain fifteenth-century Flemish and German painting. The heavy eyelids, the coifed hair, the lines around the mouth undeniably represent some particular woman, either actual or envisaged. Resemblance has usurped the iconic relationship. But with Rembrandt there is, so to speak, synthesis: the naturalistic portrait is now rendered as an icon, but an icon of a new and hitherto inconceivable kind. Similarly in a very different kind of sequence mythological faces in a certain kind of seventeenth-century French painting become aristocratic faces in the eighteenth century. Within each of these sequences at least two different kinds of good internal to the painting of human faces and bodies are achieved.

There is first of all the excellence of the products, both the excellence in performance by the painters and that of each portrait itself. This excellence—the very verb 'excel' suggests it—has to be understood historically. The sequences of development find their point and purpose in a progress towards and beyond a variety of types and modes of excellence. There are of course sequences of decline as well as of progress, and progress is rarely to be understood as straightforwardly linear. But it is in participation in the attempts to sustain progress and to respond creatively to problems that the second kind of good internal to the practices of portrait painting is to be found. For what the artist discovers within the pursuit of excellence in portrait painting—and what is true of portrait painting is true of the practice of the fine arts in general—is the good of a certain kind of life. That life may not constitute the whole of life for someone who is a painter by a very long way or it may at least for a period, Gauguin-like, absorb him or her at the expense of almost everything else. But it is the painter's living out of a greater or lesser part of his or her life *as a painter* that is the second kind of good internal to painting. And judgment upon these goods requires at the very least the kind of competence that is only to be acquired either as a painter or as someone willing to learn systematically what the portrait painter has to teach.

A practice involves standards of excellence and obedience to rules as well as the achievement of goods. To enter into a practice is to accept the authority of those standards and the inadequacy of my own performance as judged by them. It is to subject my own attitudes, choices, preferences and tastes to the standards which currently and partially define the practice. Practices of course, as I have just noticed, have a history: games, sciences and arts all have histories. Thus the standards are not themselves immune from criticism, but nonetheless we cannot be initiated into a practice without accepting the authority of the best standards realized so far. If, on starting to listen to music, I do not accept my own incapacity to judge correctly, I will never learn to hear, let alone to appreciate, Bartok's last quartets. If, on starting to play baseball, I do not accept that others know better than I when to throw a fast ball and when not, I will never learn to appreciate good pitching let alone to pitch. In the realm of practices the authority of both goods and standards operates in such a way as to rule out all subjectivist and emotivist analyses of judgment. De gustibus *est* disputandum.

We are now in a position to notice an important difference between what I have called internal and what I have called external goods. It is characteristic of what I have called external goods that when achieved they are always some individual's property and possession. Moreover characteristically they are such that the more someone has of them, the less there is for other people. This is sometimes necessarily the case, as with power and fame, and sometimes the case by reason of contingent circumstance as with money. External goods are therefore characteristically objects of competition in which there must be losers as well as winners. Internal goods are indeed the outcome of competition to excel, but it is characteristic of them that their achievement is a good for the whole community who participate in the practice. So when Turner transformed the seascape in painting or W.G. Grace advanced the art of batting in cricket in a quite new way their achievement enriched the whole relevant community.

But what does all or any of this have to do with the concept of the virtues? It turns out that we are now in a position to formulate a first, even if partial and tentative definition of a virtue: *A virtue is an acquired human quality the possession and exercise of which tends to enable us to achieve those goods which are internal to practices and the lack of which effectively prevents us from achieving any such goods*. Later this definition will need amplification and amendment. But as a first approximation to an adequate definition it already illuminates the place of the virtues in human life. For it is not difficult to show for a whole range of key virtues that without them the goods internal to practices are barred to us, but not just barred to us generally, barred in a very particular way.

It belongs to the concept of a practice as I have outlined it—and as we are all familiar with it already in our actual lives, whether we are painters or physicists or quarterbacks or indeed just lovers of good painting or first-rate experiments or a well-thrown pass—that its goods can only be achieved by subordinating ourselves within the practice in our relationship to other practitioners. We have to learn to recognize what is due to whom; we have to be prepared to take whatever self-endangering risks are demanded along the way; and we have to listen carefully to what we are told about our own inadequacies and to reply with the same carefulness for the facts. In other words we have to accept as necessary components of any practice with internal goods and standards of excellence the virtues of justice, courage and honesty. For not to accept these, to be willing to cheat as our imagined child was willing to cheat in his or her early days at chess, so far bars us from achieving the standards of excellence or the goods internal to the practice that it renders the practice pointless except as a device for achieving external goods.

We can put the same point in another way. Every practice requires a certain kind of relationship between those who participate in it. Now the virtues are those goods by reference to which, whether we like it or not, we define our relationships to those other people with whom we share the kind of purposes and standards which inform practices. Consider an example of how reference to the virtues has to be made in certain kinds of human relationship.

A, B, C, and D are friends in that sense of friendship which Aristotle takes to be primary: they share in the pursuit of certain goods. In my terms they share in a practice. D dies in obscure circumstances, A discovers how D died and tells the truth about it to B while lying to C. C discovers the lie. What A cannot then intelligibly claim is that he stands in the same relationship of friendship to both B and C. By telling the truth to one and lying to the other he has partially defined a difference in the relationship. Of course it is open to A to explain this difference in a number of ways; perhaps he was trying to spare C pain or perhaps he is simply cheating C. But some difference in the relationship now exists as a result of the lie. For their allegiance to each other in the pursuit of common goods has been put in question.

Just as, so long as we share the standards and purposes characteristic of practices, we define our relationship to each other, whether we acknowledge it or not, by reference to standards of truthfulness and trust, so we define them too by reference to standards of justice and of courage. If A, a professor, gives B and C the grades that their papers deserve, but grades D because he is attracted by D's blue eyes or is repelled by D's dandruff, he has defined his relationship to D differently from his relationship to the other members of the class, whether he wishes it or not. Justice requires that we treat others in respect of merit or desert according to uniform and impersonal standards; to depart from the standards of justice in some particular instance defines our relationship with the relevant person as in some way special or distinctive.

The case with courage is a little different. We hold courage to be a virtue because the care and concern for individuals, communities and causes which is so crucial to so much in practices requires the existence of such a virtue. If someone says that he cares for some individual, community or cause, but is unwilling to risk harm or danger on his, her or its own behalf, he puts in question the genuineness of his care and concern. Courage, the capacity to risk harm or danger to oneself, has its role in human life because of this connection with care and concern. This is not to say that a man cannot genuinely care and also be a coward. It is in part to say that a man who genuinely cares and has not the capacity for risking harm or danger has to define himself, both to himself and to others, as a coward.

I take it then that from the standpoint of those types of relationship without which practices cannot be sustained truthfulness, justice and courage—and perhaps some others—are genuine excellences, are virtues in the light of which we have to characterize ourselves and others, whatever our private moral standpoint or our society's particular codes may be. For this recognition that we cannot escape the definition of our relationships in terms of such goods is perfectly compatible with the acknowledgment that different societies have and have had different codes of truthfulness, justice and courage. Lutheran pietists brought up their children to believe that one ought to tell the truth to everybody at all times, whatever the circumstances or consequences, and Kant was one of their children. Traditional Bantu parents brought up their children not to tell the truth to unknown strangers, since they believed that this could render the family vulnerable to witchcraft. In our culture many of us have been brought up not to tell the truth to elderly great-aunts who invite us to admire their new hats. But each of these codes embodies an acknowledgment of the virtue of truthfulness. So it is also with varying codes of justice and of courage.

Practices then might flourish in societies with very different codes; what they could not do is flourish in societies in which the virtues were not valued, although institutions and technical skills serving unified purposes might well continue to flourish. (I shall have more to say about the contrast between institutions and technical skills mobilized for a unified end, on the one hand, and practices on the other, in a moment.) For the kind of cooperation, the kind of recognition of authority and of achievement, the kind of respect for standards and the kind of risk-taking which are characteristically involved in practices demand for example fairness in judging oneself and others—the kind of fairness absent in my example of the professor, a ruthless truthfulness without which fairness cannot find application—the kind of truthfulness absent in my example of A, B, C, and D—and willingness to trust the judgments of those whose achievement in the practice give them an authority to judge which presupposes fairness and truthfulness in those judgments, and from time to time the taking of self-endangering and even achievement-endangering risks. It is no part of my thesis that great violinists cannot be vicious or great chess-players mean-spirited. Where the virtues are required, the vices also may flourish. It is just that the vicious and mean-spirited necessarily rely on the virtues of others for the practices in which they engage to flourish and also deny themselves the experience of achieving those internal goods which may reward even not very good chess-players and violinists.

To situate the virtues any further within practices it is necessary now to clarify a little further the nature of a practice by drawing two important contrasts. The discussion so far I hope makes it clear that a practice, in the sense intended, is never just a set of technical skills, even when directed towards some unified purpose and even if the exercise of those skills can on occasion be valued or enjoyed for their own sake. What is distinctive in a practice is in part the way in which conceptions of the relevant goods and ends which the technical skills serve—and every practice does require the exercise of technical skills—are transformed and enriched by these extensions of human powers and by that regard for its own internal goods which are partially definitive of each particular practice or type of practice. Practices never have a goal or goals fixed for all time—painting has no such goal nor has physics—but the goals themselves are transmuted by the history of the activity. It therefore turns out not to be accidental that every practice has its own history and a history which is more and other than that of the improvement of the relevant technical skills. This historical dimension is crucial in relation to the virtues.

To enter into a practice is to enter into a relationship not only with its contemporary practitioners, but also with those who have preceded us in the practice, particularly those whose achievements extended the reach of the practice to its present point. It is thus the achievement, and *a fortiori* the authority, of a tradition which I then confront and from which I have to learn. And for this learning and the relationship to the past which it embodies the virtues of justice, courage and truthfulness are prerequisite in precisely the same way and for precisely the same reasons as they are in sustaining present relationships within practices.

It is not only of course with sets of technical skills that practices ought to be contrasted. Practices must not be confused with institutions. Chess, physics and medicine are practices; chess clubs, laboratories, universities and hospitals are institutions. Institutions are characteristically and necessarily concerned with what I have called external goods. They are involved in acquiring money and other material goods; they are structured in terms of power and status, and they distribute money, power and status as rewards. Nor could they do otherwise if they are to sustain not only themselves, but also the practices of which they are the bearers. For no practices can survive for any length of time unsustained by institutions. Indeed so intimate is the relationship of practices to institutions—and consequently of the goods external to the goods internal to the practices in question—that institutions and practices characteristically form a single causal order in which the ideals and the creativity of the practice are always vulnerable to the acquisitiveness of the institution, in which the cooperative care for common goods of the practice is always vulnerable to the competitiveness of the institution. In this context the essential function of the virtues is clear. Without them, without justice, courage and truthfulness, practices could not resist the corrupting power of institutions.

Yet if institutions do have corrupting power, the making and sustaining of forms of human community—and therefore of institutions—itself has all the characteristics of a practice, and moreover of a practice which stands in a peculiarly close relationship to the exercise of the virtues in two important ways. The exercise of the virtues is itself apt to require a highly determinate attitude to social and political issues; and it is always within some particular community with its own specific institutional forms that we learn or fail to learn to exercise the virtues. There is of course a crucial difference between the way in which the relationship between moral character and political community is envisaged from the standpoint of liberal individualist modernity and the way in which that relationship was envisaged from the standpoint of the type of ancient and medieval tradition of the virtues which I have sketched. For liberal individualism a community is simply an arena in which individuals each pursue their own self-chosen conception of the good life, and political institutions exist to provide that degree of order which makes such self-determined activity possible. Government and law are, or ought to be, neutral between rival conceptions of the good life for man, and hence, although it is the task of government to promote law-abidingness, it is on the liberal view no part of the legitimate function of government to inculcate any one moral outlook.

By contrast, on the particular ancient and medieval view which I have sketched political community not only requires the exercise of the virtues for its own sustenance, but it is one of the tasks of parental authority to make children grow up so as to be virtuous adults. The classical statement of this analogy is by Socrates in the *Crito*. It does not of course follow from an acceptance of the Socratic view of political community and political authority that we ought to assign to the modern state the moral function which Socrates assigned to the city and its laws. Indeed the power of the liberal individualist standpoint partly derives from the evident fact that the modern state is indeed totally unfitted to act as moral educator of any community. But the history of how the modern state emerged is of course itself a moral history. If my account of the complex relationship of virtues to practices and to institutions is correct, it follows that we shall be unable to write a true history of practices and institutions unless that history is also one of the virtues and vices. For the ability of a practice to retain its integrity will depend on the way in which the virtues can be and are exercised in sustaining the institutional forms which are the social bearers of the practice. The integrity of a practice causally requires the exercise of the virtues by at least some of the individuals who embody it in their activities; and conversely the corruption of institutions is always in part at least an effect of the vices.

The virtues are of course themselves in turn fostered by certain types of social institution and endangered by others. Thomas Jefferson thought that only in a society of small farmers could the virtues flourish; and Adam Ferguson with a good deal more sophistication saw the institutions of modern commercial society as endangering at least some traditional virtues. It is Ferguson's type of sociology which is the empirical counterpart of the conceptual account of the virtues which I have given, a sociology which aspires to lay bare the empirical, causal connection between virtues, practices and institutions. For this kind of conceptual account has strong empirical implications; it provides an explanatory scheme which can be tested in particular cases. Moreover my thesis has empirical content in another way; it does entail that without the virtues there could be a recognition only of what I have called external goods and not at all of internal goods in the context of practices. And in any society which recognized only external goods competitiveness would be the dominant and even exclusive feature.

We have a brilliant portrait of such a society in Hobbes's account of the state of nature; and Professor Turnbull's report of the fate of the Ik suggests that social reality does in the most horrifying way confirm both my thesis and Hobbes's.

Virtues then stand in a different relationship to external and to internal goods. The possession of the virtues—and not only of their semblance and simulacra—is necessary to achieve the latter; yet the possession of the virtues may perfectly well hinder us in achieving external goods. I need to emphasize at this point that external goods genuinely are goods. Not only are they characteristic objects of human desire, whose allocation is what gives point to the virtues of justice and of generosity, but no one can despise them altogether without a certain hypocrisy. Yet notoriously the cultivation of truthfulness, justice and courage will often, the world being what it contingently is, bar us from being rich or famous or powerful. Thus although we may hope that we can not only achieve the standards of excellence and the internal goods of certain practices by possessing the virtues *and* become rich, famous and powerful, the virtues are always a potential stumbling block to this comfortable ambition. We should therefore expect that, if in a particular society the pursuit of external goods were to become dominant, the concept of the virtues might suffer first attrition and then perhaps something near total effacement, although simulacra might abound.

The time has come to ask the question of how far this partial account of a core conception of the virtues—and I need to emphasize that all that I have offered so far is the first stage of such an account—is faithful to the tradition which I delineated. How far, for example, and in what ways is it Aristotelian? It is—happily—not Aristotelian in two ways in which a *good* deal of the rest of the tradition also dissents from Aristotle. First, although this account of the virtues is teleological, it does not require any allegiance to Aristotle's metaphysical biology. And secondly, just because of the multiplicity of human practices and the consequent multiplicity of goods in the pursuit of which the virtues may be exercised—goods which will often be contingently incompatible and which will therefore make rival claims upon our allegiance—conflict will not spring solely from flaws in individual character. But it was just on these two matters that Aristotle's account of the virtues seemed most vulnerable; hence if it turns out to be the case that this socially teleological account can support Aristotle's general account of the virtues as well as does his own biologically teleological account, these differences from Aristotle himself may well be regarded as strengthening rather than weakening the case for a generally Aristotelian standpoint.

There are at least three ways in which the account that I have given *is* clearly Aristotelian. First it requires for its completion a cogent elaboration of just those distinctions and concepts which Aristotle's account requires voluntariness, the distinction between the intellectual virtues and the virtues of character, the relationship of both to natural abilities and to the passions and the structure of practical reasoning. On every one of these topics something very like Aristotle's view has to be defended, if my own account is to be plausible.

Secondly my account can accommodate an Aristotelian view of pleasure and enjoyment, whereas it is interestingly irreconcilable with any utilitarian view and more particularly with Franklin's account of the virtues. We can approach these questions by considering how to reply to someone who, having considered my account of the differences between goods internal to and goods external to a practice enquired into which class, if either, does pleasure or enjoyment fall? The answer is, 'Some types of pleasure into one, some into the other.'

Someone who achieves excellence in a practice, who plays chess or football well or who carries through an enquiry in physics or an experimental mode in painting with success, characteristically enjoys his achievement and his activity in achieving. So does someone who, although not breaking the limit of achievement, plays or thinks or acts in a way that leads towards such a breaking of limit. As Aristotle says, the enjoyment of the activity and the enjoyment of achievement are not the ends at which the agent aims, but the enjoyment supervenes upon the successful activity in such a way that the activity achieved and the activity enjoyed are one and the same state. Hence to aim at the one is to aim at the other; and hence also it is easy to confuse the pursuit of excellence with the pursuit of enjoyment *in this specific sense*. This particular confusion is harmless enough; what is not harmless is the confusion of enjoyment *in this specific sense* with other forms of pleasure.

For certain kinds of pleasure are of course external goods along with prestige, status, power and money. Not all pleasure is the enjoyment supervening upon achieved activity; some is the pleasure of psychological or physical states independent of all activity. Such states—for example that produced on a normal palate by the closely successive and thereby blended sensations of Colchester oyster, cayenne pepper and Veuve Cliquot—may be sought as external goods, as external rewards which may be purchased by money or received in virtue of prestige. Hence the pleasures are categorized neatly and appropriately by the classification into internal and external goods.

It is just this classification which can find no place within Franklin's account of the virtues which is framed entirely in terms of external relationships and external goods. Thus although by this stage of the argument it is possible to claim that my account does capture a conception of the virtues which is at the core of the particular ancient and medieval tradition which I have delineated, it is equally clear that there is more than one possible conception of the virtues and that Franklin's standpoint and indeed any utilitarian standpoint is such that to accept it will entail rejecting the tradition and *vice versa*.

One crucial point of incompatibility was noted long ago by D.H. Lawrence. When Franklin asserts, 'Rarely use venery but for health or offspring . . .', Lawrence replies, 'Never *use* venery.' It is of the character of a virtue that in order that it be effective in producing the internal goods which are the rewards of the virtues it should be exercised without regard to consequences. For it turns out to be the case that—and this is in part at least one more empirical factual claim—although the virtues are just those qualities which tend to lead to the achievement of a certain class of goods, nonetheless unless we practice them irrespective of whether in any particular set of contingent circumstances they will produce those goods or not, we cannot possess them at all. We cannot be genuinely courageous or truthful and be so only on occasion. Moreover, as we have seen, cultivation of the virtues always may and often does hinder the achievement of those external goods which are the mark of worldly success. The road to success in Philadelphia and the road to heaven may not coincide after all.

Furthermore we are now able to specify one crucial difficulty for *any* version of utilitarianism—in addition to those which I noticed earlier. Utilitarianism cannot accommodate the distinction between goods internal to and goods external to a practice. Not only is that distinction marked by none of the classical utilitarians—it cannot be found in Bentham's writings nor in those of either of the Mills or of Sidgwick—but internal goods and external goods are not commensurable with each other. Hence the notion of summing goods—and *a fortiori* in the light of what I have said about kinds of pleasure and enjoyment the notion of summing happiness—in terms of one single formula or conception of utility, whether it is Franklin's or Bentham's or Mill's, makes no sense. Nonetheless we ought to note that although *this* distinction is alien to J.S. Mill's thought, it is plausible and in no way patronizing to suppose that something like this is the distinction which he was trying to make in *Utilitarianism* when he distinguished between 'higher' and 'lower' pleasures. At the most we can say 'something like this'; for J.S. Mill's upbringing had given him a limited view of human life and powers, had unfitted him, for example, for appreciating games just because of the way it had fitted him for appreciating philosophy. Nonetheless the notion that the pursuit of excellence in a way that extends human powers is at the heart of human life is instantly recognizable as at home in not only J.S. Mill's political and social thought, but also in his and Mrs. Taylor's life. Were I to choose human exemplars of certain of the virtues as I understand them, there would of course be many names to name, those of St. Benedict and St. Francis of Assisi and St. Theresa *and* those of Frederick Engels and Eleanor Marx and Leon Trotsky among them. But that of John Stuart Mill would have to be there as certainly as any other.

Thirdly my account is Aristotelian in that it links evaluation and explanation in a characteristically Aristotelian way. From an Aristotelian standpoint to identify certain actions as manifesting or failing to manifest a virtue or virtues is never only to evaluate; it is also to take the first step towards explaining why those actions rather than some others were performed. Hence for an Aristotelian quite as much as for a Platonist the fate of a city or an individual can be explained by citing the injustice of a tyrant or the courage of its defenders. Indeed without allusion to the place that justice and injustice, courage and cowardice play in human life very little will be genuinely explicable. It follows that many of the explanatory projects of the modern social sciences, a methodological canon of which is the separation of 'the facts'—this conception of the 'the facts' is the one which I delineated in Chapter 7—from all evaluation, are bound to fail. For the fact that someone was or failed to be courageous or just cannot be recognized as 'a fact' by those who accept that methodological canon. The account of the virtues which I have given is completely at one with Aristotle's on this point. But now the question may be raised: your account may be in many respects Aristotelian, but is it not in some respects false? Consider the following important objection.

I have defined the virtues partly in terms of their place in practices. But surely, it may be suggested, some practices—that is, some coherent human activities which answer to the description of what I have called a practice—are evil. So in discussions by some moral philosophers of this type of account of the virtues it has been suggested that torture and sado-masochistic sexual activities might be examples of practices. But how can a disposition be a virtue if it is the kind of disposition which sustains practices and some practices issue in evil? My answer to this objection falls into two parts.

First I want to allow that there *may* be practices in the sense in which I understand the concept—which simply *are* evil. I am far from convinced that there are, and I do not in fact believe that either torture or sado-masochistic sexuality answer to the description of a practice which my account of the virtues employs. But I do not want to rest my case on this lack of conviction, especially since it is plain that as a matter of contingent fact many types of practice may on particular occasions be productive of evil. For the range of practices includes the arts, the sciences and certain types of intellectual and athletic game. And it is at once obvious that any of these may under certain conditions be a source of evil: the desire to excel and to win can corrupt, a man may be so engrossed by his painting that he neglects his family, what was initially an honorable resort to war can issue in savage cruelty. But what follows from this?

It certainly is not the case that my account entails *either* that we ought to excuse or condone such evils *or* that whatever flows from a virtue is right. I do have to allow that courage sometimes sustains injustice, that loyalty has been known to strengthen a murderous aggressor and that generosity has sometimes weakened the capacity to do good. But to deny this would be to fly in the face of just those empirical facts which I invoked in criticizing Aquinas' account of the unity of the virtues. That the virtues need initially to be defined and explained with reference to the notion of a practice thus in no way entails approval of all practices in all circumstances. That the virtues—as the objection itself presupposed—*are* defined not in terms of good and right practices, but of practices, does not entail or imply that practices as actually carried through at particular times and places do not stand in need of moral criticism. And the resources for such criticism are not lacking. There is in the first place no inconsistency in appealing to the requirements of a virtue to criticize a practice. Justice may be initially defined as a disposition which in its particular way is necessary to sustain practices; it does not follow that in pursuing the requirements of a practice violations of justice are not to be condemned. Moreover I already pointed out in Chapter 12 that a morality of virtues requires as its counterpart a conception of moral law. Its requirements too have to be met by practices. But, it may be asked, does not all this imply that more needs to be said about the place of practices in some larger moral context? Does not this at least suggest that there is more to the core concept of a virtue than can be spelled out in terms of practices? I have after all emphasized that the scope of any virtue in human life extends beyond the practices in terms of which it is initially defined. What then is the place of the virtues in the larger arenas of human life?

I stressed earlier that any account of the virtues in terms of practices could only be a partial and first account. What is required to complement it? The most notable difference so far between my account and any account that could be called Aristotelian is that although I have in no way restricted the exercise of the virtues to the context of practices, it is in terms of practices that I have located their point and function. Whereas Aristotle locates that point and function in terms of the notion of a type of whole human life which can be called good. And it does seem that the question 'What would a human being lack who lacked the virtues?' must be given a kind of answer which goes beyond anything which I have said so far. For such an individual would not merely fail *in a variety of particular ways* in respect of the kind of excellence which can be achieved through participation in practices and in respect of the kind of human relationship required to sustain such excellence. His own life *viewed as a whole* would perhaps be defective; it would not be the kind of life which someone would describe in trying to answer the question 'What is the best kind of life for this kind of man or woman to live?' And that question cannot, be, answered without at least raising Aristotle's own question, 'What is the good life for man?' Consider three ways in which human life informed only by the conception of the virtues sketched so far would be defective.

It would be pervaded, first of all, by *too many* conflicts and *too much* arbitrariness. I argued earlier that it is a merit of an account of the virtues in terms of a multiplicity of goods that it allows for the possibility of tragic conflict in a way in which Aristotle's does not. But it may also produce even in the life of someone who is virtuous and disciplined too many occasions when one allegiance points in one direction, another in another. The claims of one practice may be incompatible with another in such a way that one may find oneself oscillating in an arbitrary way, rather than making rational choices. So it seems to have been with T.E. Lawrence. Commitment to sustaining the kind of community in which the virtues can flourish may be incompatible with the devotion which a particular practice—of the arts, for example—requires. So there may be tensions between the claims of family life and those of the arts—the problem that Gauguin solved or failed to solve by fleeing to Polynesia, or between the claims of politics and those of the arts—the problem that Lenin solved or failed to solve by refusing to listen to Beethoven.

If the life of the virtues is continuously fractured by choices in which one allegiance entails the apparently arbitrary renunciation of another, it may seem that the goods internal to practices do after all derive their authority from our individual choices; for when different goods summon in different and in incompatible directions, 'I' have to choose between their rival claims. The modern self with its criterionless choices apparently reappears in the alien context of what was claimed to be an Aristotelian world. This accusation might be rebutted in part by returning to the question of why both goods and virtues do have authority in our lives and repeating what was said earlier in this chapter. But this reply would only be partly successful; the distinctively modern notion of choice would indeed have reappeared, even if with a more limited scope for its exercise than it has usually claimed.

Secondly without an overriding conception of the *telos* of a whole human life, conceived as a unity, our conception of certain individual virtues has to remain partial and incomplete. Consider two examples. Justice, on an Aristotelian view, is defined in terms of giving each person his or her due or desert. To deserve well is to have contributed in some substantial way to the achievement of those goods, the sharing of which and the common pursuit of which provide foundations for human community. But the goods internal to practices, including the goods internal to the practice of making and sustaining forms of community, need to be ordered and evaluated in some way if we are to assess relative desert. Thus any substantive application of an Aristotelian concept of justice requires an understanding of goods and of the good that goes beyond the multiplicity of goods which inform practices. As with justice, so also with patience. Patience is the virtue of waiting attentively without complaint, but not of waiting thus for anything at all. To treat patience as a virtue presupposes some adequate answer to the question: waiting for what? Within the context of practices a partial, although for many purposes adequate, answer can be given: the patience of a craftsman with refractory material, of a teacher with a slow pupil, of a politician in negotiations, are all species of patience. But what if the material is just too refractory, the pupil too slow, the negotiations too frustrating? Ought we always at a certain point just to give up in the interests of the practice itself? The medieval exponents of the virtue of patience claimed that there are certain types of situation in which the virtue of patience requires that

I do not ever give up on some person or task, situations in which, as they would have put it, I am required to embody in my attitude to that person or task something of the patient attitude of God towards his creation. But this could only be so if patience served some overriding good, some *telos* which warranted putting other goods in a subordinate place. Thus it turns out that the content of the virtue of patience depends upon how we order various goods in a hierarchy and *a fortiori* on whether we are able rationally so to order these particular goods.

I have suggested so far that unless there is a *telos* which transcends the limited goods of practices by constituting the good of a whole human life, the good of a human life conceived as a unity, it will *both* be the case that a certain subversive arbitrariness will invade the moral life *and* that we shall be unable to specify the context of certain virtues adequately. These two considerations are reinforced by a third: that there is at least one virtue recognized by the tradition which cannot be specified at all except with reference to the wholeness of a human life—the virtue of integrity or constancy. 'Purity of heart,' said Kierkegaard, 'is to will one thing.' This notion of singleness of purpose in a whole life can have no application unless that of a whole life does.

It is clear therefore that my preliminary account of the virtues in terms of practices captures much, but very far from all, of what the Aristotelian tradition taught about the virtues. It is also clear that to give an account that is at once more fully adequate to the tradition and rationally defensible, it is necessary to raise a question to which the Aristotelian tradition presupposed an answer, an answer so widely shared in the pre-modern world that it never had to be formulated explicitly in any detailed way. This question is: is it rationally justifiable to conceive of *each* human life as a unity, so that we may try to specify each such life as having its good and so that we may understand the virtues as having their function in enabling an individual to make of his or her life one kind of unity rather than another?

Ideals of Human Excellence and Preserving Natural Environments*

Thomas E. Hill Jr.

I

A wealthy eccentric bought a house in a neighborhood I know. The house was surrounded by a beautiful display of grass, plants, and flowers, and it was shaded

*Thomas E. Hill Jr., "Ideals of Human Excellence and Preserving Natural Environments," *Environmental Ethics* 5 (Fall 1983): 211–24. Reprinted by permission of the author and publisher from *Environmental Ethics*.

by a huge old avocado tree. But the grass required cutting, the flowers needed tending, and the man wanted more sun. So he cut the whole lot down and covered the yard with asphalt. After all it was his property and he was not fond of plants.

It was a small operation, but it reminded me of the strip mining of large sections of the Appalachians. In both cases, of course, there were reasons for the destruction, and property rights could be cited as justification. But I could not help but wonder, "What sort of person would do a thing like that?"

Many Californians had a similar reaction when a recent governor defended the leveling of ancient redwood groves, reportedly saying, "If you have seen one redwood, you have seen them all."

Incidents like these arouse the indignation of ardent environmentalists and leave even apolitical observers with some degree of moral discomfort. The reasons for these reactions are mostly obvious. Uprooting the natural environment robs both present and future generations of much potential use and enjoyment. Animals too depend on the environment; and even if one does not value animals for their own sakes, their potential utility for us is incalculable. Plants are needed, of course, to replenish the atmosphere quite aside from their aesthetic value. These reasons for hesitating to destroy forests and gardens are not only the most obvious ones, but also the most persuasive for practical purposes. But, one wonders, is there nothing more behind our discomfort? Are we concerned solely about the potential use and enjoyment of the forests, etc., for ourselves, later generations, and perhaps animals? Is there not something else which disturbs us when we witness the destruction or even listen to those who would defend it in terms of cost/benefit analysis?

Imagine that in each of our examples those who would destroy the environment argue elaborately that, even considering future generations of human beings and animals, there are benefits in "replacing" the natural environment which outweigh the negative utilities which environmentalists cite.[1] No doubt we could press the argument on the facts, trying to show that the destruction is shortsighted and that its defenders have underestimated its potential harm or ignored some pertinent rights or interests. But is this all we could say? Suppose we grant, for a moment, that the utility of destroying the redwoods, forests, and gardens is equal to their potential for use and enjoyment by nature lovers and animals. Suppose, further, that we even grant that the pertinent human rights and animal rights, if any, are evenly divided for and against destruction. Imagine that we also concede, for argument's sake, that the forests contain no potentially useful endangered species of animals and plants. Must we then conclude that there is no further cause for moral concern? Should we then feel morally indifferent when we see the natural environment uprooted?

II

Suppose we feel that the answer to these questions should be negative. Suppose, in other words, we feel that our moral discomfort when we confront the destroyers of nature is not fully explained by our belief that they have miscalculated the best use of natural resources or violated rights in exploiting them. Suppose, in particular, we sense that part of the problem is that the natural environment is being viewed exclusively as a natural *resource*. What could be the ground of such a feeling? That is, what is there in our system of normative principles and values that could account for our remaining moral dissatisfaction?[2]

Some may be tempted to seek an explanation by appeal to the interests, or even the rights, of plants. After all, they may argue, we only gradually came to acknowledge the moral importance of all human beings, and it is even more recently that consciences have been aroused to give full weight to the welfare (and rights?) of animals. The next logical step, it may be argued, is to acknowledge a moral requirement to take into account the interests (and rights?) of plants. The problem with the strip miners, redwood cutters, and the like, on this view, is not just that they ignore the welfare and rights of people and animals; they also fail to give due weight to the survival and health of the plants themselves.

The temptation to make such a reply is understandable if one assumes that all moral questions are exclusively concerned with whether *acts* are right or wrong, and that this, in turn, is determined entirely by how the acts impinge on the rights and interests of those directly affected. On this assumption, if there is cause for moral concern, some right or interest has been neglected; and if the rights and interests of human beings and animals have already been taken into account, then there must be some other pertinent interests, for example, those of plants. A little reflection will show that the assumption is mistaken; but, in any case, the conclusion that plants have rights or morally relevant interests is surely untenable. We do speak of what is "good for" plants, and they can "thrive" and also be "killed." But this does not imply that they have "interests" in any morally relevant sense. Some people apparently believe that plants grow better if we talk to them, but the idea that the plants suffer and enjoy, desire and dislike, etc., is clearly outside the range of both common sense and scientific belief. The notion that the forests should be preserved to avoid *hurting* the trees or because they have a *right* to life is not part of a widely shared moral consciousness, and for good reason.[3]

Another way of trying to explain our moral discomfort is to appeal to certain religious beliefs. If one believes that all living things were created by a God who cares for them and entrusted us with the use of plants and animals only for limited purposes, then one has a reason to avoid careless destruction of the forests, etc., quite aside from their future utility. Again, if one believes that a divine force is immanent in all nature, then too one might have reason to care for more than sentient things. But such arguments require strong and controversial premises, and, I suspect, they will always have a restricted audience.

Early in this century, due largely to the influence of G. E. Moore, another point of view developed which some may find promising.[4] Moore introduced, or at least made popular, the idea that certain states of affairs are intrinsically valuable—not just valued, but valuable, and not necessarily because of their effects on sentient beings. Admittedly Moore came to believe that in fact the only intrinsically valuable things were conscious experiences of various sorts,[5] but this restriction was not inherent in the idea of intrinsic value. The intrinsic goodness of something, he thought, was an objective, nonrelational property of the thing, like its texture or color, but not a property perceivable by sense perception or detectable by scientific instruments. In theory at least, a single tree thriving alone in a universe without sentient beings, and even without God, could be intrinsically valuable. Since, according to Moore, our duty is to maximize intrinsic value, his theory could obviously be used to argue that we have reason not to destroy natural environments independently of how they affect human beings and animals. The survival of a forest might have worth beyond its worth *to* sentient beings.

This approach, like the religious one, may appeal to some but is infested with problems. There are, first, the familiar objections to intuitionism, on which the theory depends. Metaphysical and epistemological doubts about nonnatural, intuited properties are hard to suppress, and many have argued that the theory rests on a misunderstanding of the words *good*, *valuable*, and the like.[6] Second, even if we try to set aside these objections and think in Moore's terms, it is far from obvious that everyone would agree that the existence of forests, etc., is intrinsically valuable. The test, says Moore, is what we would say when we imagine a universe with just the thing in question, without any effects or accompaniments, and then we ask, "Would its existence be better than its nonexistence?" Be careful, Moore would remind us, not to construe this question as, "Would you *prefer* the existence of that universe to its nonexistence?" The question is, "Would its existence have the objective, nonrelational property, intrinsic goodness?"

Now even among those who have no worries about whether this really makes sense, we might well get a diversity of answers. Those prone to destroy natural environments will doubtless give one answer, and nature lovers will likely give another. When an issue is as controversial as the one at hand, intuition is a poor arbiter.

The problem, then, is this. We want to understand what underlies our moral uneasiness at the destruction of the redwoods, forests, etc., even apart from the loss of these as resources for human beings and animals. But I find no adequate answer by pursuing the questions, "Are rights or interests of plants neglected?"

"What is God's will on the matter?" and "What is the intrinsic value of the existence of a tree or forest?" My suggestion, which is in fact the main point of this paper, is that we look at the problem from a different perspective. That is, let us turn for a while from the effort to find reasons why certain *acts* destructive of natural environments are morally wrong to the ancient task of articulating our ideals of human excellence. Rather than argue directly with destroyers of the environment who say, "Show me why what I am doing is *immoral*," I want to ask, "What sort of person would want to do what they propose?" The point is not to skirt the issue with an *ad hominem*, but to raise a different moral question, for even if there is no convincing way to show that the destructive acts are wrong (independently of human and animal use and enjoyment), we may find that the willingness to indulge in them reflects the absence of human traits that we admire and regard morally important.

This strategy of shifting questions may seem more promising if one reflects on certain analogous situations. Consider, for example, the Nazi who asks, in all seriousness, "Why is it wrong for me to make lampshades out of human skin—provided, of course, I did not myself kill the victims to get the skins?" We would react more with shock and disgust than with indignation, I suspect, because it is even more evident that the question reveals a defect in the questioner than that the proposed act is itself immoral. Sometimes we may not regard an act wrong at all though we see it as reflecting something objectionable about the person who does it. Imagine, for example, one who laughs spontaneously to himself when he reads a newspaper account of a plane crash that kills hundreds. Or, again, consider an obsequious grandson who, having waited for his grandmother's inheritance with mock devotion, then secretly spits on her grave when at last she dies. Spitting on the grave may have no adverse consequences and perhaps it violates no rights. The moral uneasiness which it arouses is explained more by our view of the agent than by any conviction that what he did was immoral. Had he hestitated and asked, "Why shouldn't I spit on her grave?" it seems more fitting to ask him to reflect on the sort of person he is than to try to offer reasons why he should refrain from spitting.

III

What sort of person, then, would cover his garden with asphalt, strip mine a wooded mountain, or level an irreplaceable redwood grove? Two sorts of answers, though initially appealing, must be ruled out. The first is that persons who would destroy the environment in these ways are either shortsighted, underestimating the harm they do, or else are too little concerned for the well-being of other people. Perhaps too they have insufficient regard for animal life. But these considerations have been set aside in order to refine the controversy. Another tempting response might be that we count it a moral virtue, or at least a human ideal, to love nature. Those who value the environment only for its utility must not really love nature and so in this way fall short of an ideal. But such an answer is hardly satisfying in the present context, for what is at issue is *why* we feel moral discomfort at the activities of those who admittedly value nature only for its utility. That it is ideal to care for nonsentient nature beyond its possible use is really just another way of expressing the general point which is under controversy.

What is needed is some way of showing that this ideal is connected with other virtues, or human excellences, not in question. To do so is difficult and my suggestions, accordingly, will be tentative and subject to qualification. The main idea is that, though indifference to nonsentient nature does not *necessarily* reflect the absence of virtues, it often signals the absence of certain traits which we want to encourage because they are, in most cases, a natural basis for the development of certain virtues. It is often thought, for example, that those who would destroy the natural environment must lack a proper appreciation of their place in the natural order, and so must either be ignorant or have too little humility. Though I would argue that this is not necessarily so, I suggest that, given certain plausible empirical assumptions, their attitude may well be rooted in ignorance, a narrow perspective, inability to see things as important apart from themselves and the limited groups they associate with, or reluctance to accept themselves as natural beings. Overcoming these deficiencies will not guarantee a proper moral humility, but for most of us it is probably an important psychological preliminary. Later I suggest, more briefly, that indifference to nonsentient nature typically reveals absence of either aesthetic sensibility or a disposition to cherish what has enriched one's life and that these, though not themselves moral virtues, are a natural basis for appreciation of the good in others and gratitude.[7]

Consider first the suggestion that destroyers of the environment lack an appreciation of their place in the universe.[8] Their attention, it seems, must be focused on parochial matters, on what is, relatively speaking, close in space and time. They seem not to understand that we are a speck on the cosmic scene, a brief stage in the evolutionary process, only one among millions of species on Earth, and an episode in the course of human history. Of course, they know that there are stars, fossils, insects, and ancient ruins; but do they have any idea of the complexity of the processes that led to the natural world as we find it? Are they aware how much the forces at work within their own bodies are like those which govern all living things and even how much they have in common with inanimate bodies? Admittedly scientific knowledge is limited and no one can master it all; but could one who had a broad and deep understanding of his place in nature really be indifferent to the destruction of the natural environment?

This first suggestion, however, may well provoke a protest from a sophisticated anti-environmentalist.[9] "Perhaps *some* may be indifferent to nature from ignorance," the critic may object, "but *I* have studied astronomy, geology, biology, and biochemistry, and I still unashamedly regard the nonsentient environment as simply a resource for our use. It should not be wasted, of course, but what should be preserved is decidable by weighing long-term costs and benefits." "Besides," our critic may continue, "as philosophers you should know the old Humean formula, 'You cannot derive an *ought* from an *is*.' All the facts of biology, biochemistry, etc., do not entail that I ought to love nature or want to preserve it. What one understands is one thing; what one values is something else. Just as nature lovers are not necessarily scientists, those indifferent to nature are not necessarily ignorant."

Although the environmentalist may concede the critic's logical point, he may well argue that, as a matter of fact, increased understanding of nature tends to heighten people's concern for its preservation. If so, despite the objection, the suspicion that the destroyers of the environment lack deep understanding of nature is not, in most cases, unwarranted, but the argument need not rest here.

The environmentalist might amplify his original idea as follows: "When I said that the destroyers of nature do not appreciate their place in the universe, I was not speaking of intellectual understanding alone, for, after all, a person can *know* a catalog of facts without ever putting them together and seeing vividly the whole picture which they form. To see oneself as just one part of nature is to look at oneself and the world from a certain perspective which is quite different from being able to recite detailed information from the natural sciences. What the destroyers of nature lack is this perspective, not particular information."

Again our critic may object, though only after making some concessions: "All right," he may say, "*some* who are indifferent to nature may lack the cosmic perspective of which you speak, but again there is no *necessary* connection between this failing, if it is one, and any particular evaluative attitude toward nature. In fact, different people respond quite differently when they move to a wider perspective. When *I* try to picture myself vividly as a brief, transitory episode in the course of nature, I simply get depressed. Far from inspiring me with a love of nature, the exercise makes me sad and hostile. You romantics think only of poets like Wordsworth and artists like Turner, but you should consider how differently Omar Khayyam responded when he took your wider perspective. His reaction, when looking at his life from a cosmic viewpoint, was 'Drink up, for tomorrow we die.' Others respond in an almost opposite manner with a joyless Stoic resignation, exemplified by the poet who pictures the wise man, at the height of personal triumph, being served a magnificent banquet, and then consummating his marriage to his beloved, all the while reminding himself, 'Even this shall pass away.'"[10] In sum, the critic may object, "Even if one should try to see oneself as one small transitory part of nature, doing so does not dictate any particular normative attitude. Some may come to love nature, but others are moved to live for the moment; some sink into sad resignation; others get depressed or angry. So indifference to nature is not necessarily a sign that a person fails to look at himself from the larger perspective."

The environmentalist might respond to this objection in several ways. He might, for example, argue that even though some people who see themselves as part of the natural order remain indifferent to nonsentient nature, this is not a common reaction. Typically, it may be argued, as we become more and more aware that we are parts of the larger whole we come to value the whole independently of its effect on ourselves. Thus, despite the possibilities the critic raises, indifference to nonsentient nature is still in most cases a sign that a person fails to see himself as part of the natural order.

If someone challenges the empirical assumption here, the environmentalist might develop the argument along a quite different line. The initial idea, he may remind us, was that those who would destroy the natural environment fail to *appreciate* their place in the natural order. "Appreciating one's place" is not simply an intellectual appreciation. It is also an attitude, reflecting what one values as well as what one knows. When we say, for example, that both the servile and the arrogant person fail to *appreciate* their place in a society of equals, we do not mean simply that they are ignorant of certain empirical facts, but rather that they have certain objectionable attitudes about their importance relative to other people. Similarly, to fail to appreciate one's place in nature is not merely to lack knowledge or breadth of perspective, but to take a certain attitude about what matters. A person who *understands* his place in nature but still views nonsentient nature merely as a resource takes the attitude that nothing is *important* but human beings and animals. Despite first appearances, he is not so much like the pre-Copernican astronomers who made the intellectual error of treating the Earth as the "center of the universe" when they made their calculations. He is more like the racist who, though well aware of other races, treats all races but his own as insignificant.

So construed, the argument appeals to the common idea that awareness of nature typically has, and should have, a humbling effect. The Alps, a storm at sea, the Grand Canyon, towering redwoods, and "the starry heavens above" move many a person to remark on the comparative insignificance of our daily concerns and even of our species, and this is generally taken to be a quite fitting response.[11] What seems to be missing, then, in those who understand nature but remain unmoved is a proper humility.[12] Absence of proper humility is not the same as selfishness or egoism, for one can be devoted to self-interest while still viewing one's own pleasures and projects as trivial and unimportant.[13] And one can have an exaggerated view of one's own importance while grandly sacrificing for those one views as inferior. Nor is the lack of humility identical with belief that one has power and influence, for a person can be quite puffed up about himself while believing that the foolish world will never acknowledge him. The humility we miss seems not so much a belief about one's relative effectiveness and recognition as an attitude which measures the importance of things independently of their relation to oneself or to some narrow group with which one identifies.

A paradigm of a person who lacks humility is the self-important emperor who grants status to his family because it is *his*, to his subordinates because *he* appointed them, and to his country because *he* chooses to glorify it. Less extreme but still lacking proper humility is the elitist who counts events significant solely in proportion to how they affect his class. The suspicion about those who would destroy the environment, then, is that what they count important is too narrowly confined insofar as it encompasses only what affects beings who, like us, are capable of feeling.

This idea that proper humility requires recognition of the importance of nonsentient nature is similar to the thought of those who charge meat eaters with "species-ism." In both cases it is felt that people too narrowly confine their concerns to the sorts of beings that are most like them. But, however intuitively appealing, the idea will surely arouse objections from our non-environmentalist critic. "Why," he will ask, "do you suppose that the sort of humility I *should* have requires me to acknowledge the importance of nonsentient nature aside from its utility? You cannot, by your own admission, argue that nonsentient nature *is* important, appealing to religious or intuitionist grounds. And simply to assert, without further argument, that an ideal humility requires us to view nonsentient nature as important for its own sake begs the question at issue. If proper humility is acknowledging the relative importance of things as one should, then to show that I must lack this you must first establish that one *should* acknowledge the importance of nonsentient nature."

Though some may wish to accept this challenge, there are other ways to pursue the connection between humility and response to nonsentient nature. For example, suppose we grant that proper humility requires only acknowledging a due status to sentient beings. We must admit, then, that it is logically possible for a person to be properly humble even though he viewed all nonsentient nature simply as a resource. But this logical possibility may be a psychological rarity. It may be that, given the sort of beings we are, we would never learn humility before persons without developing the general capacity to cherish, and regard important, many things for their own sakes. The major obstacle to humility before persons is self-importance, a tendency to measure the significance of everything by its relation to oneself and those with whom one identifies. The processes by which we overcome self-importance are doubtless many and complex, but it seems unlikely that they are exclusively concerned with how we relate to other people and animals. Learning humility requires learning to feel that something matters besides what will affect oneself and one's circle of associates. What leads a child to care about what happens to a lost hamster or a stray dog he will not see again is likely also to generate concern for a lost toy or a favorite tree where he used to live.[14] Learning to value things for their own sake, and to count what affects them important aside from their utility, is not the same as judging them to have some intuited objective property, but it is necessary to the development of humility and it seems likely to take place in experiences with nonsentient nature as well as with people and animals. If a person views all nonsentient nature merely as a resource, then it seems unlikely that he has developed the capacity needed to overcome self-importance.

IV

This last argument, unfortunately, has its limits. It presupposes an empirical connection between experiencing nature and overcoming self-importance, and this may be challenged. Even if experiencing nature promotes humility before others, there may be other ways people can develop such humility in a world of concrete, glass, and plastic. If not, perhaps all that is needed is limited experience of nature in one's early, developing years; mature adults, having overcome youthful self-importance, may live well enough in artificial surroundings. More importantly, the argument does not fully capture the spirit of the intuition that an ideal person stands humbly before nature. That idea is not simply that experiencing nature tends to foster proper humility before other people; it is, in part, that natural surroundings encourage and are appropriate to an ideal sense of oneself as part of the natural world. Standing alone in the forest, after months in the city, is not merely good as a means of curbing one's arrogance before others; it reinforces and fittingly expresses one's acceptance of oneself as a natural being.

Previously we considered only one aspect of proper humility, namely, a sense of one's relative importance with respect to other human beings. Another aspect, I think, is a kind of *self-acceptance*. This involves acknowledging, in more than a merely intellectual way, that we are the sort of creatures that we are. Whether one is self-accepting is not so much a matter of how one attributes *importance* comparatively to oneself, other people, animals, plants, and other things as it is a matter of understanding, facing squarely, and responding appropriately to who and what one is, e.g., one's powers and limits, one's affinities with other beings and differences from them, one's unalterable nature and one's freedom to change. Self-acceptance is not merely intellectual awareness, for one can be intellectually aware that one is growing old and will eventually die while nevertheless behaving in a thousand foolish ways that reflect a refusal to acknowledge these facts. On the other hand, self-acceptance is not passive resignation, for refusal to pursue what one truly wants within one's limits is a failure to accept the freedom and power one has. Particular behaviors, like dying one's gray hair and dressing like those twenty years younger, do not *necessarily* imply lack of self-acceptance, for there could be reasons for acting in these ways other than the wish to hide from oneself what one really is. One fails to accept oneself when the patterns of behavior and emotion are rooted in a desire to disown and deny features of oneself, to pretend to oneself that they are not there. This is not to say that a self-accepting person makes no value judgments about himself, that he likes all facts about himself, wants equally to develop and display them; he can, and should feel remorse for his past misdeeds and strive to change his current vices. The point is that he does not disown them, pretend that they do not exist or are facts about something other than himself. Such pretense is incompatible with proper humility because it is seeing oneself as better than one is.

Self-acceptance of this sort has long been considered a human excellence, under various names, but what has it to do with preserving nature? There is, I think, the following connection. As human beings we are part of nature, living, growing, declining, and dying by natural laws similar to those governing other living beings; despite our awesomely distinctive human powers, we share many of the needs, limits, and liabilities of animals and plants. These facts are neither good nor bad in themselves, aside from personal preference and varying conventional values. To say this is to utter a truism which few will deny, but to accept these facts, as facts about oneself, is not so easy—or so common. Much of what naturalists deplore about our increasingly artificial world reflects, and encourages, a denial of these facts, an unwillingness to avow them with equanimity.

Like the Victorian lady who refuses to look at her own nude body, some would like to create a world of less transitory stuff, reminding us only of our intellectual and social nature, never calling to mind our affinities with "lower" living creatures. The "denial of death," to which psychiatrists call attention,[15] reveals an attitude incompatible with the sort of self-acceptance which philosophers, from the ancients to Spinoza and on, have admired as a human excellence. My suggestion is not merely that experiencing nature causally promotes such self-acceptance, but also that those who fully accept themselves as part of the natural world lack the common drive to disassociate themselves from nature by replacing natural environments with artificial ones. A storm in the wilds helps us to appreciate our animal vulnerability, but, equally important, the reluctance to experience it may *reflect* an unwillingness to accept this aspect of ourselves. The person who is too ready to destroy the ancient redwoods may lack humility, not so much in the sense that he exaggerates his importance relative to others, but rather in the sense that he tries to avoid seeing himself as one among many natural creatures.

V

My suggestion so far has been that, though indifference to nonsentient nature is not itself a moral vice, it is likely to reflect either ignorance, a self-importance, or a lack of self-acceptance which we must overcome to have proper humility. A similar idea might be developed connecting attitudes toward nonsentient nature with other human excellences. For example, one might argue that indifference to nature reveals a lack of either an aesthetic sense or some of the natural roots of gratitude.

When we see a hillside that has been gutted by strip miners or the garden replaced by asphalt, our first reaction is probably, "How ugly!" The scenes assault our aesthetic sensibilities. We suspect that no one with a keen sense of beauty could have left such a sight. Admittedly not everything in nature strikes us as beautiful, or even aesthetically interesting, and sometimes a natural scene is replaced with a more impressive architectural masterpiece. But this is not usually the situation in the problem cases which environmentalists are most concerned about. More often beauty is replaced with ugliness.

At this point our critic may well object that, even if he does lack a sense of beauty, this is no moral vice. His cost/benefit calculations take into account the pleasure others may derive from seeing the forests, etc., and so why should he be faulted?

Some might reply that, despite contrary philosophical traditions, aesthetics and morality are not so distinct as commonly supposed. Appreciation of beauty, they may argue, is a human excellence which morally ideal persons should try to develop. But, setting aside this controversial position, there still may be cause for moral concern about those who have no aesthetic response to nature. Even if aesthetic sensibility is not itself a moral virtue, many of the capacities of mind and heart which it presupposes may be ones which are also needed for an appreciation of other people. Consider, for example, curiosity, a mind open to novelty, the ability to look at things from unfamiliar perspectives, empathetic imagination, interest in details, variety, and order, and emotional freedom from the immediate and the practical. All these, and more, seem necessary to aesthetic sensibility, but they are also traits which a person needs to be fully sensitive to people of all sorts. The point is not that a moral person must be able to distinguish beautiful from ugly people; the point is rather that unresponsiveness to what is beautiful, awesome, dainty, dumpy, and otherwise aesthetically interesting in nature probably reflects a lack of the openness of mind and spirit necessary to appreciate the best in human beings.

The anti-environmentalist, however, may refuse to accept the charge that he lacks aesthetic sensibility. If he claims to appreciate seventeenth-century miniature portraits, but to abhor natural wildernesses, he will hardly be convincing. Tastes vary, but aesthetic sense is not *that* selective. He may, instead, insist that he *does* appreciate natural beauty. He spends his vacations, let us suppose, hiking in the Sierras, photographing wildflowers, and so on. He might press his argument as follows: "I enjoy natural beauty as much as anyone, but I fail to see what this has to do with preserving the environment independently of human enjoyment and use. Nonsentient nature is a resource, but one of its best uses is to give us pleasure. I take this into account when I calculate the costs and benefits of preserving a park, planting a garden, and so on. But the problem you raised explicitly set aside the desire to preserve nature as a means to enjoyment. I say, let us enjoy nature fully while we can, but if all sentient beings were to die tomorrow, we might as well blow up all plant life as well. A redwood grove that no one can use or enjoy is utterly worthless."

The attitude expressed here, I suspect, is not a common one, but it represents a philosophical challenge. The beginnings of a reply may be found in the following. When a person takes joy in something, it is a common (and perhaps natural) response to come to cherish it. To cherish something is not simply to be happy with it at the moment, but to care for it for its own sake. This is not to say that one necessarily sees it as having feelings and so wants it to feel good; nor does it imply that one judges the thing to have Moore's intrinsic value. One simply wants the thing to survive and (when appropriate) to thrive, and not simply for its utility. We see this attitude repeatedly regarding mementos. They are not simply valued as a means to remind us of happy occasions; they come to be valued for their own sake. Thus, if someone really took joy in the natural environment, but was prepared to blow it up as soon as sentient life ended, he would lack this common human tendency to cherish what enriches our lives. While this response is not itself a moral virtue, it may be a natural basis of the virtue we call "gratitude." People who have no tendency to cherish things that give them pleasure may be poorly disposed to respond gratefully to persons who are good to them. Again the connection is not one of logical necessity, but it may nevertheless be important. A nonreligious person unable to "thank" anyone for the beauties of nature may nevertheless feel "grateful" in a sense; and I suspect that the person who feels no such "gratitude" toward nature is unlikely to show proper gratitude toward people.

Suppose these conjectures prove to be true. One may wonder what is the point of considering them. Is it to disparage all those who view nature merely as a resource? To do so, it seems, would be unfair, for, even if this attitude typically stems from deficiencies which affect one's attitudes toward sentient beings, there may be exceptions and we have not shown that their view of nonsentient nature is itself blameworthy. But when we set aside questions of blame and inquire what sorts of human traits we want to encourage, our reflections become relevant in a more positive way. The point is not to insinuate that all anti-environmentalists are defective, but to see that those who value such traits as humility, gratitude, and sensitivity to others have reason to promote the love of nature.

Notes

Department of Philosophy, University of California, Los Angeles, CA 90024. Hill's research interests include Kant's moral philosophy and current moral issues. The author thanks Gregory Kavka, Catherine Harlow, the participants at a colloquium at the University of Utah, and the referees for *Environmental Ethics*, Dale Jamieson and Donald Scherer, for helpful comments on earlier drafts of this paper.

1. When I use the expression "the natural environment," I have in mind the sort of examples with which I began. For some purposes it is important to distinguish cultivated gardens from forests, virgin forests from replenished ones, irreplaceable natural phenomena from the replaceable, and so on; but these distinctions, I think, do not affect my main points here. There is also a broad sense, as Hume and Mill noted, in which all that occurs, miracles aside, is "natural." In this sense, of course, strip mining is as natural as a beaver cutting trees for his dam, and, as parts of nature, we cannot destroy the "natural" environment but only alter it. As will be evident, I shall use *natural* in a narrower, more familiar sense.

2. This paper is intended as a preliminary discussion in *normative* ethical theory (as opposed to *metaethics*). The task, accordingly, is the limited, though still difficult, one of articulating the possible basis in our beliefs and values for certain particular moral judgments. Questions of ultimate justification are set aside. What makes the task difficult and challenging is not that conclusive proofs from the foundation of morality are attempted; it is rather that the particular judgments to be explained seem at first not to fall under the most familiar moral principles (e.g., utilitarianism, respect for rights).

3. I assume here that having a right presupposes having interests in a sense which in turn presupposes a capacity to desire, suffer, etc. Since my main concern lies in another direction, I do not argue the point, but merely note that some regard it as debatable. See, for example, W. Murray Hunt, "Are *Mere Things* Morally Considerable?" *Environmental Ethics* 2 (1980): 59–65; P Kenneth E. Goodpaster, "On Stopping at Everything," *Environmental Ethics* 2 (1980): 288–94; Joel Feinberg, "The Rights of Animals and Unborn Generations," in William Blackstone, ed., *Philosophy and Environmental Crisis* (Athens: University of Georgia Press, 1974), pp. 43–68; Tom Regan, "Feinberg on What Sorts of Beings Can Have Rights," *Southern Journal of Philosophy* (1976): 485–98; Robert Elliot, "Regan on the Sort of Beings that Can Have Rights," *Southern Journal of Philosophy* (1978): 701–05; Scott Lehmann, "Do Wildernesses Have Rights?" *Environmental Ethics* 2 (1981): 129–46.

4. G. E. Moore, *Principia Ethica* (Cambridge: Cambridge University Press, 1903); *Ethics* (London: H. Holt, 1912).

5. G. E. Moore, "Is Goodness a Quality?" *Philosophical Papers* (London: George Allen and Unwin, 1959), pp. 95–97.

6. See, for example, P. H. Nowell-Smith, *Ethics* (New York: Penguin Books, 1954).

7. The issues I raise here, though perhaps not the details of my remarks, are in line with Aristotle's view of moral philosophy, a view revitalized recently by Philippa Foot's *Virtue and Vice* (Berkeley: University of California Press, 1979), Alaistair McIntyre's *After Virtue* (Notre Dame: Notre Dame Press, 1981), and James Wallace's *Virtues and Vices* (Ithaca and London: Cornell University Press, 1978), and other works. For other reflections on relationships between character and natural environments, see John Rodman, "The Liberation of Nature," *Inquiry* (1976):83–131 and L. Reinhardt, "Some Gaps in Moral Space: Reflections on Forests and Feelings," in Mannison, McRobbie, and Routley, eds., *Environmental Philosophy* (Canberra: Australian National University Research School of Social Sciences, 1980).

8. Though for simplicity I focus upon those who do strip mining, etc., the argument is also applicable to those whose utilitarian calculations lead them to preserve the redwoods, mountains, etc., but who care for only sentient nature for its own sake. Similarly the phrase "indifferent to nature" is meant to encompass those who are indifferent *except* when considering its benefits to people and animals.

9. For convenience I use the labels *environmentalist* and *anti-environmentalist* (or *critic*) for the opposing sides in the rather special controversy I have raised. Thus, for example, my "environmentalist" not only favors conserving the forests, etc., but finds something objectionable in wanting to destroy them even aside from the costs to human beings and animals. My "anti-environmentalist" is not simply one who wants to destroy the environment; he is a person who has no qualms about doing so independent of the adverse effects on human beings and animals.

10. "Even this shall pass away," by Theodore Tildon, in *The Best Loved Poems of the American People*, ed. Hazel Felleman (Garden City, N.Y.: Doubleday & Co., 1936).

11. An exception, apparently, was Kant, who thought "the starry heavens" sublime and compared them with "the moral law within," but did not for all that see our species as comparatively insignificant.

12. By "*proper* humility" I mean that sort and degree of humility that is a morally admirable character trait. How precisely to define this is, of course, a controversial matter; but the point for present purposes is just to set aside obsequiousness, false modesty, underestimation of one's abilities, and the like.

13. I take this point from some of Philippa Foot's remarks.

14. The causal history of this concern may well depend upon the object (tree, toy) having given the child pleasure, but this does not mean that the object is then valued only for further pleasure it may bring.

15. See, for example, Ernest Becker, *The Denial of Death* (New York: Free Press, 1973).

Study Questions

1. Why does Aristotle state that happiness is the highest good and ultimate end of human life? In your opinion, must human life have one highest good or one ultimate end? Is the happy person necessarily virtuous? Discuss.

2. To live a good life, Aristotle recommends that we live by the motto "Nothing in excess, everything in moderation." The moral virtues help us to lead the good life by enabling us to desire and choose "the mean between extremes," with the mean relative to each individual. Do you agree with Aristotle that the life of moderation leads to happiness? Does Aristotle's doctrine of the "individual mean" lead to moral relativism? Are there some feelings or actions that are always right or always wrong? Explain your answer with reasons to support your view.

3. Confucian ethical philosophy is rooted in an attempt at perfecting the human being and human society through education in moral self-cultivation. Through this education, the superior person (*junzi*) learns to respect and honor the well-being of others, the past, society's traditions and customs and one's ancestors and one's parents and is always polite, courteous and proper. Do you agree? Is Confucius too conservative and too elitist a thinker?

4. Compare the virtue ethics of Confucius to that of Aristotle. What are some similarities? What are some differences? Are these two incompatible conceptions of human excellence or could one be both Confucian and Aristotelian?

5. What specific examples of virtue and vice does Hume give? For each of these, try to determine whether he thinks that it is a character trait that is immediately agreeable or whether it is one that is useful to its possessor or useful to others. Consider in each case whether you agree with Hume that a given example is indeed a virtue or a vice.

6. Compare MacIntyre's conception of the virtues with Aristotle's. Do you think MacIntyre's attempt to revive virtue ethics without adopting Aristotle's views on the natural "function" of human beings is successful? Why or why not?

7. Hill offers a kind of indirect argument against doing harm to nature by suggesting that persons who are indifferent to the environment lack certain virtues

most of us would deem desirable to possess. Do you find Hill's strategy an effective one? Explain.

For Further Reading

Anscombe, Elizabeth. "Modern Moral Philosophy." In *Ethics, Religion and Politics*. Vol. 3 of *The Collected Philosophical Papers of G. E. M. Anscombe*. Minneapolis: University of Minnesota Press, 1981: 26–42.

Foot, Philippa. *Virtues and Vices and Other Essays in Moral Philosophy*. Berkeley: University of California Press, 1978.

Hardie, W. F. R. *Aristotle's Ethical Theory*. Oxford: Clarendon Press, 1980.

Hursthouse, Rosalind. *On Virtue Ethics*. Oxford: Oxford University Press, 2002.

Ivanhoe, Philip J. *Confucian Moral Self-Cultivation*. 2nd ed. Indianapolis: Hackett, 2000.

MacIntyre, Alasdair. *Three Rival Versions of Moral Enquiry: Encyclopaedia, Genealogy, and Tradition*. Notre Dame, IN: University of Notre Dame Press, 1991.

Mackie, J. L. *Hume's Moral Theory*. London: Routledge, 1980.

Sandler, Ronald, and Philip Cafaro, eds. *Environmental Virtue Ethics*. Lanham, MD: Rowman & Littlefield, 2005.

CHAPTER EIGHT

Challenges to Traditional Moral Theory

In recent years there have been a number of challenges to traditional moral theory. Some of these challenges have arisen as a result of changes in contemporary culture, while others are recent variants of perennial philosophical debates. Moral theory, indeed all or almost all of philosophy, has until well into the twentieth century been the bastion of "dead white males." As society becomes more culturally diverse and gender inclusive, we have heard an increasing number of voices in the field of ethics that are not male and are not of European ancestry. These voices have often introduced diverse ethical perspectives and have, in turn, called into question not only specific moral assertions, but also whole moral theories long dominant in academic discourse. At the same time, white male philosophers from within the "mainstream" of the academy have, for somewhat different reasons, questioned the very enterprise of moral theory, as well as the very notion of morality itself.

The selection from Bernard Williams's *Ethics and the Limits of Philosophy* is an example of the latter. Williams, a very prominent late twentieth-century British philosopher, was critical of both Kantian and utilitarian moral theories, the two established alternatives in modern moral philosophy. (See chapter 5 for Williams's critique of utilitarianism.) In "Morality, the Peculiar Institution," Williams is critical of what he describes as the "morality system." For Williams, the morality system is a narrower development of the more general area of the *ethical*. While the ethical considers how best to live, taking into account many differing types of considerations, the morality system focuses on the special notion of obligation above all else. While Williams is particularly skeptical of the philosophical urge to fit all ethical matters into one systematic moral theory, he recognizes that the morality system does not belong only to moral philosophers but is largely shared by all of us. Williams is especially troubled by certain features of the morality system. These include morality's insistence that: (1) "ought implies can" (i.e., that one should be able to act on any obligation); (2) particular obligations should be backed up by more general obligations; (3) obligations cannot conflict; (4) obligations are categorical or unconditional, that is, that one "must" meet an obligation or else incur blame; (5) as many relevant ethical considerations as possible should be made into obligations; and (6) the "purity of morality" entails that moral judgments are impersonal considerations abstracted from emotional and social contexts and conditions.

Williams argues that each of these features of the morality system stems from a common mistake: ignoring the fact that obligations are just "one type of ethical consideration." In general, Williams finds the ethical life to be too complex to be reduced to one ethical concept, and too rooted in particular circumstances, personal desires, and individual points of view to adopt the impartial and abstract perspective advocated by the morality system. In asking these things of us, the morality system risks our uniqueness as persons. As a result, for Williams, we would be better off without morality.

A century before Williams, German philosopher Friedrich Nietzsche offered a forceful and wide-ranging challenge to Enlightenment moral theories. The selection from *Beyond Good and Evil* is representative of his thought. For Nietzsche, Kantian and utilitarian moral theories are attempts to establish universal and necessary moral laws and absolute moral values grounded in reason alone. But, in fact, Nietzsche maintains, they are nothing more than Western Christian morality wrapped up in the garb of "objective" rationality. Far from being universal and necessary, these moral systems arise out of particular and contingent historical and cultural contexts. He predicts that as modern Western culture increasingly loses its religion, there will no longer be any basis for traditional Western morality. In the absence of an absolute divine perspective, for Nietzsche, there are only human perspectives and as many truths and moralities as there are perspectives.

While there are many moralities, Nietzsche focuses on the fundamental distinction between two types of morality: *master morality* and *slave morality*. According to Nietzsche, the master morality is the older of the two. This moral system expresses the perspective of the nobles or the elite who distinguish between "good" (that which is strong or noble) and "bad" (that which is despicable or common). As such, the master morality is self-affirming and value creating. The slave morality, on the contrary, is based on the reaction of resentment toward the masters. It distinguishes between "good" (that which is weak or humble) and "evil" (that which is powerful, dangerous and strong), and has a negative attitude toward human beings and the human situation. While master morality is individualistic and life-affirming, for Nietzsche, slave morality is the morality of the herd and emphasizes such character traits as gentleness, kindness, pity, moderation and weakness.

According to Nietzsche, traditional Western values—a hybrid of Judeo-Christian "slave morality" and Greek rationality—are otherworldly and unhealthy in that they deny the forces of life and nature. They are the expressions of a decadent type of human being, exemplified by the priest and the philosopher, who is unable to embrace fully the "will to power" that governs all of nature and, instead, seeks to escape life for an imaginary world beyond matter and time. For Nietzsche, we must "re-evaluate" these values and go beyond the Judeo-Christian distinction of good and evil by creating a new value system, one that is true to the earth and natural instincts, accepts the ultimate meaninglessness of existence and embraces suffering as a means toward personal transformation.

In the last few decades of the twentieth century, and the first decade of the twenty-first, the academy has both welcomed and debated the idea of many perspectives and many moralities. One example in philosophy has been the various ethical theories arising from feminism. According to feminists, previous moral philosophies have expressed the male perspective: feminist ethical theory articulates the women's perspective. In the selection entitled "Feminism and Moral Theory," American moral philosopher Virginia Held suggests we take the experience of women rather than men as the starting point for moral theorizing, in particular, the experience of mothering. When the mother-child relationship replaces the "buyer-seller" relationship as paradigmatic of human interactions, then a morality rooted in the particulars of relating to and caring for others emerges as an alternative to a morality of universal rules and generalized obligations. For Held, however, such an ethic of caring need not abandon general ethical principles or the demands of justice, for this would weaken the feminist case for equal rights. Rather, a feminist ethic of caring, a perspective that takes seriously women's experience, could complement the traditional male ethical perspective, leading to a kind of ethical pluralism with "a division of moral labor" as different moral theories are applied to different problems. But Held also holds out the possibility that feminist moral theory might be more adequate to the ethical concerns of the present day than traditional male theories.

Multiculturalism is another recent movement in the academy that celebrates different voices. Multiculturalism asserts not only women's perspectives but also the perspectives of historically marginalized groups: ethnic groups such as blacks, Hispanics, and Native Americans, as well as gays and lesbians, among others. Members of these groups need and deserve a hearing. Following Nietzsche, proponents of multiculturalism challenge the assumption that there is one value system for all people. That assumption has served simply to impose one value system—the one that belongs to the dominant culture—on others. Following Nietzsche and the social philosophers Karl Marx and Michel Foucault, multiculturalism proposes that all theories, including moral theories, serve interests of power, and, as such, the moral cannot be separated from the political. In this sense, everything is political, including the search for truth and goodness.

Indeed, the philosopher Charles Taylor has described multiculturalism as the "politics of recognition." While we do not include a selection from Taylor, his ideas are important to understand, both in themselves and as background for the selections we have included by Kwame Anthony Appiah and Cornel West. According to Taylor, the politics of recognition is the attempt by marginalized groups within a culture to right the wrong of certain "misrecognitions" on the part of the dominant group that have served to belittle or oppress or otherwise cause harm to the marginalized groups. Multiculturalism champions the perspective of the "other" within society as a way of affirming and celebrating the identity of the sub-dominant group. Taylor calls for an "ethics of authenticity," each community recognizing its authentic self by embracing and expressing its identity as *this* particular people with *this* particular perspective. In the political realm, this might be referred to as "identity politics." But Taylor sees a moral dimension to the politics of recognition, for it springs from the ethics of authenticity combined with a moral outrage at the arrogance of those who oppress and marginalize the cultures or values of others.

The selection from African-American philosopher Kwame Anthony Appiah challenges some aspects of multiculturalism as described by Taylor. In *The Ethics of Identity*, Appiah expresses the concern that identifying oneself in terms of a particular group, whether ethnic, racial, religious or sexual, risks losing the significance of the individual. But this would undermine the very ethics of authenticity that Taylor sees as the basis of the moral dimension of multiculturalism. Appiah suggests, instead, that we focus on the uniqueness of individual persons rather than on "peoples," and in recent writings has called for a new form of "cosmopolitanism" as a kind of "global ethics" that includes both respect for cultural differences and respect for individual freedom.

The final selection is an example of the ethics of authenticity applied to a real world problem. This section is by another African-American philosopher, Appiah's colleague at Princeton University, Cornel West. In the essay "Nihilism in Black America," from the book *Race Matters*, West addresses inner-city despair in black communities in America. His essay challenges the prevailing political solutions to the problem, for he contends neither liberal nor conservative models get to the root of the problem. Instead, West maintains that the loss of meaning, hope and love in black America requires a moral solution. In this way, West, too, challenges the traditional distinction between the political and the moral, for his solution, a "politics of conversion," requires a "love ethic" at its center. While a progressive thinker, West challenges standard notions of what this means, since his "love ethic" reaches back to very traditional moral sources, even if he eschews traditional moral theories.

Morality, the Peculiar Institution*

Bernard Williams

Earlier I referred to morality as a special system, a particular variety of ethical thought. I must now explain what I take it to be, and why we would be better off without it.

The important thing about morality is its spirit, its underlying aims, and the general picture of ethical life it implies. In order to see them, we shall need to look carefully at a particular concept, *moral obligation*. The mere fact that it uses a notion of obligation is not what makes morality special. There is an everyday notion of obligation, as one consideration among others, and it is ethically useful. Morality is distinguished by the special notion of obligation it uses, and by the significance it gives to it. It is this special notion that I shall call "moral obligation." Morality is not one determinate set of ethical thoughts. It embraces a range of ethical outlooks; and morality is so much with us that moral philosophy spends much of its time discussing the differences between those outlooks, rather than the difference between all of them and everything else. They are not all equally typical or instructive examples of the morality system, though they do have in common the idea of moral obligation. The philosopher who has given the purest, deepest, and most thorough representation of morality is Kant But morality is not an invention of philosophers. It is the outlook, or, incoherently, part of the outlook, of almost all of us.

In the morality system, moral obligation is expressed in one especially important kind of deliberative conclusion—a conclusion that is directed toward what to do, governed by moral reasons, and concerned with a particular situation. (There are also general obligations, and we shall come back to them later.) Not every conclusion of a particular moral deliberation, even within the morality system, expresses an obligation. To go no further, some moral conclusions merely announce that you *may* do something. Those do not express an obligation, but they are in a sense still governed by the idea of obligation: you ask whether you are under an obligation, and decide that you are not.

---

*Reprinted by permission of the publisher from *Ethics and the Limits of Philosophy* by Bernard Williams, pp. 174–96, Cambridge, MA: Harvard University Press.

This description is in terms of the output or conclusion of moral deliberation. The moral considerations that go into a deliberation may themselves take the form of obligations, but one would naturally say that they did not need to do so. I might, for instance, conclude that I was under an obligation to act in a certain way, because it was for the best that a certain outcome should come about and I could bring it about in that way. However, there is a pressure within the morality system to represent every consideration that goes into a deliberation and yields a particular obligation as being itself a general obligation; so if I am now under an obligation to do something that would be for the best, this will be because I have some general obligation, perhaps among others, to do what is for the best. We shall see later how this happens.

The fact that moral obligation is a kind of practical conclusion explains several of its features. An obligation applies to someone with respect to an action—it is an obligation to do something—and the action must be in the agent's power. "*Ought* implies *can*" is a formula famous in this connection. As a general statement about *ought* it is untrue, but it must be correct if it is taken as a condition on what can be a particular obligation, where that is practically concluded. If my deliberation issues in something I cannot do, then I must deliberate again. The question of what counts as in the agent's power is notoriously problematical, not only because of large and unnerving theories claiming that everything (or everything psychological) is determined, but also because it is simply unclear what it means to say that someone can act, or could have acted, in a certain way. To say anything useful about these problems needs a wide-ranging discussion that I shall not attempt in this book.[1] What I shall have to say here, however, will suggest that morality, in this as in other respects, encounters the common problems in a peculiarly acute form.

Another feature of moral obligations in this sense is that they cannot conflict, ultimately, really, or at the end of the line. This will follow directly from the last point, that what I am obliged to do must be in my power, if one grants a further principle (it has been called the "agglomeration principle"), that if I am obliged to do X and obliged to do Y, then I am obliged to do X and Y. This requirement, too, reflects the practical shape of this notion of obligation. In an ordinary sense of "obligation," not controlled by these special requirements, obligations obviously can conflict. One of the most common occasions of mentioning them at all is when they do.[2]

The philosopher David Ross invented a terminology, still sometimes used, for discussing the conflict of obligations, which distinguished *between prima facie* and actual obligations. A *prima facie* obligation is a conclusion, supported by moral considerations, which is a candidate for being one's actual obligation. It will be the proper conclusion of one's moral deliberation if it is not outweighed by another obligation. Ross tried to explain (without much success) why a merely *prima facie* obligation—one that is eventually outweighed—is more than an apparent obligation. It is to be seen as exerting some force on the place of decision, but not enough, granted the competition, to get into that place. The effect, in more concrete terms, is that the considerations that supported the defeated *prima facie* obligation can come to support some other, actual, obligation. If I have for good and compelling reasons broken a promise, I may acquire an actual obligation to do something else because of that, such as compensate the person who has been let down.

It is not at all clear why I should be under this further obligation, since it is one's own business, on this view of things, to observe one's obligations, and I shall have done that. No actual obligation has been broken. This has a comforting consequence, that I should not blame myself. I may blame myself for something else, such as getting into the situation, but it is mistaken to blame or reproach myself for not doing the rejected action: self-reproach belongs with broken obligations, and, it has turned out, there was no obligation. It is conceded that I may reasonably feel bad about it, but this feeling is distinguished by the morality system from remorse or self-reproach, for instance under the title "regret," which is not a moral feeling. This reclassification is important, and very characteristic of what happens when the ethical is contracted to the moral. To say that your feelings about something done involuntarily, or as the lesser of two evils, are to be understood as regret, a non moral feeling, implies that you should feel toward those actions as you feel toward things that merely happen, or toward the actions of others. The thought *I did it* has no special significance; what is significant is whether I voluntarily did what I ought to have done. This turns our attention away from an important dimension of ethical experience, which lies in the distinction simply between what one has done and what one has not done. That can be as important as the distinction between the voluntary and the nonvoluntary.[3]

Moral obligation is inescapable. I may acquire an obligation voluntarily, as when I make a promise: in that case, indeed, it is usually said that it has to be voluntarily made to be a promise at all, though there is a gray area here, as with promises made under constraint. In other cases, I may be under an obligation through no choice of mine. But, either way, once I am under the obligation, there is no escaping it, and the fact that a given agent would prefer not to be in this system or bound by its rules will not excuse him; nor will blaming him be based on a misunderstanding. Blame is the characteristic reaction of the morality system. The remorse or self-reproach or guilt I have already mentioned is the characteristic first-personal reaction within the system, and if an agent never felt such sentiments, he would not belong to the morality system or be a full moral agent in its terms. The system also involves blame between persons, and unless there were such a thing, these first-personal reactions would doubtless not be found, since they are formed by internalization. But it is possible for particular agents who belong to the system never to blame anyone, in the sense of expressing blame and perhaps even of feeling the relevant sentiments. They might, for instance, be scrupulously skeptical about what was in other people's power. The point that self-blame or remorse requires one's action to have been voluntary is only a special application of a general rule, that blame of anyone is directed to the voluntary. The moral law is more exigent than the law of an actual liberal republic, because it allows no emigration, but it is unequivocally just in its ideas of responsibility.

In this respect, utilitarianism is a marginal member of the morality system. It has a strong tradition of thinking that blame and other social reactions should be allocated in a way that will be socially useful, and while this might lead to their being directed to the voluntary, equally it might not. This follows consistently from applying the utilitarian criterion to all actions, including the social actions of expressing blame and so forth. The same principle can be extended to unexpressed blame and critical thoughts; indeed, at another level, a utilitarian might well ask whether the most useful policy might not be to forget that the point of blame, on utilitarian grounds, was usefulness. These maneuvers do seem to receive a check when it comes to self-reproach and the sense of moral obligation. Utilitarians are often immensely conscientious people, who work for humanity and give up meat for the sake of the animals. They think this is what they morally ought to do and feel guilty if they do not live up to their own standards. They do not, and perhaps could not, ask: How useful is it that I think and feel like this? It is because of such motivations, and not only because of logical features, that utilitarianism in most versions is a kind of morality, if a marginal one.

The sense that moral obligation is inescapable, that what I am obliged to do is what I *must* do, is the first-personal end of the conception already mentioned, that moral obligation applies to people even if they do not want it to. The third-personal aspect is that moral judgment and blame can apply to people even if, at the limit, they want to live outside that system altogether, from the perspective of morality, there is nowhere outside the system, or at least nowhere for a responsible agent. Taking Kant's term, we may join these two aspects in saying that moral obligation is *categorical*.

I shall come back later to people outside the system. There is more that needs to be said first about what a moral obligation is for someone within the system. It is hard to agree that the course of action which, on a given occasion, there is most moral reason to take must necessarily count as a moral obligation. There are actions (also policies, attitudes, and so on) that are either more or less than obligations. They may be heroic or very fine actions, which go beyond what is obligatory or demanded. Or they may be actions that from a ethical point of view it would be agreeable or worthwhile or a good idea to do, without one's being required to do them. The point is obvious in terms of people's reactions. People may be greatly admired, or merely well thought of, for actions they would not be blamed for omitting. How does the morality system deal with the considerations that seemingly do not yield obligations?

One way in which the central, deontological, version of morality deals with them is to try to make as many as possible into obligations. (It has a particular motive for the reductivist enterprise of trying to make all ethical considerations into one type.) There are some instructive examples of this in the work of Ross, whose terminology *of prima facie* obligations I have already mentioned. He lists several types of what he regards as general obligations or, as he also calls them, duties.[4] The first type includes what everyone calls an obligation, keeping promises and, by a fairly natural extension, telling the truth. The second class involves "duties of gratitude" to do good to those who have done services for you. But it is not really clear that these are *duties*, unless the benefactor (as the word "services" may imply) has acquired a right to expect a return—in which case, it will follow from some implied promise, and the obligation will belong with the first type. Good deeds I have not asked for may indeed be oppressive, but I should not simply take that oppression for obligation.[5]

What Ross is trying to force into the mold of obligation is surely a different ethical idea, that it is a sign of good character to want to return benefits. This characteristic is not the same thing as a disposition to do what one is morally obliged to do. A different ethical thought, again, is disguised in Ross's third class, which he calls "duties of justice." What he says about this is extraordinary:

> [these duties] rest on the fact or possibility of a distribution of pleasure or happiness or the means thereto which is not in accordance with the merits of the persons concerned; in which case there arises a duty to upset or prevent such a distribution.

There are such things as duties or obligations of justice, but this incitement to insurrection against the capitalist economy (or any other, come to that) can hardly be the right account of what they are. The requirements of justice concern, in the first place, *what ought to happen*. The way in which a given requirement of justice relates to what a given person has reason to do, or more specifically is under an obligation to do, is a matter of how that person stands to the requirement. In politics, the question of how far personal action stands from the desirable—the *utopia measure*, as it might be called—is itself one of the first, and one of the first ethical, questions.

It is a mistake of morality to try to make everything into obligations. But the reasons for the mistake go deep. Here we should recall that what is *ordinarily* called an obligation does not necessarily have to win in a conflict of moral considerations. Suppose you are under an everyday obligation—to visit a friend, let us say (a textbook example), because you have promised to. You are then presented with a unique opportunity, at a conflicting time and place, to further significantly some important cause. (To make the example realistic, one should put in more detail; and, as often in moral philosophy, if one puts in the detail the example may begin to dissolve. There is the question of your friend's attitude toward the cause and also toward your support of the cause. If he or she favors both, or merely the second, and would release you from the promise if you could get in touch, only the stickiest moralist would find a difficulty. If the friend would not release you, you may wonder what sort of friend you have . . . But it should not be hard for each person reading this to find some example that will make the point.) You may reasonably conclude that you should take the opportunity to further the cause.[6] But obligations have a moral stringency, which means that breaking them attracts blame. The only thing that can be counted on to cancel this, within the economy of morality, is that the rival action should represent another and more stringent obligation. Morality encourages the idea, *only an obligation can beat an obligation*.[7]

Yet how can this action of yours have been an obligation, unless it came from some more general obligation? It will not be easy to say what the general obligation is. You are not under an unqualified obligation to pursue this cause, nor to do everything you possibly can for causes you have adopted. We are left with the limp suggestion that one is under an obligation to assist some important cause on occasions that are specially propitious for assisting it. The pressure of the demand within the morality system to find a general obligation to back a particular one—what may be called the *obligation-out, obligation-in* principle—has a clearer result in those familiar cases where some general ethical consideration is focused on to a particular occasion by an emergency, such as the obligation to try to assist someone in danger. I am not under an obligation to assist all people at risk, or to go round looking for people at risk to assist. Confronted[8] with someone at risk, many feel that they are under an obligation to try to help (though not at excessive danger to themselves, and so on: various sensible qualifications come to mind). In this case, unlike the last, the underlying obligation seems ready made. The immediate claim on me, "In this emergency, I am under an obligation to help," is thought to come from, "One is under this general obligation: to help in an emergency." If we add the thought that many, perhaps any, moral considerations could overrule some obligation on some occasion, we find that many, perhaps all, such considerations are related to some general obligations, even if they are not the simple and unqualified ones suggested by Ross's reductionism.

Once the journey into more general obligations has started, we may begin to get into trouble—not just philosophical trouble, but conscience trouble—with finding room for morally indifferent actions. I have already mentioned the possible moral conclusion that one *may* take some particular course of action. That means that there is nothing else I am obliged to do. But if we have accepted general and indeterminate obligations to further various moral objectives, as the last set of thoughts encourages us to do, they will be waiting to provide work for idle hands, and the thought can gain a footing (I am not saying that it has to) that I could be better employed than in doing something I am under no obligation to do, and, if I could be, then I ought to be: I am under an obligation not to waste time in doing things I am under no obligation to do. At this stage, certainly, only an obligation can beat an obligation, and in order to do what I wanted to do, I shall need one of those fraudulent items, a duty to myself. If obligation is allowed to structure ethical thought, there are several natural ways in which it can come to dominate life altogether.

In order to see around the intimidating structure that morality has made out of the idea of obligation, we need an account of what obligations are when they are rightly seen as merely one kind of ethical consideration among others. This account will help to lead us away from morality's special notion of moral obligation, and eventually out of the morality system altogether.

We need, first, the notion of *importance*. Obviously enough, various things are important to various people (which does not necessarily mean that those things are important for those people's interests). This involves a relative notion of importance, which we might also express by saying that someone *finds* a given thing important. Beyond this merely relative idea, we have another notion, of something's being, simply, important (important *überhaupt*, as others might put it, or important *period*). It is not at all clear what it is for something to be, simply, important. It does not mean that it is important to the universe: in that sense, nothing is important. Nor does it mean that it is as a matter of fact something that most human beings find important; nor that it is something people ought to find important. I doubt that there can be an incontestable account of this idea; the explanations people give of it are necessarily affected by what they find important.

It does not matter for the present discussion that this notion is poorly understood. I need only three things of it. One is that there is such a notion. Another is that if something is important in the relative sense to somebody, this does not necessarily imply that he or she thinks it is, simply, important. It may be of the greatest importance to Henry that his stamp collection be completed with a certain stamp, but even Henry may see that it is not, simply, important. A significant ideal lies in this: people should find important a number of things that are, simply, important, as well as many things that are not, and they should be able to tell the difference between them.

The third point is that the question of importance, and above all the question of what is, simply, important, needs to be distinguished from questions of *deliberative priority*. A consideration has high deliberative priority for us if we give it heavy weighting against other considerations in our deliberations. (This includes two ideas, that when it occurs in our deliberations, it outweighs most other considerations, and also that it occurs in our deliberations. There are some reasons for treating the second idea separately, and I shall touch on one later, but in general it is simpler to consider them together.)

Importance has some connections with deliberative priority, but they are not straightforward. There are many important things that no one can do much about, and very many that a given person can do nothing about. Again, it may not be that person's business to do anything: there is a deliberative division of labor. Your deliberations are not connected in a simple way even with what is important to you. If you find something important, then that will affect your life in one way or another, and so affect your deliberations, but those effects do not have to be found directly in the content of your deliberations.

A consideration may have high deliberative priority for a particular person, for a group of people, or for everyone. In this way priority is relativized, to people. But it should not be relativized in another way: it should not be marked for subject matter, so that things will have moral or prudential deliberative priority. This would be a misunderstanding. It may be said that moral considerations have a high priority from a moral point of view. If this is so, what it will mean is that someone within the moral system gives those considerations a high priority. It does not define a kind of priority. A major point about deliberative priority is that it can relate considerations of different types.[9] The same thing is true of importance. In a sense, there are kinds of importance, and we naturally say that some things are morally important, others aesthetically important, and so on. But there must be a question at the end, in a particular case or more generally, whether one kind of importance is more important than another kind.

Those who are within the morality system usually think that morality is important. Moreover, morality has by definition something to do with personal conduct, so here importance is likely to have something to do with deliberation. But what it has to do with it depends crucially on the way one understands morality and morality's importance. For utilitarians, what is important is that there should be as much welfare as possible. The connection with deliberation is a subsequent question, and it is entirely open. We saw when we considered indirect utilitarianism how the question is open of what moral considerations should occur in a utilitarian agent's deliberations. More than that, it is open whether any moral considerations at all should occur in them. Some kinds of utilitarian thought have supposed that the best results would follow if people did not think in moral terms at all, and merely (for instance) acted selfishly. With less faith in the invisible hand, others give moral considerations some priority, and some of them, as we have seen, take a highly conscientious line. But for any utilitarian it should always be an empirical question: What are the implications for deliberation of welfare's being important? In this respect, however, there are many utilitarians who belong to the morality system first and are utilitarians second.

At the other extreme, the purest Kantian view locates the importance of morality in the importance of moral motivation itself. What is important is that people should give moral considerations the highest deliberative priority. This view was relentlessly and correctly attacked by Hegel, on the grounds that it gave moral thought no content and also that it was committed to a double-mindedness about the improvement of the world. The content of the moral motivation was the thought of obligation to do certain things, as against mere inclination; the need for that thought implied that individuals were not spontaneously inclined to do those things; its supreme importance implied that it was better so.

Neither view is adequate, and a better view is not going to consist of any simple compromise. Ethical life itself is important, but it can see that things other than itself are important. It contains motivations that indeed serve these other ends but at the same time be seen from within that life as part of what make it worth living. On any adequate showing, ethical motivations are going to be important, and this has consequences for how we should deliberate. One consequence is that some kinds of ethical consideration will have high deliberative priority. This is only one way in which ethical motivations may affect people's deliberations. They may equally affect their style and their occasion, among other things.[10]

There is one kind of ethical consideration that directly connects importance and deliberative priority, and this is obligation. It is grounded in the basic issue of what people should be able to rely on. People must rely as far as possible on not being killed or used as a resource, and on having some space and objects and relations with other people they can count as their own. It also serves their interests if, to some extent at least, they can count on not being lied to. One way in which these ends can be served, and perhaps the only way, is by some kind of ethical life; and, certainly, if there is to be ethical life, these ends have to be served by it and within it. *One* way in which ethical life serves them is by encouraging certain motivations, and *one* form of this is to instill a disposition to give the relevant considerations a high deliberative priority—in the most serious of these matters, a virtually absolute priority, so that certain courses of action must come first, while others are ruled out from the beginning. An effective way for actions to be ruled out is that they never come into thought at all, and this is often the best way. One does not feel easy with the man who in the course of a discussion of how to deal with political or business rivals says, "Of course, we could have them killed, but we should lay that aside right from the beginning." It should never have come into his hands to be laid aside. It is characteristic of morality that it tends to overlook the possibility that some concerns are best embodied in this way, in deliberative silence.

Considerations that are given deliberative priority in order to secure reliability constitute obligations; corresponding to those obligations are rights, possessed by people who benefit from the obligations. One type of obligations is picked out by the basic and standing importance of the interests they serve. These are all negative in force, concerning what we should not do. Another, and now positive, sort involves the obligations of immediacy. Here, a high deliberative priority is imposed by an emergency, such as the rescue case we considered before. A general ethical recognition of people's vital interests is focused into a deliberative priority by immediacy, and it is immediacy to *me* that generates *my* obligation, one I cannot ignore without blame. Two connected things follow from understanding the obligations of emergency in this way. First, we do not after all have to say that the obligation comes from a more general obligation. The point of the negative obligations does lie in their being general; they provide a settled and permanent pattern of deliberative priorities. In the positive kind of case, however, the underlying disposition is a general concern, which is not always expressed in deliberative priority, and what produces an obligation from it is, precisely, the emergency. We need not accept the *obligation-out, obligation-in* principle.

More important, there are ethical consequences of understanding these obligations in this way. Some moralists say that if we regard immediacy or physical nearness as relevant, we must be failing in rationality or imagination; we are irrational if we do not recognize that those starving elsewhere have as big a claim on us as those starving here. These moralists are wrong, at least in trying to base their challenge simply on the structure of obligations. Of course this point does not dispose of the challenge itself. We should be more concerned about the sufferings of people elsewhere. But a correct understanding of what obligation is will make it clearer how we should start thinking about the challenge. We should not banish the category of immediacy, but we must consider what for us, in the modern world, should properly count as immediacy, and what place we have in our lives for such concerns when they are not obligations.

The obligations considered so far involve (negatively) what is fundamentally important and (positively) what is important and immediate. They are both based ultimately on one conception, that each person has a life to lead. People need help but (unless they are very young, very old, or severely handicapped) not all the time. All the time they need not to be killed, assaulted, or arbitrarily interfered with. It is a strength of contractualism to have seen that such positive and negative obligations will follow from these basic interests.[11]

The obligations that are most familiarly so called, those of promises, differ from both of these because what I am obliged to do, considered in itself, may not be important at all. But just because of that, they are an example of the same connection, between obligation and reliability. The institution of promising operates to provide portable reliability, by offering a formula that will confer high deliberative priority on what might otherwise not receive it. This is why it is odd for someone to promise not to kill you—if he does not already give it high priority, why should his promising be relied upon to provide it? (There are answers to this question, in special cases, and considering what they might be will help to show how the system works.)

Obligation works to secure reliability, a state of affairs in which people can reasonably expect others to behave in some ways and not in others. It is only one among other ethical ways of doing this. It is one that tries to produce an expectation *that* through an expectation *of*. These kinds of obligation very often command the highest deliberative priority and also present themselves as important—in the case of promises, because they are promises and not simply because of their content. However, we can also see how they need not always command the highest priority even in ethically well-disposed agents. Reflecting that some end is peculiarly important, and the present action importantly related to it, an agent can reasonably conclude that the obligation may be broken on this occasion, as we noticed before, and indeed this conclusion may be acceptable,[12] in the sense that he can explain within a structure of ethical considerations why he decided as he did. But there is no need for him to call this course another and more stringent obligation. An obligation is a special kind of consideration, with a general relation to importance and immediacy. The case we are considering is simply one in which there is a consideration important enough to outweigh this obligation on this occasion,[13] and it is cleaner just to say so. We should reject morality's other maxim, that only an obligation can beat an obligation.

When a deliberative conclusion embodies a consideration that has the highest deliberative priority and is also of the greatest importance (at least to the agent), it may take a special form and become the conclusion not merely that one should do a certain thing, but that one *must*, and that one cannot do anything else. We may call this a conclusion of practical necessity. Sometimes, of course, "must" in a practical conclusion is merely relative and means only that some course of action is needed for an end that is not at all a matter of "must." "I must go now" may well be completed ". . . if I am to get to the movies" where there is no suggestion that I have to go to the movies: I merely am going to the movies. We are not concerned with this, but with a "must" that is unconditional and *goes all the way down*.

It is an interesting question, how a conclusion in terms of what we must do, or equally of what we cannot do, differs from a conclusion expressed merely in terms of what we have most reason to do; in particular, how it can be stronger, as it seems to be. (How, in deliberation, can anything stronger be concluded in favor of a course of action than that we have most reason to take it?) I shall not try to discuss this question here.[14] What is immediately relevant is that practical necessity is in no way peculiar to ethics. Someone may conclude that he or she unconditionally must do a certain thing, for reasons of prudence, self-protection, aesthetic or artistic concern, or sheer self-assertion. In some of these cases (basic self-defense, for instance), an ethical outlook may itself license the conclusion. In others, it will disapprove of it. The fundamental point is that a conclusion of practical necessity is the same sort of conclusion whether it is grounded in ethical reasons or not.

Practical necessity, and the experience of reaching a conclusion with that force, is one element that has gone into the idea of moral obligation (this may help to explain the sense, which so many people have, that moral obligation is at once quite special and very familiar). Yet practical necessity, even when it is grounded in ethical reasons, does not necessarily signal an obligation. The course of action the agent "must" take may not be associated with others' expectations, or with blame for failure. The ethically outstanding or possibly heroic actions I mentioned before, in being more than obligations, are not obligatory, and we cannot usually be asked to do them or be blamed for not doing them. But the agent who does such a thing may feel that he must do it, that there is no alternative for him, while at the same time recognizing that it would not be a demand on others. The thought may come in the form that it is a demand on him, but not on others, because he is different from others; but the difference will then typically turn out to consist in the fact that he is someone who has this very conviction. His feelings indeed, and his expectations of feelings he will have if he does not act, may well be like those associated with obligations (more like them than morality admits[15]).

I have already mentioned Kant's description of morality as categorical. When he claimed that the fundamental principle of morality was a Categorical Imperative, Kant was not interested in any purely logical distinction between forms of what are literally imperatives. He was concerned with the recognition of an *I must* that is unconditional and goes all the way down, but he construed this unconditional practical necessity as being peculiar to morality. He thought it was unconditional in the sense that it did not depend on desire at all: a course of action presented to us with this kind of necessity was one we had reason to take *whatever we might happen to want*, and it was only moral reasons that could transcend desire in that way. As I have introduced it, however, practical necessity need not be independent of desire in so strong a sense. I distinguished a "must" that is unconditional from one that is conditional on a desire *that the agent merely happens to have*; but a conclusion of practical necessity could itself be the expression of a desire, if the desire were not one that the agent merely happened to have, but was essential to the agent and had to be satisfied. The difference between this conception of practical necessity and Kant's is not of course merely a matter of definition or of logical analysis. Kant's idea of practical necessity is basically this more familiar one, but it is given a particularly radical interpretation, under which the only necessary practical conclusions are those absolutely unconditioned by any desire. For Kant there could be a practical conclusion that was radically unconditioned in this way, because of his picture of the rational self as free from causality, and because there were reasons for action which depended merely on rational agency and not on anything (such as a desire) that the agent might not have had.[16]

Kant also describes the conclusion of practical necessity, understood as peculiar to morality, as a recognition of the demands of moral law, and when he speaks of this in psychological terms, he refers to a special feeling or sentiment, a "sense of reverence for the law." Modern moralists are not likely to use those words, but they do not find it hard to recognize what Kant was describing. (Some of them still want to invoke a conception of moral law. Others, reluctant to do so, are using ideas that implicitly involve it.) Kant did not think that the compelling sense of moral necessity, regarded as a feeling, was itself what provided the reason for moral action. As a feeling, it was just a feeling and had no more rational power than any other merely psychological item had. The reason lay not in what that feeling was, but in what it represented, the truth that moral universality was a requirement of practical reason itself.

That truth, as Kant took it to be, meant that morality had an objective foundation, and he took the experience of the moral demand to represent this foundation. However, it must be said that it also significantly misrepresents it. The experience is like being *confronted* with something, a law that is part of the world in which one lives.[17] Yet the power of the moral law, according to Kant, does not lie and could not conceivably lie in anything outside oneself. Its power lies in its objective foundation, and no experience could adequately represent that kind of objectivity. The objectivity comes from this, that the requirements of practical reason will be met only by leading a life in which moral considerations play a basic and characteristic role; and that role is one they perform only if, unlike other motivations, they present themselves in the form of an objective demand. But then what is it for a consideration to present itself as an objective demand? It cannot consist in its presenting itself as so related to that very argument. It must have some other psychological form, and the form will be, to that extent, misleading.

On Kant's assumptions, however, one can at least come to understand how, and why, such an experience is bound to be misleading, and this will help to make it stable to reflection. If Kant is right, I can come to understand what the "sense of reverence for the law" is, and not lose my respect for it or for the moral law. This stability is helped by a further thought, that there is one sense in which the law is rightly represented by the experience as being outside me: it is equally in other people. The moral law is the law of the notional republic of moral agents. It is a notional republic, but they are real agents and, because it is rationally self-imposed by each of them, it is a real law.

Once we have ceased to believe in Kant's own foundation or anything like it, we cannot read this experience in this way at all. It is the conclusion of practical necessity, no more and no less, and it seems to come "from outside" in the way that conclusions of practical necessity always seem to come from outside—from deeply inside. Since ethical considerations are in question, the agent's conclusions will not usually be solitary or unsupported, because they are part of an ethical life that is to an important degree shared with others. In this respect, the morality system itself, with its emphasis on the "purely moral" and personal sentiments of guilt and self-reproach, actually conceals the dimension in which ethical life lies outside the individual.

When we know what the recognition of obligation is, if we still make it the special center of ethical experience, we are building ethical life around an illusion. Even in Kant's own view, this experience involves a misrepresentation, but it is a necessary and acceptable one, a consequence of transposing objectivity from the transcendental level to the psychological. But if this experience is special only in the psychological mode, then it is worse than a misrepresentation: there is nothing (or nothing special) for it to represent.

Kant's construction also explains how the moral law can unconditionally apply to all people, even if they try to live outside it. Those who do not accept his construction, but still accept the morality system, need to say how moral obligation binds those who refuse it. They need to say how there can be a moral *law* at all.[18] The fact that a law applies to someone always consists in more than a semantic relation; it is not merely that the person falls under some description contained in the law. The law of a state applies to a person because he belongs to a state that can apply power. The law of God applied because God applied it. Kant's moral law applied because as a rational being one had a reason to apply it to oneself. For the moral law to apply now, it can only be that we apply it.

When we say that someone ought to have acted in some required or desirable way in which he has not acted, we sometimes say that *there was a reason* for him to act in that way—he had promised, for instance, or what he actually did violated someone's rights. Although we can say this, it does not seem to be connected in any secure way with the idea that *he had a reason* to act in that way. Perhaps he had no reason at all. In breaking the obligation, he was not necessarily behaving irrationally or unreasonably, but badly. We cannot take for granted that he had a reason to behave well, as opposed to our having various reasons for wishing that he would behave well. How do we treat him? We recognize in fact, very clumsily in the law, less clumsily in informal practice, that there are many different ways in which people can fail to be what we would ethically like them to be. At one extreme there is general deliberative incapacity. At another extreme is the sincere and capable follower of another creed. Yet again there are people with various weaknesses or vices, people who are malicious, selfish, brutal, inconsiderate, self-indulgent, lazy, greedy. All these people can be part of our ethical world. No ethical world has ever been free of those with such vices (though their classification will be a matter of the culture in question); and any individual life is lined by some of them. There are, equally, various negative reactions to them, from hatred and horror in the most extreme cases, to anger, regret, correction, blame. When we are not within the formal circumstances of the state's law, there is the further dimension of who is reacting: not everyone can or should sustain every complaint. It is another consequence of the fiction of the moral law that this truth does not occur to us. It is as if every member of the notional republic were empowered to make a citizen's arrest.

Within all this there is a range, quite a wide one, of particular deviations that we treat with the machinery of everyday blame. They include many violations of obligations, but not all of them: some of the most monstrous proceedings, which lie beyond ordinary blame, involve violations of basic human rights. Nor, on the other hand, is there blame only for broken obligations; particularly in bringing up children, actions that merely manifest imperfect dispositions are blamed. But blame always tends to share the particularized, practical character of moral obligation in the technical sense. Its negative reaction is focused closely on an action or omission, and this is what is blamed. Moreover—though there are many inevitable anomalies in its actual working—the aspiration of blame is that it should apply only to the extent that the undesired outcome is the product of voluntary action on the particular occasion.

This institution, as opposed to other kinds of ethically negative or hostile reaction to people's doings (it is vital to remember how many others there are), seems to have something special to do with the idea that the agent had a reason to act otherwise. As I have already said, this is often not so.[19] The institution of blame is best seen as involving a fiction, by which we treat the agent as one for whom the relevant ethical considerations are reasons. The "ought to have" of blame can be seen as an extension into the unwilling of the "ought to have" we may offer, in advice, to those whose ends we share. This fiction has various functions. One is that if we treat the agent as someone who gives weight to ethical reasons, this may help to make him into such a person.

The device is specially important in helping to mediate between two possibilities in people's relations. One is that of shared deliberative practices, where to a considerable extent people have the same dispositions and are helping each other to arrive at practical conclusions. The other is that in which one group applies force or threats to constrain another. The fiction underlying the blame system helps at its best to make a bridge between these possibilities, by a process of continuous recruitment into a deliberative community. At its worst, it can do many bad things, such as encouraging people to misunderstand their own fear and resentment—sentiments they may quite appropriately feel—as the voice of the Law.

The fiction of the deliberative community is one of the positive achievements of the morality system. As with other fictions, it is a real question whether its working could survive a clear understanding of how it works. This is part of the much larger question of what needs to be, and what can be, restructured in the light of a reflective and nonmythical understanding of our ethical practices. It is certain that the practices of blame, and more generally the style of people's negative ethical reactions to others, will change. The morality system, in my view, can no longer help them to do so in a desirable way. One reason is that morality is under too much pressure on the subject of the voluntary.

To the extent that the institution of blame works coherently, it does so because it attempts less than morality would like it to do. When we ask whether someone acted voluntarily, we are asking, roughly, whether he really acted, whether he knew what he was doing, and whether he intended this or that aspect of what happened. This practice takes the agent together with his character, and does not raise questions about his freedom to have chosen some other character. The blame system, most of the time, closely concentrates on the conditions of the particular act; and it is able to do this because it does not operate on its own. It is surrounded by other practices of encouragement and discouragement, acceptance and rejection, which work on desire and character to shape them into the requirements and possibilities of ethical life.

Morality neglects this surrounding and sees only that focused, particularized judgment. There is a pressure within it to require a voluntariness that will be total and will cut through character and psychological or social determination, and allocate blame and responsibility on the ultimately fair basis of the agent's own contribution, no more and no less. It is an illusion to suppose that this demand can be met (as opposed to the less ambitious requirements of Voluntariness that take character largely as given). This fact is known to almost everyone, and it is hard to see a long future for a system committed to denying it. But so long as morality itself remains, there is danger in admitting the fact, since the system itself leaves us, as the only contrast to rational blame, forms of persuasion it refuses to distinguish in spirit from force and constraint.

In truth, almost all worthwhile human life lies between the extremes that morality puts before us. It starkly emphasizes a series of contrasts: between force and reason, persuasion and rational conviction, shame and guilt, dislike and disapproval, mere rejection and blame. The attitude that leads it to emphasize all these contrasts can be labeled its *purity*. The purity of morality, its insistence on abstracting the moral consciousness from other kinds of emotional reaction or social influence, conceals not only the means by which it deals with deviant members of its community, but also the virtues of those means. It is not surprising that it should conceal them, since the virtues can be seen as such only from outside the system, from a point of view that can assign value to it, whereas the morality system is closed in on itself and must consider it an indecent misunderstanding to apply to the system any values other than those of morality itself.

The purity of morality itself represents a value. It expresses an ideal, presented by Kant, once again, in a form that is the most unqualified and also one of the most moving: the ideal that human existence can be ultimately just. Most advantages and admired characteristics are distributed in ways that, if not unjust, are at any rate not just, and some people are simply luckier than others. The ideal of morality is a value, moral value, that transcends luck. It must therefore lie beyond any empirical determination. It must lie not only in trying rather than succeeding, since success depends partly on luck, but in a kind of trying that lies beyond the level at which the capacity to try can itself be a matter of luck. The value must, further, be supreme. It will be no good if moral value is merely a consolation prize you get if you are not in worldly terms happy or talented or good-humoured or loved. It has to be what ultimately matters.

This is in some ways like a religious conception. But it is also unlike any real religion, and in particular unlike orthodox Christianity. The doctrine of grace in Christianity meant that there was no calculable road from moral effort to salvation; salvation lay beyond merit, and men's efforts, even their moral efforts, were not the measure of God's love.[20] Moreover, when it was said by Christianity that what ultimately mattered was salvation, this was thought to involve a difference that anyone would recognize as a difference, as *the* difference. But the standpoint from which pure moral value has its value is, once more, only that of morality itself. It can hope to transcend luck only by turning in on itself.

The ideals of morality have without doubt, and contrary to a vulgar Marxism that would see them only as an ideology of unworldliness, played a part in producing some actual justice in the world and in mobilizing power and social opportunity to compensate for bad luck in concrete terms. But the idea of a value that lies beyond all luck is an illusion, and political aims cannot continue to draw any conviction from it. Once again, the other conceptions of morality cannot help us. They can only encourage the idea, which always has its greedy friends, that when these illusions have gone there can be no coherent ideas of social justice, but only efficiency, or power, or uncorrected luck.

Many philosophical mistakes are woven into morality. It misunderstands obligations, not seeing how they form just one type of ethical consideration. It misunderstands practical necessity, thinking it peculiar to the ethical. It misunderstands ethical practical necessity, thinking it peculiar to obligations. Beyond all this, morality makes people think that, without its very special obligation, there is only inclination; without its utter voluntariness, there is only force; without its ultimately pure justice, there is no justice. Its philosophical errors are only the most abstract expressions of a deeply rooted and still powerful misconception of life.

Notes

1. I touch briefly on some points later in this chapter. Most discussions of free will do not pay enough attention to the point that causal explanation may have a different impact on different parts of our thought about action and responsibility. It is worth consideration that deliberation requires only *can*, while blame requires *could have*.

2. I have discussed the question of conflict in several essays, in *Problems of the Self* and *Moral Luck*. It is important that, if it were logically impossible for two actual obligations to conflict, I could not get into a situation of their conflicting even through my own fault. What is it supposed that I get into?

3. This point is discussed in my essay "Moral Luck," in the book of that title. It illustrates the general point that the morality system lays particularly heavy weight on the unsure structure of voluntariness.

4. W. D. Ross, *The Right and the Good* (Oxford: Clarendon Press, 1930), pp. 21ff.

5. This is so even when the good deeds are part of a general practice that others hope I will join. The point is admirably pressed by Robert Nozick in *Anarchy, State and Utopia* (New York: Basic Books, 1974), chap. 5.

6. The example is of a conflict between an obligation and a consideration that is not at first sight an obligation. It may very readily represent another conflict as well, between private and public. For various considerations on this, and particularly on the role of utilitarian considerations in public life, see the essays in Stuart Hampshire, ed., *Public and Private Morality* (New York: Cambridge University Press, 1978).

7. Morality encourages the idea, certainly in cases of this kind, but it does not always insist on it, at least in the form that an obligation of mine can be overridden only by another obligation of mine. If some vital interest of mine would have to be sacrificed in order to carry out a promise, particularly if the promise were relatively unimportant, even the severest moralist may agree that I would have the right to break the promise, without requiring that I would be under an obligation to do so (I owe this point to Gilbert Harman). This is correct but, unless the promise is very trivial, the severe moralist will agree, I suspect, only if the interests involved are indeed vital. This suggests an interpretation under which my obligation would indeed be beaten by an obligation, but not one of mine. In insisting that only vital interests count, it is likely that the moralist, when he says that I have the right to safeguard my interest, does not mean simply that I may do that, but that I have what has been called a claim-right to do so: that is to say, others are under an obligation not to impede me in doing so. Then my original obligation will be canceled by an obligation *of the promissee*, to waive his or her right to performance.

8. What counts as being confronted is a real question, and a very practical one for doctors in particular. I touch on the question later, in giving an account of immediacy which does not need the *obligation-out, obligation-in* principle. This is notoriously a kind of obligation increasingly unrecognized in modern cities, to the extent that it is not saluted even by people guiltily leaving the scene.

9. The point is related to the discussion of deliberative questions in Chapter 1.

10. It is relevant to recall, as well, a point made in Chapter 1: the deliberative considerations that go with a given ethical motivation, such as a virtue, may not be at all simply related to it.

11. The reference to contractualism brings out the point that the account is, in a certain sense, individualist.

12. It is a mistake to suppose that it has to be equally acceptable to everyone. Some may have a greater right than others to complain.

13. This *kind* of occasion? Yes. But particularizing facts, such as that this is the second time (to her, this year), can certainly be relevant.

14. I have made a suggestion about it in "Practical Necessity," *Moral Luck*, pp. 124–132.

15. How alike? This touches on an important question that I cannot pursue here, the distinction between guilt and shame. There is such a distinction, and it is relevant to ethics, but it is much more complex than is usually thought. Above all, it is a mistake to suppose that guilt can be distinguished as a mature and autonomous reaction that has a place in ethical experience, whereas shame is a more primitive reaction that does not. Morality tends to deceive itself about its relations to shame. For some suggestive remarks on the distinction, see Herbert Morris, "Guilt and Shame," in *On Guilt and Innocence* (Berkeley: University of California Press, 1976).

16. This is connected with the differing conceptions of the self entertained by Kant and by Hegelian critics: see Chapter 1, note 6. It is important here to distinguish two different ideas. Other people, and indeed I myself, can have an "external" idea of different ideals and projects that I might have had, for instance if I had been brought up differently: there are few reasons for, and many reasons against, saying that if I had been brought up differently, it would not have been me. This is the area of metaphysical necessity. But there is a different area, of practical necessity, concerned with what are possible lines of action and possible projects for me, granted that I have the ideals and character I indeed have. This is the level at which we must resist the Kantian idea that the truly ethical subject is one for whom nothing is necessary except agency itself. This is also closely related to the matter of real interests, discussed in Chapter 3.

17. The model of a moral law helps to explain why the system should have the difficulties it has with those ethical acts that, as I put it before, are more or less than obligations. It is not surprising that something interpreted as law should leave only the three categories of the required, the forbidden and the permitted. Kant's own attempts to deal with some problems of these other ethical motives within his framework of duty involve his interpretations (which changed over time) of the traditional distinction between perfect and imperfect duties. On this, see M. J. Gregor, *Laws of Freedom* (New York: Barnes & Noble, 1963), chaps. 7–11.

18. The question of a categorical imperative and its relation to reasons for action has been pursued by Philippa Foot in several papers, collected in *Virtues and Vices*. I am indebted to these, though our conclusions are different. The moral *ought* was one of several targets assaulted by G. E. M. Anscombe in her vigorous "Modern Moral Philosophy," reprinted in *Ethics, Religion and Politics*, vol. 3 of her *Collected Papers* (Minneapolis: University of Minnesota Press, 1981).

19. Of course, much depends on what is to count as having a reason. I do not believe that there can be an absolutely "external" reason for action, one that does not speak to any motivation the agent already has (as I have stressed, Kant did not think so either). There are indeed distinctions between, for instance, simply drawing an agent's attention to a reason he already has and persuading him to act in a certain way. But it is basically important that a spectrum is involved, and such distinctions are less clear than the morality system and other rationalistic conceptions require them to be. See "Internal and External Reasons," in my *Moral Luck*.

20. This is why I said in Chapter 4 that Kant's conception was like that of the Pelagian heresy, which did adjust salvation to merit.

The Natural History of Morals*

Friedrich Nietzsche

186. The moral sentiment in Europe at present is perhaps as subtle, belated, diverse, sensitive, and refined, as the "Science of Morals" belonging thereto is recent, initial, awkward, and coarse-fingered:—an interesting contrast, which sometimes becomes incarnate and obvious in the very person of a moralist. Indeed, the expression, "Science of Morals" is, in respect to what is designated thereby, far too presumptuous and counter to *good* taste,—which is always a foretaste of more modest expressions. One ought to avow with the utmost fairness *what* is still necessary here for a long time, *what* is alone proper for the present: namely, the collection of material, the comprehensive survey and classification of an immense domain of delicate sentiments of worth, and distinctions of worth, which live, grow, propagate, and perish—and perhaps attempts to give a clear idea of the recurring and more common forms of these living crystallizations—as preparation for a *theory of types* of morality. To be sure, people have not hitherto been so modest. All the philosophers, with a pedantic and ridiculous seriousness, demanded of themselves something very much higher, more pretentious, and ceremonious, when they concerned themselves with morality as a science: they wanted to *give a basis* to morality—and every philosopher

*From Friedrich Nietzsche, *Beyond Good and Evil*. Translated by Helen Zimmern in *The Complete Works of Friedrich Nietzsche*, edited by Oscar Levy (Edinburgh and London: T. N. Foulis, 1909).

hitherto has believed that he has given it a basis; morality itself, however, has been regarded as something "given." How far from their awkward pride was the seemingly insignificant problem—left in dust and decay—of a description of forms of morality, notwithstanding that the finest hands and senses could hardly be fine enough for it! It was precisely owing to moral philosophers' knowing the moral facts imperfectly, in an arbitrary epitome, or an accidental abridgement—perhaps as the morality of their environment, their position, their church, their Zeitgeist, their climate and zone—it was precisely because they were badly instructed with regard to nations, eras, and past ages, and were by no means eager to know about these matters, that they did not even come in sight of the real problems of morals—problems which only disclose themselves by a comparison of *many* kinds of morality. In every "Science of Morals" hitherto, strange as it may sound, the problem of morality itself has been *omitted*: there has been no suspicion that there was anything problematic there! That which philosophers called "giving a basis to morality," and endeavoured to realize, has, when seen in a right light, proved merely a learned form of good *faith* in prevailing morality, a new means of its *expression*, consequently just a matter-of-fact within the sphere of a definite morality, yea, in its ultimate motive, a sort of denial that it is *lawful* for this morality to be called in question—and in any case the reverse of the testing, analyzing, doubting, and vivisecting of this very faith. . .

187. Apart from the value of such assertions as "there is a categorical imperative in us," one can always ask: What does such an assertion indicate about him who makes it? There are systems of morals which are meant to justify their author in the eyes of other people; other systems of morals are meant to tranquilize him, and make him self-satisfied; with other systems he wants to crucify and humble himself, with others he wishes to take revenge, with others to conceal himself, with others to glorify himself and gave superiority and distinction,—this system of morals helps its author to forget, that system makes him, or something of him, forgotten, many a moralist would like to exercise power and creative arbitrariness over mankind, many another, perhaps, Kant especially, gives us to understand by his morals that "what is estimable in me, is that I know how to obey—and with you it *shall* not be otherwise than with me!" In short, systems of morals are only a *sign-language of the emotions*.

188. In contrast to laisser-aller, every system of morals is a sort of tyranny against "nature" and also against "reason", that is, however, no objection, unless one should again decree by some system of morals, that all kinds of tyranny and unreasonableness are unlawful. What is essential and invaluable in every system of morals, is that it is a long constraint. In order to understand Stoicism, or Port Royal, or Puritanism, one should remember the constraint under which every language has attained to strength and freedom—the metrical constraint, the tyranny of rhyme and rhythm. How much trouble have the poets and orators

of every nation given themselves!—not excepting some of the prose writers of today, in whose ear dwells an inexorable conscientiousness—"for the sake of a folly," as utilitarian bunglers say, and thereby deem themselves wise—"from submission to arbitrary laws," as the anarchists say, and thereby fancy themselves "free," even free-spirited. The singular fact remains, however, that everything of the nature of freedom, elegance, boldness, dance, and masterly certainty, which exists or has existed, whether it be in thought itself, or in administration, or in speaking and persuading, in art just as in conduct, has only developed by means of the tyranny of such arbitrary law, and in all seriousness, it is not at all improbable that precisely this is "nature" and "natural"—and not laisser-aller! Every artist knows how different from the state of letting himself go, is his "most natural" condition, the free arranging, locating, disposing, and constructing in the moments of "inspiration"—and how strictly and delicately he then obeys a thousand laws, which, by their very rigidness and precision, defy all formulation by means of ideas (even the most stable idea has, in comparison therewith, something floating, manifold, and ambiguous in it). The essential thing "in heaven and in earth" is, apparently (to repeat it once more), that there should be long *obedience* in the same direction, there thereby results, and has always resulted in the long run, something which has made life worth living; for instance, virtue, art, music, dancing, reason, spirituality—anything whatever that is transfiguring, refined, foolish, or divine. The long bondage of the spirit, the distrustful constraint in the communicability of ideas, the discipline which the thinker imposed on himself to think in accordance with the rules of a church or a court, or conformable to Aristotelian premises, the persistent spiritual will to interpret everything that happened according to a Christian scheme, and in every occurrence to rediscover and justify the Christian God:—all this violence, arbitrariness, severity, dreadfulness, and unreasonableness, has proved itself the disciplinary means whereby the European spirit has attained its strength, its remorseless curiosity and subtle mobility; granted also that much irrecoverable strength and spirit had to be stifled, suffocated, and spoilt in the process (for here, as everywhere, "nature" shows herself as she is, in all her extravagant and *indifferent* magnificence, which is shocking, but nevertheless noble). That for centuries European thinkers only thought in order to prove something—nowadays, on the contrary, we are suspicious of every thinker who "wishes to prove something"—that it was always settled beforehand what *was to be* the result of their strictest thinking, as it was perhaps in the Asiatic astrology of former times, or as it is still at the present day in the innocent, Christian-moral explanation of immediate personal events "for the glory of God," or "for the good of the soul":—this tyranny, this arbitrariness, this severe and magnificent stupidity, has *educated* the spirit; slavery, both in the coarser and the finer sense, is apparently an indispensable means even of spiritual education and discipline.

One may look at every system of morals in this light: it is "nature" therein which teaches to hate the laisser-aller, the too great freedom, and implants the need for limited horizons, for immediate duties—it teaches the *narrowing of perspectives*, and thus, in a certain sense, that stupidity is a condition of life and development. "Thou must obey some one, and for a long time; *otherwise* thou wilt come to grief, and lose all respect for thyself"—this seems to me to be the moral imperative of nature, which is certainly neither "categorical," as old Kant wished (consequently the "otherwise"), nor does it address itself to the individual (what does nature care for the individual!), but to nations, races, ages, and ranks; above all, however, to the animal "man" generally, to *mankind*.

189. Industrious races find it a great hardship to be idle: it was a master stroke of *English* instinct to hallow and begloom Sunday to such an extent that the Englishman unconsciously hankers for his week—and work-day again:—as a kind of cleverly devised, cleverly intercalated *fast*, such as is also frequently found in the ancient world (although, as is appropriate in southern nations, not precisely with respect to work). Many kinds of fasts are necessary; and wherever powerful influences and habits prevail, legislators have to see that intercalary days are appointed, on which such impulses are fettered, and learn to hunger anew. Viewed from a higher standpoint, whole generations and epochs, when they show themselves infected with any moral fanaticism, seem like those intercalated periods of restraint and fasting, during which an impulse learns to humble and submit itself—at the same time also to *purify* and *sharpen* itself; certain philosophical sects likewise admit of a similar interpretation (for instance, the Stoa, in the midst of Hellenic culture, with the atmosphere rank and overcharged with Aphrodisiacal odours).—Here also is a hint for the explanation of the paradox, why it was precisely in the most Christian period of European history, and in general only under the pressure of Christian sentiments, that the sexual impulse sublimated into love (amour-passion).

190. There is something in the morality of Plato which does not really belong to Plato, but which only appears in his philosophy, one might say, in spite of him: namely, Socratism, for which he himself was too noble. "No one desires to injure himself, hence all evil is done unwittingly. The evil man inflicts injury on himself; he would not do so, however, if he knew that evil is evil. The evil man, therefore, is only evil through error; if one free him from error one will necessarily make him—good."—This mode of reasoning savours of the *populace*, who perceive only the unpleasant consequences of evil-doing, and practically judge that "it is *stupid* to do wrong"; while they accept "good" as identical with "useful and pleasant," without further thought. As regards every system of utilitarianism, one may at once assume that it has the same origin, and follow the scent: one will seldom err.—Plato did all he could to interpret something refined and noble into the tenets of his teacher, and above all to interpret himself into

them—he, the most daring of all interpreters, who lifted the entire Socrates out of the street, as a popular theme and song, to exhibit him in endless and impossible modifications—namely, in all his own disguises and multiplicities . . .

191. The old theological problem of "Faith" and "Knowledge," or more plainly, of instinct and reason—the question whether, in respect to the valuation of things, instinct deserves more authority than rationality, which wants to appreciate and act according to motives, according to a "Why," that is to say, in conformity to purpose and utility—it is always the old moral problem that first appeared in the person of Socrates, and had divided men's minds long before Christianity. Socrates himself, following, of course, the taste of his talent—that of a surpassing dialectician—took first the side of reason; and, in fact, what did he do all his life but laugh at the awkward incapacity of the noble Athenians, who were men of instinct, like all noble men, and could never give satisfactory answers concerning the motives of their actions? In the end, however, though silently and secretly, he laughed also at himself: with his finer conscience and introspection, he found in himself the same difficulty and incapacity. "But why"—he said to himself—"should one on that account separate oneself from the instincts! One must set them right, and the reason *also*—one must follow the instincts, but at the same time persuade the reason to support them with good arguments." This was the real *falseness* of that great and mysterious ironist; he brought his conscience up to the point that he was satisfied with a kind of self-outwitting: in fact, he perceived the irrationality in the moral judgment.—Plato, more innocent in such matters, and without the craftiness of the plebeian, wished to prove to himself, at the expenditure of all his strength—the greatest strength a philosopher had ever expended—that reason and instinct lead spontaneously to one goal, to the good, to "God"; and since Plato, all theologians and philosophers have followed the same path—which means that in matters of morality, instinct (or as Christians call it, "Faith," or as I call it, "the herd") has hitherto triumphed. Unless one should make an exception in the case of Descartes, the father of rationalism (and consequently the grandfather of the Revolution), who recognized only the authority of reason: but reason is only a tool, and Descartes was superficial.

194. The difference among men does not manifest itself only in the difference of their lists of desirable things—in their regarding different good things as worth striving for, and being disagreed as to the greater or less value, the order of rank, of the commonly recognized desirable things:—it manifests itself much more in what they regard as actually *having* and *possessing* a desirable thing. As regards a woman, for instance, the control over her body and her sexual gratification serves as an amply sufficient sign of ownership and possession to the more modest man; another with a more suspicious and ambitious thirst for possession, sees the "questionableness," the mere apparentness of such

ownership, and wishes to have finer tests in order to know especially whether the woman not only gives herself to him, but also gives up for his sake what she has or would like to have—only *then* does he look upon her as "possessed." A third, however, has not even here got to the limit of his distrust and his desire for possession: he asks himself whether the woman, when she gives up everything for him, does not perhaps do so for a phantom of him; he wishes first to be thoroughly, indeed, profoundly well known; in order to be loved at all he ventures to let himself be found out. Only then does he feel the beloved one fully in his possession, when she no longer deceives herself about him, when she loves him just as much for the sake of his devilry and concealed insatiability, as for his goodness, patience, and spirituality. One man would like to possess a nation, and he finds all the higher arts of Cagliostro and Catalina suitable for his purpose. Another, with a more refined thirst for possession, says to himself: "One may not deceive where one desires to possess"—he is irritated and impatient at the idea that a mask of him should rule in the hearts of the people: "I must, therefore, *make* myself known, and first of all learn to know myself!" Among helpful and charitable people, one almost always finds the awkward craftiness which first gets up suitably him who has to be helped, as though, for instance, he should "merit" help, seek just *their* help, and would show himself deeply grateful, attached, and subservient to them for all help. With these conceits, they take control of the needy as a property, just as in general they are charitable and helpful out of a desire for property. One finds them jealous when they are crossed or forestalled in their charity. Parents involuntarily make something like themselves out of their children—they call that "education"; no mother doubts at the bottom of her heart that the child she has borne is thereby her property, no father hesitates about his right to *his own* ideas and notions of worth. Indeed, in former times fathers deemed it right to use their discretion concerning the life or death of the newly born (as among the ancient Germans). And like the father, so also do the teacher, the class, the priest, and the prince still see in every new individual an unobjectionable opportunity for a new possession. The consequence is . . .

195. The Jews—a people "born for slavery," as Tacitus and the whole ancient world say of them; "the chosen people among the nations," as they themselves say and believe—the Jews performed the miracle of the inversion of valuations, by means of which life on earth obtained a new and dangerous charm for a couple of millenniums. Their prophets fused into one the expressions "rich," "godless," "wicked," "violent," "sensual," and for the first time coined the word "world" as a term of reproach. In this inversion of valuations (in which is also included the use of the word "poor" as synonymous with "saint" and "friend") the significance of the Jewish people is to be found; it is with *them* that the *slave-insurrection in morals* commences.

197. The beast of prey and the man of prey (for instance, Caesar Borgia) are fundamentally misunderstood, "nature" is misunderstood, so long as one seeks a "morbidness" in the constitution of these healthiest of all tropical monsters and growths, or even an innate "hell" in them—as almost all moralists have done hitherto. Does it not seem that there is a hatred of the virgin forest and of the tropics among moralists? And that the "tropical man" must be discredited at all costs, whether as disease and deterioration of mankind, or as his own hell and self-torture? And why? In favour of the "temperate zones"? In favour of the temperate men? The "moral"? The mediocre?—This for the chapter: "Morals as Timidity."

198. All the systems of morals which address themselves with a view to their "happiness," as it is called—what else are they but suggestions for behaviour adapted to the degree of *danger* from themselves in which the individuals live; recipes for their passions, their good and bad propensities, insofar as such have the Will to Power and would like to play the master; small and great expediencies and elaborations, permeated with the musty odour of old family medicines and old-wife wisdom; all of them grotesque and absurd in their form—because they address themselves to "all," because they generalize where generalization is not authorized; all of them speaking unconditionally, and taking themselves unconditionally; all of them flavoured not merely with one grain of salt, but rather endurable only, and sometimes even seductive, when they are over-spiced and begin to smell dangerously, especially of "the other world." That is all of little value when estimated intellectually, and is far from being "science," much less "wisdom"; but, repeated once more, and three times repeated, it is expediency, expediency, expediency, mixed with stupidity, stupidity, stupidity—whether it be the indifference and statuesque coldness towards the heated folly of the emotions, which the Stoics advised and fostered; or the no-more-laughing and no-more-weeping of Spinoza, the destruction of the emotions by their analysis and vivisection, which he recommended so naively; or the lowering of the emotions to an innocent mean at which they may be satisfied, the Aristotelianism of morals; or even morality as the enjoyment of the emotions in a voluntary attenuation and spiritualization by the symbolism of art, perhaps as music, or as love of God, and of mankind for God's sake—for in religion the passions are once more enfranchised, provided that . . . ; or, finally, even the complaisant and wanton surrender to the emotions, as has been taught by Hafis and Goethe, the bold letting-go of the reins, the spiritual and corporeal *licentia morum* in the exceptional cases of wise old codgers and drunkards, with whom it "no longer has much danger."—This also for the chapter: "Morals as Timidity."

199. Inasmuch as in all ages, as long as mankind has existed, there have also been human herds (family alliances, communities, tribes, peoples, states, churches), and always a great number who obey in proportion to the small

number who command—in view, therefore, of the fact that obedience has been most practiced and fostered among mankind hitherto, one may reasonably suppose that, generally speaking, the need thereof is now innate in everyone, as a kind of *formal conscience* which gives the command "Thou shalt unconditionally do something, unconditionally refrain from something", in short, "Thou shalt". This need tries to satisfy itself and to fill its form with a content, according to its strength, impatience, and eagerness, it at once seizes as an omnivorous appetite with little selection, and accepts whatever is shouted into its ear by all sorts of commanders—parents, teachers, laws, class prejudices, or public opinion. The extraordinary limitation of human development, the hesitation, protractedness, frequent retrogression, and turning thereof, is attributable to the fact that the herd-instinct of obedience is transmitted best, and at the cost of the art of command. If one imagine this instinct increasing to its greatest extent, commanders and independent individuals will finally be lacking altogether, or they will suffer inwardly from a bad conscience, and will have to impose a deception on themselves in the first place in order to be able to command just as if they also were only obeying. This condition of things actually exists in Europe at present—I call it the moral hypocrisy of the commanding class. They know no other way of protecting themselves from their bad conscience than by playing the role of executors of older and higher orders (of predecessors, of the constitution, of justice, of the law, or of God himself), or they even justify themselves by maxims from the current opinions of the herd, as "first servants of their people," or "instruments of the public weal". On the other hand, the gregarious European man nowadays assumes an air as if he were the only kind of man that is allowable, he glorifies his qualities, such as public spirit, kindness, deference, industry, temperance, modesty, indulgence, sympathy, by virtue of which he is gentle, endurable, and useful to the herd, as the peculiarly human virtues. In cases, however, where it is believed that the leader and bell-weather cannot be dispensed with, attempt after attempt is made nowadays to replace commanders by the summing together of clever gregarious men all representative constitutions, for example, are of this origin. In spite of all, what a blessing, what a deliverance from a weight becoming unendurable, is the appearance of an absolute ruler for these gregarious Europeans—of this fact the effect of the appearance of Napoleon was the last great proof the history of the influence of Napoleon is almost the history of the higher happiness to which the entire century has attained in its worthiest individuals and periods.

200. The man of an age of dissolution which mixes the races with one another, who has the inheritance of a diversified descent in his body—that is to say, contrary, and often not only contrary, instincts and standards of value, which struggle with one another and are seldom at peace—such a man of late culture and broken lights, will, on an average, be a weak man. His fundamental

desire is that the war which is *in him* should come to an end; happiness appears to him in the character of a soothing medicine and mode of thought (for instance, Epicurean or Christian); it is above all things the happiness of repose, of undisturbedness, of repletion, of final unity—it is the "Sabbath of Sabbaths," to use the expression of the holy rhetorician, St. Augustine, who was himself such a man.—Should, however, the contrariety and conflict in such natures operate as an *additional* incentive and stimulus to life—and if, on the other hand, in addition to their powerful and irreconcilable instincts, they have also inherited and indoctrinated into them a proper mastery and subtlety for carrying on the conflict with themselves (that is to say, the faculty of self-control and self-deception), there then arise those marvelously incomprehensible and inexplicable beings, those enigmatical men, predestined for conquering and circumventing others, the finest examples of which are Alcibiades and Caesar (with whom I should like to associate the *first* of Europeans according to my taste, the Hohenstaufen, Frederick the Second), and among artists, perhaps Leonardo da Vinci. They appear precisely in the same periods when that weaker type, with its longing for repose, comes to the front; the two types are complementary to each other, and spring from the same causes.

201. As long as the utility which determines moral estimates is only gregarious utility, as long as the preservation of the community is only kept in view, and the immoral is sought precisely and exclusively in what seems dangerous to the maintenance of the community, there can be no "morality of love to one's neighbour." Granted even that there is already a little constant exercise of consideration, sympathy, fairness, gentleness, and mutual assistance, granted that even in this condition of society all those instincts are already active which are latterly distinguished by honourable names as "virtues," and eventually almost coincide with the conception "morality": in that period they do not as yet belong to the domain of moral valuations—they are still *ultra-moral.* A sympathetic action, for instance, is neither called good nor bad, moral nor immoral, in the best period of the Romans; and should it be praised, a sort of resentful disdain is compatible with this praise, even at the best, directly the sympathetic action is compared with one which contributes to the welfare of the whole, to the *res publica.* After all, "love to our neighbour" is always a secondary matter, partly conventional and arbitrarily manifested in relation to our *fear of our neighbor.* After the fabric of society seems on the whole established and secured against external dangers, it is this fear of our neighbour which again creates new perspectives of moral valuation. Certain strong and dangerous instincts, such as the love of enterprise, foolhardiness, revengefulness, astuteness, rapacity, and love of power, which up till then had not only to be honoured from the point of view of general utility—under other names, of course, than those here given—but had to be fostered and cultivated (because they were perpetually

required in the common danger against the common enemies), are now felt in their dangerousness to be doubly strong—when the outlets for them are lacking—and are gradually branded as immoral and given over to calumny. The contrary instincts and inclinations now attain to moral honour, the gregarious instinct gradually draws its conclusions. How much or how little dangerousness to the community or to equality is contained in an opinion, a condition, an emotion, a disposition, or an endowment—that is now the moral perspective, here again fear is the mother of morals. It is by the loftiest and strongest instincts, when they break out passionately and carry the individual far above and beyond the average, and the low level of the gregarious conscience, that the self-reliance of the community is destroyed, its belief in itself, its backbone, as it were, breaks, consequently these very instincts will be most branded and defamed. The lofty independent spirituality, the will to stand alone, and even the cogent reason, are felt to be dangers, everything that elevates the individual above the herd, and is a source of fear to the neighbour, is henceforth called *Evil*, the tolerant, unassuming, self-adapting, self-equalizing disposition, the *mediocrity* of desires, attains to moral distinction and honour. Finally, under very peaceful circumstances, there is always less opportunity and necessity for training the feelings to severity and rigour, and now every form of severity, even in justice, begins to disturb the conscience, a lofty and rigorous nobleness and self-responsibility almost offends, and awakens distrust, "the lamb," and still more "the sheep," wins respect. There is a point of diseased mellowness and effeminacy in the history of society, at which society itself takes the part of him who injures it, the part of the *criminal*, and does so, in fact, seriously and honestly. To punish, appears to it to be somehow unfair—it is certain that the idea of "punishment" and "the obligation to punish" are then painful and alarming to people. "Is it not sufficient if the criminal be rendered *harmless*? Why should we still punish? Punishment itself is terrible!"—with these questions gregarious morality, the morality of fear, draws its ultimate conclusion. If one could at all do away with danger, the cause of fear, one would have done away with this morality at the same time, it would no longer be necessary, it *would not consider itself* any longer necessary!—Whoever examines the conscience of the present-day European, will always elicit the same imperative from its thousand moral folds and hidden recesses, the imperative of the timidity of the herd "we wish that some time or other there may be *nothing more to fear*!" Some time or other—the will and the way *thereto* is nowadays called "progress" all over Europe.

202. Let us at once say again what we have already said a hundred times, for people's ears nowadays are unwilling to hear such truths—*our* truths. We know well enough how offensive it sounds when any one plainly, and without metaphor, counts man among the animals, but it will be accounted to us almost a *crime*, that it is precisely in respect to men of "modern ideas" that we have

constantly applied the terms "herd," "herd-instincts," and such like expressions. What avail is it? We cannot do otherwise, for it is precisely here that our new insight is. We have found that in all the principal moral judgments, Europe has become unanimous, including likewise the countries where European influence prevails in Europe people evidently *know* what Socrates thought he did not know, and what the famous serpent of old once promised to teach—they "know" today what is good and evil. It must then sound hard and be distasteful to the ear, when we always insist that that which here thinks it knows, that which here glorifies itself with praise and blame, and calls itself good, is the instinct of the herding human animal, the instinct which has come and is ever coming more and more to the front, to preponderance and supremacy over other instincts, according to the increasing physiological approximation and resemblance of which it is the symptom. *Morality in Europe at present is herding-animal morality*, and therefore, as we understand the matter, only one kind of human morality, beside which, before which, and after which many other moralities, and above all *higher* moralities, are or should be possible. Against such a "possibility," against such a "should be," however, this morality defends itself with all its strength, it says obstinately and inexorably "I am morality itself and nothing else is morality!" Indeed, with the help of a religion which has humoured and flattered the sublimest desires of the herding-animal, things have reached such a point that we always find a more visible expression of this morality even in political and social arrangements: the *democratic* movement is the inheritance of the Christian movement. That its *tempo*, however, is much too slow and sleepy for the more impatient ones, for those who are sick and distracted by the herding-instinct, is indicated by the increasingly furious howling, and always less disguised teeth-gnashing of the anarchist dogs, who are now roving through the highways of European culture. Apparently in opposition to the peacefully industrious democrats and Revolution-ideologues, and still more so to the awkward philosophasters and fraternity—visionaries who call themselves Socialists and want a "free society," those are really at one with them all in their thorough and instinctive hostility to every form of society other than that of the *autonomous* herd (to the extent even of repudiating the notions "master" and "servant"—*ni dieu ni maitre*, says a socialist formula); at one in their tenacious opposition to every special claim, every special right and privilege (this means ultimately opposition to *every* right, for when all are equal, no one needs "rights" any longer); at one in their distrust of punitive justice (as though it were a violation of the weak, unfair to the *necessary* consequences of all former society); but equally at one in their religion of sympathy, in their compassion for all that feels, lives, and suffers (down to the very animals, up even to "God"—the extravagance of "sympathy for God" belongs to a democratic age); altogether at one in the cry and impatience of their sympathy, in their deadly hatred of suffering generally, in their almost feminine incapacity for witnessing it or *allowing* it; at one in their involuntary beglooming and heart-softening, under the spell of which Europe seems to be threatened with a new Buddhism; at one in their belief in the morality of *mutual* sympathy, as though it were morality in itself, the climax, the *attained* climax of mankind, the sole hope of the future, the consolation of the present, the great discharge from all the obligations of the past; altogether at one in their belief in the community as the *deliverer*, in the herd, and therefore in "themselves."

203. We, who hold a different belief—we, who regard the democratic movement, not only as a degenerating form of political organization, but as equivalent to a degenerating, a waning type of man, as involving his mediocrising and depreciation: where have *we* to fix our hopes? In *new philosophers*—there is no other alternative: in minds strong and original enough to initiate opposite estimates of value, to transvalue and invert "eternal valuations"; in forerunners, in men of the future, who in the present shall fix the constraints and fasten the knots which will compel millenniums to take *new* paths. To teach man the future of humanity as his *will*, as depending on human will, and to make preparation for vast hazardous enterprises and collective attempts in rearing and educating, in order thereby to put an end to the frightful rule of folly and chance which has hitherto gone by the name of "history" (the folly of the "greatest number" is only its last form)—for that purpose a new type of philosopher and commander will some time or other be needed, at the very idea of which everything that has existed in the way of occult, terrible, and benevolent beings might look pale and dwarfed. The image of such leaders hovers before *our* eyes:—is it lawful for me to say it aloud, ye free spirits? The conditions which one would partly have to create and partly utilize for their genesis; the presumptive methods and tests by virtue of which a soul should grow up to such an elevation and power as to feel a *constraint* to these tasks; a transvaluation of values, under the new pressure and hammer of which a conscience should be steeled and a heart transformed into brass, so as to bear the weight of such responsibility; and on the other hand the necessity for such leaders, the dreadful danger that they might be lacking, or miscarry and degenerate:—these are *our* real anxieties and glooms, ye know it well, ye free spirits! these are the heavy distant thoughts and storms which sweep across the heaven of *our* life. There are few pains so grievous as to have seen, divined, or experienced how an exceptional man has missed his way and deteriorated; but he who has the rare eye for the universal danger of "man" himself *deteriorating*, he who like us has recognized the extraordinary fortuitousness which has hitherto played its game in respect to the future of mankind—a game in which neither the hand, nor even a "finger of God" has participated!—he who divines the fate that is hidden under the idiotic unwariness and blind confidence of "modern ideas," and still more under the whole of Christo-European

morality—suffers from an anguish with which no other is to be compared. He sees at a glance all that could still *be made out of man* through a favourable accumulation and augmentation of human powers and arrangements; he knows with all the knowledge of his conviction how unexhausted man still is for the greatest possibilities, and how often in the past the type man has stood in presence of mysterious decisions and new paths:—he knows still better from his painfulest recollections on what wretched obstacles promising developments of the highest rank have hitherto usually gone to pieces, broken down, sunk, and become contemptible. The *universal degeneracy of mankind* to the level of the "man of the future"—as idealized by the socialistic fools and shallow-pates—this degeneracy and dwarfing of man to an absolutely gregarious animal (or as they call it, to a man of "free society"), this brutalizing of man into a pigmy with equal rights and claims, is undoubtedly *possible*! He who has thought out this possibility to its ultimate conclusion knows *another* loathing unknown to the rest of mankind—and perhaps also a new *mission*!

Feminism and Moral Theory*

Virginia Held

The tasks of moral inquiry and moral practice are such that different moral approaches may be appropriate for different domains of human activity. I have argued in a recent book that we need a division of moral labor.[1] In *Rights and Goods*, I suggest that we ought to try to develop moral inquiries that will be as satisfactory as possible for the actual contexts in which we live and in which our experience is located. Such a division of moral labor can be expected to yield different moral theories for different contexts of human activity, at least for the foreseeable future. In my view, the moral approaches most suitable for the courtroom are not those most suitable for political bargaining; the moral approaches suitable for economic activity are not those suitable for relations within the family, and so on. The task of achieving a unified moral field theory covering all domains is one we may do well to postpone, while we do our best to devise and to "test" various moral theories in actual contexts and in light of our actual moral experience.

What are the implications of such a view for women? Traditionally, the experience of women has been located to a large extent in the context of the

*Virginia Held, "Feminism and Moral Theory" in *Women and Moral Theory*, edited by Eva Feder Kittay and Diana T. Meyers, pp. 112–28.

family. In recent centuries, the family has been thought of as a "private" domain distinct not only from that of the "public" domain of the polis, but also from the domain of production and of the marketplace. Women (and men) certainly need to develop moral inquiries appropriate to the context of mothering and of family relations, rather than accepting the application to this context of theories developed for the marketplace or the polis. We can certainly show that the moral guidelines appropriate to mothering are different from those that now seem suitable for various other domains of activity as presently constituted. But we need to do more as well: we need to consider whether distinctively feminist moral theories, suitable for the contexts in which the experience of women has or will continue to be located, are better moral theories than those already available, and better for other domains as well.

The Experience of Women

We need a theory about how to count the experience of women. It is not obvious that it should count equally in the construction or validation of moral theory. To merely survey the moral views of women will not necessarily lead to better moral theories. In the Greek thought that developed into the Western philosophical tradition,[2] reason was associated with the public domain from which women were largely excluded. If the development of adequate moral theory is best based on experience in the public domain, the experience of women so far is less relevant. But that the public domain is the appropriate locus for the development of moral theory is among the tacit assumptions of existing moral theory being effectively challenged by feminist scholars. We cannot escape the need for theory in confronting these issues. We need to take a stand on what moral experience is. As I see it, moral experience is "the experience of consciously choosing, of voluntarily accepting or rejecting, of willingly approving or disapproving, of living with these choices, and above all of acting and of living with these actions and their outcomes. . . . Action is as much a part of experience as is perception."[3] Then we need to take a stand on whether the moral experience of women is as valid a source or test of moral theory as is the experience of men, or on whether it is more valid.

Certainly, engaging in the process of moral inquiry is as open to women as it is to men, although the domains in which the process has occurred has been open to men and women in different ways. Women have had fewer occasions to experience for themselves the moral problems of governing, leading, exercising power over others (except children), and engaging in physically violent conflict. Men, on the other hand, have had fewer occasions to experience the moral problems of family life and the relations between adults and children. Although vast amounts of moral experience are open to all human beings who make the effort to become conscientious moral inquirers, the contexts in which experience is obtained may make a difference. It is essential that we avoid taking a given moral theory, such as a Kantian one, and deciding that those who fail to develop toward it are deficient, for this procedure imposes a theory on experience, rather than letting experience determine the fate of theories, moral and otherwise.

We can assert that as long as women and men experience different problems, moral theory ought to reflect the experience of women as fully as it reflects the experience of men. The insights and judgments and decisions of women as they engage in the process of moral inquiry should be presumed to be as valid as those of men. In the development of moral theory, men ought to have no privileged position to have their experience count for more. If anything, their privileged position in society should make their experience more suspect rather than more worthy of being counted, for they have good reasons to rationalize their privileged positions by moral arguments that will obscure or purport to justify these privileges.[4]

If the differences between men and women in confronting moral problems are due to biological factors that will continue to provide women and men with different experiences, the experience of women should still count for at least as much as the experience of men. There is no justification for discounting the experience of women as deficient or underdeveloped on biological grounds. Biological "moral inferiority" makes no sense.

The empirical question of whether and to what extent women think differently from men about moral problems is being investigated.[5] If, in fact, women approach moral problems in characteristic ways, these approaches should be reflected in moral theories as fully as are those of men. If the differing approaches to morality that seem to be displayed by women and by men are the result of historical conditions and not biological ones, we could assume that in nonsexist societies, the differences would disappear, and the experience of either gender might adequately substitute for the experience of the other.[6] Then feminist moral theory might be the same as moral theory of any kind. But since we can hardly imagine what a nonsexist society would be like, and surely should not wait for one before evaluating the experience of women, we can say that we need feminist moral theory to deal with the differences of which we are now aware and to contribute to the development of the nonsexist society that might make the need for a distinctively feminist moral theory obsolete. Specifically, we need feminist moral theory to deal with the regions of experience that have been central to women's experience and neglected by traditional moral theory. If the resulting moral theory would be suitable for all humans in all contexts, and thus could be thought of as a human moral theory or a universal moral theory, it would be a feminist moral theory as well if it adequately reflected the experience and standpoint of women.

That the available empirical evidence for differences between men and women with respect to morality is tentative and often based on reportage and interpretation, rather than on something more "scientific,"[7] is no problem at all for the claim that we need feminist moral theory. If such differences turn out to be further substantiated, we will need theory to evaluate their implications, and we should be prepared now for this possibility (or, as many think, probability). If the differences turn out to be insignificant, we still need feminist moral theory to make the moral claim that the experience of women is of equal worth to the experience of men, and even more important, that women themselves are of equal worth as human beings. If it is true that the only differences between women and men are anatomical, it still does not follow that women are the moral equals of men. Moral equality has to be based on moral claims. Since the devaluation of women is a constant in human society as so far developed, and has been accepted by those holding a wide variety of traditional moral theories, it is apparent that feminist moral theory is needed to provide the basis for women's claims to equality.

We should never forget the horrors that have resulted from acceptance of the idea that women think differently from men, or that men are rational beings, women emotional ones. We should be constantly on guard for misuses of such ideas, as in social roles that determine that women belong in the home or in educational programs that discourage women from becoming, for example, mathematicians. Yet, excessive fear of such misuses should not stifle exploration of the ways in which such claims may, in some measure, be true. As philosophers, we can be careful not to conclude that whatever tendencies exist ought to be reinforced. And if we succeed in making social scientists more alert to the naturalistic fallacy than they would otherwise be, that would be a side benefit to the development of feminist moral theory.

Mothering and Markets

When we bring women's experience fully into the domain of moral consciousness, we can see how questionable it is to imagine contractual relationships as central or fundamental to society and morality. They seem, instead, the relationships of only very particular regions of human activity.[8]

The most central and fundamental social relationship seems to be that between mother or mothering person and child. It is this relationship that creates and recreates society. It is the activity of mothering which transforms biological entities into human social beings. Mothers and mothering persons produce children and empower them with language and symbolic representations. Mothers and mothering persons thus produce and create human culture.

Despite its implausibility, the assumption is often made that human mothering is like the mothering of other animals rather than being distinctively human. In accordance with the traditional distinction between the family and the polis, and the assumption that what occurs in the public sphere of the polis is distinctively human, it is assumed that what human mothers do within the family belongs to the "natural" rather than to the "distinctively human" domain. Or, if it is recognized that the activities of human mothers do not resemble the activities of the mothers of other mammals, it is assumed that, at least, the difference is far narrower than the difference between what animals do and what humans who take part in government and industry and art do. But, in fact, mothering is among the most human of human activities.

Consider the reality. A human birth is thoroughly different from the birth of other animals, because a human mother can choose not to give birth. However extreme the alternative, even when abortion is not a possibility, a woman can choose suicide early enough in her pregnancy to consciously prevent the birth. A human mother comprehends that she brings about the birth of another human being. A human mother is then responsible, at least in an existentialist sense, for the creation of a new human life. The event is essentially different from what is possible for other animals.

Human mothering is utterly different from the mothering of animals without language. The human mother or nurturing person constructs with and for the child a human social reality. The child's understanding of language and of symbols, and of all that they create and make real, occurs in interactions between child and caretakers. Nothing seems more distinctively human than this. In comparison, government can be thought to resemble the governing of ant colonies, industrial production to be similar to the building of beaver dams, a market exchange to be like the relation between a large fish that protects and a small fish that grooms, and the conquest by force of arms that characterizes so much of human history to be like the aggression of packs of animals. But the imparting of language and the creation within and for each individual of a human social reality, and often a new human social reality, seems utterly human.

An argument is often made that art and industry and government create new human reality, while mothering merely "reproduces" human beings, their cultures, and social structures. But consider a more accurate view: in bringing up children, those who mother create new human *persons*. They change persons, the culture, and the social structures that depend on them, by creating the kinds of persons who can continue to transform themselves and their surroundings. Creating new and better persons is surely as "creative" as creating new and better objects or institutions. It is not only bodies that do not spring into being unaided and fully formed; neither do imaginations, personalities, and minds.

Perhaps morality should make room first for the human experience reflected in the social bond between mothering person and child, and for the human projects of nurturing and of growth apparent for both persons in the relationship. In comparison, the transactions of the marketplace seem peripheral; the authority of weapons and the laws they uphold, beside the point.

The relation between buyer and seller has often been taken as the model of all human interactions.[9] Most of the social contract tradition has seen this relation of contractual exchange as fundamental to law and political authority as well as to economic activity. And some contemporary moral philosophers see the contractual relation as the relation on which even morality itself should be based. The marketplace, as a model for relationships, has become so firmly entrenched in our normative theories that it is rarely questioned as a proper foundation for recommendations extending beyond the marketplace. Consequently, much moral thinking is built on the concept of rational economic man. Relationships between human beings are seen as arising, and as justified, when they serve the interests of individual rational contractors.

In the society imagined in the model based on assumptions about rational economic man, connections between people become no more than instrumental. Nancy Hartsock effectively characterizes the worldview of these assumptions, and shows how misguided it is to suppose that the relationship between buyer and seller can serve as a model for all human relations: "the paradigmatic connections between people [on this view of the social world] are instrumental or extrinsic and conflictual, and in a world populated by these isolated individuals, relations of competition" and domination come to be substitutes for a more substantial and encompassing community."[10]

Whether the relationship between nurturing person (who need not be a biological mother) and child should be taken as itself paradigmatic, in place of the contractual paradigm, or whether it should be seen only as an obviously important relationship that does not fit into the contractual framework and should not be overlooked, remains to be seen. It is certainly instructive to consider it, at least tentatively, as paradigmatic. If this were done, the competition and desire for domination thought of as acceptable for rational economic man might appear as a very particular and limited human connection, suitable perhaps, if at all, only for a restricted marketplace. Such a relation of conflict and competition can be seen to be unacceptable for establishing the social trust on which public institutions must rest,[11] or for upholding the bonds on which caring, regard, friendship, or love must be based.[12]

The social map would be fundamentally altered by adoption of the point of view here suggested. Possibly, the relationship between "mother" and child would be recognized as a much more promising source of trust and concern than any other, for reasons to be explored later. In addition, social relations would be seen as dynamic rather than as fixed-point exchanges. And assumptions that human beings are equally capable of entering or not entering into the contractual relations taken to characterize social relations generally would be seen for the distortions they are. Although human mothers could do other than give birth, their choices to do so or not are usually highly constrained. And children, even human children, cannot choose at all whether to be born.

It may be that no human relationship should be thought of as paradigmatic for all the others. Relations between mothering persons and children can become oppressive for both, and relations between equals who can decide whether to enter into agreements may seem attractive in contrast. But no mapping of the social and moral landscape can possibly be satisfactory if it does not adequately take into account and provide appropriate guidance for relationships between mothering persons and children.

Between the Self and the Universal

Perhaps the most important legacy of the new insights will be the recognition that more attention must be paid to the domain *between* the self—the ego, the self-interested individual—on the one hand, and the universal—everyone, others in general—on the other hand. Ethics traditionally has dealt with these poles, trying to reconcile their conflicting claims. It has called for impartiality against the partiality of the egoistic self, or it has defended the claims of egoism against such demands for a universal perspective.

In seeing the problems of ethics as problems of reconciling the interests of the self with what would be right or best for everyone, moral theory has neglected the intermediate region of family relations and relations of friendship, and has neglected the sympathy and concern people actually feel for particular others. As Larry Blum has shown, "contemporary moral philosophy in the Anglo-American tradition has paid little attention to [the] morally significant phenomena" of sympathy, compassion, human concern, and friendship.[13]

Standard moral philosophy has construed personal relationships as aspects of the self-interested feelings of individuals, as when a person might favor those he loves over those distant because it satisfies his own desires to do so. Or it has let those close others stand in for the universal "other," as when an analysis might be offered of how the conflict between self and others is to be resolved in something like "enlightened self-interest" or "acting out of respect for the moral law," and seeing this as what should guide us in our relations with those close, particular others with whom we interact.

Owen Flanagan and Jonathan Adler provide useful criticism of what they see as Kohlberg's "adequacy thesis"—the assumption that the more formal the moral reasoning, the better.[14] But they themselves continue to construe the tension in ethics as that between the particular self and the universal. What feminist moral theory will emphasize, in contrast, will be the domain of particular others in relations with one another.

The region of "particular others" is a distinct domain, where it can be seen that what becomes artificial and problematic are the very "self" and "all others" of standard moral theory. In the domain of particular others, the self is already closely entwined in relations with others, and the relation may be much more real, salient, and important than the interests of any individual self in isolation. But the "others" in the picture are not "all others," or "everyone," or what a universal point of view could provide. They are particular flesh and blood others for whom we have actual feelings in our insides and in our skin, not the others of rational constructs and universal principles.

Relationships can be characterized as trusting or mistrustful, mutually considerate or selfish, and so forth. Where trust and consideration are appropriate, we can find ways to foster them. But doing so will depend on aspects of what can be understood only if we look at relations between persons. To focus on either self-interested individuals or the totality of all persons is to miss the qualities of actual relations between actual human beings.

Moral theories must pay attention to the neglected realm of particular others in actual contexts. In doing so, problems of egoism vs. the universal moral point of view appear very different, and may recede to the region of background insolubility or relative unimportance. The important problems may then be seen to be how we ought to guide or maintain or reshape the relationships, both close and more distant, that we have or might have with actual human beings.

Particular others can, I think, be actual starving children in Africa with whom one feels empathy or even the anticipated children of future generations, not just those we are close to in any traditional context of family, neighbors, or friends. But particular others are still not "all rational beings" or "the greatest number."

In recognizing the component of feeling and relatedness between self and particular others, motivation is addressed as an inherent part of moral inquiry. Caring between parent and child is a good example.[15] We should not glamorize parental care. Many mothers and fathers dominate their children in harmful or inappropriate ways, or fail to care adequately for them. But when the relationship between "mother" and child is as it should be, the caretaker does not care for the child (nor the child for the caretaker) because of universal moral rules. The love and concern one feels for the child already motivate much of what one does. This is not to say that morality is irrelevant. One must still decide what one ought to do. But the process of addressing the moral questions in mothering and of trying to arrive at answers one can find acceptable involves motivated acting, not just thinking. And neither egoism nor a morality of universal rules will be of much help.

Mothering is, of course, not the only context in which the salient moral problems concern relations between particular others rather than conflicts between egoistic self and universal moral laws; all actual human contexts may be more like this than like those depicted by Hobbes or Kant. But mothering may be one of the best contexts in which to make explicit why familiar moral theories are so deficient in offering guidance for action. And the variety of contexts within mothering, with the different excellences appropriate for dealing with infants, young children, or adolescents, provide rich sources of insight for moral inquiry.

The feelings characteristic of mothering;—that there are too many demands on us, that we cannot do everything that we ought to do—are highly instructive. They give rise to problems different from those of universal rule vs. self-interest. They require us to weigh the claims of one self-other relationship against the claims of other self-other relationships, to try to bring about some harmony between them, to see the issues in an actual temporal context, and to act rather than merely reflect.

For instance, we have limited resources for caring. We cannot care for everyone or do everything a caring approach suggests. We need moral guidelines for ordering our priorities. The hunger of our own children comes before the hunger of children we do not know. But the hunger of children in Africa ought to come before some of the expensive amusements we may wish to provide for our own children. These are moral problems calling to some extent for principled answers. But we have to figure out what we ought to do when actually buying groceries, cooking meals, refusing the requests of our children for the latest toy they have seen advertised, and sending money to UNICEF. The context is one of real action, not of ideal thought.

Principles and Particulars

When we take the context of mothering as central, rather than peripheral, for moral theory, we run the risk of excessively discounting other contexts. It is a commendable risk, given the enormously more prevalent one of excessively discounting mothering. But I think that the attack on principles has sometimes been carried too far by critics of traditional moral theory.

Noddings, for instance, writes that "To say, 'It is wrong to cause pain needlessly,' contributes nothing by way of knowledge and can hardly be thought likely to change the attitude or behavior of one who might ask, 'Why is it wrong?' . . . Ethical caring . . . depends not upon rule or principle" but upon the development of a self "in congruence with one's best remembrance of caring and being cared-for."[16]

We should not forget that an absence of principles can be an invitation to capriciousness. Caring may be a weak defense against arbitrary decisions, and the person cared for may find the relation more satisfactory if both persons, but especially the person caring, are guided, to some extent, by principles concerning obligations and rights. To argue that no two cases are ever alike is to invite moral chaos. Furthermore, for one person to be in a position of caretaker means that that person has the power to withhold care, to leave the other without it. The person cared for is usually in a position of vulnerability. The moral significance of this needs to be addressed along with other aspects of the caring relationship. Principles may remind a giver of care to avoid being capricious or domineering. While most of the moral problems involved in mothering contexts may deal with issues above and beyond the moral minimums that can be covered by principles concerning rights and obligations, that does not mean that these minimums can be dispensed with.

Noddings's discussion is unsatisfactory also in dealing with certain types of questions, for instance those of economic justice. Such issues cry out for relevant principles. Although caring may be needed to motivate us to act on such principles, the principles are not dispensable. Noddings questions the concern people may have for starving persons in distant countries, because she sees universal love and universal justice as masculine illusions. She refrains from judging that the rich deserve less or the poor more, because caring for individuals cannot yield such judgments. But this may amount to taking a given economic stratification as given, rather than as the appropriate object of critical scrutiny that it should be. It may lead to accepting that the rich will care for the rich and the poor for the poor, with the gap between them, however unjustifiably wide, remaining what it is. Some important moral issues seem beyond the reach of an ethic of caring, once caring leads us, perhaps through empathy, to be concerned with them.

On ethical views that renounce principles as excessively abstract, we might have few arguments to uphold the equality of women. After all, as parents can care for children recognized as weaker, less knowledgeable, less capable, and with appropriately restricted rights, so men could care for women deemed inferior in every way. On a view that ethics could satisfactorily be founded on caring alone, men could care for women considered undeserving of equal rights in all the significant areas in which women have been struggling to have their equality recognized. So an ethic of care, essential as a component of morality, seems deficient if taken as an exclusive preoccupation.

That aspect of the attack on principles which seems entirely correct is the view that not all ethical problems can be solved by appeal to one or a very few simple principles. It is often argued that all more particular moral rules or principles can be derived from such underlying ones as the Categorical Imperative or the Principle of Utility, and that these can be applied to all moral problems. The call for an ethic of care may be a call, which I share, for a more pluralistic view of ethics, recognizing that we need a division of moral labor employing different moral approaches for different domains, at least for the time being.[17] Satisfactory intermediate principles for areas such as those of international affairs, or family relations, cannot be derived from simple universal principles, but must be arrived at in conjunction with experience within the domains in question.

Attention to particular Others will always require that we respect the particularity of the context, and arrive at solutions to moral problems that will not give moral principles more weight than their due. But their due may remain considerable. And we will need principles concerning relationships, not only concerning the actions of individuals, as we will need evaluations of kinds of relationships, not only of the character traits of individuals.

Birth and Valuing

To a large extent, the activity of mothering is potentially open to men as well as to women. Fathers can conceivably come to be as emotionally close, or as close through caretaking, to children as are mothers. The experience of relatedness, of responsibility for the growth and empowerment of new life, and of responsiveness to particular others, ought to be incorporated into moral theory, and will have to be so incorporated for moral theory to be adequate. At present, in this domain, it is primarily the experience of women (and of children) that has not been sufficiently reflected in moral theory and that ought to be so reflected. But this is not to say that it must remain experience available only to women. If men came to share fully and equitably in the care of all persons who need care—especially children, the sick, the old—the moral values that now arise for women in the context of caring might arise as fully for men.

There are some experiences, however, that are open only to women: menstruating, having an abortion, giving birth, suckling. We need to consider their possible significance or lack of significance for moral experience and theory. I will consider here only one kind of experience not open to men but of obviously great importance to women: the experience of giving birth or of deciding not to. Does the very experience of giving birth, or of deciding not to exercise the capacity to do so, make a significant difference for moral experience and moral theory? I think the answer must be perhaps.

Of course birthing is a social as well as a personal or biological event. It takes place in a social context structured by attitudes and arrangements that deeply affect how women experience it: whether it will be accepted as "natural," whether it will be welcomed and celebrated, or whether it will be fraught with fear or shame. But I wish to focus briefly on the conscious awareness women can have of what they are doing in giving birth, and on the specifically personal and biological aspects of human birthing.

It is women who give birth to other persons. Women are responsible for the existence of new persons in ways far more fundamental than are men. It is not bizarre to recognize that women can, through abortion or suicide choose not to give birth. A woman can be aware of the possibility that she can act to prevent a new person from existing, and can be aware that if this new person exists, it is because of what she has done and made possible.

In the past we have called attention to the extent to which women do not control their capacity to give birth. They are under extreme economic and social pressure to engage in intercourse, to marry, and to have children. Legal permission to undergo abortion is a recent, restricted, and threatened capacity. When the choice not to give birth requires grave risk to life, health, or well-being, or requires suicide, we should be careful not to misrepresent the situation when we speak of a woman's "choice" to become a mother, or of how she "could have done other" than have a child, or that "since she chose to become a mother, she is responsible for her child." It does not follow that because women are responsible for creating human beings, they should be held responsible by society for caring for them, either alone, primarily, or even at all. These two kinds of responsibility should not be confused, and I am speaking here only of the first. As conscious human beings, women can do other than give birth, and if they do give birth, they are responsible for the creation of other human beings. Though it may be very difficult for women to avoid giving birth, the very familiarity of the literary image of the woman who drowns herself or throws herself from a cliff rather than bear an illegitimate child should remind us that such eventualities are not altogether remote from consciousness.

Women have every reason to be justifiably angry with men who refuse to take responsibility for their share of the events of pregnancy and birth, or for the care children require. Because, for so long, we have wanted to increase the extent to which men would recognize their responsibilities for causing pregnancy, and would share in the long years of care needed to bring a child to independence, we have tended to emphasize the ways in which the responsibilities for creating a new human being are equal between women and men.[18] But in fact, men produce sperm and women produce babies and the difference is enormous. Excellent arguments can be made that boys and men suffer "womb envy"; indeed, men lack a wondrous capacity that women possess.[19]

Of all the human capacities, it is probably the capacity to create new human beings that is most worth celebrating. We can expect that a woman will care about and feel concern for a child she has created as the child grows and develops, and that she feels responsible for having given the child life. But her concern is more than something to be expected. It is, perhaps, justifiable in certain ways unique to women.

Children are born into actual situations. A mother cannot escape ultimate responsibility for having given birth to this particular child in these particular circumstances. She can be aware that she could have avoided intercourse, or used more effective contraception, or waited to get pregnant until her circumstances were different; that she could have aborted this child and had another later; or that she could have killed herself and prevented this child from facing the suffering or hardship of this particular life. The momentousness of all these decisions about giving or not giving life can hardly fail to affect what she experiences in relation to the child.

Perhaps it might be thought that many of these issues arise in connection with infanticide, and that if one refrains from killing an infant, one is responsible for giving the infant life. Infanticide is as open to men as to women. But to kill or refrain from killing a child, once the child is capable of life with caretakers different from the person who is responsible for having given birth to the child, is a quite different matter from creating or not creating this possibility, and I am concerned in this discussion with the moral significance of giving birth.

It might also be thought that those, including the father, who refrain from killing the mother, or from forcing her to have an abortion, are also responsible for not preventing the birth of the child.[20] But unless the distinction between suicide and murder, and between having an abortion and forcing a woman to have an abortion against her will, are collapsed completely, the issues would be very different. To refrain from murdering someone else is not the same as deciding not to kill oneself. And to decide not to force someone else to have an abortion is different from deciding not to have an abortion when one could. The person capable of giving birth who decides not to prevent the birth is the person responsible, in the sense of "responsible" I am discussing, for creating another human being. To create a new human being is not the same as to refrain from ending the life of a human being who already exists.

Perhaps there is a tendency to want to approve of or to justify what one has decided with respect to giving life. In deciding to give birth, perhaps a woman has a natural tendency to approve of the birth, to believe that the child ought to have been born. Perhaps this inclines her to believe whatever may follow from this: that the child is entitled to care, and that feelings of love for the child are appropriate and justified. The conscious decision to create a new human being may provide women with an inclination to value the child and to have hope for the child's future. Since, in her view, the child ought to have been born, a woman may feel that the world ought to be hospitable to the child. And if the child ought to have been born, the child ought to grow into an admirable human adult. The child's life has, and should continue to have, value that is recognized.

Consider next the phenomenon of sacrifice. In giving birth, women suffer severe pain for the sake of new life. Having suffered for the child in giving the child life, women may have a natural tendency to value what they have endured pain for. There is a tendency, often noted in connection with war, for people to feel that because sacrifices have been made, the sacrifice should have been "worth it," and if necessary, other things ought to be done so that the sacrifice "shall not have been in vain." There may be a similar tendency for those who have suffered to give birth to assure themselves that the pain was for the good reason of creating a new life that is valuable and that will be valued.

Certainly, this is not to say that there is anything good or noble about suffering, or that merely because people want to believe that what they suffered for was worthwhile, it was. A vast amount of human suffering has been in vain, and could and should have been avoided. The point is that once suffering has already occurred and the "price," if we resort to such calculations, has already been paid, it will be worse if the result is a further cost, and better if the result is a clear benefit that can make the price, when it is necessary for the result, validly "worth it."

The suffering of the mother who has given birth will more easily have been worthwhile if the child's life has value. The chance that the suffering will be outweighed by future happiness is much greater if the child is valued by the society and the family into which the child is born. If the mother's suffering yields nothing but further suffering and a being deemed to be of no value, her suffering may truly have been in vain. Anyone can have reasons to value children. But the person who has already undergone the suffering needed to create one has a special reason to recognize that the child is valuable and to want the child to be valued so that the suffering she has already borne will have been, truly, worthwhile.

These arguments can be repeated for the burdens of work and anxiety normally expended in bringing up a child. Those who have already borne these burdens have special reasons for wanting to see the grown human being for whom they have cared as valuable and valued. Traditionally, women have not only borne the burdens of childbirth, but, with little help, the much greater burdens of child rearing. Of course, the burdens of child rearing could be shared fully by men, as they have been partially shared by women other than natural mothers. Although the concerns involved in bringing up a child may greatly outweigh the suffering of childbirth itself, this does not mean that giving birth is incidental.

The decision not to have children is often influenced by a comparable tendency to value the potential child.[21] Knowing how much care the child would deserve and how highly, as a mother, she would value the child, a woman who gives up the prospect of motherhood can recognize how much she is losing. For such reasons, a woman may feel overwhelming ambivalence concerning the choice.

Consider, finally, how biology can affect our ways of valuing children. Although men and women may share a desire or an instinctive tendency to wish to reproduce, and although these feelings may be equally strong for both men and women, such feelings might affect their attitudes toward a given child very differently. In terms of biological capacity, a mother has a relatively greater stake in a child to which she has given birth. This child is about one-twentieth or one twenty-fifth of all the children she could possibly have, whereas a man could potentially have hundreds or thousands of other children. In giving birth, a woman has already contributed a large amount of energy and effort toward the production of this particular child, while a man has, biologically, contributed only a few minutes. To the extent that such biological facts may influence attitudes, the attitudes of the mother and father toward the "worth" or "value" of a particular child may be different. The father might consider the child more easily replaceable in the sense that the father's biological contribution can so easily and so painlessly be repeated on another occasion or with another woman; for the mother to repeat her biological contribution would be highly exhausting and painful. The mother, having already contributed so much more to the creation of this particular child than the father, might value the result of her effort in proportion. And her pride at what she has accomplished in giving birth can be appropriately that much greater. She has indeed "accomplished" far more than has the father.

So even if instincts or desires to reproduce oneself or one's genes, or to create another human being, are equally powerful among men and women, a given child is, from the father's biological standpoint, much more incidental and interchangeable: any child out of the potential thousands he might sire would do. For the mother, on the other hand, if this particular child does not survive and grow, her chances for biological reproduction are reduced to a much greater degree. To suggest that men may think of their children as replaceable is offensive to many men, and women. Whether such biological facts as those I have mentioned have any significant effect on parental attitudes is not known. But arguments from biological facts to social attitudes, and even to moral norms, have a very long history and are still highly popular; we should be willing to examine the sorts of unfamiliar arguments I have suggested that can be drawn from biological facts. If anatomy is destiny, men may be "naturally" more indifferent toward particular children than has been thought.

Since men, then, do not give birth, and do not experience the responsibility, the pain, and momentousness of childbirth, they lack the particular motives to value the child that may spring from this capacity and this fact. Of course, many other reasons for valuing a child are felt by both parents, by caretakers of either gender, and by those who are not parents, but the motives discussed, and others arising from giving birth, may be morally significant. The long years of child care may provide stronger motives for valuing a child than do the relatively short months of pregnancy and hours of childbirth. The decisions and sacrifices involved in bringing up a child can be more affecting than those normally experienced in giving birth to a child. So the possibility for men to acquire such motives through child care may outweigh any long-term differences in motivation between women and men. But it might yet remain that the person responsible for giving birth would continue to have a greater sense of responsibility for how the child develops, and stronger feelings of care and concern for the child.

That adoptive parents can feel as great concern for and attachment to their children as can biological parents may indicate that the biological components in valuing children are relatively modest in importance. However, to the extent that biological components are significant, they would seem to affect men and women in different ways.

Morality and Human Tendencies

So far, I have been describing possible feelings rather than attaching any moral value to them. That children are valued does not mean that they are valuable, and if mothers have a natural tendency to value their children, it does not follow that they ought to. But if feelings are taken to be relevant to moral theory, the feelings of valuing the child, like the feelings of empathy for other persons in pain, may be of moral significance.

To the extent that a moral theory takes natural male tendencies into account, it would at least be reasonable to take natural female tendencies into account. Traditional moral theories often suppose it is legitimate for individuals to maximize self-interest, or satisfy their preferences, within certain constraints based on the equal rights of others. If it can be shown that the tendency to want to pursue individual self-interest is a stronger tendency among men than among women, this would certainly be relevant to an evaluation of such theory. And if it could be shown that a tendency to value children and a desire to foster the developing capabilities of the particular others for whom we care is a stronger tendency among women than among men, this too would be relevant in evaluating moral theories.

The assertion that women have a tendency to value children is still different from the assertion that they ought to. Noddings speaks often of the "natural" caring of mothers for children.[22] I do not intend to deal here with the disputed empirical question of whether human mothers do or do not have a strong natural tendency to love their children. And I am certainly not claiming that natural mothers have greater skills or excellences in raising children than have others, including, perhaps, men. I am trying, rather, to explore possible "reasons" for mothers to value children, reasons that might be different for mothers and potential mothers than they would be for anyone else asking the question: why should we value human beings? And it does seem that certain possible reasons for valuing living human beings are present for mothers in ways that are different from what they would be for others. The reason, if it is one, that the child should be valued because I have suffered to give the child life is different from the reason, if it is one, that the child should be valued because someone unlike me suffered to give the child life. And both of these reasons are different from the reason, if it is one, that the child should be valued because the continued existence of the child satisfies a preference of a parent, or because the child is a bearer of universal rights, or has the capacity to experience pleasure.

Many moral theories, and fields dependent on them such as economics, employ the assumption that to increase the utility of individuals is a good thing to do. But if asked *why* it is a good thing to increase utility, or satisfy desire, or produce pleasure, or *why* doing so counts as a good reason for something, it is very difficult to answer. The claim is taken as a kind of starting assumption for which *no further* reason can be given. It seems to rest on a view that people seek pleasure, or that we can recognize pleasure as having intrinsic value. But if women recognize quite different assumptions as more likely to be valid, that would certainly be of importance to ethics. We might then take it as one of our starting assumptions that creating good relations of care and concern and trust between ourselves and our children, and creating social arrangements in which children will be valued and well cared for, are more important than maximizing individual utilities. And the moral theories that might be compatible with such assumptions might be very different from those with which we are familiar.

A number of feminists have independently declared their rejection of the Abraham myth.[23] We do not approve the sacrifice of children out of religious duty. Perhaps, for those capable of giving birth, reasons to value the actual life of the born will, in general, seem to be better than reasons justifying the sacrifice of such life.[24] This may reflect an accordance of priority to caring for particular others over abstract principle. From the perspectives of Rousseau, of Kant, of Hegel, and of Kohlberg, this is a deficiency of women. But from a perspective of what is needed for late twentieth century survival, it may suggest a superior morality. Only feminist moral theory can offer a satisfactory evaluation of such suggestions, because only feminist moral theory can adequately understand the alternatives to traditional moral theory that the experience of women requires.

Notes

1. See Virginia Held, *Rights and Goods: Justifying Social Action* (New York: Free Press, Macmillan, 1984).

2. See Genevieve Lloyd, *The Man of Reason: "Male" and "Female" in Western Philosophy* (Minneapolis: University of Minnesota Press, 1984).

3. Virginia Held, *Rights and Goods*, p. 272. See also V. Held, "The Political 'Testing' of Moral Theories," *Midwest Studies in Philosophy* 7 (1982): 343–63.

4. For discussion, see especially Nancy Hartsock, *Money, Sex, and Power* (New York: Longman, 1983), chaps. 10, 11.

5. Lawrence Kohlberg's studies of what he claimed to be developmental stage in moral reasoning suggested that girls progress less well and less far than boy through these

stages. See his *The Philosophy of Moral Development* (San Francisco: Harper & Row, 1981); and L. Kohlberg and R. Kramer, "Continuities and Discontinuities in Child and Adult Moral Development," *Human Development* 12 (1969): 93–120. James R. Rest, on the other hand, claims in his study of adolescents in 1972 and 1974 that "none of the male-female differences on the Defining Issues Test . . . and on the Comprehension or Attitudes tests were significant." See his "Longitudinal Study of the Defining Issues Test of Moral Judgment: A Strategy for Analyzing Developmental Change," *Developmental Psychology* (Nov. 1975): 738–48; quotation at 741. Carol Gilligan's *In A Different Voice* (Cambridge: Harvard University Press 1982) suggests that girls and women tend to organize their thinking about moral problems somewhat differently from boys and men; her subsequent work support the view that whether people tend to construe moral problems in terms of rules of justice or in terms of caring relationships is at present somewhat associated with gender (Carol Gilligan, address at Conference on Women and Moral Thought SUNY Stony Brook, March 21, 1985). Other studies have shown that females are significantly more inclined than males to cite compassion and sympathy as reasons for their moral positions; see Constance Boucher Holstein, "Irreversible, Stepwise Sequence in the Development of Moral Judgment: A Longitudinal Study of Male and Females." *Child Development* 47, no. 1 (March 1976): 51–61.

6. For suggestions on how Gilligan's stages, like Kohlberg's, might be thought to be historically and culturally, rather than more universally, based, see Lind. Nicholson, "Women, Morality, and History," *Social Research* 50, no. 3 (Autumn 1983): 514–36.

7. See, e.g., Debra Nails, "Social-Scientific Sexism: Gilligan's Mismeasure of Man," *Social Research* 50, no. 3 (Autumn 1983): 643–64.

8. I have discussed this in a paper that has gone through several major revisions and changes of title, from its presentation at a conference at Loyola University on April 18, 1983, to its discussion at Dartmouth College, April 2, 1984. I will, refer to it as "Non-Contractual Society: A Feminist Interpretation." See also Carole Pateman, "The Fraternal Social Contract: Some Observations on Patriarchy," paper presented at American Political Science Association meeting, Aug. 30–Sept. 2 1984, and "The Shame of the Marriage Contract," in *Women's Views of the Political, World of Men*, edited by Judith Hicks Stiehm (Dobbs Ferry, N.Y.: Transnational Publishers, 1984).

9. For discussion, see especially Nancy Hartsock, *Money, Sex, and Power*.

10. Ibid., p. 39.

11. See Held, *Rights and Goods*, chap. 5.

12. Ibid., chap. 11.

13. Lawrence A. Blum, *Friendship, Altruism and Morality* (London: Routledge and Kegan Paul, 1980), p. 1.

14. Owen J. Flanagan, Jr., and Jonathan E. Adler, "Impartiality and Particularity," *Social Research* 50, no. 3 (Autumn 1983): 576–96.

15. See, e.g., Nell Noddings, *Caring: A Feminine Approach to Ethics and Moral Education* (Berkeley: University of California Press, 1984) pp. 91–94.

16. Ibid., pp. 91–94.

17. Participants in the conference on Women and Moral Theory offered the helpful term "domain relativism" for the version of this view that I defended.

18. See, e.g., Virginia Held, "The Obligations of Mothers and Fathers," repr. in *Mothering: Essays in Feminist Theory*, edited by Joyce Trebilcot (Totowa, N.J.: Rowman and Allanheld, 1984).

19. See Eva Kittay, "Womb Envy: An Explanatory Concept," in *Mothering*, edited by Joyce Trebilcot. To overcome the pernicious aspects of the "womb envy" she skillfully identifies and describes, Kittay argues that boys should be taught that their "procreative contribution is of equal significance" (p. 123). While boys should certainly be told the truth, the truth may remain that, as she states elsewhere, "there is the . . . awesome quality of creation itself—the transmutation performed by the parturient woman" (p. 99).

20. This point was made by Marcia Baron in correspondence with me.

21. In exploring the values involved in birth and mothering, we need to develop views that include women who do not give birth. As Margaret Simons writes, "we must define a feminist maternal ethic that supports a woman's right not to have children." See Margaret A. Simons, "Motherhood, Feminism and Identity," *Hypatia, Women's Studies International Forum* 7, 5 (1984): 353.

22. E.g., Noddings, *Caring*, pp. 31, 43, 49.

23. See Gilligan, *In a Different Voice*, p. 104; Held, "Non-Contractual Society: A Feminist Interpretation;" and Noddings, *Caring*, p. 43.

24. That some women enthusiastically send their sons off to war may be indicative of a greater than usual acceptance of male myths rather than evidence against this claim, since the enthusiasm seems most frequent in societies where women have the least influence in the formation of prevailing religious and other beliefs.

The Demands of Identity*

Kwame Anthony Appiah

Ethical individualism, it may be worth spelling out, has no simple friend-or-foe relation to "recognition"; and careful readers of Hegel, such as Charles Taylor and Axel Honneth, are surely right that much of modern social and political life turns on such questions of recognition. In our liberal tradition, of course, we see recognition largely as a matter of acknowledging individuals and their identities: and we have the notion, which comes (as Taylor says) from the ethics of authenticity, that, other things being equal, people have the right to be acknowledged publicly as what they already really are. It is because someone is already authentically Jewish or gay that we deny him something in requiring him to hide this fact, to "pass," as we say, for something that he is not. As has often been observed, though, the way much discussion of recognition proceeds is at odds with the individualistic thrust of talk of authenticity.[1] In particular, attending to the oppositional aspects

*From K. Anthony Appiah, *The Ethics of Identity* © 2005 Princeton University Press. Reprinted by permission of Princeton University Press.

of authenticity would complicate the picture, because it would bring sharply into focus the difference between two levels of authenticity that the contemporary politics of recognition seems to conflate.

. . . It is, among other things, your being, say, an African American that shapes the authentic self that you seek to express. And it is, in part, because you seek to express your self that you seek recognition of an African American identity. This is what makes problems for Lionel Trilling's notion of the "opposing self": for recognition as an African American means social acknowledgment of that collective identity, which requires not just recognizing its existence but actually demonstrating respect for it. If, in understanding yourself as African American, you see yourself as resisting white norms, mainstream American conventions, the racism (and, perhaps, the materialism or the individualism) of "white culture," why should you at the same time seek recognition from these white others?

There is, in other words, at least an irony in the way that an ideal of authenticity—you will recognize it if I call it the Bohemian ideal—requiring us to reject much that is conventional in our society, is turned around and made the basis of a "politics of recognition."[2] Now, you may be skeptical of the Bohemian ideal, or see it as a mere indulgence or affectation; but the notion that identities are founded in antagonism should by now be an unsurprising one.

I used the example of African Americans just now, and it might seem that this complaint cannot be lodged against an American black nationalism: African American identity, it might be said, is shaped by African American society, culture, and religion. Here is how the argument might be framed: "It is dialogue with these black others that shapes the black self; it is from these black contexts that the concepts through which African-Americans shape themselves are derived. The white society, the white culture, over against which an African-American nationalism of the counter-conventional kind poses itself, is therefore not part of what shapes the collective dimension of the individual identities of black people in the United States."

This claim seems to me to be simply false. What shows that it is false is the fact that it is in part a recognition of a black identity by "white society" that is demanded by nationalism of this form. And "recognition" here means what Taylor means by it, not mere acknowledgment of one's existence. African American identity (like all other American ethnoracial identities) is centrally shaped by American society and institutions: it cannot be seen as constructed solely within African American communities, any more than whiteness is made only by whites.

There is another error in the standard framing of authenticity as an ideal, and that is the philosophical realism (which is nowadays usually called "essentialism") that seems inherent in the way questions of authenticity are normally posed. Authenticity speaks of the real self buried in there, the self one has to dig out and express. It is only later, after romanticism, that the idea develops that one's self is something that one creates, makes up, like a work of art. . . . [N]either the picture in which there is just an authentic nugget of selfhood, the core that is distinctively me, waiting to be dug out, nor the notion that I can simply make up any self I choose, should tempt us. We make up selves from a tool kit of options made available by our culture and society. . . . [W]e do make choices, but we don't, individually, determine the options among which we choose. To neglect this fact is to ignore Taylor's "webs of interlocution," to fail to recognize the dialogical construction of the self, and thus to commit what Taylor calls the "monological" fallacy.

If you agree with this, you will wonder to what extent we should acknowledge authenticity in our political morality: and that will depend, surely, on whether an account of it can be developed that isn't monological. It would be too large a claim that the identities that cry out for recognition in the multicultural chorus *must* be monological. But it seems to me that one reasonable ground for suspicion of much contemporary multicultural talk is that the conceptions of collective identity they presuppose are indeed remarkably unsubtle in their understandings of the processes by which identities, both individual and collective, develop. And I am not sure whether Taylor would agree with me that collective identities disciplined by historical knowledge and philosophical reflection would be radically unlike the identities that now parade before us for recognition, and would raise, as a result, questions different from the ones he addresses. In a rather unphilosophical nutshell: my suspicion is that Taylor is happier with the collective identities that actually inhabit our globe than I am: and that may be one of the reasons why I am more hesitant to make the concessions to them that he does. For an ethics of identity must confront two distinct though not wholly separable questions: how existing identities should be treated; and what sort of identities there should be.

. . . [T]he large collective identities that call for recognition come with notions of how a proper person of that kind behaves: it is not that there is *one* way that gay people or blacks should behave, but that there are gay and black modes of behavior. These notions provide loose norms or models, which play a role in shaping the ground projects of those for whom these collective identities are central to their individual identities. Collective identities, again, provide what I have been calling scripts: narratives that people use in shaping their pursuits and in telling their life stories. And that is why, as we've seen, the personal dimensions of identity work differently from the collective ones.

How does this general idea apply to our current situation in the West? We live in societies in which certain individuals have not been treated with equal dignity because they were, for example, women, homosexuals, blacks, Catholics. Because, as Taylor observes, our identities are dialogically shaped, people who have these characteristics find them central—often, negatively central—to their identities. Nowadays there is widespread agreement that the insults to their dignity and the limitations of their autonomy imposed in the name of these collective identities are seriously wrong. One way the stigmatized have responded has been to uphold these collective identities not as sources of limitation and insult but as a central and valuable part of what they are. Because the ethics of authenticity requires us to express what we centrally are, they move, next, to the demand that they be recognized in social life *as* women, homosexuals, blacks, Catholics. Because there was no good reason to treat people of these sorts badly, and because society continues to provide degrading images of them nevertheless, they demand that we work to resist the stereotypes, to challenge the insults, to lift the restrictions.

These old restrictions suggested life-scripts for the bearers of these identities, but they were, in substantial part, negative ones. . . . [O]ne does not construct a social identity *ab ovo*, that our choices are at once constrained and enabled by existing practices and beliefs; but neither do we always "play it as it lays." And there have been historical moments where we see groups contesting and transforming the meaning of their identities with seismic vigor. Certainly this has been a notable dimension of the grand identity movements of the late twentieth century. In order to construct a life with dignity, it has seemed natural to take the collective identity and construct positive life-scripts instead. An African American after the Black Power movement takes the old script of self-hatred, the script in which he or she is a nigger, and works, in community with others, to construct a series of positive black life-scripts. In these life-scripts, being a Negro is recoded as being black: and for some this may entrain, among other things, refusing to assimilate to white norms of speech and behavior. And if one is to be black in a society that is racist, then one has constantly to deal with assaults on one's dignity. In this context, insisting on the right to live a dignified life will not be enough. It will not even be enough to require that one be treated with equal dignity despite being black: for that would suggest that being black counts to some degree against one's dignity. And so one will end up asking to be respected *as a black*.

Let me rewrite this paragraph as a paragraph about gay identity: An American homosexual after Stonewall and gay liberation takes the old script of self-hatred, the script of the closet, and works, in community with others, to construct a series of positive gay life-scripts. In these life-scripts, being a faggot is recoded as being gay: and this requires, among other things, refusing to stay in the closet. And if one is to be out of the closet in a society that deprives homosexuals of equal dignity and respect, then one has constantly to deal with assaults on one's dignity. In this context, the right to live as an "open homosexual" will not be enough. It will not even be enough to be treated with equal dignity despite being homosexual: for that would suggest that being homosexual counts to some degree against one's dignity. And so one will end up asking to be respected *as a homosexual*.

I hope I seem sympathetic to the stories of gay and black identity I have just told, distilling those identity movements of the 1960s and 1970s. I see how the story goes. It may even be historically, strategically necessary for the story to go this way. But I think we need to go on to the next step, which is to ask whether the identities constructed in this way are ones we can be happy with in the longer run. Demanding respect for people *as blacks* and *as gays* can go along with notably rigid strictures as to how one is to be an African American or a person with same-sex desires. In a particularly fraught and emphatic way, there will be proper modes of being black and gay: there will be demands that are made; expectations to be met; battles lines to be drawn. It is at this point that someone who takes autonomy seriously may worry whether we have replaced one kind of tyranny with another. We know that acts of recognition, and the civil apparatus of such recognition, can sometimes ossify the identities that are their object. Because here a gaze can turn to stone, we can call this the Medusa Syndrome. The politics of recognition, if pursued with excessive zeal, can seem to require that one's skin color, one's sexual body, should be politically acknowledged in ways that make it hard for those who want to treat their skin and their sexual body as personal dimensions of the self. And personal, here, does not mean secret or (*per impossible*) wholly unscripted or innocent of social meanings; it means, rather, something that is not too tightly scripted, not too resistant to our individual vagaries. Even though my race and my sexuality may be elements of my individuality, someone who demands that I organize my life around these things is not an ally of individuality. Because identities are constituted in part by social conceptions and by treatment—as, in the realm of identity there is no bright line between recognition and imposition.

Note

1. The identities whose recognition Taylor discusses are largely what we can call "collective social identities": religion, gender, ethnicity, race, sexuality. This list is somewhat heterogeneous: such collective identities matter to their bearers and to others in very different ways. Religion, for example, unlike all the others, entails attachments to creeds or commitment to practices. Gender and sexuality, unlike the rest, are both grounded in the sexual body; both are differently experienced at different places and times; still, everywhere that I know of, gender identity proposes norms of behavior, of dress, of character. And, of course, gender and sexuality are, despite these abstract similarities, in many ways profoundly different. In our society, for example, passing as a woman or a man is hard, passing as straight (or gay) is relatively easy. There are other collective identities—disabled people, for example—that have sought recognition, modeling themselves sometimes on racial minorities (with whom they share the experience of discrimination and insult), or (as with deaf people) on ethnic groups. And there are castes, in South Asia; and clans on every continent; and classes, with enormously varying degrees of class-consciousness, all over the industrialized world. But the major collective identities that demand recognition in North America currently go under the rubrics of religion, gender, ethnicity (or nationality), race, and sexuality; and that they matter to us for reasons so heterogeneous should, I think, make us want to be careful not to assume that what goes for one goes for the others.

2. Irony is not the bohemian's only problem. As we saw in chapter 1, this notion of authenticity has built into it a series of errors of philosophical anthropology. It is, first of all, wrong in failing to see what Taylor—or, indeed, George Herbert Mead—so clearly recognized, namely, the way in which the self is, as Taylor says, dialogically constituted. The rhetoric of authenticity proposes not only that I have a way of being that is all my own, but that in developing it I must fight against the family, organized religion, society, the school, the state—all the forces of convention. This is wrong, however, not only because I develop a conception of my own identity in dialogue with other people's understandings of who I am (Taylor's point), but also because my identity is crucially constituted through concepts and practices made available to me by religion, society, school, and state, and mediated by varying degrees by the family. Dialogue shapes the identity I develop as I grow up: but the very material out of which I form it is provided, in part, by my society, by what Taylor calls its language "in a broad sense," including the language of art, of gesture, and so forth. I shall borrow and extend Taylor's term "monological" here to describe views of authenticity that make these connected errors.

Nihilism in Black America*

Cornel West

We black folk, our history and our present being, are a mirror of all the manifold experiences of America. What we want, what we represent, what we endure is what America *is*. If we black folk perish, America will perish. If America has forgotten her past, then let her look into the mirror of our consciousness and she will see the *living* past living in the present, for our memories go back, through our black folk of today, through the recollections of our black parents, and through the tales of slavery told by our black grandparents, to the time when none of us, black or white, lived in this fertile land. The differences between black folk and white folk are not blood or color, and the ties that bind us are deeper than those that separate us.

The common road of hope which we all traveled has brought us into a stronger kinship than any words, laws, or legal claims.

—Richard Wright, *12 Million Black Voices* (1941)

Recent discussions about the plight of African Americans—especially those at the bottom of the social ladder—tend to divide into two camps. On the one hand, there are those who highlight the *structural* constraints on the life chances of black people. Their viewpoint involves a subtle historical and sociological analysis of slavery, Jim Crowism, job and residential discrimination,

*From *Race Matters* by Cornel West, pp. 11–20. Copyright © 1993 by Beacon Press. Reproduced with permission of Beacon Press in the format Textbook via Copyright Clearance Center.

skewed unemployment rates, inadequate health care, and poor education. On the other hand, there are those who stress the *behavioral* impediments on black upward mobility. They focus on the waning of the Protestant ethic—hard work, deferred gratification, frugality, and responsibility—in much of black America.

Those in the first camp—the liberal structuralists—call for full employment, health, education, and child-care programs, and broad affirmative action practices. In short, a new, more sober version of the best of the New Deal and the Great Society: more government money, better bureaucrats, and an active citizenry. Those in the second camp—the conservative behaviorists—promote self-help programs, black business expansion, and non-preferential job practices. They support vigorous "free market" strategies that depend on fundamental changes in how black people act and live. To put it bluntly, their projects rest largely upon a cultural revival of the Protestant ethic in black America.

Unfortunately, these two camps have nearly suffocated the crucial debate that should be taking place about the prospects for black America. This debate must go far beyond the liberal and conservative positions in three fundamental ways. First, we must acknowledge that structures and behavior are inseparable, that institutions and values go hand in hand. How people act and live are shaped—though in no way dictated or determined—by the larger circumstances in which they find themselves. These circumstances can be changed, their limits attenuated, by positive actions to elevate living conditions.

Second, we should reject the idea that structures are primarily economic and political creatures—an idea that sees culture as an ephemeral set of behavioral attitudes and values. Culture is as much a structure as the economy or politics; it is rooted in institutions such as families, schools, churches, synagogues, mosques, and communication industries (television, radio, video, music). Similarly, the economy and politics are not only influenced by values but also promote particular cultural ideals of the good life and good society.

Third, and most important, we must delve into the depths where neither liberals nor conservatives dare to tread, namely, into the murky waters of despair and dread that now flood the streets of black America. To talk about the depressing statistics of unemployment, infant mortality, incarceration, teenage pregnancy, and violent crime is one thing. But to face up to the monumental eclipse of hope, the unprecedented collapse of meaning, the incredible disregard for human (especially black) life and property in much of black America is something else.

The liberal conservative discussion conceals the most basic issue now facing black America: *the nihilistic threat to its very existence*. This threat is not simply a matter of relative economic deprivation and political powerlessness—though economic well-being and political clout are requisites for meaningful black progress. It is primarily a question of speaking to the profound sense of psychological depression, personal worthlessness, and social despair so widespread in black America.

The liberal structuralists fail to grapple with this threat for two reasons. First, their focus on structural constraints relates almost exclusively to the economy and politics. They show no understanding of the structural character of culture. Why? Because they tend to view people in egoistic and rationalist terms according to which they are motivated primarily by self-interest and self-preservation. Needless to say, this is partly true about most of us. Yet, people, especially degraded and oppressed people, are also hungry for identity, meaning, and self-worth.

The second reason liberal structuralists overlook the nihilistic threat is a sheer failure of nerve. They hesitate to talk honestly about culture, the realm of meanings, and values, because doing so seems to lend itself too readily to conservative conclusions in the narrow way Americans discuss race. If there is a hidden taboo among liberals, it is to resist talking *too much* about values because such discussions remove the focus from structures and especially because they obscure the positive role of government. But this failure by liberals leaves the existential and psychological realities of black people in the lurch. In this way, liberal structuralists neglect the battered identities rampant in black America.

As for the conservative behaviorists, they not only misconstrue the nihilistic threat but inadvertently contribute to it. This is a serious charge, and it rests upon several claims. Conservative behaviorists talk about values and attitudes as if political and economic structures hardly exist. They rarely, if ever, examine the innumerable cases in which black people do act on the Protestant ethic and still remain at the bottom of the social ladder. Instead, they highlight the few instances in which blacks ascend to the top, as if such success is available to all blacks, regardless of circumstances. Such a vulgar rendition of Horatio Alger in blackface may serve as a source of inspiration to some—a kind of model for those already on the right track. But it cannot serve as a substitute for serious historical and social analysis of the predicaments of and prospects for all black people, especially the grossly disadvantaged ones.

Conservative behaviorists also discuss black culture as if acknowledging one's obvious victimization by white supremacist practices (compounded by sexism and class condition) is taboo. They tell black people to see themselves as agents, not victims. And on the surface, this is comforting advice, a nice cliché for downtrodden people. But inspirational slogans cannot substitute for substantive historical and social analysis. While black people have never been simply victims, wallowing in self-pity and begging for white giveaways, they have been—and are—*victimized*. Therefore, to call on black people to be agents makes sense only if we also examine the dynamics of this victimization against which their agency will, in part, be exercised. What is particularly naive and peculiarly vicious about the conservative behavioral outlook is that it tends to deny the lingering effect of black history—a history inseparable from though not reducible to victimization. In this way, crucial and indispensable themes of self-help and personal responsibility are wrenched out of historical context and contemporary circumstances—as if it is all a matter of personal will.

This ahistorical perspective contributes to the nihilistic threat within black America in that it can be used to justify right-wing cutbacks for poor people struggling for decent housing, child care, health care, and education. As I pointed out above, the liberal perspective is deficient in important ways, but even so liberals are right on target in their critique of conservative government cutbacks for services to the poor. These ghastly cutbacks are one cause of the nihilist threat to black America.

The proper starting point for the crucial debate about the prospects for black America is an examination of the nihilism that increasingly pervades black communities. *Nihilism is to be understood here not as a philosophic doctrine that there are no rational grounds for legitimate standards or authority; it is, far more, the lived experience of coping with a life of horrifying meaninglessness, hopelessness, and (most important) lawlessness.* The frightening result is a numbing detachment from others and a self-destructive disposition toward the world. Life without meaning, hope, and love breeds a coldhearted, mean-spirited outlook that destroys both the individual and others.

Nihilism is not new in black America. The first African encounter with the New World was an encounter with a distinctive form of the Absurd. The initial black struggle against degradation and devaluation in the enslaved circumstances of the New World was, in part, a struggle against nihilism. In fact, the major enemy of black survival in America has been and is neither oppression nor exploitation but rather the nihilistic threat—that is, loss of hope and absence of meaning. For as long as hope remains and meaning is preserved, the possibility of overcoming oppression stays alive. The self-fulfilling prophecy of the nihilistic threat is that without hope there can be no future, that without meaning there can be no struggle.

The genius of our black foremothers and forefathers was to create powerful buffers to ward off the nihilistic threat, to equip black folk with cultural armor to beat back the demons of hopelessness, meaninglessness, and lovelessness. These buffers consisted of cultural structures of meaning and feeling that created and sustained communities; this armor constituted ways of life and struggle that embodied values of service and sacrifice, love and care, discipline and excellence. In other words, traditions for black surviving and thriving under usually adverse New World conditions were major barriers against the nihilistic threat. These traditions consist primarily of black religious and civic institutions that sustained familial and communal networks of support. If cultures are, in part, what human beings create (out of antecedent fragments of other cultures) in order to convince themselves not to commit suicide, then black foremothers and forefathers are to be applauded. In fact, until the early seventies black Americans had the lowest suicide rate in the United States. But now young black people lead the nation in suicides.

What has changed? What went wrong? The bitter irony of integration? The cumulative effects of a genocidal conspiracy? The virtual collapse of rising expectations after the optimistic sixties? None of us fully understands why the cultural structures that once sustained black life in America are no longer able to fend off the nihilistic threat. I believe that two significant reasons why the threat is more powerful now than ever before are the saturation of market forces and market moralities in black life and the present crisis in black leadership. The recent market-driven shattering of black civil society—black families, neighborhoods, schools, churches, mosques—leaves more and more black people vulnerable to daily lives endured with little sense of self and fragile existential moorings.

Black people have always been in America's wilderness in search of a promised land. Yet many black folk now reside in a jungle ruled by a cutthroat market morality devoid of any faith in deliverance or hope for freedom. Contrary to the superficial claims of conservative behaviorists, these jungles are not primarily the result of pathological behavior. Rather, this behavior is the tragic response of a people bereft of resources in confronting the workings of U.S. capitalist society. Saying this is not the same as asserting that individual black people are not responsible for their actions—black murderers and rapists should go to jail. But it must be recognized that the nihilistic threat contributes to criminal behavior. It is a threat that feeds on poverty and shattered cultural institutions and grows more powerful as the armors to ward against it are weakened.

But why is this shattering of black civil society occurring? What has led to the weakening of black cultural institutions in asphalt jungles? Corporate market institutions have contributed greatly to their collapse. By corporate market institutions I mean that complex set of interlocking enterprises that have a disproportionate amount of capital, power, and exercise a disproportionate influence on how our society is run and how our culture is shaped. Needless to say, the primary motivation of these institutions is to make profits, and their basic strategy is to convince the public to consume. These institutions have helped create a seductive way of life, a culture of consumption that capitalizes on every opportunity to make money. Market calculations and cost-benefit analyses hold sway in almost every sphere of U.S. society.

The common denominator of these calculations and analyses is usually the provision, expansion, and intensification *of pleasure*. Pleasure is a multivalent term; it means different things to many people. In the American way of life pleasure involves comfort, convenience, and sexual stimulation. Pleasure, so defined, has little to do with the past and views the future as no more than a repetition of a hedonistically driven present. This market morality stigmatizes others as objects for personal pleasure or bodily stimulation. Conservative behaviorists have alleged that traditional morality has been undermined by radical feminists and the cultural radicals of the sixties. But it is clear that corporate market institutions have greatly contributed to undermining traditional morality in order to stay in business and make a profit. The reduction of individuals to objects of pleasure is especially evident in the culture industries—television, radio, video, music—in which gestures of sexual foreplay and orgiastic pleasure flood the marketplace.

Like all Americans, African Americans are influenced greatly by the images of comfort, convenience, machismo, femininity, violence, and sexual stimulation that bombard consumers. These seductive images contribute to the predominance of the market-inspired way of life over all others and thereby edge out non-market values—love, care, service to others—handed down by preceding generations. The predominance of this way of life among those living in poverty-ridden conditions, with a limited capacity to ward off self-contempt and self-hatred, results in the possible triumph of the nihilistic threat in black America.

A major contemporary strategy for holding the nihilistic threat at bay is a direct attack on the sense of worthlessness and self-loathing in black America. This *angst* resembles a kind of collective clinical depression in significant pockets of black America. The eclipse of hope and collapse of meaning in much of black America is linked to the structural dynamics of corporate market institutions that affect all Americans. Under these circumstances black existential *angst* derives from the lived experience of ontological wounds and emotional scars inflicted by white supremacist beliefs and images permeating U.S. society and culture. These beliefs and images attack black intelligence, black ability, black beauty, and black character daily in subtle and not-so-subtle ways. Toni Morrison's novel *The Bluest Eye*, for example, reveals the devastating effect of pervasive European ideals of beauty on the self-image of young black women. Morrison's exposure of the harmful extent to which these white ideals affect the black self-image is a first step toward rejecting these ideals and overcoming the nihilistic self-loathing they engender in blacks.

The accumulated effect of the black wounds and scars suffered in a white-dominated society is a deep-seated anger, a boiling sense of rage, and a passionate pessimism regarding America's will to justice. Under conditions of slavery and Jim Crow segregation, this anger, rage, and pessimism remained relatively muted because of a well-justified fear of brutal white retaliation. The major breakthroughs of the sixties—more psychically than politically—swept this fear away. Sadly, the combination of the market way of life, poverty-ridden conditions, black existential *angst*, and the lessening of fear of white authorities has directed most of the anger, rage, and despair toward fellow black citizens, especially toward black women who are the most vulnerable in our society and in black communities. Only recently has this nihilistic threat—and its ugly inhumane outlook and actions—surfaced in the larger American society. And its appearance surely reveals one of the many instances of cultural decay in a declining empire.

What is to be done about this nihilistic threat? Is there really any hope, given our shattered civil society, market-driven corporate enterprises, and white supremacism? If one begins with the threat of concrete nihilism, then one must talk about some kind of *politics of conversion*. New models of collective black leadership must promote a version of this politics. Like alcoholism and drug addiction, nihilism is a disease of the soul. It can never be completely cured, and there is always the possibility of relapse. But there is always a chance for conversion—a chance for people to believe that there is hope for the future and a meaning to struggle. This chance rests neither on an agreement about what justice consists of nor on an analysis of how racism, sexism, or class subordination operate. Such arguments and analyses are indispensable. But a politics of conversion requires more. Nihilism is not overcome by arguments or analyses; it is tamed by love and care. Any disease of the soul must be conquered by a turning of one's soul. This turning is done through one's own affirmation of one's worth—an affirmation fueled by the concern of others. A love ethic must be at the center of a politics of conversion.

A love ethic has nothing to do with sentimental feelings or tribal connections. Rather it is a last attempt at generating a sense of agency among a downtrodden people. The best exemplar of this love ethic is depicted on a number of levels in Toni Morrison's great novel *Beloved*. Self-love and love of others are both modes toward increasing self-valuation and encouraging political resistance in one's community. These modes of valuation and resistance are rooted in a subversive memory—the best of one's past without romantic nostalgia—and guided by a universal love ethic. For my purposes here, *Beloved* can be construed as bringing together the loving yet critical affirmation of black humanity found in the best of black nationalist movements, the perennial hope against hope for trans-racial coalition in progressive movements, and the painful struggle for self-affirming sanity in a history in which the nihilistic threat *seems* insurmountable.

The politics of conversion proceeds principally on the local level—in those institutions in civil society still vital enough to promote self-worth and self-affirmation. It surfaces on the state and national levels only when grassroots democratic organizations put forward a collective leadership that has earned the love and respect of and, most important, has proved itself *accountable* to these organizations. This collective leadership must exemplify moral integrity, character, and democratic statesmanship within itself and within its organizations.

Like liberal structuralists, the advocates of a politics of conversion never lose sight of the structural conditions that shape the sufferings and lives of people. Yet, unlike liberal structuralism, the politics of conversion meets the nihilistic threat head-on. Like conservative behaviorism, the politics of conversion openly confronts the self-destructive and inhumane actions of black people. Unlike conservative behaviorists, the politics of conversion situates these actions within inhumane circumstances (but does not thereby exonerate them). The politics of conversion shuns the limelight—a limelight that solicits status seekers and ingratiates egomaniacs. Instead, it stays on the ground among the toiling everyday people, ushering forth humble freedom fighters—both followers and leaders—who have the audacity to take the nihilistic threat by the neck and turn back its deadly assaults.

Study Questions

1. What does Bernard Williams mean by the "morality system" and why does he want to do away with it? Do you agree with Williams's contention that the ethical life cannot be systematized in one all-encompassing moral theory? If so, how are we to make moral judgments? If not, what problems do you have with Williams's views?

2. Friedrich Nietzsche contends that moral values are not absolute and universal, but have a definite history traceable to some particular origin. Discuss Nietzsche's analysis of the origin of moral values and his critique of Western morality, making reference to particular moral theories found in this book. Does Nietzsche's critique of morality lead to moral relativism? Explain your answer with reference to the selections from chapter 3. Finally, provide an assessment of Nietzsche's philosophy. Is he convincing? Is he a liberator of humanity or a danger to humanity? With what do you agree and with what do you disagree? Explain.

3. Virginia Held argues that because men's and women's life experiences differ so markedly, there may not be a single unified moral theory that would do justice to both male and female moral thinking. More and more women now have work lives that are very similar to what Held ascribes only to men. Women are now corporate executives, senators, construction workers, soldiers. More men are opting for being the primary caretaker of their young children, or sharing equally in child rearing with their wives. Do you think that Held's arguments are still valid in the twenty-first century? Discuss.

4. Comment on Kwame Anthony Appiah's response to the ethics of multiculturalism. Do you think Appiah fairly represents this perspective in his critique? With what in Appiah's essay do you agree and with what do you disagree?

5. What does Cornel West mean by the problem of "nihilism" within black America? Discuss West's proposed solution to the problem. How does his position challenge the distinctions between moral and political, liberal and conservative, progressive and traditional ways of thinking? Finally, do you agree with West's assessment of the situation and its solution? Why or why not?

For Further Reading

Appiah, Kwame Anthony. *Cosmopolitanism: Ethics in a World of Strangers*. New York: W. W. Norton, 2006.

Caputo, John. *Against Ethics: Contributions to a Poetics of Obligation with Constant Reference to Deconstruction*. Bloomington: Indiana University Press, 1993.

Leiter, Brian, and Neil Sinhababu, eds. *Nietzsche and Morality*. New York: Oxford University Press, 2007.

Noddings, Nel. *Caring: A Feminine Approach to Ethics and Moral Education*. Berkeley and Los Angeles: University of California Press, 1984.

Sartre, Jean-Paul. *Existentialism Is a Humanism*. Trans. Carol Macomber. New Haven, CT: Yale University Press, 2007.

Stocker, Michael. "The Schizophrenia of Modern Ethical Theories." *The Journal of Philosophy* 73 (1976): 453–66.

Taylor, Charles, et al., *Multiculturalism: Examining the Politics of Recognition*. Princeton, NJ: Princeton University Press, 1994.

Tong, Rosemarie. *Feminine and Feminist Ethics*. Belmont, CA: Wadsworth Publishing Company, 1993.

Wolf, Susan. "Moral Saints." *The Journal of Philosophy* 79 (1982): 419–39.

CHAPTER NINE

Living a Good Life

The conception of ethics as the quest for the good life is as old as philosophy itself. The focus here is not so much on the rightness or wrongness of specific acts, or the solving of difficult moral problems or quandaries, but rather the overall character of one's life. This was the view of Pythagoras, who in the sixth century B.C.E. first coined the term "philosophy" to describe a way of life devoted to the pursuit of wisdom and goodness, a way of life he considered the best for human beings. The contemplative life, the philosophical life; this is Pythagoras's answer to the question that is at the heart of ethics—"How should I live?"

The conception of ethics as the quest for the best way to live also motivated the most influential of ancient Greek philosophers, Socrates. Taking to heart the inscription at the temple of the Oracle at Delphi, "Know thyself," Socrates became the living example of one who devotes his life to self-scrutiny and self-improvement, teaching and exhorting others also to take "care of the soul" above all else. Facing death at the hands of the state, Socrates proclaims that "the unexamined life is not worth living" and that "it is not life, but the good life" that ultimately matters. Philosophers ever since have devoted themselves to discovering and teaching how to live a good life.

There is some overlap between traditional virtue ethics and ethics of the good life. Both might be regarded as eudaimonistic ethics in that they aim at *eudaimonia*, a term usually translated from the Greek as "happiness," but which means something like "living well." But, unlike virtue ethics, the ethics of the good life need not be focused on specific character traits or skills of excellence. Rather, it is concerned with the general way one lives. In this view, e at the achievement of a certain desirable state of being through living a certain way of life. Often a dominant metaphor is used as a guide. "Be like a rock," urged the Stoic philosopher Marcus Aurelius, so that one may enjoy a state of inner peace, unaffected by negative outside influences. "Be like water," urged the Taoists of ancient China, in order that one may be one with the Tao or the Way. And while the focus is primarily personal, the ethics of the good life also includes an altruistic component. Plato aims at a harmonious soul not only because this is best for the individual, but also because the balanced or just soul treats others with justice. The Buddhist seeks individual peace of mind through the achievement of the state of *nirvana*, yet the Buddhist way of life requires that one have compassion for all sentient beings.

In the first selection of this chapter, the French historian-philosopher Pierre Hadot contends that ancient philosophy was primarily a way of life. Even theoretical speculation on metaphysical questions concerning the nature of reality had a practical bearing on how to live one's life. According to Hadot, philosophy as a way of life made use of practices designed to help one to live the good life. Hadot regards these practices as "spiritual exercises," a form of *ascesis* (ascetic training) aimed at the transformation of the individual into a sage, that is, a person who experiences peace of mind, inner freedom and a "cosmic consciousness." Even the writings of the philosophers are to be used in a "therapeutic" way, that is, as exercises that help one to work on oneself and make progress in the art of living. In this sense, *philosophy* as a form of practice is distinguished from *discourse about philosophy* as mere theory. As in the *Enchiridion* of Epictetus, philosophical writing takes the form of a "handbook" of useful advice for how to live the good life.

The selections that follow from Plato come from two of his mature dialogues, the *Phaedo* and the *Republic*. In the *Phaedo*, we find Socrates awaiting the poison that will end his life. As he awaits his fate, he philosophizes about the nature of death, for learning how to face death teaches us a great deal about life and how to live. Socrates makes the bold claim that philosophy is nothing but practicing for death; that is, philosophy is a way of life that is a kind of preparation for death. Socrates understands death to be the separation of the soul from the body. Similarly, philosophy also separates the soul from the body, for in its search for eternal wisdom it must wean the soul from the body and its desires for temporal (and temporary) things. And this is why the philosopher does not fear death. In freeing the soul from the body, the philosopher is already living life from the perspective of eternity, from the point of view of what ultimately matters.

In the *Republic*, Plato brings his philosophy back to Earth as Socrates attempts to refute the Sophistic idea, put forth by Thrasymachus and Glaucon, that the unjust (or immoral) life is better than the just life. Socrates aims to show that, contrary to popular opinion, the life of virtue is the best life for the individual since it leads to both personal and societal flourishing. He does this presenting an alternative view of justice in terms of an analogy between three parts of the *polis* or city-state (craftspeople, warriors and rulers) and three parts of the soul—bodily appetites, the *thumos* or emotional or spirited element, and the mind or reason—along with their corresponding virtues—*sophrosune* or self-control or temperance, courage or fortitude, and wisdom. Justice is the virtue that emerges when all parts of the state or soul perform their own function well. Since justice is harmony or balance of the three parts—a healthy state of being—and since health is intrinsically good or desirable, it follows that the just or virtuous life is better than the unjust life. Virtue is its own reward. The good life is the best life for human beings.

The Platonic model of the good life emphasizes the importance of wisdom above the other virtues since it is reason that must rule both the self and the state. One must be able to comprehend the Form or Idea of the Good in order to form oneself in its image. The philosopher, above all others, can achieve this lofty aim of subjecting the passions to the rule of reason in order to know the good and to balance the soul. Plato illustrates this in the *Republic* through his famous "Allegory of the Cave." Only the philosopher is able to break the chains of the desires and see beyond the shadows of the bodily senses by a journey of the mind into the light of truth. After enlightenment, the philosopher must return to the cave (society) to lead the other prisoners. For Plato, the philosopher, then, is best suited to rule the state. The good life, therefore, requires not only harmony within oneself, but also harmony between the eternal and the temporal, the self and society, the theoretical and the practical.

The emphasis on the good life as the life of reason is strong in the Western tradition. We see it at work in another ancient Greek school of thought, Stoicism. Our representative Stoic philosopher is Epictetus, who lived from approximately 50 to 130 C.E. Epictetus was born a slave in Asia Minor and was owned by an administrative secretary to the Emperor Nero. He was freed by his master in 68 and studied Stoicism, of which he became an influential teacher. Stoicism developed during the Hellenistic period, after Athens declined as a military power and center of culture, but when Greek influences were spread throughout the Mediterranean world and beyond by the conquests of Alexander the Great. The Hellenistic period was one where life was uncertain for most people and where expectations for the fulfillment of personal ambitions were low. Stoicism's teaching that one could and should live in harmony with nature (the interconnected system that made up the cosmos) no matter what happened was widely appealing during this period. The breadth of Stoicism's appeal is illustrated by the fact that two of its most famous teachers were Epictetus—a lame former slave—and Marcus Aurelius—an emperor of Rome.

Unlike earlier Stoics who emphasized logic and a theoretical understanding of physical reality as a means to living in harmony with nature, Epictetus puts his emphasis on describing how to live an excellent human life. Like Socrates, he did not write anything himself, but students of his recorded his teachings. The secret of living well, according to him, is to develop complete control of one's attitude and to realize that one's attitude is, in fact, the only thing one *can* control. If one cares deeply about things that are beyond one's control, one's happiness will be hostage to external circumstances. In contrast, the Stoic strives to accept the role that nature has given him and to remain tranquil come what may.

The philosophies of Asia have also concerned themselves with the ethics of the good life. The selection from the *Tao Te Ching (The Power of the Way)* expresses some of the key ideas of Taoism, a philosophy originating in ancient China. Its author is said to be Lao-Tzu, or "Old Master," an older contemporary of Confucius. The *Tao Te Ching* has had an enormous influence on Chinese culture and thought, forming an essential complement to Confucianism and coloring the way Buddhism would be received and transmitted. The main concept of Taoism is the Tao or the Way. It can refer to the way of nature or the mysterious ultimate reality that transcends nature, gives rise to it and permeates it. It can also refer to the way of life that is in harmony with the Tao. Unlike Confucianism, which stresses education, self-cultivation and following the ways of society, Taoism teaches that one should let go of all that is artificial, including society's norms and rituals, and return to one's natural state. This letting go allows one to act by not-acting (*wu-wei*). For Taoism, the way to do is to be. Simplicity is key. As opposed to the Confucian advice to carve and polish oneself, Lao-Tzu advises that we remain *p'u*, an "uncarved block" of wood.

Like the Chinese landscape paintings that reflect Taoist influence, the clearest way to be in harmony with the Tao is to recede into nature. For this reason, the *Tao Te Ching* praises humility as the highest virtue. We should be gentle, yielding and soft rather than strong, unyielding and hard. We should be more feminine rather than masculine and more like flexible infants than crusty adults. One should be as "selfless as melting ice," as empty of self as cups, windows and doorways, which are useful precisely because of their emptiness. "The best man is like water," claims Lao-Tzu, for water is soft, yielding, flowing. The Taoist learns to go with the flow.

The final selection of this section is from the fourteenth Dalai Lama, the present supreme religious and political leader of the Tibetan people. In his *Ethics for the New Millennium*, the Dalai Lama puts forth a contemporary version of Buddhism as a way of life. Buddhism originates in ancient India with the basic teachings of Siddhartha Gautama (563–483 B.C.E), known by his followers as the Buddha or "awakened one." Its main aim is therapeutic: to free human beings from suffering. In order to become free from the cyclic patterns of unsatisfied longing that characterize the human condition, Buddhism teaches that one needs to overcome one's desires for earthly pleasure and worldly gain, and, ultimately, one's own egocentric nature. The way to liberation, to the "other shore" of *nirvana*—the state of supreme peace and contentment—is presented in the Buddha's teaching of the Four Noble Truths, which assert: (1) life is suffering, (2) desire or craving is the cause of suffering, (3) suffering can be ended, (4) the Eight-Fold Path is the way to end suffering and achieve nirvana. The Eight-Fold Path is typically broken down into three main parts: wisdom (right views and right intention), morality (right speech, right conduct, right livelihood), and meditation (right effort, right mindfulness, right concentration).

While the teachings that constitute morality are most clearly concerned with the development of moral character, the entire Buddhist path is one of inner spiritual development. For the Hinayana or Theravada Buddhist tradition, the highest virtue is wisdom, the insight into the true nature of reality and the self. In this tradition, wisdom may be seen as both the beginning and end of the Buddhist path, although the degree of wisdom is greater in the final state of enlightenment. For the Mahayana Buddhist tradition, which the Dalai Lama represents, the highest virtue is compassion, the fruit of wisdom, and is exemplified most fully in the *Bodhisattva*, one who forgoes his or her own liberation for the sake of relieving the suffering of others. As the Dalai Lama explains, such "great compassion" includes both sympathy with other people's suffering and a sense of responsibility to help those in need. It requires moving beyond selfishness and partiality since it is an unconditional love for all beings. According to the Dalai Lama, compassion for others is both the root of virtue and the source of our happiness, for living compassionately promotes both external and internal peace. As for Plato, for the Dalai Lama, the good life is also the best life for human beings.

Philosophy as a Way of Life*

Pierre Hadot

Every person—whether Greek or Barbarian—who *is in training for wisdom*, leading a blameless, irreproachable life, chooses neither to commit injustice nor return it unto others, but to avoid the company of busybodies, and hold in contempt the

---

*From Pierre Hadot, *Philosophy as a Way of Life: Spiritual Exercises from Socrates to Foucault*, edited by Arnold Davidson, translated by Michael Chase, pp. 264–76.

places where they spend their time—courts, councils, marketplaces, assemblies—in short, every kind of meeting or reunion of thoughtless people. As their goal is a life of peace and serenity, they contemplate nature and everything found within her: they attentively explore the earth, the sea, the air, the sky, and every nature found therein. In thought, they accompany the moon, the sun, and the rotations of the other stars, whether fixed or wandering. Their bodies remain on earth, but they give wings to their souls, so that, rising into the ether, they may observe the powers which dwell there, as is fitting for those who have truly become citizens of the world. Such people consider the whole world as their city, and its citizens are the companions of wisdom; they have received their civic rights from virtue, which has been entrusted with presiding over the universal common-wealth. Thus, filled with every excellence, they are accustomed no longer to take account of physical discomforts or exterior evils, and they train themselves to be indifferent to indifferent things; they are armed against both pleasures and desires, and, in short, they always strive to keep themselves above passions . . . they do not give in under the blows of fate, because they have calculated its attacks in advance (for foresight makes easier to bear even the most difficult of the things that happen against our will; since then the mind no longer supposes what happens to be strange and novel, but its perception of them is dulled, as if it had to do with old and worn-out things). It is obvious that people such as these, who find their joy in virtue, celebrate a festival their whole life long. To be sure, there is only a small number of such people; they are like embers of wisdom kept smouldering in our cities, so that virtue may not be altogether snuffed out and disappear from our race. But if only people everywhere felt the same way as this small number, and became as nature meant for them to be: blameless, irreproachable, and *lovers of wisdom*, rejoicing in the beautiful just because it *is* beautiful, and considering that there is no other good besides it . . . then our cities would be brimful of happiness. They would know nothing of the things that cause grief and fear, but would be so filled with the causes of joy and well-being that there would be no single moment in which they would not lead a life full of joyful laughter; indeed, the whole cycle of the year would be a festival for them.[1]

In this passage from Philo of Alexandria, inspired by Stoicism, one of the fundamental aspects of philosophy in the Hellenistic and Roman eras comes clearly to the forefront. During this period, philosophy was a *way of life*. This is not only to say that it was a specific type of moral conduct; we can easily see the role played in the passage from Philo by the contemplation of nature. Rather, it means that philosophy was a mode of existing-in-the-world, which had to be practiced at each instant, and the goal of which was to transform the whole of the individual's life.

For the ancients, the mere word *philo-sophia*—the love of wisdom—was enough to express this conception of philosophy. In the *Symposium*, Plato had shown that Socrates, symbol of the philosopher, could be identified with Eros, the son of Poros (expedient) and of Penia (poverty). Eros lacked wisdom, but he did know how to acquire it.[2] Philosophy thus took on the form of an exercise of the thought, will, and the totality of one's being, the goal of which was to achieve a state practically inaccessible to mankind: wisdom. Philosophy was a method of spiritual progress which demanded a radical conversion and transformation of the individual's way of being.

Thus, philosophy was a way of life, both in its exercise and effort to achieve wisdom, and in its goal, wisdom itself. For real wisdom does not merely cause us to know: it makes us "be" in a different way. Both the grandeur and the paradox of ancient philosophy are that it was, at one and the same time, conscious of the fact that wisdom is inaccessible, and convinced of the necessity of pursuing spiritual progress. In the words of Quintillian: "We must . . . strive after that which is highest, as many of the ancients did. Even though they believed that no sage had ever yet been found, they nevertheless continued to teach the precepts of wisdom."[3] The ancients knew that they would never be able to realize wisdom within themselves as a stable, definitive state, but they at least hoped to accede to it in certain privileged moments, and wisdom was the transcendent norm which guided their action.

Wisdom, then, was a way of life which brought peace of mind (*ataraxia*), inner freedom (*autarkeia*), and a cosmic consciousness. First and foremost, philosophy presented itself as a therapeutic, intended to cure mankind's anguish. This concept is stated explicitly in Xenocrates,[4] and in Epicurus:[5] "We must not suppose that any other object is to be gained from the knowledge of the phenomena of the sky . . . than peace of mind and a sure confidence." This was also a prominent idea for the Stoics[6] and for the Skeptics, apropos of whom Sextus Empiricus[7] utilizes the following splendid image:

> Apelles, the famous painter, wished to reproduce the foam from a horse's mouth in a painting. He was not able to get it right, and decided to give up. So, he threw the sponge he used to wipe his brushes against the painting. When the sponge hit the painting, it produced nothing other than an imitation of a horse's foam. In the same way, the Skeptics start off like the other philosophers, seeking peace of mind in firmness and confidence in their judgments. When they do not achieve it, they suspend their judgment. No sooner do they do this than, by pure chance, peace of mind accompanies the suspension of judgment, like a shadow follows a body.

Philosophy presented itself as a method for achieving independence and inner freedom (*autarkeia*), that state in which the ego depends only upon itself. We encounter this theme in Socrates,[8] among the Cynics, in Aristotle—for whom only the contemplative life is independent[9]—in Epicurus,[10] and among the Stoics.[11] Although their methodologies differ, we find in all philosophical schools the same awareness of the power of the human self to free itself from everything which is alien to it, even if, as in the case of the Skeptics, it does so via the mere refusal to make any decision.

In Epicureanism and in Stoicism, cosmic consciousness was added to these fundamental dispositions. By "cosmic consciousness," we mean the consciousness that we are a part of the cosmos, and the consequent dilation of our self throughout the infinity of universal nature. In the words of Epicurus' disciple Metrodorus: "Remember that, although you are mortal and have only a limited life-span, yet you have risen, through the contemplation of nature to the infinity of space and time, and you have seen all the past and all the future."[12] According to Marcus Aurelius: "The rational soul . . . travels through the whole universe and the void that surrounds it . . . it reaches out into the boundless extent of infinity, and it examines and contemplates the periodic rebirth of all things."[13] At each instant, the ancient sage was conscious of living in the cosmos, and he placed himself in harmony with the cosmos.

In order better to understand in what way ancient philosophy could be a way of life, it is perhaps necessary to have recourse to the distinction proposed by the Stoics,[14] between *discourse about* philosophy and *philosophy itself*. For the Stoics, the parts of philosophy—physics, ethics, and logic—were not, in fact, parts of philosophy itself, but rather parts of philosophical *discourse*. By this they meant that when it comes to teaching philosophy, it is necessary to set forth a theory of logic, a theory of physics, and a theory of ethics. The exigencies of discourse, both logical and pedagogical, require that these distinctions be made. But philosophy itself—that is, the philosophical way of life—is no longer a theory divided into parts, but a unitary act, which consists in *living* logic, physics, and ethics. In this case, we no longer study logical theory—that is, the theory of speaking and thinking well—we simply think and speak well. We no longer engage in theory about the physical world, but we contemplate the cosmos. We no longer theorize about moral action, but we act in a correct and just way.

Discourse about philosophy is not the same thing as *philosophy*. Polemon, one of the heads of the Old Academy, used to say:

> we should exercise ourselves with realities, not with dialectical speculations, like a man who has devoured some textbook on harmonics, but has never put his knowledge into practice. Likewise, we must not be like those who can astonish their onlookers by their skill in syllogistic argumentation, but who, when it comes to their own lives, contradict their own teachings.[15]

Five centuries later, Epictetus echoed this view:

> A carpenter does not come up to you and say, "Listen to me discourse about the art of carpentry," but he makes a contract for a house and builds it. . . . Do

> the same thing yourself. Eat like a man, drink like a man . . . get married, have children, take part in civic life, learn how to put up with insults, and tolerate other people.[16]

We can immediately foresee the consequences of this distinction, formulated by the Stoics but admitted by the majority of philosophers, concerning the relationship between theory and practice. An Epicurean saying puts it clearly: "Vain is the word of that philosopher which does not heal any suffering of man."[17] Philosophical theories are in the service of the philosophical life. That is why, in the Hellenistic and Roman periods, they were reduced to a theoretical, systematic, highly concentrated nucleus, capable of exercising a strong psychological effect, and easy enough to handle so that it might always be kept close at hand (*procheiron*).[18] Philosophical discourse was not systematic because it wanted to provide a total, systematic explanation of the whole of reality. Rather, it was systematic in order that it might provide the mind with a small number of principles, tightly linked together, which derived greater persuasive force and mnemonic effectiveness precisely from such systematization. Short sayings summed up, sometimes in striking form, the essential dogmas, so that the student might easily relocate himself within the fundamental disposition in which he was to live.

Does the philosophical life, then, consist only in the application, at every moment, of well-studied theorems, in order to resolve life's problems? As a matter of fact, when we reflect on what the philosophical life implies, we realize that there is an abyss between philosophical theory and philosophizing as living action. To take a similar case: it may seem as though artists, in their creative activity, do nothing but apply rules, yet there is an immeasurable distance between artistic creation and the abstract theory of art. In philosophy, however, we are not dealing with the mere creation of a work of art. The goal is rather to transform *ourselves*. The act of living in a genuinely philosophical way thus corresponds to an order of reality totally different from that of philosophical discourse.

In Stoicism, as in Epicureanism, philosophizing was a continuous act, permanent and identical with life itself, which had to be renewed at each instant. For both schools, this act could be defined as an orientation of the attention.

In Stoicism, attention was oriented toward the purity of one's intentions. In other words, its objective was the conformity of our individual will with reason, or the will of universal nature. In Epicureanism, by contrast, attention was oriented toward pleasure, which is, in the last analysis, the pleasure of existing. In order to realize this state of attention, however, a number of exercises were necessary: intense meditation on fundamental dogmas, the ever-renewed awareness of the finitude of life, examination of one's conscience, and, above all, a specific attitude toward time.

Both the Stoics and the Epicureans advised us to live *in the present*, letting ourselves be neither troubled by the past, nor worried by the uncertainty of the future. For both these schools of thought, the present sufficed for happiness, because it was the only reality which belongs to us and depends on us. Stoics and Epicureans agreed in recognizing the infinite value of each instant: for them, wisdom is just as perfect and complete in one instant as it is throughout an eternity. In particular, for the Stoic sage, the totality of the cosmos is contained and implied in each instant. Moreover, we not only *can* but we *must* be happy *right now*. The matter is urgent, for the future is uncertain and death is a constant threat: "While we're waiting to live, life passes us by."[19] Such an attitude can only be understood if we assume that there was, in ancient philosophy, a sharp awareness of the infinite, incommensurable value of existence. Existing within the cosmos, in the unique reality of the cosmic event, was held to be infinitely precious.

Thus, as we have seen, philosophy in the Hellenistic and Greek period took on the form of a way of life, an art of living, and a way of being. This, however, was nothing new; ancient philosophy had had this character at least as far back as Socrates. There was a Socratic style of life (which the Cynics were to imitate), and the Socratic dialogue was an exercise which brought Socrates' interlocutor to put himself in question, to take care of himself, and to make his soul as beautiful and wise as possible.[20] Similarly, Plato defined philosophy as a training for death, and the philosopher as the person who does not fear death, because he contemplates the totality of time and of being.[21]

It is sometimes claimed that Aristotle was a pure theoretician, but for him, too, philosophy was incapable of being reduced to philosophical discourse, or to a body of knowledge. Rather, philosophy for Aristotle was a quality of the mind, the result of an inner transformation. The form of life preached by Aristotle was the life according to the mind.[22]

We must not, therefore, as is done all too often, imagine that philosophy was completely transformed during the Hellenistic period, whether after the Macedonian domination over the Greek cities, or during the imperial period. On the one hand, it is not the case, as tenacious, widely-held clichés would have us believe, that the Greek city-state died after 330 BC, and political life along with it. Above all, the conception of philosophy as an art and form of living is not linked to political circumstances, or to a need for escape mechanisms and inner liberty, in order to compensate for lost political freedom. Already for Socrates and his disciples, philosophy was a mode of life, and a technique of inner living. Philosophy did not change its essence throughout the entire course of its history in antiquity.

In general, historians of philosophy pay little attention to the fact that ancient philosophy was, first and foremost, a way of life. They consider philosophy as, above all, philosophical discourse. How can the origins of this prejudice be explained? I believe it is linked to the evolution of philosophy itself in the Middle Ages and in modern times.

Christianity played a considerable role in this phenomenon. From its very beginnings—that is, from the second century AD on—Christianity had presented itself as a philosophy: the Christian way of life.[23] Indeed, the very fact that Christianity was able to present itself as a philosophy confirms the assertion that philosophy was conceived in antiquity as a way of life. If to do philosophy was to live in conformity with the law of reason, so the argument went, the Christian was a philosopher, since he lived in conformity with the law of the Logos—divine reason.[24] In order to present itself as a philosophy, Christianity was obliged to integrate elements borrowed from ancient philosophy. It had to make the Logos of the gospel according to John coincide with Stoic cosmic reason, and subsequently also with the Aristotelian or Platonic intellect. It also had to integrate philosophical spiritual exercises into Christian life. The phenomenon of integration appears very clearly in Clement of Alexandria, and was intensely developed in the monastic movement, where we find the Stoico/Platonic exercises of attention to oneself (*prosoche*), meditation, examination of conscience, and the training for death. We also re-encounter the high value accorded to peace of mind and impassibility.

The Middle Ages was to inherit the conception of monastic life as Christian philosophy, that is, as a Christian way of life. As Dom Jean Leclerq has written: "As much as in antiquity, *philosophia* in the monastic Middle Ages designates not a theory or a way of knowing, but a lived wisdom, a way of living according to reason."[25] At the same time, however, the medieval universities witnessed the elimination of the confusion which had existed in primitive Christianity between theology, founded on the rule of faith, and traditional philosophy, founded on reason. Philosophy was now no longer "the supreme science, but the "servant of theology;" it supplied the latter with the conceptual, logical, physical, and metaphysical materials it needed. The Faculty of Arts became no more than a preparation for the Faculty of Theology.

If we disregard, for the moment, the monastic usage of the word *philosophia*, we can say that philosophy in the Middle Ages had become a purely theoretical and abstract activity. It was no longer a way of life. Ancient spiritual exercises were no longer a part of philosophy, but found themselves integrated into Christian spirituality. It is in this form that we encounter them once again in the *Spiritual Exercises* of Saint Ignatius.[26] Neoplatonic mysticism was prolonged into Christian mysticism, especially among such Rhineland Dominicans as Meister Eckhardt.

Thus, the Middle Ages saw a radical change in the content of philosophy as compared to antiquity. Moreover, from the medieval period on, theology and philosophy were taught in those universities which had been creations of the medieval church. Even though attempts have been made to use the word "university" in reference to ancient educational institutions, it appears that neither the notion nor the reality of the university ever existed during antiquity, with the possible exception of the Orient near the end of the late antique period.

One of the characteristics of the university is that it is made up of professors who train professors, or professionals training professionals. Education was thus no longer directed toward people who were to be educated with a view to becoming fully developed human beings, but to specialists, in order that they might learn how to train other specialists. This is the danger of "Scholasticism," that philosophical tendency which began to be sketched at the end of antiquity, developed in the Middle Ages, and whose presence is still recognizable in philosophy today.

The scholastic university, dominated by theology, would continue to function up to the end of the eighteenth century, but from the sixteenth to the eighteenth centuries, genuinely creative philosophical activity would develop *outside* the university, in the persons of Descartes, Spinoza, Malebranche, and Leibniz. Philosophy thus reconquered its autonomy vis-è-vis theology, but this movement—born as a reaction against medieval Scholasticism—was situated on the same terrain as the latter. In opposition to one kind of theoretical philosophical discourse, there arose yet another theoretical discourse.

From the end of the eighteenth century onward, a new philosophy made its appearance within the university, in the persons of Wolff, Kant, Fichte, Schelling, and Hegel. From now on, with a few rare exceptions like Schopenhauer or Nietzsche, philosophy would be indissolubly linked to the university. We see this in the case of Bergson, Husserl, and Heidegger. This fact is not without importance. Philosophy—reduced, as we have seen, to philosophical discourse—develops from this point on in a different atmosphere and environment from that of ancient philosophy. In modern university philosophy, philosophy is obviously no longer a way of life or form of life—unless it be the form of life of a professor of philosophy. Nowadays, philosophy's element and vital milieu is the state educational institution; this has always been, and may still be, a danger for its independence. In the words of Schopenhauer:

> Generally speaking, university philosophy is mere fencing in front of a mirror. In the last analysis, its goal is to give students opinions which are to the liking of the minister who hands out the Chairs. . . . As a result, this state-financed philosophy makes a joke of philosophy. And yet, if there is one thing desirable in this world, it is to see a ray of light fall onto the darkness of our lives, shedding some kind of light on the mysterious enigma of our existence.[27]

Be this as it may, modern philosophy is first and foremost a discourse developed in the classroom, and then consigned to books. It is a text which requires exegesis.

This is not to say that modern philosophy has not rediscovered, by different paths, some of the existential aspects of ancient philosophy. Besides, it must be added that these aspects have never completely disappeared. For example, it was no accident that Descartes entitled one of his works *Meditations*. They are indeed meditations—*meditatio* in the sense of exercise—according to the spirit of the Christian philosophy of St Augustine, and Descartes recommends that they be practiced over a certain period of time. Beneath its systematic, geometrical form, Spinoza's *Ethics* corresponds rather well to what systematic philosophical discourse could mean for the Stoics. One could say that Spinoza's discourse, nourished on ancient philosophy, teaches man how to transform, radically and concretely, his own being, and how to accede to beatitude. The figure of the sage, moreover, appears in the final lines of the *Ethics*: "the sage, in so far as he is regarded as such, is scarcely at all disturbed in spirit, but, being conscious of himself, and of God, and of things, by a certain eternal necessity, never ceases to be, but always possesses true acquiescence of the spirit."[28] The philosophies of Nietzsche and of Schopenhauer are also invitations to radically transform our way of life. Both men were, moreover, thinkers steeped in the tradition of ancient philosophy.

According to the Hegelian model, human consciousness has a purely historical character; and the only lasting thing is the action of the spirit itself, as it constantly engenders new forms. Under the influence of Hegel's method, the idea arose among Marx and the young Hegelians that theory cannot be detached from practice, and that it is man's action upon the world which gives rise to his representations. In the twentieth century, the philosophy of Bergson and the phenomenology of Husserl appeared less as systems than as methods for transforming our perception of the world. Finally, the movement of thought inaugurated by Heidegger and carried on by existentialism seeks—in theory and in principle—to engage man's freedom and action in the philosophical process, although, in the last analysis, it too is primarily a philosophical discourse.

One could say that what differentiates ancient from modern philosophy is the fact that, in ancient philosophy, it was not only Chrysippus or Epicurus who, just because they had developed a philosophical discourse, were considered philosophers. Rather, every person who lived according to the precepts of Chrysippus or Epicurus was every bit as much of a philosopher as they. A politician like Cato of Utica was considered a philosopher and even a sage, even though he wrote and taught nothing, because his life was perfectly Stoic. The same was true of Roman statesmen like Rutilius Rufus and Quintus Mucius Scaevola Pontifex, who practiced Stoicism by showing an exemplary disinterestedness and humanity in the administration of the provinces entrusted to them. These men were not merely examples of morality, but men who lived the totality of Stoicism, speaking like Stoics (Cicero tells us explicitly[29] that they refused to use a certain type of rhetoric in the trials in which they testified), and looking at the world like Stoics; in other words, trying to live in accord with cosmic reason. They sought to realize the ideal of Stoic wisdom: a certain way of being human, of living according to reason, within the cosmos and along with other human beings. What constituted the object of their efforts was not merely ethics, but the human being as a whole.

Ancient philosophy proposed to mankind an art of living. By contrast, modern philosophy appears above all as the construction of a technical jargon reserved for specialists.

Everyone is free to define philosophy as he likes, to choose whatever philosophy he wishes, or to invent—if he can—whatever philosophy he may think valid. Descartes and Spinoza still remained faithful to the ancient definition: for them, philosophy was "the practice of wisdom."[30] If, following their example, we believe that it is essential for mankind to try to accede to the state of wisdom, we shall find in the ancient traditions of the various philosophical schools—Socratism, Platonism, Aristotelianism, Epicureanism, Stoicism, Cynicism, Skepticism—models of life, fundamental forms in accordance with which reason may be applied to human existence, and archetypes of the quest for wisdom. It is precisely this plurality of ancient schools that is precious. It allows us to compare the consequences of all the various possible fundamental attitudes of reason, and offers a privileged field for experimentation. This, of course, presupposes that we reduce these philosophies to their spirit and essence, detaching them from their outmoded cosmological or mythical elements, and disengaging from them the fundamental propositions that they themselves considered essential. This is not, by the way, a matter of choosing one or the other of these traditions to the exclusion of the others. Epicureanism and Stoicism, for example, correspond to two opposite but inseparable poles of our inner life: the demands of our moral conscience, and the flourishing of our joy in existing.[31]

Philosophy in antiquity was an exercise practiced at each instant. It invites us to concentrate on each instant of life, to become aware of the infinite value of each present moment, once we have replaced it within the perspective of the cosmos. The exercise of wisdom entails a cosmic dimension. Whereas the average person has lost touch with the world, and does not see the world qua world, but rather treats the world as a means of satisfying his desires, the sage never ceases to have the whole constantly present to mind. He thinks and acts within a cosmic perspective. He has the feeling of belonging to a whole which goes beyond the limits of his individuality. In antiquity, this cosmic consciousness was situated in a different perspective from that of the scientific knowledge of the universe that could be provided by, for instance, the science of astronomical phenomena. Scientific knowledge was objective and mathematical, whereas cosmic consciousness was the result of a spiritual exercise, which consisted in becoming aware of the place of one's individual existence within the great current of the cosmos and the perspective of the whole, *toti se inserens mundo*, in the words of Seneca.[32] This exercise was situated not in the absolute space of exact science, but in the lived experience of the concrete, living, and perceiving subject.

We have here to do with two radically different kinds of relationship to the world. We can understand the distinction between these two kinds by recalling the opposition pointed out by Husserl[33] between the rotation of the earth, affirmed and proved scientifically, and the earth's immobility, postulated both by our day-to-day experience and by transcendental/constitutive consciousness. For the latter, the earth is the immobile ground of our life, the reference point of our thought, or, as Merleau-Ponty put it, "the womb of our time and of our space."[34] In the same way, nature and the cosmos are, for our living perception, the infinite horizon of our lives, the enigma of our existence which, as Lucretius said, inspires us with *horror et divina voluptas*, a shudder and a divine pleasure. As Goethe put it in admirable verses:

> The best part of man is the shudder.
> However dearly the world makes him pay for this emotion,
> He is seized by amazement when he feels the Prodigious.[35]

Ancient philosophical traditions can provide guidance in our relationship to ourselves, to the cosmos, and to other human beings. In the mentality of modern historians, there is no cliché more firmly anchored, and more difficult to uproot, than the idea according to which ancient philosophy was an escape mechanism, an act of falling back upon oneself. In the case of the Platonists, it was an escape into the heaven of ideas, into the refusal of politics in the case of the Epicureans, into the submission to fate in the case of the Stoics. This way of looking at things is, in fact, doubly false. In the first place, ancient philosophy was always a philosophy practiced in a group, whether in the case of the Pythagorean communities, Platonic love, Epicurean friendship, or Stoic spiritual direction. Ancient philosophy required a common effort, community of research, mutual assistance, and spiritual support. Above all, philosophers—even, in the last analysis, the Epicureans—never gave up having an effect on their cities, transforming society, and serving their citizens, who frequently accorded them praise, the vestiges of which are preserved for us by inscriptions. Political ideas may have differed from school to school, but the concern for having an effect on city or state, king or emperor, always remained constant. This is particularly true of Stoicism, and can easily be seen in many of the texts of Marcus Aurelius. Of the three tasks which must be kept in mind at each instant, alongside vigilance over one's thoughts and consent to the events imposed by destiny, an essential place is accorded to the duty always to act in the service of the human community; that is, to act in accordance with justice. This last requirement is, moreover, intimately linked to the two others. It is one and the same wisdom which conforms itself to cosmic wisdom and to the reason in which human beings participate. This concern for living in the service of the human community, and for acting in accordance with justice, is an essential element of every philosophical life. In other words, the philosophical life normally entails a communitary engagement. This last is probably the hardest part to carry out. The trick is to maintain oneself on the level of reason, and not allow oneself to be blinded by political passions, anger, resentments, or prejudices. To be sure, there is an equilibrium—almost impossible to achieve—between the inner peace brought about by wisdom, and the passions to which the sight of the injustices, sufferings, and misery of mankind cannot help but give rise. Wisdom, however, consists in precisely such an equilibrium, and inner peace is indispensable for efficacious action.

Such is the lesson of ancient philosophy: an invitation to each human being to transform himself. Philosophy is a conversion, a transformation of one's way of being and living, and a quest for wisdom. This is not an easy matter. As Spinoza wrote at the end of the *Ethics:*

> If the way which I have pointed out as leading to this result seems exceedingly hard, it may nevertheless be discovered. It must indeed be hard, since it is so seldom found. How would it be possible, if salvation were easy to find, and could without great labour be found, that it should be neglected by almost everybody? But all excellent things are as difficult as they are rare.[36]

Notes

1. Philo Judaeus, *On the Special Laws*, 2, 44–8.
2. Cf. above.
3. Quintillian, *Oratorical Institutions*, bk I, Preface, 19–20.
4. Xenocrates, fr. 4 Heinze.
5. Epicurus, *Letter to Pythocles*, §85.
6. Marcus Aurelius, *Meditations*, 9, 31.
7. Sextus Empiricus, *Outlines of Pyrrhonism*, I, 28.
8. Xenophon, *Memorabilia*, I, 2, 14.
9. Aristode, *Nicomachean Ethics*, 10, 7, 1178b3.
10. Epicurus, *Gnomologicum Vaticanum*, §77.
11. Epictetus, *Discourses*, 3, 13, 7.
12. Cf. above.
13. Marcus Aurelius, *Meditations*, 11, 1.
14. E.g. Diogenes Laertius, *Lives of the Philosophers*, 7, 39.
15. Ibid, 4, 18.
16. Epictetus, *Discourses*, 3, 21, 4—6.
17. Cf. below.
18. On the concept of *procheiron*, see above.

19. Seneca, *Letters to Lucilius*, I, 1.
20. Plato, *Apology*, 29elff.
21. Plato, *Republic*, 486a.
22. Aristode, *Nicomachean Ethics*, 10, 7, 1178aff.
23. Cf. below.
24. Justin, *Apology*, I, 46, 1–4.
25. J. Leclerq, "Pour l'histoire de l'expression 'philosophie chrétienne'," *Mélanges de Science Religieuse* 9 (1952), p. 221.
26. Cf. below.
27. A. Schopenhauer, *The World as Will and Representation*, trans. E.F.J. Payne, 2 vols, Indian Hills CO 1958, London/Toronto 1909, ch. 17, vol. 2, pp. 163–4.
28. Spinoza, *Ethics*, Part 5, Prop. 42, p. 270 Elwes.
29. Cicero, *On Oratory*, I, 229ff.
30. René Descartes, *Principii philosophiae*, Foreword to Picot.
31. See the references from Kant, Goethe, and Jaspers cited above.
32. "Plunging oneself into the totality of the world." Seneca, *Letters to Lucilius*, 66.
33. E. Husserl, "Grundlegende Untersuchungen zum phanomenologiscen Urspung der Räumlichkeit der Natur" (= Umsturz der Kopernikanischen Lehre), in Marvin Faber, ed., *Philosophical Essays in Memory of E. Husserl*, Cambridge MA 1940, p. 132.
34. M. Merleau-Ponty, *Éloge de la philosophic et autres essais*, Paris 1953, p. 285.
35. Johann Wolfgang von Goethe, *Faust*, 6272ff.
36. Spinoza, *Ethics*, pp. 270–1.

*Phaedo**

Plato

. . . And now, O my judges, I desire to prove to you that the real philosopher has reason to be of good cheer when he is about to die, and that after death he may hope to obtain the greatest good in the other world. And how this may be, Simmias and Cebes, I will endeavour to explain. For I deem that the true votary of philosophy is likely to be misunderstood by other men; they do not perceive that he is always pursuing death and dying; and if this be so, and he has had the desire of death all his life long, why when his time comes should he repine at that which he has been always pursuing and desiring?

Simmias said laughingly: Though not in a laughing humour, you have made me laugh, Socrates; for I cannot help thinking that the many when they hear your words will say how truly you have described philosophers, and our people at home will likewise say that the life which philosophers desire is in reality death, and that they have found them out to be deserving of the death which they desire.

*Reprinted from *The Dialogues of Plato*, translated by Benjamin Jowett (Macmillan and Co., 1892).

And they are right, Simmias, in thinking so, with the exception of the words 'they have found them out'; for they have not found out either what is the nature of that death which the true philosopher deserves, or how he deserves or desires death. But enough of them:—let us discuss the matter among ourselves: Do we believe that there is such a thing as death?

To be sure, replied Simmias.

Is it not the separation of soul and body? And to be dead is the completion of this; when the soul exists in herself, and is released from the body and the body is released from the soul, what is this but death?

Just so, he replied.

There is another question, which will probably throw light on our present inquiry if you and I can agree about it:—Ought the philosopher to care about the pleasures—if they are to be called pleasures—of eating and drinking?

Certainly not, answered Simmias.

And what about the pleasures of love—should he care for them?

By no means.

And will he think much of the other ways of indulging the body, for example, the acquisition of costly raiment, or sandals, or other adornments of the body? Instead of caring about them, does he not rather despise anything more than nature needs? What do you say?

I should say that the true philosopher would despise them.

Would you not say that he is entirely concerned with the soul and not with the body? He would like, as far as he can, to get away from the body and to turn to the soul.

Quite true.

In matters of this sort philosophers, above all other men, may be observed in every sort of way to dissever the soul from the communion of the body.

Very true.

Whereas, Simmias, the rest of the world are of opinion that to him who has no sense of pleasure and no part in bodily pleasure, life is not worth having; and that he who is indifferent about them is as good as dead.

That is also true.

What again shall we say of the actual acquirement of knowledge?—is the body, if invited to share in the enquiry, a hinderer or a helper? I mean to say, have sight and hearing any truth in them? Are they not, as the poets are always telling us, inaccurate witnesses? and yet, if even they are inaccurate and indistinct, what is to be said of the other senses?—for you will allow that they are the best of them?

Certainly, he replied.

Then when does the soul attain truth?—for in attempting to consider anything in company with the body she is obviously deceived.

True.

Then must not true existence be revealed to her in thought, if at all?

Yes.

And thought is best when the mind is gathered into herself and none of these things trouble her—neither sounds nor sights nor pain nor any pleasure,—when she takes leave of the body, and has as little as possible to do with it, when she has no bodily sense or desire, but is aspiring after true being?

Certainly.

And in this the philosopher dishonours the body; his soul runs away from his body and desires to be alone and by herself?

That is true.

Well, but there is another thing, Simmias: Is there or is there not an absolute justice?

Assuredly there is.

And an absolute beauty and absolute good?

Of course.

But did you ever behold any of them with your eyes?

Certainly not.

Or did you ever reach them with any other bodily sense?—and I speak not of these alone, but of absolute greatness, and health, and strength, and of the essence or true nature of everything. Has the reality of them ever been perceived by you through the bodily organs? or rather, is not the nearest approach to the knowledge of their several natures made by him who so orders his intellectual vision as to have the most exact conception of the essence of each thing which he considers?

Certainly.

And he attains to the purest knowledge of them who goes to each with the mind alone, not introducing or intruding in the act of thought sight or any other sense together with reason, but with the very light of the mind in her own clearness searches into the very truth of each; he who has got rid, as far as he can, of eyes and ears and, so to speak, of the whole body, these being in his opinion distracting elements which when they infect the soul hinder her from acquiring truth and knowledge—who, if not he, is likely to attain the knowledge of true being?

What you say has a wonderful truth in it, Socrates, replied Simmias.

And when real philosophers consider all these things, will they not be led to make a reflection which they will express in words something like the following? 'Have we not found,' they will say, 'a path of thought which seems to bring us and our argument to the conclusion, that while we are in the body, and while the soul is infected with the evils of the body, our desire will not be satisfied? and our desire is of the truth. For the body is a source of endless trouble to us by reason of the mere requirement of food; and is liable also to diseases which overtake and impede us in the search after true being: it fills us full of loves, and lusts, and fears, and fancies of all kinds, and endless foolery, and in fact, as men say, takes away from us the power of thinking at all. Whence come wars, and fightings, and factions? whence but from the body and the lusts of the body? wars are occasioned by the love of money, and money has to be acquired for the sake and in the service of the body; and by reason of all these impediments we have no time to give to philosophy; and, last and worst of all, even if we are at leisure and betake ourselves to some speculation, the body is always breaking in upon us, causing turmoil and confusion in our enquiries, and so amazing us that we are prevented from seeing the truth. It has been proved to us by experience that if we would have pure knowledge of anything we must be quit of the body—the soul in herself must behold things in themselves: and then we shall attain the wisdom which we desire, and of which we say that we are lovers, not while we live, but after death; for if while in company with the body, the soul cannot have pure knowledge, one of two things follows—either knowledge is not to be attained at all, or, if at all, after death. For then, and not till then, the soul will be parted from the body and exist in herself alone. In this present life, I reckon that we make the nearest approach to knowledge when we have the least possible intercourse or communion with the body, and are not surfeited with the bodily nature, but keep ourselves pure until the hour when God himself is pleased to release us. And thus having got rid of the foolishness of the body we shall be pure and hold converse with the pure, and know of ourselves the clear light everywhere, which is no other than the light of truth.' For the impure are not permitted to approach the pure. These are the sort of words, Simmias, which the true lovers of knowledge cannot help saying to one another, and thinking. You would agree; would you not?

Undoubtedly, Socrates.

But, O my friend, if this is true, there is great reason to hope that, going whither I go, when I have come to the end of my journey, I shall attain that which has been the pursuit of my life. And therefore I go on my way rejoicing, and not I only, but every other man who believes that his mind has been made ready and that he is in a manner purified.

Certainly, replied Simmias.

And what is purification but the separation of the soul from the body, as I was saying before; the habit of the soul gathering and collecting herself into herself from all sides out of the body; the dwelling in her own place alone, as in another life, so also in this, as far as she can;—the release of the soul from the chains of the body?

Very true, he said.

And this separation and release of the soul from the body is termed death?

To be sure, he said.

And the true philosophers, and they only, are ever seeking to release the soul. Is not the separation and release of the soul from the body their especial study?

That is true.

And, as I was saying at first, there would be a ridiculous contradiction in men studying to live as nearly as they can in a state of death, and yet repining when it comes upon them.

Clearly.

And the true philosophers, Simmias, are always occupied in the practice of dying, wherefore also to them least of all men is death terrible. Look at the matter thus:—if they have been in every way the enemies of the body, and are wanting to be alone with the soul, when this desire of theirs is granted, how inconsistent would they be if they trembled and repined, instead of rejoicing at their departure to that place where, when they arrive, they hope to gain that which in life they desired—and this was wisdom—and at the same time to be rid of the company of their enemy. Many a man has been willing to go to the world below animated by the hope of seeing there an earthly love, or wife, or son, and conversing with them. And will he who is a true lover of wisdom, and is strongly persuaded in like manner that only in the world below he can worthily enjoy her, still repine at death? Will he not depart with joy? Surely he will, O my friend, if he be a true philosopher. For he will have a firm conviction that there and there only, he can find wisdom in her purity. And if this be true, he would be very absurd, as I was saying, if he were afraid of death.

He would, indeed, replied Simmias.

And when you see a man who is repining at the approach of death, is not his reluctance a sufficient proof that he is not a lover of wisdom, but a lover of the body, and probably at the same time a lover of either money or power, or both?

Quite so, he replied.

And is not courage, Simmias, a quality which is specially characteristic of the philosopher?

Certainly.

There is temperance again, which even by the vulgar is supposed to consist in the control and regulation of the passions, and in the sense of superiority to them—is not temperance a virtue belonging to those only who despise the body, and who pass their lives in philosophy?

Most assuredly.

For the courage and temperance of other men, if you will consider them, are really a contradiction.

How so?

Well, he said, you are aware that death is regarded by men in general as a great evil.

Very true, he said.

And do not courageous men face death because they are afraid of yet greater evils?

That is quite true.

Then all but the philosophers are courageous only from fear, and because they are afraid; and yet that a man should be courageous from fear, and because he is a coward, is surely a strange thing.

Very true.

And are not the temperate exactly in the same case? They are temperate because they are intemperate—which might seem to be a contradiction, but is nevertheless the sort of thing which happens with this foolish temperance. For there are pleasures which they are afraid of losing; and in their desire to keep them, they abstain from some pleasures, because they are overcome by others; and although to be conquered by pleasure is called by men intemperance, to them the conquest of pleasure consists in being conquered by pleasure. And that is what I mean by saying that, in a sense, they are made temperate through intemperance.

Such appears to be the case.

Yet the exchange of one fear or pleasure or pain for another fear or pleasure or pain, and of the greater for the less, as if they were coins, is not the exchange of virtue. O my blessed Simmias, is there not one true coin for which all things ought to be exchanged?—and that is wisdom; and only in exchange for this, and in company with this, is anything truly bought or sold, whether courage or temperance or justice. And is not all true virtue the companion of wisdom, no matter what fears or pleasures or other similar goods or evils may or may not attend her? But the virtue which is made up of these goods, when they are severed from wisdom and exchanged with one another, is a shadow of virtue only, nor is there any freedom or health or truth in her; but in the true exchange there is a purging away of all these things, and temperance, and justice, and courage, and wisdom herself are the purgation of them. The founders of the mysteries would appear to have had a real meaning, and were not talking nonsense when they intimated in a figure long ago that he who passes unsanctified and uninitiated into the world below will lie in a slough, but that he who arrives there after initiation and purification will dwell with the gods. For 'many,' as they say in the mysteries, 'are the thyrsus-bearers, but few are the mystics,'—meaning, as I interpret the words, 'the true philosophers.' In the number of whom, during my whole life, I have been seeking, according to my ability, to find a place;—whether I have sought in a right way or not, and whether I have succeeded or not, I shall truly know in a little while, if God will, when I myself arrive in the other world—such is my belief. And therefore I maintain that I am right, Simmias and Cebes, in not grieving or repining at parting from you and my masters in this world, for I believe that I shall equally find good masters and friends in another world. But most men do not believe this saying; if then I succeed in convincing you by my defense better than I did the Athenian judges, it will be well.

*Republic**

Plato

Book IV

. . . First let us complete the old investigation, which we began, as you remember, under the impression that, if we could previously examine justice on the larger scale, there would be less difficulty in discerning her in the individual. That larger example appeared to be the State, and accordingly we constructed as good a one as we could, knowing well that in the good State justice would be found. Let the discovery which we made be now applied to the individual—if they agree, we shall be satisfied; or, if there be a difference in the individual, we will come back to the State and have another trial of the theory. The friction of the two when rubbed together may possibly strike a light in which justice will shine forth, and the vision which is then revealed we will fix in our souls.

That will be in regular course; let us do as you say.

I proceeded to ask: When two things, a greater and less, are called by the same name, are they like or unlike in so far as they are called the same?

Like, he replied.

The just man then, if we regard the idea of justice only, will be like the just State?

He will.

And a State was thought by us to be just when the three classes in the State severally did their own business; and also thought to be temperate and valiant and wise by reason of certain other affections and qualities of these same classes?

True, he said.

And so of the individual; we may assume that he has the same three principles in his own soul which are found in the State; and he may be rightly described in the same terms, because he is affected in the same manner?

---

*Reprinted from *The Dialogues of Plato*, translated by Benjamin Jowett (Macmillan and Co., 1892).

Certainly, he said.

Once more, then, O my friend, we have alighted upon an easy question—whether the soul has these three principles or not?

An easy question! Nay, rather, Socrates, the proverb holds that hard is the good.

Very true, I said; and I do not think that the method which we are employing is at all adequate to the accurate solution of this question; the true method is another and a longer one. Still we may arrive at a solution not below the level of the previous inquiry.

May we not be satisfied with that? he said; under the circumstances, I am quite content. I, too, I replied, shall be extremely well satisfied.

Then faint not in pursuing the speculation, he said.

Must we not acknowledge, I said, that in each of us there are the same principles and habits which there are in the State; and that from the individual they pass into the State?—how else can they come there? Take the quality of passion or spirit; it would be ridiculous to imagine that this quality, when found in States, is not derived from the individuals who are supposed to possess it, e.g., the Thracians, Scythians, and in general the Northern nations; and the same may be said of the love of knowledge, which is the special characteristic of our part of the world, or of the love of money, which may, with equal truth, be attributed to the Phoenicians and Egyptians.

Exactly so, he said.

There is no difficulty in understanding this.

None whatever.

But the question is not quite so easy when we proceed to ask whether these principles are three or one; whether, that is to say, we learn with one part of our nature, are angry with another, and with a third part desire the satisfaction of our natural appetites; or whether the whole soul comes into play in each sort of action—to determine that is the difficulty.

Yes, he said; there lies the difficulty.

Then let us now try and determine whether they are the same or different.

How can we? he asked.

I replied as follows: The same thing clearly cannot act or be acted upon in the same part or in relation to the same thing at the same time, in contrary ways; and therefore whenever this contradiction occurs in things apparently the same, we know that they are really not the same, but different.

Good.

For example, I said, can the same thing be at rest and in motion at the same time in the same part?

Impossible.

Still, I said, let us have a more precise statement of terms, lest we should hereafter fall out by the way. Imagine the case of a man who is standing and also moving his hands and his head, and suppose a person to say that one and the same person is in motion and at rest at the same moment—to such a mode of speech we should object, and should rather say that one part of him is in motion while another is at rest.

Very true.

And suppose the objector to refine still further, and to draw the nice distinction that not only parts of tops, but whole tops, when they spin round with their pegs fixed on the spot, are at rest and in motion at the same time (and he may say the same of anything which revolves in the same spot), his objection would not be admitted by us, because in such cases things are not at rest and in motion in the same parts of themselves; we should rather say that they have both an axis and a circumference; and that the axis stands still, for there is no deviation from the perpendicular; and that the circumference goes round. But if, while revolving, the axis inclines either to the right or left, forward or backward, then in no point of view can they be at rest.

That is the correct mode of describing them, he replied.

Then none of these objections will confuse us, or incline us to believe that the same thing at the same time, in the same part or in relation to the same thing, can act or be acted upon in contrary ways.

Certainly not, according to my way of thinking.

Yet, I said, that we may not be compelled to examine all such objections, and prove at length that they are untrue, let us assume their absurdity, and go forward on the understanding that hereafter, if this assumption turn out to be untrue, all the consequences which follow shall be withdrawn.

Yes, he said, that will be the best way.

Well, I said, would you not allow that assent and dissent, desire and aversion, attraction and repulsion, are all of them opposites, whether they are regarded as active or passive (for that makes no difference in the fact of their opposition)?

Yes, he said, they are opposites.

Well, I said, and hunger and thirst, and the desires in general, and again willing and wishing—all these you would refer to the classes already mentioned. You would say—would you not?—that the soul of him who desires is seeking after the object of his desire; or that he is drawing to himself the thing which he wishes to possess: or again, when a person wants anything to be given him, his mind, longing for the realization of his desire, intimates his wish to have it by a nod of assent, as if he had been asked a question?

Very true.

And what would you say of unwillingness and dislike and the absence of desire; should not these be referred to the opposite class of repulsion and rejection?

Certainly.

Admitting this to be true of desire generally, let us suppose a particular class of desires, and out of these we will select hunger and thirst, as they are termed, which are the most obvious of them?

Let us take that class, he said.

The object of one is food, and of the other drink?

Yes.

And here comes the point: is not thirst the desire which the soul has of drink, and of drink only; not of drink qualified by anything else; for example, warm or cold, or much or little, or, in a word, drink of any particular sort: but if the thirst be accompanied by heat, then the desire is of cold drink; or, if accompanied by cold, then of warm drink; or, if the thirst be excessive, then the drink which is desired will be excessive; or, if not great, the quantity of drink will also be small: but thirst pure and simple will desire drink pure and simple, which is the natural satisfaction of thirst, as food is of hunger?

Yes, he said; the simple desire is, as you say, in every case of the simple object, and the qualified desire of the qualified object.

But here a confusion may arise; and I should wish to guard against an opponent starting up and saying that no man desires drink only, but good drink, or food only, but good food; for good is the universal object of desire, and thirst being a desire, will necessarily be thirst after good drink; and the same is true of every other desire.

Yes, he replied, the opponent might have something to say.

Nevertheless I should still maintain, that of relatives some have a quality attached to either term of the relation; others are simple and have their correlatives simple.

I do not know what you mean.

Well, you know of course that the greater is relative to the less?

Certainly.

And the much greater to the much less?

Yes.

And the sometime greater to the sometime less, and the greater that is to be to the less that is to be?

Certainly, he said.

And so of more or less, and of other correlative terms, such as the double and the half, or, again, the heavier and the lighter, the swifter and the slower; and of hot and cold, and of any other relatives; is not this true of all of them?

Yes.

And does not the same principle hold in the sciences? The object of science is knowledge (assuming that to be the true definition), but the object of a particular science is a particular kind of knowledge; I mean, for example, that the science of house-building is a kind of knowledge which is defined and distinguished from other kinds and is therefore termed architecture.

Certainly.

Because it has a particular quality which no other has?

Yes.

And it has this particular quality because it has an object of a particular kind; and this is true of the other arts and sciences?

Yes.

Now, then, if I have made myself clear, you will understand my original meaning in what I said about relatives. My meaning was, that if one term of a relation is taken alone, the other is taken alone; if one term is qualified, the other is also qualified. I do not mean to say that relatives may not be disparate, or that the science of health is healthy, or of disease necessarily diseased, or that the sciences of good and evil are therefore good and evil; but only that, when the term "science" is no longer used absolutely, but has a qualified object which in this case is the nature of health and disease, it becomes defined, and is hence called not merely science, but the science of medicine.

I quite understand, and, I think, as you do.

Would you not say that thirst is one of these essentially relative terms, having clearly a relation—

Yes, thirst is relative to drink.

And a certain kind of thirst is relative to a certain kind of drink; but thirst taken alone is neither of much nor little, nor of good nor bad, nor of any particular kind of drink, but of drink only?

Certainly.

Then the soul of the thirsty one, in so far as he is thirsty, desires only drink; for this he yearns and tries to obtain it?

That is plain.

And if you suppose something which pulls a thirsty soul away from drink, that must be different from the thirsty principle which draws him like a beast to drink; for, as we were saying, the same thing cannot at the same time with the same part of itself act in contrary ways about the same.

Impossible.

No more than you can say that the hands of the archer push and pull the bow at the same time, but what you say is that one hand pushes and the other pulls.

Exactly so, he replied.

And might a man be thirsty, and yet unwilling to drink?

Yes, he said, it constantly happens.

And in such a case what is one to say? Would you not say that there was something in the soul bidding a man to drink, and something else forbidding him, which is other and stronger than the principle which bids him?

I should say so.

And the forbidding principle is derived from reason, and that which bids and attracts proceeds from passion and disease?

Clearly.

Then we may fairly assume that they are two, and that they differ from one another; the one with which a man reasons, we may call the rational principle of the soul; the other, with which he loves, and hungers, and thirsts, and feels the flutterings of any other desire, may be termed the irrational or appetitive, the ally of sundry pleasures and satisfactions?

Yes, he said, we may fairly assume them to be different.

Then let us finally determine that there are two principles existing in the soul. And what of passion, or spirit? Is it a third, or akin to one of the preceding?

I should be inclined to say—akin to desire.

Well, I said, there is a story which I remember to have heard, and in which I put faith. The story is, that Leontius, the son of Aglaion, coming up one day from the Piraeus, under the north wall on the outside, observed some dead bodies lying on the ground at the place of execution. He felt a desire to see them, and also a dread and abhorrence of them; for a time he struggled and covered his eyes, but at length the desire got the better of him; and forcing them open, he ran up to the dead bodies, saying, Look, ye wretches, take your fill of the fair sight.

I have heard the story myself, he said.

The moral of the tale is, that anger at times goes to war with desire, as though they were two distinct things.

Yes; that is the meaning, he said.

And are there not many other cases in which we observe that when a man's desires violently prevail over his reason, he reviles himself, and is angry at the violence within him, and that in this struggle, which is like the struggle of factions in a State, his spirit is on the side of his reason; but for the passionate or spirited element to take part with the desires when reason decides that she should not be opposed, is a sort of thing which I believe that you never observed occurring in yourself, nor, as I should imagine, in anyone else?

Certainly not.

Suppose that a man thinks he has done a wrong to another, the nobler he is, the less able is he to feel indignant at any suffering, such as hunger, or cold, or any other pain which the injured person may inflict upon him—these he deems to be just, and, as I say, his anger refuses to be excited by them.

True, he said.

But when he thinks that he is the sufferer of the wrong, then he boils and chafes, and is on the side of what he believes to be justice; and because he suffers hunger or cold or other pain he is only the more determined to persevere and conquer. His noble spirit will not be quelled until he either slays or is slain; or until he hears the voice of the shepherd, that is, reason, bidding his dog bark no more.

The illustration is perfect, he replied; and in our State, as we were saying, the auxiliaries were to be dogs, and to hear the voice of the rulers, who are their shepherds.

I perceive, I said, that you quite understand me; there is, however, a further point which I wish you to consider.

What point?

You remember that passion or spirit appeared at first sight to be a kind of desire, but now we should say quite the contrary; for in the conflict of the soul spirit is arrayed on the side of the rational principle.

Most assuredly.

But a further question arises: Is passion different from reason also, or only a kind of reason; in which latter case, instead of three principles in the soul, there will only be two, the rational and the concupiscent; or rather, as the State was composed of three classes, traders, auxiliaries, counsellors, so may there not be in the individual soul a third element which is passion or spirit, and when not corrupted by bad education is the natural auxiliary of reason?

Yes, he said, there must be a third.

Yes, I replied, if passion, which has already been shown to be different from desire, turn out also to be different from reason.

But that is easily proved: We may observe even in young children that they are full of spirit almost as soon as they are born, whereas some of them never seem to attain to the use of reason, and most of them late enough.

Excellent, I said, and you may see passion equally in brute animals, which is a further proof of the truth of what you are saying. And we may once more appeal to the words of Homer, which have been already quoted by us, "He smote his breast, and thus rebuked his soul;" for in this verse Homer has clearly supposed the power which reasons about the better and worse to be different from the unreasoning anger which is rebuked by it.

Very true, he said.

And so, after much tossing, we have reached land, and are fairly agreed that the same principles which exist in the State exist also in the individual, and that they are three in number.

Exactly.

Must we not then infer that the individual is wise in the same way, and in virtue of the same quality which makes the State wise?

Certainly.

Also that the same quality which constitutes courage in the State constitutes courage in the individual, and that both the State and the individual bear the same relation to all the other virtues?

Assuredly.

And the individual will be acknowledged by us to be just in the same way in which the State is just?

That follows of course.

We cannot but remember that the justice of the State consisted in each of the three classes doing the work of its own class?

We are not very likely to have forgotten, he said.

We must recollect that the individual in whom the several qualities of his nature do their own work will be just, and will do his own work?

Yes, he said, we must remember that too.

And ought not the rational principle, which is wise, and has the care of the whole soul, to rule, and the passionate or spirited principle to be the subject and ally?

Certainly.

And, as we were saying, the united influence of music and gymnastics will bring them into accord, nerving and sustaining the reason with noble words and lessons, and moderating and soothing and civilizing the wildness of passion by harmony and rhythm?

Quite true, he said.

And these two, thus nurtured and educated, and having learned truly to know their own functions, will rule over the concupiscent, which in each of us is the largest part of the soul and by nature most insatiable of gain; over this they will keep guard, lest, waxing great and strong with the fulness of bodily pleasures, as they are termed, the concupiscent soul, no longer confined to her own sphere, should attempt to enslave and rule those who are not her natural-born subjects, and overturn the whole life of man?

Very true, he said.

Both together will they not be the best defenders of the whole soul and the whole body against attacks from without; the one counselling, and the other fighting under his leader, and courageously executing his commands and counsels?

True.

And he is to be deemed courageous whose spirit retains in pleasure and in pain the commands of reason about what he ought or ought not to fear?

Right, he replied.

And him we call wise who has in him that little part which rules, and which proclaims these commands; that part too being supposed to have a knowledge of what is for the interest of each of the three parts and of the whole?

Assuredly.

And would you not say that he is temperate who has these same elements in friendly harmony, in whom the one ruling principle of reason, and the two subject ones of spirit and desire, are equally agreed that reason ought to rule, and do not rebel?

Certainly, he said, that is the true account of temperance whether in the State or individual.

And surely, I said, we have explained again and again how and by virtue of what quality a man will be just.

That is very certain.

And is justice dimmer in the individual, and is her form different, or is she the same which we found her to be in the State?

There is no difference, in my opinion, he said.

Because, if any doubt is still lingering in our minds, a few commonplace instances will satisfy us of the truth of what I am saying.

What sort of instances do you mean?

If the case is put to us, must we not admit that the just State, or the man who is trained in the principles of such a State, will be less likely than the unjust to make away with a deposit of gold or silver? Would anyone deny this?

No one, he replied.

Will the just man or citizen ever be guilty of sacrilege or theft, or treachery either to his friends or to his country?

Never.

Neither will he ever break faith where there have been oaths or agreements.

Impossible.

No one will be less likely to commit adultery, or to dishonor his father and mother, or to fail in his religious duties?

No one.

And the reason is that each part of him is doing its own business, whether in ruling or being ruled?

Exactly so.

Are you satisfied, then, that the quality which makes such men and such States is justice, or do you hope to discover some other?

Not I, indeed.

Then our dream has been realized; and the suspicion which we entertained at the beginning of our work of construction, that some divine power must have conducted us to a primary form of justice, has now been verified?

Yes, certainly.

And the division of labor which required the carpenter and the shoemaker and the rest of the citizens to be doing each his own business, and not another's, was a shadow of justice, and for that reason it was of use?

Clearly.

But in reality justice was such as we were describing, being concerned, however, not with the outward man, but with the inward, which is the true self and concernment of man: for the just man does not permit the several elements within him to interfere with one another, or any of them to do the work of others—he sets in order his own inner life, and is his own master and his own law, and at peace with himself; and when he has bound together the three principles within him, which may be compared to the higher, lower, and middle notes of the scale, and the intermediate intervals—when he has bound all these together, and is no longer many, but has become one entirely temperate and perfectly adjusted nature, then he proceeds to act, if he has to act, whether in a matter of property, or in the treatment of the body, or in some affair of politics or private business; always thinking and calling that which preserves and co-operates with this harmonious condition just and good action, and the knowledge which presides over it wisdom, and that which at any time impairs this condition he will call unjust action, and the opinion which presides over it ignorance.

You have said the exact truth, Socrates.

Very good; and if we were to affirm that we had discovered the just man and the just State, and the nature of justice in each of them, we should not be telling a falsehood?

Most certainly not.

May we say so, then?

Let us say so.

And now, I said, injustice has to be considered.

Clearly.

Must not injustice be a strife which arises among the three principles—a meddlesomeness, and interference, and rising up of a part of the soul against the whole, an assertion of unlawful authority, which is made by a rebellious subject against a true prince, of whom he is the natural vassal—what is all this confusion and delusion but injustice, and intemperance, and cowardice, and ignorance, and every form of vice?

Exactly so.

And if the nature of justice and injustice be known, then the meaning of acting unjustly and being unjust, or, again, of acting justly, will also be perfectly clear?

What do you mean? he said.

Why, I said, they are like disease and health; being in the soul just what disease and health are in the body.

How so? he said.

Why, I said, that which is healthy causes health, and that which is unhealthy causes disease.

Yes.

And just actions cause justice, and unjust actions cause injustice?

That is certain.

And the creation of health is the institution of a natural order and government of one by another in the parts of the body; and the creation of disease is the production of a state of things at variance with this natural order?

True.

And is not the creation of justice the institution of a natural order and government of one by another in the parts of the soul, and the creation of injustice the production of a state of things at variance with the natural order?

Exactly so, he said.

Then virtue is the health, and beauty, and well-being of the soul, and vice the disease, and weakness, and deformity, of the same?

True.

And do not good practices lead to virtue, and evil practices to vice?

Assuredly.

Still our old question of the comparative advantage of justice and injustice has not been answered: Which is the more profitable, to be just and act justly and practise virtue, whether seen or unseen of gods and men, or to be unjust and act unjustly, if only unpunished and unreformed?

In my judgment, Socrates, the question has now become ridiculous. We know that, when the bodily constitution is gone, life is no longer endurable, though pampered with all kinds of meats and drinks, and having all wealth and all power; and shall we be told that when the very essence of the vital principle is undermined and corrupted, life is still worth having to a man, if only he be allowed to do whatever he likes with the single exception that he is not to acquire justice and virtue, or to escape from injustice and vice; assuming them both to be such as we have described?

Yes, I said, the question is, as you say, ridiculous . . .

Book VII

And now, I said, let me show in a figure how far our nature is enlightened or unenlightened: Behold! human beings living in an underground den, which has a mouth open toward the light and reaching all along the den; here they have been from their childhood, and have their legs and necks chained so that they cannot move, and can only see before them, being prevented by the chains from turning round their heads. Above and behind them a fire is blazing at a distance, and between the fire and the prisoners there is a raised way; and you will see, if you look, a low wall built along the way, like the screen which marionette-players have in front of them, over which they show the puppets.

I see.

And do you see, I said, men passing along the wall carrying all sorts of vessels, and statues and figures of animals made of wood and stone and various materials, which appear over the wall? Some of them are talking, others silent.

You have shown me a strange image, and they are strange prisoners.

Like ourselves, I replied; and they see only their own shadows, or the shadows of one another, which the fire throws on the opposite wall of the cave?

True, he said; how could they see anything but the shadows if they were never allowed to move their heads?

And of the objects which are being carried in like manner they would only see the shadows?

Yes, he said.

And if they were able to converse with one another, would they not suppose that they were naming what was actually before them?

Very true.

And suppose further that the prison had an echo which came from the other side, would they not be sure to fancy when one of the passers-by spoke that the voice which they heard came from the passing shadow?

No question, he replied.

To them, I said, the truth would be literally nothing but the shadows of the images.

That is certain.

And now look again, and see what will naturally follow if the prisoners are released and disabused of their error. At first, when any of them is liberated and compelled suddenly to stand up and turn his neck round and walk and look toward the light, he will suffer sharp pains; the glare will distress him, and he will be unable to see the realities of which in his former state he had seen the shadows; and then conceive someone saying to him, that what he saw before was an illusion, but that now, when he is approaching nearer to being and his eye is turned toward more real existence, he has a clearer vision—what will be his reply? And you may further imagine that his instructor is pointing to the objects as they pass and requiring him to name them—will he not be perplexed? Will he not fancy that the shadows which he formerly saw are truer than the objects which are now shown to him?

Far truer.

And if he is compelled to look straight at the light, will he not have a pain in his eyes which will make him turn away to take refuge in the objects of vision which he can see, and which he will conceive to be in reality clearer than the things which are now being shown to him?

True, he said.

And suppose once more, that he is reluctantly dragged up a steep and rugged ascent, and held fast until he is forced into the presence of the sun himself, is he not likely to be pained and irritated? When he approaches the light his eyes will be dazzled, and he will not be able to see anything at all of what are now called realities.

Not all in a moment, he said.

He will require to grow accustomed to the sight of the upper world. And first he will see the shadows best, next the reflections of men and other objects in the water, and then the objects themselves; then he will gaze upon the light of the moon and the stars and the spangled heaven; and he will see the sky and the stars by night better than the sun or the light of the sun by day?

Certainly.

Last of all he will be able to see the sun, and not mere reflections of him in the water, but he will see him in his own proper place, and not in another; and he will contemplate him as he is.

Certainly.

He will then proceed to argue that this is he who gives the season and the years, and is the guardian of all that is in the visible world, and in a certain way the cause of all things which he and his fellows have been accustomed to behold?

Clearly, he said, he would first see the sun and then reason about him.

And when he remembered his old habitation, and the wisdom of the den and his fellow-prisoners, do you not suppose that he would felicitate himself on the change, and pity him?

Certainly, he would.

And if they were in the habit of conferring honors among themselves on those who were quickest to observe the passing shadows and to remark which of them went before, and which followed after, and which were together; and who were therefore best able to draw conclusions as to the future, do you think that he would care for such honors and glories, or envy the possessors of them? Would he not say with Homer,

"Better to be the poor servant of a poor master,"

and to endure anything, rather than think as they do and live after their manner?

Yes, he said, I think that he would rather suffer anything than entertain these false notions and live in this miserable manner.

Imagine once more, I said, such a one coming suddenly out of the sun to be replaced in his old situation; would he not be certain to have his eyes full of darkness?

To be sure, he said.

And if there were a contest, and he had to compete in measuring the shadows with the prisoners who had never moved out of the den, while his sight was still weak, and before his eyes had become steady (and the time which would be needed to acquire this new habit of sight might be very considerable), would he not be ridiculous? Men would say of him that up he went and down he came without his eyes; and that it was better not even to think of ascending; and if anyone tried to loose another and lead him up to the light, let them only catch the offender, and they would put him to death.

No question, he said.

This entire allegory, I said, you may now append, dear Glaucon, to the previous argument; the prison-house is the world of sight, the light of the fire is the sun, and you will not misapprehend me if you interpret the journey upward to be the ascent of the soul into the intellectual world according to my poor belief, which, at your desire, I have expressed—whether rightly or wrongly, God knows. But, whether true or false, my opinion is that in the world of knowledge the idea of good appears last of all, and is seen only with an effort; and, when seen, is also inferred to be the universal author of all things beautiful and right, parent of light and of the lord of light in this visible world, and the immediate source of reason and truth in the intellectual; and that this is the power upon which he who would act rationally either in public or private life must have his eye fixed.

I agree, he said, as far as I am able to understand you.

Moreover, I said, you must not wonder that those who attain to this beatific vision are unwilling to descend to human affairs; for their souls are ever hastening into the upper world where they desire to dwell; which desire of theirs is very natural, if our allegory may be trusted.

Yes, very natural.

And is there anything surprising in one who passes from divine contemplations to the evil state of man, misbehaving himself in a ridiculous manner; if, while his eyes are blinking and before he has become accustomed to the surrounding darkness, he is compelled to fight in courts of law, or in other places, about the images or the shadows of images of justice, and is endeavoring to meet the conceptions of those who have never yet seen absolute justice?

Anything but surprising, he replied. Anyone who has common-sense will remember that the bewilderments of the eyes are of two kinds, and arise from two causes, either from coming out of the light or from going into the light, which is true of the mind's eye, quite as much as of the bodily eye; and he who remembers this when he sees anyone whose vision is perplexed and weak, will not be too ready to laugh; he will first ask whether that soul of man has come out of the brighter light, and is unable to see because unaccustomed to the dark, or having turned from darkness to the day is dazzled by excess of light. And he will count the one happy in his condition and state of being, and he will pity the other; or, if he have a mind to laugh at the soul which comes from below into the light, there will be more reason in this than in the laugh which greets him who returns from above out of the light into the den.

That, he said, is a very just distinction.

But then, if I am right, certain professors of education must be wrong when they say that they can put a knowledge into the soul which was not there before, like sight into blind eyes.

They undoubtedly say this, he replied.

Whereas, our argument shows that the power and capacity of learning exists in the soul already; and that just as the eye was unable to turn from darkness to light without the whole body, so too the instrument of knowledge can only by the movement of the whole soul be turned from the world of becoming into that of being, and learn by degrees to endure the sight of being, and of the brightest and best of being, or, in other words, of the good.

Very true.

And must there not be some art which will effect conversion in the easiest and quickest manner; not implanting the faculty of sight, for that exists already, but has been turned in the wrong direction, and is looking away from the truth?

Yes, he said, such an art may be presumed.

And whereas the other so-called virtues of the soul seem to be akin to bodily qualities, for even when they are not originally innate they can be implanted later by habit and exercise, the virtue of wisdom more than anything else contains a divine element which always remains, and by this conversion is rendered useful and profitable; or, on the other hand, hurtful and useless. Did you never observe the narrow intelligence flashing from the keen eye of a clever rogue—how eager he is, how clearly his paltry soul sees the way to his end; he is the reverse of blind, but his keen eyesight is forced into the service of evil, and he is mischievous in proportion to his cleverness?

Very true, he said.

But what if there had been a circumcision of such natures in the days of their youth; and they had been severed from those sensual pleasures, such as eating and drinking, which, like leaden weights, were attached to them at their birth, and which drag them down and turn the vision of their souls upon the things that are below—if, I say, they had been released from these impediments and turned in the opposite direction, the very same faculty in them would have seen the truth as keenly as they see what their eyes are turned to now.

Very likely.

Yes, I said; and there is another thing which is likely, or rather a necessary inference from what has preceded, that neither the uneducated and uninformed of the truth, nor yet those who never make an end of their education, will be able ministers of the State; not the former, because they have no single aim of duty which is the rule of all their actions, private as well as public; nor the latter, because they will not act at all except upon compulsion, fancying that they are already dwelling apart in the islands of the blessed.

Very true, he replied.

Then, I said, the business of us who are the founders of the State will be to compel the best minds to attain that knowledge which we have already shown to be the greatest of all—they must continue to ascend until they arrive at the good; but when they have ascended and seen enough we must not allow them to do as they do now.

What do you mean?

I mean that they remain in the upper world: but this must not be allowed; they must be made to descend again among the prisoners in the den, and partake of their labors and honors, whether they are worth having or not.

But is not this unjust? he said; ought we to give them a worse life, when they might have a better?

You have again forgotten, my friend, I said, the intention of the legislator, who did not aim at making any one class in the State happy above the rest; the happiness was to be in the whole State, and he held the citizens together by persuasion and necessity, making them benefactors of the State, and therefore benefactors of one another; to this end he created them, not to please themselves, but to be his instruments in binding up the State.

True, he said, I had forgotten.

Observe, Glaucon, that there will be no injustice in compelling our philosophers to have a care and providence of others; we shall explain to them that in other States, men of their class are not obliged to share in the toils of politics: and this is reasonable, for they grow up at their own sweet will, and the government would rather not have them. Being self-taught, they cannot be expected to show any gratitude for a culture which they have never received. But we have brought you into the world to be rulers of the hive, kings of yourselves and of the other citizens, and have educated you far better and more perfectly than they have been educated, and you are better able to share in the double duty. Wherefore each of you, when his turn comes, must go down to the general underground abode, and get the habit of seeing in the dark. When you have acquired the habit, you will see ten thousand times better than the inhabitants of the den, and you will know what the several images are, and what they represent, because you have seen the beautiful and just and good in their truth. And thus our State, which is also yours, will be a reality, and not a dream only, and will be administered in a spirit unlike that of other States, in which men fight with one another about shadows only and are distracted in the struggle for power, which in their eyes is a great good. Whereas the truth is that the State in which the rulers are most reluctant to govern is always the best and most quietly governed, and the State in which they are most eager, the worst.

Quite true, he replied.

And will our pupils, when they hear this, refuse to take their turn at the toils of State, when they are allowed to spend the greater part of their time with one another in the heavenly light?

Impossible, he answered; for they are just men, and the commands which we impose upon them are just; there can be no doubt that every one of them will take office as a stern necessity, and not after the fashion of our present rulers of State.

Yes, my friend, I said; and there lies the point. You must contrive for your future rulers another and a better life than that of a ruler, and then you may have a well-ordered State; for only in the State which offers this, will they rule who are truly rich, not in silver and gold, but in virtue and wisdom, which are the true blessings of life. Whereas, if they go to the administration of public affairs, poor and hungering after their own private advantage, thinking that hence they are to snatch the chief good, order there can never be; for they will be fighting about office, and the civil and domestic broils which thus arise will be the ruin of the rulers themselves and of the whole State.

Most true, he replied.

And the only life which looks down upon the life of political ambition is that of true philosophy. Do you know of any other?

Indeed, I do not, he said.

And those who govern ought not to be lovers of the task? For, if they are, there will be rival lovers, and they will fight.

No question. Who, then, are those whom we shall compel to be guardians? Surely they will be the men who are wisest about affairs of State, and by whom the State is best administered, and who at the same time have other honors and another and a better life than that of politics?

They are the men, and I will choose them, he replied.

And now shall we consider in what way such guardians will be produced, and how they are to be brought from darkness to light—as some are said to have ascended from the world below to the gods?

By all means, he replied.

The process, I said, is not the turning over of an oystershell, but the turning round of a soul passing from a day which is little better than night to the true day of being, that is, the ascent from below, which we affirm to be true philosophy?

Quite so.

The Enchiridion, or Manual*

Epictetus

I. Of things some are in our power, and others are not. In our power are opinion, movement toward a thing, desire, aversion (turning from a thing); and in a word, whatever are our own acts: not in our power are the body, property, reputation, offices (magisterial power), and in a word, whatever are not our own acts. And the things in our power are by nature free, not subject to restraint nor hindrance: but the things not in our power are weak, slavish, subject to restraint, in the control of others. Remember then that if you think the things which are by nature slavish to be free, and the things which are in the power of others to be your own, you will be hindered, you will lament, you will be disturbed, you will blame both gods and men: but if you think that only which is your own to be your own, and if you think that what is another's, as it really is, belongs to another, no man will ever compel you, no man will hinder you, you will never blame any man, you will accuse no man, you will do nothing involuntarily (against your will), no man will harm you, you will have no enemy, for you will not suffer any harm.

III. In everything which pleases the soul, or supplies a want, or is loved, remember to add this to the (description, notion); what is the nature of each thing, beginning from the smallest? If you love an earthen vessel, say it is an earthen vessel which you love; for when it has been broken, you will not be disturbed. If you are kissing your child or wife, say that it is a human being whom you are kissing, for when the wife or child dies, you will not be disturbed.

IV. When you are going to take in hand any act, remind yourself what kind of an act it is. If you are going to bathe, place before yourself what happens in the bath: some splashing the water, others pushing against one another, others abusing one another, and some stealing; and thus with more safety you will undertake the matter, if you say to yourself, I now intend to bathe, and to maintain my will in a manner conformable to nature. And so you will do in every act: for thus if any hindrance to bathing shall happen, let this thought be ready; it was not this only that I intended, but I intended also to maintain my will in a way conformable to nature; but I shall not maintain it so, if I am vexed at what happens.

V. Men are disturbed not by the things which happen, but by the opinions about the things: for example, death is nothing terrible, for if it were, it would have seemed so to Socrates; for the opinion about death, that it is terrible, is the

*From *The Discourses of Epictetus, with the Encheridion and Fragments*, translated by George Long (George Bell, 1877).

terrible thing. When then we are impeded or disturbed or grieved, let us never blame others, but ourselves, that is, our opinions. It is the act of an ill-instructed man to blame others for his own bad condition; it is the act of one who has begun to be instructed, to lay the blame on himself; and of one whose instruction is completed, neither to blame another, nor himself.

VIII. Seek not that the things which happen should happen as you wish; but wish the things which happen to be as they are, and you will have a tranquil flow of life.

XI. Never say about anything, I have lost it, but say I have restored it. Is your child dead? It has been restored. Is your wife dead? She has been restored. Has your estate been taken from you? Has not then this also been restored? But he who has taken it from me is a bad man. But what is it to you, by whose hands the giver demanded it back? So long as he may allow you, take care of it as a thing which belongs to another, as travelers do with their inn.

XIV. If you would have your children and your wife and your friends to live forever, you are silly; for you would have the things which are not in your power to be in your power, and the things which belong to others to be yours. So if you would have your slave to be free from faults, you are a fool; for you would have badness not to be badness, but something else. But if you wish not to fail in your desires, you are able to do that. Practice then this which you are able to do. He is the master of every man who has the power over the things, which another person wishes or does not wish, the power to confer them on him or to take them away. Whoever then wishes to be free, let him neither wish for anything nor avoid anything which depends on others: if he does not observe this rule, he must be a slave.

XIX. You can be invincible, if you enter into no contest in which it is not in your power to conquer. Take care then when you observe a man honored before others or possessed of great power or highly esteemed for any reason, not to suppose him happy, and be not carried away by the appearance. For if the nature of the good is in our power, neither envy nor jealousy will have a place in us. But you yourself will not wish to be a general or senator or consul, but a free man: and there is only one way to this, to despise (care not for) the things which are not in our power.

XX. Remember that it is not he who reviles you or strikes you, who insults you, but it is your opinion about these things as being insulting. When then a man irritates you, you must know that it is your own opinion which has irritated you. Therefore especially try not to be carried away by the appearance. For if you once gain time and delay, you will more easily master yourself.

XXI. Let death and exile and every other thing which appears dreadful be daily before your eyes; but most of all death: and you will never think of anything mean nor will you desire anything extravagantly.

XXII. If you desire philosophy, prepare yourself from the beginning to be ridiculed, to expect that many will sneer at you, and say, He has all at once returned to us as a philosopher; and whence does he get this supercilious look for us? Do you not show a supercilious look; but hold on to the things which seem to you best as one appointed by God to this station. And remember that if you abide in the same principles, these men who first ridiculed will afterward admire you: but if you shall have been overpowered by them, you will bring on yourself double ridicule.

XXIII. If it should ever happen to you to be turned to externals in order to please some person, you must know that you have lost your purpose in life. Be satisfied then in everything with being a philosopher; and if you wish to seem also to any person to be a philosopher, appear so to yourself, and you will be able to do this.

XXXIII. Immediately prescribe some character and some form to yourself, which you shall observe both when you are alone and when you meet with men.

And let silence be the general rule, or let only what is necessary be said, and in few words. And rarely and when the occasion calls we shall say something; but about none of the common subjects, nor about gladiators, nor horse-races, nor about athletes, nor about eating or drinking, which are the usual subjects; and especially not about men, as blaming them or praising them, or comparing them. If then you are able, bring over by your conversation the conversation of your associates to that which is proper; but if you should happen to be confined to the company of strangers, be silent.

Let not your laughter be much, nor on many occasions, nor excessive.

Refuse altogether to take an oath, if it is possible: if it is not, refuse as far as you are able.

Avoids banquets which are given by strangers and by ignorant persons. But if ever there is occasion to join in them, let your attention be carefully fixed, that you slip not into the manners of the vulgar (the uninstructed). For you must know, that if your companion be impure, he also who keeps company with him must become impure, though he should happen to be pure.

Take (apply) the things which relate to the body as far as the bare use, as food, drink, clothing, house, and slaves: but exclude everything which is for show or luxury.

As to pleasure with women, abstain as far as you can before marriage: but if you do indulge in it, do it in the way which is conformable to custom. Do not however be disagreeable to those who indulge in these pleasures, or reprove them; and do not often boast that you do not indulge in them yourself.

XXXV. When you have decided that a thing ought to be done and are doing it, never avoid being seen doing it, though the many shall form an unfavorable opinion about it. For if it is not right to do it, avoid doing the thing; but if it is right, why are you afraid of those who shall find fault wrongly?

XXXVIII. In walking about as you take care not to step on a nail or to sprain your foot, so take care not to damage your own ruling faculty: and if we observe this rule in every act, we shall undertake the act with more security.

XLIV. These reasonings do not cohere: I am richer than you, therefore I am better than you; I am more eloquent than you, therefore I am better than you. On the contrary these rather cohere, I am richer than you, therefore my possessions are greater than yours: I am more eloquent than you, therefore my speech is superior to yours. But you are neither possession nor speech.

XLVIII. The condition and characteristic of an uninstructed person is this: he never expects from himself profit (advantage) nor harm, but from externals. The condition and characteristic of a philosopher is this: he expects all advantage and all harm from himself. The signs (marks) of one who is making progress are these: he censures no man, he praises no man, he blames no man, he accuses no man, he says nothing about himself as if he were somebody or knew something; when he is impeded at all or hindered, he blames himself: if a man praises him, he ridicules the praiser to himself: if a man censures him, he makes no defense: he goes about like weak persons, being careful not to move any of the things which are placed, before they are firmly fixed: he removes all desire from himself, and he transfers aversion to those things only of the things within our power which are contrary to nature: he employs a moderate movement toward everything: whether he is considered foolish or ignorant, he cares not: and in a word he watches himself as if he were an enemy and lying in ambush.

The Tao Te Ching*

Lao-Tzu

Part I

1

1. The Tao that can be trodden is not the enduring and unchanging Tao. The name that can be named is not the enduring and unchanging name.

2. (Conceived of as) having no name, it is the Originator of heaven and earth; (conceived of as) having a name, it is the Mother of all things.

*From *The Texts of Taoism*, translated by James Legge in *Sacred Books of the East*, edited by Max Müller (Oxford: Clarendon Press, 1891).

3. Always without desire we must be found,
If its deep mystery we would sound;
But if desire always within us be,
Its outer fringe is all that we shall see.

4. Under these two aspects, it is really the same; but as development takes place, it receives the different names. Together we call them the Mystery. Where the Mystery is the deepest is the gate of all that is subtle and wonderful.

2

1. All in the world know the beauty of the beautiful, and in doing this they have (the idea of) what ugliness is; they all know the skill of the skilful, and in doing this they have (the idea of) what the want of skill is.

2. So it is that existence and non-existence give birth the one to (the idea of) the other; that difficulty and ease produce the one (the idea of) the other; that length and shortness fashion out the one the figure of the other; that (the ideas of) height and lowness arise from the contrast of the one with the other; that the musical notes and tones become harmonious through the relation of one with another; and that being before and behind give the idea of one following another.

3. Therefore the sage manages affairs without doing anything, and conveys his instructions without the use of speech.

4. All things spring up, and there is not one which declines to show itself; they grow, and there is no claim made for their ownership; they go through their processes, and there is no expectation (of a reward for the results). The work is accomplished, and there is no resting in it (as an achievement). The work is done, but how no one can see; 'Tis this that makes the power not cease to be.

3

1. Not to value and employ men of superior ability is the way to keep the people from rivalry among themselves; not to prize articles which are difficult to procure is the way to keep them from becoming thieves; not to show them what is likely to excite their desires is the way to keep their minds from disorder.

2. Therefore the sage, in the exercise of his government, empties their minds, fills their bellies, weakens their wills, and strengthens their bones.

3. He constantly (tries to) keep them without knowledge and without desire, and where there are those who have knowledge, to keep them from presuming to act (on it). When there is this abstinence from action, good order is universal.

4

1. The Tao is (like) the emptiness of a vessel; and in our employment of it we must be on our guard against all fulness. How deep and unfathomable it is, as if it were the Honoured Ancestor of all things!

2. We should blunt our sharp points, and unravel the complications of things; we should attemper our brightness, and bring ourselves into agreement with the obscurity of others. How pure and still the Tao is, as if it would ever so continue!

3. I do not know whose son it is. It might appear to have been before God.

5

1. Heaven and earth do not act from (the impulse of) any wish to be benevolent; they deal with all things as the dogs of grass are dealt with. The sages do not act from (any wish to be) benevolent; they deal with the people as the dogs of grass are dealt with.

2. May not the space between heaven and earth be compared to a bellows?

'Tis emptied, yet it loses not its power;
'Tis moved again, and sends forth air the more.
Much speech to swift exhaustion lead we see;
Your inner being guard, and keep it free.

6

The valley spirit dies not, aye the same; The female mystery thus do we name. Its gate, from which at first they issued forth, Is called the root from which grew heaven and earth. Long and unbroken does its power remain, Used gently, and without the touch of pain.

7

1. Heaven is long-enduring and earth continues long. The reason why heaven and earth are able to endure and continue thus long is because they do not live of, or for, themselves. This is how they are able to continue and endure.

2. Therefore the sage puts his own person last, and yet it is found in the foremost place; he treats his person as if it were foreign to him, and yet that person is preserved. Is it not because he has no personal and private ends, that therefore such ends are realised?

8

1. The highest excellence is like (that of) water. The excellence of water appears in its benefiting all things, and in its occupying, without striving (to the contrary), the low place which all men dislike. Hence (its way) is near to (that of) the Tao.

2. The excellence of a residence is in (the suitability of) the place; that of the mind is in abysmal stillness; that of associations is in their being with the virtuous; that of government is in its securing good order; that of (the conduct

of) affairs is in its ability; and that of (the initiation of) any movement is in its timeliness.

3. And when (one with the highest excellence) does not wrangle (about his low position), no one finds fault with him.

9

1. It is better to leave a vessel unfilled, than to attempt to carry it when it is full. If you keep feeling a point that has been sharpened, the point cannot long preserve its sharpness.

2. When gold and jade fill the hall, their possessor cannot keep them safe. When wealth and honours lead to arrogancy, this brings its evil on itself. When the work is done, and one's name is becoming distinguished, to withdraw into obscurity is the way of Heaven.

10

1. When the intelligent and animal souls are held together in one embrace, they can be kept from separating. When one gives undivided attention to the (vital) breath, and brings it to the utmost degree of pliancy, he can become as a (tender) babe. When he has cleansed away the most mysterious sights (of his imagination), he can become without a flaw.

2. In loving the people and ruling the state, cannot he proceed without any (purpose of) action? In the opening and shutting of his gates of heaven, cannot he do so as a female bird? While his intelligence reaches in every direction, cannot he (appear to) be without knowledge?

3. (The Tao) produces (all things) and nourishes them; it produces them and does not claim them as its own; it does all, and yet does not boast of it; it presides over all, and yet does not control them.This is what is called 'The mysterious Quality' (of the Tao).

11

1. The thirty spokes unite in the one nave; but it is on the empty space (for the axle), that the use of the wheel depends. Clay is fashioned into vessels; but it is on their empty hollowness, that their use depends. The door and windows are cut out (from the walls) to form an apartment; but it is on the empty space (within), that its use depends. Therefore, what has a (positive) existence serves for profitable adaptation, and what has not that for (actual) usefulness.

14

1. We look at it, and we do not see it, and we name it 'the Equable.' We listen to it, and we do not hear it, and we name it 'the Inaudible.' We try to grasp it, and do not get hold of it, and we name it 'the Subtle.' With these three

qualities, it cannot be made the subject of description; and hence we blend them together and obtain The One.

2. Its upper part is not bright, and its lower part is not obscure. Ceaseless in its action, it yet cannot be named, and then it again returns and becomes nothing. This is called the Form of the Formless, and the Semblance of the Invisible; this is called the Fleeting and Indeterminable.

3. We meet it and do not see its Front; we follow it, and do not see its Back. When we can lay hold of the Tao of old to direct the things of the present day, and are able to know it as it was of old in the beginning, this is called (unwinding) the clue of Tao.

15

1. The skilful masters (of the Tao) in old times, with a subtle and exquisite penetration, comprehended its mysteries, and were deep (also) so as to elude men's knowledge. As they were thus beyond men's knowledge, I will make an effort to describe of what sort they appeared to be.

2. Shrinking looked they like those who wade through a stream in winter; irresolute like those who are afraid of all around them; grave like a guest (in awe of his host); evanescent like ice that is melting away; unpretentious like wood that has not been fashioned into anything; vacant like a valley, and dull like muddy water.

3. Who can (make) the muddy water (clear)? Let it be still, and it will gradually become clear. Who can secure the condition of rest? Let movement go on, and the condition of rest will gradually arise.

4. They who preserve this method of the Tao do not wish to be full (of themselves). It is through their not being full of themselves that they can afford to seem worn and not appear new and complete.

16

1. The (state of) vacancy should be brought to the utmost degree, and that of stillness guarded with unwearying vigour. All things alike go through their processes of activity, and (then) we see them return (to their original state). When things (in the vegetable world) have displayed their luxuriant growth, we see each of them return to its root. This returning to their root is what we call the state of stillness; and that stillness may be called a reporting that they have fulfilled their appointed end.

2. The report of that fulfilment is the regular, unchanging rule. To know that unchanging rule is to be intelligent; not to know it leads to wild movements and evil issues. The knowledge of that unchanging rule produces a (grand) capacity and forbearance, and that capacity and forbearance lead to a community (of feeling with all things).

From this community of feeling comes a kingliness of character; and he who is king-like goes on to be heaven-like. In that likeness to heaven he possesses the Tao. Possessed of the Tao, he endures long; and to the end of his bodily life, is exempt from all danger of decay.

18

1. When the Great Tao (Way or Method) ceased to be observed, benevolence and righteousness came into vogue. (Then) appeared wisdom and shrewdness, and there ensued great hypocrisy.

2. When harmony no longer prevailed throughout the six kinships, filial sons found their manifestation; when the states and clans fell into disorder, loyal ministers appeared.

19

1. If we could renounce our sageness and discard our wisdom, it would be better for the people a hundredfold. If we could renounce our benevolence and discard our righteousness, the people would again become filial and kindly. If we could renounce our artful contrivances and discard our (scheming for) gain, there would be no thieves nor robbers.

2. Those three methods (of government)
Thought olden ways in elegance did fail
And made these names their want of worth to veil;
But simple views, and courses plain and true
Would selfish ends and many lusts eschew.

20

1. When we renounce learning we have no troubles.
The (ready) 'yes,' and (flattering) 'yea;'—
Small is the difference they display.
But mark their issues, good and ill;—
What space the gulf between shall fill?

What all men fear is indeed to be feared; but how wide and without end is the range of questions (asking to be discussed)!

2. The multitude of men look satisfied and pleased; as if enjoying a full banquet, as if mounted on a tower in spring. I alone seem listless and still, my desires having as yet given no indication of their presence. I am like an infant which has not yet smiled. I look dejected and forlorn, as if I had no home to go to. The multitude of men all have enough and to spare. I alone seem to have lost everything. My mind is that of a stupid man; I am in a state of chaos.

Ordinary men look bright and intelligent, while I alone seem to be benighted. They look full of discrimination, while I alone am dull and confused.

I seem to be carried about as on the sea, drifting as if I had nowhere to rest. All men have their spheres of action, while I alone seem dull and incapable, like a rude borderer. (Thus) I alone am different from other men, but I value the nursing-mother (the Tao).

21

The grandest forms of active force
From Tao come, their only source.
Who can of Tao the nature tell?
Our sight it flies, our touch as well.
Eluding sight, eluding touch,
The forms of things all in it crouch;
Eluding touch, eluding sight,
There are their semblances, all right.
Profound it is, dark and obscure;
Things' essences all there endure.
Those essences the truth enfold
Of what, when seen, shall then be told.
Now it is so; 'twas so of old.
Its name—what passes not away;
So, in their beautiful array,
Things form and never know decay.

How know I that it is so with all the beauties of existing things? By this (nature of the Tao).

22

1. The partial becomes complete; the crooked, straight; the empty, full; the worn out, new. He whose (desires) are few gets them; he whose (desires) are many goes astray.

2. Therefore the sage holds in his embrace the one thing (of humility), and manifests it to all the world. He is free from self-display, and therefore he shines; from self-assertion, and therefore he is distinguished; from self-boasting, and therefore his merit is acknowledged; from self-complacency, and therefore he acquires superiority. It is because he is thus free from striving that therefore no one in the world is able to strive with him.

3. That saying of the ancients that 'the partial becomes complete' was not vainly spoken:—all real completion is comprehended under it.

24

He who stands on his tiptoes does not stand firm; he who stretches his legs does not walk (easily). (So), he who displays himself does not shine; he who asserts his own views is not distinguished; he who vaunts himself does not find his merit acknowledged; he who is self-conceited has no superiority allowed to him. Such conditions, viewed from the standpoint of the Tao, are like remnants of food, or a tumour on the body, which all dislike. Hence those who pursue (the course) of the Tao do not adopt and allow them.

25

1. There was something undefined and complete, coming into existence before Heaven and Earth. How still it was and formless, standing alone, and undergoing no change, reaching everywhere and in no danger (of being exhausted)! It may be regarded as the Mother of all things.

2. I do not know its name, and I give it the designation of the Tao (the Way or Course). Making an effort (further) to give it a name I call it The Great.

3. Great, it passes on (in constant flow). Passing on, it becomes remote. Having become remote, it returns. Therefore the Tao is great; Heaven is great; Earth is great; and the (sage) king is also great. In the universe there are four that are great, and the (sage) king is one of them.

4. Man takes his law from the Earth; the Earth takes its law from Heaven; Heaven takes its law from the Tao. The law of the Tao is its being what it is.

28

1.

Who knows his manhood's strength,
Yet still his female feebleness maintains;
As to one channel flow the many drains,
All come to him, yea, all beneath the sky.
Thus he the constant excellence retains;
The simple child again, free from all stains.
Who knows how white attracts,
Yet always keeps himself within black's shade,
The pattern of humility displayed,
Displayed in view of all beneath the sky;
He in the unchanging excellence arrayed,
Endless return to man's first state has made.
Who knows how glory shines,
Yet loves disgrace, nor e'er for it is pale;
Behold his presence in a spacious vale,
To which men come from all beneath the sky.
The unchanging excellence completes its tale;
The simple infant man in him we hail.

2. The unwrought material, when divided and distributed, forms vessels. The sage, when employed, becomes the Head of all the Officers (of government); and in his greatest regulations he employs no violent measures.

33

1. He who knows other men is discerning; he who knows himself is intelligent. He who overcomes others is strong; he who overcomes himself is mighty. He who is satisfied with his lot is rich; he who goes on acting with energy has a (firm) will.

2. He who does not fail in the requirements of his position, continues long; he who dies and yet does not perish, has longevity.

34

1. All-pervading is the Great Tao! It may be found on the left hand and on the right.

2. All things depend on it for their production, which it gives to them, not one refusing obedience to it. When its work is accomplished, it does not claim the name of having done it. It clothes all things as with a garment, and makes no assumption of being their lord;—it may be named in the smallest things. All things return (to their root and disappear), and do not know that it is it which presides over their doing so;—it may be named in the greatest things.

3. Hence the sage is able (in the same way) to accomplish his great achievements. It is through his not making himself great that he can accomplish them.

37

1. The Tao in its regular course does nothing (for the sake of doing it), and so there is nothing which it does not do.

2. If princes and kings were able to maintain it, all things would of themselves be transformed by them.

3. If this transformation became to me an object of desire, I would express the desire by the nameless simplicity.

> Simplicity without a name
> Is free from all external aim.
> With no desire, at rest and still,
> All things go right as of their will.

Part II

40

1.
> The movement of the Tao
> By contraries proceeds;
> And weakness marks the course
> Of Tao's mighty deeds.

2. All things under heaven sprang from It as existing (and named); that existence sprang from It as non-existent (and not named).

41

1. Scholars of the highest class, when they hear about the Tao, earnestly carry it into practice. Scholars of the middle class, when they have heard about it, seem now to keep it and now to lose it.

Scholars of the lowest class, when they have heard about it, laugh greatly at it. If it were not (thus) laughed at, it would not be fit to be the Tao.

2. Therefore the sentence-makers have thus expressed themselves:—

'The Tao, when brightest seen, seems light to lack;
Who progress in it makes, seems drawing back;
Its even way is like a rugged track.
Its highest virtue from the vale doth rise;
Its greatest beauty seems to offend the eyes;
And he has most whose lot the least supplies.
Its firmest virtue seems but poor and low;
Its solid truth seems change to undergo;
Its largest square doth yet no corner show
A vessel great, it is the slowest made;
Loud is its sound, but never word it said;
A semblance great, the shadow of a shade.'

3. The Tao is hidden, and has no name; but it is the Tao which is skilful at imparting (to all things what they need) and making them complete.

42

1. The Tao produced One; One produced Two; Two produced Three; Three produced All things. All things leave behind them the Obscurity (out of which they have come), and go forward to embrace the Brightness (into which they have emerged), while they are harmonised by the Breath of Vacancy.

2. What men dislike is to be orphans, to have little virtue, to be as carriages without naves; and yet these are the designations which kings and princes use for themselves. So it is that some things are increased by being diminished, and others are diminished by being increased.

3. What other men (thus) teach, I also teach. The violent and strong do not die their natural death. I will make this the basis of my teaching.

43

1. The softest thing in the world dashes against and overcomes the hardest; that which has no (substantial) existence enters where there is no crevice. I know hereby what advantage belongs to doing nothing (with a purpose).

2. There are few in the world who attain to the teaching without words, and the advantage arising from non-action.

47

1. Without going outside his door, one understands (all that takes place) under the sky; without looking out from his window, one sees the Tao of Heaven. The farther that one goes out (from himself), the less he knows.

2. Therefore the sages got their knowledge without travelling; gave their (right) names to things without seeing them; and accomplished their ends without any purpose of doing so.

48

1. He who devotes himself to learning (seeks) from day to day to increase (his knowledge); he who devotes himself to the Tao (seeks) from day to day to diminish (his doing).

2. He diminishes it and again diminishes it, till he arrives at doing nothing (on purpose). Having arrived at this point of non-action, there is nothing which he does not do.

3. He who gets as his own all under heaven does so by giving himself no trouble (with that end). If one take trouble (with that end), he is not equal to getting as his own all under heaven.

52

1. (The Tao) which originated all under the sky is to be considered as the mother of them all.

2. When the mother is found, we know what her children should be. When one knows that he is his mother's child, and proceeds to guard (the qualities of) the mother that belong to him, to the end of his life he will be free from all peril.

3. Let him keep his mouth closed, and shut up the portals (of his nostrils), and all his life he will be exempt from laborious exertion.

Let him keep his mouth open, and (spend his breath) in the promotion
of his affairs, and all his life there will be no safety for him.

4. The perception of what is small is (the secret of clear-sightedness; the guarding of what is soft and tender is (the secret of) strength.

5. Who uses well his light,
Reverting to its (source so) bright,
Will from his body ward all blight,
And hides the unchanging from men's sight.

55

1. He who has in himself abundantly the attributes (of the Tao) is like an infant. Poisonous insects will not sting him; fierce beasts will not seize him; birds of prey will not strike him.

2. (The infant's) bones are weak and its sinews soft, but yet its grasp is firm. It knows not yet the union of male and female, and yet its virile member may be excited;—showing the perfection of its physical essence. All day long it will cry without its throat becoming hoarse;—showing the harmony (in its constitution).

3. To him by whom this harmony is known,
(The secret of) the unchanging (Tao) is shown,
And in the knowledge wisdom finds its throne.
All life-increasing arts to evil turn;
Where the mind makes the vital breath to burn,
(False) is the strength, (and o'er it we should mourn.)

4. When things have become strong, they (then) become old, which may be said to be contrary to the Tao. Whatever is contrary to the Tao soon ends.

56

1. He who knows (the Tao) does not (care to) speak (about it); he who is (ever ready to) speak about it does not know it.

2. He (who knows it) will keep his mouth shut and close the portals (of his nostrils). He will blunt his sharp points and unravel the complications of things; he will attemper his brightness, and bring himself into agreement with the obscurity (of others). This is called 'the Mysterious Agreement.'

3. (Such an one) cannot be treated familiarly or distantly; he is beyond all consideration of profit or injury; of nobility or meanness:—he is the noblest man under heaven.

70

1. My words are very easy to know, and very easy to practise; but there is no one in the world who is able to know and able to practise them.

2. There is an originating and all-comprehending (principle) in my words, and an authoritative law for the things (which I enforce). It is because they do not know these, that men do not know me.

3. They who know me are few, and I am on that account (the more) to be prized. It is thus that the sage wears (a poor garb of) hair cloth, while he carries his (signet of) jade in his bosom.

76

1. Man at his birth is supple and weak; at his death, firm and strong. (So it is with) all things. Trees and plants, in their early growth, are soft and brittle; at their death, dry and withered.

2. Thus it is that firmness and strength are the concomitants of death; softness and weakness, the concomitants of life.

3. Hence he who (relies on) the strength of his forces does not conquer; and a tree which is strong will fill the out-stretched arms, (and thereby invites the feller.)

4. Therefore the place of what is firm and strong is below, and that of what is soft and weak is above.

81

1. Sincere words are not fine; fine words are not sincere. Those who are skilled (in the Tao) do not dispute (about it); the disputatious are not skilled in it. Those who know (the Tao) are not extensively learned; the extensively learned do not know it.

2. The sage does not accumulate (for himself). The more that he expends for others, the more does he possess of his own; the more that he gives to others, the more does he have himself.

3. With all the sharpness of the Way of Heaven, it injures not; with all the doing in the way of the sage he does not strive.

The Ethic of Compassion*

The Dalai Lama

All the world's major religions stress the importance of cultivating love and compassion. In the Buddhist philosophical tradition, different levels of attainment are described. At a basic level, compassion *(nying je)* is understood mainly in terms of empathy—our ability enter into and, to some extent, share others' suffering. But Buddhists—and perhaps others—believe that this can be developed to such a degree that not only does our compassion arise without any effort, but it is unconditional, undifferentiated, and universal in scope. A feeling of intimacy toward all other sentient beings, including of course those who would harm us, is generated, which is likened in the literature to the love a mother has for her only child.

But this sense of equanimity toward all others is not seen as an end in itself. Rather, it is seen as the springboard to a love still greater. Because our capacity for empathy is innate, and because the ability to reason is also an innate faculty, compassion shares the characteristics of consciousness itself. The potential we have to develop it is therefore stable and continuous. It is not a resource which can be used up—as water is used up when we boil it. And though it can be

*From *Ethics for the New Millennium* by Dalai Lama and Alexander Norman. Copyright © 1999 by His Holiness The Dalai Lama. Used by permission of Riverhead Books, an imprint of Penguin Group (USA) Inc.

described in terms of activity, it is not like a physical activity which we train for, like jumping, where once we reach a certain height we can go no further. On the contrary, when we enhance our sensitivity toward others' suffering through deliberately opening ourselves up to it, it is believed that we can gradually extend out compassion to the point where the individual feels so moved by even the subtlest suffering of others that they come to have an overwhelming sense of responsibility toward those others. This causes the one who is compassionate to dedicate themselves entirely to helping others overcome both their suffering and the causes of their suffering. In Tibetan, this ultimate level of attainment is called *nying je chenmo*, literally "great compassion."

Now I am not suggesting that each individual must attain these advanced states of spiritual development in order to lead an ethically wholesome life, I have described *nying je chenmo* not because it is a precondition of ethical conduct but rather because I believe that pushing the logic of compassion to the highest level can act as a powerful inspiration. If we can just keep the aspiration to develop *nying je chenmo*, or great compassion, as an ideal, it will naturally have a significant impact on our outlook. Based on the simple recognition that, just as I do, so do all others desire to be happy and not to suffer, it will serve as a constant reminder against selfishness and partiality. It will remind us that if we reserve ethical conduct for those whom we feel close to, the danger is that we will neglect our responsibilities toward those outside this circle. It will remind us that there is little to be gained from being kind and generous because we hope to win something in return. It will remind us that actions motivated by the desire to create a good name for ourselves are still selfish, however much they may appear to be acts of kindness. It will also remind us that there is nothing exceptional about acts of charity toward those we already feel close to. And it will help us to recognize that the bias we naturally feel toward our families and friends is actually a highly unreliable thing on which to base ethical conduct.

Why is this? So long as the individuals in question continue to meet our expectations, all is well. But should they fail to do so, someone we consider a dear friend one day can become our sworn enemy the next. As we saw earlier, we have a tendency to react badly to all who threaten fulfillment of our cherished desires, though they may be our closest relations. For this reason, compassion and mutual respect offer a much more solid basis for our relations with others. This is also true of partnerships. Likewise, if our love for someone is based largely on attraction, whether it be their looks or some other superficial characteristic, our feelings for that person are liable, over time, to evaporate. When they lose the quality we found alluring, or when we find ourselves no longer satisfied by it, the situation can change completely, this despite their being the same person. This is why relationships based purely on attraction are almost always unstable. On the other hand, when we begin to perfect our compassion, neither the other's appearance nor their behavior affects our underlying attitude.

Consider, too, that habitually our feelings toward others depend very much on their circumstances. Most people, when they see someone who is handicapped, feel sympathetic toward that person. But then when they see others who are wealthier, or better educated, or better placed socially, they immediately feel envious and competitive toward them. Our negative feelings prevent us from seeing the sameness of ourselves and all others. We forget that just like us, whether fortunate or unfortunate, distant or near, they desire to be happy and not to suffer.

The struggle is thus to overcome these feelings of partiality. Certainly, developing genuine compassion for our loved ones is the obvious and appropriate place to start. The impact our actions have on our close ones will generally be much greater than on others, and therefore our responsibilities toward them are greater. Yet we need to recognize that, ultimately, there are no grounds for discriminating in their favor. In this sense, we are all in the same position as a doctor confronted by ten patients suffering the same serious illness. They are each equally deserving of treatment. The reader should not suppose that what is being advocated here is a state of detached indifference, however. The further essential challenge, as we begin to extend our compassion toward all others, is to maintain the same level of intimacy as we feel toward those closest to us. In other words, what is being suggested is that we need to strive, for even-handedness in our approach toward all others, a level ground into which we can plant the seed of *nying je chenmo*, of great love and compassion.

If we can begin to relate to others on the basis of such equanimity, our compassion will not depend on the fact that so and so is my husband, my wife, my relative, my friend. Rather, a feeling of closeness toward all others can be developed based on the simple recognition that, just like myself, all wish to be happy and to avoid suffering. In other words, we will start to relate to others on the basis of their sentient nature. Again, we can think of this in terms of an ideal, one which it is immensely difficult to attain. But, for myself, I find it one which is profoundly inspiring and helpful.

Let us now consider the role of compassionate love and kind-heartedness in our daily lives. Does the ideal of developing it to the point where it is unconditional mean that we must abandon our own interests entirely? Not at all. In fact, it is the best way of serving them—indeed, it could even be said to constitute the wisest course for fulfilling self-interest. For if it is correct that those qualities such as love, patience, tolerance, and forgiveness are what happiness consists in, and if it is also correct that *nying je*, or compassion, as I have defined it, is both the source and the fruit of these qualities, then the more we are compassionate, the more we provide for our own happiness. Thus, any idea that concern for others, though a noble quality, is a matter for our private lives only, is simply shortsighted. Compassion belongs to every sphere of activity, including, of course, the workplace.

Here, though, I must acknowledge the existence of a perception—shared by many, it seems—that compassion is, if not actually an impediment, at least irrelevant to professional life. Personally, I would argue that not only is it relevant, but that when compassion is lacking, our activities are in danger of becoming destructive. This is because when we ignore the question of the impact our actions have on others' well-being, inevitably we end up hurting them. The ethic of compassion helps provide the necessary foundation and motivation for both restraint and the cultivation of virtue. When we begin to develop a genuine appreciation of the value of compassion, our outlook on others begins automatically to change. This alone can serve as a powerful influence on the conduct of our lives. When, for example, the temptation to deceive others arises, our compassion for them will prevent us from entertaining the idea. And when we realize that our work itself is in danger of being exploited to the detriment of others, compassion will cause us to disengage from it. So to take an imaginary case of a scientist whose research seems likely to be a source of suffering, they will recognize this and act accordingly, even if this means abandoning the project.

I do not deny that genuine problems can arise when we dedicate ourselves to the ideal of compassion. In the case of a scientist who felt unable to continue in the direction their work was taking them, this could have profound consequences both for themselves and for their families. Likewise, those engaged in the caring professions—in medicine, counseling, social work, and so on—or even those looking after someone at home may sometimes become so exhausted by their duties that they feel overwhelmed. Constant exposure to suffering, coupled occasionally with a feeling of being taken for granted, can induce feelings of helplessness and even despair. Or it can happen that individuals may find themselves performing outwardly generous actions merely for the sake of it—simply going through the motions, as it were. Of course this is better than nothing. But when left unchecked, this can lead to insensitivity toward others' suffering. If this starts to happen, it is best to disengage for a short while and make a deliberate effort to reawaken that sensitivity. In this it can be helpful to remember that despair is never a solution. It is, rather, the ultimate failure. Therefore, as the Tibetan expression has it, even if the rope breaks nine times, we must splice it back together a tenth time. In this way, even if ultimately we do fail, at least there will be no feelings of regret. And when we combine this insight with a clear appreciation of our potential to benefit others, we find that we can begin to restore our hope and confidence.

Some people may object to this ideal on the grounds that by entering into others' suffering, we bring suffering on ourselves. To an extent, this is true. But I suggest that there is an important qualitative distinction to be made between experiencing one's own suffering and experiencing suffering in the course of sharing in others'. In the case of one's own suffering, given that it is involuntary, there is a sense of oppression: it seems to come from outside us. By contrast, sharing in someone else's suffering must at some level involve a degree of voluntariness, which itself is indicative of a certain inner strength. For this reason, the disturbance it may cause is considerably less likely to paralyze us than our own suffering.

Of course, even as an ideal, the notion of developing unconditional compassion is daunting. Most people, including myself, must struggle even to reach the point where putting others' interests on a par with our own becomes easy. We should not allow this to put us off, however. And while undoubtedly there will be obstacles on the way to developing a genuinely warm heart, there is the deep consolation of knowing that in doing so we are creating the conditions for our own happiness. As I mentioned earlier, the more we truly desire to benefit others, the greater the strength and confidence we develop and the greater the peace and happiness we experience. If this still seems unlikely, it is worth asking ourselves how else we are to do so. With violence and aggression? Of course not. With money? Perhaps up to a point, but no further. But with love, by sharing in others' suffering, by recognizing ourselves clearly in all others—especially those who are disadvantaged and those whose rights are not respected—by helping them to be happy: yes. Through love, through kindness, through compassion we establish understanding between ourselves and others. This is how we forge unity and harmony.

Compassion and love are not mere luxuries. As the source both of inner and external peace, they are fundamental to the continued survival of our species. On the one hand, they constitute non-violence in action. On the other, they are the source of all spiritual qualities: of forgiveness, tolerance, and all the virtues. Moreover, they are the very thing that gives meaning to our activities and makes them constructive. There is nothing amazing about being highly educated; there is nothing amazing about being rich. Only when the individual has a warm heart do these attributes become worthwhile.

So to those who say that the Dalai Lama is being unrealistic in advocating this ideal of unconditional love, I urge them to experiment with it nonetheless. They will discover that when we reach beyond the confines of narrow self-interest, our hearts become filled with strength. Peace and joy become our constant companion. It breaks down barriers of every kind and in the end destroys the notion of my interest as independent from others' interest. But most important, so far as ethics is concerned, where love of one's neighbor, affection, kindness, and compassion live, we find that ethical conduct is automatic. Ethically wholesome actions arise naturally in the context of compassion.

Study Questions

1. Comment on Hadot's understanding of philosophy as a way of life. Does his view of the nature of philosophy conflict with your experience in the classroom? Do you find any of the ideas and practices described by Hadot to be helpful to your own attempt at living a good life? Why or why not?

2. In the *Phaedo*, what does Socrates mean by the idea that "philosophy is practicing death"? Do you find this philosophy of life to be too dismissive of the body and material things, or is it a useful corrective to our culture's obsession with them? In what ways, in general, can reflecting on one's death lead one to live a better life?

3. The notion of a tripartite soul is a prominent feature of Plato's moral psychology in the *Republic*. Do you think the self has three parts (reason, will, desires)? Does this explain why we are sometimes "at war" with ourselves? Do you strive for balance or harmony in your life as a way of reaching peace within yourself? Explain.

4. Comment on Plato's "Allegory of Cave" as a basis for forming a philosophy of life. Do you think we are prisoners in a cave? If so, what do you think we are prisoners of? What does the cave represent for you?

5. What things does Epictetus think are "in our power"? What things are not "in our power"? How would your life be changed if you took the attitude that Epictetus recommends to your body, reputation and social position? Do you think your life would improve? Why or why not?

6. Do you find Taoism be a form of otherworldly mysticism or a practical moral philosophy of life? Could it be both? Explain your answer.

7. Comment on the Dalai Lama's claim that living compassionately is beneficial both to others and to oneself. Do you agree with this claim? Compare the Dalai Lama's views to that of Plato in the *Republic* and Jesus in the Sermon on the Mount (see chapter 2). In what ways are they similar and in what ways are they different?

For Further Reading

Annas, Julia. *Platonic Ethics, Old and New*. Ithaca, NY: Cornell University Press, 1999.

Cicero. *On the Good Life*. Trans. Michael Grant. London: Penguin, 1971.

Cottingham, John. *On the Meaning of Life*. London: Routledge, 2003.

Hadot, Pierre. *The Inner Citadel: The Meditations of Marcus Aurelius*. Trans. Michael Chase. Cambridge, MA: Harvard University Press, 1998.

Keown, Damien. *The Nature of Buddhist Ethics*. New York: St. Martin's Press, 1992.

McGhee, Michael. *Transformations of Mind: Philosophy as Spiritual Practice*. Cambridge: Cambridge University Press, 2000.

Nusbaum, Martha C. *The Therapy of Desire: Theory and Practice in Hellenistic Ethics*. Princeton, NJ: Princeton University Press, 1994.

Watts, Alan. *Tao: The Watercourse Way*. With the collaboration of Al Chung-liang Huang. New York: Pantheon, 1975.

About the Editors

Andrew J. Dell'Olio is professor of philosophy at Hope College. He is the author of *Foundations of Moral Selfhood: Aquinas on Divine Goodness and the Connection of the Virtues* (2003) and has published numerous articles on ethics and the philosophy of religion.

Caroline J. Simon is John and Jeanne Jacobson Professor of Philosophy at Hope College. She is the author of *The Disciplined Heart: Love, Destiny and Imagination* (1997) and has published many articles on moral knowledge, virtue ethics, friendship, and sexuality. She has also published books and numerous articles on higher education.

Made in the USA
San Bernardino, CA
18 September 2018